Cinema Expanded

Cinema Expanded

Avant-Garde Film in the Age of Intermedia

Jonathan Walley

OXFORD

UNIVERSITY PRESS

OXFORD
UNIVERSITY PRESS

Oxford University Press is a department of the University of Oxford. It furthers
the University's objective of excellence in research, scholarship, and education
by publishing worldwide. Oxford is a registered trade mark of Oxford University
Press in the UK and certain other countries.

Published in the United States of America by Oxford University Press
198 Madison Avenue, New York, NY 10016, United States of America.

Library of Congress Cataloging-in-Publication Data
Names: Walley, Jonathan, author.
Title: Cinema expanded : avant-garde film in the age of intermedia / [Jonathan Walley].
Description: New York, NY : Oxford University Press, [2019] |
Includes bibliographical references and index.
Identifiers: LCCN 2019058177 (print) | LCCN 2019058178 (ebook) |
ISBN 9780190938635 (hardback) | ISBN 9780190938642 (paperback) |
ISBN 9780190938666 (epub) | ISBN 9780190938673 (online) | 9780190938659 (updf)
Subjects: LCSH: Experimental films—History and criticism. |
Intermediality. | New media art.
Classification: LCC PN1995.9.E96 W26 2020 (print) |
LCC PN1995.9.E96 (ebook) | DDC 791.43/611—dc23
LC record available at https://lccn.loc.gov/2019058177
LC ebook record available at https://lccn.loc.gov/2019058178

1 3 5 7 9 8 6 4 2

Paperback printed by Marquis, Canada
Hardback printed by Bridgeport National Bindery, Inc., United States of America

Contents

Acknowledgments

This book is the culmination of nearly 20 years of research and writing on expanded cinema. As such, it has benefited from the contributions—direct and indirect—from countless artists and filmmakers, critics and scholars, curators, programmers, and archivists, not to mention family members and friends. And I do mean countless; to try and name them all would be as hopeless an endeavor as cataloging every work of expanded cinema. I want to identify some standouts here, and to apologize to anyone I may have inadvertently omitted.

Special thanks for images, information, ideas, emails, phone calls, conversations, criticisms, corrections, support, and so on are due to Craig Baldwin, Erika Balsom, Dianna Barrie, Marilyn Brakhage, Bill Brand, Fred Camper, Esperanza Collado, Tony Conrad, Louise Curham, Gill Eatherley, Cate Elwes, Keith Evans, Christian Farrell, Brian Frye, David Gatten, J. Ronald Green, Nicky Hamlyn, James Hansen, Tony Hill, Chrissie Iles, Lucas Ihlein, Ken Jacobs, Nisi Jacobs, Kim Knowles, Malcolm Le Grice, William Raban, A. L. Rees, Lucy Reynolds, Lynn Sachs, Christopher Sieving, Christopher Sharits, Guy Sherwin, Mary Stark, Chris Stults, Tess Takahashi, Richard Tuohy, Malcolm Turvey, Mark Webber, Duncan White, Federico Windhausen, Gregory Zinman, and Mike Zryd. Thanks also to Norm Hirschy, my patient and encouraging editor at Oxford University Press.

Most of the images in this book were generously provided by the artists themselves. Others were provided by galleries, museums, archives, estates, and other film and art organizations and institutions. These are credited in the captions, but I would like to thank some of the individuals behind these institutions for working with me on obscure image acquisitions and sometimes complicated copyright clearances: Steven Ball (British Artists' Film and Video Study Collection), Michael Blair (Electronic Arts Intermix), Broc Blegen (Castelli Gallery), Elle Burchill (Microscope Gallery), Cathleen Chaffee (Albright-Knox Art Gallery), Peter Corina (Division of Rare and Manuscript Collections, Cornell University), Joyce Faust (Art Resource, Inc.), George Habeeb (Greene Naftali), Martha Fleming-Ives (Greene Naftali), Genevieve Fong (Eames Office), Elyse Goldberg (Estate of Robert Smithson), Sigrid Guggenberger (Atelier Valie EXPORT), Linda Gustavson (ArtSite), Tullis Johnson (Burchfield Penney Art Center), Fredericka Hunter (ARTPIX), Margarete Krueger (VISUM), Lynn Maliszewski (Callicoon Fine Arts), Julie Martin (Experiments in Art and Technology), Tom Martinelli (Holt/Smithson Foundation), Bryony MacIntyre (Arika), Barbara Moore (Peter Moore Archive), Tessa Moorefield (Paula Cooper Gallery), Hannah Pacious (Nam June Paik Archive), Scott Propeack (Burchfield Penney Art Center), Tina Rivers Ryan (Albright-Knox Art Gallery), Enrica Sampong (Fondazione Bonotto), Raquel Scherr (the *Berkley Barb* Project), Pat Seymour (The

Andy Warhol Museum), and Chelsea Spengemann (Stan VanDerBeek Archive). Thanks also to Artists Rights Society.

I also want to single out several filmmakers who have been especially stalwart advocates of my work over many years and in some cases have become good friends: Alan Berliner, Roger Beebe, Bradley Eros, Sandra Gibson, Sally Golding, Kerry Laitala, Jeanne Liotta, Anthony McCall, Bruce McClure, Luis Recoder, and Al Wong.

Adolfas Mekas and John Pruitt, two of my professors in the Film Department at Bard College and the two people who kindled my interest in expanded cinema in the first place, died while I was working on this book. Adolfas saw cinema everywhere in the world, as if it was a natural phenomenon, while John taught me (and hundreds of other students across his career) to love avant-garde cinema; my first experience of expanded cinema was a screening of *Line Describing a Cone* in 1991, which John screened after I told him how much I wanted to see it. I am especially sorry that John, who died in the spring of 2019, did not live to see this book completed, as it owes a tremendous lot to his influence.

My grandmother, Anne Turner Henry, died as I was completing this book, a week short of her 102nd birthday. Her extraordinary life will always be an inspiration. I would like to think this book would have made her proud.

My wife, Jane M. Greene, has taught me at least as much about cinema as any of the brilliant teachers I studied with in college and graduate school. More importantly, she has immeasurably enriched every other part of my life, and indeed has given me the best, most fun, and fullest life I could ever have hoped for. Without that I could not have done this.

My parents, Craig and Connie Walley, have always enthusiastically supported and nurtured my creative and scholarly efforts—successful and unsuccessful. I dedicate this book to them, with much gratitude and love.

Columbus, Ohio
Autumn 2019

Introduction

The Persistence of Cinema

Since I'm being outrageous, I might as well be totally outrageous and refer to the whole history of art as either a series of prefigurations or a series of footnotes to film.

—Hollis Frampton (1974)

Cinema has not yet been invented!

—André Bazin (1946)

Creative Histories and Strange Ontologies

In 2009, amid a flurry of sweeping, literally millennial prognostications about cinema's future, archeologists at Cambridge University made a startling claim about its past. According to Christopher Chippindale and Frederick Baker, Copper Age rock carvings found throughout Western Europe were in fact a form of proto-cinema. Images of hunting, religious rituals, and scenes of daily life, hewn into the rock in serial form, play out stages of action like the individual frames of a strip of film (figs. I.1 and I.2). Illuminated by the sun, acting as "projector," the carvings cast shadows that create the illusion of three-dimensionality. Baker—who is also a filmmaker—writes of the "revelatory" experience of seeing these ancient figures "leap out and then disappear" as the sun passed over and set behind them.[1] What is more, archeo-acoustic studies reveal that the mountainous surroundings where the carvings are typically found possess special sonic properties, converting cliff walls into massive "open air cinemas."[2] Prehistoric viewers, then, experienced immersive, "multi-screen" audiovisual performances over 5,000 years before surround sound, 3D, and IMAX.

---

[1] "Major Motion Pictures from Our Prehistoric Past," http://www.cam.ac.uk/research/features/major-motion-pictures-from-our-prehistoric-past. May 17, 2013. Also see Damien Gayle, "The Caveman Cartoons: How Prehistoric Artists Make Their Paintings MOVE," http://www.dailymail.co.uk/science-tech/article-2207596/A-night-pictures-caveman-style-Prehistoric-artists-used-cartoon-like-techniques-make-paintings-move.html. September 3, 2012. ; Chelsea Wald, "Valley of Echoes," *New Scientist* 212, no. 2834, p. 53; "32,000 Years of Special Effects," http://www.cam.ac.uk/research/news/32000-years-of-special-effects. October 15, 2011; "Cinema in 2500 BC," http://www.science20.com/news_articles/cinema_2500_bc. June 29, 2010; and http://www.pitoti.org/, the website for the Prehistoric Picture Project.
[2] "Scientists Say Prehistoric Man Enjoyed 3D Cinema Too," http://artdaily.com/news/39125/Scientists-Say-Prehistoric-Man-Enjoyed-3D-Cinema-Too.

Cinema Expanded. Jonathan Walley, Oxford University Press (2020). © Oxford University Press.
DOI: 10.1093/oso/9780190938635.001.0001

Fig. I.1. Copper Age rock carvings at Valcamonica.
Photograph ©Alan Denney.

Fig. I.2. Copper Age rock carvings at Valcamonica.
Photograph ©Alan Denney.

Fig. I.3. 3D-Pitoti, an EU- supported project for extensive 3D mapping of ancient rock art in Valcamonica. Capo di Ponte, province of Brescia, Lombardy, Italy. July 8, 2013. Photograph ©Marc Steinmetz/VISUM.

Chippindale and Baker are the co-founders of the "Prehistoric Picture Project," which merges archeological research and state-of-the-art digital filmmaking techniques. With researchers and artists from Cambridge, St. Pölten University of Applied Sciences, and the Bauhaus-Universität Weimar, they have begun to transform these images into interactive animated digital installations (fig. I.3), one of which was included in the 2012 Milan Triennale as a work of "ambient cinema."[3] Animating digital scans of these sequential images reveals that their makers captured details of movement—birds in flight, the arc of a spear—with naturalistic accuracy, with Baker going so far as to make an analogy to neo-realist cinema: "We animated an image of a bird, and not only got it to fly in an absolutely naturalistic sense, but found that concentric arcs inside its body were not plumage but follow the graphic logic of a bird's beating wings."[4] His participation in the Prehistoric Picture Project eventually led to a greater interest in 3D moving image mapping, with Baker producing films designed for projection onto specific architectural sites. *The Return of Harry Lime* (2014), a short film based on the scene in *The Third Man* in which the Orson Welles character reappears after being presumed dead, was mapped onto the Bridge of Sighs at St John's College and viewed by spectators in boats floating on the River Cam (fig. I.4). Baker's work updates the primitive cinematic aspirations of Chalcolithic rock

---

[3] See "Pitoti: Digital Rock Art from Ancient Europe," http://triennale.org/en/exhibitions/next/1329-pitoti-digital-rock-art-from-ancient-europe.
[4] "Major Motion Pictures from Our Prehistoric Past."

Fig. I.4. Frederick Baker, *The Return of Harry Lime* (2014). Performance view at the Bridge of Sighs, St John's College of Cambridge University, May 5, 2015.
Photograph by Hamish Park.

artists, while the Prehistoric Picture Project released their images from centuries of stasis imposed only by the lack of proper technology.

Leaping ahead now from Copper Age Europe to 20th-century New York—specifically Tribeca on June 18, 1975. Avant-garde artist-turned-filmmaker Anthony McCall "premiered" his *Long Film for Ambient Light* at the Idea Warehouse, an abandoned industrial building *cum* makeshift artists' space at 22 Reade Street (fig. I.5). McCall's film "ran" from noon of the 18th to noon the following day, during which time spectators could come and go as they pleased and move about the space at will. Viewers arriving to see *Long Film for Ambient Light* encountered a large, bare, industrial-looking room with a bank of windows along one wall covered by diffusion paper; by night, a single bare bulb hanging from the ceiling provided the only light. A timeline marking off 50 days in one-hour increments ran along one wall, the 24-hour duration of the film in mid-June bracketed in the center (fig. I.6). Next to it was an artist's statement entitled "Notes in Duration," which proclaimed that these elements—the space, light, timeline, and statement—along with the coming and going of spectators, comprised the work. There was no film, no projector, no movie screen, no rows of seats; rather, McCall claimed a specific location during a specific time as "a film," suggesting that the necessary and sufficient conditions for a work of cinema consisted of the modulation of light in space and time (the timeline on the wall additionally indicated the "fluctuations of darkness and daylight"), and the

Fig. I.5. Anthony McCall, *Long Film for Ambient Light* (1975). Installation view at Idea Warehouse, New York, 2pm, June 18, 1975.
Photograph by Anthony McCall.

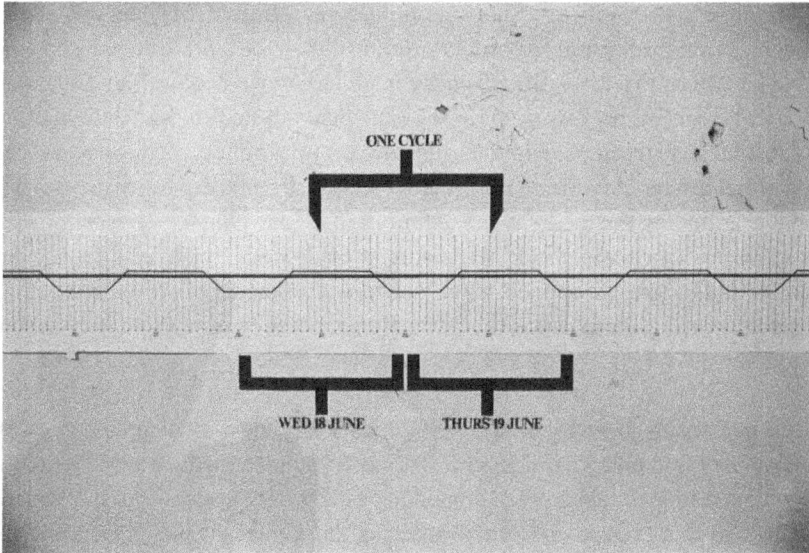

Fig. I.6. Anthony McCall, *Long Film for Ambient Light* (1975). Time schema installation view at Idea Warehouse, New York, 1975.
Photograph by Anthony McCall.

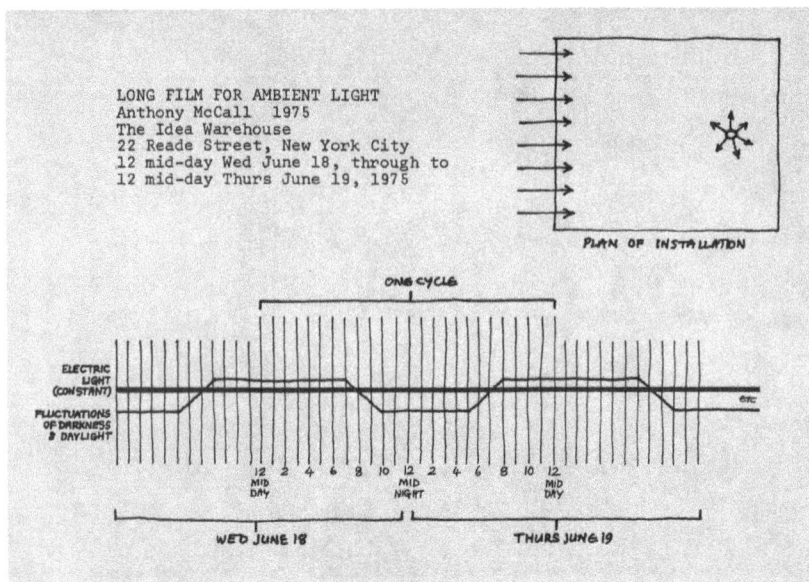

Fig. I.7. Anthony McCall, *Long Film for Ambient Light* (1975). Announcement, The Idea Warehouse, New York, 1975.
Photograph by Anthony McCall.

actions of spectators within such conditions (fig. I.7). Indeed, the only way an independent, avant-garde filmmaker could afford to make a 24-hour film in the first place would have been to jettison the expensive materials of the medium, particularly film stock and chemical processing. McCall's statement attested to this, claiming that it was possible to make films "without using the customary photochemical and electromechanical processes (which have the disadvantage of being expensive, i.e. slow)."[5]

But abandoning the medium did not mean that *Long Film for Ambient Light* was not a film or "cinematic" work. To be sure, it made nods to a hybrid artistic pedigree; McCall's statement connected the work to the aesthetics of process art and minimalism, rejecting, for instance, the distinction between temporal and non-temporal art forms:

This film sits deliberately on a threshold, between being considered a work of movement and being considered a static condition. Formalist art criticism has continued to maintain a stern, emphatic distinction between these two states, a division that I consider absurd. Everything that occurs, including the (electrochemical) process of thinking, occurs in time.[6]

[5] Anthony McCall, "Notes in Duration," reprinted in P. Adams Sitney, ed., *The Avant-Garde Film: A Reader of Theory and Criticism* (New York: Anthology Film Archives, 1987), p. 253.
[6] Ibid., p. 252.

Despite his adaptation of concepts from the other arts, however, McCall explicitly framed his "film" in terms of ideas and aims specific to cinema, and to the cinematic avant-garde in particular. *Long Film for Ambient Light* was not a work of multimedia or "intermedia," not a happening or event lacking a specific artistic identity. That film itself was missing from the "film" didn't matter; in fact, it allowed McCall to explore fundamentals of cinema all the more directly: "I do not rule out the possibility of continuing to make 'films.' However, for the time being I intend to concentrate less on the physical process of production and more on the presuppositions behind film as an art activity."[7]

We have moved from a latent cinema, made long before the requisite technologies were invented, to a cinema that dispensed with those technologies the better to retrieve some elusive essential quality, some primordial origin. Two instances of a radically other cinema mirror each other across thousands of years.

The Prehistoric Picture Project and *Long Film for Ambient Light* raise intriguing questions. What does it mean to call these objects "cinema"? Painted or carved prehistoric images have usually been thought of as the earliest instances of painting, or sculpture, or narrative art. Why now re-christen them as part of *cinema's* ancestry? In the milieu of 1970s avant-garde art, *Long Film for Ambient Light* would have been easily accepted as a sculptural installation, or a work of light art, or a conceptual art piece. But a film? Does this mean that cinema is, in fact, a painterly, or sculptural, or performative art? If so, what are the implications of this for our understanding of the nature of these art forms and their relationship to cinema?

We might object to a definition of cinema so broad as to include ancient rock carvings or a room full of light. If these things are cinema, what *isn't* cinema? What are the necessary and sufficient conditions for something to be "cinematic"? And how do the assertions that millennia-old rock art and an entirely film-less "film" count as instances of cinema affect our understanding of the materials and practices of conventional cinema? This conventional cinema—call it "cinema as we know it"—has existed for over a century, and archeologists have been aware of primitive rock carvings for even longer. Why is it only now that someone has thought to re-cast prehistoric art of which we have long known in cinematic terms? Has something happened to enable this redefinition both of cinema and past art? Might McCall's work offer a key to answering this question?

The Prehistoric Picture Project's reclamation of rock carvings in the name of cinema, while creative, is not new. Sergei Eisenstein found essentially cinematic properties in the very language and visual culture of Japan, while André Bazin traced cinema's lineage to mummification and statuary in ancient Egypt.[8] In his essay "The Myth of Total Cinema," Bazin argued, "It would be a reversal . . . of the concrete order of

[7] Ibid., p. 254.
[8] Sergei Eisenstein, "The Cinematographic Principle and the Ideogram," in *Film Form*, translated by Jay Leyda (San Diego: Harcourt Brace Jovanovich, 1949), pp. 28–32; André Bazin, "The Ontology of the Photographic Image," in *What Is Cinema?* vol. 1, translated by Hugh Gray (Berkeley: University of California Press, 1967), pp. 9–10.

causality, at least psychologically, to place the scientific discoveries or the industrial techniques that have loomed so large in its development at the source of the cinema's invention."[9] Bazin's point was that a fully formed idea of cinema preexisted the technological experiments that eventually coalesced to form the film medium, where "cinema as we know it" began. The teleological claim that the spirit of cinema was present, at least as a concept, dream, or myth, in the earliest instances of statuary and painting (Bazin), or the linguistic principles of Japanese (Eisenstein), or in prehistoric rock art (Chippindale and Baker), raises all sorts of implications for the relationship between cinema and the other arts. For one thing, it undermines the belief that cinema is the youngest of the arts, as well as attendant ideas about its relative maturity and thus its significance and expressive power.

To discover cinema in the ancient world, or in a work that entirely abandons any form of moving image media, requires a conception of that art form distinct from any specific materials or necessary exhibition format. At the same time, though, it requires some internally consistent idea of cinema into which such seemingly "noncinematic" objects can be included. Otherwise, what makes the claim that ancient rock art or the furthest-out instances of post-minimal installation are works of cinema any more tenable than the claim that they are sculpture, painting, or anything else? Why identify specific art forms at all? The assertion that such objects are cinema, then, involves a dialectic between a conception of an art form that is quite open and heterogeneous and one that is still delimited enough to be recognizable: inclusive, but still limiting (or vice-versa). Each position is fraught with peril. The inclusive position can quickly become overly so, undermining the very purpose of defining art forms in the first place—the "what *isn't* cinema?" problem. And the limiting impulse can devolve into arbitrary artistic purism, which is always vulnerable to exceptions and counter-examples, not to mention art's historical restlessness and resistance to definition, which we often take to be some of its essential qualities.

Both the Prehistoric Picture Project and *Long Film for Ambient Light* juggle these two positions. The former relies upon metaphors of "projection" (the sun), the interplay of flatness and depth (the shadows of the carvings creating "3D" effects), multiple "screens" (the numerous carved rock faces simultaneously visible to an observer), and of "stills" and "animation" (actions represented serially), connecting ancient rock carvings to familiar material features of cinema as we know it. But cinema is also understood as an inherently multiple art form, integrating sound, narrative, and performance with painterly or sculptural imagery. So multiple, in fact, as to make one wonder whether the designation "cinema" for these objects doesn't stretch the category to the point of meaninglessness.

Similarly, McCall's "film" made its claim as a work of cinema by way of analogies to more conventional filmmaking: the row of windows resembles the frames of a strip of film, as do the increments on the timeline; shifts from daylight to electric light might

---

[9] "The Myth of Total Cinema," in *What Is Cinema?*, vol. 1, pp. 21–22.

suggest long dissolves or fades, or even the flickering—in extreme slow motion—of a film projector; McCall referred to the paper-covered windows as "screens" (fig. I.8). McCall's "presuppositions behind film as an art activity," removed from the "customary photochemical and electro-mechanical processes" of the medium, echoes in reverse the unrealized cinematic desires of primitive rock artists waiting for receptive materials to come along. In each case, cinema, or "the cinematic," is independent of

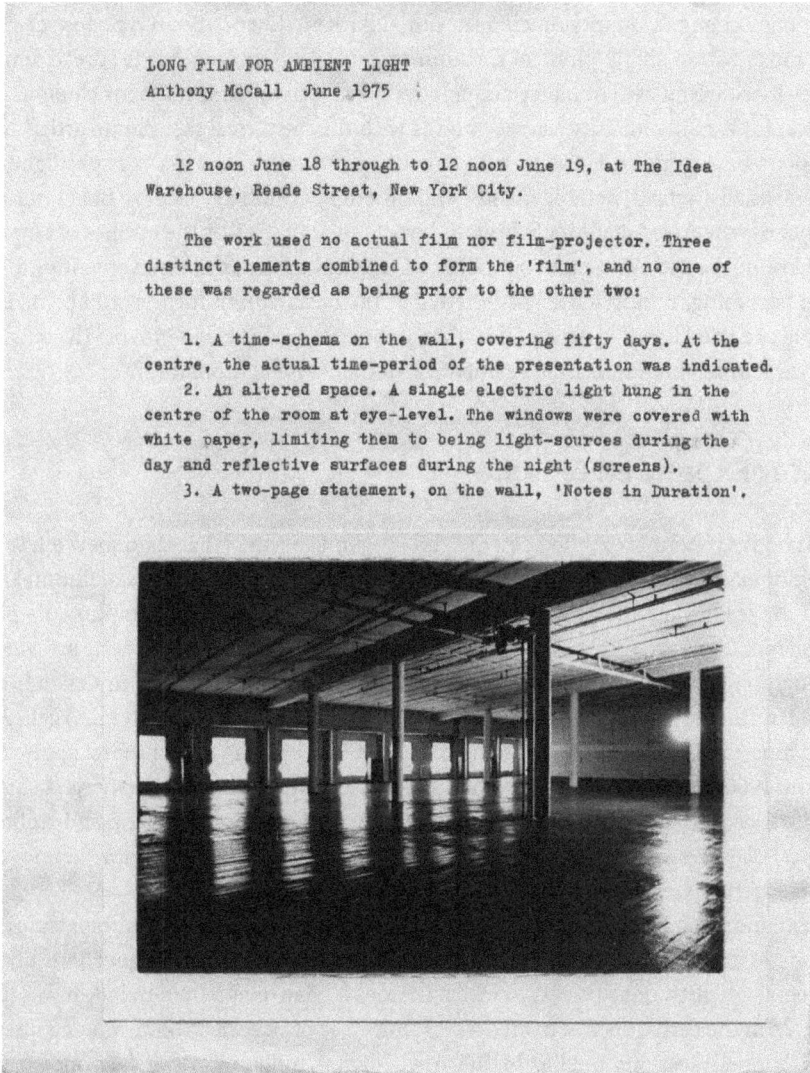

Fig. I.8. Anthony McCall, notes for *Long Film for Ambient Light* (1975) analogizing covered windows to light sources and "screens." Offset lithography, vintage gelatin silver print mounted on typing paper, 28 × 21.6 cm, 11 × 8½ in.
Photograph by Anthony McCall.

specific materials. And like his ancient predecessors, McCall produced a work that was at once specifically cinematic, trading as it did in cinema's "presuppositions," and curiously hybrid: sculptural, spatial, discursive, performative.

So, *qu'est-ce que le cinéma*? Bazin's famous question has become more and more complicated in the decades since his death. To answer it, as Bazin and many others attempted to do, is to identify an art form's nature or essence, one of the defining endeavors of film theory up to the 1960s. Since then, however, the idea has faced increased skepticism. The proliferation of new moving image media since the 1960s has made cinema's identity much more difficult to pin down, since it is no longer synonymous with a single physical medium or exhibition format, but is spread across an ever-widening field of materials, practices, and spaces. The search for cinema's essence, for a stable identity, seems at odds with this historical fact. Some artists and scholars have gone so far as to take cinema as *the* emblem of art's *un*specifiability, as essentially hybrid, heterogeneous, and inherently multiple. George Baker, for instance, has declared that McCall's work "proclaimed that it was the essence of cinema to have no essence. Cinema could only be particularized as the movement of form into becoming, multiplicity, and difference. The basis of film form would be its undoing of a fixed basis."[10] An equivocation, to be sure, but one that mirrors the tension between limit and limitlessness evident in McCall's film without film.

Enter Expanded Cinema

This book is about "expanded cinema," moving image works that claim new territory for cinema, beyond the bounds of the familiar materials and practices of filmmaking and the traditional theatrical exhibition space. Multi-screen films, multimedia performance, light art, moving image environments and installations, kinetic art, video, holography, and computer-generated imagery have all been placed under the "expanded cinema" umbrella at one time or other. It broke out of the theater into galleries and museums, and took shape as objects, environments, and actions. First appearing in the 1960s amid seismic shifts in all the arts, expanded cinema re-emerged with a vengeance at the dawn of the new millennium, as widespread artistic and technological changes once more opened a vast new horizon of possibility for the moving image, perhaps even heralding the end of "cinema as we know it."

Expanded cinema is the most radical manifestation of cinema's ontological restlessness, instability, and alleged essence-less-ness. It raises vexing questions about cinema's identity, not the least of which is: does it have one? When the term was first coined in the early 1960s, it named a dizzying array of new electronic, moving image, and communications media. In the new, "digital millennium," it has once again been put to that use, covering a constantly growing and mutating field of forms and

[10] George Baker, "Film Beyond Its Limits," in Helen Legg, ed., *Anthony McCall: Film Installations* (exhibition catalogue) (Warwick: Mead Gallery, 2004), pp. 22–23.

mediums. Not surprisingly, since it names a process whereby cinema grows beyond recognizable limits, the term has meant different things to different people; that is, the term itself has been as mutable as the thing it attempts to name—a problem in which this book intervenes. Broadly speaking, however, it refers to the belief that neither specific physical media (e.g., "celluloid" film) nor conventional exhibition practices (e.g., theatrical exhibition) define cinema or exhaust its possibilities.[11] Rather, the traditional materials and practices of the history of cinema up to 1960 represent only one very narrow range of options for the art form; by the mid-sixties, many saw this range of options as arbitrarily constraining, especially as new moving image media were appearing as rapidly as new ideas about the nature of art.

Sheldon Renan, one of the earliest critics to write about expanded cinema, described it in these very open terms:

> Expanded cinema is not the name of a particular style of filmmaking. It is a name for a spirit of inquiry that is leading in many different directions. It is cinema expanded to include many different projectors in the showing of one work. It is cinema expanded to include computer-generated images and electronic manipulation of images on television. It is cinema expanded to the point at which the effect of film may be produced without the use of film at all.[12]

Renan alludes to several forms that the term expanded cinema encompassed: multi-screen projection, new moving image and media technologies like video, television, and computers, and film-less films like McCall's (though Renan wrote this in 1967, nearly a decade before *Long Film for Ambient Light*). Multi-projection works like Andy Warhol's two-screen *The Chelsea Girls* (1966) (fig. I.9) or Charles and Ray Eames's seven-screen *Glimpses of the U.S.A.* (1959) and massive 22-screen THINK (1964; see chapter 3), film-performance hybrids by Nam June Paik and Robert Whitman, video and television works by Paik and Stan VanDerBeek (fig. I.10), computer films by John Whitney, multimedia performances and environments by the intermedia collective USCO (The Company of Us), and psychedelic light shows, color projection instruments, shadowplays, and kinetic sculptures all fall under the heading of expanded cinema. Moreover, Renan conveys the spirit of boundary breaking, of the refusal of tradition and convention that, for some, defined expanded cinema above and beyond any specific forms individual expanded works took. Renan implies that, whatever it looked like in 1967, expanded cinema—as a "spirit of inquiry that is leading in many different directions"—was, by definition, ever changing, unpredictable, and completely contrary to the idea that cinema could be specified.

---

[11] Throughout this book I will use the term "celluloid film" as shorthand for the medium of analog, photochemical, mechanical film, including film stock, cameras, and projectors. Film stock has not been made of celluloid for decades, but the term has stuck even with professional filmmakers.

[12] Sheldon Renan, *An Introduction to the American Underground Film* (New York: E.P Dutton & Co., Inc., 1967), p. 227.

Fig. I.9. Andy Warhol, *The Chelsea Girls* (1966). 16mm film, black and white and color, sound, 204 minutes in double screen.

Fig. I.10. Stan VanDerBeek in Studio 46, WNET, NY producing *Newsreel of Dreams* (1973).

Courtesy Stan VanDerBeek Archive.

Gene Youngblood, whose 1970 book *Expanded Cinema* remains one of the defining accounts of the subject, echoed Renan but went even further in detaching expanded cinema from any particular medium, and from any art form at all:

When we say expanded cinema we actually mean expanded consciousness. Expanded cinema does not mean computer films, video phosphors, atomic light, or spherical projections. Expanded cinema isn't a movie at all: like life it's a process of becoming, man's ongoing historical drive to manifest his consciousness outside of his mind, in front of his eyes.[13]

Such anti-essentialist positions vis-à-vis cinema, echoed by scores of artists and critics at the time, paralleled the general conception of art that developed after the Second World War. In this context, the very notion of artistic specificity, whether defined by particular physical media, by formal traits or conventions, or by broader historical traditions, came under siege. "Young artists of today need no longer say, 'I am a painter' or 'a poet' or 'a dancer,'" Allan Kaprow declared in 1958; "They are simply 'artists.' All of life will be open to them."[14] A decade later, Joseph Kosuth wrote:

> Being an artist now means to question the nature of art. If one is questioning the nature of painting, one cannot be questioning the nature of art . . . That's because the word "art" is general and the word "painting" is specific. Painting is a kind of art. If you make paintings you are already accepting (not questioning) the nature of art.[15]

Such declarations of war on Modernism's ideal of specificity fueled extensive experiments with cross-fertilization and forays into the gray areas between art forms. Inasmuch as it was possible for traditional arts like painting or sculpture even to exist in this environment, they did so in an increasingly diffuse state, in a greatly expanded field of media and activities. Hence the birth of the term "expanded arts," one of a family of concepts that identified the attempts to escape from the gravitational pull of artistic tradition: "multimedia," "synaesthesia," "art process," "dematerialization," "intermedia." The latter term is usually credited to the Fluxus artist Dick Higgins, for whom intermedia meant those artworks occupying a liminal space "between media," rejecting an "essentially mechanistic approach" to categorizing art forms (one could substitute "medium specific" for "mechanistic" here) and progressively resisting rigid categorizations that Higgins saw as an extension of class divisions.[16] Intermedia art mirrored the "classless society" Higgins believed was on the horizon in 1965, and which required forms of thought that were not "compartmentalized." This hints at the appeal of expanded cinema to the counterculture. The sense of utter rule-lessness, of freedom from restrictions whether technological, aesthetic, or social, permeates references to expanded cinema in the underground press (fig. I.11), a point to which we shall return in chapter 1. College campuses and youth culture venues like

---

[13] Gene Youngblood, *Expanded Cinema* (New York: E.P. Dutton & Co., Inc., 1970), p. 41.

[14] Allan Kaprow, "The Legacy of Jackson Pollock," *ArtNews* (October 1958), p. 57.

[15] Joseph Kosuth, "Art After Philosophy," in Gabriele Cuercio, ed., *Art After Philosophy and After: Collected Writings, 1966–1990* (Cambridge: MIT Press, 1991), p. 18. "Art After Philosophy" originally appeared in *Studio International* (October 1969), and Kosuth first made this statement in Arthur R. Rose, "Four Interviews," *Arts Magazine* 43, no. 4 (February 1969), p. 23.

[16] Dick Higgins, "Synesthesia and Intersenses: Intermedia," originally published in *Something Else Newsletter* 1, no. 1 (Something Else Press, 1966).

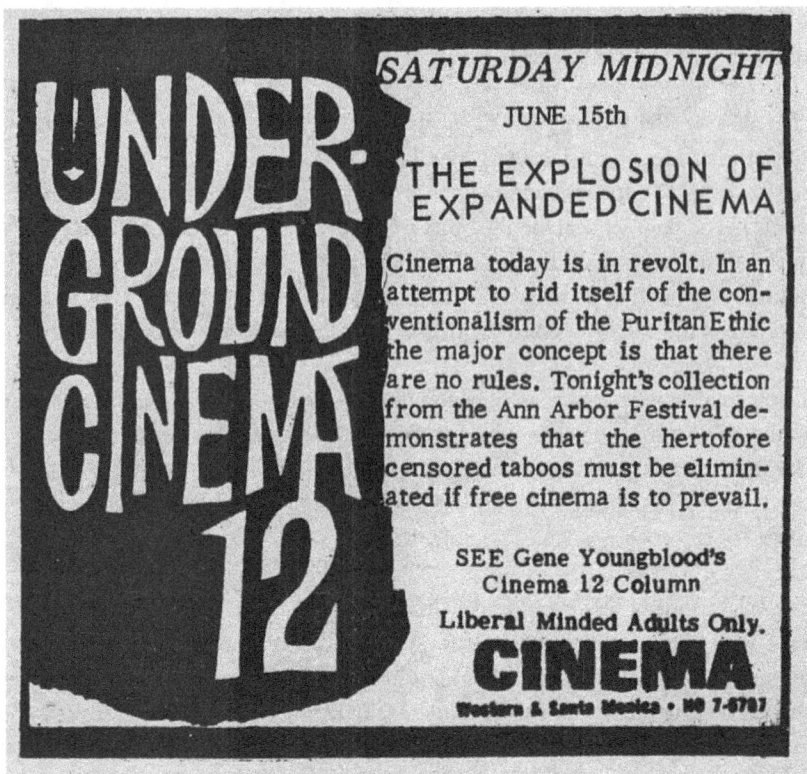

Fig. I.11. Advertisement in the *Los Angeles Free Press* for expanded cinema event in Los Angeles, referencing Gene Youngblood's writings on the subject in the same newspaper. June 14, 1968.

discotheques and coffee houses hosted the earliest works of expanded cinema almost as often as did museums, galleries, and cinematheques (fig. I.12).

Such "expansive" thinking has gone on in all the arts since the 1960s. The most recent variant of the line of thinking that denies traditional media their ontological pride of place is Rosalind Krauss's "post-medium condition," wherein artists invent their own art forms rather than inheriting them, discovering untapped aesthetic possibilities in new materials.[17] But it is cinema that has arguably been subject to more radical reconception and destabilization than any other art form. Indeed, one could claim that it has never been a stable art form, as Baker does. Chrissie Iles has articulated a similar view, that cinema was "always already" expanded, never really

---

[17] See Rosalind Krauss, *"A Voyage on the North Sea": Art in the Age of the Post-medium Condition* (London: Thames & Hudson, 2000); "Reinventing the Medium," *Critical Inquiry* 25, no. 2 (Winter 1999), pp. 289–305; and "'. . . And Then Turn Away?' An Essay on James Coleman," *October* 81 (Summer 1997), p. 5.

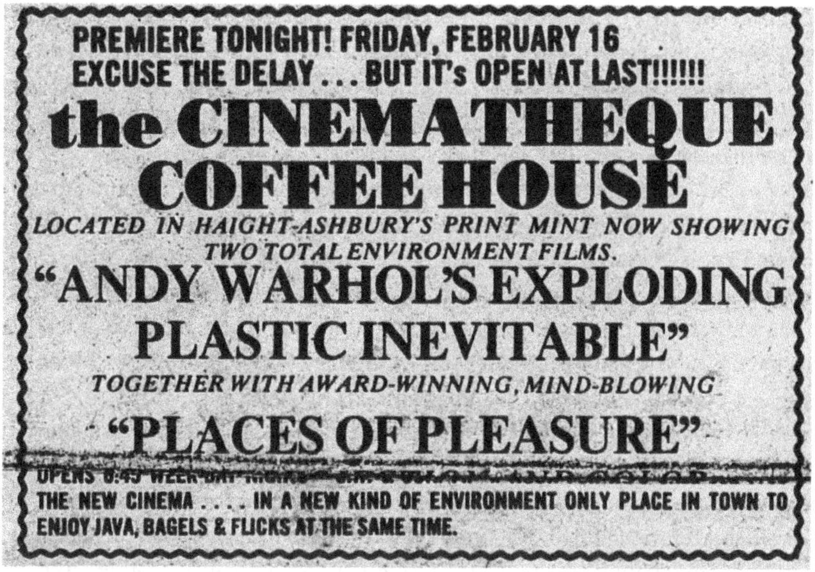

Fig. I.12. Advertisement for screening of *Andy Warhol's Exploding Plastic Inevitable* (Ronald Nameth, 1966) and the dual-screen *Palace of Pleasure* (John Hoffsess, 1966; title misspelled in ad) at the Cinematheque Coffee House in Haight-Ashbury, San Francisco.
From *The Berkley Barb* 6, no. 7 (131), February 16–22, 1968.

coalescing around a stable technological base or presentation format, or only doing so temporarily before taking on new forms. This would suggest that the endeavor to discover and maintain an autonomous, stable identity for cinema is too limiting, ahistorical, and idealistic in the light of artistic expansion, intermedia, and the post-medium condition. By this account, the "expanded" in "expanded cinema" is redundant; the use of the term as a proper noun—"Expanded Cinema"—simply throws into relief the fact of cinema's identity-less-ness in general.[18]

I take quite a different position in this book. I argue that expanded cinema neither abandoned the project of specifying cinema and distinguishing it from other art forms, nor cast off cinema's historical traditions, formal conventions, or familiar materials. After an initial, and rather brief, wave of expanded cinema that equated the term with intermedia and promoted the belief that cinema could be anything, a shift occurred whereby cinema's unwieldy and unlimited expansion encountered a reassertion of cinema's specificity and artistic autonomy by filmmakers and critics. Expanded

---

[18] Chrissie Iles, "Inside Out: Expanded Cinema and Its Relationship to the Gallery in the 1970s," a lecture given at the Tate Modern conference "Expanded Cinema, Activating the Space of Reception," April 17–19, 2009. Video documentation of Iles's talk can be found at http://www.rewind.ac.uk/expanded/Narrative/Tate_Doc_Session_2_-CI.html.

cinema became part of this countermovement against the unfettered broadening of artistic categories. Particularly in light of more recent events, including an international resurgence of expanded work since the mid-1990s, expanded cinema is best seen, I argue, as negotiating between cinema's technological and aesthetic heterogeneity on the one hand, and its specificity and historical continuity on the other. Part of this process has involved artists claiming qualities and effects for cinema that were usually thought of as belonging to other art forms (a process that chapters 3 through 6 trace out in detail). And so cinema, though expanded, remains cinema.

Hence the title of this book, which reverses that of Youngblood's decidedly intermedial and *non*-specific account, privileging, one could say, the "expanded" over the "cinema." My version is precisely an inversion of this, privileging the "cinema" as much as the "expanded" and arguing for the continuity of artistic identity even as filmmakers pushed toward the furthest reaches of their art and explored forms like the performance, the sculptural, the conceptual, the musical, and the painterly. I intend to show that, even as they did so, they did not intend their work as intermedia but as cinema, just expanded. The book's subtitle takes "intermedia" both as the word was initially understood and as a blanket signifier for all manner of other "inter-s" as well: interdisciplinarity, inter-arts, multimedia (another version of the categorical in-betweenness of post-WWII avant-garde art)—in a word, the interstitiality so prized in academia and the art world and believed to have displaced a conservative and philosophically untenable approach to art marked by purism, essentialism, medium specificity. This displacement is signaled by a parallel cluster of prefixes, the "posts": the postmodern, the post-medium condition, and the post-cinematic. The "intermedia age" of my title, then, incorporates all of these. As a whole, the book intervenes in the general situation these terms denote.

My revision of expanded cinema is at once categorical and historical; one revision entails the other. Contrary to previous accounts that privilege the expanded arts *milieu* as the source of expanded cinema's development, I want to return my subject to what I take to be its more proximate and proper historical context, which is the history of avant-garde/experimental cinema. My account connects expanded cinema much more directly to this branch of cinematic practice, which is no less a wellspring of creative histories and strange ontologies than the expanded arts scene in general, but one that has nevertheless grounded expansive thinking and artmaking in a model of (cinematic) specificity. Indeed, I claim that expanded cinema extends the tradition of film-ontological meditations that constitutes one of avant-garde cinema's defining features, a tradition represented most clearly in the theory and practice of "structural" and "structural-materialist" film, but certainly not limited to these. Perhaps even more importantly, I identify expanded cinema as part of a longer and still ongoing effort by filmmakers and critics not only to claim cinema's autonomy among the other arts, but also to promote and defend the values of avant-garde film culture itself. The nature of these values, and the ways they shaped works of expanded cinema, are two of this book's major subjects. Expanded cinema provides us with a rich case study of the ways that filmmakers and critics have confronted the complexities of cinema's nature and history, its relationship to specific media and exhibition formats, and its place among the other arts, questions that come to the forefront during periods of major technological and artistic change.

The distinction between two avant-gardes, "one that would isolate, if not purify, the intrinsic attributes of a particular medium, and another which would miscegenate with the other media," was as much a part of avant-garde film criticism as it was of art world discourses more generally.[19] The tendency has been to associate expanded cinema with the latter, as a radical break from the traditions and conventions of cinema as we know it, and the opposite of avant-garde film's "isolating" and "purifying" impulses. This has marginalized expanded cinema, as though it is not *really* a cinematic practice and thus not part of the purview of cinema studies or the study of avant-garde film in particular. That the most prominent artists in early accounts of expanded cinema were already well established in other art forms— Warhol, Whitman, Paik—confirms this, making expanded cinema a condition of what was happening in the art world rather than in the film world. More recent studies of expanded cinema often locate it outside of the familiar spaces of cinema, in world's fairs, discotheques, and art galleries, as a manifestation of technological, aesthetic, and political developments outside the sphere of avant-garde cinema.[20] I do not deny that, at least initially, expanded cinema was a very broad concept relevant to a variety of contexts. But I would add two qualifications: first, expanded cinema's intimate connection to avant-garde film culture has been a blind spot for a number of previous writers on the subject, something this book corrects; second, as the term is used contemporaneously, it refers almost exclusively to work produced within the cinematic avant-garde, by artists who self-identify with that tradition, as *filmmakers*. Thus, from our contemporary perspective, we can now see a historical trajectory in which the concept of expanded cinema has been narrowed and specified. From this perspective, we can revise our understanding of the expanded cinema of the 1960s and 1970s. This is precisely what this book will do: revise "expanded cinema" as a concept, reclaiming it for a more narrowly and thus clearly defined group of works. My account attempts to stabilize the concept without closing it off to the ongoing processes of cinematic change to which it refers. The ultimate goal is to reinvest the term with meaning, finding a middle point between a conception of expanded cinema that is so vague and inclusive as to be useless, and one so narrow and inflexible as to be blind to cinema's historical dynamism. This book, then, is a new assertion of what expanded cinema was and still is, and of the answers it has offered to questions about cinema's identity that have been so central to the art form's history, and which have taken on new meaning since the 1960s.

[19] Richard Kostelanetz, *Metamorphosis in the Arts: A Critical History of the 1960s* (New York: Assembling Press, 1980), p. 11.
[20] See, for instance, Andrew V. Uroskie, *Between the Black Box and the White Cube: Expanded Cinema and Postwar Art* (Chicago: University of Chicago Press, 2014), and Janine Marchessault and Susan Lord, eds., *Fluid Screens, Expanded Cinema (Digital Futures)* (Toronto: University of Toronto Press, 2008).

Cinematic Specificity, Expanded

It should be clear by now that "specificity" will be a central concept of this book. The practitioners of expanded cinema propose variations on the notions of cinema's specificity rather than rejecting the idea altogether, as the earliest accounts of expanded cinema would have us believe.

My emphasis on cinematic specificity evokes the specter of "medium specificity," the belief that art forms (e.g., cinema) are determined by the raw physical materials of a given medium (e.g., "celluloid" film). I indeed argue that film has remained central for avant-garde filmmakers, including those who make expanded cinema. I further argue that medium specificity of the sort I just described is actually a much more complex and subtle concept, one that does not reduce to "cinema is determined by the materials of a physical medium." But the idea of cinematic specificity that animates this book is not the same as "medium specificity" as that term is normally construed. I identify three distinct, though interrelated, levels of specificity.

The first of these is the specificity of a physical material: here, "celluloid" film, meaning not only photochemical film stock but the machines and processes that make up what Krauss has called the "aggregate" medium of film: cameras, projectors, analog editing equipment like film splicers and flatbed editing machines, photochemical processing, and so on.[21] When I refer to "film" in this book, it will be to that medium, that aggregate of materials and processes (or to a work that utilizes these, as in "a film by . . ."). "Medium specificity" will refer to the idea that different physical materials have unique properties that carry aesthetic and even political consequences, thus making distinctions between media like film and digital video important even though the critical rhetoric of remediation claims otherwise.[22] The physical specificity of such media, though not absolutely determinative of the cinematic, has figured crucially in the formation of that latter concept. This remains true even as we hear more and more often of the "death" of film, and as avant-garde filmmakers with reputations for filmic purism utilize digital video.[23] Looking more closely at medium specificity throughout this book, I show that it is no theoretical monolith or simplistic technological determinism, but a field of answers to questions about the relationship between physical material, technical craft, and artmaking. At times these answers are

---

[21] Krauss, "A Voyage on the North Sea," pp. 24–25.

[22] I discuss the terms "remediation" and "media convergence" in the second chapter. The former was introduced by David Jay Bolter and Richard Grusin in their book *Remediation: Understanding New Media* (Cambridge: MIT Press, 1999), and is based upon Marshall McLuhan's idea that new media imitate older media or take these media as their initial content. Remediation is essentially what allows convergence to take place, according to a number of theorists of new media, as film scholar Erika Balsom explains: " . . . 'convergence' designates the operation by which media lose their medium-specific qualities by being remediated or transcoded to data based in binary code." See Erika Balsom, *Exhibiting Cinema in Contemporary Art* (Amsterdam: Amsterdam University Press, 2013), pp. 13–15.

[23] On this subject, see Federico Windhausen, "Assimilating Video," *October*, 137 (Summer 2011), pp. 69–83.

conflicting and competing. The assertions of the film medium's specific characteristics comprise a multifaceted and richly layered conception of the nature of that physical medium, which has provided the conceptual basis even for works that dispensed with it, as *Long Film for Ambient Light* does (fig. I.13). Since expanded cinema meant, among other things, that analog film was no longer cinema's privileged material form, it is worth considering the ramifications of this for artists who nevertheless continued to use that medium, and examining their beliefs about it. One of these beliefs, often tacit, was that film was as much a field of possibilities as a set of limitations or restrictions, many of them unexplored. Thinking of the medium in a certain way could generate expanded cinema even though that concept pointed to a cinema beyond film; as Renan put it, "the effect of film can be created without the use of film at all."

A second level of specificity we can identify is that of cinema, understood as an art form not necessarily embodied in a specific material substrate like celluloid film or digital video. This actually pitches the concept of "cinematic specificity" at a fairly high level of generality; it becomes less abstract through differentiations between cinema and the other arts. Above and beyond material differences between media, cinema can be distinguished from the other arts by identifying central concepts or areas of aesthetic investigation that have defined cinema as a unique form of art, one

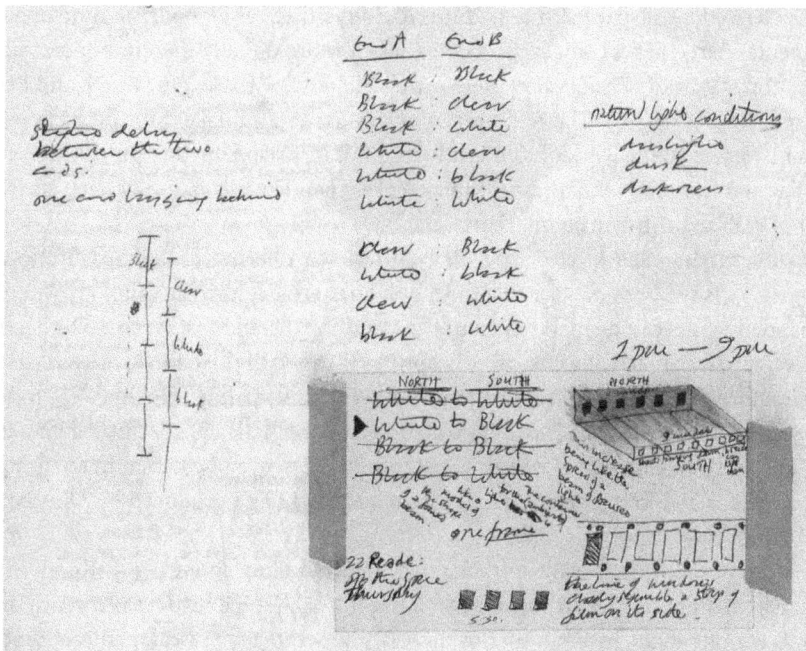

Fig. I.13. Anthony McCall, *Long Film for Ambient Light* (1975). Installation drawing (from May 1–June 26, 1975 notebook). Detail showing McCall's analogy between line of windows and strip of film.
Courtesy Anthony McCall.

different from theater, literature, or music. These concepts or areas constitute a kind of shared language of filmmakers, even if different types of filmmakers speak it in very different dialects. In his essay "A Pentagram for Conjuring the Narrative," Hollis Frampton proposed three "inevitable conditions" of cinema, three irreducible elements of all cinema, whether popular or avant-garde: "all the celluloid that has ever cascaded through the projector's gate."[24] These were the frame, photographic illusion, and narrative (by which Frampton, in his characteristically expansive manner of thinking, seems to have meant any kind of temporal structure). Frampton's argument is deliberately provocative, but we could probably agree on certain core, non-medium-specific elements of cinema such as framing, editing, light, and the effects of lens optics, as well as cinema's distinct forms of temporal organization. These are fundamental elements that cut across different moving image media, shaping the work of all filmmakers whether a Maya Deren, a Jean-Luc Godard, or a Steven Spielberg. Indeed, avant-garde cinema's long tradition of critiquing mainstream film is only possible where the concerns of the two "camps" overlap. For instance, Deren's radical reconfiguration of continuity editing conventions in films like *Meshes of the Afternoon* (1943) and *At Land* (1944) can only be recognized in comparison to popular films in which continuity editing is used in the standard realistic manner. Warhol's stable of superstars can only be meaningful to a viewer who is at least marginally aware of the Hollywood star system. Filmmakers and critics have often tacitly characterized avant-garde films as "films like any other," as embodying fundamental elements shared across cinematic modes, albeit more directly than in popular films (e.g., Tony Conrad's *The Flicker* [1966], Michael Snow's *Wavelength* [1967], and Ernie Gehr's *History* [1970]). The tendency of avant-garde filmmakers to revisit popular film history, as in the work of Ken Jacobs and Bill Morrison, further indicates a sense of shared tradition, even if these filmmakers see their work as radically separate from that of their mainstream counterparts.

In identifying this level of specificity, I am not offering my own definition of cinema. I wish to be very clear that this book does not put forth an ontology whereby expanded works can be made to "count" as genuine instances of cinema. Rather, my project is to trace such ontological conceptions through the discourses of avant-garde film culture. By the logic of these discourses, works of expanded cinema were indeed considered to be cinema. Thus, my isolation of "cinematically specific" elements is not an assertion that said elements constitute "the essence of cinema" in some strict ontological sense, but a synthesis of discourses on cinema produced by filmmakers and critics.

Before proceeding, I want to make two further points about my distinction between a medium and an art form. First, it might strike some readers as roughly similar to the one made by a number of theorists between a "physical medium" and an "artistic medium." The former is simply a raw material, a "stuff" that may or may not

---

[24] Hollis Frampton, "A Pentagram for Conjuring the Narrative," in Sitney, ed., *The Avant-Garde Film*, p. 284.

be used to produce a work of art; for instance, painting a house is not artmaking, while painting a picture is, even though the material being used is the same in each instance. What allows us to identify a particular use of a physical material as a work of art are the artistic conventions to which that material has been subject, which are independent of that material, the argument goes. David Davies summarizes the distinction:

> In the case of paintings, for example, the physical medium consists of pigments (oil, tempera, water colors) applied to a surface (wood, canvas, glass), while the artistic medium is "a purposeful system of brushstrokes." Similarly, in talking about dance, the physical medium of bodily movements is to be distinguished from the artistic medium of articulated steps . . . The artist characteristically works *in* a particular artistic medium when *working* a physical medium.[25]

Krauss's work on what she calls the "post-medium condition" takes up this distinction between physical and artistic medium. She argues that many contemporary artists, finding traditional art forms like painting and sculpture to be exhausted, have invented their own mediums by discovering aesthetic possibilities in obsolete technologies not originally designed to make art. These artists create systems of formal conventions out of the internal structural logic of such "artless" physical mediums; while these conventions—"*artistic* media"—are related to their physical substrates— "*physical* media"—they are not identical, according to Krauss. That is, art is not defined by a physical material, but by formal systems that may be generated within them. She cites the work of James Coleman, who has worked with slide-tape machines first used in educational and industrial contexts, which is to say *not* to make art. Now that digital slide presentation programs like PowerPoint have rendered the slide-tape machine obsolete, it may be rediscovered and repurposed by artists like Coleman, whose work brings out aesthetic potentials not intentionally designed into the technology. This act of invention is more than "the mere adoption of a novel technical support," Krauss writes, but the creation and re-creation, over time, of a singular artistic tradition, limited to the work of a single artist but nonetheless providing the necessary condition for the recognition and appreciation of artworks: a base upon which to "test the meaningfulness of forms":[26] "For centuries," Krauss asserts, "it was only within and against the tradition encoded by a medium that innovation could be measured, just as it was in relation to its reservoir of meanings that new ranges of feeling could be tested."[27]

The relevance of the distinction between physical and artistic media to expanded cinema should be clear. The idea that cinema is not identical with, or constrained

---

[25] David Davies, "Medium in Art," in Jerrold Levinson, ed., *The Oxford Handbook of Aesthetics* (Oxford: Oxford University Press, 2005), p. 183.

[26] Rosalind Krauss, ". . . And Then Turn Away?," p. 9.

[27] Ibid., p. 5.

by, a specific physical material is the core principle of expanded cinema. And Krauss's argument that obsolescence is prerequisite for an industrial technology to become the basis for a new artistic medium has obvious bearing on cinema given that art form's basis in such technologies, and that the film medium is reportedly all but obsolete. The problem with the concept of artistic medium, however, is that its defenders are often unclear in defining it, and about how general or specific it is. For example, identifying the artistic medium of painting as "a purposeful system of brushstrokes," in addition to returning us to a physical material with which some, though not all, paintings are made, also seems quite limiting. What of color, the organization of elements with the frame, and so on? It also raises the question of how many such systems there might be and whether different systems constitute different artistic media. Do the paintings of Giatto di Bondone, Charles Courtney Curran, and Helen Frankenthaler each instantiate different artistic media? Can an artistic medium be unique to a single work or artist, an intrinsic norm not applicable to works by any other artists? Krauss argues that Coleman has invented his own artistic medium, which seems to suggest that these media can be limited in that way, though in the same essay she identifies picture novels, comic books, and films as influences on Coleman's aesthetics. If some of the formal conventions of these art forms are to be found in Coleman's work, then should we say that he works in multiple artistic media in each piece? Doesn't any work of art, and any art form, mobilize multiple conventions, some inextricable from specific physical media, others more or less independent of them? With this in mind, what is the artistic medium of cinema? In any film we might see systems of editing, cinematography, lighting, and temporal organization, not to mention systems deriving from the physical material of celluloid or digital video. Certainly cinema exceeds any single formal system.

My point here is not to resolve these questions about artistic media, but to distinguish that concept from the broader notion of "art form" in this book. An art form is not the same as a particular formal system or convention, but comprises instead many such systems, beyond any one instantiation or specific systematization of its broad range of aesthetic possibilities. We might think of cinema as being defined by a loose cluster of traits or qualities, which returns us once more to such things as editing, cinematography, light and color, and the temporal articulation of shots. These are not systems, but broad spheres of possibility that accommodate a very wide range of specific systems and conventions that utilize these traits in many different ways. Art forms are also social and discursive, which do not seem to be traits of artistic media as theorists normally use that term. They are created and sustained by the collective action of artists, critics, and appreciators who self-identify with them and invest in them personally, often across the distinctions between narrower branches within art forms (e.g., avant-garde film, art cinema, Hollywood film, documentary). They are made up not only of works that systematize aesthetic traits, but of assertions as well, discourses that make the contours of an art form visible, often by comparing and contrasting them with other art forms. This play of independence and interdependence is central to this book, as is the inextricability of the material, formal, social, and discursive in the creation of art forms.

The second point to bear in mind concerning the distinction between a physical medium and an art form is that it does not entail an absolute break between the two. While specific media do not strictly delimit art forms, they do play a critical and often underappreciated role in shaping them. Part I will set forth this argument in more detail, at least as it has been advanced from within avant-garde cinema. Here I only wish to signal the importance of specific physical media, and particularly "celluloid" film, for expanded cinema. Insofar as expanded cinema has been theorized as the earliest manifestation of what has come to be called "new media," my revisionist account of expanded cinema also criticizes some of the tenets of new media theory, particularly that field's tendency to downplay the importance and autonomy of specific media and art forms. This book at once revises the concept of medium specificity and defends it, illustrating its continued validity for filmmaking and cinema scholarship alike, even where the most expanded, "furthest out" forms of cinema are concerned. I agree with Murray Smith's claim, in his own defense of medium specificity:

> artworks are by definition objects which are realized through some material substance and process, that is, some "medium," the work thus becoming available for perception by an audience. As Hegel put it, the work of art is the "the sensuous embodiment of the idea." The medium is the material bridgehead between the artist and the appreciator; it is what allows the artwork to be sensed.[28]

By "idea," Smith means the concept an individual artwork represents, implying that such an idea is not fully separable from the manner in which it is realized within a physical medium. I suggest that we can take this premise further, extending the constitutive function of physical media to the very "idea" of cinema itself, not only to the perception of a particular work of art but to the recognition of an art form. Throughout this book, in my discussions of both expanded cinema works and non-expanded avant-garde films, I track the dialectic between "liberation" from the familiar structure of the film medium and references back to that structure. Film—understood, again, as an aggregate medium—has provided avant-garde filmmakers with a rich field of metaphors, which become the basis for works that at once exceed film and reaffirm it. As Pavle Levi has argued with reference to both the historical avant-garde and filmmakers working in the 1960s and 1970s:

> many of the most innovative 1960s and 1970s endeavors to differentiate the concept of cinema from the actual cinematographic apparatus were at least as strongly expressive of their practitioners' radicalized—even perverse—*fidelity* to the notion of medium-specificity.[29]

---

[28] Murray Smith, "My Dinner with Noël; or, Can We Forget the Medium?" *Film Studies* 8 (Summer 2006), p. 142.

[29] Pavle Levi, *Cinema by Other Means* (Oxford: Oxford University Press, 2012), p. 29.

Levi's point is that, in their desire to produce work that did not employ the film medium but was nonetheless recognizably "cinematic," many avant-garde filmmakers worked from an abstract "ideal of cinema," a concept of the art form that could be called "dematerialized" in that it did not require one specific physical medium for its embodiment. In considering precursors to expanded cinema, Levi identifies works like Raoul Hausmann's newspaper collage *Gurk* (1919) and Aleksandar Vučo and Dušan Matic's collage construction *The Frenzied Marble* (1930) as examples of the "ideal of cinema" in non-filmic artworks. He argues, however, that such works evince an "unorthodox devotion to medium-specificity" by referencing, even mimicking, structural features of the cinematographic apparatus.[30] This is because the idea of cinema as art form was only fully legible in the light of that apparatus; though not absolutely bound to the film medium, nor was the art of cinema entirely independent of it. Referencing creative historical reversals like Bazin's, Levi writes:

> For if the Idea, or the dream, of cinema may, indeed, be said to have preceded and motivated the invention of the film medium, it seems equally necessary to recognize, in a true dialectical reversal . . . that this Idea acquired sufficient conceptual precision—that it gained its own, albeit immaterial, specificity—only after the cinematographic apparatus had already been invented.[31]

I would add that if the ideal of cinema gains precision from the material of film, something like the reverse is also true: the material of film gains layers of abstract meaning from the idea of cinema. One way this process has developed is by filmmakers and historians identifying an ever-growing field of forms and practices as part of cinema's prehistory, including magic lantern shows, camera obscuras, Victorian-era optical illusion and motion toys, and prehistoric art. These could only be brought into cinema's genealogy in retrospect, after the invention of the film medium and the standardization of cinematic exhibition, in a process Levi calls "retrograde remediation."[32] This retroactively evolving genealogy introduces an expanding family tree of cinematic objects and experiences, to be sure, but just as importantly it links the machines of cinema as we know it to the expanded field of historical associations linked to these objects and experiences. The result is a model of medium specificity that invests cinematic media with a much wider range of meanings than critics have typically attributed to them.

Consider the following interpretation of Andy Warhol's *Sleep* (1963) written in 1964 by Metropolitan Museum curator Henry Geldzahler:

> In painting in the past fifty years we have become increasingly aware of the limitations and special qualities of the medium: texture, two-dimensionality,

---

[30] Ibid., p. 31.

[31] Ibid., pp. 31–32.

[32] Ibid., pp. 42–43.

brushstroke, etc. And Warhol's film, in which we are constantly aware of the filmic process, sometimes even seeing the frames that end the reels, frames that any so-phisticated movie maker would edit out, makes us aware exactly of the limitations and qualities of film itself.[33]

Take this as an example of the standard application of medium-specificity theory in cinema; avant-garde films, in one way or another, make us aware of the physical qual-ities of the film medium. Whatever content we see represented on screen, we also see the structure of film itself, in flash frames, emulsion grain, the flicker of the shutter, and so on. These express no other meaning than the literal: "this is film." Put another way, the physical elements of the film medium are made meaningful in and of them-selves in the standard version of medium-specific criticism. They represent nothing; they simply are. However, if artists and critics invest physical media with deeper, more abstract meanings, then medium-specific interpretations are no longer limited to the literal proposition that film X is solely about the material properties of its me-dium. I show in this book that avant-garde filmmakers have done just this, "concep-tualizing" the film medium, making its material elements representative of broader artistic and political meanings and values. These have enabled much richer and sub-tler medium-specific interpretations than the sort represented by the above passage.

An anecdote Annette Michelson shares in a 1974 essay on Paul Sharits provides a paradigm of this more robust interpretive framework. Michelson recounts her struggle to choose just the right image for the cover of a catalogue for "New Forms in Film," an exhibition of recent North American avant-garde cinema screened at the Lausanne Museum of Art in Montreux, Switzerland in 1974 (fig. I.14). What single image could possible serve as an emblem of "a decade's most significant work?"

I faltered, while my printer waited . . . until a friend in softest perfidy suggested, "And why not an empty film frame, its shape and composition that of the screen itself?" To which my reply, exploding in the immediate relief of laughter, could only be: "But then, whose frame or screen is it to be? To which filmmaker do I go, to Brakhage, Snow, Jacobs, or Frampton? To Breer, Mekas, Kubelka, Sharits?"[34]

Michelson reminds us of both the extent to which avant-garde cinema has taken the materials of filmmaking as its symbols and the diverse ways they have used these materials. The empty frame is never just a frame but Brakhage's frame, or Frampton's, or Kubelka's, each one representative of a distinct vision of its meanings and effects. It symbolizes not a singularity but a plurality. Appeal to the notion of medium

---

[33] Henry Geldzahler, "Some Notes on Sleep," *Film Culture* 32 (1964), p. 13.
[34] Annette Michelson, "Paul Sharits and the Critique of Illusionism: An Introduction," *Film Culture* 65–66 (1978), p. 83. This essay originally appeared in *Projected Images: Peter Campus, Rockne Krebs, Paul Sharits, Michael Snow, Ted Victoria, Robert Whitman*, catalogue for an exhibition at the Walker Art Center, Minneapolis, MN, September 21–November 3, 1974.

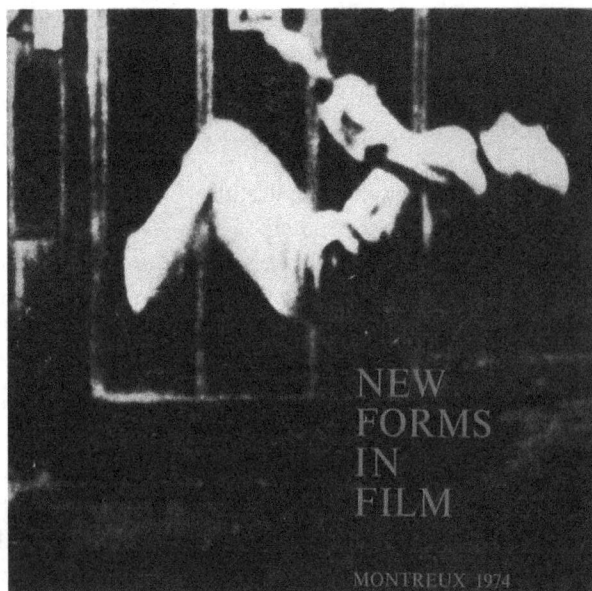

Fig. I.14. "New Forms in Film" catalogue cover featuring a still from *Tom, Tom, the Piper's Son* (Ken Jacobs, 1969)
Imprimereie Corbaz 1974.

specificity, to avant-garde cinema's reflexive attention to its materials, need not flatten out this diverse field of possibilities.

Talk of the dialectic between "the material of film and the idea of cinema" should not lose sight of the fact that the former has been construed in much broader terms than simply the nuts and bolts of celluloid, cameras, and projectors.[35] By the late 1960s, an expanded view of materialism reached beyond the physical stuff of the film medium to the social and institutional aspects of cinema that inform our experience and understanding of it. As elements of a revised notion of cinema's materiality, they have also shaped filmmaking practice and expanded cinema. This leads us to the third level of cinematic specificity: that of a distinct branch of cinema history, in this case avant-garde/experimental film. All of the terms used to designate this tradition have come under fire: "avant-garde" for being elitist and too historically specific; "experimental" for its scientific connotation and the suggestion that filmmakers are "just experimenting" rather than producing mature work; and "underground" because that term seems appropriate only for certain branches of the tradition (e.g., punk and no wave films, the "Cinema of Transgression"). But whatever objections have been

---

[35] The phrase "the material of film and the idea of cinema" comes from my own earlier work on paracinema, a branch of expanded cinema that will get further attention elsewhere in this book (and upon which Pavle Levi is building in the section of his book cited in note 29). See Jonathan Walley, "The Material of Film and the Idea of Cinema: Contrasting Practices in Sixties and Seventies Avant-Garde Film," *October* 103 (Winter 2003), pp. 15–30.

raised to the labels, no one disputes the existence of the cinema to which they refer. I will use "avant-garde" and "experimental" interchangeably to refer to this tradition, which I identify as a "mode of film practice."

David Bordwell, Janet Staiger, and Kristin Thompson introduced the term "mode of film practice" in their groundbreaking book *The Classical Hollywood Cinema: Film Style and Mode of Production to 1960*. It refers to the cluster of historically bound institutions, practices, and concepts that form a specific context within which cinematic media are used:

> The concept of a mode of film practice situates textual processes in their most pertinent and proximate collective context. This context includes both a historically defined group of films and the material practices that create and sustain that group . . . A mode of film practice, then, consists of a set of widely held stylistic norms sustained by and sustaining an integral mode of film production . . . these formal and stylistic norms will be created, shaped, and supported within a mode of film production—a characteristic ensemble of economic aims, a specific division of labor, and particular ways of conceiving and executing the work of filmmaking.[36]

The authors note that a mode of film practice is not limited to the concepts and methods that animate production, but extends to the channels of distribution, venues and conventions of exhibition, and viewing strategies that characterize each mode and distinguish one from another. For instance, Bordwell identifies art cinema (as in films by Godard, Fellini, Bergman) as a mode of film practice "possessing a definite historical existence, a set of formal conventions, and implicit viewing procedures" distinct from classical Hollywood cinema.[37] Smith has applied the term to avant-garde cinema, identifying it as a mode distinguishable from both Hollywood and art cinema: "Such a practice is defined by an integrated set of economic, institutional, and aesthetic norms."[38] A mode of film practice, then, is a historical, institutional, and discursive context constituted by norms of production, distribution, exhibition and reception of cinematic art. These four categories interact. The ideas, statements, and activities of artists inform critical reception, which in turn feeds back into the pool of concepts to which artists relate. Assumptions about the exhibition contexts in which works will be seen affect both artistic production and critical reception. Changes in media technologies, or novel uses of existing technologies (a practice common in expanded cinema) at once shape and are shaped by the aims of artists.

There are *cinemas* rather than cinema, then, different cinematic traditions identifiable formally, institutionally, and historically. While there can be areas of aesthetic overlap between them, the larger scope of their historical and institutional identities

---

[36] David Bordwell, Janet Staiger, and Kristin Thompson, *The Classical Hollywood Cinema: Film Style and Mode of Production to 1960* (New York: Columbia University Press, 1985), p. xiv.

[37] David Bordwell, "Art Cinema as a Mode of Film Practice," *Film Criticism* 1, no. 4 (Fall 1979), p. 56.

[38] Murray Smith, "Modernism and the Avant-Gardes," in John Hill and Pamela Church Gibson, eds., *The Oxford Guide to Film Studies* (Oxford: Oxford University Press, 1998), p. 395.

differentiate them, providing backdrops against which to view apparent similarities in their formal tendencies. We can pick out several distinct modes of film practice: commercial studio cinema, documentary, the international "art" or "festival" cinema, avant-garde film, and artists' film/video, the latter denoting moving image works produced within the context of the art world by artists like Matthew Barney, Shirin Neshat, Douglas Gordan, and Tacita Dean. Avant-garde cinema has long staked out its unique identity primarily in contradistinction to "Hollywood," that word functioning as shorthand for popular/commercial cinema in general. I will show that avant-garde film culture has also defined itself against moving image art in the gallery context.[39] The relationship between these two modes bears particularly on works of expanded cinema, which have often occupied gallery and museum spaces and taken on forms assumed to be those of the other arts.

I will elaborate upon the characteristics of avant-garde cinema as mode of film practice throughout this book, making an argument for their significance for expanded cinema. A brief list of the most prominent traits will suffice for the moment. The working methods of avant-garde filmmakers can best be described as artisanal; production is independent of the kind of economic structures and division of labor found in most other modes, which is why the term "filmmaker" is indeed appropriate for the avant-garde. Roles such as director, screenwriter, cinematographer, editor, and producer are simply not part of what Ed Small calls the "acollaborative" approach to production in avant-garde film.[40] This helps explain another key trait, which is avant-garde film's preoccupation with the concept of cinematic specificity and the specificity of the film medium, an investment in these ideas and in the material of film itself, which are much less evident in other modes. That the individual avant-garde filmmaker is responsible for the totality of production, sometimes even hand-processing and personally projecting their work, requires a broad mastery of cinematic craft distinct from other modes, which delegate specified tasks to more narrowly focused professionals. Avant-garde filmmakers therefore have a very different perspective on that craft, a depth of involvement with the cinema's materials and processes that finds its expression in a medium-specific, reflexive cinema.

Turning to distribution and exhibition, avant-garde film culture does not conceive of the film print (or digital file, or any other object in which a cinematic work might be embodied) as an art object in the sense of something with market value in and of itself. This is true of other modes of film practice, as well, with the important exception being moving image work in the art world. There, despite the fact that any moving image medium affords easy copying, the aura of individual film prints or digital discs is maintained via enforced scarcity. These objects are handled more or less like any other object in the art market, their value determined in large part by the notoriety of

---

[39] Also see Jonathan Walley, "Modes of Film Practice in the Avant-Garde," in Tanya Leighton, ed., *Art and the Moving Image: A Critical Reader* (London: Tate Publishing, 2008), pp. 182–199.

[40] Ed Small, *Direct Theory: Experimental Film/Video as Major Genre* (Carbondale: Southern Illinois University Press, 1994).

the artist. Film prints, DVDs, or digital files of avant-garde films, on the other hand, are rented to screening venues, either by cooperatively run distribution companies or individually by the filmmakers themselves. These differences in perception of the cinematic work as physical object will come under consideration in chapters 4 and 5. Avant-garde films are generally exhibited outside of commercial cinema venues, including screening spaces dedicated to experimental film, museums and galleries, university classrooms, film festivals, and microcinemas. What these varied spaces have in common is that they usually provide contextualizing information. While not necessarily required, it has become standard practice in avant-garde cinema and an expectation of audiences. Concomitantly, the viewing expectations among audiences are quite different than in other modes. This is not to say that the audience for avant-garde cinema is literally made up of different people than the audience for popular cinema or art films, but that the exhibition practices of that cinema in effect creates a different kind of audience. For one thing, that audience is usually both expected and willing to be more critically engaged with the work rather than receiving it passively. The nature of avant-garde film practice is such that it allows a closer, more self-aware relationship between filmmaker and viewer. Filmmakers are more accessible; they are not celebrities like Quentin Tarantino or Martin Scorsese, and are part of a cinematic tradition in which exchanges between artist and audience are common and part of the point. Frequently the filmmakers themselves are the source of contextualizing information at a screening.

Of course there are exceptions to this general outline of traits. Several works of expanded cinema complicate this model, which is not the same as saying they upend it or prove the concept of modes of film practice invalid. Works of expanded cinema designed for gallery spaces and/or presented as objects (as in "art objects") are an example, but it is in the very act of questioning or otherwise troubling some of avant-garde film's characteristic traits that such works of expanded cinema become interesting, and make the idea of cinematic modes all the more useful.

The specificity of a particular mode of film practice sits somewhere between the very narrow specificity of a physical medium and the more general sense of the identity of an art form. Broadly defined features of "the cinematic," like editing, are more sharply defined by the activities of filmmakers working within a specific mode. Depending upon the significance of medium specificity within a given mode of film practice, conceptions of these features may be further honed. In fact, the very perception of a physical medium differs from one mode to another, which is to say that "the film medium" is in part constituted discursively within each mode of film practice. Thus, these three levels of specificity interpenetrate, providing us with a complex tripartite framework though which we can interpret individual works and general trends in avant-garde cinema. I analyze works of expanded cinema according to this framework, taking them not merely as propositions about the physical nature of film or the qualities and effects of the art of cinema, but as assertions of avant-garde cinema's central concepts and defining values as well. Consider projection performance, for example, a form of expanded cinema in which the filmmaker's live manipulation

Fig. I.15. Bruce McClure, 16mm film projection performance at OK-LÀ, Montreal, July 14, 2018.
Photo credit Yannick Grandmont.

of projectors is itself the act of creation (fig. I.15). Projection performance is medium specific in emphasizing the unique mechanical and material facets of film and projector. It reflects on the nature of cinema as an art form by reconceiving it as performative rather than mechanical and automatic, challenging boundaries between art forms, often through analogies to early cinematic practices like itinerant projection. This latter rhetorical strategy suggests the shared heritage of all cinemas, before such distinctions as "narrative/non-narrative," "fictional/documentary," and "popular/avant-garde" came to be. Finally, projection performance enacts certain historically consistent traits of exhibition and film/filmmaker/audience relations that are unique to avant-garde cinema as a mode of film practice, putting these values on display all the more vividly by making cinema a live performance (fig. I.16).

The initial period of expanded cinema coincided with a moment during which avant-garde film consolidated itself as a cinematic culture. Certainly avant-garde films had existed prior to this, but an international movement toward developing an institutional infrastructure for this cinema reached a state of critical mass during the early-to-mid-1960s. This was one manifestation of the general rise in cinema's status as a legitimate art form, and was paralleled by the growth of film festivals, the creation of critical language that took film art seriously, and the rise of cinema studies in academia. Similar developments unfolded within avant-garde cinema; by the start of the 1960s, avant-garde film had its own distribution companies and exhibition venues, critical journals, defining historical and theoretical explications, and a canon of major

Fig. I.16. Sally Golding and Spatial, *Spatial-Golding* (2016). Performance documentation. 16mm film projectors, motorized shutters, camera flash units, laboratory strobe light, mixing desk feedback, custom software, synthesizers. Serralves Museum of Contemporary Art, Porto, 2016.
Photograph by Pedro Figueiredo, Fundação de Serralves, Porto. Courtesy of Sally Golding.

artists and works. Important art critics wrote about it in the pages of *Artforum* and the *New York Times*, addressing it in the same language with which they would modern painting, literature, or music (and with the same reverence). In this respect, the validating critical discourses that coalesced around avant-garde cinema were especially interesting. On the one hand, they drew analogies between cinema and the other arts meant to demonstrate the artistic worthiness of the former; but on the other hand, they asserted cinema's artistic autonomy by identifying *uniquely cinematic* aesthetic traits. Avant-garde filmmakers have straddled these two poles, making films equivalent to contemporaneous movements in the other arts while exploring and promoting the idea of the "specifically cinematic." Specificity itself was an inter-arts concept, a paradox of which numerous filmmakers have taken note, as in Maya Deren's well-known proclamation:

> If cinema is to take its place beside the others as a full-fledged art form, it must cease to merely record realities that owe nothing of their actual existence to the film instrument. Instead, it must create a total experience so much out of the very nature of the instrument as to be inseparable from its means.[41]

[41] Maya Deren, "Cinematography: The Creative Use of Reality," in Sitney, ed., *The Avant-Garde Film*, p. 72.

Paul Sharits made much the same point just over a decade later, taking note more explicitly of the irony of artistic "self-definition:"

> If film is to be "an art," it will measure itself in terms of the maturity, rigor, and complexity of the "other arts" (advanced painting, dance, sculpture, music, and so on). Although the specific problems of film (temporal) are not the same as the problems of, say, sculpture (spatial), there seems to be some general aesthetic interests shared by contemporary arts (one of which is, "paradoxically" self-definition— "Painting as the subject of painting," etc.).[42]

The history of avant-garde cinema begins with artists using film to extend work they had done as painters, sculptors, composers, photographers, and poets. It continues through the emergence of designations like "poetic films" and "cine-plastics," through the promotion of avant-garde films by art world institutions like the Museum of Modern Art, into the high modernist period in which it took up the endeavor of defining itself in relation to the other arts. Contemporary developments include the increased presence of film and video in art galleries and hybrid film-digital practices by avant-garde filmmakers. Expanded cinema embodies this complex, sometimes contradictory history, and so gives us the richest possible case study of it.

Histories and Modalities of Expansion

Cinema Expanded is in two parts. Part I, "Histories of Expanded Cinema(s)," offers a historical account of expanded cinema from its emergence in the early 1960s to the present day, which has seen a resurgence of interest in expanded cinema among artists and scholars alike. Chapter 1, "The Two Expanded Cinemas," covers the 1960s and 1970s; chapter 2, "Expanded Cinema Revis(it)ed" picks up in the mid-1990s, when a new generation of avant-garde filmmakers once again began experimenting with expanded forms and the generation that had pioneered expanded cinema revisited their earlier work, in some cases producing new work.

Part II, "Modes of Expansion," divides expanded cinema into three broad and overlapping categories, each corresponding to another art form: cinema as performance, as object (i.e., "sculptural" object), and as idea or concept. Framing my argument in terms of these artistic categories allows me plumb the depths of expanded cinema's process of negotiation between cinema's independence and its multiple connections to the other arts.

This negotiation is both an overarching historical process traceable from the 1960s to the present, and a feature of specific works of expanded cinema that embody this dialectic on a smaller scale. My book provides a historical framework for the full

---

[42] Paul Sharits, "Words per Page," *Film Culture* 65–66 (1978), p. 29. Originally printed in *Afterimage* 4 (Autumn 1972).

sweep of expanded cinema history and an analytical framework for illuminating individual works, artists, and critical writings. Hence, the two parts of *Cinema Expanded* are two sides of the same coin, each end of expanded cinema's defining ontological and institutional dialectic. Structuring the book into these two parts is intended to throw this feature of expanded cinema into relief.

Readers unfamiliar with expanded cinema will find an orientation in the first two chapters, a survey of the history of expanded cinema that establishes context for the more localized historical arguments I make later. These chapters trace the history of the term and survey important early writings on the subject, illuminating its changing contexts and analyzing several prominent works. Central to this orientation, however, is a re-orientation of sorts, as I restore avant-garde film as expanded cinema's most proximate historical context, providing a new account of the stakes of artistic expansion and new moving image media for that particular mode of film practice. This re-orientation is the basis for another revisionist move I make: identifying three distinct historical phases of expanded cinema. During the initial phase, the term "expanded cinema" was more or less synonymous with "intermedia" and related ideas of hybridity, the dissolution of artistic boundaries, and the attack upon traditional art forms. Within a few years, however, the term was reclaimed by filmmakers whose work extended avant-garde cinema's tradition of specifying the cinematic. This phase of expanded cinema lasted through the 1970s into the first few years of the 1980s. A third wave began in the mid-1990s and continues as of this writing. This wave once again emerges from the theory and practice of avant-garde cinema. As such, it reflects skepticism toward contemporary ideas about new media, media convergence, and the end of cinema as we know it.

I characterize the transition from first phase to second as a shift towards a more "cine-centric" notion of expanded cinema, a turn from centrifugal forms that escaped cinema to a more centripetal one. This introduces the historical process of negotiation between cinema's specificity and its connections to the other arts, a process that works of expanded cinema enact. And a critical dimension of this process was a perceived tension between two ontological conceptions of cinema—as material (as in "materialist") and as ephemeral ("immaterial" or "dematerialized"). We can think of specific instances of expanded cinema as sitting somewhere on a continuum between utterly material and elusively ephemeral, of playing out a back and forth between these two qualities in myriad ways. Sharits described this in terms of an "object/projection dualism":

in film [in contrast to other art forms] we have a case where we can experience both a changing and enduring existence—we can look at the "same" film as an *object*, before or after projection (and it is not a "score"; it is "the film"), and as temporal *process*, while it is being projected . . . This equivocality of object/projection is further complicated when we admit that there are occasions when we are looking at a screen and we don't know whether we are or are not seeing "a film"; we cannot distinguish "the movie" from "the projection."[43]

---

[43] Ibid., p. 35.

More recently, projection performers Sandra Gibson and Luis Recoder expressed this duality in terms of the metaphysical and phenomenological, invoking the metaphor of life and death that resonates with film and cinema's current situation as obsolete forms:

> To ask about cinema is not the same to ask about film. Cinema is the metaphysical idea (of cinema) and not the phenomenological "thing itself." It is bereft of materiality in its escape into a dream-like immateriality. Cinema is not film. It is the death of film (from the moment darkness settles in, the materials disappear in the dark fabric of an abysmal masking device). Film is not cinema. Film goes up against the grain (but it has no grain) of cinema. It is the rotting flesh made up of bones and other corporal beasts lurking in the dark, suspended in a murky substance.[44]

Sharits's version of film's object/projection dualism is literal, Gibson and Recoder's metaphorical. Either way, the reciprocal movement they describe between the material and ephemeral is a key factor in expanded cinema's formal mutability, its charting of the limits of cinema, and articulation of its interfaces with the other arts.

Part II follows on these themes of specificity, materiality, and ephemerality, and the negotiation of cinema's relationship to other art forms. Chapters 3 through 6 examine three modalities of expanded cinema: cinema as performance, object, and concept. While not organized chronologically, each chapter pays close attention to the ways that these modalities of expanded cinema have changed over time, in relation to art historical developments, shifts in moving image technology, and major trends in the fields of cinema studies and art history. My central argument really takes shape in these chapters, as they survey works of expanded cinema that take forms thought to belong to performance, sculpture and installation, and conceptual art.

Live cinematic performance, the subject of chapter 3, was arguably the first form of expanded cinema. Cinematic performance occupies the territory between the materiality of film as object/technology and the ephemerality of cinema in projection. The tactility of film and projector are often on display, as is the performer. But alongside these markers of cinema's objecthood and physical presence is the ephemerality of live performance. Non-repeatable, site-specific, and aleatory instead of mechanistically automatic, expanded cinema performance is centered upon the moment when the material of film is transformed into the far less tactile play of light, shadow, and illusion, and when objects give way to processes and experiences.

Performance's integration into cinema was initially a reflection of "the blurring of art and life," to use Allan Kaprow's phrase, which was one of the basic tenets of intermedia and the expanded arts. In a very general sense, this ethos continued to inform cinematic performance in the later phases of expanded cinema. The presence of the filmmaker, engaging in an act of filmmaking before the audience's eyes, refuses

---

[44] Sandra Gibson and Luis Recoder, "Cinema/Film," *World Picture Journal* 2 (Autumn 2008), n.p.

the absorbed, hermetically sealed illusionary world on screen, situating cinema very much in the room, in the present, in the real world. But unlike film-theater hybrids of the first wave of expanded cinema, subsequent projection performances claimed a performative dimension for cinema itself, rather than thinking of it as an alien form grafted onto film in a new intermedia format. Thus, projection performance became an expression of cinematic specificity.

Chapters 4 and 5 look at works of expanded cinema that emphasize what could be called cinema's "sculptural" properties, particularly its physicality and spatiality. The sculptural characteristics of such works, which often requires that they be exhibited in the "white cube" of the gallery rather than the "black box" of the movie theater, suggests that they are intermedia hybrids of cinema and sculpture. But this hybridity is only apparent, I argue. In fact, these works were asserted and understood within the context of avant-garde film culture as primarily, if not solely, cinematic.

Chapter 4 addresses works of expanded cinema that isolate one material element of the film medium, such as the filmstrip, screen, or projector, removing it from its place in a system of machines and displaying it as an object in its own right. In doing so, such works break apart the unified machine of the cinematic apparatus, pulling the objects that constitute that apparatus out of the shadows. In normal cinematic exhibition, these objects disappear, replaced by the ephemeral experience of watching the illusory images of light and shadow that they invisibly produce. Object-based works of expanded cinema reverse this process, returning the sense of mass, weight, and gravity to the materials of the medium and forcing a new consideration of the possibilities film offers for direct, sensuous physical experience. These include direct displays of filmstrips and projectors.

In other cases, filmmakers developed strategies for heightening awareness of cinema's spatiality, and of the fact that the entire apparatus of cinema indeed occupied real space beyond the illusory "space" on screen. The major form here is film installation, which, rather than exploding the cinematic apparatus as the above-mentioned object-based works do, brings that apparatus out of the dark, presenting it in its totality for contemplation and analysis in a way that conventional film exhibition intentionally thwarts.

Chapters 4 and 5 consider major historical factors during both the early-to-mid '70s and the last two decades that informed the conception of cinema as object. During the 1960s and '70s, the attention given to cinema's physical properties was related to the anti-illusionist aims of avant-garde filmmakers for whom "materiality" included the very space of cinematic exhibition and the ideological ramifications of that space: the very term "cinematic apparatus" develops from this movement. More recently, the impending obsolescence of analog film and the presumed ephemerality of digital media have resulted in the former's physical or object properties taking on new meaning and importance.

Chapter 6 examines works of expanded cinema that push even further into the territory of the ephemeral and the transitory explored by live cinema. This can be called "conceptual cinema." "Conceptual," here, refers to the belief that cinema was ultimately a conceptual phenomenon even when it took forms that seemed decidedly material. The term, or variants of it, was used in the 1960s and '70s to refer to "imaginary" films, films planned or written but purposely never executed, unprojected or unprojectable films, and objects of cinematic ephemera—on paper, for instance. There are parallels between such conceptual cinematic works and conceptual art. In both cases, concepts, intentions, imagination, and language are taken to be as constitutive of art works as materials and physical processes. The objects of the film medium were, and continue to be, de-centered in favor of these less tangible conceptual or discursive dimensions of cinematic practice.

While conceptual art will be a point of reference, I will also show that a concept-based ontology of cinema emerged organically from within the avant-garde film world. That is, it should not be thought of simply as a delayed response by filmmakers to prior art world developments, as if playing catch-up with their fellow artists. And, perhaps ironically, though conceptual cinema seems to take cinema's ephemerality as far as it can go, it also tends to assume cinematic essences, returning such works to the firmer ground of a specific art form. The works in this chapter best exemplify what the cine-centric second and third phases of expanded cinema have in common: they embody a complex paradigm of cinema that accommodated expansion but prevented complete dissolution, making each work legible as an instance of the cinematic in spite of their wide range of formal traits: performative, sculptural, conceptual.

These three modalities—cinema as performance, object, and concept—are broad heuristics, general frameworks for the analysis of individual works and larger trends in the history of expanded cinema. They are meant to be open and adaptable, encompassing a variety of forms and practices. They will be sharpened when put into the service of specific analyses and rounded out with historical context and further theoretical concepts. They are also not mutually exclusive. Their flexibility and overlapping edges are intended to accommodate expanded cinema's heterogeneity, shifting historical meaning, and frequently paradoxical ontological status.

Disciplines, Traditions, and Limits

Moderating a panel discussion on expanded cinema in 1965, Henry Geldzahler argued for the most open and accommodating possible definition of the term:

> The nice thing about the topic "Expanded Cinema" is that it makes everybody feel like he's talking about his own work . . . I think the phrase "expanded cinema" isn't something that should pin us down . . . There are several directions in which a phrase like "expanded cinema" can move us but I think we should try to move in all those directions.[45]

---

[45] From a transcript of the "Expanded Cinema Symposium" in *Film Culture*, no. 43 (Winter 1966), p. 1. This was a special edition of *Film Culture* called "Expanded Arts."

Nearly 40 years later, art historian Liz Kotz lamented that, as a result of such a position, expanded cinema had yet to be adequately theorized or historicized. It was, in a word, undisciplined:

> [the] quest for more diverse and robust histories that would allow for a fuller account of multiscreen and performative cinemas to emerge is often unable to articulate a set of terms—historical trajectories, defining conditions or artistic principles—that would give multiscreen work some kind of historical or aesthetic grounding: in effect, to provide it with some kind of discipline.[46]

While the ensuing decade has seen some progress on this score, one still finds significant resistance to the idea of "disciplining" expanded cinema, to use Kotz's words. This resistance is just part of the widespread skepticism toward both artistic and disciplinary specificity in cinema studies, art history, and media studies. Ironically, avant-garde cinema is one area in which filmmakers and scholars alike have sought to restore a sense of such specificity and connect expanded cinema to historical tradition. Recent scholarship on avant-garde film, including expanded cinema, has helped clarify what has become too fuzzily outlined, shoring up boundaries that have become too permeable and installing a sense of continuity between historical and contemporary work. That spirit very much animates this book. In belonging to everyone, expanded cinema has ultimately been claimed by no one. The position that expanded cinema—or cinema itself for that matter—is anything other than inherently hybrid, inter-art, multidisciplinary, and impossible to pin down is historically myopic. I hope to show that linking expanded cinema to tradition in no way deprives it of the categorical elusiveness prized by certain commentators. Traditional cinema need not be seen as an anchor; it has tended instead to function as a wide and varied set of enabling parameters within which most practitioners of expanded cinema have worked.

Hence, some of the work that was called "expanded cinema" in the mid-1960s will not appear in this book. Many forms of art involving light, projection, or moving images differentiated themselves from cinema, and were in many cases never intended as cinema in the first place. This is not an arbitrary narrowing of expanded cinema's definition, though it does make the category less unwieldy. I show that this revised notion of expanded cinema more accurately reflects how the term has been used since it first appeared, and what the term has really meant to filmmakers and critics in the avant-garde. Putting it simply, "expanded cinema" is reserved for works that, while indeed expanded, are nonetheless still intended, claimed, and legible *as cinema*. My ultimate goal is to show how, in periods of expansion, convergence, remediation, intermediality, and interdisciplinarity, *cinema persists*.

---

[46] Liz Kotz, "Disciplining Expanded Cinema," in Matthias Michalka, ed., *X-Screen: Film Installations and Actions in the 1960s and 1970s* (Cologne: Walther König, 2004), p. 44.

PART I
HISTORIES OF EXPANDED CINEMA(S)

1

The Two Expanded Cinemas

The aim of the revolution is, ironically, liberation from film itself. Already there have been experiments in which other materials—colored cellophane, old socks, draft cards—have been joined and projected. The best idea yet: look briefly into a bright light and rub your eyes. Eyeball cinema is as pure as it is personal, the last, abstract gas.

—Vincent Canby (1966)

So the avant-garde artists, who are working in a more classical tradition of cinema, are asking themselves what this new gush of light-motion art will do to their work. Have no fear, cried the captain! No good "old" art is ever invalidated by the "new" art ... with five, six, seven years perspective, these far-far-out anti-art works begin to fall into the same thousand-year-old treasury of all art.

—Jonas Mekas (1965)

A "Little History" of Expanded Cinema?

If ever a subject placed an author in the position of Walter Benjamin's angel of history, driven backward into the future by the winds of progress while struggling to make sense of a growing pile of debris in the ever-receding past, expanded cinema is that subject. Expanded cinema is elusive. Works are often site specific and ephemeral, hence difficult to see. Documentation can be hard to come by, and when it exists, can mediate the work to the point that the record bears little resemblance to the original. The term "expanded cinema" has covered a dizzying array of media and art forms across more than 60 years, and recent scholarship has pointed to precursors dating back to the earliest cinematic experiments of the European avant-garde. Constant fluctuations of existing moving image technologies trouble definitions and categorical boundaries. And a large portion of my book addresses contemporary work, produced during yet another period of artistic upheaval and seismic technological change. My attempt to begin historicizing it before the dust has settled may therefore strike some readers as premature.

In "For a Metahistory of Film: Commonplace Notes and Hypotheses," Hollis Frampton contrasts historians and metahistorians of cinema. The historian of cinema, he claims, is "responsible for every frame of film in existence. For the history of cinema consists precisely of every film that has ever been made, for any purpose

Cinema Expanded. Jonathan Walley, Oxford University Press (2020). © Oxford University Press.
DOI: 10.1093/oso/9780190938635.001.0001

whatever," including "instructional films, sing-alongs, endoscopic cinematography."[1] Historians cannot be selective, according to Frampton, cannot ignore non-artistic uses of film in favor of canonical works of cinematic art. But the metahistorian of cinema is not only concerned exclusively with such works, but may also *produce* them if it is necessary for the clarity and cohesiveness of the metahistory:

> The metahistorian ... is occupied with inventing a tradition, that is, a coherent wieldy set of discrete monuments, meant to inseminate resonant consistency into the growing body of his art. Such works may not exist, and then it is his duty to make them.[2]

The historian objectively chronicles what already exists; the metahistorian creatively intervenes to produce what does not, or at least not completely: a legible artistic tradition of cinema. Clearly Frampton's metahistorian is a filmmaker, and we can think of the makers of expanded cinema as doing exactly what Frampton describes as the metahistorian's task, which is to create the missing works of an imagined or unexplored cinematic tradition, possibly even outside the limits of the film medium and of "every film that has ever been made."

If the metahistorian of cinema is an artist unbound by the factual record of what film has been in the past, then the historian must be the cinema scholar, envisioned here as an empiricist in the extreme. I doubt that any practicing historians would grant Frampton's claim that their work attempts to be so totalizing, or that selection and invention (understood as acts of creation, not falsification) play no role in their histories. While cinema historians do not add to the body of work they study as filmmakers do, they are nevertheless in search of those "monuments" that resonate with the wider range of films and ideas that form their historical contexts. And expanded cinema is desperately in need of that "resonant consistency" Frampton described, if it is to be intelligible as a field of work or an artistic tradition, or useful as a categorical designation. Such consolidation is one of the goals of this book.

"Expanded cinema" and "expanded arts" are spatial metaphors, characterizing the processes of artistic and technological change in terms of categories spreading out past old boundaries to occupy new territories. It comes as no surprise, then, to find maps of expanded cinema and the expanded arts. George Maciunas's well-known 1966 "Expanded Arts Diagram" (fig. 1.1) looks like a subway map, with a central line of major "stops," all of which are expanded variants of theater: "Neo-Haiku Theatre," "Acoustic Theatre," "Kinesthetic Theatre," "Neo-Baroque Theatre," and "Verbal Theatre."[3] Criss-crossing through each form of theater are more specific

---

[1] Hollis Frampton, "For a Metahistory of Film: Commonplace Notes and Hypotheses," in Bruce Jenkins, ed., *On the Camera Arts and Consecutive Matters: The Writings of Hollis Frampton* (Cambridge, MA: MIT Press, 2009), p. 136.

[2] Ibid.

[3] Maciunas's map first appeared in the "Expanded Arts" edition of *Film Culture*, no. 23 (Winter 1966), p. 7.

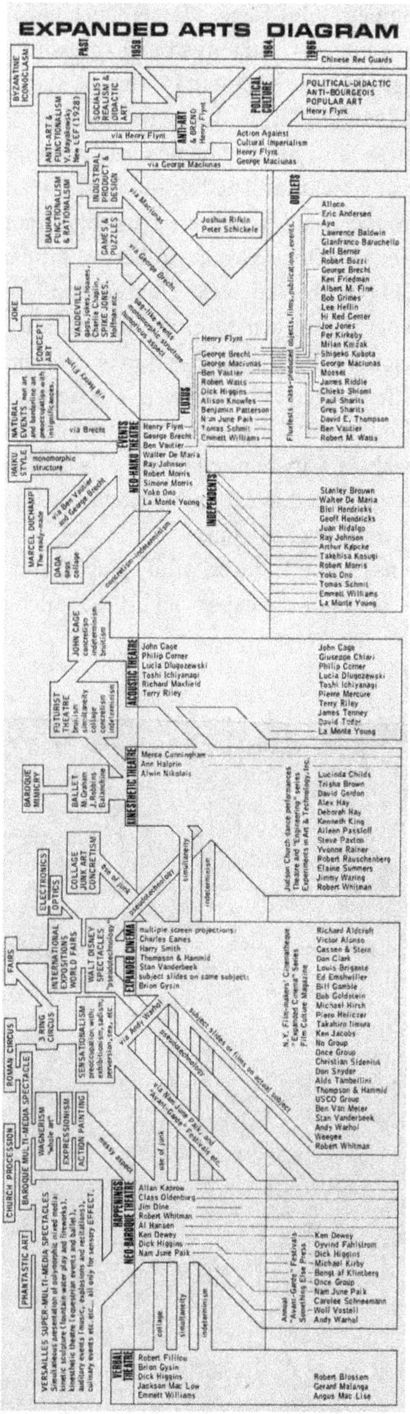

Fig. 1.1. George Maciunas, "Expanded Arts Diagram" (1966).
©2019 George Maciunas Foundation/Artists Rights Society (ARS), New York.

categories, including names (John Cage, Marcel Duchamp), types of events (fairs, church processions), movements (Dada, Abstract Expressionism), and traits (collage, indeterminism). Tellingly, expanded cinema is one of Maciunas's large-scale theatrical categories, placed between "Kinesthetic Theatre" and "Neo-Baroque Theatre," the latter being Maciunas's idiosyncratic name for happenings. Many of the approximately two dozen artists Maciunas listed in the expanded cinema box engaged in moving image performance, and were self-avowedly "intermedia artists" rather than filmmakers per se: the Once Group, Robert Whitman, Andy Warhol, Stan VanDerBeek, and USCO (Gerd Stern, Steve Durkee, and Michael Callahan). A slew of often undefined and perplexing artistic crosscurrents flow in and out of each form of theater; expanded cinema sits at the intersection of "international expos," "pseudo-technology," "multimedia spectacles," "circuses," "electronics," "optics," "collage junk art concretism," and "simultaneity" (fig. 1.2). Only two brief references to avant-garde film culture, the Filmmakers' Cinematheque and *Film Culture* magazine, appear in Maciunas's diagram, suggesting that expanded cinema was primarily a condition of art world developments outside of cinema.

The design of Maciunas's map is purposefully playful and chaotic, disrupting the reader's ability to make sense of the expanded arts as much as aiding it. More than

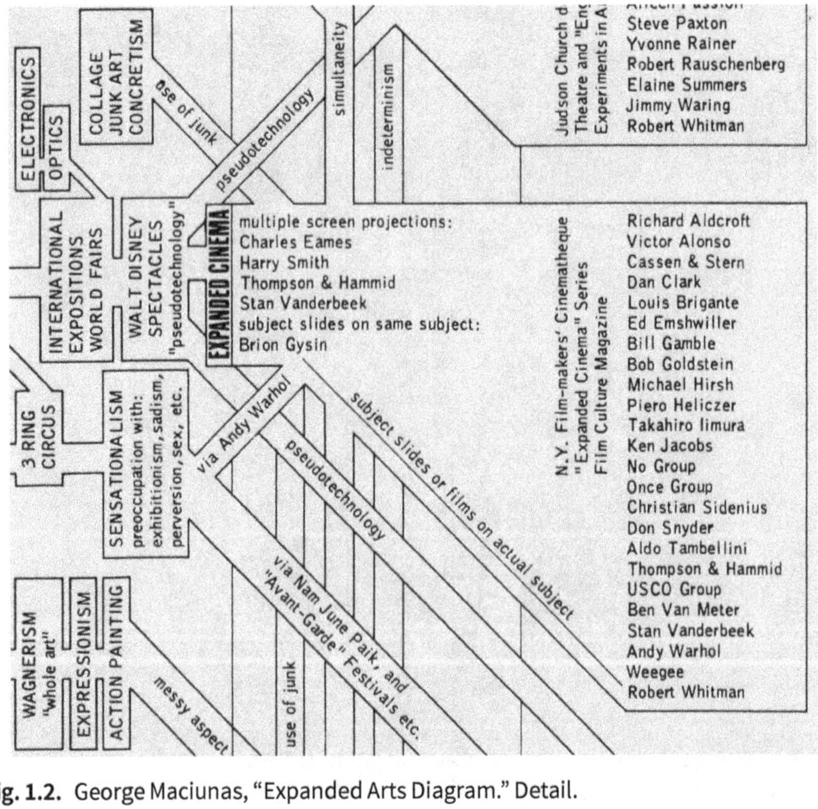

Fig. 1.2. George Maciunas, "Expanded Arts Diagram." Detail.

Fig. 1.3. Duncan White, "Expanded Cinema Map" (2009). Detail.
Design © Jonathan Hares.

forty years later, film scholar Duncan White offered a revised diagram, "an attempt to map the key coordinates of Expanded Cinema … meant to give a sense of the various histories, connections and developments that make up the polymorphous nature of practices associated with 'Expanded Cinema'" (fig. 1.3).[4] Like Maciunas's diagram, White's chart is impressive, ambitious, and sprawling, a work of art in its own right. Unlike the Maciunas diagram, however, it does not "anchor" its subject in major forms as Maciunas did with his variations of theater. White's categorical approach is more haphazard; a category might be a specific name (Cage, Carolee Schneemann, Peter Weibel), event (Expo '67 in Montreal, the 1975 "Video Show" at the Serpentine Gallery), movement (Punk Film, Fluxus), or very broad artistic form or quality (intermedia, "interactive," and internet art). Behind the boxes containing these various categories is a nexus of crisscrossing lines, implying that the map is also a kind of family tree and that the map's user can trace historical or formal connections among individuals, events, and movements. Attempting to do this, however, often reveals dead ends, inexplicable associations, or unmade links. For instance, the link between Punk cinema and VJ concerts is perplexing, while the unmade connection between

---

4 Duncan White, "Expanded Cinema," *Vertigo Magazine* 4, no. 2 (Winter–Spring 2009), https://www.closeupfilmcentre.com/vertigo_magazine/volume-4-issue-2-winter-spring-20091/expanded-cinema/.

Ken Jacobs and "creative projection," despite the fact that Jacobs was a pioneer of projection performance, seems like a major oversight.

Both of these maps represent expanded cinema's history as the accumulation of specific works, types of work, individuals, movements, events, and very general traits. They visualize taxonomies, of which there has been no shortage for expanded cinema. The subcategories that turn up, especially in the early accounts I will discuss in this chapter, seem endless: "Synaesthetic Cinema," "Cybernetic Cinema," "Computer Films," "Teledynamic Environments," "Holographic Cinema," "Intermedia Theatre," "Film/Dance," "Light Shows," "Kinetic Art," "Light Art," "Color Instruments," "variations on the theme of film," and on and on.[5] Thus, the attempt to organize expanded cinema into categories has tended to focus on specific surface features, listing the subgenres of expanded cinema according to the technological media used (video, projected light, computers) and the forms that come to be associated with these media (video art, light shows, computer films). This approach to sorting expanded cinema doesn't account for the broader causal forces at work in artistic expansion, such as the specific historical and institutional contexts in which expanded cinema has been made, and the widely varying film, art, and media discourses with which expanded works resonate. In short, the shifting ontological contours of moving image media at any given time, which lie beneath the surface of particular technologies, works, and forms, remain untraced. In this chapter, I take an alternative approach, bringing these broader contours to light and tracking the underlying conceptions of cinema and media that have animated specific instances of expanded cinema rather than exhaustively itemizing every one of those instances. Throughout this book, I will nuance the large-scale historical account I offer here, zeroing in on more local factors that will sharpen the global picture I paint in this chapter. I begin by tracing what has been perhaps the most significant historical dialectic expanded cinema manifests: between two very different conceptions of the relationship between expanded work and artistic tradition.

Expanded Cinema: Liberation

It is not clear who first coined the term "expanded cinema," or when; various commentators have identified the originator of the term as Jonas Mekas, Stan VanDerBeek, and John Brockman, once manager of the Filmmakers' Cinematheque and coordinator, with Mekas, of the "Festival of Expanded Cinema" (sometimes referred to as the "New Cinema Festival") in 1965 (fig. 1.4).[6] What is clear is that there was a concentrated period between 1964 and 1967 of expanded cinema work, which was

---

[5] I draw this list of terms primarily from Renan's *An Introduction to the American Underground Film*, pp. 227–257; and Youngblood's *Expanded Cinema*.

[6] Brockman also claims to have invented the word "intermedia," though the artist Dick Higgins is usually—and probably correctly—credited as the first to use it. On Brockman and "intermedia," see Elenor Lester, "So What Happens After Happenings," *New York Times*, September 4, 1966, pp. 9 and 17.

Fig. 1.4. Advertisement for a performance of USCO's *HUBBUB* (1965) with Carolee Schneemann at the New Cinema Festival (aka the Festival of Expanded Cinema) at the Filmmakers' Cinematheque.
From *The New York Times*, November 17, 1965.

accompanied by widespread coverage in the popular press, one of many things that differentiates this wave of expanded cinema from subsequent ones. The earliest writings on expanded cinema appeared during this period. That these are still the most frequently cited also helps explain the continued dominance of this wave in more recent scholarship on the subject; Renan's book was published in 1967, Youngblood's in 1970, drawn mostly from articles Youngblood had written for the *Los Angeles Free Press* between 1967 and 1969 (fig. 1.5). Mekas wrote several essays on expanded cinema for his "Movie Journal" column in the *Village Voice*, all between early 1964 and 1966.

During this initial period, "expanded cinema" was often used more or less interchangeably with terms like "intermedia," "multi-" or "mixed media," and "new theater." Artists and the popular press alike explicitly linked expanded cinema with major developments across the arts, particularly happenings, assemblage or collage, "the theater of mixed means," and psychedelia and the counterculture generally. Expanded cinema was characterized as immersive, technologically advanced, and

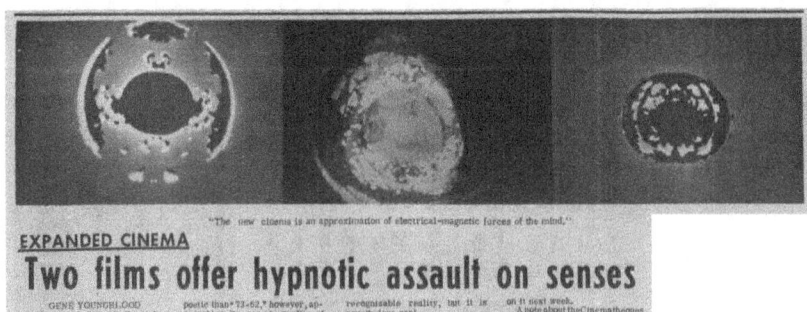

Fig. 1.5. Headline for "Expanded Cinema: Two Films Offer Hypnotic Assault on Senses." Gene Youngblood, *The Los Angeles Free Press*, July 26, 1968.

spectacular.[7] As Renan, one of expanded cinema's first chroniclers, wrote, "Its work is more spectacular, more technological, and more diverse in form that that of avant-garde/experimental/underground film so far. But it is less personal."[8]

These traits—technological spectacle, impersonality, imbrication within general trends in the other arts, impersonality, and popular appeal—distanced this wave of expanded cinema from what one might expect to have been the most proximate point of reference for practices that so thoroughly challenged cinematic norms: avant-garde film. It wasn't that critics didn't recognize expanded cinema as avant-garde, but that they did not see it as an outgrowth of that branch of cinema specifically. And during this period the avant-garde, in cinema and everywhere else, was more closely aligned with popular interests and artistic tastes that it had ever been. All this would begin to change by the end of the 1960s.

Two related senses of the term "expanded cinema" predominated in the 1960s and '70s, and continue to hold sway today. The first was that cinema was expanding beyond the bounds of the materials and forms that had defined it since its invention, in particular the medium of film and standard theatrical exhibition. Previously, making cinema had meant working within these parameters, even in the avant-garde. As Renan pointed out:

> Avant-garde/experimental/underground films are produced primarily in the way that all films have been produced (in the way that even the films of Lumière and Méliès were produced). They are (1) conceived, (2) directed and photographed, (3) edited into a more or less permanent form, (4) projected for an audience from one projector onto one screen. And as rich in potential as this time-honored process is, it is still limited. Therefore, the artists have attacked it, have fragmented it,

[7] "The theater of mixed means" was a term popularized, and possibly invented, by the critic Richard Kostelanetz. See *The Theatre of Mixed Means: An Introduction to Happenings, Kinetic Environments, and Other Mixed-Means Performances* (New York: Dial Press, 1968).

[8] Renan, *An Introduction to the American Underground Film*, p. 227.

and have destroyed the old idea—that the motion picture is a static work, that it is exactly the same every time it is shown, and that motion pictures should be made to universal specifications so that they may be shown on given machines under given and never changing conditions.[9]

The rejection of "universal specifications," "given machines," and "never changing conditions" opened up cinema to video and television, light art, shadow plays, computer imaging technologies, and holography, to name only a few. Thus, expanded cinema encompassed several nascent art forms, a point to which I shall return. For Renan, this expansion was liberatory; cinema was freed "from the concept of standardization."[10] Such notion not only appealed to a generation of artists more interested in multi- and inter-media than medium-specificity, but to a counterculture challenging traditional values and social mores. As expanded cinema saw media coverage in places like *The New York Times, The Nation*, and *Newsweek*, it was most heavily covered in these early years by the alternative press: *The Village Voice, The East Village Other, The Berkeley Barb*, and, of course, *The Los Angeles Free Press*, which published Gene Youngblood's articles on the subject. This enthusiasm for cinema's new freewheeling heterogeneity in the wake of new technologies and artistic ideas hints at the other major idea embodied in the term "expanded cinema": the belief that cinema and newer media would play a major role in the "expansion" of human consciousness. The new, expanded, cinema would augment human perception, increasing its sensitivity by giving it a kind of electronic extension. It is this sense of the potential of new electronic media that informs Youngblood's, still the best-known account of the subject.

Youngblood's book and Renan's discussion, which is the final chapter of his 1967 book *An Introduction to the American Underground Film*, are the earliest studies of expanded cinema and the most often cited. Generally speaking, both authors worked from the same definition of expanded cinema I have already surveyed: art historical developments, technological changes, and emerging ideas about proliferating electronic media collectively fueled a formidable challenge to conventional assumptions about the nature of moving image media, not to mention a much greater variety of "cinematic" works. Both authors mentioned unconventional work in the film medium, such as avant-garde films by Andy Warhol, Michael Snow, and Ken Jacobs. But they dedicated much more space to computer-generated films, television and video art, multimedia environments, performances involving moving images or projected light, holographic imagery, and other new forms of electronic (multi-) media. And, again, Youngblood and Renan alike characterized expanded cinema in terms of the liberation of both art and consciousness. "Expanded cinema isn't a movie at all" but was "like life," Youngblood had written. And Renan had claimed, "Artists now want their works to be environments, to be big as life, and in many cases, literally to be

---

[9] Ibid.
[10] Ibid., pp. 227–228.

life."[11] Such statements are representative of yet another assault on artistic specificity: the "blurring" of art and life, as Allan Kaprow put it.[12] Like distinctions between
art forms, the very idea of art as a separate sphere from everyday life was suspect.
A parallel predilection for blurring emerged in the study of new communications
media, taking the form of organic metaphors for media and their effects: "the global
village," and technology as "simulation of consciousness" and "extensions of man."[13]

Though Renan and Youngblood posited different contexts for the emergence of
expanded cinema, they agreed that it was something quite apart from filmmaking in
its traditional form, even from the radical manifestations of that form that came from
the avant-garde. For Renan, the post-WWII art world was expanded cinema's major
context, especially the move toward mixed media, intermedia, and other ephemeral
and hard-to-define art forms. Suggestively, Renan's chapter on expanded cinema
comes at the end of a book otherwise dedicated exclusively to the world of "underground" or avant-garde film, as if Renan imagined cinema expanding not just beyond
the bounds of the film medium and traditional exhibition practices, but also beyond
the province of the distinct cinematic culture that the rest of his book chronicled.
By his lights, expanded cinema was largely an art world phenomenon, motivated
by inter-arts activity traceable to "action" interpretations of Abstract Expressionist
painting, the ideas of John Cage, and Kaprow's happenings. Filmmaking, as in a distinct technical craft, art form, or tradition, was only one "mutating factor" in Renan's
chapter, and a relatively minor one at that: "avant-garde/experimental/underground
film is only one of the sources of expanded cinema. What has changed cinema to expanded cinema has been nothing less than the development of whole new conditions
and sensibilities spreading across all the arts."[14] The terms "intermedia," "media-mix,"
and "media combine" pepper Renan's account, which is divided into subsections such
as "Light Art," "Color Instruments," "Film/Dance and Film/Theatre," "Light Shows,"
and "Kinetic Sculpture." What these latter terms have in common is that all connote
theatricality and liveness, a powerful new sense of dynamism, and the preponderance of light and light effects in early works of expanded cinema. Insofar as projected,
flickering, and moving light were (1) not unique to any one art form, and (2) could be
used to create an immersive and sensorially overpowering field of color and motion
(to be occupied by spectator-participants), its appeal to expanded cinema artists was
undeniable.

The work of USCO provides some especially good examples. *Fanflashtick* (1968), a
multimedia strobe light environment, was breathlessly described by Elenor Lester as
"a 10-foot-high shimmering transparent vinyl gazebo, exploding with rock music and

[11] Ibid., p. 228.
[12] Allan Kaprow, *Essays on the Blurring of Art and Life* (Berkeley: University of California Press, 2003).
Kaprow had been espousing this notion since the end of the 1950s, most famously in "The Legacy of
Jackson Pollock."
[13] The references are Marshall McLuhan's, of course, from his seminal book *Understanding
Media: Extensions of Man* (New York: McGraw Hill, 1964).
[14] Renan, *An Introduction to the American Underground Film*, p. 228.

Fig. 1.6. USCO, *Fanflashtick* (1968).
Image courtesy Gerd Stern and Intermedia Foundation.

grimacing, laughing, dancing, prancing people, tossing balloons and confetti while they were being visually fragmented by flashing strobes" (fig. 1.6).[15] The discotheque-like frenzy of such a work is captured in the title of USCO's *HUBBUB* (1966), a multimedia event advertised in *The Village Voice* as "Expanded Cinema! Psychedelic Cinema! Media Mix! Marshall McLuhan! Timothy Leary! Film, oscilloscopes, stroboscopes, computerized, kinetic and live images. A visual feast." Such associations of expanded cinema with the counterculture, specifically psychedelia and the use of mind-expanding drugs, was common, especially in the underground press, for whom expanded cinema was one manifestation of the assault upon rules and social convention that Leary and LSD culture represented (fig. 1.7). Dick Preston's review of *HUBBUB* in *The East Village Other* identified it as the Filmmakers' Cinematheque's "selection as the best show" from its "Expanded Cinema survey" (also called "The Festival of Expanded Cinema" or "The New Cinema Festival"), and noted the film's assault on both the senses and traditional cinema. In light of works like *HUBBUB*, "the traditional type of cinema, with its relatively diminutive screen set clunk in the

---

[15] Elenor Lester, "Tune In, Turn On—And Walk Out?," *New York Time Magazine*, May 12, 1968, p. 30.

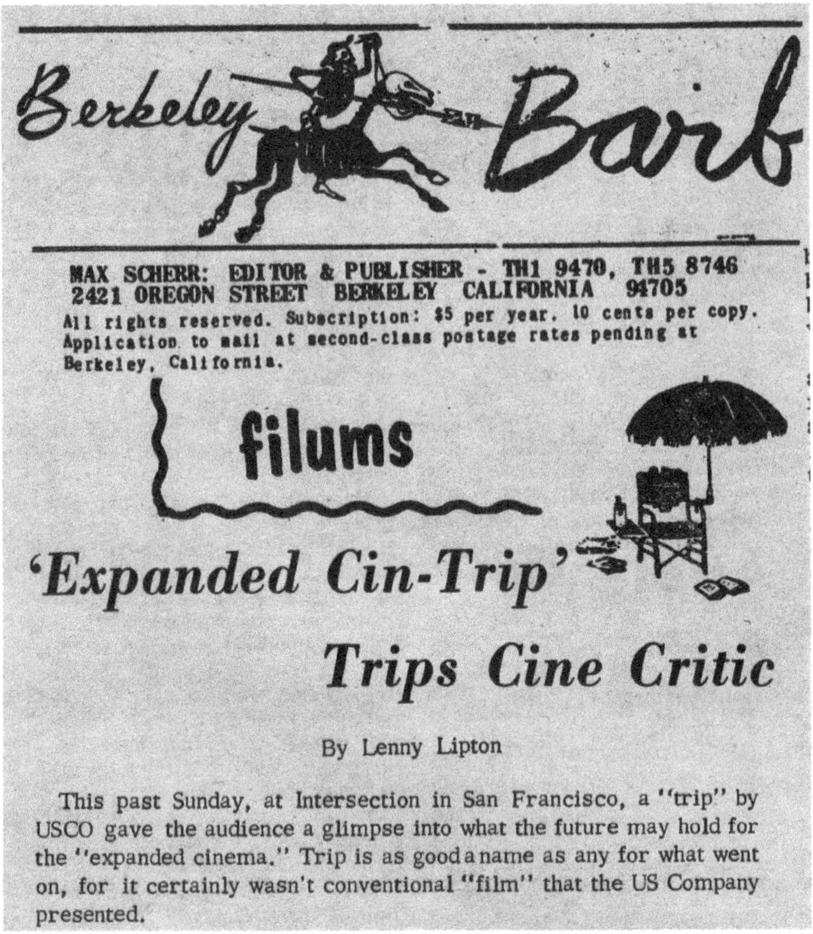

Berkeley Barb

MAX SCHERR: EDITOR & PUBLISHER - TH1 9470, TH5 8746
2421 OREGON STREET BERKELEY CALIFORNIA 94705
All rights reserved. Subscription: $5 per year. 10 cents per copy. Application to mail at second-class postage rates pending at Berkeley, California.

filums

'Expanded Cin-Trip' Trips Cine Critic

By Lenny Lipton

This past Sunday, at Intersection in San Francisco, a "trip" by USCO gave the audience a glimpse into what the future may hold for the "expanded cinema." Trip is as good a name as any for what went on, for it certainly wasn't conventional "film" that the US Company presented.

Fig. 1.7. Headline of a review of a USCO "trip" (presumably *HUBBUB*) by Lenny Lipton. From *The Berkeley Barb* 2, no. 26, July 1, 1966.

place where they've had the stage for the past Christ knows how many hundred years, has got to go . . . Going to a movie should be one hell of an experience, not just an entertainment."[16]

Ultimately, Renan did reconnect expanded cinema to cinema's "basic materials," grounding it in some concept of a specific art form rather than a hybrid one: "It is only light and time that link all the forms of cinema, past, present, and future."[17] But this is awfully vague, leaving one to wonder what, by this model, *wasn't* cinema. Light and time may indeed by the basic materials of cinema, but by the expanded logic of the 1960s avant-garde, painting, sculpture, performance, et cetera could also claim

[16] Dick Preston, untitled review, *The East Village Other* 1, no. 6, February 15–March 1, 1966, p. 11.
[17] Renan, *An Introduction to the American Underground Film*, p. 257.

these as fundamental elements. Were color instruments musical or cinematic? Was a "film/dance" a dance or a work of cinema? Was kinetic sculpture still sculpture, or did the ever-expanding cinema absorb it as a type of "moving image?" And so we return to the questions about the identities of art forms raised by the Prehistoric Picture Project.

Where Renan emphasized developments in the art world (and to some extent psychedelic drugs), for Youngblood expanded cinema's primary motivating forces were new communications media and scientific and sociological theories related to these, with Marshall McLuhan an obvious source of inspiration. *Expanded Cinema* is an early account of what would eventually be called "new media," a theory of media convergence *avant la lettre*. Like Renan, then, Youngblood de-emphasized the autonomy of individual technologies and art forms in favor of hybrid ones, but in terms of "synergy," a word that would eventually become a corporatized expression of media convergence.[18] And while Renan's definition of expanded cinema connected it to traditional cinema, albeit very loosely, Youngblood's use of the term was plainly metaphorical: expanded cinema manifested humankind's attempt to project the image of itself onto the screen of the outside world. "Cinema" was the metaphor for this image, and a blanket term for convergent media.

Not only was Youngblood's model of cinema convergent, his very methodology could also be described as hybrid, weaving together references from media theory, art history, the sciences, sociology, theology, psychology, and philosophy. A seven-page chapter called "Art, Entertainment, Entropy" begins with quotes from Wallace Stevens and D. H. Lawrence, then cites Alfred Hitchcock, Krishnamurti, and the avant-garde filmmaker Ken Kelman; it moves on to communication theory and the first and second laws of thermodynamics, then finishes with references to Buckminster Fuller and the engineer J. R. Pierce. This is not merely an idiosyncrasy of Youngblood's writing, but indication of the bias against specialization adopted from McLuhan, for whom such specialization was a relic of the machine age. The Yale University art collective Pulsa, though only briefly mentioned in Youngblood's book, stands out as a key example of the kind of work Youngblood most favored, and which he contrasted favorably with traditional cinema, even in its avant-garde forms. Like USCO, Pulsa created highly technological multimedia environments, but while USCO aimed at sensory overload and immersion, Pulsa's work literally interfaced with the natural world and sought to draw spectator's attention to the integration of that world and new media technologies that increasingly defined human experience (fig. 1.8). An article on Pulsa's large-scale light and sound installation in Boston's Public Garden in October of 1968, Pulsa member Michael Cain articulated the goal of the project: "to incorporate many other phenomenon of the technological world into this sort of 'natural conception,' giving some kind of aesthetic quality to the interaction of man and machine to make men more aware of the planet on which they live."[19] Yates McKee

---

[18] Youngblood, *Expanded Cinema*, pp. 109–111.
[19] "Pulsa Pulsates: New Art Form Tried at Yale." *New Haven Journal-Courier*, Wednesday, November 13, 1968. No author identified.

Fig. 1.8. Pulsa, untitled Yale Golf Course installation (1969). Strobe lights, poly-planar speakers, computer, analog-digital synthesizer control system, and punched-paper tape reader. New Haven, Connecticut, January 1969.
©Pulsa. Photograph by William Crosby, courtesy of David Rumsey.

makes the remarkable parallels between Pulsa's and Youngblood's ideas, noting that both "conceived the artist as an intermedia 'ecologist' facilitating the design of open systems, structures, and spaces amenable to collective participation and transformation over and against the 'closed system' strictures of modernist medium-specificity in art and architecture alike."[20] Breaking the bounds of medium-specific specialization, Pulsa's work could "open up" as it were into forms that could integrate with everyday life. As Youngblood wrote:

> Today when one speaks of cinema one implies a metamorphosis in human perception ... While personal films, videotapes, and light shows will continue to expand human communication on one level, organizations such as PULSA at Yale University, and the various national chapters of Experiments in Art and Technology (E.A.T.) are suffusing art, science, and the eco-system of earth itself at that point where all converge within the purview of modern technology.[21]

---

[20] Yates McKee, "The Public Sensoriums of Pulsa: Cybernetic Abstraction and the Biopolitics of Urban Survival," *Art Journal* 67 (Fall 2008), p. 48.

[21] Youngblood, *Expanded Cinema*, pp. 415–416.

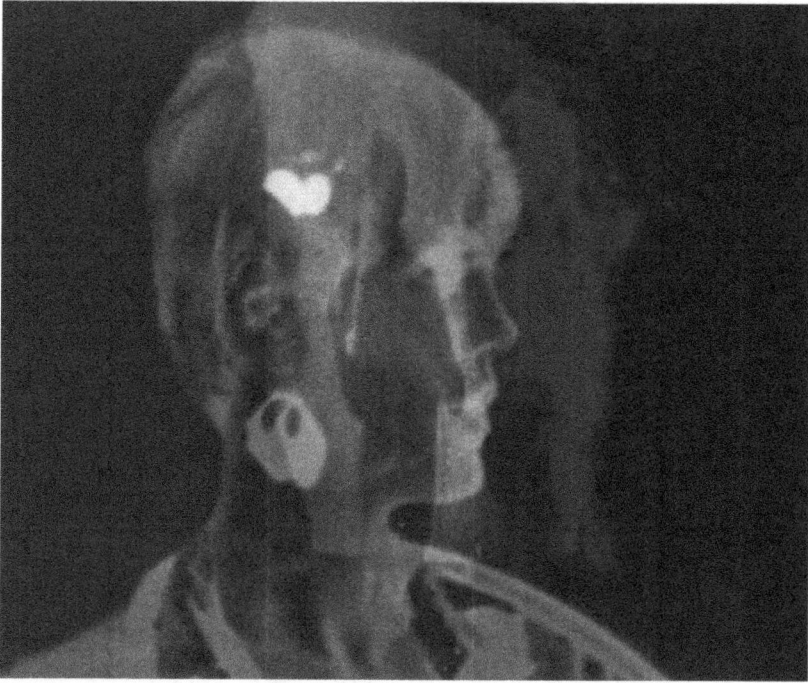

Fig. 1.9. Ronald Nameth, *Andy Warhol's Exploding Plastic Inevitable* (1966). Frame enlargement.

As interested in mass media as he was in the fine arts, Youngblood devoted well over half of his book to computer imaging, video, holography, and multimedia, his blanket term for these being "cybernetic cinema." The term suggests an inherently hybrid ontology, a "cyborg" cinema made up of mechanical, electronic, and organic parts. But further, the designation privileges new technology over old by implying that cinema was advancing through its affiliations with newer media just as the cyborgs Youngblood claimed to be already living among us were evidence of humankind's evolution toward a more perfect state.[22] And while an early section of *Expanded Cinema* dealt with filmmakers working in the conventional film format (albeit making unconventional, avant-garde films), it notably ignored work by such filmmakers that posed alternatives to the traditional forms of film production and exhibition. For instance, Youngblood briefly mentioned Warhol's *Exploding Plastic Inevitable* performances, though only in the context of an analysis of Ronald Nameth's 1966 film of the same name (fig. 1.9), never discussing Warhol's dual screen films or film installations. A long chapter on Jordan Belson only notes Belson's famous multi-projection

---

[22] Ibid., p. 52.

Fig. 1.10. Michael Snow, *Wavelength* (1967). Frame enlargements. 16mm film, 45 minutes, color, sound.
Courtesy of Michael Snow.

Vortex concerts in passing. And while Youngblood wrote a close analysis of Michael Snow's *Wavelength* (1967) (fig. 1.10), he did not address Snow's work in other media, including installation. His interpretation of *Wavelength* is telling: while he briefly acknowledged the particular context of Snow's film, the preoccupation evident in those films with the specificities of cinematic language was only important insofar as a command of that language was the necessary first step in the expansion of human consciousness:

> Snow emphasizes that editing is an abstraction of reality by alternating times of day with each cut, and by cutting rarely. Thus he achieves what Mondrian called the "relations" of abstract nature. The theory of relativity reduces everything to relations; it emphasizes structure, not material. We've been taught by modern science that the so-called objective world is a relationship between the observer and the observed, so that ultimately we are able to know nothing but that relationship. Extra-objective art replaces object-consciousness with metaphysical relation-consciousness.[23]

In this way, Youngblood reoriented *Wavelength*'s exploration of properties specific to cinema, such as editing, toward a very different interpretation that made Snow's film an object lesson on media's relationship to expanded consciousness. The film's connection to the narrower tradition of avant-garde film and its foregrounding of specifically cinematic traits and effects were nudged aside.

For avant-garde filmmakers of the sixties and seventies, the differentiation of cinema from the other arts was a major concern, a point upon which I will elaborate later in this chapter. For Youngblood, distinctions between media were much less important: "In the language of synaesthetics we have our structural paradigm."[24]

---

[23] Ibid., p. 127.
[24] Ibid., p. 135.

According to him, all media were converging into an electronic environment that encircled the earth and penetrated every facet of human society, which Youngblood called the "noosphere" after the philosopher Teilhard de Chardin.[25] Youngblood characterized the noosphere as a single intermedia technology, a view that informs his decidedly hybrid, or cyborg, conception of cinema. Stan VanDerBeek, an early adopter of expanded cinema, and according to some the term's inventor, expressed the same sentiment in a 1966 symposium on the subject:

> when I talk about expanded cinema, I'm talking about an expanded cinema that quite literally circles, you know, the world, in one form or another. In other words, communications systems that just aren't peculiar—you know, they are particular to each culture, they are not peculiar to the total world culture and I think that that sort of thing is something we're coming into ... I have a term for it, I call it culture intercom.[26]

For both Youngblood and VanDerBeek, "cinema" was a catch-all term for any and all technological communication systems that transmitted sound and image. VanDerBeek's primary aim as a maker of expanded cinema seemed to be the re-creation of the noosphere on a smaller scale, in essence acclimating viewers to this relatively new feature of their environment and awakening them to its possibilities and their role as participants in it. Since this process involved all world cultures, written/spoken language was inadequate: "man does not have means to talk to other men ... the world hangs by a thread of nouns and verbs," VanDerBeek wrote in his landmark manifesto "CULTURE: Intercom and Expanded Cinema."[27] The responsibility of the artist was to create a new image language that was free from the bounds of specific nations and cultures, and forms of presentation within which viewers could learn this new image language through direct experience of the noosphere. VanDerBeek's most famous attempt at such a "culture intercom" was his *Movie Drome* (1965) in Stony Point, New York (figs. 1.11 and 1.12). The *Movie Drome* was an exhibition space in which multiple film, video, and slide images were projected on the interior of a grain silo's dome, which the audience viewed by laying on the floor. The purpose of this planetarium/happening hybrid was precisely to overwhelm the viewer with images and sounds from multiple cultures and historical periods, "the course of western civilization since the time of the Egyptians to the present," as VanDerBeek described it.[28] The immersive experience of the *Movie Drome* was intended to force each audience member to experience the images and draw conclusions from them in his or her own way, making them active participants in communication rather than passive receivers of spectacle.

[25] Ibid., p. 57.
[26] From the transcript of the "Expanded Cinema Symposium," *Film Culture* 43 (Winter 1966), p. 1.
[27] Stan VanDerBeek, "CULTURE: Intercom and Expanded Cinema," *Film Culture* 40 (1966), pp. 15–18.
[28] Ibid., p. 17.

Fig. 1.11. Stan VanDerBeek, *Movie Drome* (1965). Design-In, Central Park, New York, NY, 1967.

Photograph by Bob Hanson. Courtesy Stan VanDerBeek Archive.

Video, television, and computers were VanDerBeek's privileged technologies, as they allowed instantaneous transmission of images, something that differentiated them from the film medium. That film was indeed a machine, "the last machine" in Hollis Frampton's words, has special implications given Youngblood's and VanDerBeek's views of media technology.[29] Considering their proclamations about the democratizing, unifying, and consciousness-raising potentials of new electronic media, the film medium must have struck them as very limited. Films like Belson's or Stan Brakhage's might symbolize the new expanded consciousness Youngblood prophesized, but the film medium itself was inadequate to the task of bringing it about. Films were not instantaneously transmittable, and thus lacked electronic media's freedom of movement. Traditional cinematic exhibition required the audience to come to the theater, while electronic media came to the viewer. In this conventional exhibition format, cinema did not allow for interaction (it was one of McLuhan's "hot" media), whereas new electronic media were, at least potentially, interactive (video, for example, being a "cool" medium). Thus, cinema in its standard

---

[29] Frampton, "For a Metahistory of Film," p. 136.

Fig. 1.12. Stan VanDerBeek standing inside the *Movie Drome* (1965). Stony Point, NY, 1966.

Photograph by Richard Raderman. Courtesy Stan VanDerBeek Archive.

medium and presentational format could not play as important a role as electronic media in the sweeping sociological changes that expanded cinema was making possible. As Youngblood wrote:

> We've followed the evolution of image language to its limits: the end of fiction, drama, and realism as they have been traditionally understood. Conventional cinema can be pushed no further. To explore new dimensions of awareness requires new technological extensions. Just as the term "man" is coming to mean man/plant/machine, so the definition of cinema must be expanded to include videotronics, computer science, atomic light.[30]

Scientific references like these recur throughout Youngblood's book and are a major theme in VanDerBeek's writings. Because Youngblood believed that media comprised a feature of the environment, it was subject to the same natural laws, such as the first and second laws of thermodynamics. He did not employ these concepts metaphorically; such phenomena as synergy and entropy literally applied to mass

---

[30] Youngblood, *Expanded Cinema*, p. 135.

media. Popular film and television, for instance, were entropic because they were formulaic, thus redundant, and thus contributed nothing to the development of human society. Youngblood characterized expanded cinema as "negentropic," or self-regenerative, its practitioners "design scientists" who created "a new language of conceptual design information with which we arrive at a new and more complete understanding of old facts, thus expanding out of control over the interior and exterior environments."[31]

But as far as this might seem from the art world language of Renan, both authors took expanded cinema as something entirely other than traditional cinema, the latter being rapidly displaced by forces emanating from the art world and the spheres of mass media and the sciences. And this is where expanded cinema's rhetoric of liberation met with a quite different set of ideas, and encountered skepticism about expanded cinema's implications rather than celebration of its liberating potential.

Expanded Cinema: Identity Crisis

Given Renan's and Youngblood's respective emphases upon the post-minimal, intermedia arts and McLuhan-esque theories of new media, one might wonder about the position in the expanded cinema landscape of filmmakers, film critics, and film theory—that is, the history and theory of cinema as it had been known for more than half a century. Youngblood had said, "Expanded cinema isn't a movie at all." If the liberation of cinema from standardization and the confines of singular media opened a door onto an exciting new horizon of possibilities, it also provoked anxiety among filmmakers and critics over their art form's identity.

Annette Michelson's seminal essay "Film and the Radical Aspiration" was an early expression of concern over this very question. Initially given as a paper in connection with the fourth New York Film Festival in 1966 and shortly thereafter published in *Film Culture*, Michelson's essay criticized the intermedia art of expanded cinema artists like Robert Whitman and Ken Dewey, whose work appeared in the festival. Having examined cinema's relationship to the other arts in such contexts as Soviet Russia and post-WWII France, Michelson concluded her essay by turning to expanded cinema:

The questioning of the values of formal autonomy has led to an attempted dissolution of distinctions or barriers between media ... Cinema, on the verge of winning the battle for the recognition of its specificity—and every major filmmaker and critic in the last half-century has fought that battle—is now engaged in a reconsideration of its aims. The Victor now questions his Victory. The emergence of new "intermedia," the revival of the old dream of synaesthesia, the cross-fertilization of

---

[31] Ibid., p. 71.

dance, theater, and film … constitute a syndrome of that radicalism's crisis, both formal and social.[32]

Notably, Michelson did not distinguish among more specific branches of cinematic practice: "every major filmmaker," avant-garde or otherwise, had played a part in articulating cinema's specificity and thus its artistic legitimacy. Interestingly, Youngblood made a similar move. In those relatively rare moments when he allowed that a conventionally made film constituted an instance of expanded cinema, he made no distinction between mass-market films, art cinema, and the avant-garde. Expanded cinema could refer to a commercial feature like Stanley Kubrick's *2001: A Space Odyssey* (1968), an art film like Jean-Luc Godard's *Pierrot le Fou* (1965), or an avant-garde film like *Wavelength*, as well as the plethora of other media forms available to artists *and popular entertainers* in the sixties and seventies.

At the time Michelson's essay was published, cinema was for the first time enjoying broad public acceptance as a fine art form and a subject worthy of serious consideration. The emergence of "new waves" and "young cinemas" in the United States, Europe, and Asia was a key factor, but the new appreciation of cinema was not limited to rarified forms of the international art film or the avant-garde. Hollywood cinema gained artistic legitimacy when viewed through new critical frameworks such as the auteur theory and structuralism. These discourses were linked to a growing institutional infrastructure devoted to cinema, including newly formed cinema studies programs in academia, independent screening venues, specialized film distributors, and a growing number of scholarly journals devoted to film. The latter included *Film Culture*, which, though best known as an avant-garde film journal, focused as much on Hollywood and art cinema in its early years. In sum, as the recognition of cinema as a legitimate art form transcended genres and filmmaking modes, concerns over the destabilization of cinema's identity in a moment of artistic expansion applied to all cinemas, not just those with obviously modernist aesthetics. The critical language of cinematic specificity crystallized as much around mainstream cinema as around the films of Godard or Brakhage. Expanded cinema was taken as an assault on this widely shared critical value.

But Michelson's plea for maintaining cinema's autonomy was neither a blanket condemnation of cross-fertilization nor an argument in favor of filmmakers jealously guarding some idealized purity of their art form. By her account, art forms could fruitfully interact. She acknowledged the potential for film to thrive by drawing upon the other arts, naming Alain Resnais, Robert Breer, Jacques Tati, and Godard as filmmakers whose work exemplified "the possibility of these convergences and cross-fertilizations."[33] But the success of such convergences required that said forms be secure in their "respective ontologies," something she argued had

---

[32] Annette Michelson, "Film and the Radical Aspiration," in P. Adams Sitney, ed., *Film Culture Reader* (New York: Cooper Square Press, 2000), p. 420.
[33] Ibid., p. 419.

occurred in post-WWII France in the case of film and literature.[34] That is, artistic mixing depended upon reciprocity, the interacting art forms in a mutually sustaining relationship rather than one parasitically feeding on the other. Michelson criticized Brakhage for analogizing his films to Abstract Expressionist painting on the grounds that this rhetorical move blocked cinema's quest for its own aesthetic, capitulating to the "authority" of "Abstract Expressionist orthodoxy" and naively reproducing action painting's Romantic discourse of the artist as "moral hero."[35] But this specific example did not upend the general principle that art forms could benefit from interactions with one another. The implication of the Brakhage example simply seemed to be that cinema, as the youngest art form, was the most susceptible to losing its identity and independence through interaction with the other arts because its ontology was still maturing. Expanded cinema threatened this process as it represented an idea of cross-fertilization in which the individuality of art forms no longer mattered.

Michelson's text was early in noting the existence and potential ramifications of expanded cinema, but in terms of the history of film theory, it is a rather late example of the modernist commitment to the idea of cinematic specificity. Classical film theorists had been preoccupied with distinguishing cinema from the other arts since the teens, but by the time Michelson wrote her essay film theory was abandoning the belief in cinematic essentialism on the grounds that it was idealist, ahistorical, and formalist. But classical theories of cinema's ontology, while validating film as an art form by identifying those qualities it shared with no other, also tended to outline the conditions under which cinema could benefit from connections with those other arts. Rudolf Arnheim's work is the exemplary case; while Arnheim's primary aim was to contrast the qualities of the filmic image from those of ordinary human perception, the distinctions he made also separated film from the other arts. His defense of silent black and white films on the grounds that they most fully departed from natural perception was, at the same time, a denial of sound, dialogue, and color—traits of music, theater, and painting, respectively. His emphasis of film's "projection of solids upon a plane surface," which is to say its elimination of depth, simultaneously distanced cinema from a defining quality of both reality *and sculpture*.[36] Only when the boundaries between cinema and the other arts were clearly delimited could the former intermingle with the latter in such a way that each art form retained its identity and contributed meaningfully to a composite whole: "artistic media combine ... as separate and complete forms ... Their combination resembles a successful marriage, where similarity and adaptation make for unity but where the personality of the two partners remains intact, nevertheless."[37] Arnheim differentiated the individual "married" art forms from a hypothetical "child" of such a union, in whom the distinct traits of each form would be indistinguishable. Like Michelson, Arnheim and other early

---

[34] Ibid., p. 419.
[35] Ibid., p. 417.
[36] Rudolf Arnheim, *Film as Art* (Berkeley: University of California Press, 1957), p. 9.
[37] Ibid., pp. 207–208.

film theorists favored a model of artistic compositeness that maintained rather than dissolved boundaries between art forms.

Expanded cinema, then, was a reminder of the extent to which cinema's ontology had always been staked out in relation to the other arts. More to the point, the characteristics of these other arts have shaped the very language of cinematic specificity: cinema has been "painting with light," "sculpting in time," "writing in movement." It has been analogized to music, poetry, dance, and language. Expanded cinema was perhaps the culmination of the paradoxes that dogged the essentialist quest since the earliest speculative writings on cinema. But while it may have been perceived as a threat to this quest by "every major filmmaker and critic," expanded cinema entailed special consequences for one cinematic tradition in particular: avant-garde or experimental film. It was in the avant-garde film world that questions of cinema's identity and its relationship to the other arts were explored in the greatest depth, the process becoming one of that branch of filmmaking's defining traits. To complicate matters, avant-garde cinema was also historically interconnected with the other arts in ways that mainstream cinemas weren't, making it more difficult to define against the backdrop of media-focused expanded and inter-arts practices. The line Michelson drew between mutually beneficial artistic exchanges that would clarify ontological outlines and synaesthetic mash-ups that would destabilize them has not always been so easy to make out amid the play of radical forms and inter-arts references characteristic of avant-garde film's history. This goes to the very roots of experimental cinema, borne as it was of the early forays into filmmaking by visual artists like Fernand Léger, Hans Richter, Marcel Duchamp, Salvador Dali, Man Ray, and László Moholoy-Nagy. The body of films variously named "structural," "materialist," and "structural-materialist" reiterated this apparent contradiction in the sixties and seventies, as they aggressively asserted cinema's material and formal uniqueness despite frequently being made by artists who first worked in other media. Expanded cinema was the newest and most direct expression of the belief that cinema was an essentially essence-less art form, in which all the arts intersected, and that avant-garde film was an inherently mixed tradition. But it was from within this tradition, with which Michelson identified despite the broad purview of her essay, that filmmakers countered this belief and resisted the absorption of their art into the welter of intermedia.

As Andrew Uroskie has pointed out, Michelson's essay came at a critical moment for expanded cinema.[38] It began its long life as a lecture entitled "Radicalism in Film, Europe and the United States" at an event organized by Amos Vogel as part of the 1966 New York Film Festival. Shortly after the lecture, also connected to the festival, a symposium on expanded cinema took place featuring VanDerBeek, Whitman, Dewey, critic John Gruen, and moderator Henry Geldzahler, then curator of American art at the Metropolitan Museum. Michelson's essay, newly christened, appeared later that year in *Film Culture* #42; the very next issue of *Film Culture*, also published in

---

[38] Andrew V. Uroskie, *Between the Black Box and the White Cube: Expanded Cinema and Postwar Art* (Chicago: University of Chicago Press, 2014), pp. 145–146.

1966, was a special edition devoted to the expanded arts, which began with a transcription of the expanded cinema symposium. Calling attention to Michelson's status as a critic and noting "the force of [her] rhetoric," Uroskie suggests that Michelson's essay single-handedly dampened interest among filmmakers and critics in expanded cinema; "Michelson gave voice," Uroskie writes, "to a widespread suspicion that serious art practice was giving way to populist, technophilic kitsch."[39]

But Michelson was by no means the only one to express skepticism about expanded cinema, nor was the main concern she and others raised one of technophilia, spectacle, and populism. Indeed, as I shall suggest later in this chapter, the popularity of early expanded cinema had its benefits. Michelson's main criticism of intermedia—she never used the term expanded cinema in her essay—was that it undermined cinema's quest for autonomy, blocking its development of a distinct formal language and reconnecting it to the very art form from which it had sought to differentiate itself: theater. Looking at entries from Jonas Mekas's "Movie Journal" in the *Village Voice* between 1964 and 1966, one finds similar reservations despite the fact that Mekas was supportive of expanded cinema. He participated in the symposium and wrote much of the material in the special edition of *Film Culture*, of which he was, of course, editor.

Mekas's commentary on expanded cinema during this brief period is not directly critical, as Michelson's was. Rather, it seems to embody a tension between Mekas's characteristically enthusiastic promotion of this "new cinema" and a desire to reconcile it with the traditions of avant-garde and art cinema with which he was primarily occupied as artist, critic, and organizer. These attempts at reconciliation are often critical of expanded cinema works, frequently returning to well-established filmmakers like Brakhage, Kenneth Anger, Gregory Markopolous, and Harry Smith as barometers of genuine cinematic art. As often as expanded cinema and multimedia artists like USCO, Whitman, Paik, and Charles and Ray Eames turned up in Mekas's *Village Voice* column, and as appreciative as Mekas *sometimes* was of their work, names from the roster of avant-garde filmmakers of the 1950s and 1960s appeared much more often. For Mekas, they represented the standard of excellence in cinematic art in both its expanded and traditional forms. For instance, reviewing a 1965 program entitled "Psychedelic Explorations" at the New Theatre on East 54th Street (fig. 1.13), Mekas lamented that a portion of the program devoted to slide projections was "sometimes pretty" but fell drastically short of the purely visual artistry evident in Brakhage's films. "An artist's temperament and intelligence was needed to organize [the images] in time and space into 'life-sustaining forces,'" Mekas wrote, attributing the final phrase to Robert Kelly, himself commenting on Brakhage's work.[40] But

[39] Ibid., p. 146.

[40] Mekas, "Movie Journal," *Village Voice*, July 22, 1965, [p. 11]. All of Mekas's "Movie Journal" entries on expanded cinema from February 1964 to June 1966 were collected in the "Expanded Arts" edition of *Film Culture* referenced in this chapter's note 3. The page numbers listed in these footnotes refer to that issue.

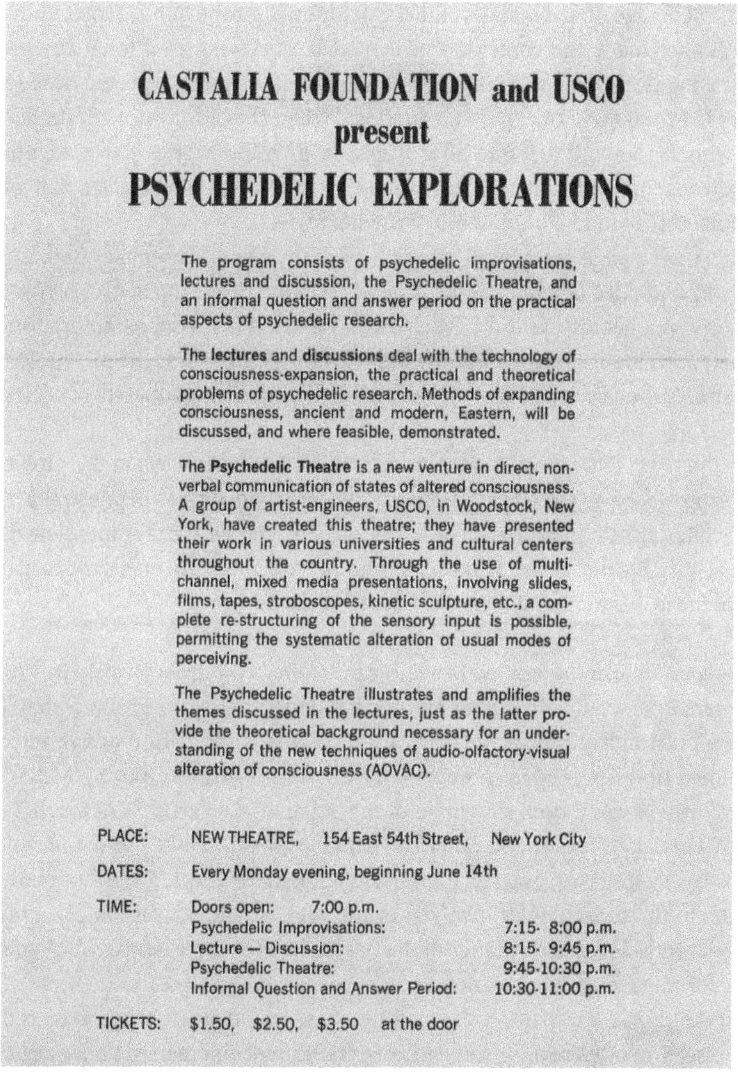

CASTALIA FOUNDATION and USCO
present
PSYCHEDELIC EXPLORATIONS

The program consists of psychedelic improvisations, lectures and discussion, the Psychedelic Theatre, and an informal question and answer period on the practical aspects of psychedelic research.

The **lectures** and **discussions** deal with the technology of consciousness-expansion, the practical and theoretical problems of psychedelic research. Methods of expanding consciousness, ancient and modern, Eastern, will be discussed, and where feasible, demonstrated.

The **Psychedelic Theatre** is a new venture in direct, non-verbal communication of states of altered consciousness. A group of artist-engineers, USCO, in Woodstock, New York, have created this theatre; they have presented their work in various universities and cultural centers throughout the country. Through the use of multi-channel, mixed media presentations, involving slides, films, tapes, stroboscopes, kinetic sculpture, etc., a complete re-structuring of the sensory input is possible, permitting the systematic alteration of usual modes of perceiving.

The Psychedelic Theatre illustrates and amplifies the themes discussed in the lectures, just as the latter provide the theoretical background necessary for an understanding of the new techniques of audio-olfactory-visual alteration of consciousness (AOVAC).

PLACE: NEW THEATRE,   154 East 54th Street,   New York City

DATES: Every Monday evening, beginning June 14th

TIME: Doors open: 7:00 p.m.
Psychedelic Improvisations: 7:15- 8:00 p.m.
Lecture — Discussion: 8:15- 9:45 p.m.
Psychedelic Theatre: 9:45-10:30 p.m.
Informal Question and Answer Period: 10:30-11:00 p.m.

TICKETS: $1.50, $2.50, $3.50   at the door

Fig. 1.13. Flier for "Psychedelic Explorations." The New Theatre, 154 East 54th Street, New York, NY. June 1965.
From the Timothy Leary Manuscripts and Ephemera, 1940–1986 collection, Division of Rare and Manuscript Collections, Cornell University. John McWhinnie, collector.

disorganization seems to have been the purpose of the kind of work staged during the "Psychedelic Explorations" event, which was organized by Timothy Leary and featured multimedia performances by USCO. "The psychedelic theatre attempts to stimulate multiple levels of consciousness by audio-visual bombardment," Howard Junker wrote in a review of the event, who characterized USCO's "multi-channel media mix" as a "barrage of films, slides, kinetic sculpture, strobe lights, tapes, and live ac-tors."[41] Junker made the contrast between such work and traditional cinema clear, paraphrasing USCO and articulating a position that would be repeated over and over during the initial wave of expanded cinema: "while the old-fashioned, single-screen movie with its sequential, frame-after-frame progression, worked once, we now need simultaneous, multiple images. More than that, we need a new theatre that will pro-vide a total art, a grand combination of media."[42]

Mekas was often at least implicitly critical of the theatrical quality of many inter-media and expanded cinema events. A strong sense of the performative seems to have struck him as a liability, as it did Michelson. Of the "Psychedelic Explorations" pro-gram just described, he wrote that the best part of the show was the pre-performance preparation, when the artists set up and tested their machines un-self-consciously:

I like the part which preceded the program proper—I mean, when the projectors and slide machines were being tested, lights arranged; flashes of unusually beau-tiful whites; fleeting glimpses of an imperfectly placed slide; the empty slide frame full of light. Like that Oriental musician who went to a Western music concert, I pre-ferred the instrument tuning period to the real concert.[43]

Mekas expressed similar ambivalence toward Robert Whitman's work, in which live performers interacted with filmed images of themselves, on the grounds that it relied too often on simple gimmickry (see chapter 3). The combination of live actors with their filmed doubles created moments of humor and surprise, but by Mekas's reck-oning Whitman was more a showman or magician than an artist.[44] Across his "Movie Journal" entries on expanded cinema, Mekas uses terms like "showmanship" and "virtuosity" to indicate a sacrifice of artistry for mere effect, a kind of show-offish approach to the technologies involved in the performances, again implying that the overly self-conscious performance of the possibilities of these new technologies was a liability for much expanded work.

Most striking about Mekas's chronicling of expanded cinema, however, is the per-sistent assertion of its relationship to more traditional cinema. As I have argued, this context was not especially significant for the first wave of expanded cinema artists, who often did not think of themselves as "filmmakers." But for a filmmaker and avant-garde cinema devotee like Mekas, and film critic like Michelson, this was a crucial point. In a June 1965 "Movie Journal" entry, Mekas called himself the "lonely histo-rian of the new [expanded] cinema."[45] Certainly Mekas was not the only one writing about expanded cinema—articles on the subject even appeared in the *New York Times* throughout 1966 and 1967. But Mekas does seem to have been the only one at the

---

[41] Howard Junker, "LSD: 'The Contact High,'" in *The Nation*, July 5, 1965, p. 25.
[42] Ibid., p. 26.
[43] Mekas, "Movie Journal," *Village Voice*, July 22, 1965, [p. 11].
[44] Mekas, "Movie Journal," *Village Voice*, December 2, 1965, [p. 12].
[45] Mekas, "Movie Journal," *Village Voice*, June 3, 1965, [p. 11].

time who was particularly concerned about the implications of expanded cinema for what he called "cinema as we know it," and the extent to which the former could be reconciled with the latter. The potential for intermedia to displace traditional cinema appears to have troubled him just as it did Michelson. A June 1964 entry that begins "There are very strange things happening in cinema," went on to provide a little history of the art form beginning with the Lumieres' *Train Arriving at a Station* (1895), running through the innovations of the first and second generations of avant-garde filmmakers, and into the most recent work in expanded cinema, drawing a line of continuity from cinema's origins to work that seemed quite distant from these.[46] To lessen this distance, Mekas made the rhetorical move, familiar by now, of retrograde remediation, positing cinema as an ancient art form in existence long before the invention of film, a strategy for re-familiarizing film-less forms of expanded cinema that only employed lights, shadows, vapors, hallucinations, and dreams.

The most direct expressions of Mekas's ambivalence toward expanded cinema are found in his "Movie Journal" coverage of the New Cinema Festival of November and December 1965. Its very name, alternately the "Festival of Expanded Cinema" and the "New Cinema Festival" depending on when it was referred to and by whom, represented the indeterminate status of works of expanded cinema, at least by Mekas's reckoning. In an entry from November 11, Mekas wrote, "Not all that's happening at the Filmmakers' Cinematheque this month can be called cinema."[47] The rest of the entry plumbs this question of what in the festival was cinema and what was not and how this could be determined. "The medium of cinema is breaking out and taking over and is going blindly and by itself. Where to—nobody knows."[48] While enthusiastically proclaiming that expanded cinema artists like Paik and Angus McLise "dissolved the edges of this art called cinema into a frontiersland mystery," much of the rest of his entry takes up the work of reining this process back in.[49] "The cinema aspect ... dominate[s] these works," Mekas wrote, adding the statement about cinematic tradition that begins this chapter: "No good 'old' art is ever invalidated by the 'new' art ... with five, six, seven years perspective, these far-far-out anti-art works begin to fall into the same thousand-year-old treasury of all art."[50] Mekas thus completes the loop implied in the article, in which the "mystery" of expanded cinema's identity is solved by historical perspective and the continuity of cinematic tradition.

Michelson's and Mekas's commentary takes on new meaning when we consider the unique historical circumstances in which avant-garde film culture found itself during this initial period of expanded cinema. At this moment avant-garde cinema saw for the first time the possibility of reaching, if not a mass audience, at least a much larger one. The interests of avant-garde film momentarily dovetailed with those of cinema in general, with people like Mekas seeing an opportunity in the sudden sea change

---

[46] Mekas, "Movie Journal," *Village Voice*, June 25, 1964, [p.11].
[47] Mekas, "Movie Journal," *Village Voice*, November 11, 1965, [p.11].
[48] Ibid.
[49] Ibid.
[50] Ibid.

in the popular perception of cinema as art. The establishment of the New American Cinema Group, Filmmakers' Cinematheque, Filmmakers' Co-op, and New York Film Festival, all of which took place concurrently with cinema's sudden expansion, point to the avant-garde's brief alignment with more popular trends in cinema. *Film Culture*, founded by Jonas and Adolfas Mekas in 1955, was, until the early '60s, dedicated as much to European and American auteurs like Joseph von Sternberg and Orson Welles as to avant-garde filmmakers. The auteur theory was first articulated in English within its pages.[51] "The First Statement of the New American Cinema Group" of 1962 never mentioned Brakhage, Deren, Anger, and the like, but filmmakers like Shirley Clarke, John Cassavetes, Robert Frank, and Mekas, who had produced a series of feature length narrative films on budgets that were high by avant-garde film standards.[52] Though railing against the "official" cinema, Mekas and others saw in that cinema a model for a parallel infrastructure for the avant-garde, and made and promoted this series of more mainstream "new" films in relation to the development of this infrastructure.

In short, this was a period in which the champions of avant-garde cinema briefly sought to hook their interests to the larger cause for cinema's mass appreciation as an art form, seeing a chance to take advantage of a cultural situation in which innovation and radicalism in cinema could find a large and appreciative audience. This new appreciation extended to coverage in the mainstream media, which had taken interest in expanded cinema by 1966. Tellingly, a September 1967 *New York Times* article on the New York Film Festival implicitly linked expanded cinema with the larger question of film's artistic status: "there are the multi-media or expanded cinema people, who would like to turn the festival into an Expo 67 Movie Drome. And ... there are still some diehard intellectuals who have not yet admitted films to the realm of art and see no point at all in the film festival."[53] The statement offers a snapshot of the perception of cinema as well as expanded cinema's role in changing that perception, contrasting those who resisted the claim that cinema was a legitimate art form with those who were advancing that claim in even bolder and more aggressive terms. Some went so far as to claim that expanded cinema made other avant-garde or underground films obsolete. Writing for *The Nation* in 1965, Howard Junker asked, "How many ill-conceived, half-baked, technically incompetent, faggoty, poetic films can anyone see before announcing, 'I've made that scene. And never mind about the art form of the age?'" Expanded cinema, by contrast, was where it was at: "single-screen movies are well and good, but the art form of the age is something else. Too much is happening, we have too great a data-processing capability, for the single image to monopolize our eye."[54]

---

[51] *Film Culture* published Andrew Sarris's landmark essay "Notes on the Auteur Theory in 1962" in issue 27 (Winter 1962–1963).

[52] "The First Statement of the New American Cinema Group," *Film Culture* 22–23 (Summer 1961).

[53] Elenor Lester, "The Movie Buffs Gather—To See and Be Seen," *New York Times*, September 17, 1967, p. 21.

[54] Howard Junker, "Films—The Underground Renaissance," *The Nation*, December 27, 1965, pp. 539–540.

We can think of the first wave of expanded cinema, then, as one means of staging film's parity with the other arts, perhaps even its superiority as *the* art form of the twentieth century, during a period in which film had become, in Bruce Jenkins's words, "a sort of lingua franca for the avant-garde."[55] If this was the case, then the attention it received from the mainstream press was beneficial; articles about intermedia in the popular press also mentioned avant-garde or underground films and film venues. In a 1966 *New York Times* article on the New York Film Festival, festival director Amos Vogel wrote, "several accomplished [avant-garde] works (including some 'mixed media' presentations) represent a genuine American contribution to world cinema."[56] But the elevated profile of avant-garde film during this period, including that of expanded cinema, was a double-edged sword. In a scathing critique of the New American Cinema Group written in 1967, Vogel repeatedly pointed to expanded cinema as a sign of a "dangerous new age" for avant-garde film. He saw it as both symptom of popular co-optation, with "discotheques and coffeehouses utilizing film-oriented mixed media techniques," and aesthetic exhaustion: "Thematic liberation is no guarantee of quality. Nor is the use of five simultaneously-operating projectors." "Mixed media" had devolved into one of a handful of "publicizable new techniques."[57]

The first wave of expanded cinema revealed both the promises and perils of expansion to avant-garde filmmakers: the promise of new avenues for cinematic radicalism and new grounds upon which to assert film's equal footing with the other arts; the peril of losing cinema entirely within a gaseous field of intermedia, where it was shut off from the historical traditions in which filmmakers found meaning. Expanded cinema's popularity might have helped draw attention to avant-garde film, but it simultaneously connoted the kind of faddishness that the avant-garde wanted to avoid. Mekas's ambivalence toward expanded cinema, and Michelson's broadside against it, set forth what the terms and challenges would be for the next wave of such work.

Return of the Suppressed: Re-claiming Cinema in Expanded Cinema

Shortly after participating in a tape-recorded interview with Mekas and film critic P. Adams Sitney, Michael Snow wrote them a follow-up letter, which begins:

---

[55] Bruce Jenkins, "The 'Other' Cinema: American Avant-Garde Film of the 1960s," in Russell Ferguson, ed., *Art and Film Since 1945: Hall of Mirrors* (Los Angeles: The Museum of Contemporary Art, Los Angeles, 1996), p. 202.

[56] Amos Vogel, "The Onus Is Not on the Artist; It Is We Who Must Learn," *New York Times*, September 11, 1966, p. 24.

[57] Amos Vogel, "Thirteen Confusions," *Evergreen Review*, June 1967, reprinted in Scott MacDonald, ed., *Cinema 16: Documents Toward History of the Film Society* (Philadelphia: Temple University Press, 1966), pp. 428–435.

> Some ramblings occasioned by things unsaid: feel there to be some submerged
> issue about my work in other media and wish we had a couple of days to go into
> their connections. If I were a "mixed media" artist perhaps it would be easier. Have
> been, not opposed but the general won't cancel the specific.[58]

"The general won't cancel the specific"; though Snow was an artist who worked in
multiple media, he was not, by his own account, a multimedia artist. *Wavelength*
was decidedly about cinema: the physical traits of the film medium, the experience
of time in film viewing, the nature of narrative, and film/viewer relations. While
Youngblood read *Wavelength* as representative of the consciousness-raising possibilities of expanded cinema, and "paleocybernetic" society's increasing awareness of the
"relational" nature of so-called objective reality, the film has been much more commonly read as signaling the emergence of something else entirely: a new assertion of
cinematic specificity.

During the first wave of expanded cinema, a new phase in avant-garde cinema
was also beginning, a sharp turn from the "Baudelairean" narratives, "poetic"
films, and beat cinema of the 1950s and early 1960s, to what Sitney famously labeled "structural film."[59] Though Sitney's conception of structural film was idiosyncratic, taking it as the continuation of a uniquely American avant-garde
aesthetic tradition, the term very soon came to stand for a cluster of international
movements that plumbed the depths of cinematic modernism. Though most of
the filmmakers Sitney labeled "structural" also worked in media other than film,
structural film clearly declared cinema's autonomy. It represented a turning away
both from the ideals of intermedia and the relative accessibility of New American
Cinema filmmakers like Clarke, Cassavettes, and, to a certain extent, Warhol.
Structural film was thus a condition of avant-garde film culture's institutional consolidation as a phenomenon distinct from the art world and mainstream cinema
alike. This will be important to bear in mind as we turn our attention to the next
waves of expanded cinema.

As if following Kosuth's dictum about the primacy of "art in general," the first wave
of expanded cinema conceived of cinema at such a high level of generality as to cancel
out the cinematic traditions that had come before, avant-garde or otherwise. The next
wave would return cinematic specificity to expanded cinema. This second wave began
around 1967 and ran more or less through the next decade, with some filmmakers

---

[58] Michael Snow, "Two Letters and Notes on Films," in P. Adams Sitney, ed., *The Avant-Garde Film: A Reader of Theory and Criticism* (New York: Anthology Film Archives, 1987), p. 184. Snow's letter is dated August 21, 1968.

[59] "Baudelairean Cinema" was Jonas Mekas's term, "A world of flowers of evil, of illuminations, of torn and tortured flesh, a poetry which is at once beautiful and terrible, good and evil, delicate and dirty." See "On the Baudelairean Cinema," *Village Voice*, May 2, 1966, reprinted in Mekas, *Movie Journal: The Rise of the New American Cinema, 1959-1971* (New York: Macmillan, 1972), pp. 85–86. "Structural Film" was Sitney's invention, first described in Sitney, "Structural Film," *Film Culture*, no. 47 (Summer 1969), pp. 1–10.

continuing to produce expanded work during the first few years of the 1980s. During this second wave expanded cinema became a preoccupation of the avant-garde film world, moving underground, so to speak. Mainstream media coverage of expanded cinema was waning by 1968 as the novelty of technological spectacles and immersive, happening-esque inter-arts events of the first wave wore off. If the new expanded cinema built upon some of the formal innovations of the first wave, it differentiated itself sharply from its major forms, was animated by a very different set of values, and had markedly more limited appeal.

Rather than abandoning the idea of cinematic specificity, the next wave of expanded cinema stepped directly into the breach between cinema's claims for autonomy and its historical entwining with the other arts. In contrast to the conceptions of cinema's expansion held by authors like Renan and Youngblood and artists like VanDerBeek, expanded cinema by the end of the 1960s resisted cinema's absorption into a mass of mixed forms, whether conceived in terms of intermedia (Renan) or media convergence (Youngblood). One could say that the first wave of expanded cinema emphasized the "expanded": the liberation of cinema from the materials and forms that had defined it for 70 years. Where Renan looked outside avant-garde film for the factors that precipitated cinema's expansion—the art world, the drug culture, new communications technologies—the second wave was the result of an expansion *from within*, a continuation of avant-garde film's tradition of theorizing cinema's ontology and distinguishing it from other art forms. Privileging the "cinema" in expanded cinema, it was an outgrowth of the autocritical tendency that has defined avant-garde film throughout its history. The artists who produced this work were self-identified "filmmakers," and asserted their works, however far from conventional cinema they appeared to be, as "cinema." Recall, for instance, that Anthony McCall spoke of *Long Film for Ambient Light* as a meditation on cinema's presuppositions, a model of cinematic first principles. Elsewhere, he differentiated his work from "light spectacles," a branch of expanded cinema à la Youngblood and Renan, entirely unlike the psychedelic performances of the Joshua Light Show, works like *Fanflashtick*, or Pulsa's 1969 light Yale Golf Course installation.[60] Later generations of filmmakers making expanded work have similarly emphasized their connection to the traditions of filmmaking rather than those of multi- or inter-media, as we shall see. These latter two terms were synonymous with expanded cinema during the mid-sixties, while work produced subsequently was decidedly *cinema*.

During the initial phase of expanded cinema, the term was a convenient designation for a rapidly emerging field of new media and artistic forms that were time-based and employed light and/or moving images. Cinema was a proximate point of reference for a group of nascent art forms that did not yet have their own languages, much less

[60] Anthony McCall, "Formalist Cinema and Politics," *Performing Arts Journal* 1, no. 3 (Winter 1977), p. 59.

their own institutions and histories. But this situation could only be temporary. As time passed, these embryonic art forms specified their practices and developed their own histories defined by major artists and works, supporting institutions, and distinct critical languages. "Expanded cinema" was a handy catch-all term, a placeholder for what we would very soon come to know as video art, media art and activism, performance art, experimental and alternative TV, light art, and the electronic arts and new media.

One way to describe this new wave of expanded cinema is to say that it took Mekas's "cinema as we know it" as its basis rather than a foil, thus tempering any apparent hybridity or ontological indeterminacy by hooking itself to the well-established contours of a specific art form. This is the opposite of Renan's liberatory model, with artists "attacking" and ultimately rejecting cinema as we know it and thus escaping the putatively limiting parameters of that tradition. One key implication of this is that expanded cinema was no longer at the opposite end of the spectrum from experimental film's history of reflexive, medium-specific aesthetics. Rather than conceiving it as anathema to avant-garde film's modernism, expanded cinema since the late 1960s has been another manifestation of it. This, in turn, has produced a more nuanced model of cinematic modernism than has previously been acknowledged.

European avant-garde filmmakers were the first to construe the term "expanded cinema" more narrowly, setting themselves apart from the ideas of intermedia and expanded consciousness that shaped American expanded cinema. Valie EXPORT and Peter Weibel in Austria, Wilhelm and Birgit Hein and Werner Nekes in Germany, and several filmmakers connected with the London Filmmakers' Cooperative and the Filmaktion group (Malcolm Le Grice, William Raban, Gill Eatherley, and others) spoke explicitly of an expanded cinema that was, in the words of Le Grice, "a direct development from what was known variously as experimental, underground, structural, or avant-garde film," rather than simply "the broad extension of the media boundaries in art" in general (fig. 1.14).[61] Raban has made a similar distinction between American and European expanded cinemas, connecting the latter specifically to the reflexive practices of avant-garde film.[62]

I would argue that the main reason for this is the prominence of Youngblood's book, which made the term synonymous with intermedia and gave it its associations with psychedelia, the counterculture, and the utopian, quasi-scientific theories of new media like McLuhan's. These associations stuck even as the second wave of expanded cinema was emerging in Europe, and a few years later in the United States. Le Grice addressed this indirectly in 1977:

Youngblood's book was published in 1970, but Peter Weibel in Austria had used the term about his own work as early as 1967. Wherever it originated,

---

[61] Malcolm Le Grice, "Mapping in Multi-Space—Expanded Cinema to Virtuality," in Le Grice, *Experimental Cinema in the Digital Age* (London: BFI, 2001), p. 274.

[62] William Raban, "Reflexivity and Expanded Cinema: A Cinema of Transgression?" in A. L. Rees, David Curtis, Duncan White, and Steven Ball, eds., *Expanded Cinema: Art, Performance, Film* (London: Tate Publishing, 2011), pp. 98–107.

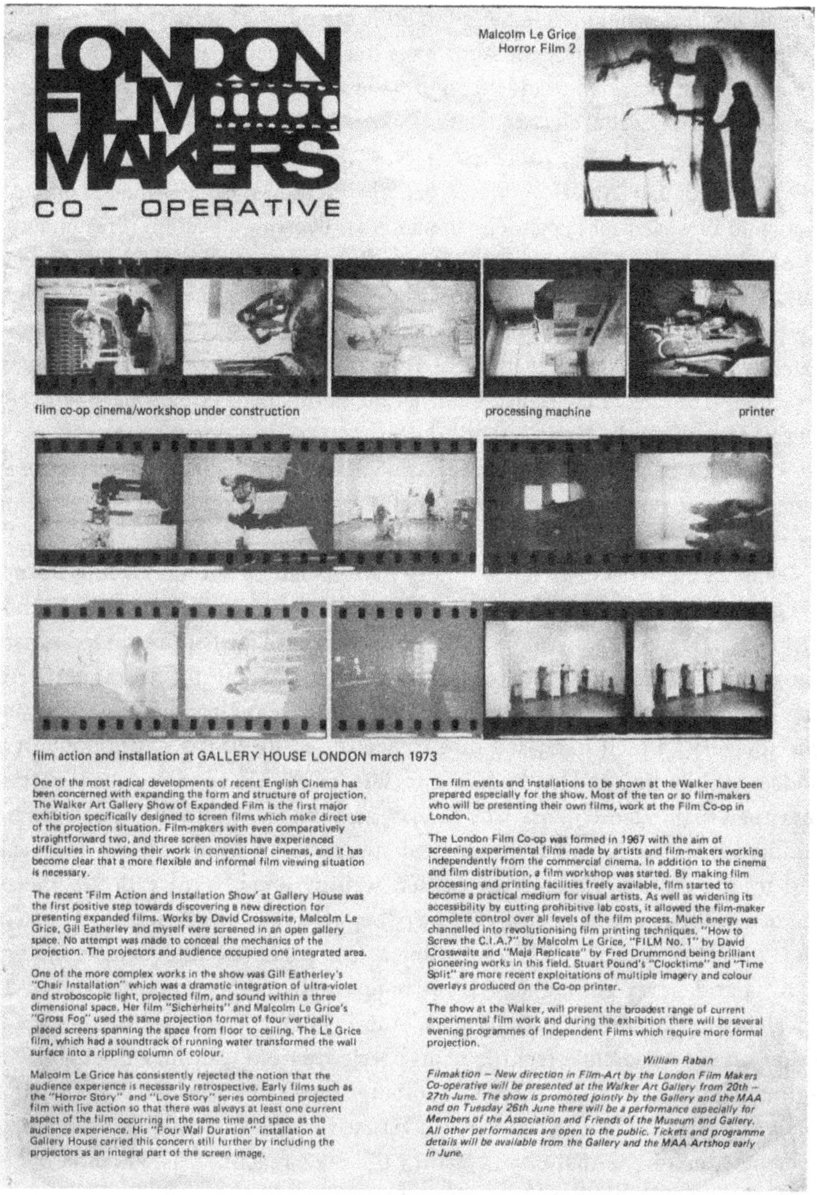

LONDON FILM MAKERS CO – OPERATIVE

Malcolm Le Grice
Horror Film 2

film co-op cinema/workshop under construction

processing machine

printer

film action and installation at GALLERY HOUSE LONDON march 1973

One of the most radical developments of recent English Cinema has been concerned with expanding the form and structure of projection. The Walker Art Gallery Show of Expanded Film is the first major exhibition specifically designed to screen films which make direct use of the projection situation. Film-makers with even comparatively straightforward two, and three screen movies have experienced difficulties in showing their work in conventional cinemas, and it has become clear that a more flexible and informal film viewing situation is necessary.

The recent 'Film Action and Installation Show' at Gallery House was the first positive step towards discovering a new direction for presenting expanded films. Works by David Crosswaite, Malcolm Le Grice, Gill Eatherley and myself were screened in an open gallery space. No attempt was made to conceal the mechanics of the projection. The projectors and audience occupied one integrated area.

One of the more complex works in the show was Gill Eatherley's "Chair Installation" which was a dramatic integration of ultra-violet and stroboscopic light, projected film, and sound within a three dimensional space. Her film "Sicherheits" and Malcolm Le Grice's "Gross Fog" used the same projection format of four vertically placed screens spanning the space from floor to ceiling. The Le Grice film, which had a soundtrack of running water transformed the wall surface into a rippling column of colour.

Malcolm Le Grice has consistently rejected the notion that the audience experience is necessarily retrospective. Early films such as the "Horror Story" and "Love Story" series combined projected film with live action so that there was always at least one current aspect of the film occurring in the same time and space as the audience experience. His "Four Wall Duration" installation at Gallery House carried this concern still further by including the projectors as an integral part of the screen image.

The film events and installations to be shown at the Walker have been prepared especially for the show. Most of the ten or so film-makers who will be presenting their own films, work at the Film Co-op in London.

The London Film Co-op was formed in 1967 with the aim of screening experimental films made by artists and film-makers working independently from the commercial cinema. In addition to the cinema and film distribution, a film workshop was started. By making film processing and printing facilities freely available, film started to become a practical medium for visual artists. As well as widening its accessibility by cutting prohibitive lab costs, it allowed the film-maker complete control over all levels of the film process. Much energy was channelled into revolutionising film printing techniques. "How to Screw the C.I.A.?" by Malcolm Le Grice, "FILM No. 1" by David Crosswaite and "Maja Replicate" by Fred Drummond being brilliant pioneering works in this field. Stuart Pound's "Clocktime" and "Time Split" are more recent exploitations of multiple imagery and colour overlays produced on the Co-op printer.

The show at the Walker, will present the broadest range of current experimental film work and during the exhibition there will be several evening programmes of Independent Films which require more formal projection.

William Raban

Filmaktion – New direction in Film-Art by the London Film Makers Co-operative will be presented at the Walker Art Gallery from 20th – 27th June. The show is promoted jointly by the Gallery and the MAA and on Tuesday 26th June there will be a performance especially for Members of the Association and Friends of the Museum and Gallery. All other performances are open to the public. Tickets and programme details will be available from the Gallery and the MAA Artshop early in June.

Fig. 1.14. Flier for London Filmmakers' Cooperative event featuring the work of Filmaktion. Gallery House, London. March 1973.
Courtesy of William Raban.

its connotations for Youngblood do not fit the extensive amount of European work being done in this area. Youngblood understands it mainly in terms of American West Coast abstraction . . . In Europe, on the other hand, it is seen as a development of the formal issues of cinema and a concern with the reality of the projection situation itself. A quite arbitrary point of contact is in the field of multi-projection: European aims have been almost exclusively formal, frequently conceptual and didactic, and have nothing in common with experiments in "total" visual environments.[63]

Le Grice's claim that "American West Coast abstraction" was the primary context for Youngblood's variant of expanded cinema is an oversimplification. Presumably Le Grice had in mind the admixture of Eastern religion and iconography, hallucinogenic drugs, and psychedelic light and music shows that defined the California counterculture at the time rather than the narrower context of West Coast abstract painting. Certainly the almost mystical flavor of Youngblood's ideas would have rubbed the more literal minded materialist avant-garde filmmakers of Europe like Weibel, Valie EXPORT, and Le Grice himself the wrong way. In any event, the assumption that American expanded cinema necessarily meant intermedia in the service of idealistic consciousness expansion meant that bright lines were drawn between North American and European work.

Mekas, like Le Grice, took a similarly nationalistic position. Having attended the Festival of Avant-Garde Film at London's National Film Theatre in September 1973 (fig. 1.15), Mekas wrote a little dismissively of British expanded cinema, "of course, New York went through it 10 years ago."[64] But for Mekas, American expanded cinema consisted primarily of multimedia environments and "psychedelic imagery," which likely led him to see the more film-specific body of expanded work in England, and a few years later in the United States, as something other than expanded cinema. For Mekas, and other critics, "expanded cinema" connoted intermedia and technological spectacle, of which Mekas had clearly tired by the early 1970s. A year earlier, writing about VanDerBeek's *Violence Sonata* (1970) and *Newsreel of Dreams* (begun 1963, continued into the early '70s), Mekas had expressed exhaustion at American expanded cinema's technophilia and never ending search for bigger and more immersive audiovisual experiences: "For almost two decades, Stan [VanDerBeek] has been engaged in mastering every possible technique and style that one can find in cinema," including the use of multiple screens, computer imagery, and video. "The big question is: is it possible to do a concentrated creative work and still follow and master every new technique that comes within the eye's reach?"[65] The comments that follow clearly indicate that Mekas thought not.

Violence Sonata and *Newsreel of Dreams* utilized film, video, live performance, and audience participation and interaction. The former additionally involved telephone,

---

[63] Malcolm Le Grice, *Abstract Film and Beyond* (Cambridge, MA: MIT Press, 1977).

[64] Mekas, "Movie Journal," *Village Voice*, September 4, 1973, reprinted in Rees, et al., *Expanded Cinema*, p. 72.

[65] Mekas, "Movie Journal," *Village Voice*, July 6, 1972, p. 50.

Fig. 1.15. Poster for the Expanded Cinema event during the Festival of Avant-Garde Film. National Film Theatre, London, September 1973.
Courtesy of British Artists' Film and Video Study Collection, Central Saint Martins, University of the Arts London.

television, radio broadcasts, and print media. Both also extended VanDerBeek's *Movie Drome* experiments and longstanding interest in collage. The individual films and video reels shown as part of *Violence Sonata* and *Newsreel of Dreams* were culled together from footage VanDerBeek had both made and found; they were further collaged by being projected in a multi-screen format. Finally, the projection of these collage reels was part of a larger event that included live, real time manipulation of the source material in immersive, participatory multimedia events, often of long duration. *Violence Sonata* took place over several days in both print and on television, while a revised version of *Newsreel of Dreams*, renamed *Cine-Dreams*, was an eight-hour overnight event held in the Strasenburgh Planetarium in Rochester, New York, in 1972 (fig. 1.16). Mark Bartlett describes the complexity of *Violence Sonata* (fig. 1.17), which took place at the WGBH studio in Boston on January 12, 1970:

In the days leading up to its broadcast, *Violence Sonata* was announced in the form of a "pre-event" in print and on the radio, and on the day the work was produced, it was "simulcast" to home audiences asked to place two television sets side-by-side, each tuned to different channels, one showing the in-studio events, and the other, presenters commenting on them. Telephone call-ins were broadcast live as part of the TV-Theatre, which included an audience of

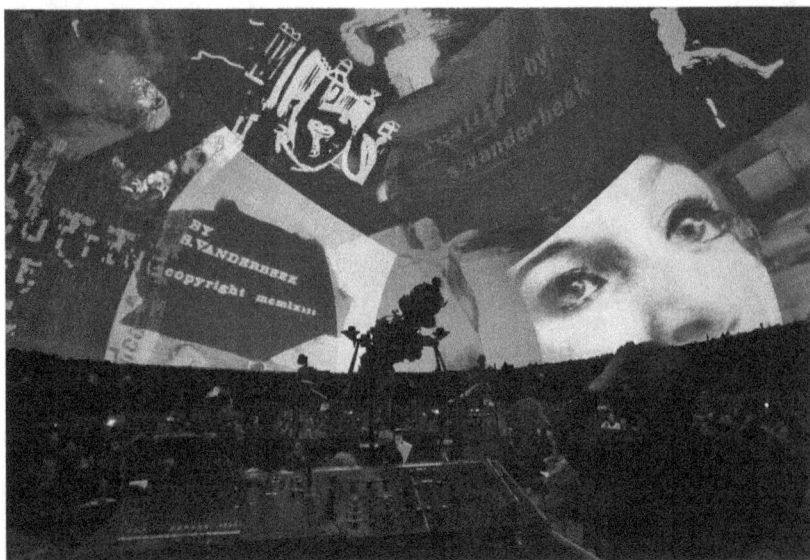

Fig. 1.16. Stan VanDerBeek, *Cine-Dreams* (1972). Civico Planetario Ulrico Hoepli, Milan, 2014.
Photograph by Marco De Scalzi. Courtesy Stan VanDerBeek Archive and Fondazione Nicola Trussardi.

Fig. 1.17. Stan VanDerBeek, *Violence Sonata* (1970). WGBH Studio, Boston, MA, 1970.
Courtesy Stan VanDerBeek Archive.

three hundred in the WGHB studio, staged intermedia, expanded cinema, happenings and other theatrical events which now functioned at the level of mass broadcasting.[66]

---

[66] Mark Bartlett, "Socialimagestics and the Visual Acupuncture of Stan VanDerBeek's Expanded Cinema," in Rees, et al., *Expanded Cinema*, p. 55.

VanDerBeek envisioned both pieces as co-opting mainstream media, at once to critique it and offer more progressive alternatives to the authoritarian, unidirectional,
non-participatory forms of commercial communication media. Not to oversimplify
VanDerBeek's fascinating work, but these were clearly instantiations of McLuhan's
claim "the medium is the message." The social-political content of VanDerBeek's
work was not only, or even mostly, in its imagery, but in the ways it re-imagined the
structure of media technologies and their uses by the masses. According to Bartlett,
"VanDerBeek described [*Violence Sonata*] as an 'information concert' with a Dada
political aesthetic, and as the first work of anti-TV in which the walls of mass media
were torn down and converted into a 'People's Park TV.' "[67] Thus, it represents exactly
the kind of work and political ethos at the core of Youngblood's conception of expanded cinema, particularly his claim that expanded cinema artists were "ecologists,"
and that the ecosystem now included the "noosphere," the layer of communications
technologies encircling the earth.

Mekas had seen the first two parts of a single-screen version of *Newsreel of Dreams*
at The Kitchen in June of 1972, where VanDerBeek had claimed that the work consisted of eight parts intended to be viewed simultaneously on eight screens. Mekas's
response: "a full aesthetic experience of one screen is worth 1000 half-experiences
on eight screens."[68] While the expanded cinema Mekas saw in London the following year did include multi-screen work, ultimately he saw little continuity between American expanded cinema à la VanDerBeek and the British work of a few
years later: "I came to the conclusion that they are not repeating history."[69] Mekas
often noted the austerity of European expanded cinema, its simplicity relative to
American expanded work, at least as Mekas understood it. He described it in terms
of "classicism," suggesting that, as I have argued, the next wave of expanded cinema
that Mekas witnessed emerging in Europe was more cinema-centered, an intervention in traditional filmmaking and exhibition rather than a complete escape from
or abandonment of it.[70]

The historical distinctions made by Le Grice and Mekas between American and
European expanded cinema need to be muddied. On the one hand, the U.S./Europe
split has occluded national and regional differences among expanded practices on
each side of the Atlantic, not to mention the work by Japanese, Australian, and South
American filmmakers. On the other hand, it has also tended to obscure parallels between work by European expanded cinema makers and avant-garde film artists in
North America. Work by Ken Jacobs, Tony Conrad, Paul Sharits, Frampton, Snow,
and McCall (an Englishman who moved to New York in 1973), to name just a few, was

---

[67] Ibid.

[68] Mekas, "Movie Journal," *Village Voice*, July 6, 1972, p. 50.

[69] Mekas, "Movie Journal," *Village Voice*, September 4, 1973, reprinted in Rees, et al., *Expanded
Cinema*, p. 72.

[70] See Mekas, "Movie Journal," *Village Voice*, October 11, 1973, in which Mekas refers to Le Grice's projector performance *Horror Film #1* as "classical." Reprinted in Rees, et al., *Expanded Cinema*, p. 78. I discuss
Horror Film 1 in chapter 3.

not usually referred to as "expanded cinema" despite the obvious appropriateness of the term for it.

Mekas's sharp criticisms of VanDerBeek reveal his exasperation at the seemingly unstoppable ambition of the expansion of cinema, at its increasing unwieldiness and distance from cinematic tradition. The waves of expanded cinema that followed, however, represented as much a consolidation of cinema as a departure from it, an enactment of the "specifically cinematic" as that cluster of qualities has been formulated explicitly and implicitly within avant-garde film. As such, it can be thought of as at once an expansion and contraction of cinema, adding new forms to the category of cinema without mutating that category to the point of unrecognizability or meaningless over-accommodation. Several commentators on expanded cinema have invoked the idea of contraction as a kind of complementary movement or process taking place across cinema's history. Addressing the challenge of defining expanded cinema, Chrissie Iles spoke of an "ongoing expansion and contraction of the cinema" that could be traced to the precinematic past, at least as far back as experiments with anamorphism during the baroque period. Expanded Cinema ("capital 'E' capital 'C,'" as Iles put it), had been "a specific historical moment" growing out of structural and structural/materialist film, just one phase of a larger process by which cinema's ontology is constantly redefined and re-historicized.[71] The phrase "expansion and contraction" denotes the tension between a centrifugal "moving out" of cinema from its traditional forms and a centripetal crystallization of an essential cinematic core, though one that can take many different shapes.

"Contracted cinema" might sound like an apt descriptor for structural and structural-materialist films, since these were said to take some material or formal quality of the film medium as the basis for an entire work. As David James has described it, each structural film "develops principles of construction peculiar to the specific area of the filmic process it de-signs." That is, in detaching filmic elements from signification—"de-signing" them—structural films make those elements their primary meaning.[72] This is an act of contraction, a reduction of cinema to the materials of a specific medium. But taken far enough, avant-garde film's radical reductionism has resulted in works that resist any simplistic medium-specific explications. For instance, McCall's desire to explore the "presuppositions behind film as an art activity" produced an entirely film-less work; in a 1986 interview with McCall, Scott MacDonald said of *Long Film for Ambient Light*, "it's as though filmmaking had led you out of film."[73] In other words, the reductionism of avant-garde filmmaking in the sixties and seventies could ultimately lead to its opposite. Conceiving cinema as fundamentally about light, space, and time opened up the art form rather than closing it down. This was also the case with expanded works that took structural film's method

---

[71] Iles, "Inside Out."

[72] David James, *Allegories of Cinema: American Film in the Sixties* (Princeton: Princeton University Press, 1989), p. 244.

[73] Scott MacDonald, "Anthony McCall," in *A Critical Cinema 2: Interviews with Independent Filmmakers* (Berkeley: University of California Press, 1992), p. 165.

of "positing a film constructed to manifest each moment in an atomized model of the entire cinematic process," as James explains it, to its logical conclusion, isolating individual elements of the medium in ways that necessitated a mode of exhibition unlike that of conventional cinema.[74] The act of purification whereby a single film is entirely "about" zooming (*Wavelength*), or the shutter (Conrad's 1966 *The Flicker* or Sharits's films), or photographic re-printing (J. J. Murphy's 1974 *Print Generation*), or any other material or formal trait could suggest a kind of expanded cinema. For instance, Sharits, Peter Kubelka, and Takahiko Iimura were all preoccupied in the 1960s and 1970s with the individual film frame, producing a series of films that made that frame their main subject. But this obsession with the frame took all three filmmakers further, to the point of displaying the filmstrip itself as the sole object of contemplation, in Sharits's *Frozen Film Frames* series, Kubelka's wall-mounted installation of *Arnulf Rainer* (1960) and *Antiphon* (2012), and Iimura's 16mm film loops encased in Plexiglas boxes (2007). Nekes made a series of what he called "contracted-expanded film performances" in 1967. In one, a strip of 16mm film was cut lengthwise down the middle, the two pieces projected simultaneously side-by-side, the projectionists attempting to reconnect the two halved images on screen. In another piece, *Standing Film/Moving Film*, Nekes projected a single frame of moldy film onto a wall; as the projector's lamp heated the frame, the microbes of mold moved, causing the colors in the frame to shift.[75]

More recently, a new generation of filmmakers, including Jennifer Reeves, Sandra Gibson, Luis Recoder, and Joel Schlemowitz, has employed the same exhibition format (see chapter 4). The filmmaker Bradley Eros has revived the term "contracted cinema," positing a historical process of expansion and contraction for which film's literal elasticity as a length of plastic is the basis for a metaphor for cinema's "mutability": "this malleable material, this sculptural aspect, combined with its translucency, is what gives it the great potentiality to mutate as an art form."[76] But this mutability is not entirely open; Eros characterizes cinema as "breathing," expanding and contracting in a historical loop. This dualism also finds a metaphor in the physical makeup of the film medium, which Eros describes as at once resolutely material and elusively ephemeral, which is to say both (medium) specific and non-specific, a "tabula rasa" open to the influences and qualities of other art forms. In a passage that at once invokes Youngblood's vision of expanded cinema and its opposite, Eros writes that film "mirrors both the mind-expanding and the concise-focused in human consciousness."[77]

Eros's live projection performance *Burn (or, The 2nd Law of Thermodynamics* (2004) puts this dialectic into practice (fig. 1.18). Eros pulls sections of an 8mm

[74] James, *Allegories of Cinema*, p. 243.
[75] Werner Nekes, "Some Notes on Some Expanded Films," in Rees, et al., *Expanded Cinema*, pp. 182–184.
[76] Bradley Eros, "There Will Be Projections in All Dimensions," *Millennium Film Journal* nos. 43/44 (Summer/Fall 2005), p. 66.
[77] Ibid.

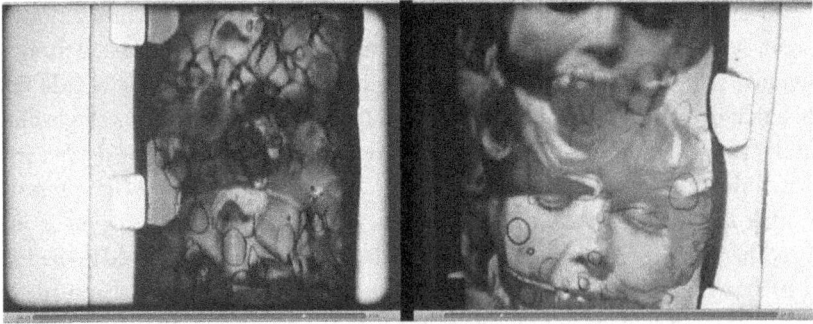

Fig. 1.18. Bradley Eros, *Burn (or, The 2nd Law of Thermodynamics)* (2004). Stills from digital version. Originally super-8mm in a 16mm projector, found-footage hand-manipulated in the gate, color, sound. 5:15 min. (v.1)/6:30 min. (v.2)/5:35 min. (v.3)// 17:20 TRT). Composed and performed by Bradley Eros.
Image courtesy of the artist.

pornographic film by hand through the gate of a 16mm projector. The projector's gate, designed for a film frame twice the size of 8mm's, reveals multiple still frames at once rather than isolating single frames and animating them into illusory movement as in normal projection. The film's passage through the projector is inconsistent, as Eros allows segments of the film to linger in the gate until they begin to bubble and melt in the heat of the projector lamp. Robert DeNiro's brooding voiceover narration from the film *Taxi Driver* accompanies the performance. As Travis Bickle, he speaks of cleansing and purification in brutal terms appropriate to the spectacle unfolding on screen. Eros describes *Burn*, and contracted cinema in general, as "a separation (or purification) of medium-specific filmic elements to concentrate on a singular material or mechanical property. The elimination of superfluous or extraneous means. Precise focus."[78] Contrast this with the all-encompassing models of expanded cinema offered by Renan and Youngblood. But ironically, such resolutely materialist, radically reductive practices open onto expanded cinema, which is to say cinema in an expanded range of possible materials or configurations of those materials. Eros's "precise focus" on the film frame, on its fragility and plasticity, on sprocket holes and aperture gates, emulsion grains and framelines, takes a form completely distinct from conventional cinema. Contracted cinema passes through a kind of conceptual wormhole to expanded cinema.

Hence, the brand of medium specificity on view in works of "contracted" expanded cinema was not about the reification of the film medium or the unquestioning acceptance of the parameters constituted by its standard uses. Rather, it articulated the

---

[78] Ibid., p. 75.

medium's inherent material and formal multiplicity without losing a sense of its specificity and the enabling limitations this entailed. I shall elaborate on this version of filmic medium specificity in the next chapter, while "contracted" works like those of McCall, Iimura, and Eros will appear throughout this book. For now, the point to make is that the film medium and the traditional theatrical mode of cinematic exhibition were links between expanded cinema after 1967 and "cinema as we know it." They provided a heuristic by which expanded work was made recognizable as cinema rather than another art form or work of intermedia. *Long Film for Ambient Light*, for instance, played on the idea of the camera obscura, analogized windows to screens, and suggested temporal articulations like fades and dissolves on the greatly extended temporal scale of the merging of day into night.

Reflecting in 2003 upon her own expanded cinema work of the late 1960s, EXPORT invoked similar ideas and motivations:

> In Expanded Cinema, the film phenomenon is initially split up into its formal components, and then put back together again in a new way. The operations of the collective union which is film, such as the screen, the cinema theatre, the projector, light and celluloid, are partially replaced by reality in order to install new signs of the real ... The formal arrangement of the elements of film, whereby elements are exchanged or replaced by others—for example, electric light by fire, celluloid by reality, a beam of light by rockets—had an effect which was artistically liberating and yielded a wealth of new possibilities, such as film installations and the film-environment.[79]

EXPORT's most notorious effort to replace elements of film with "signs of the real" was *TAPP UND TAST KINO* (*Touch Cinema*, with Peter Weibel, 1968), which engaged the political resonances of what EXPORT called the "body as screen," fiercely critiquing the film industry's use of images of female sexuality to reproduce and reinforce ideological norms governing that sexuality. In this performance, conducted in a street outside a movie theater in Vienna, EXPORT wore a cardboard box over her naked torso as Weibel encouraged onlookers to reach into the box to touch EXPORT's bare breasts (fig. 1.19). The box functioned as a miniature movie theater, complete with a set of makeshift curtains at the front behind which the erotic spectacle lay.

Two other works enacted EXPORT's belief that, "In the production of the film medium, celluloid is only one aspect that could (also) be deleted. Instead of the projected image, the film strip itself can become a site for expanding the medium."[80] In *Abstract Film No. 1* (1967–1968) flashlight beams cast light on mirrors over which EXPORT poured various liquids, and which reflected the light onto a nearby

[79] Valie EXPORT, "Expanded Cinema: Expanded Reality," in Rees, et al., *Expanded Cinema*, p. 290.
[80] Ibid., p. 291.

Fig. 1.19. Valie EXPORT, *TAPP UND TAST KINO* (*Touch Cinema*, with Peter Weibel, 1968). Photograph courtesy of Valie EXPORT Atelier.

screen (fig. 1.20). *Instant Film* (1968) was simply a piece of transparent PVC foil, which EXPORT referred to as "screen, projector, and camera all in one" and which could be displayed on a wall, cut or perforated, or peered through by the spectator-turned-filmmaker.[81] Text accompanying a photograph of EXPORT demonstrating *Instant Film* in 1968 (fig. 1.21) reads:

> The installation is the task of the viewer. He can hang the foil on the 4 walls of his house—his own four canvases—with four different color backgrounds. He can put the foil in front of an object, to create his own collage and superimpositions that way. He can turn "Reality" into "film" by holding the foil in front of his eyes. The canvas format enlarges when the distance from the pair of eyes increases. A prepared foil (with scissors, cigarette, sharpies . . .) conveys "hints" or "insights" anytime. Live turns "transparent" and "clear." If the user draws his "worldview" on the foil, he will see the world according to his views.[82]

EXPORT and Weibel's expanded cinema performances and installations constitute a veritable catalogue of possibilities for the model I've described, wherein

---

[81] Ibid., p. 291.
[82] I am grateful to Helmut Berthold and Kevlin Haire for this translation from the original German.

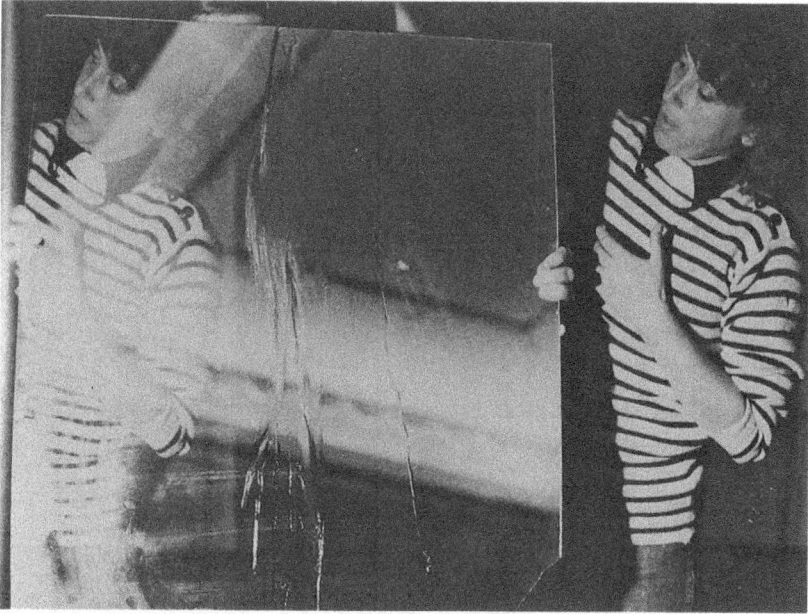

Fig. 1.20. Valie EXPORT, *Abstract Film No. 1* (1967–1968).
Photograph courtesy of Valie EXPORT Atelier.

elements of cinema as we know it are reconfigured or replaced. EXPORT and
Weibel negotiated between the pure physical materiality of the film medium and
social and political complexities of reality in the spirit of the blurring of art and
life. But they did so without sacrificing a connection to cinema's specificity. In fact,
to be recognizable and thus meaningful as interventions in conventional cinema
as EXPORT and Weibel intended, these works needed to be legible as cinema,
however expanded. Furthermore, EXPORT and Weibel explored the implications
of the varied new forms expanded cinema could take—performative, sculptural,
painterly—illustrating that filmmakers could continue to assert the autonomy of
their art form without cutting it off from the others. EXPORT has stated that her
use of natural materials such as water, light, and the body created "unexpected and
yet fundamentally illuminating connections with minimal art, land art, *arte po-
vera*."[83] EXPORT's conception of expanded cinema thus signaled the return of a
cinema-centered interpretive framework: the "atomization" of cinema's materials,
the dialectic of expansion and contraction, and the desire to preserve cinema's autonomy in the period of Kosuth's "art in general."

Two more facets of EXPORT's work and the concept of cinematic expansion
it represents are worth noting here. First, EXPORT promoted a breakdown of the

---

[83] Ibid., p. 295.

INSTANT FILM   1968

objektfilm, zus. mit p. weibel
material : durchsichtige pvc-folie

die montage ist die sache des zuschauers. er kann die folie zu hause
auf seine eigenen 4 wände – seine eigenen 4 leinwände– auf einen jeweils
verschiedenen farbhintergrund hängen. er kann die folie vor ein objekt
geben, solcherart seine eigenen collagen und superimpositions ausführen.
er kann die "wirklichkeit" zu einem "film" machen, indem er die folie
vor seine augen hält. der gesichtsraum (=leinwandformat) verlängert sich
durch die entfernung vom augenpaar. eine präparierte folie (durch schere,
zigarette, filzstifte.) vermittelt jederzeit "durcgblicke" oder "ein =
blicke". das leben wird "durchschaubar", "überschaubar". zeichnet der
benutzer sein "weltbild" auf die folie, sieht er die welt nach seinem
"bilde".

aktionsfoto, göteborg, 1968.

Fig. 1.21. Valie EXPORT, ephemera for *Instant Film* (1968), with EXPORT holding PVC foil (right).
Courtesy of Valie EXPORT Atelier.

distinction between art and life, as Renan and Youngblood did following Kaprow and Cage. But in her model, life, or what she calls "the real," was shaped by traditional cinematic materials and conventions. Cinema as we know it was a model that structured the performative, participatory forms that EXPORT's expanded cinema took, a pattern we will see in the work of dozens of other artists. Second, like the artists of expanded cinema's first wave, EXPORT speaks of intermedia practices as liberatory:

> the expanded concept of art … made it possible to engage individually in every element of the collective form "cinema" to re-form and re-interpret context in such a way that not only the apparative art is liberated from the confining mechanism; rather, it also frees image-connected thought from its constraints.[84]

But the liberation offered by artistic expansion in general is not seen here in terms of abandonment of tradition. Rather, EXPORT thinks of it as liberation from arbitrary, unnecessary, or harmful aspects of conventional cinema, in EXPORT's case illusionism and the technologically deterministic constraints of a physical medium. EXPORT thus sees that medium as simultaneously constraining and enabling, both an arbitrary mechanical limitation and a creatively generative system that can be adjusted to produce novel cinematic forms. This stance toward medium specificity will turn up again and again in the expanded cinema works surveyed in this book.

It should also be noted that EXPORT combines two different meanings of "material" in her phrase "material film." Though the work is rooted in the material elements of the medium like celluloid and screen, the replacement of these with real bodies and actions rather than illusory ones leads to another kind of materialist cinema. "Material" in this sense of the word extends beyond the raw materials of film technology to the routinized practices and institutions of filmmaking, exhibition, and spectatorship that had coalesced over 70 years of cinema history. EXPORT and Weibel's expanded cinema was intended as much as an intervention in the dominant patterns of cinema spectatorship as it was as an investigation of the film medium's specificity. The attack "on the continuity of the phases of production," EXPORT claimed, "robs the production companies of their conventional success."[85] Contemporary avant-garde cinema, to which I turn in the next chapter, continues in this interventional spirit, though conditions in the environments of cinema, art, and media have changed in significant ways.

Whither Expanded Cinema?

If Eros and Iles are right that the history of expanded cinema is really the history of cinema's expansion *and contraction*, then it would be fair to say that the late seventies was a moment in which the latter took place. By the end of the decade, the excitement expanded cinema generated for many filmmakers and critics seems to have died down, with many of the form's major figures turning their attentions elsewhere, often

---

[84] Ibid., p. 290.
[85] Ibid., p. 293.

returning to filmmaking in its conventional format. Expanded cinema didn't exactly disappear; elsewhere in this book we will encounter artists making expanded cinema into the mid-1980s, though they were much more the exception than the rule by that time. Once the methods and forms of expanded cinema were introduced, subsequent artists could employ them as they could any other format. The historical question is why these forms, once made available, became so much less prominent by the end of the 1970s. What happened to expanded cinema? To my knowledge, no other critical account has attempted an answer. To conclude this chapter, I sketch some possible explanations.

Many new artistic forms initially labeled as expanded cinema became something else, as the impulse to define and differentiate them, abandoned by the first wave of expanded cinema, took over again. Even in Youngblood's book, the language of medium-specificity and artistic autonomy rears its head. Interestingly, most citations of *Expanded Cinema* in scholarly literature come from the early chapters of the book, where Youngblood makes the boldest philosophical claims about media convergence and intermedia. By the latter half of the book, Youngblood and many of the artists he examines delve back into the distinct possibilities of new physical media like video and computers. Youngblood's McLuhan-esque language of interactive and passive media is, in the final analysis, about the physical characteristics of new media technologies and their promise of new aesthetic and social experiences. His discussion of video artist Loren Sears is instructive. "Loren Sears regards television as an extension of the central nervous system, and thus employs the term 'neuro-aesthetics' to indicate *the unique character* of videographic art," Youngblood writes (italics mine). He then quotes Sears himself:

Every medium has a fundamental means of operation. In film it's sprocket holes, registration, optics, frames. The characteristics of television are different. In both cases, however, there's a strategic way of using the medium effortlessly.[86]

Analogies to the human nervous system or to the environment, which pepper *Expanded Cinema*, can be made in the first place because of the physical nature of the technologies under discussion, in which physical differences become especially important.

Sears later invokes the muses of the arts, advancing an argument for television's uniqueness in much the same way that generations of filmmakers had for film. Sears claims:

Any medium can be transformed by the user. The paradigm for it all is music. There's the music of the medium, which means it also has a muse. We can learn

---

[86] Youngblood, *Expanded Cinema*, p. 291.

from it. Television has been used as an attraction, a come-on, an effect. Nothing used for effect is an art.[87]

Sears's use of the term "attraction" for "non-artistic" uses of a new medium recalls Tom Gunning's concept of "the cinema of attractions."[88] To rephrase Gunning's argument in Sears's vocabulary, once the new medium of film was no longer merely a "come-on" or "effect," which is to say an "attraction," it became cinema as we know it, an art form undergoing a process of both standardization and consolidation. Gunning's essay concludes with an acknowledgement that the attractions of the cinema of attractions became the basis for avant-garde film. What is important here is the idea that a new technology's artistic potential can only be realized when it stops being a marvel and is mined for distinct artistic possibilities, which displace the purely technological effects as the center of the spectator's attention. If, as I have claimed, "expanded cinema" was a vaporous catch-all term for the wave of new visual and communications media that crested in the 1960s, it was also a term that connoted spectacle, novelty, and technological side-shows. No coincidence that world's fairs were an early home to many forms of expanded cinema. The exhaustion expressed by Mekas in response to VanDerBeek's multi-screen and multimedia extravaganzas, and the cautionary tone sounded by Michelson that expanded cinema was merely another *gesamtkunstwerk*, point precisely to skepticism over expanded cinema's "spectacularity." Such perceptions must have further stoked artists' desire to distinguish their developing work in video, television, and computer art from cinema. That is, both cinema and expanded cinema were loaded with historical and conceptual baggage that most practitioners of new media art did not want to carry. It was time, by the mid-1970s at the latest, to cultivate the mature ontological identities of these new media that would transform them from "come-on" to art form.

In 1974, the Museum of Modern Art hosted "Open Circuits: An International Conference on the Future of Television," attended by a veritable who's-who of avant-garde moving image and electronic art makers (including Paik, VanDerBeek, Snow, Frampton, Frank Gillette, Richard Serra, Joan Jonas, Vito Acconci, and Shigeko Kubota) (figs. 1.22 and 1.23). Papers and talks delivered at the conference appeared in the edited volume *The New Television: A Public/Private Art* in 1977. "The future of television" and "the new television" announce the agenda of the artists in attendance, and of many other television and video artists at the time: the prescription, if loose, of video art's unique path, which would necessarily lead away from cinema, expanded or otherwise. The texts in *The New Television* play out a dialectic of differentiation and analogy, explicitly distinguishing video from cinema, its most proximate "other," while paralleling it with painting, sculpture, happenings, and performance art.[89] For

---

[87] Ibid., p. 292.

[88] Tom Gunning, "The Cinema of Attractions: Early Film, Its Spectator, and the Avant-Garde," *Wide Angle* 8, nos. 3 & 4 (Fall 1986).

[89] See, especially, Hollis Frampton, "The Withering Away of the State of the Art" and Wulf Herzogenrath, "Notes on Video as an Artistic Medium," in Douglas Davis and Allison Simmons, eds., *The New Television: A Public/Private Art* (Cambridge, MA: MIT Press, 1977), pp. 24–35 and 88–93, respectively.

Fig. 1.22. Participants in a panel during "Open Circuits" (left to right: Michael Snow, Jane Livingston, James Herithas, Lydia Vitale.
Photograph by Leonardo LeGrand. Courtesy of Electronic Arts Intermix (EAI), New York.

cinema, the "other" had been theater, and more broadly reality itself, something that will become important in chapter 3. The new television could be in the museum or gallery, could be sculptural, painterly, a variant of visual music, a collage form, a kind of participatory or conceptual art, but not cinema. Tellingly, there are no references to expanded cinema anywhere in the book. The term simply doesn't appear, despite the fact that *Expanded Cinema* had been published only four years earlier and that many of the artists at the conference were significant figures in Youngblood's book. A chronology included in *The New Television* reveals that "Open Circuits" was just one of a series of events centered on televisual and video art, many of which followed a similar agenda.[90]

By the late 1970s, then, there was less expanded cinema, which is to say that fewer art forms fell under that heading. This set the stage for the narrower, more cinecentric model that contemporary expanded cinema represents. Many avant-garde filmmakers, among them Sharits, Conrad, McCall, and members of the London

---

[90] These included "Television as a Creative Medium" at the Howard Wise Gallery in New York (1969), "A Special Videotape Show" at the Whitney Museum (1971), and "Collector's Video Art" at the Los Angeles County Museum of Art (1974), to name only a few.

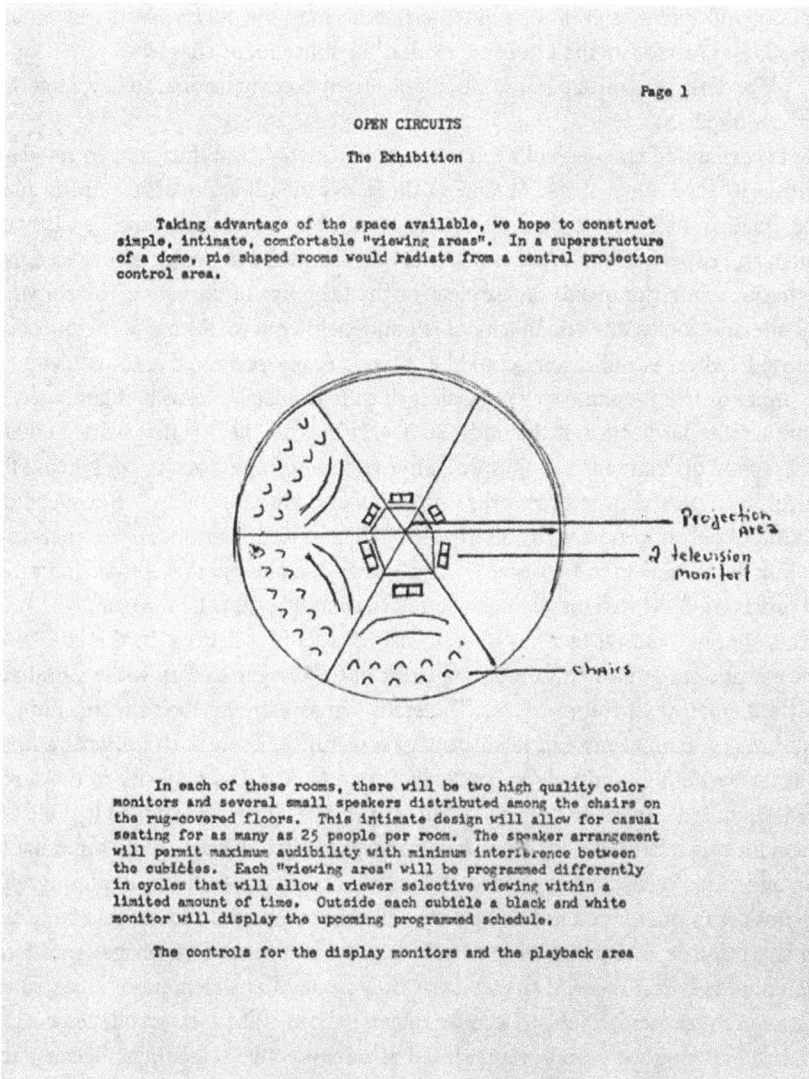

Fig. 1.23. Layout plan for "Open Circuits." From "Open Circuits: Art at the Beginning of the Electronic Age: Project Proposal" (1972).
Courtesy of Electronic Arts Intermix (EAI), New York.

Filmmakers' Cooperative, continued to make film-based installations, objects, and performances. Implicitly or explicitly, these filmmakers distanced their work from the idea of expanded cinema, likely because its connotations of utopia, the global village, and the breakdown of cinema's ontological identity were still too proximate. Undoubtedly, though, these are works of expanded cinema in the narrower sense that necessarily resulted from filmmakers' desire to re-secure the bounds of their art form and contemporaneous efforts by video artists to map out theirs. Works by Sharits, Conrad, and others, as shall become evident in subsequent chapters, were propositions of and meditations upon the cinematic tested via expansion into new materials, forms, and spaces.

But if expanded cinema had been usefully contracted, and thus concentrated and clarified, it faced other obstacles. One of these was the difficulty of sustaining an artistic practice that did not produce a permanent object, one that could be easily circulated and experienced the same way every time and did not require concessions to the unique exhibition needs of the piece or the presence of the artist. The ephemerality, site-specificity, and singularity of expanded cinema works made them difficult to present, whereas a film print could be shipped easily, projected automatically, and seen more or less the same way regardless of time or place. Mekas had lamented the medium's standardization in the mid-1960s, arguing that the best new work could not be "wrapped up, canned, and shipped," after encountering difficulty convincing film festivals to show multi-screen works by Warhol and Barbara Rubin.[91] But sustaining the kind of output produced by Sharits, McCall, and Ken Jacobs was extremely difficult long term, and so the positive traits of expanded cinema that Renan and others had proclaimed as liberatory came to be seen as liabilities as time wore on.

This simple material fact has crucial historical consequences. In the late 1970s, we see avant-garde film culture taking stock of its 60-year history while simultaneously anticipating its future course. The historical assessment took the form of a series of major exhibitions and retrospective screenings, along with important books on avant-garde film and new journals dedicated to it.[92] The majority of these relegated expanded cinema to the role of outlier practice, if they addressed it at all. One reason for this relative lack of representation was likely the dearth of documentation. Film and video records of expanded cinema events were rare, and still photographs, also not common, tended to be of poor quality in comparison to the relatively clear and sharp frame enlargements from standard-format films. Still images could provide only the barest sense of the work, as they isolated one element of an expanded cinema event or performance. Because they were difficult to (re-)produce, works of expanded cinema were underrepresented at retrospective screenings. Because they were often one-time events, often undocumented, they were underrepresented in scholarly studies. Expanded cinema became, in a sense, avant-garde film scholarship's "lost object," lost precisely because it did not produce an object in the first place. Other factors I have already outlined must have played a part in expanded cinema's marginalization—its connotations of techno-fetishism and naïve utopianism, its

[91] Mekas, *Movie Journal*, pp. 249–250.

[92] The retrospective screenings include Documenta 6, "*Film als Film*," a major festival of expanded cinema at London's ICA, "Perspectives on British Avant-Garde Film" at The Hayward Gallery in 1977, and a 1976 American Federation of Arts retrospective of American avant-garde cinema. The books include Sitney, *The Avant-Garde Film*; Le Grice, *Abstract Film and Beyond*; Peter Gidal, ed., *Structural Film Anthology* (London: BFI Press, 1976). *Camera Obscura* and *Wide Angle* appeared in 1976, and *Millennium Film Journal* began publishing in 1978, immediately offering major reconsiderations of avant-garde film's history.

challenges to cinematic essentialism and its apparently unstable identity, its wanderings into non-cinematic exhibition spaces. But the ramifications of its material elusiveness cannot be understated.

Avant-garde cinema's new trajectory was nicely articulated by Tony Conrad in 2005. Reflecting on his expanded cinema *Yellow Movies* series of the early 1970s (see chapter 6), Conrad concludes that they "ultimately failed as an intervention, since they were not cogently legible at the time within either film or art" and that they "were occluded by the more relevant feminist interventions of the mid 1970s."[93] The failure, to use Conrad's word, was the result of their "illegibility" as a specific art form, which is another way of describing the problem of expanded cinema's indeterminate artistic identity. But it is the "occlusion" of expanded cinema by "more relevant" work that concerns me here. The feminist films of the 1970s to which Conrad refers, by filmmakers like Yvonne Rainer and Laura Mulvey (with Peter Wollen), reflected a larger trend wherein avant-garde cinema turned its attentions from the nature of cinema to the social and political realities of the period. In doing so, it additionally took up narrative, as well as representational "content" more broadly. It also abandoned expanded forms and returned to the conventional single screen theatrical mode. Conrad's own filmmaking followed this trajectory immediately after a prolific period of producing expanded cinema. Anthony McCall and Valie EXPORT would do the same, as would many others who had spent years charting cinema's expanded field.

Historians have often marked a fairly clean break from structural film to "the New Talkie," from the centripetal mode of reflexivity and medium-specificity to a centrifugal one where film re-engaged with real life, with people and their personal and political lives.[94] Inasmuch as expanded cinema was an outgrowth of the former, and thus a variant of modernism, it seemed ill suited for grappling with the new political preoccupations of the avant-garde. Its anti-illusionism and self-awareness, especially, were perceived as blocking filmmakers who wanted to look outward onto the real world rather than inward to the forms and mechanisms of cinema *qua* cinema. In sum, the turn I am describing here was not simply a matter of one tendency replacing another in a natural cycle of shifting dominants. The ontological, essentializing bent of structural film and expanded cinema were anathema to the emerging political aspirations of avant-garde film. The latter was not only a replacement of the former, but a correction of its formalism and ahistoricism, and its putative blindness to gender and cultural difference.

But we should not make *too* clean a break here. The return of narrative as a vehicle for political expression did not so much displace the modernism of structural film and expanded cinema as absorb it and re-orient it toward new aims. Filmmakers now used the lessons they had learned from a rigorously reflexive film practice to make

---

[93] Tony Conrad, "Is This Penny Ante or a High Stakes Game? An Interventionist Approach to Experimental Filmmaking," *Millennium Film Journal* 43/44 (Summer/Fall 2005), pp. 104–105.

[94] Annette Michelson, "The New Talkies," *October* 17 (Summer 1981), pp. 2–4. The entire issue of *October* was dedicated to "the New Talkies."

films that could represent reality without falling into the traps of representational filmmaking as usually understood—illusionism, lack of critical distance, spectatorial passivity. For this to happen, narrative itself had to be scrutinized. As a form for political representation it had to be analyzed in the same way film itself had been by structural filmmakers and practitioners of expanded cinema. Hence, narrative form displaced the cinematic medium as the primary object of avant-garde filmmakers' reflexive, analytical attentions. And the trait of narrative that came under the most scrutiny was temporality. In the new narrative films, the literal time of structural film and expanded cinema became externally referential, figurative time.

Of structural films, and much the same could be said for many of the works of expanded cinema discussed in this book, David James has written, "each develops principles of construction peculiar to the specific area of the filmic process it *de-signs*."[95] James's unusual usage of "design" points to the refusal of reflexive avant-garde film works to reference anything other than their medium, each film detaching the elements of cinema from signification, literally "de-signing" them. This included the signification of time, the crux of cinematic storytelling, as continental post-structuralist film theorists pointed out contemporaneously with structural film's rise. Our comprehension of narrative causality, for instance, which is the basis for our perception of any higher-level connotative meanings, is predicated upon the signification of time. As Christian Metz had put it in 1967:

> the pioneers of "cinematographic language"—Melies, Porter, Griffith—couldn't care less about "formal" research conducted for its own sake; what is more (except for occasional naïve and confused attempts), they cared little about the symbolic, philosophical or human "messages" of their films. Men of denotation rather than of connotation, they wanted above all to tell a story; they were not content unless they could subject the continuous, analogical material of photographic duplication to the *articulations*—however rudimentary—of a narrative discourse.[96]

"The continuous, analogical material of photographic duplication" means, simply, celluloid film, which passes through camera and projector continuously, in real, linear time. "Articulating" that material meant joining "disarticulated" pieces of film—shots—in such a way that signified something other than this literal time. Hence, early filmmakers learned how to use continuous material to signify *discontinuousness*: simultaneity, flashbacks and flashforwards, temporal ellipses, and so on. They also learned to create the appearance of continuousness when none existed, reassembled multiple shots taken out of order into apparent temporal continuity via matches-on-action, eyeline matches, and shot/reverse-shots. Structural film did the

[95] James, *Allegories of Cinema*, p. 244.
[96] Christian Metz, "Problems of Denotation in the Fiction Film," in Leo Braudy and Marshall Cohen, eds., *Film Theory and Criticism*, 6th ed. (Oxford: Oxford University Press, 2004), p. 67.

reverse, unyoking film from temporal signification and returning it to its "pure" state, the literal time so often referenced by avant-garde filmmakers and critics.

We shall see in chapter 3 that the simple antinomy of "structural realism vs. narrative illusion," of literal time vs. signified time, was not so simple in practice. Even an apparently staunch cinematic literalist like Sharits explored temporal signification, albeit in ways that did not produce the illusions of popular cinema. Sharits was alive to a tradition in avant-garde film that ran parallel to the one Metz had described, an underground, shadow tradition of avant-garde filmmakers subjecting "the continuous, analogical material" of film to alternative temporal articulations, or counter-representations of time. Those avant-garde filmmakers who took up narrative form in the 1970s took up this tradition, which was resistant to linearity, simple causality, and the seemingly natural flow of narrative, making films that represented fictional or semi-fictional events but in ways that retained avant-garde cinema's temporal radicalism. Structural film and expanded cinema provided a specific model for these filmmakers: the "time shape." It was Sharits's term, but analogies can be found throughout the writings of contemporaneous avant-garde filmmakers and critics. It referred to forms of temporal representation wherein time, in theory at least, could be apprehended all at once, as a shape.[97]

The concept of the "time shape" is a variant of an idea about duration abroad in avant-garde film culture during the 1970s. In this context, duration did not mean running time, but referred instead to the simultaneously temporal *and spatial* experience that certain films were said to produce, especially structural films. Michael Snow had written of *Wavelength*:

> I was thinking of, planning for a time monument in which the beauty and sadness of equivalence would be celebrated, thinking of trying to make a definitive statement of pure Film space and time, a balancing of "illusion" and "fact," all about seeing. The space starts at the camera's (spectator's) eye, is in the air, then is on the screen, then is within the screen (the mind).... The room (and the zoom) are interrupted by four human events including a death.[98]

Snow's characterization of *Wavelength* as a "time monument" signals the belief in the inextricability of temporal and spatial in avant-garde cinema. His tracing of real and illusionistic spaces suggests a web or nexus running through real and representational space, a series of relays from both on and "within" the screen to the spectators and their imaginations. His fusion of "room and zoom" further elaborates this notion. *Wavelength* thus articulates a web or nexus, or shape. That so many analyses of *Wavelength* and other structural films employs a language of vectors, trajectories, fields, and volumes also attests to the predominance of the "time shape" in the

---

[97] Paul Sharits, "Words Per Page," *Film Culture* 65/66 (1978; a special issue dedicated entirely to Sharits), pp. 36–39.

[98] Quoted in Annette Michelson, "Toward Snow," in Sitney, ed., *Avant-Garde Film* (1987), p. 173.

discourses of avant-garde film culture, the interpenetration of space and time under the term "duration."[99]

Later chapters will expand upon this conception of cinematic time, but for now its relevance to expanded cinema should be clear. Works of expanded cinema literally spatialized film, taking a quality of cinematic experience that was latent or implied by structural films in the standard exhibition format and giving it physical, external form. The arrangement of screens, projectors, and spectators within this space was one of the defining tasks of the production of a work of expanded cinema. But even in the more streamlined, simplified form of filmic objects, expanded cinema literally took shape, finding a static form that nonetheless implied movement and change in time (e.g., filmstrips displayed directly without the mediation of projection, which are the subject of chapter 3). In such works, cinema was laid out before the viewer all of a piece, as an object, field, matrix, or map. Which is to say that cinema's first expansion was from the temporal into the spatial, which entailed it taking architectural form whereby cinema was schematized, given physically embodied models and diagrammatic representations.

Thus, expanded cinema and structural film provided a model for filmmakers who "returned to narrative" in the mid-1970s, including Rainer, Mulvey and Wollen, Le Grice, and Lis Rhodes. As Simon Field wrote of Le Grice's *Tense Alignment/Blackbird Descending* (1977): "Malcolm Le Grice is tiptoeing so gingerly backwards into that forbidden zone for the English 'Structural' filmmaker that is known as 'Narrative.'" But, Field noted,

> It is absolutely not a question of a "return" to narrative; it is more a wholly new approach made possible by the investigation of "first things," the foregrounding of cinematic procedures, characteristic of Le Grice's work—and that of other avant-garde filmmakers—over the last ten years.[100]

Building upon the lessons learned by the "investigation of 'first things,'" filmmakers who turned from structural film and expanded cinema to narrative or quasi-narrative films muted the sense of linearity and causality in those films by constructing them in ways that connoted objecthood.

A thorough review of this aspect of avant-garde film after expanded cinema is not within the purview of this book. Hopefully one example of how object analogies

[99] This point will be elaborated in subsequent chapters. For another discussion of this interpretation of "duration," see Jonathan Walley, "Anthony McCall," *Luxonline* (http://www.luxonline.org.uk/artists/anthony_mccall/essay%281%29.html), 2007. Snow's explication of *Wavelength* resonates with what would shortly thereafter be defined as the cinematic *dispositif* or apparatus. As theorized by Jean-Louis Baudry, the apparatus was a kind of conceptual web that held the spectator in place, "positioning" them within a set of relays in space both real and illusory: between the (implied) camera and the pro-filmic event, between projector and screen, and between the characters in the fiction. See Jean-Louis Baudry, "Ideological Effects of the Basic Cinematographic Apparatus," *Film Quarterly* 28, no. 2 (Winter 1974–1975), pp. 39–47.

[100] Simon Field, from the London Filmmakers' Co-op Catalogue, 1997. Reprinted in *Luxonline*, http://www.luxonline.org.uk/artists/malcolm_le_grice/blackbird_descending_-_tense_alignment.html.

guided filmmaking during this period will be both instructive and suggestive of other possibilities. One compositional approach that predominated in the so-called "New Talkies" was a variation on the tableau, something more commonly associated with pre-avant-garde painting, melodramatic theater, and early cinema à la Griffith.[101] A tableau is a static image of a moment in time, a frozen instant that nonetheless implies temporality by suggesting both the events that have led up to it and those that might follow. Though emblematizing a state of affairs within a story, the tableau also disrupts narrative, halting time for the purpose of visual spectacle. It is a sculptural or painterly element inserted into a temporal form. Thus, a tableau is at least semi-independent of the larger narrative, a free standing visual "object." The variation of the tableau by avant-garde filmmakers in the mid-to-late 1970s consisted of a cluster of interrelated formal traits: single-shot composition, a sense of formal isolation from the surrounding actions or scenes, and highly stylized staging and set design. The first trait, in essence the equation of scene with shot, produces the impression of spatio-temporal unity, implying that the scene is an autonomous object in the overall formal architecture of the film. The famous central section of Mulvey and Wollen's *Riddles of the Sphinx* (1977) is composed of 13 scenes, each consisting of a single panning shot of the main character going about her daily routine. Scott MacDonald likens these shots/scenes to a series of complete short films, aptly characterizing the way they diminish the impression both of temporality and causality via their tableau construction.[102]

Yvonne Rainer employed the term "paratactic" to describe the disjunctive construction of her own narrative films.[103] Paratactic is a grammatical term referring to the combination of phrases or clauses without the use of conjunctions. What Rainer meant was that scenes in films like *Lives of Performers* (1972), *Film About a Woman Who . . .* (1974), and *Kristina Talking Pictures* (1976) were not so much "linked" causally but simply arranged in sequence. This sequence could be re-ordered in multiple ways and still achieve the same effect, as if the scenes were laid out on a surface in different combinations as in a collage. In other words, paratactic filmmaking was partly detemporalized and thus resistant to narrativization, and thereby granted each scene a degree of autonomy rather than conceiving of them as points along a narrative line.

The organization of mise-en-scène in these tableau scenes further heightens their sense of formal autonomy. Their visual compositions diagrammatically represent, or schematize, whatever concept the scene represents. That concept exhausts the entire scene. While the scene necessarily unfolds in time, as it must in any film, the image

---

[101] The term tableau turns up frequently in descriptions of these films, especially Rainer's. See, for instance, Scott MacDonald, *Avant-Garde Film: Motion Studies* (Cambridge: Cambridge University Press, 1993), p. 157. David Curtis applies the term to *Riddles of the Sphinx* in *A History of Artists' Film and Video in Britain* (London: BFI, 2007), p. 186.

[102] Specifically, MacDonald refers to each scene as a "minifilm." See *Avant-Garde Film*, p. 85.

[103] See Camera Obscura Collective, "Yvonne Rainer: An Introduction: Appendix: Rainer's Descriptions of Her Films," *Camera Obscura*, no. 1 (Fall 1976), p. 72. For further discussion of the effects of this construction on narrative continuity, see Yvonne Rainer, *A Woman Who . . . Essays, Interviews, Scripts* (Baltimore & London: Johns Hopkins University Press, 1999), p. 93

Fig. 1.24. Anthony McCall and Andrew Tyndall, *Argument* (1978). Film still.
Courtesy of Anthony McCall.

functions as an instantaneously perceivable sign of its animating concept. The image is thus a sort of frieze, though a conceptual rather than narrative one, not a *tableau vivant* but a *tableau conceptuel*. Anthony McCall and Andrew Tyndall's *Argument* (1978) offers an example. The film dramatizes the complex relationship between film-making and economics and the difficult position of the filmmaker in this relationship. It elaborates this idea by creating an often contradictory matrix of written and spoken critiques of contemporaneous avant-garde cinema and written, spoken, and visual analyses of fashion advertisements as well as print and television news.[104] A central scene, in that it is both near the middle of the film and a crucial moment, features a man reading a detailed statement about the film's production while another man changes out of a punk rock outfit into business attire (fig. 1.24). The man reading the film's technical and financial details stands in closeup in the right foreground, while the man changing clothes is visible in full body in the left background.

The concept being visualized here is the contrast between the financial realities of filmmaking with the Romantic view of the artist operating outside those realities.

---

[104] This brief description does not nearly do the film justice. For a more comprehensive discussion of *Argument*'s multiple theoretical and political agendas, see Anthony McCall and Andrew Tyndall, eds., *Argument* (an anthology of statements and essays accompanying the film) (New York: Jay Street Project, 1976) and McCall and Tyndall, "Sixteen Working Statements," *Millennium Film Journal* 1, no. 2 (Spring–Summer 1978), pp. 29–37.

The scene pits materialism against idealism, collaborative production in a division of labor against the Romantic visionary artist concerned only with the representation of his/her consciousness. The scene also critiques structural film specifically, revealing the repressed of structural film's medium-specificity and reflexivity, including the drab facts of film financing and technical labor, including film processing, and the reality of financing institutions and the corporations that make cameras and film stock.

The scene takes time to unfold, of course, running about four minutes. But it does not develop as a narrative scene must. The process of narration in a conventional narrative film is one wherein states of affairs transform moment-by-moment as the causal chain develops. This happens across the film, and is reproduced on a smaller scale in each scene. Films like *Argument* were primarily about concepts, which lack this developmental structure, as Le Grice pointed out:

> In a sense, all our perceptions and consciousness take place in a "timeline" but it is evident that from these discrete temporal elements—our perceptions—we are able to construct concepts which are not themselves fundamentally temporal. For example, from our temporal perceptions we can model spatial relationships, or link temporal events to construct a hierarchy which is not itself linearly causal.[105]

This is not to say that a viewer's grasp of a concept illustrated by a film like *Argument* occurred instantaneously. The scene's "atemporality" is implied, as the viewer encounters less a process than an idea for which the scene provides a relatively static analogy. Critics have seized upon this quality of the new narrative films of the 1970s, frequently describing them in a language of shapes. MacDonald likens *Riddles . . .* to both a grid and a pyramid,[106] and A. L. Rees similarly attributes a "pyramidical structure" to the film.[107] Rakhee Balaram describes it as a loop, the "beginning and end of the film [joined]."[108] *Riddles of the Sphinx* and *Argument* were scripted in diagram or chart form, further supporting the idea that they are to be imagined as shapes, as if perceivable all at once.

McCall and Tyndall screened *Argument* in a series of small group workshops, where the film was intended to catalyze discussion among invited members of New York's art and film communities (fig. 1.25). A book of statements by the filmmakers, critical responses by other authors, collages of images from the film, and an image of the diagrammatical script accompanied these screenings (fig. 1.26). The film itself, then, was not the center of attention, but immersed into a larger discursive context that required the participation of filmmakers and audience members alike, and

---

[105] Malcolm Le Grice, *Experimental Cinema in the Digital Age* ("A Non-Linear Tradition—Experimental Film and Digital Cinema" [1997]) (London: BFI, 2001), p. 292.

[106] MacDonald, *Avant-Garde Film*, pp. 84 and 87, respectively. He attributes the pyramid description to Mulvey herself.

[107] A. L. Rees, *A History of Experimental Film and Video* (London: British Film Institute, 1999), p. 91.

[108] Rakhee Balaram, "Laura Mulvey and Peter Wollen," Luxonline (http://www.luxonline.org.uk/artists/laura_mulvey_and_peter_wollen/essay%281%29.html).

Fig. 1.25. Anthony McCall and Andrew Tyndall leading a discussion of *Argument* at the Millennium Film Workshop, New York. October 1978.

Courtesy of Anthony McCall.

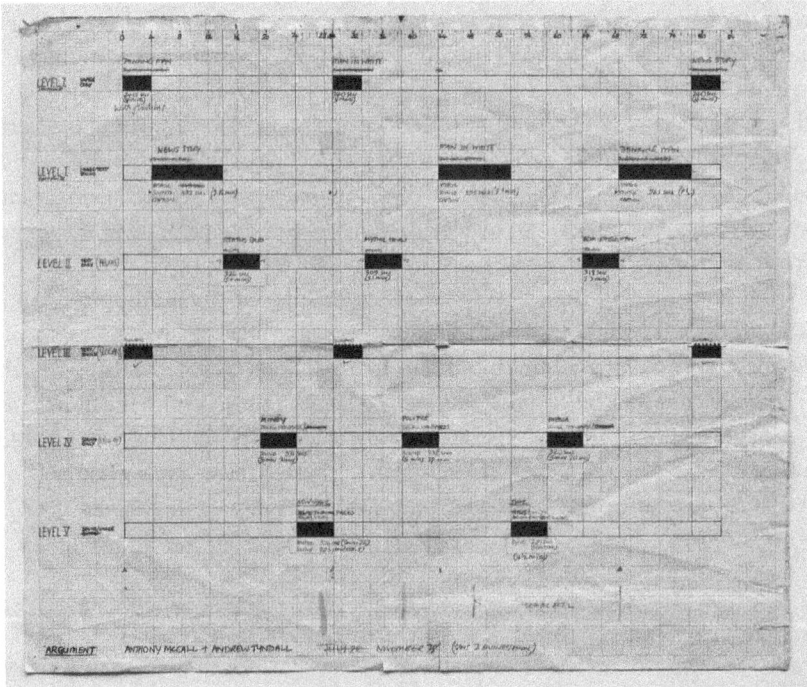

Fig. 1.26. Anthony McCall and Andrew Tyndall, *Argument* (1978). Schematic drawing of the film's structure. 55.9 × 67.3 cm, 22 × 26.5 in.

Courtesy of Anthony McCall.

a tool in a larger non-filmic event. Hence, in addition to the object-based method of its construction, *Argument* adapted expanded cinema's strategies for making the space of exhibition and the activity within that space part of the work. My claim is not that *Argument* counts as expanded cinema, but that it reveals how the "first things" learned during expanded cinema's prominence were subsequently re-oriented.[109]

One of the defining aspirations of avant-garde filmmakers has been to represent time and space in ways that did not follow the example of commercial cinema. If I am right that expanded cinema was not only a modernist, reflexive cinematic practice but a variation on this theme of film time and space as well, then expanded cinema moves from outlier practice toward the center of avant-garde film history. The first wave of expanded cinema, heralded by Youngblood, VanDerBeek, and others, appeared to be anathema to the notion of cinematic tradition, occurring as it did during what Mekas has recently called a "nervous breakdown" experienced by all the arts at the time.[110] But the subsequent work of expanded cinema's second wave was decidedly more cine-centric. The sense of urgency that animated the search for Field's "first things" and McCall's "first principles" diminished by the late 1970s, it seems, but the lessons learned in that search continued to figure in more conventionally produced and exhibited avant-garde films.[111] If the foregoing helps to explain why expanded cinema became less prominent as the 1970s wound down, the next question to answer is why did it re-emerge with such force two decades later?

[109] And, of course, the "solid light" films McCall produced between 1973 and 1975, such as *Line Describing a Cone* (1973) and *Conical Solid* (1974) were very much about shape, and the interplay of temporality and non-temporality (see chapter 4).

[110] Mekas made this comment in a panel discussion during "Never Twice," an exhibition of expanded cinema at Microscope Gallery, Brooklyn, December 11, 2015–January 10, 2016.

[111] Anthony McCall and the critic Deke Dusinberre both employed the term "first principles" in reference to expanded cinema, McCall in "Two Statements," in Sitney, ed., *Avant-Garde Film*, p. 254 and Dusinberre in "On Expanding Cinema," *Studio International*, no. 190 (November–December 1975), p. 220.

2
Expanded Cinema Revis(it)ed

Expanded cinema is an open question: Beyond what possibility did you imagine? With fiber optics in your veins, computer chips in your retina, digital in place of your digits, or an evocation of the dual terms of consciousness that allows for analytical reflection *and* the drift of experience ... "Like a patient etherized upon a table" *and*, at the same time, fully conscious of the theater of operations, a cinema comes into being as a "form that thinks" constantly re-inventing itself as a neurophysiological, image-restructuring, sonic-synaptic system.

—Bradley Eros (2005)

Expanded Cinema: the picture would show a balloon and the reflection of a rectangle distorted by the projection onto the curved membrane. Usually in cartoons this shape is understood to be the light of a window and has four quadrants representing the cartoon panes of glass.
Aspect ratio as you please.
2012: as the balloon rises, atmospheric pressure drops.
Expanding to its limit—it pops.

—Bruce McClure (2012)

Always in the Present

Friday, March 16, 1973, approximately 8pm at the short-lived but highly influential artists' space Gallery House, South Kensington, London. British filmmaker William Raban stands at a microphone in front of a film screen lit by the beam of an empty 16mm projector. He announces the date, time, and location, and adds: "A camera is filming an audience watching the blank screen. Sounds of the projection and of the audience's responses are being recorded." So began the unusual premier of Raban's now well-known work of live expanded cinema, *2'45"* (fig. 2.1). Unusual because the work did not exist prior to the screening, *2'45"* was by design a perpetually incomplete work-in-progress that came into being in the moment of its exhibition and would never be the same film twice.

As Raban indicated in his opening announcement, a 16mm camera mounted next to the projector captured the view from the back of the space: Raban on stage standing to one side of the empty screen, and the surrounding space including the backs of the audience members' heads. Once the 100-foot roll of film was spent, projector and

Cinema Expanded. Jonathan Walley, Oxford University Press (2020). © Oxford University Press.
DOI: 10.1093/oso/9780190938635.001.0001

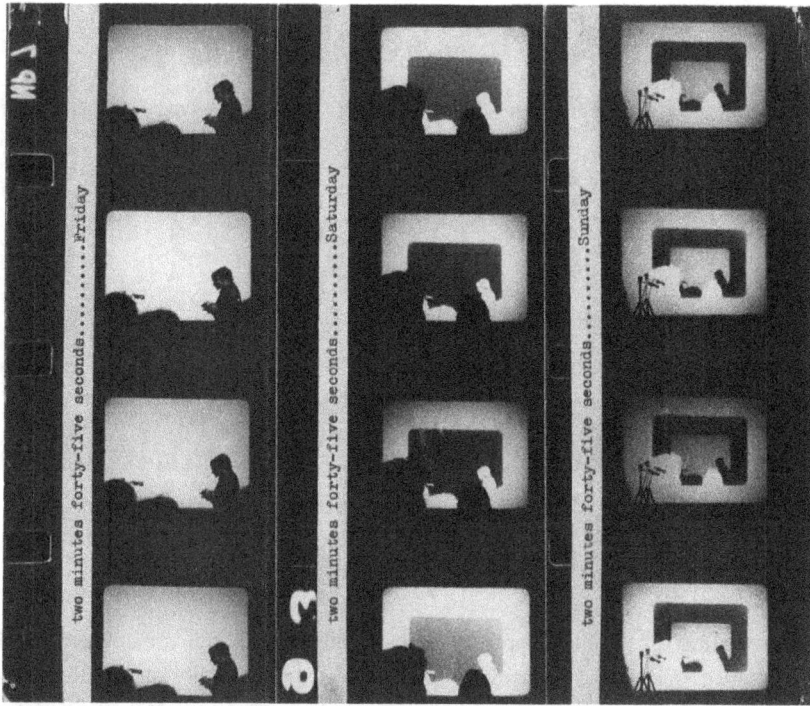

Fig. 2.1. William Raban, *2'45"* (1973). Performance documentation. Friday–Sunday, March 16–18, 1973. Performed during Film Action and Installation Show, Gallery House, London.
Courtesy of William Raban.

camera were turned off and the work was complete—for the time being. Raban developed the roll overnight, and the following day repeated the process I have just described for a new audience, only this time projecting the filmed record of the prior evening's event rather than leaving the projector empty. Once again Raban took the stage and made his announcement, now slightly altered: "A camera is filming an audience watching yesterday's audience watching the blank screen. Sounds of the projection and of the audience's responses are being recorded." The Gallery House attendees watched the image of the prior audience watching the blank screen. Because Raban did not make positive prints for projection, the image was in negative. The sounds and images were again recorded, Raban once more processed the film overnight and screened it the following day for a third instantiation of the work, a new layer of image and sound added to the earlier two. As each new roll of film was shot and developed, the roll from the prior performance was destroyed, so even as more and more temporal layers were recorded the duration of the work remained the same: 2 minutes and 45 seconds, the approximate length of a single 100-foot roll of 16mm film at the standard shooting and projection speed of 24 frames per second. Each

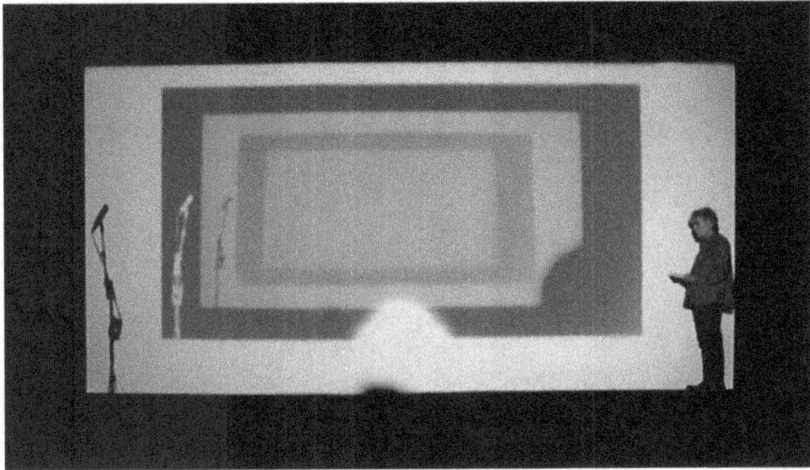

Fig. 2.2. William Raban, *4′22″*, expanded cinema performance (35mm version of *2′45″*). Performed December 1–6, 2008 during "The Live Record," BFI Southbank, London.

new realization displaced the previous ones, in effect "pushing" the images of earlier performances back into a deepening tunnel of nested frames, alternating positive and negative, receding from the surface of the screen like images endlessly reflected in opposing mirrors.

Raban's own description of the work glosses over its technical complexity the better to capture its formal and philosophical elegance: "the successive negative and positive images receding into the depths of the depths of the screen ... form a *mise en abyme* to build a picture comprised solely of the layers of space and time of the film's coming into being."[1] The work's merging of time and space parallels its dissolving of present into past, the echoing of temporal layers. "Expanded cinema is, of course, cinema in the present tense where film production and film exhibition become conjoined within the same time frame," Raban has written, the phrase "time frame" a poetic evocation of the work's spatialization of time.[2] As a model of expanded cinema "in the present tense," *2′45″*, Raban stipulated, "could only be shown if it was being re-filmed."[3] It is fitting, then, that *2′45″* has become a contemporary work, with Raban and others reproducing it numerous times since 2007. At a 2008 symposium on expanded cinema at BFI Southbank, Raban participated in a re-creation of *2′45″* in 35mm color film, re-titling it *4′22″* (the length of a 400-foot reel of 35mm) (fig. 2.2), and in 2014 he produced a version in digital video for the Oberhausen Film Festival.

---

[1] Raban, "Reflexivity and Expanded Cinema," p. 103.

[2] Ibid.

[3] Raban filmed/performed several versions of *2′45″* during the 1970s, including a relatively well-documented iteration as part of the expanded cinema section of the Festival of International Avant-Garde Film organized by David Curtis and Simon Field at the Institute of Contemporary Arts in London.

Fig. 2.3. Teaching and Learning Cinema's 2007 re-enactment of William Raban's *2′45″*, as *Six Minutes*. Performance documentation.
Courtesy of Louise Curham and Lucas Ihlein.

Digital documentation of the 35mm version made for the BFI event subsequently screened in at least two film festivals, though without the element of live performance.

Raban's re-makes were predated by a six-minute digital video version staged in 2007 by Australian artists Lucas Ihlein and Louis Curham, operating under the collective moniker Teaching and Learning Cinema (fig. 2.3). The extension of the work's duration and the seemingly heretical decision to use digital video instead of film were motivated by Ihlein and Curham's desire to retrieve the "experiential essence" of *2′45″* rather than produce a shallow simulacrum of the original.[4] Digital video, they reasoned, was the contemporary equivalent to 16mm as it was cheap, accessible, and easy to use. To shoot on film simply because Raban did in 1973 would have lent the re-creation a "nostalgic feel" that Ihlein and Curham wished to avoid: "To re-enact 1970s Expanded Cinema is not, we would argue, to produce a 'cover version'—a lesser imprint of an 'original' which retains its authenticity even in the face of its corporeal degradation—but rather it is to engage in an ongoing chain of remediation initiated

---

[4] Lucas Ilhein and Louise Curham, "Re-enacting Expanded Cinema: Three Case Studies," a "research report" written as part of Ilhein and Curham's re-enactment of *Man With Mirror* (as *Woman With Mirror*) in 2009. See http://www.teachingandlearningcinema.org/wp-content/uploads/2012/03/TLC-Reenacting-expanded-cinema-three-case-studies.pdf, p. 4.

(and indeed called into being!) by the work itself."[5] The implication of these varying re-enactments is that if there is any guarantee of "authenticity" it is not in the slavish reproduction of the original in the "correct" medium. Though Raban saw his expanded cinema pieces in terms of the reflexive attention to the materiality of film that characterized contemporaneous structural-materialist filmmaking in the United Kingdom, those pieces simultaneously assert the centrality of the social and institutional dimensions of cinema. Raban's work requires a process, space, and group of spectator-participants as much as a specific moving image technology. The choice of video or film becomes less important in this context than the re-creation of the circumstances of avant-garde cinema's uniquely social, interactive and participatory exhibition mode, which is what *2'45"* is ultimately about.

Digital video's alleged superiority to film as a documenting medium lies in its relative accessibility and user-friendliness, its ability to capture events in greater detail and the ease and speed with which it circulates. Raban's film makes these irrelevant, as it must be experienced live by an audience in the unique time and place of its exhibition. "I always thought the film was meaningless unless it was being re-filmed. So I've always resisted showing old versions as documentation," Raban has said.[6] Perhaps this explains the sense that the screening of digital documentation in recent festivals without Raban's presence and without re-shooting seems facile, a capitulation to the presumed inevitability of digital's replacement of film that entirely misses the point the work makes about cinema's social dimensions. What is lost is not a specific medium, but the dialectic of past and present, of lived event and recorded image, and of interaction between filmmaker and audience. Screening only the digital documentation of *2'45"* isolates it from the social situation that gives the work its meaning.

Thus *2'45"*, sometimes dated 1973–ongoing, is the perfect emblem for contemporary expanded cinema. An image of oscillating past and present tenses, which Malcolm Le Grice described as a "time corridor"; live experience and record in a loop; the play of continuity and discontinuity across its perpetual re-creation.[7] Any account of contemporary work in expanded cinema would be incomplete without mention of such re-stagings, which have become regular occurrences since the early 2000s. *Shoot Shoot Shoot: The First Decade of the London Film-Makers' Co-operative and British Avant Garde Film 1966–76* opened at Tate Modern in May 2002 and traveled across Europe, Australia, and the United States, and featured works of expanded cinema by Raban, McCall, and Le Grice. *Shoot Shoot Shoot* curator Mark Webber also organized *Expanded Cinema: Film as Spectacle, Event, and Performance* and *Expanded Cinema: Space/Time/Structure* (2004 and 2006, respectively). The 35mm re-creation

[5] Lucas Ilhein, "Medium-Specificity and Sociality in Expanded Cinema Re-Enactment," in K. Cleland, L. Fisher, and R. Harley, eds., *Proceedings of the 19th International Symposium of Electronic Art*, ISEA2013, Sydney. http://ses.library.usyd.edu.au/handle/2123/9475, p. 2.

[6] Duncan White and William Raban, "Interview of William Raban by Duncan White," 2008, from the website Rewind: Artists' Film and Video in the '70s and '80s, http://www.rewind.ac.uk/expanded/Narrative/Interviews_files/RabanTS.pdf.

[7] Le Grice, *Abstract Film and Beyond*, p. 150.

Fig. 2.4. Teaching and Learning Cinema's 2007 re-enactment of Anthony McCall's *Long Film for Ambient Light* (1975). The Performance Space, Sydney, March 16–17, 2007. Courtesy of Louise Curham and Lucas Ihlein.

of *2'45"* was part of *Expanded Cinema: The Live Record*, a 2008 symposium on expanded cinema held at BFI Southbank. *The Live Record* was one of several symposia and screenings in the United Kingdom leading up to Tate Modern's controversial 2009 conference *Expanded Cinema: Activating the Space of Reception*, undoubtedly the highest profile and most frequently discussed expanded cinema event since those in New York in the 1960s and London in the early 1970s. All these expanded cinema events included re-enactments of historical work and new performances by a younger generation of filmmakers working in multi-projection, film performance, and installation. Ihlein and Curham's Teaching and Learning Cinema has re-enacted Anthony McCall's *Long Film for Ambient Light* (fig. 2.4), Malcolm Le Grice's *Horror Film 1*, and Guy Sherwin's *Man With Mirror* (fig. 2.5), in each instance working with the original artists.

Such revisitings have provoked criticisms of nostalgia, at best, historical blindness and avant-garde hagiography, at worst. The historicizing aims of the Tate conference, especially, raised the specter of those "other" histories marginalized or ignored in favor of promoting the standard story, the same old works by the same old artists in the all-too-frequently re-tread golden age of avant-garde cinema. This criticism of the Tate event merged with another: that by burying its head in the historical sand of the 1960s and '70s, it ignored the contemporary "expansion" of cinema in digital media

Fig. 2.5. Louise Curham of Teaching and Learning Cinema re-enacting *Man With Mirror* (Guy Sherwin, 1976), as *(Wo)man With Mirror* (2009). Performance documentation. Courtesy of Louise Curham and Lucas Ihlein.

in laptops, cell phone videos, the internet, YouTube, and social media. According to one particularly vituperative review, which called the conference a "funeral parlour," attendees were "visibly more interested in how expanded cinema is inherited in contemporary visual culture rather than a mere saccadic recreation of an invented history of this practice."[8] Another reviewer assented: "frustration came from those for whom the conference title had promised a broader exploration of moving image culture, on our phones, laptops and throughout the urban environment." The same reviewer then asked:

> What happens to the self-definition of the experimental filmmaker when their techniques are proliferated and advanced throughout a larger culture that is unwilling to see what they do as particularly important or interesting? Do conferences like this, at their worst, become guarded zones for the preservation of self-importance?[9]

[8] Esperanza Collado and Chevalier Vassard, "Cinema Now Wants a Body or The Politics of The Red Carpet," *Experimental Conversations*, no. 4 (Summer 2009), http://www.experimentalconversations.com/review/147/.

[9] David Berridge, "Expanded Cinema: The Tale of Tate Modern and the Virgin Megastore," from the *More Milk Yvette* blog, http://moremilkyvette.blogspot.com/2009/05/expanded-cinema-tale-of-tate-modern-and.html. May 20, 2009.

Unwittingly, perhaps, these critics reveal the stakes for contemporary filmmakers producing expanded cinema and critics both reassessing the past and trying to understand new work. If most people are more interested in social media and some abstraction called "contemporary visual culture" than the narrower history of avant-garde cinema, and if the avant-garde's co-opted innovations are "proliferated" in a culture indifferent to the historical source of those innovations, then what is necessary is precisely the act of "inventing" the history of expanded cinema and promoting it through a venue (i.e., Tate Modern) where its importance can be asserted forcefully. I would argue that such an act is better understood as self-preservation than "self-importance," as a historically misunderstood and marginalized cinematic culture struggles to define and sustain itself. The "saccadic recreation of an invented history" can be recast in positive terms as a metahistorical intervention, the forging of what Le Grice once called "the history we need," which "implies a recognition that a neutral and inclusive history is broadly impossible and that the historical enterprise should be aimed at aiding the development of contemporary practice."[10]

With the corridor of reverberating temporal layers in *2'45"* once more in mind, we can see the rediscovery of historical works of expanded cinema and the taking up of expanded forms by a younger generation of filmmakers as twin phenomena, paired responses to circumstances that are in some respects new but in many others familiar. Critics who attacked the Tate conference on the grounds that it ignored the revolutionary potential of social media revive the totalizing notions of media and moving image practices of the first wave of expanded cinema, apparently unaware of their own historical shortsightedness. We shall see that such uber-conceptions of "cinema," or "the moving image," or "media" are insensitive to material and social differences among art forms, and will encounter contemporary avant-garde film culture's attempts to restore such sensitivity. It will hopefully be clear by now that such is one of the aims of this chapter, which provides broad historical background for the emergence of a third wave of expanded cinema that began in the mid-1990s and continues at the time of this writing. And if this introduction has struck readers as polemical, it sets the tone for what is to come. This chapter's polemical edge is sharper because it is addressing historical conditions that directly affect its author as both scholar and teacher of cinema. While Le Grice's "history we need" is perhaps overly partisan, its exclusionary impulse and sensitivity to the contours of a specific set of artistic practices are necessary antidotes to all-inclusive histories and theories of the moving image that the "expansion" of cinema has too often licensed.

In the last chapter I argued that the second wave of expanded cinema was in part a reaction against the ideas and critical rhetoric of the first. Something similar can be said of the third wave. In the last two decades a set of historical conditions has arisen that are strikingly similar to those that framed the initial appearance and theorization of expanded cinema. So it comes as no surprise

---

[10] Malcolm Le Grice, "The History We Need," in *Film as Film: Formal Experiment in Film, 1910–1975* (exhibition catalogue), Hayward Gallery, Arts Council of Great Britain, 1979, p. 113.

that contemporary avant-garde film culture has responded in ways similar to its second-wave predecessors, countering trends in moving image practice and criticism that are antithetical to its values and diminish avant-garde cinema historically. In this light, we can see a connection between the third wave of expanded cinema and contemporary avant-garde film in general, just as the second wave of expanded cinema extended rather than abandoned the aesthetics of structural and structural-materialist film.

A few writers have begun to turn their gaze toward more recent work, but it still suffers from a lack of critical attention, especially formal analysis and historical contextualization. One sign of this is the proliferation of terms and labels: "cinema by other means," "the idea (or ideal) of cinema," "paracinema," "film beyond its limits," even the "explosion" of cinema.[11] Perhaps scholars are hesitant to use the term expanded cinema for new work (and in some cases historical work) because Youngblood's book is still so prominent. Its animating concepts of intermedia and synaesthesia, along with its associations with psychedelia and techno-utopianism, embarrass some critics and artists. But in its forms and aesthetics, social values and politics, and major historical and theoretical contexts, this new wave of work is undoubtedly in continuity with the second wave of expanded cinema. Like that work, contemporary expanded cinema takes unconventional forms that resonate with the other arts but that nonetheless are intended as meditations on, interventions in, or re-inventions of cinema as we know it. That is, its emphasis is once again as much on "cinema" as on "expansion," and negotiates once more between an art form's autonomy and interdependence, between artistic specificity and intermedial generality.

The next three sections of this chapter—on digital media, the notion of "craft" in contemporary experimental film, and the issue of what and how films make meaning—trace out in some detail the historical context for the third wave of expanded cinema. These sections primarily address conventionally made, *non*-expanded, experimental films. This might strike some readers as a rather long digression. But to dis-integrate expanded cinema from avant-garde film culture more broadly would be to repeat the mistake of earlier scholarship, which has made expanded cinema an outlier when in fact, I am arguing, it is part and parcel of the avant-garde film tradition. Never has this been more true than for contemporary expanded cinema, which I hope to show (especially in the section on microcinemas later in this chapter) is thoroughly imbricated within experimental film culture of today, a fact that ties it to the second wave of expanded cinema while starkly contrasting it from the first.

---

[11] The term "paracinema" was most likely Ken Jacobs's invention around 1970, and refers to works identified by their makers as "cinematic" despite not using any conventional moving image medium (specifically film, as Jacobs coined the term before video was a viable alternative to celluloid for filmmakers). I will discuss paracinema in chapter 6; also see Walley, "The Material of Film and the Idea of Cinema,"; and "The 'Paracinema' of Anthony McCall and Tony Conrad," in Alexander Graf and Dietrich Scheunemann, eds., *Avant-Garde Film* (Amsterdam: Rodopi, 2007), pp. 355–382.

Avant-Garde Cinema in the Expanded Field of Digital

The most obvious large-scale historical development to consider is the rapid spread of digital technology into all facets of the moving image: the production, distribution, exhibition, and reception of films and videos. In several respects, of course, "films" made entirely digitally continue the familiar narrative forms and visual style of cinema as it has been made for over a century. Digital technology has reached the point where digital images are indistinguishable from filmed ones, even to the trained eye. But it is not simply a matter of production practices. The ways in which films are circulated and exhibited have changed significantly as a result of the widespread adoption of digital and the forced obsolescence of celluloid film. Part of this is the increased availability of the moving image, and images in general, through digital means. That is, technological change has been accompanied by cultural changes in the perception of moving images that echo some of those voiced by artists and critics during expanded cinema's first wave. As I claimed in this chapter's introduction, much of the rhetoric around social media and digital image making rehearses the same utopian claims about the political potential of new media expressed by Youngblood (via McLuhan) and VanDerBeek. The ready availability of digital cameras, thanks to smart phones, implies that moving images are more democratically available and that content can be shared across a new digital "noosphere." This is especially the case in some of the more enthusiastic discussions of social media, whose very name suggests that it fulfills the promise of VanDerBeek's culture intercom, or, for that matter, McLuhan's global village.[12] To digital media activists who believe Facebook and Twitter are potential tools of the revolution, the relative formalism and asceticism of works like McCall's or Nekes's will likely appear apolitical and outdated. The inability of film and analog video to be circulated as easily as digital code and engaged interactively by users is seen as a liability, just as film's mechanical nature put it at a disadvantage compared to broadcast video and public lumia displays for critics like Youngblood. Digital media is in the streets, available to everyone with a phone or laptop; historical works of expanded cinema require the traditional spaces of theater or museum, not to mention the rarefied aesthetic sensibilities such spaces putatively expect of their attendees.

But the shift in perceptions of the moving image I have just glossed is not limited to the popular sphere. In contemporary academia, theories of new media and

---

[12] A good recent example of this is the coverage of social media's role in the Egyptian Spring. See, for instance, Jose Antonio Vargas, "Spring Awakening: How an Egyptian Revolution Began on Facebook," *New York Times*, February 17, 2012, http://www.nytimes.com/2012/02 /19/books/review/how-an-egyptian-revolution-began-on-facebook.html?pagewanted=all&_r=0, and Tanja Aitamurto, "How Social Media Is Keeping the Egyptian Revolution Alive," http://www.pbs.org/mediashift/2011/09/how-social-media-is-keeping-the-egyptian-revolution-alive256/. Youngblood continues to characterize the internet in this way; see his lecture, "Secession From the Broadcast: The Internet and the Crisis of Social Control," http:// www. secessionfromthebroadcast.org/2013/10/29/secession-broadcast-internet-crisis-social-control/.

media convergence, and the concomitant obsessions with new technology and inter-disciplinarity, similarly deny the importance of cinematic specificity, relegating it to the status of historical relic. Curiously, even the privileging of cinema by certain new media theorists mutes its specificity by reconceiving it as essentially a multimedia art form. Lev Manovich writes that cinema "was the original modern 'multimedia,'" because "filmmakers were already combining moving images, sound, and text" long before multimedia became a recognizable phenomenon.[13] Cinema plays a critical role in Manovich's influential theories of new media because it provides a template for these media, a position that D. N. Rodowick calls "comforting to film theorists, since [Manovich] places so much emphasis on the importance of cinema as a 'cultural interface.'"[14] But it must be remembered that Manovich's model of cinema's nature is inherently intermedial, and as a consequence sweepingly general. By his account cinema is simply one step in a long historical process that also encompasses still photography and analytical computing and whose aims are now being realized by digital media, which merges photography and cinema with the computer. He writes,

> A hundred years after cinema's birth, cinematic ways of seeing the world, of structuring time, of narrating a story, of linking one experience to the next, have become the basic means by which computer users access and interact with all cultural data. In this respect, the computer fulfills the promise of the cinema as a visual Esperanto.[15]

In making this historical argument, Manovich must oversimplify the "cinematic," ignoring differences among cinematic media like film and video, and limiting his view of it to narrative film and linearity in general. In "What Is Digital Cinema?" Manovich goes further, placing both traditional *and* digital cinema in the larger historical context of painting and animation, reducing the aesthetics of traditional cinema—again, construed *very* broadly—to one option among many.[16]

Manovich's argument is teleological, positing new media as "fulfill[ing] the promise of the cinema," in essence realizing the latter's true aims, which the limitations of its technology prevented it from attaining. While this implicitly elevates traditional cinema's cultural position by making it a crucial precursor to new media, and thus "comforting" cinema scholars, it only does so at the cost of eliding material and aesthetic differences among moving image media and practices. And as Kim Knowles has argued, positions like Manovich's participate in the fetishization of new technology, grafting a narrative of progress onto the shift from film to digital and limiting the possibilities of both by emphasizing continuity over difference.

[13] Lev Manovich, *The Language of New Media* (Cambridge, MA: MIT Press, 2001), p. 67.
[14] D. N. Rodowick, *The Virtual Life of Film* (Cambridge, MA: Harvard University Press, 2007), p. 95.
[15] Manovich, *The Language of New Media*, p. 87.
[16] Manovich, "What Is Digital Cinema," http://manovich.net/index.php/projects/what-is-digital-cinema, n.p. 1995.

New media theorists rarely tackle the intricate dialectics of media change beyond an historical-theoretical standpoint that reinforces the cultural dominance
of the new ... Often, this is couched in narratives of continuity from the analog
to the digital, which see new media as furthering the goals of "old" practices, not
simply replacing them, but realizing their desires through necessary technological
progress.[17]

And while Rodowick is critical of Manovich's position and often more alert to the
specificities of different media and cinematic traditions, he makes the same kind of
claim: that "the history of cinema has been only a long digression in the more cultur-
ally significant merging of the history of electronic screens with the history of com-
putational processes."[18] Ultimately, the two theorists advance totalizing arguments
about what cinema was *really* about, so to speak. Digital media allow us to see cinema
less as a distinct art form or medium and more as one manifestation among many of
much larger phenomena in the history of visual and electronic media.

   This totalizing effect results from the pairing of two major concepts in new media
theory: remediation and media convergence. "Remediation," introduced in 1999 by
media scholars Jay David Bolter and Richard Grusin, refers to the process of one medium modeling itself on the forms of another. By this definition the incorporation of
live performance in certain works of expanded cinema could be an example of film's
remediation of theater. Remediation need not be a linear historical progression, in
both the literal and evaluative senses of the word, wherein new media pick up and
advance the forms of the old. Rather, it is a nexus of associations among all media,
new and old. "Our culture conceives of each medium or constellation of media as it
responds to, redeploys, competes with, and reforms other media," Bolter and Grusin
write, referring to "a genealogy of affiliations."[19] Thus, from one perspective, the concept of remediation itself re-mediates the spirit of hybridity, cross-fertilization, and
intermedia that animated so much art in the 1960s and '70s. The concept was indeed
intended to counter the "modernist myth of the new," the assumption "that digital
technologies ... must divorce themselves from earlier media for a new set of aesthetic
and cultural principles," further evidence of the parallel between remediation and the
reigning theoretical paradigms of intermedia art.[20]

   It is at this point that media convergence enters the frame. It may be that all media
have had a tendency to converge in the many cycles of remediation Bolter and Grusin
describe, but digital media embodies this process uniquely, as all media can be
transcoded into binary. Digital is thus both a medium on its own and a uniquely flexible "platform" for other media, one that fundamentally alters our experience of those

---

[17] Kim Knowles, "Analog Obsolescence and the 'Death of Cinema' Debate: The Case of Experimental
Film." MiT7 Conference: "Unstable Platforms: The Promise and Peril of Transition," May 2011, Cambridge,
MA. <web.mit.edu/comm-forum/mit7/papers/Knowles_ analog_obsolescence.pdf>.
[18] Rodowick, *The Virtual Life of Film*, p. 96.
[19] Bolter and Grusin, *Remediation*, p. 55.
[20] Ibid., backmatter.

media. Erika Balsom eloquently describes the process and suggests the ramifications for cinema as it becomes "available on an increasing number of viewing platforms":

> If, for decades, the elements of the cinematic apparatus had been relatively tightly sutured together to form a discernible entity, recent years have seen these elements dispersed across the field of culture, shattering the cinema into a multiplicity of attributes that separate, recombine, mutate, and enter into aggregate formations with other media.[21]

Here we encounter the curiously contradictory logic in the joining of remediation and media convergence. On one hand, all media are reduced to the same medium, "old" media converging under the umbrella of digital remediation. On the other, new media technology is "expansive" because it provides so many new platforms for the circulation and exhibition of images. Interestingly, Maya Deren diagnosed a similar condition of the film medium in 1960:

> The photographic medium is, as a matter of fact, so amorphous that it is not merely unobtrusive but virtually transparent, and so becomes, more than any other medium, susceptible of servitude to any and all the others ... its own character is as a latent image which can become manifest only if no other image is imposed upon it to obscure it.[22]

That an avant-garde filmmaker at the beginning of the 1960s, before cinema's first expansion, implied that celluloid film was a kind of neutral platform for all other art forms belies claims that such "servitude" is a unique condition of digital media and therefore a genuinely new phenomenon. Deren's solution, that cinema be specified, has indeed been taken to heart by artists exploring ways in which digital media are unique. One reason that theories of new media fail to account for Knowles's "intricate dialectics of media change" is that they rely on a fuzzy conception of a medium. In the theoretical accounts I've parsed, the following things are called mediums: film, cinema, painting, theater, literature, and, of course, "the digital." This is surely too monolithic a notion of the nature of mediums to be meaningful, just as the more accommodating definitions of expanded cinema expand it past the point of usefulness.

Theories of new media such as these reflect the wider trend in academia toward interdisciplinarity, particularly in the study of art and media. Of course, cinema studies has always been interdisciplinary, drawing upon all manner of other fields. But recent calls for a greater degree of interdisciplinarity in the study of cinema are unique in their insistence that *any* version of cinematic specificity must be rejected, and that to believe in such specificity is necessarily also to assume that there are no connections between cinema and the other arts. Janet Staiger puts forth this idea

[21] Balsom, *Exhibiting Cinema in Contemporary Art*, p. 14.
[22] Deren, "Cinematography," p. 60.

when she writes, "While I believe fully that the concept of media specificity exists, being sheltered by studying only film is to work with blinders on. Film as a business and an art was never isolated from the other entertainments or from the political and aesthetic expressions with which it competed."[23] This statement conflates the belief in the specificity of a medium with the study of that medium in complete isolation not only from other media but from cultural context as well. This is a variant of a long-standing bias against formalism in cinema studies, where formalism is caricatured as entirely apolitical and thus suspect. A related fallacy plaguing the contemporary version of interdisciplinarity in academic cinema studies is the belief that the emergence of digital technology somehow proves the bankruptcy of cinematic specificity as a concept. Rick Altman, recently calling for "increased efforts to explode the very idea of film studies as a viable notion," argues that cinema studies faculty of the older generation are "ill-prepared" for teaching in the digital age because their "film education stressed cinematic specificity rather than methods for handling the extraordinary variety of materials now available with a few keystrokes."[24] Like Staiger, Altman conflates a belief in cinema's specificity with studying it in a vacuum. But he further conflates interdisciplinarity with digital technology, implying that what he calls "non-film" research resources were born with the Internet, or that a commitment to specificity is anathema to utilizing such resources.

Hence, in the contemporary moment, interdisciplinarity and intermediality have become conjoined, with digital media providing an emblem of both. The "transcoding" of other, older media via digital technology can be taken as a symbol of the breaking down and ultimate erasure of boundaries between media, art forms, and academic disciplines. The belief that each medium or art form has unique properties distinguishing them from others and that anyone studying said medium or art form ought to be familiar with these properties bolsters the very disciplinary boundaries that the insistence on interdisciplinarity in academia seeks to break down. That digital media are said to make the medium of film obsolete is part of this larger picture. If, as Knowles claims, ideas about new media posit digital technology as the fulfillment of film's promise, doing everything film could do but more easily and cheaply, then film becomes unnecessary. Furthermore, as cinema studies is a primarily analytical and hermeneutic discipline, the nuts-and-bolts material differences between physical media aren't terribly important for many scholars. Those aspects of a moving image work to which analysis and interpretation generally attend—narrative or non-narrative structure, editing, cinematography, sound/image relationships, star personae, implicit and/or ideological meanings, and so on—can be appreciated regardless of the medium in which the work is made or viewed. And even when cinema scholars turn from the formal to the historical, the material and aesthetic qualities of a cinematic work in a given medium can be passed over in the new interdisciplinary,

---

[23] Janet Staiger, "The Future of the Past," *Cinema Journal* 44, no. 1 (Autumn 2004), p. 127.
[24] Rick Altman, "Whither Film Studies (In a Post–Film Studies World)?," *Cinema Journal* 49, no. 1 (Fall 2009), p. 135.

intermedial regime of media studies. As David Bordwell notes, close examination of technique in other artistic disciplines "constitutes a good part of the core knowledge demanded of every professional. Film studies may be rare in encouraging historians of an art medium to ignore matters of form and style."[25]

There are multiple countervailing movements, by no means limited to the cinematic avant-garde. In the academy, prominent cinema scholars like Bordwell, Rodowick, Mary Ann Doane, and Tom Gunning have called for more sensitivity among their peers to differences among physical media, and to the unique craft practices in which filmmakers engage and the ways that differences among cinematic media shape these practices.[26] In the realm of mainstream cinema, professional cinematographers have expressed serious concern over the implications of the digital intermediate for their ability to control their images once a film enters postproduction.[27] Fears about the longevity of digital film restoration and preservation have made strange bedfellows of Hollywood directors, cinema historians, and archivists. But the main locus of apprehension over current conditions, as well as resistance to them, has been avant-garde film culture. In 2004, McCall referred to "a fierce rear guard action against digital media" mounted by avant-garde filmmakers.[28] There is some truth to this, but the claim must be qualified in two respects. First, avant-garde filmmakers have not simply refused to use digital video, but have slowly and carefully assimilated it into their practice. Second, the anti-digital sentiment one does find within the avant-garde reduces neither to a stubborn commitment to film nor a simplistic and historically doomed medium specificity or celluloid Luddism.

As Federico Windhausen has shown, even avant-garde filmmakers once considered film purists have begun to shoot, edit, and distribute their work digitally.[29] This has been a process of assimilation of digital to the kinds of uses that have characterized avant-garde filmmaking for decades. One of Windhausen's examples is Ernie Gehr's use of "flicker" effects in *Crystal Palace* (2002), which are not caused by the actions of a mechanical shutter but by image scanning errors unique to interlaced video. Kerry Laitala, whose work I will examine in later chapters, admitted digital video into her filmmaking practice when a relatively affordable DSLR allowed her to manually adjust focus and thus "explore depth," something earlier generations of

---

[25] David Bordwell, "Film and the Historical Return," http://www.davidbordwell.net/ essays/return.php. March 2005.

[26] See Mary Ann Doane, "The Indexical and the Concept of Medium Specificity," *differences: A Journal of Feminist Cultural Studies* 18, no. 1, pp. 128–152, and Tom Gunning, "Moving Away From the Index: Cinema and the Impression of Reality," pp. 29–52 of the same journal.

[27] See John Dailey, ASC, "The DI Dilemma, or, Why I Still Love Celluloid," *American Cinematographer* 89, no. 6 (June 2008), pp. 92–97; John Toll, ASC, "Letters: Another 'Grumpy Cinematographer' Speaks Out," *American Cinematographer* 89, no. 11 (November 2008), p. 12; and Roger Deakins, ASC and BSC, "Filmmakers' Forum: The DI, Luddites, and Other Musings," *American Cinematographer* 89, no. 10 (October 2008), pp. 78–83. Also see *The Digital Dilemma: Strategic Issues in Archiving and Accessing Digital Motion Picture Materials*, a publication of the Science and Technology Council of the Academy of Motion Picture Arts and Sciences, 2007.

[28] Jonathan Walley, "An Interview with Anthony McCall," *The Velvet Light Trap*, no. 54 (Fall 2004), p. 70.

[29] Windhausen, "Assimilating Video," pp. 69–83.

DV cameras did not allow.[30] Previously her work had been resolutely filmic, her writings often polemically anti-digital: "Cinema as a medium of reflection worthy of the same consideration that one would pay to the 'plastic arts' is in immediate danger as too many think that there is no difference between light sensitive mediums and digital or electronic mediums."[31] But as changes in digital technology made cameras like the DSLR more amenable to at least some of Laitala's working methods and formal interests, she adjusted her position vis-à-vis digital to an extent, and currently shoots, edits, and distributes *some* work digitally. In some cases a filmmaker's decision to utilize digital technology is practical: cost, the potential for easier and wider distribution, and the necessity of having good digital versions of work for submission to film festivals. But the larger assimilation of digital video by avant-garde film culture is never merely pragmatic, nor an unquestioning acceptance of digital. Rather, it is a process of negotiation, of reconciling the new medium with a cinematic tradition that existed long before it and which historically relied upon and emphasized the materials of an older medium. In works like *Crystal Palace*, a dialectic unfolds in which prominent formal devices of avant-garde cinema are both reiterated and reinvented through the distinct capacities *and flaws* of digital. This is, additionally, a process of negotiation between medium specificity and literally inter-media connections. In digital video's unique variant of the flicker, for instance, Gehr has found a device that is at once "a reflexive, medium-specific feature of video" and a "possible iteration of a cross-media optical effect," as Windhausen states it.[32] Such a process requires precisely the kind of sensitivity to the specific qualities of digital video and film and to the differences and similarities between them so often lacking in the discourses of new media.

The point to be made here is that while avant-garde filmmakers have not adopted digital video completely and continue to regard it with some skepticism, neither have they rejected it simply on the grounds that it is not celluloid. Their stance toward digital cannot be characterized as mere nostalgia or fetishism. The process of assimilation of digital is complicated because avant-garde filmmakers share a complex conception of the specificity of cinematic media. In commercial cinema, the nearly completed shift from film to digital has been enabled in part by the fact that films made and projected digitally are putatively indistinguishable from those made and projected on celluloid (something that is often reduced entirely to image resolution). Attentive as they are to the specificities of film and digital imagery, many avant-garde filmmakers do not acknowledge that this is true to begin with and do not desire digital simply to replace film in this manner. But more importantly, formal similarity or even identity of film and digital video, the ability of the latter to "remediate" the former, is not the measure of digital's acceptability to avant-garde filmmakers. Zoe Beloff describes digital's ability to mimic such filmic traces as emulsion grains or scratches as "ersatz

[30] Jonathan Walley, "Interview with Kerry Laitala," *Speaking Directly: Oral Histories of the Moving Image (Cinematograph 7)* (San Francisco: San Francisco Cinematheque Books, 2013), p. 102.

[31] Kerry Laitala, "Cinema as Material Presence," *Otherzine* 7 (Fall 2004), n.p. See http://www.othercinema.com/otherzine/archives/index.php?issueid=1&article_id=8.

[32] Windhausen, "Assimilating Video," p. 80.

authenticity."[33] Discussing the use of end flares in his 16mm films and digital video's ability to re-create such "filmic" effects, Ken Jacobs states:

> that's to make nonsense out of this stuff. The flameouts—I kept them in my films for a number of reasons. I wanted to say, 'This is the end; I can't shoot anymore, because I have no other roll of film.' But I also wanted to say, 'This is film; this is the character of film. What I'm showing you are unedited rolls from a camera; I left the flash frames in'—that was part of the statement. And now you can make it happen digitally, *and it doesn't connote anything. It doesn't signify.* It's just an effect.[34] [emphasis added]

Thus, the assimilation of digital video by avant-garde filmmakers is not simply predicated upon digital's ability to re-create such favored visual devices as flicker, film grain, or distressed celluloid. This is because these visual qualities or effects are not the endgame of avant-garde filmmaking practice even in its most apparently medium-specific and reflexive forms. Jacobs's comment reveals deeper values at stake in a filmmaker's choice to use one medium or the other. Were this not the case, avant-garde film culture's commitment to film and its more recent attention to the specific properties of digital video would indeed be nothing more than fetishism. But what must be understood, and too frequently it is not, is how intricately linked the constitutive aesthetic and ideological values of avant-garde cinema are to analog film. Or, to put it more accurately, to avant-garde cinema's unique conception of the properties and processes of analog film. This conception is a condition of the distinctive relationship between artist and material that characterizes avant-garde cinema as a mode of film practice, providing it with an inherent sense of identity and thus a basis upon which to distinguish it from other modes. The raw materials of film, or of any physical medium, are not in and of themselves as important as the artisanal model of filmmaking that has emerged through decades of literally independent avant-garde filmmakers working with those materials. Avant-garde cinema's artisanal mode of working, which is radically different from what we find in commercial film and moving image art in the gallery, is what makes any particular physical element of a cinematic medium meaningful.

The Art—and Craft—of Cinema

This point might gain some clarity if we view it through the lens of the concept of craft, and the significance of that concept in a period marked by aesthetic Postmodernism

[33] Heather Hendershot, "Of Ghosts and Machines: An Interview with Zoe Beloff," *Cinema Journal* 44, no. 3 (Spring 2006), p. 131.
[34] Flo Jacobs, Ken Jacobs, et al., "Roundtable on Digital Experimental Filmmaking," *October*, no. 137 (Summer 2011), p. 59.

and its minimization of the importance of specific media in both art theory and practice. Alison Pearlman defines craft as "artists' depth of involvement with their media over time ... craft-based artists demonstrate a commitment to exploring the possibilities of one medium or a very limited number of media."[35] She contrasts craft-based artists with "concept-based" ones who "refuse such specialization," taking up whatever materials seem called for by each new idea, often outsourcing the necessary craft labor required by the materials with which they happen to be working. Pearlman traces this "nomadic" approach to art-making from Duchamp's ready-mades, through the first stirrings of intermedia in the work of John Cage and Robert Rauschenberg, through Minimalism and conceptual art, into Rosalind Krauss's era of the "post-medium condition." For Pearlman, the marginalization of craft in the post-minimal and post-medium period is unfortunate because it devalues the close study of form and the consideration of aesthetic issues that are still vital to an education in the arts. But she further argues that the disparagement of craft is politically harmful, devaluing technical skill and work, reinforcing a hierarchy of intellect over material labor, and even inadvertently reproducing corporate capitalism's practice of outsourcing. In short, this conception of craft is not simply synonymous with technical skill, but stands for a set of positive aesthetic and political values. As Pearlman states it, the craft-based approach "requires an artist to develop, over time, attention to and respect for a material other than his or her ego, an empathy with another matter's distinct properties, laws, or conventions."[36] Gregory Zinman, also drawing upon Pearlman's work in his study of "handmade" avant-garde films, adds: "the word 'craft' connotes a qualitative valence, a level of skill with respect to the tools and materials at hand—the 'well-made-ness' of an object."[37]

By this definition, craft is where a physical medium intersects with the shared values of a community of users. More to the point, the medium and those values, while not indistinguishable from each other, are also not separable. And though Pearlman does not discuss moving image work in her essay, her comments regarding craft certainly describe the defining work ethic of avant-garde film culture. Furthermore, it is precisely what distinguishes avant-garde cinema from commercial film. Zinman makes the connection for us, referring to avant-garde cinema as "artisanal": "the rubric of craft helps position artisanal cinema as an oppositional practice ... Constructed with small budgets and preoccupied with formal innovation and abstract imagery, handmade-film practices carry economic and even political valences with respect to mainstream film production.[38]

But not only with respect to mainstream cinema, I would venture. Pearlman's concept-based approach is intended to describe recent and contemporary

[35] Alison Pearlman, "Craft Matters," *Afterimage* 32, no. 1 (July/August 2004), p. 6. I am very grateful to Greg Zinman for making me aware of this reference.

[36] Ibid.

[37] Gregory Zinman, "Handmade: The Moving Image in the Artisanal Mode" (PhD diss., New York University, 2012), pp. 7–8.

[38] Ibid., p. 9.

developments in the art world, and there we do indeed find a method of moving image making that parallels Hollywood's. The increasing ambition and scale of many gallery moving image works require quite sizable production crews and financial investment, and thereby call for a mode of working in which labor is dispersed over a (sometimes quite large) number of personnel with the requisite specialized skills for executing the work of instantiating the idea in the chosen media.

This working method is antithetical to the artisanal, craft-based approach of avant-garde cinema. And it is this method and its concomitant artistic and political values that are at stake for avant-garde filmmakers working in a period of media convergence, not just the survival of the specific medium of celluloid film. Reservations about digital video among avant-garde filmmakers are ultimately about digital's amenability to the artisanal mode of production, a manner of working for which film is very well-suited, as a more "hands-on" mechanical medium. The assimilation process described above, then, is one of negotiation in which artists explore the possibilities of adapting digital media to their artisanal working method. We can compare this to EXPORT's "replacement" model of expanded cinema, which does not dispense with film completely but intervenes in those aspects of the medium seen as ideologically harmful. Contemporary avant-garde filmmakers working with digital video attempt to exorcize, as it were, those features of the new medium that run against the grain of avant-garde film culture's values.

This is difficult, however, because digital is resistant to the ideals of avant-garde cinema in several ways. This resistance is a sign of the corporate capitalist values that many filmmakers believe are designed into digital hardware and software. If they are to assimilate digital into their cinematic practice, they must find ways to subvert those traits of the technology that manifest these suspect values. The avant-garde filmmaker and critic Nicky Hamlyn expresses this in no uncertain terms, referring to digital moving image technology as "a kind of revenge of technocracy on creative approaches which examine the specificity of the medium":

> The democratization of moving image technology [made possible by digital media] is achieved at a high price: the idiot-proofing of all aspects of production, resulting in cameras which effortlessly, relentlessly generate perfectly focused, exposed, and colour-balanced images, stands as a metaphor for the increasingly administered and conformist world in which we live, wherein harmless protest is encouraged but true dissenters are demonized or ridiculed.[39]

Hamlyn's reference to its "perfectly focused, exposed, and colour-balanced images" links digital video to what generations of avant-garde filmmakers have taken as the defining tendency of commercial cinema: the occlusion of medium and craft for the purposes of creating a seamless illusion of reality consumed passively by an

---

[39] Nicky Hamlyn, *Film Art Phenomenon* (London: BFI, 2003), p. 14.

unthinking mass audience. With analog film, hiding filmmaking craft from viewers ironically took significant technical skill; with digital, the act is designed into the medium itself, so that production is potentially as passive and unthinking as consumption. The filmmaker Lynne Sachs summarizes this view of digital media:

> The shame of the digital world is that as the machinery gets more and more advanced, there is an attempt to mirror reality as closely as possible. That's what I find so disturbing, whereas the avant-garde is not trying to mirror reality. We're trying to shape, investigate, play with, and sculpt it. High-definition is so unappealing to me because of that.[40]

Sachs's mention of high-definition is telling. Digital's ability to remediate and successfully replace film is often reduced to its ability to reach film's resolution, something 4K digital video is said to have finally achieved. Digital technology offers, at last, the ultimate fulfillment of commercial cinema's realist aesthetics and thereby serves the ideological goals behind those aesthetics. Anyone paying attention to the ways in which digital video has been integrated into the practices of commercial filmmakers will know that its realism is its primary selling point. Hence, digital does not only remediate film, but furthermore fulfills the promise described by André Bazin in his essay "The Myth of Total Cinema." According to Bazin, the "guiding myth" behind the invention and development of cinematic technologies was "an integral realism, a recreation of the world in its own image, an image unburdened by the *freedom of interpretation of the artist*"[41] Bazin's theory has become newly relevant in the midst of the digital turn, not surprising given the association of digital with increased realism— its ability, for instance, to create apparently seamless spaces and spans of time even though these were not part of the profilmic event. Bazin's narrative of progress from a primordial human need for "integral realism" to technologies that increasingly meet that need might indicate that he would have welcomed digital, especially because, as Sachs puts it, digital closes down on modernist filmmakers' desire to "shape, investigate, play with, and sculpt" reality.

For avant-garde filmmakers, however, the remediation of film by digital is actually only an extension of one particular aesthetic and ideological preoccupation. Other cinematic traditions, such as the avant-garde, have not shared those preoccupations, and so express anxiety over the ramifications of film's enforced obsolescence in the wake of digital technology's advance. While many avant-garde filmmakers once believed that film was too automatic—Kodak's slogan, after all, was "You push the button, we do the rest"—in comparison to digital media, film's shortcomings as a mimetic medium have become increasingly apparent. Hence the emphasis of its recalcitrance and resistance to automatic, seamless illusion: its user *un*friendliness. Avant-garde cinema has even offered its own counter-reading of realism ala Bazin

---

[40] Flo Jacobs, Ken Jacobs, et al., "Roundtable on Digital Experimental Filmmaking," p. 53.
[41] André Bazin, "The Myth of Total Cinema," p. 21. Italics mine.

to validate its film-specific and thoroughly abstract practices over the automatic realism of digital. Recall that photochemical film's indexicality was central to Bazin's
realist theory and was the basis for analogies he made between film and the natural
world: "Photography affects us like a phenomenon in nature, like a flower or a snow-
flake whose vegetable or earthly origins are an inseparable part of their beauty."[42]
Seizing upon this conception of the indexical, Tess Takahashi has brilliantly argued
that contemporary handmade avant-garde films like David Gatten's series *What the
Water Said* (parts 1–3 made in 1998, 4–6 in 2007; see pp. 165–166) abandon realism
as it is usually understood for an authenticity based on their indexical connection to
the natural world.[43] As Takahashi points out, according to the discourses of avant-
garde film culture film possesses a physicality and tactility that digital media lack.
These qualities provide a link between the brute raw material of film and the larger
ideology of artisanal filmmaking, including the range of alternative meaning systems
that handmade films like Gatten's are ultimately about. Takahashi describes the col-
laboratively made *Quarry Movie* (1999, produced by Greta Snider); a group of filmmakers shot 16mm footage of a quarry, buried that footage in earth in spots around
the quarry for several weeks, then unearthed the footage, hand-processed it, and
combined it to form the finished film. Following Snider's lead, Takahashi interprets
the film as a document of the quarry despite the fact that its images are frequently unrecognizable as such. But these very abstractions were produced by the conditions of
the film's production, so provide an indexical record of weather and soil conditions in
the titular quarry in the same way that Gatten's film is a record of its own encounters
with the sea.[44] In short, these films represent the real world precisely through their
abstraction, their lack of iconic realism. The scratches and blotches of color are artifacts of place and process just as striations on a rock wall are records of glacial movements from the distant past.

"... like a phenomenon in nature": Jeanne Liotta's 2017 projection performance
Path of Totality strays even further from conventional mimetic filmmaking methods,
into the realm of expanded cinema, in the quest for a more genuine and compelling
image of the natural world (fig. 2.6). Liotta projects abstract flickering 16mm film
loops through crystals and glassware, some filled with colored liquid, which diffuse
and diffract the projector's light, casting beyond the bounds of the screen and into
the room. A thin rod extends from the projector, seated just above its lens, at the end
of which Liotta has affixed a metal ring in the center of which dangles a small hollow
sphere made of three interlocked circular bands. The work was "precipitated by the
solar eclipse event of August 21, 2017," in Liotta's words, and more to the point by the
filmmaker's frustration with "the inability of photographic imagery to render those

---

[42] Bazin, "The Ontology of the Photographic Image," p. 13.
[43] Tess Takahashi, "After the Death of Film: Writing the Natural World in the Digital Age," *Visible
Language* (2008), pp. 44–69.
[44] Ibid., pp. 58–60.

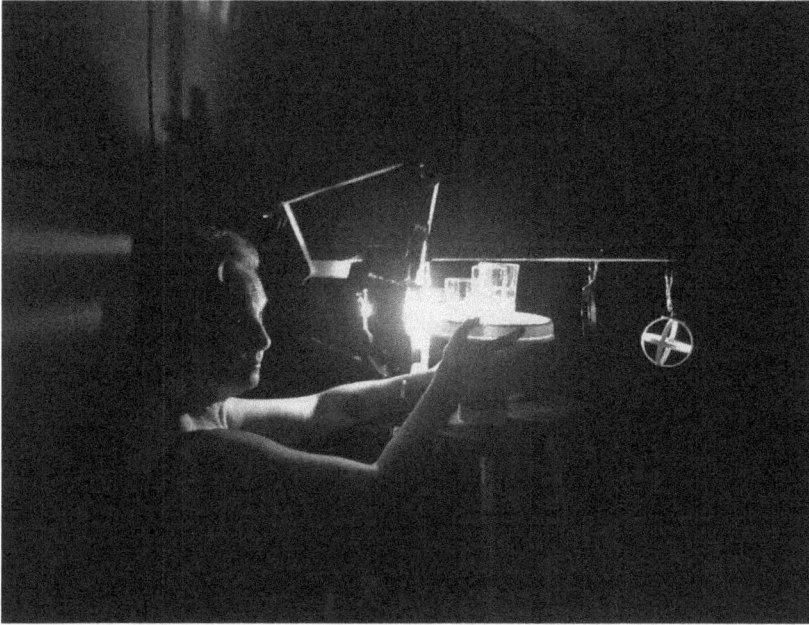

Fig. 2.6. Jeanne Liotta, *Path of Totality* (2017). Performance documentation.
Courtesy of Jeanne Liotta and Microscope Gallery.

particular light conditions."[45] The title refers to the trajectory of the moon's shadow across the surface of the earth during an eclipse, astronomical events and information being a particular interest of Liotta's. Her description of an earlier film, *Eclipse* (2005), hints at the kind of thinking that would lead to *Path of Totality*:

> The lunar eclipse event of November 2003 is observed, documented, and trans-lated via the light-sensitive medium of Kodachrome film. In the 4th c BCE Aristotle founded The Lyceum, a school for the study of all natural phenomena pursued without the aid of mathematics, which was considered too perfect for application on this imperfect terrestrial sphere. By eye and hand then, in the spirit of.[46]

Eclipse, like *Path of Totality*, is abstract, the familiar image of the titular event "lost in translation" as it is converted to the distinctive structural logic of film optics and chemistry the better to capture the essence of the visual experience. In her program

---

[45] From program notes for Liotta's performance of *Path of Totality* during Microscope Gallery's 2019 exhibition series "Scrapbook (or, Why Can't We Live Together)," https://microscopegallery.com/scrapbook-beloff-liotta/.

[46] Jeanne Liotta, notes for *Eclipse*, http://www.jeanneliotta.net/filmpages/eclipse.html.

notes for the first performances of the work, Liotta quotes the author Annie Dillard's famous and oft-reprinted 1982 essay "Total Eclipse":

> The sky snapped over the sun like a lens cover. The hatch in the brain slammed. Abruptly it was dark night, on the land and in the sky. In the night sky was a tiny ring of light. The hole where the sun belongs is very small. A thin ring of light marked its place. There was no sound. The eyes dried, the arteries drained, the lungs hushed. There was no world. We were the world's dead people rotating and orbiting around and around, embedded in the planet's crust, while the earth rolled down. Our minds were light-years distant, forgetful of almost everything. Only an extraordinary act of will could recall to us our former, living selves and our contexts in matter and time. We had, it seems, loved the planet and loved our lives, but could no longer remember the way of them. We got the light wrong. In the sky was something that should not be there. In the black sky was a ring of light. It was a thin ring, an old, thin silver wedding band, an old, worn ring. It was an old wedding band in the sky, or a morsel of bone. There were stars. It was all over.[47]

Elsewhere in the essay Dillard likens her experience to watching "a faded color print of a movie filmed in the Middle Ages," another instance of the filmic metaphor that likens sky to lens cover. In short, a film that could not possibly exist, one of many ways the author attempts to express what she refers to above as the "wrongness" of the light, and the terrifying sublimity of the event. Dillard must avail herself of the imaginative language of fiction in her non-fictional account in order to reproduce the spirit of the event even as she sacrifices realism. Liotta does much the same in *Path of Totality*, constructing a tiny model of the eclipse she witnessed, its three-dimensional—literally expanded—filmic form necessary to preserve what is essentially the experience of perceiving shadow, a shadow being an indexical image whose appearance may depart dramatically from that of the object casting it.

We may seem to have strayed an awfully long way from "Bazinian" realism and the aesthetics of Renoir, Wyler, or De Sica. But there is precedent in Bazin for reading visual abstraction in terms of indexical authenticity. Bazin argued that a photograph honored its indexical guarantee "no matter how fuzzy, distorted, or discolored, no matter how lacking in documentary value" that photograph was.[48] No matter how badly the photograph was taken, "those grey or sepia shadows, phantomlike and almost undecipherable," nevertheless retain their "charm," their psychological power, because they are indexical records of the people or places in them.[49] Bazin's descriptions of botched photographs, "fuzzy, distorted, or discolored," "phantomlike and almost undecipherable," could just as easily apply to films like *Quarry Movie*, *What the*

---

[47] Annie Dillard, "Total Eclipse," originally published in *Teaching a Stone to Talk: Expeditions and Encounters* (New York: Harper and Row, 1982), revised edition published by Harper Perennial in 2013, pp. 17–18.

[48] Bazin, "The Ontology of the Photographic Image," p. 14.

[49] Ibid.

Water Said, or hundreds of other avant-garde films whose primary power is not in their resemblance to the world in front of the camera but in their direct physical link to that world and to a way of working with the medium.

Facile realism is not digital's only liability, however. What Hamlyn calls "the idiot-proofing of all aspects of production" is a consequence of digital video's merging of moving image making and computerization. The computer by this view is the impenetrable black box that thinks for its user, a condition of digital media utterly at odds with a filmmaking tradition in which artists are used to exercising precise control over practically every facet of film production. Frampton presciently described the passing of the film medium into obsolescence, and so into the realm of art, in almost identical terms in 1971. While most critics saw video as the invention that ended "the age of machines" and thus made film obsolete, Frampton found this "imprecise": "I prefer radar, which replaced the mechanical reconnaissance aircraft with a static anonymous black box."[50] Note that Frampton's characterization of radar includes the fact that it obviates a human user, the pilot of the reconnaissance aircraft who presumably possesses both the skills to operate the machine and fly it in such a way as to avoid detection. The contrast is between a craftsperson operator and an automated machine inside a mysterious black box. Contemporary avant-garde filmmakers and critics contrast film and digital video in much the same way, emphasizing the skills required of filmmakers while pointing out that digital media render those skills unnecessary. Beloff, for instance, connects analog filmmaking to a larger spirit of mechanical wherewithal, of tinkering and inventiveness, and digital media to the opposite:

> In the early part of the twentieth century people were really interested in how things worked and how to fix them when they broke. Today, nobody cares what's inside a computer, as long as it works, and when it doesn't work you throw it away and you buy another one. That's managed obsolescence.[51]

Beloff's critique extends from the technology of digital to the ideology of the corporate culture it is designed to serve. The impenetrability of digital media, the "anonymous black box" of the computer, fosters passivity in its users and causes their craft muscles to atrophy, allowing manufacturers to drastically condense the life cycles of digital cameras, editing platforms, and projectors. The rhetoric of "the new," which elevates every new version of software or hardware to practically revolutionary status, helps mask these unpleasant truths about planned obsolescence.

Such value-laden distinctions between film and digital video permeate the discourses of avant-garde film culture. To digital's automaticity is contrasted film's demand of technical skill. To digital's apparent seamlessness is contrasted film's difficulty, recalcitrance, and downright mechanical clunkiness. And against the corporate

---

[50] Frampton, "For a Metahistory of Film," p. 136.
[51] Hendershot, "Of Ghosts and Machines," p. 137.

ideology behind these problematic traits of digital stand the qualities of sensitivity, inventiveness, discipline, and Pearlman's "empathy," all meanings that contemporary avant-garde filmmakers and critics routinely ascribe to the film medium. The following statement, from Brisbane, Australia's Otherfilm Collective, is representative:

> Within a contemporary economics of digital superfluity, the very inconvenience of film requires, of necessity, a discipline of its creators. No other medium demands as much resort to complex formulae related to light, distance, time and chemistry: despite the evanescence of the projected image, no other medium can advance the conceit that it embodies the physical universe upon so complete a scale.[52]

According to this view, the "evanescence" of film in the form of the ephemeral projected image is only apparent. It is, in fact, a thoroughly tactile medium in contrast to digital's genuine ungraspability and transience. As Eros expresses it, also hooking film to the natural world, "The digital realm is a hidden operation, a literal sleight of hand, whereby all tricks are now concealed in a truly encrypted language. Though film may have once had elements of the veiled, compared to the latest technologies, it now seems absolutely lapidarian."[53]

These conceptions of film are most apparent in a recent wave of avant-garde films that are in some way handmade: made without cameras or shot with homemade ones, hand-processed, projected on alternative, D-I-Y projection machines, sewn, scratched, painted or etched upon, hole-punched, buried in earth, submerged in water, and so on. Countering the seamlessness of the digital image, these films evince all sorts of "mistakes" arising from the contingencies of mechanical filmmaking at such a hands-on, artisanal level: flares, chemical burns, scratches, and inconsistencies of color and exposure caused by hand-processing. They point up the recalcitrance of the film medium so prized by avant-garde filmmakers and by some accounts central to the concept of craft in general.[54]

Gatten's aforementioned *What the Water Said* is an oft-cited example of contemporary avant-garde filmmakers' preoccupation with the contingencies and errors that attend working with analog film (figs. 2.7 and 2.8). To make the six films that compose the series Gatten submerged unexposed rolls of 16mm film stock in the

---

[52] The Otherfilm Collective, at the time this statement was issued, included filmmaker Sally Golding, sound artist Joel Stern, and scholar Danni Zuvela. See Jim Knox, "Beyond Play," *RealTime*, no. 83 (February/March 2008), p. 20. Accessible online at http://www.realtimearts.net/article/issue83/8873. Golding's work, both individually and as part of the projection performance duo Abject Leader (with Stern), will come under consideration in chapter 4.

[53] Bradley Eros, "Elastic Film, Mercurial Cinema," originally published in *Whitney Biennial 2006: Day for Night* (New York: Whitney Museum of American Art, 2006). Accessible at http://www.no-w-here.org.uk/index.php?cat=7&subCat=docdetail&id=171.

[54] See Davies, "Medium in Art"), p. 182: "the recalcitrance of the medium in which an artist works enters crucially into the creative process, and into the sorts of qualities we attend to and value in appreciating works."

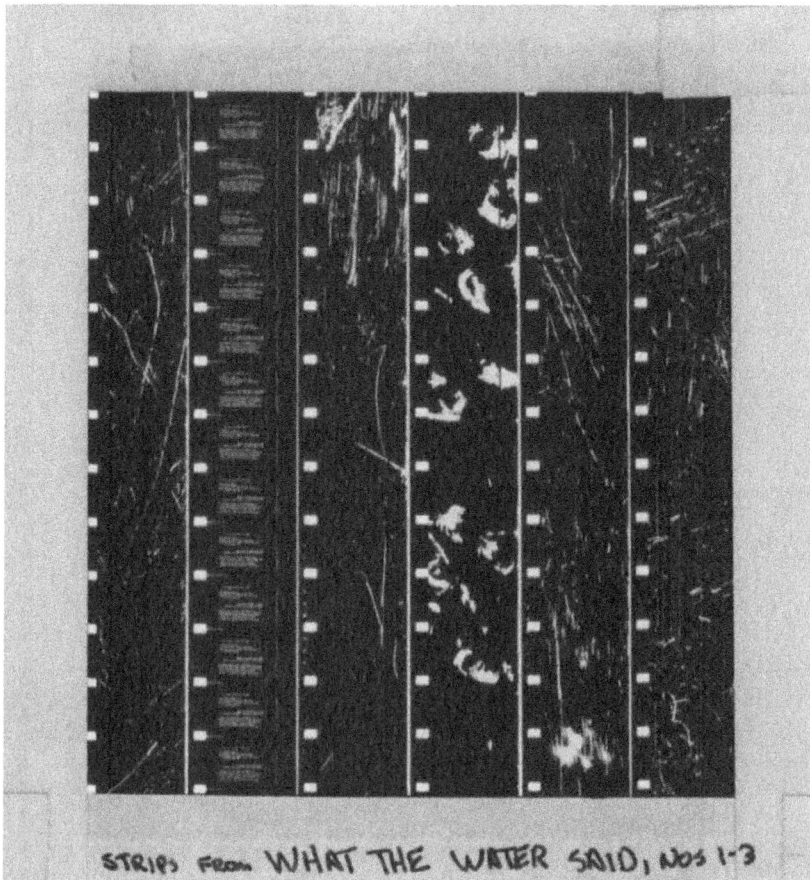

STRIPS FROM WHAT THE WATER SAID, NOS 1-3

Fig. 2.7. David Gatten, filmstrips from *What the Water Said Nos. 1–3* (1998).
Courtesy of David Gatten.

waters off the coast of South Carolina, in some cases leaving them in lobster cages, in others stringing long strips of unspooled film into the water like fishing line. The chemical reactions and wear-and-tear resulting from the filmstrips' contact with salt water and oceanic detritus produced all the abstract images and sounds of the films. Gatten also claims that some of the marks on the strip of film were made by sea animals chewing on them. No camera or chemical processing entered into the process except when prints were made of the originals, which were far too fragile to pass through a projector. Each film, then, is an indexical record of "what the water said," of the actions of the water and its contents on the film stock and of conditions like temperature and tidal movement. The narrative of *What the Water Said*'s production process is one of the avant-garde filmmaker's unique relationship to their materials and resulting sensitivity to their possibilities. And of the demands of the artisanal approach: though Gatten's method was partly aleatoric, making the results viewable

Fig. 2.8. David Gatten, filmstrips from *What the Water Said Nos. 4–6* (2007). Courtesy of David Gatten.

required remarkable technical skills not required or even conceivable in other film-making modes, such as piecing together hundreds of film fragments that washed onto the shore after a reel was lost in the ocean. Along with the contextual knowledge about their making that is always provided at screenings, the films put on display the materials of the medium and the craft ethos of the filmmaker and the cinematic community with which he identifies.

Jennifer Reeves's work is another prominent example both of artisanal method in avant-garde film and the linking of medium and process to the theme of the natural world. *When It Was Blue* (2008) consists of meticulously edited images of nature

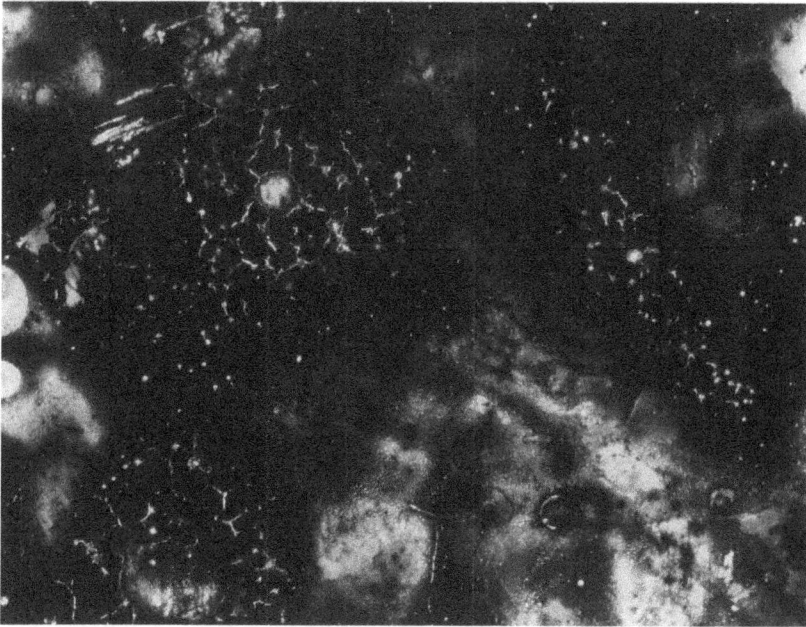

Fig. 2.9. Jennifer Reeves, *When It Was Blue* (2008). Frame enlargement.
Courtesy of Jennifer Reeves.

Reeves took while traveling the world, further subject to what Reeves describes as "direct-on-film" techniques such as painting individual frames by hand and distressing portions of the film by scratching or rubbing them (fig. 2.9). Not wanting to waste the copious outtakes from *When It Was Blue*, Reeves buried them for a time in a landfill, then painted or otherwise hand-worked them into a new film, *Landfill 16* (2011) (fig. 2.10). Like *What the Water Said, When It Was Blue* and *Landfill 16* were produced through a "collaboration with nature," to use Gatten's words, an incorporation of the natural world's materials and means into each filmmaker's already rugged, hands-on manner of working.[55] Such works extend, indeed merge, two avant-garde filmmaking traditions. The first is the intensive, often lyrical contemplation of nature in the films of, say, Peter Hutton, Chris Welsby, James Benning, Margaret Tait, and Brakhage. The second is the camera-less film, from Man Ray and Len Lye to the silt collective, Lynn Loo, and Guy Sherwin (see chapter 3). That so many recent avant-garde films take nature as a theme is no coincidence, but an expression of the increasingly widespread conception of the film medium as natural rather than industrial. The proposition might sound shaky given that the medium has historically been an

[55] Quoted in Takahashi, "After the Death of Film," p. 63.

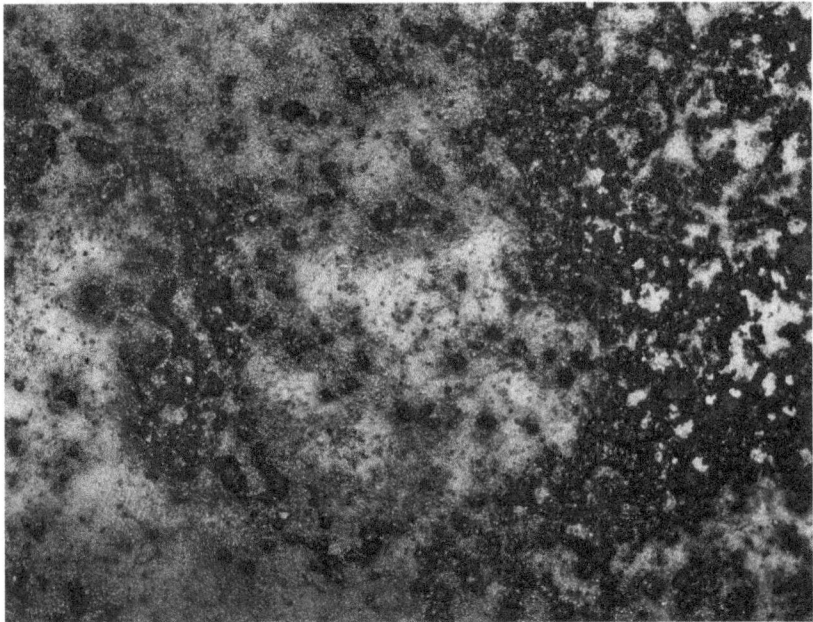

Fig. 2.10. Jennifer Reeves, *Landfill 16* (2011). Frame enlargement.
Courtesy of Jennifer Reeves.

industrial product through and through, and one whose materials are potentially hazardous to the environment. But the notion becomes ever more plausible as avant-garde filmmakers extricate themselves from the structures and materials of industrial filmmaking.

The term "industrial filmmaking" has two meanings here. It refers to the commercial film industry: its aesthetics, characteristic mode of production, and politics. Resistance to this capitalist and illusionist other has shaped avant-garde filmmaking across its history, of course, but so has ambivalence toward film's industrial heritage. This is the second sense of "industrial filmmaking," film's reliance on machines and processes created by corporations toward specific ideological ends. As these corporations abandon film, artists who wish to work with the medium must find ways to do so entirely outside of the standard mechanical and chemical methods, something they are prepared to do because they are already part of a tradition that has found escape hatches from these industrial strictures. One such escape hatch leads out into the natural world. Nature stands in opposition to industry, providing alternative chemical processes, sources of light, and image- and sound-making strategies. And within what might be called the ethics of avant-garde filmmaking are values also associated with nature, such as preservation (i.e., of film), recycling/re-use (as in found footage films), and small-scale organic manufacture (artisanal filmmaking as equivalent to family farming). Nature, then, is more than a rich source of the lyrical imagery of much avant-garde cinema. As a concept in opposition to the industrial it resonates with the very artisanal means of avant-garde filmmaking, providing a conceptual frame of reference that imbues highly materialist filmmaking practices like Gatten's and Reeves's with artistic, ethical, and political meanings that standard medium-specific interpretations of such work cannot acknowledge.

Ed Halter's review of *When It Was Blue* reveals this discursive process in action:

> Among contemporary 16-mm film artists, Reeves is not alone in her desire to engage with the natural world ... No doubt the fragile stuff of film, made newly strange in an age of immaterial electronic images, encourages the contemplation of change and chance, birth and death; such notions are registered through utterly physical means by Reeves in the fractal cracks of distressed pigment that adorn some of her hand-edited frames and in the tidal flows of thick, opalescent paint, sometimes dotted with stellar bubbles of captured air, that wash across other moments.... But *When It Was Blue* should not be understood as a half century's echo of [Brakhage's] *Dog Star Man* (1961–64); here, Reeves looks not mythically inward but phenomenally outward, attempting to embrace and commune with a realm seemingly beyond human experience that has nevertheless been made poignantly precious through its rapid endangerment.[56]

Different levels of meaning interrelate here, from the purely material to the meta-phoric. Films like *When It Was Blue* and *What the Water Said* are indeed about the materials of film, but more importantly they are also about a unique conception of the medium defined by a particular way of working with those materials and the relationship between artist and medium it entails. Parallels with nature amplify and nuance these meanings, elevating medium specificity to an ethos that resonates with other fields of meaning beyond the simplistic, circular meaning "this film is about film itself." Reeves herself echoes Halter's interpretation, saying of 16mm film, "I think it actually has this connection to the human body ... the skin, the aging, the imperfection, the color, the beauty. It's more surprising, organic, imperfect."[57] Nature is only one such field of meanings. Other filmmakers, including those who produce expanded cinema, associate their work to alchemy, the paranormal, the history of pre-industrial cinema, and the human body. We will see this association of avant-garde filmmaking practices with these semantic fields frequently in the next four chapters. Each field of association provides a parallel to an artistic practice that is non- or pre-industrial, artisanal or craft-based, marginalized, obsolete, threatened, fragile, misunderstood.

[56] Ed Halter, "Outward Bound," Artforum.com, October 27, 2008, http://artforum.com/ film/id=21328.
[57] Sophie Mayer, "The Skin, the Aging, the Imperfection, the Colour, the Beauty," *Vertigo* 4, no. 2 (Winter–Spring 2009), n.p., https://www.closeupfilmcentre.com/vertigo_magazine/ volume-4-issue-2-winter-spring-20091/the-skin-the-aging-the-imperfection-the-colour-the-beauty/.

The Meaning of Meaning

Contemporary avant-garde filmmakers' connection of their work to these fields of meaning makes that work referential, a quality not usually associated with medium-specific filmmaking practice and indeed prohibited by the stricter strains of materialist cinema in the 1960s and '70s. Peter Gidal's model of structural-materialist film, for instance, proscribed any reference other than self-reference, linking the representation of anything other than the processes of film production and spectatorship to a nexus of ideologically suspect traits: illusionism, narrative, escapism, and the mystification of filmmaking labor. Though Gidal's films and theoretical writings were probably the most polemical of this period, it is clear that, for many filmmakers and theoreticians of the period, external reference was a threat to the broadly modernist, auto-critical aims of structural cinema. Meaning was the enemy, and a "purist" film aesthetics did not necessarily defeat it: "There is this representational 'reality' one is aiming the camera at. This remains true even if for example the representational content is pared down to the filmstrip itself being pulled through the printer."[58] Representation, in other words, was unavoidable, even if it was constrained to a cinematic literalism in the self-referential image of film itself. "The assertion of film as material is, in fact, predicated upon representation, in as much as 'pure' empty acetate running through the projector gate without image ... merely sets off another level of abstract (or non-abstract) associations." Simply revealing film as material was not enough to escape illusion or to demystify the filmmaking process. " 'Empty screen' is no less significatory than 'carefree happy smile.' "[59]

Gidal criticized American structural film precisely on the grounds that its reflexivity and anti-illusionism were false, coopted by systems of referential meaning. Its "empty screens" and other materialist images served either "romanticism," as in P. Adams Sitney's claim that structural film continued the Romantic individualist thrust of American avant-garde cinema since Deren, or "pseudo-narrative investigations" of filmic processes rather than the more direct instantiations of these in European structural-materialist film.[60]

But as Gidal was formulating these ideas and putting them into practice along with many other European avant-garde filmmakers, a countermovement arose on both sides of the Atlantic. Certain critics and filmmakers began to express exhaustion at structural film's asceticism and materialist literalism. The critic Deke Dusinberre warned that such a rigorously self-referential filmmaking practice ran "the risk of lapsing into meaninglessness," arbitrarily limiting cinema's potential for expression

---

[58] Peter Gidal, "Theory and Definition of Structural/Materialist Film," in Gidal, ed., *Structural Film Anthology* (London: BFI, 1976), p. 2.

[59] Ibid., pp. 2–3.

[60] Ibid., p. 86, in an editor's note that comes at the end of Lois Mendelson and Bill Simon's essay on Ken Jacobs's *Tom, Tom, the Piper's Son* (1969). Gidal included that essay in his *Structural Film Anthology* as an example of a "misunderstanding" of materialism.

to the tautological proposition: "a film is a film," as in the favorite modernist critical formulation "a film about film."[61] Dusinberre and others acknowledged that reflexive, medium-specific film had yielded important insights from which ongoing cinematic practice would benefit, and that a continued commitment to reflexivity was necessary for avant-garde film to oppose dominant cinema. But a new system of meaning was necessary as an escape from what Dusinberre called "the formalist impasse," the endless reiteration of film itself, reminding the viewer over and over that they were watching a film. The way around this impasse was an "analogical" mode wherein each film's reflexive investigation of the medium took a form analogous to another meaning system. Dusinberre cited the example of the phenomenological interpretation of *Wavelength*, by which that film was "a metaphor for the intentionality of consciousness," in the words of Annette Michelson.[62] The analogical mode accommodated a reflexive examination of cinema's materials and spectatorial routines but broke the tautological loop by opening up reflexive filmmaking to other meanings that remained oppositional to conventional structures of cinematic representation.

If my account of contemporary avant-garde cinema is accurate, then clearly filmmakers have embraced this model of reflexivity and medium specificity, finding meaning systems external to film that nonetheless bear structural similarities to it and whose values resonate with those of avant-garde cinema as a mode of film practice. Gatten, criticizing Gidal's prescriptive model of political filmmaking, claims, "if you followed this program to its conclusion, you actually couldn't make films. Everyone that tries to follow it is painted into a corner."[63] The "corner" Gatten has in mind is Gidal's strict ban on meaning, representation, and narrative, though he might also include visual pleasure, which was forbidden under the strictest variants of materialist filmmaking. Descriptions of contemporary avant-garde films, especially handmade works like Gatten's and Reeves's, frequently make reference to their sensuous qualities and visual beauty. The filmmaker Bryan Frye writes of the reconciliation of pleasure with a filmmaking practice that remains rigorously reflexive and materialist, comically referencing the politics of structural-materialist film as expressed by theorists like Gidal:

> In the 1990s experimental filmmakers learned to stop worrying and love the movies. Or rather, some film students put down their Adorno and Lacan texts and returned to the movie theater.... Long-deferred aesthetic questions began to reemerge and demand answers—questions about film, what it looks like, how it works. Young filmmakers started to realize that asking how people experience

---

[61] Deke Dusinberre, "The Ascetic Task: Peter Gidal's *Room Film 1973*," in *Structural Film Anthology*, p. 111. Also see Dusinberre, "St. George in the Forest: The English Avant-Garde," *Afterimage*, no. 6 (Summer 1976), pp. 14–17.

[62] Dusinberre, "The Ascetic Task," pp. 110–111. Michelson's interpretation of *Wavelength* is in her essay "Toward Snow," in Sitney, ed., *The Avant-Garde Film*, pp. 172–183.

[63] William Rose, ed., "The Responsibility of Forms: David Gatten and Fred Worden in Conversation," *Millennium Film Journal*, no. 58 (Fall 2013), p. 166.

movies could be a real line of inquiry and not just a pre-text for wacky crypto-Marxism.... Once again filmmakers explored the plastic qualities of motion picture film, but this time they didn't feel obliged to make believe that doing so consti-tuted ideological subversion.[64]

Such generational distinctions are not absolute, however. We shall see in the fol-lowing chapters that many avant-garde filmmakers putatively engaging in the kind of purist and ascetic materialism of the 1960s and '70s nevertheless made reference to external, non-filmic meaning systems exactly as Dusinberre advocated, making them important precursors to contemporary filmmakers who have unashamedly embraced meaning. This practice extended to expanded cinema works by Sharits, Iimura, Annabel Nicolson, and several others. The point I wish to make for now is that neither connotative richness nor sensuous pleasure are at odds with medium-specific filmmaking. And expanded cinema, as the remaining chapters will show, was not a rejection of some caricature of medium specificity but the enactment of the broadened model of the concept I have tried to illuminate thus far.

I also hope the foregoing summary of the contemporary situation of avant-garde cinema gives the lie to any claim that recent work—expanded or otherwise—is moti-vated by mere nostalgia or the fad for all things analog, or that the renewed interest among filmmakers and scholars in medium specificity is willfully blind to the realities of contemporary art and media. Avant-garde cinema has responded directly to these realities: the oversimplification of the concept of artistic specificity, an untenably absolutist version of interdisciplinarity in academia, and the rhetoric of new media according to which film is obsolete and differences among media are unimportant. While claims of the "death of film" and critiques of medium specificity have often been made in the name of progressive abandonment of arbitrarily limiting concep-tions of cinema's possibilities, we must recognize how they inadvertently serve the interests of media corporations essentially imposing film's obsolescence upon it for financial reasons. This is the situation in which contemporary avant-garde film cul-ture intervenes, often with more sensitivity and nuance than many cinema and media scholars.

Re-enter Expanded Cinema

We can now see where expanded cinema fits into the larger picture of contempo-rary avant-garde film and why it has once again become such a popular mode of working among filmmakers. As a form that puts the materials and processes of film-making on display so directly, expanded cinema extends the craft or artisanal values

---

[64] Bryan Frye, "The New Science of the Cinema," in Steven Anker, Kathy Geritz, and Steve Seid, eds., *Radical Light: Alternative Film and Video in the San Francisco Bay Area, 1945–2000* (Berkeley: University of California Press, 2010), p. 290.

Fig. 2.11. *Machine Gut* (2011), curated by Katherine Bauer. The Commons Gallery, NYU Steinhardt, 2011. Photograph by Joel Schlemowitz.
Courtesy of the artist and Microscope Gallery.

of avant-garde film culture. These values have already been thrown into sharper relief by film's digital other, and especially by the ways in which popular discourses around digital media represent it. The forms of expanded cinema are particularly well suited to counteract the negative qualities avant-garde filmmakers attribute to digital media, such as their automaticity, effortless illusionism, and ease-of-use. More than simply anti-digital or anti-realist, these works represent something more, a manner of working and a relationship between artist and material that are unique, and a range of extra-cinematic meanings and principles by which avant-garde cinema identifies itself.

Consider, as just one among countless recent examples, the collaborative film performance/installation *Machine Gut* (2011) organized by the filmmaker Katherine Bauer and held at New York University's Commons Gallery in Brooklyn (figs. 2.11 and 2.12). Visitors who passed through the rooms of the gallery encountered what looked more like a filmmaker's studio or equipment storage space than a screening. A variety of analog projectors—8 and 16mm, slide and antique magic lantern projectors—littered the space, some stacked on A/V carts, others placed haphazardly on the floor. Dozens of small, mostly empty film reels were strewn about, as were strips of film and multicolored leader, film splicers, gelled lights, and bits of filmic ephemera like daylight spools and empty boxes of film. Long loops of film were threaded through multiple 16mm projectors, running from one to the next across film reels mounted

Fig. 2.12. *Machine Gut* (2011). Photograph by Joel Schlemowitz.
Courtesy of the artist and Microscope Gallery.

on podia, while other loops spun unprojected, running between one projector's takeup reel and another like a fan belt. Strips of film purposely misloaded into projectors slipped out of the gate, lost focus, and were chewed up by sprocket wheels. The event's collaborators, including Bauer, Eros, Joel Schlemowitz, M. M. Serra, and Sarah Halpern, roved about the space changing reels, making improvisatory splices, and adjusting the equipment. The piece unfolded in what Schlemowitz called "a splendidly Rube Goldberg contraption-like fashion."[65] The phrase calls up a flurry of associations: the artisanal, industrial age tinkerer; the sense of the film medium as an infernal machine, difficult to operate and ever on the verge of malfunctioning or falling apart entirely; a device that performs a simple task in an overly complicated fashion—in light of digital media, film is experienced as just such a device. Works of expanded cinema like *Machine Gut* enact these associations and thus the deeper values of contemporary avant-garde film culture.

Schlemowitz has produced a series of film installations in a similar Rube Goldberg spirit himself. His "filmscrolls" combine strips of 16mm film with non-filmic machines that connote the archaic and arcane alike. Strips of film on editing rewinds pass through a typewriter, child's sewing machine, or microscope's viewing plate (figs. 2.13 and 2.14).

---

[65] Joel Schlemowitz, "*Machine Gut*," from Schlemowitz's blog Cine-Soiree!! http://cinesoiree. blogspot. com/2011/09/machine-gut.html.

Fig. 2.13. Joel Schlemowitz, *Filmscroll 8 (Film Typer)* (2000). Two metal rewinds mounted on oak board, two metal film reels with 16mm film, Remington manual typewriter. 13 in. × 22 in. × 7¾ in.
Courtesy of the artist and Microscope Gallery.

Fig. 2.14. Joel Schlemowitz, *Filmscroll 5 (Film Sewing Machine)* (2000). Two metal rewinds mounted on oak board, two metal film reels with 16mm film, Singer Model 20 child's sewing machine. 8½ in. × 24 in. × 8½ in.
Courtesy of the artist and Microscope Gallery.

One filmscroll lays over the surface of a Ouija board "for divination of the film." The works' strange hybridity is surreal in one of that word's original senses, Ducasse's "chance meeting on a dissecting table of a sewing machine and an umbrella." Schlemowitz's filmscrolls place film and cinema in the presence of their turn-of-the-century cousins, signaling the curious intersection of science, pseudoscience, and cinema that informs expanded work by a number of other filmmakers, including Eros, Beloff, Jeanne Liotta, and Kerry Laitala. The filmscrolls reference the rationalizing forces of science and technology that constitute part of film's historical lineage, via the microscope or the

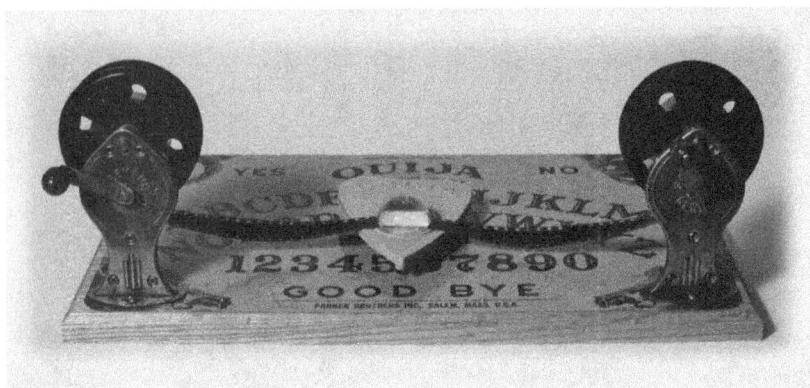

Fig. 2.15. Joel Schlemowitz, *Filmscroll 4 (Ouija Board)* (2000). Two metal rewinds mounted on oak Ouija Board, two metal film reels with 16mm film, plastic message indicator. 12 in. × 18 in. × 6¾ in.
Courtesy of the artist and Microscope Gallery.

sewing machine, for example. But they simultaneously subvert these forces, serving as emblems of the misuse of machinery and the purposeful breaking down of the proper functioning of technology seen in so much contemporary avant-garde film. The magical or mystical connotations of the work, as in the Ouija board filmscroll, are further signs of avant-garde cinema's subversion of the automaticity designed into moving image technologies (fig. 2.15). Filmmakers are attracted to paranormal or pseudoscientific meaning systems like magic(k), the occult, and alchemy, because these are creative forces whose logic cannot be understood or predicted. Skill in these practices combines mastery over craft with imagination and the willingness to embrace the irrational, mysterious, and unpredictable. Expanded works like Bauer's and Schlemowitz's are the most direct manifestation of avant-garde cinema's longstanding resistance to the "you push the button, we do the rest" ethos, expressed here years earlier by James Broughton.

> In the dark of his laboratory the cinematic alchemist works for hours, days, months, years, seeking the seemingly impossible goal of metamorphosis. With his paraphernalia he tries to transform the invisible into the visible ... He searches for that continuously flowing Light which will transform his leaden fragments into a single glowing jewel. Often enough, alas, his "original chaos" remains unredeemed.[66]

Recalling Dusinberre's criticism of structural-materialist film, this version of cinematic essentialism refracts cinema's specificity through the lens of alternative meaning systems at once analogous to cinema (film as alchemy in this instance) and

---

[66] James Broughton, *Making Light of It* (San Francisco: City Lights Books, 1977), pp. 74–75.

oppositional to cultural norms (alchemy as arcane religious practice associated with witchcraft). Expanded cinema works that explore contingency, chance, and even failure are examples of Broughton's unredeemed "original chaos."

Little surprise, then, that the most prominent form of expanded cinema among contemporary avant-garde filmmakers is projection performance. Although precedents can be found throughout the history of avant-garde film in the form of variants of "live cinema," projection performance is no longer on the fringe but a common practice even among filmmakers not known as creators of expanded cinema. The performance of cinema has become a central feature of avant-garde film exhibition, frequently part of screenings not identified as expanded cinema events per se. It is undoubtedly the fullest realization of expanded cinema's celebration of contingency, chance, and failure, but its prominence in the avant-garde film world is likely due to the fact that it so completely embodies the assault on automaticity, seamless illusion, ease-of-use, and passive spectatorship while also showcasing cinematic craft.

As I will show in chapter 3, the performance of projection is additionally a performance of cinema's history, particularly its very early and pre-history. More than the use of superannuated cameras or projectors, which is a feature of some projection performances, or the allusions to "itinerant projection" by filmmakers like Laitala and Bruce McClure, live cinema is part of a much broader historical turn in expanded cinema that re-enacts "primitive" cinema, reimagining it as a model for current and future avant-garde film practice. Countless recent works of expanded cinema have used or re-created devices retroactively brought into cinema's genealogy by film historians, such as magic lanterns, pinhole cameras, handcranked projectors, and camera obscuras. Schlemowitz's 2014 installation "Parallax Reveries" at Brooklyn's Microscope Gallery displayed stereoscopic collages and antique stereoscopic viewers through which attendees could view them. The installation offered a palimpsest of historical imagery; through old, pre-cinematic technology, visitors gazed upon representations of even older craft practices (furniture building and Japanese tea ceremonies, among others) in 3D, a form that has recently been re-popularized by commercial cinema. Though the stereoscopic viewers were originals presumably happened upon in antique shops or on Ebay, the cards were contemporary, handmade by Schlemowitz, a collapsing of past and present that was artisanal in both form and content. "Parallax Reveries" was a subtle meditation on remediation moving in both historical directions, nested images of past art forms reimagined through newer forms and technologies, though never privileging the new over the old.

Beloff's expanded cinema performances with forgotten or soon to be forgotten media technologies—vintage Kodascope 16mm projectors, stereo slide projectors, 78 rpm hand-cranked phonographs, Theremins, hand-cranked film projectors, and magic lanterns—associate the use of such technologies with the very act of remembering and, by extension, preserving the past (fig. 2.16). This is in contrast to the ahistorical present-ness brought about by the ever condensing life cycles of digital media machines. In a statement on her expanded work *Lost* (1995), "a document of everyday life on New York's Lower East Side" employing a slide projector, hand-cranked

Fig. 2.16. Poster for Zoe Beloff and Brian Frye, "An Evening of Philosophical Toys." Robert Beck Memorial Cinema, 145 Ludlow Street, New York City, October 27, 1998.

film projector, and gramophone, Beloff equates the forgetting and tossing out of old machines with a deepening blindness to history itself: "My project for some time has been an attempt to awaken the past buried behind the present, behinds the illusion of progress by studying its scraps and remains, outdated buildings and fashions, the landscape of the everyday that has been discarded, overlooked. And at the same time exploring the ever changing relationship between technology, imagination and perception."[67] She further associates the aging technology she uses to the aging facades of buildings and storefronts; that the Lower East Side subsequently became one of the city's most trendy and heavily gentrified areas confirms Beloff's skepticism toward the rhetoric of the new and her linking of history to the representational machines that mediate it.

A filmmaker's historical references can be literal, as in the use of specific machines and early exhibition practices like live hand-cranked projection. Or they can be more creative, imagining a primordial cinema whose origins are a combination of subterranean pseudoscientific beliefs and ancient devices like camera obscuras and magic lanterns. Why is early cinema history such a significant body of knowledge at this time? What has made it so creatively generative for makers of expanded cinema? Of course, we must remember that avant-garde cinema took a historical turn long before the contemporary moment, a turn mirrored by a wave of revisionist scholarship on early cinema in academia beginning in the late 1970s. But since the mid-1990s avant-garde cinema has fiercely recommitted to this turn, making a historical *return*. What explains this? David James points us toward an answer:

> The search for an entirely literal film language ... goes further and further back through the archaeology of early cinema, past the reflexive audience confrontation and the movable shot in *The Great Train Robbery*, past the almost schematic analysis of illusion in *Uncle Josh at the Moving Picture Show*, and so to the premonition of Warhol in the earliest preserved film, *John Rice—May Irwin Kiss*. Eventually the search falls away in the filmstrips of Muybridge, in the enumeration of the components of a possible cinema, and in the speculations in which the idea of film was first broached, the first conceptual film created.[68]

James wrote this in 1989 in reference to structural films by the likes of Jacobs, Warhol, Frampton (who also made works of serial photography parodying Muybridge), the films of Fluxus, and so on. Hence, it is not unique to contemporary avant-garde film. James's claim is that in seeking out cinema's essence some structural filmmakers naturally looked to its origins. Early and pre-cinema offered a field of alternative possibilities for cinema, untraveled roads cut off by the institutionalization and commercialization of film and the creation of "cinema as we know it." By this interpretation, Warhol's early silent films like *Kiss* (1963) and *Empire* (1964) revisit the actualities of the Lumières and the period when audiences took pleasure in the novelty of the close-up. Many Fluxus films, such as *Eyeblink* (Yoko Ono) and *Smoking* (Joe Jones, both films 1966), made with a special high-speed camera that renders the titular acts in extreme slow motion, echo early "trick" films like Cecil Hepworth's *How It Feels To Be Run Over* (1900) or Méliès's *The Untamable Whiskers* (1904). But in tracing this historical turn even further back, to the earliest ideas of cinema's possibility *before*

[67] Zoe Beloff, artist's statement on *Lost* (1995). http://www.zoebeloff.com/pages/lost.html.
[68] James, *Allegories of Cinema*, p. 242.

the invention of film, James implies an expanded cinema. Followed far enough, the impulse behind structural and structural-materialist film ultimately leads to a cinema that "falls away" into strips of imagery and, eventually, into a "conceptual" phenomenon that retroactively detaches cinema from the institutional structure it was beginning to take in the mid-1900s and from the material constraints of the specific medium though which it became recognizable in the first place.

In a way, the claim repeats the one Sheldon Renan made about expanded cinema's origins, but with a difference. Here, the opening up of cinema is from within, the result of a turn to its own historical sources and genealogical lines (both real and imagined) rather than to external art world influences. Filmmakers' growing awareness of their art form's historical variability is as much a factor in its expansion as their knowledge of conceptual, minimalist, or postmodern art practices. Whereas Renan and Youngblood envisioned cinema's future in new technologies and art world developments, expanded cinema of the third wave has looked to cinema's past for alternate technologies, modes of working, and exhibition structures. This should not be mistaken for an act of nostalgia, a willful ignorance of present realities on the part of filmmakers clinging to a mummified past. The point is not to recreate or relive early cinema history, but to take up the model it offers for alternative production and exhibition, which can only be recognized as such in light of what has come since—the formation of the film industry, the standardization of production and exhibition, the rise of the narrative feature to a position of dominance, and most recently the denigration of technical crafts and viewing experiences that avant-garde filmmakers deem important. As the filmmaker Alex Mackenzie states it, "the use of so-called outmoded technologies is not a harkening back to the past, but rather a way of examining the present, a reaction to modes of information processing available to us today."[69] The most successful avant-garde film work, he continues, reveals that conceptions of "good" cinema are economically and technologically determined by the industry. Hence, a *pre*-industrial filmmaking practice becomes, in the present, an *anti*-industrial one freed from its historically bound "pre-" to offer an alternative that is entirely viable in the contemporary context.

Expanded Exhibition—the Microcinema as Expanded Cinema

The strategy of mining the past for present and future options is not unique to contemporary avant-garde filmmakers. What is unique to the present moment, however, is that these filmmakers have a new kind of exhibition space that institutionalizes the more varied, open, and anarchic modes of working and viewing suggested by the historical turn. This space is the microcinema. The word is the

---

[69] Alex Mackenzie, "Hand Cranked: A Conversation with Filmmaker Lee Krist," *Millennium Film Journal*, no. 50 (Fall 2008), p. 40.

invention of filmmakers David Sherman and Rebecca Barten, founders of the Total Mobile Home Microcinema, a 30-seat screening space in the basement of their San Francisco apartment, in 1994 (fig. 2.17). Though the filmmaker Craig Baldwin's Other Cinema, a very similar sort of exhibition venue, had been in operation since the late 1970s, a microcinema movement could only be said to have begun in the mid-nineties. Digital media once more play an important role. As digital began to replace film, especially in university film programs, 16mm projectors and related equipment became cheaper. It is also likely that increased savvy among filmmakers and scholars about the institutional dimensions of avant-garde

Fig. 2.17. David Sherman and Rebecca Barten at Total Mobile Home microcinema. October 28, 1995.

Photograph ©Christine T. Anderson, 1995. Courtesy of David Sherman and Rebecca Barten.

cinema has heightened awareness of the importance of infrastructure and community building within the avant-garde. All cinemas are defined by a field of discourses, institutions, and practices that shape filmmaking and viewing alike—this is precisely what the concept of modes of film practice means. But avant-garde film culture has always been distinct in the extent to which that field is a visible force permeating the viewing experience. As a mode of film practice, avant-garde cinema uniquely privileges the communal, interactive—in a word, social—aspect of cinematic events, additionally bridging the gulf between filmmaker and viewer that is unavoidable in mass-produced and mass-consumed popular cinema. Which is to say that the artisanal ethos of avant-garde cinema extends to features of exhibition such as increased artist presence (e.g., at screenings), the closer relationships that are possible between filmmakers, critics, and "regular" viewers, and the greater amount of curiosity and knowledge about the nature of filmmaking labor and cinema history among viewers. The culture of the microcinema has dramatically amplified this trait of avant-garde film, to the point that a change in degree has arguably become a change in kind, a significant shift in film exhibition that has fed back into production and shaped critical discourse.

Not surprisingly given the name, microcinemas are small, but the "micro" means more than this. It refers to the reduction of scale appropriate to an independent artisanal filmmaking tradition. Microcinemas frequently inhabit spaces never intended for screening films, as in the case of Barten and Sherman's basement, roughly converted with folding chairs, a screen, and rudimentary projection equipment. Needless to say, they look nothing like conventional film theaters, but do resemble the ramshackle, makeshift nickelodeon theaters of cinema's early history. And like many of those theaters they serve a raucous, decidedly indecorous audience, in Baldwin's words, an "energized microcinema audience opting for the provocative images and ideas only available in a non-commercial and non-academic salon environment."[70] Reflecting on his days as co-curator of the Robert Beck Memorial Cinema in New York, which he founded in 1998, Brian Frye speaks of the same kind of viewing experience: "Our most memorable shows usually involved turning a movie into an interactive experience" (fig. 2.18)[71]

Significantly, Barten and Sherman define microcinema not so much as a kind of exhibition space but a "mode of action," which in many microcinemas is sensed as a form of collaboration between curator/operators and audiences.[72] The experience of the microcinema is one of a sometimes barely orchestrated event that exceeds the bounds of the screen. Even screenings of conventionally formatted—non-expanded—films become something like expanded cinema events. Baldwin recalls a screening at Shapeshifters, a monthly screening event in Oakland, in which

[70] From Other Cinema's website, http://www.othercinema.com/aboutoc.html.

[71] Bryan L. Frye, "On the Origins of the Robert Beck Memorial Cinema," *INCITE Journal of Experimental Media*, no. 4 (Fall 2013), p. 129.

[72] From the Total Mobile Home website, http://www.totalmobilehome.com/tmh_history.htm.

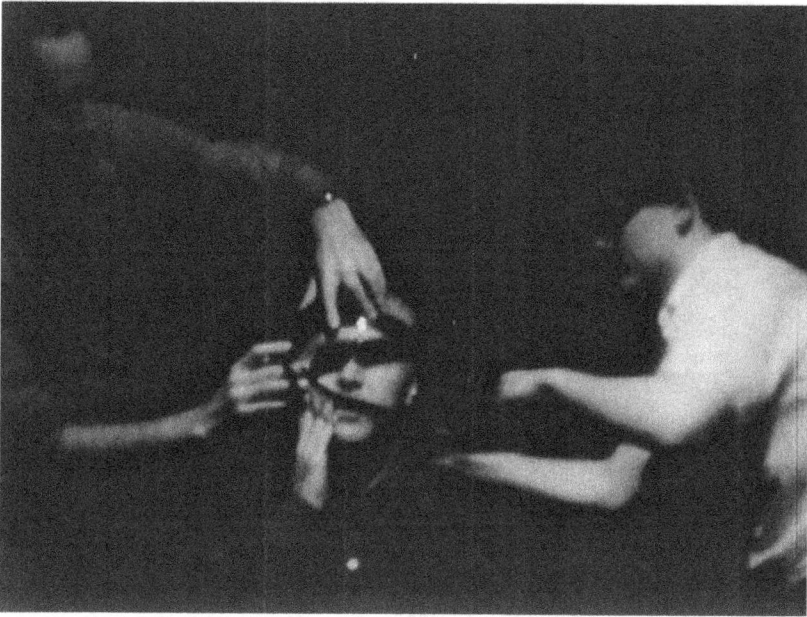

Fig. 2.18. Bradley Eros (left) and Brian Frye (right) unwrapping Stuart Sherman's head from a tangle of film. Frame enlargement from *Robert Beck Is Alive and Well and Living in NYC* (2002), 16mm film by Brian Frye and Lee Ellickson. Documentation of one of Sherman's "perfilmances" during a September 26, 2000, screening at Robert Beck Memorial Cinema, New York City.
Courtesy of Brian Frye.

projections of conventional narrative films from his storied print collection became the basis for a participatory expanded cinema performance (figs. 2.19 and 2.20):

> I had two (actually more) projectors, each w/colored filter, and on lazy susans. The material on each projector was very similar, sometimes the same film in fact (I have two prints of some titles), but of course the projectors would never be in sync, and of course we'd swing the image right and left on the lazy susans. The audience was wearing Chromadepth glasses, so we had a 3-D effect going with the red popping out in front of the blue. But I had an even bolder idea . . . to put live bodies in front of the projections, imitating the action on the screen.[73]

At the Robert Beck, Frye recalls, "we presented 'Subterranean Science Night,' in which Bradley [Eros] added smell, touch, taste, and performance elements to an assortment of science films."[74] Central to the microcinema model is that cinematic

---

[73] Email to author, October 16, 2019.
[74] Frye, "On the Origins of the Robert Beck Memorial Cinema," p. 129.

Fig. 2.19. Craig Baldwin (right, in 3D glasses) operating multiple projectors at Shapeshifters, Oakland, CA. October 13, 2013.
Courtesy of Craig Baldwin.

Fig. 2.20. Audience members participating in the "kissing montage" during Craig Baldwin's October 13, 2013, multiple-projector 3D screening at Shapeshifters.
Courtesy of Craig Baldwin.

experience and socializing become indistinguishable from one another. Adjacent to the screening room in Total Mobile Home was a wine bar; Christine Metropoulos, executive director of the San Francisco Cinematheque, recalls that her first experience at TMH was not a screening but a barbeque;[75] Michael Johnsen, one of the co-founders of Pittsburgh's Orgone Cinema, describes that microcinema as a "fun, informal, friendly atmosphere that was peppered with silliness, giveaways, corny food; all in the same room as the projection equipment."[76] Evidence of this social dimension of microcinemas, Johnsen's recollection also speaks to the fact that the polymorphous nature of microcinema events is matched by the mutability of the spaces they inhabit. Indeed, several nomadic microcinemas claim no single location as their home, but shift opportunistically to whatever spaces are available. Such spaces were not originally intended for theatrical screenings, which, rather than a shortcoming, is a benefit given that the conception of cinema that informs microcinemas is itself mutable. Microcinemas are thus staging grounds for cinema's heterogeneity, one night arranged to roughly approximate a traditional theatrical screening venue, the next set up more like a gallery, another night adjusted once more for live musical performance accompanying projection.

The curatorial approach common to microcinemas further evidences these twin traits of sociality and mutability. This could best be described as a collage approach, "polymorphous group shows" in Baldwin's words.[77] Avant-garde film screenings have historically been programs, as the films tend to be much shorter than feature length, and there has always been an art to the organization of such screenings. Once more, the microcinema builds upon this tradition within avant-garde film culture and pushes it to a new limit. This frequently means intermixing avant-garde films with documentaries, educational films, PSAs, and the like within a single screening. The films shown during the "Subterranean Science Night" screening at Robert Beck were educational films about topics like crystals, carnivorous plants, and water. Appropriately, the event was billed as an evening of "experiments with films, not experimental films," reconceiving the screening as an act of collage or found footage film but performed live and augmented by the sensory interventions Frye describes (fig. 2.21). In an essay on the "morality" of curating films, Sherman and Barten write, "every new film program is simultaneously an interpretation, a performance and an addition to a lineage of events." And, "Context is essence. Little films are very responsive to their environment."[78] The morality of microcinema programming, then, is about sensitivity to the often unpredictable interchanges that occur between programmer, film, and audience. Microcinema curating is also attuned to the sense of

---

[75] Christine Metropoulos, "A Cinematic Reverie in Five Parts: Visions of Venues in the 1990s (excerpt)," http://www.davidshermanfilms.com/Christines_TMH_writing.html.

[76] Michael Johnsen, Greg Pierce, and Adam Abrams, "Pittsburgh's Orgone Cinema: A Deadly Serious Joke," *INCITE Journal of Experimental Media*, no. 4 (Fall 2013), p. 101.

[77] From Other Cinema's website, http://www.othercinema.com/aboutoc.html.

[78] David Sherman and Rebecca Barten, "On Curating," http://www.totalmobilehome.com/ curating. htm.

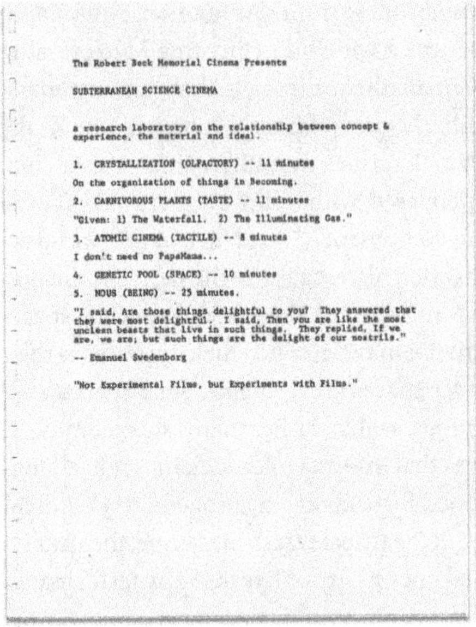

The Robert Beck Memorial Cinema Presents

SUBTERRANEAN SCIENCE CINEMA

a research laboratory on the relationship between concept & experience, the material and ideal.

1. CRYSTALLIZATION (OLFACTORY) -- 11 minutes

On the organization of things in Becoming.

2. CARNIVOROUS PLANTS (TASTE) -- 11 minutes

"Given: 1) The Waterfall. 2) The Illuminating Gas."

3. ATOMIC CINEMA (TACTILE) -- 8 minutes

I don't need no PapaMama...

4. GENETIC POOL (SPACE) -- 10 minutes

5. NOUS (BEING) -- 25 minutes.

"I said, Are those things delightful to you? They answered that they were most delightful. I said, Then you are like the most unclean beasts that live in such things. They replied, If we are, we are; but such things are the delight of our nostrils."

-- Emanuel Swedenborg

"Not Experimental Films, but Experiments with Films."

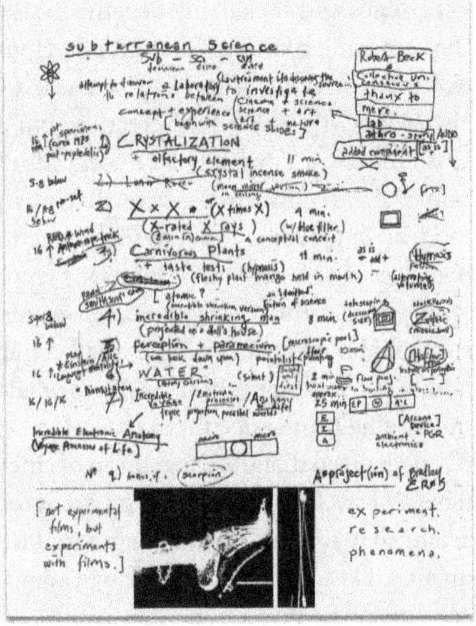

Fig. 2.21. Screening list (left) and performance instructions (right) from "Subterranean Science Night." Robert Beck Memorial Cinema, New York City. June 9, 1998.

liveness, of presence and presentness, the knowledge that the tenor of the screening is contingent on the specificity of its place, time, and audience, and could not be replicated if, say, the films were collected on a DVD for home viewing. The tendency either not to publicize their events or to do so minimally, yet another practice of commercial cinema that microcinema organizers reject, is also a sign of the ephemerality of those events. This is celebrated rather than seen as a liability. Liotta, who co-founded the outdoor garden microcinema Firefly, writes, "Whoever showed up showed up; there were no mailing lists, websites, or other advertisements. Come and go as you please. Sorry if you missed it."[79] Schlemowitz adds: "Experimental film screenings are often fleeting and transitory . . . there is often a heightened sense of the ephemerality of experience in their occurrence and passing."[80]

There are two related but distinct emotional valences here. Liotta's "sorry if you missed it" is a minor expression of regret, as if said with a shrug of the shoulders and an attitude of "*que sera, sera*." Whoever shows up, shows up; whatever happens, happens—even failure. Microcinemas accept the risks of such a patently risky, under- or unfunded, grassroots endeavor, indeed designing them into their exhibition practices. Failure is not necessarily a goal, but it is one acceptable, creatively productive possibility with its own potential rewards. The tenuousness of

[79] Jeannie Liotta, "Firefly Cinema (or Cinema for the People)," *INCITE Journal of Experimental Media*, no. 4 (Fall 2013), p. 37.

[80] Joel Schlemowitz, "Ephemeral Cinema: Mono No Aware," *Boog City* 84 (n.d., ca. 2013), p. 12.

microcinemas—sustained by word of mouth rather than press coverage and ads, by passionate commitment rather than money—becomes a point of pride, a defiant gesture toward commercial cinema and mainstream culture. On the other hand, Schlemowitz's "passing" strikes a much more somber note, suggesting death and loss. The experience of ephemerality, of an event that will never repeat itself, is a poignant one, especially as it resonates now with the possibility of film's "passing" into obsolescence. As I have tried to show, it is not just a physical medium whose passage is at issue, but core values threatened in the contemporary media environment. This darker emotional tone accompanying an ephemeral cinematic event hints at what is at stake for microcinemas and avant-garde filmmakers surviving at subsistence level, even if their public stance is one of acceptance of failure and loss. An article about the analog filmmaking and expanded cinema organization Mono No Aware strikes a balance between these two senses of the ephemerality of film and film culture: "As the existing infrastructure collapses around them, these non-profit organizations will keep making movies and they will share them with friends, neighbors, lovers and strangers."[81] "Mono no aware" can be translated as "the pathos of things," an apt phrase for the intertwined discourses of materiality and ephemerality that have historically informed avant-garde filmmaking and expanded cinema, and that manifest now in the twin aims of preserving a physical medium and the acceptance, even celebration, of the fleeting quality of cinematic experience. This might sound like waxing poetic, but it is exactly this kind of language that predominates in discussions of microcinemas and other facets of contemporary avant-garde cinema, and attentiveness to this discourse will provide us with the basis for approaching specific works of expanded cinema in the remaining chapters.

It should be clear by now where this discussion of microcinema culture is leading. More than receptive spaces for expanded cinema, microcinemas are models for it. Like expanded works, microcinemas showcase cinema's adaptability to varying spaces, its heterogeneity, and the ways it responds to its social and discursive contexts. Exhibition is a form of creative production subject to the contingencies of exhibition in a space where chance and audience participation are actively courted. In their anti-industrial stance, microcinemas and expanded cinema alike renew historical, pre-industrial technologies and techniques and align themselves with cultural values like artisanship, thrift, conservation, and grassroots collective action. It is no coincidence that the growth of the microcinema movement began in the mid-1990s, simultaneous with the emergence of the current wave of expanded cinema. This is not to say that microcinemas *caused* expanded cinema's renaissance. Rather, both developments emerged in tandem out of historical conditions that necessitated the forms of action specific to them.

The performances of Andrew Lampert throw into relief the parallels between avant-garde film programming and contemporary expanded cinema. In addition to

[81] Randy Sterling Hunter, "Why'd You Have to Take Our Kodachrome Away?," *Mono No Aware*, no. 1 (2013), p. 91.

Fig. 2.22. Andrew Lampert, *That's Undertainment* (2010). Performance documentation. Anthology Film Archives, New York City. April 6, 2010.
Courtesy of Andrew Lampert.

being a filmmaker, Lampert has engaged in critical film programming and preservation work for nearly 20 years, having served as Anthology Film Archives' archivist and curator of collections from 2002 to 2015. As part of his ongoing series "Unessential Cinema," which he has curated at Anthology since 2004, Lampert created the expanded cinema performance *That's Undertainment* in 2010 (fig. 2.22). Lampert and a group of fellow film archivists, including Stephen Parr of Oddball Film in San Francisco and Greg Pierce of Orgone Cinema in Pittsburgh (both microcinemas), projected multiple archival films simultaneously in Anthology's Courthouse Theater. The films were chosen by the participants, who had been given the mandate to "cull favorite footage that others might term tedious, difficult, dreary, lackluster, lifeless, or even uninteresting," hence the title of the performance, a play upon Anthology's long-standing "Essential Cinema" program of canonical films.[82]

Writing of Lampert's work, Ed Halter notes that, though Lampert is an archivist, "his performances, films, and audio pieces bear none of the librarianlike stuffiness usually associated with the latter profession—in fact, much of his art seems to be about undermining any assumed reverence for the preservation of media artifacts." Halter quotes Lampert—"The projector and the screen and the projectionist and the

---

[82] From Andrew Lampert's website, http://www.andrewlampert.com/thats-undertainment.

audience are together far more integral to cinema than any film running through a projector in a booth behind the audience," a sentiment that could be part of a mission statement for microcinemas, which decenters the film-as-object in a chaotic, social, participatory experience of experimental cinema's values.[83]

Consider, once more, Eros's *Burn (or, The 2nd Law of Thermodynamics)* as a case study of how these conditions shaped a specific work of expanded cinema. The piece grew out of two events at the Robert Beck Memorial Cinema, the aforementioned "Subterranean Science" program and a later event entitled "Mistakes (everything you can do wrong)." In the latter, Eros, Frye, and Liotta attempted to exhaust the possibilities in the creative misuse of projectors and found films, threading films backward or upside down into projectors, for example, or loading an 8mm film into a 16mm projector as in the case of *Burn*. Both events followed the "experiments with films, not experimental films" theme and the collage approach to programming characteristic of microcinemas, employing decidedly *non*-avant-garde educational films in a live performance so that the event itself was "experimental" even if the individual films were not. A handwritten document that looks like a set list for the Subterranean Science event refers to each film as a "specimen."[84] Via this association of the expanded use of a film with scientific method, Eros also associates cinema with the natural world, further evident in his description of *Burn* in "lapidarian" and astronomical terms: the tortured transformations of frame after frame are "jewel-like crystallizations" and "tiny supernova(s) of destruction."[85] Such references inflect filmic specificity with positive qualities; jewels are valuable, beautiful, and enduring. Eros has acknowledged the interplay of the literal and figurative: "[T]he fragility of the plastic material is both magnified and transformed, serving as a physical fact of film and a brutal metaphor."[86]

Presumably, the imagery of the 8mm film frames fluttering, melting, and burning inside the glowing 16mm projector gate could be convincingly reproduced using digital means. But such a reproduction would only be meaningful insofar as it faithfully mimicked the materials and mechanisms of film. Put another way, it would merely be an imitation, inconceivable without the prior existence of a physically distinct medium. Eros's expressive materialism requires a material with specific physical traits that digital video lacks even if it can imitate them. It is not only that film stock is plastic and can therefore be melted, but that the imagery of film is fused to a physically tangible material, so that the qualities of that material become the qualities of the image itself. And the filmmaker can intervene in the operation of film's mechanisms in ways that digital video does not allow. In short, the imagery of *Burn* results both

---

[83] Ed Halter, "Andrew Lampert," *BOMB Magazine*, July 1, 2010, https://bombmagazine.org/articles/andrew-lampert/, n.p.

[84] Bryan L. Frye, "The Robert Beck Memorial Cinema, Volume I: May 1998–October 1999." This is collection of ephemera from the first year-and-a-half of Robert Beck's operation, accessible at https://archive.org/details/TheRobertBeckMemorialCinemaVolumeIMay1998-october1999.

[85] Eros, "There Will Be Projections in All Dimensions," p. 75.

[86] Ibid., p. 76.

from the specific traits of film stock and the kind of exchanges between medium and filmmaker not possible in digital. As an instance of live cinema, *Burn* subverts the automaticity of projection and undermines the relative stability of celluloid, taking the path of *most* resistance. Thus, the work is an assault on more than celluloid, but furthermore on the ideology of digital media, that of perfect, easy illusion requiring practically no technical skill. Ironically, *Burn* demonstrates the artisanal skill of the projectionist (in the world of avant-garde cinema, frequently the filmmaker him or herself), through the knowingly erroneous use of that skill. Projection is removed from the strictures of standardized film gauges, projection speed, and proper focus, not to mention the requirement of handling the projected films with care. There is more to Eros's implied critique of digital media's rhetoric of automaticity and ease in this work, however. After documenting the three versions of the performance on digital video, Eros altered the images further, through digitally specific means. The image at times softens into blurry superimpositions of different moments in the performance. At other spots the color of the frame changes suddenly. Changes in focus, some due to the fluttering of the film in the projector gate, others to adjustments made to the digital camera's focus ring, produce disorienting layers of blurred imagery. And because the frame rate of video is different from film, the documentation exaggerates the degree of flicker and thus heightens the "filmic" quality of the work. Had Eros used digital video for the merely pragmatic purpose of documentation, he would, in effect, have been accepting the idea of digital's capacity for perfect mimesis. The effects he created in the documentation bend digital to the aesthetics and ideology of the avant-garde.

Burn is patently ephemeral, as the source material was destroyed by the deliberate misuse of the projector. And although documentation of the work is available as a digital file from the Filmmakers' Cooperative, it does not preserve the sense of liveness that would have been a substantive part of the original piece as a projection performance. We cannot see Eros wrestling with the filmstrip, or the projector, and cannot hear the sounds of that projector as the film jerks through it. As if to emphasize the ephemerality of the performance and the contingent nature of expanded cinema in general, Eros presents three different instantiations in the digital documentation, three different segments of 8mm film running through the projector, each time with different results. By its nature, *Burn* is not documentable because it is not "a" work—it is inextricable from the singular circumstances of each iteration, and assuming Eros did not retain a copy of the found film he used for the performance, it will eventually be impossible to reproduce.

Lastly, in laying claim to a performative dimension in cinema, *Burn* asserts that cinema is something we did not customarily believe it to be. If we are to take the work as an instance of cinema rather than a film-theater hybrid, then several things follow: if cinema can be a live art form, it can also be interactive and participatory insofar as it can acknowledge and integrate the realities of its social situation, the specificities of audience and space. With that in mind, one of the most striking things about microcinemas and expanded cinema both is that they display so explicitly the

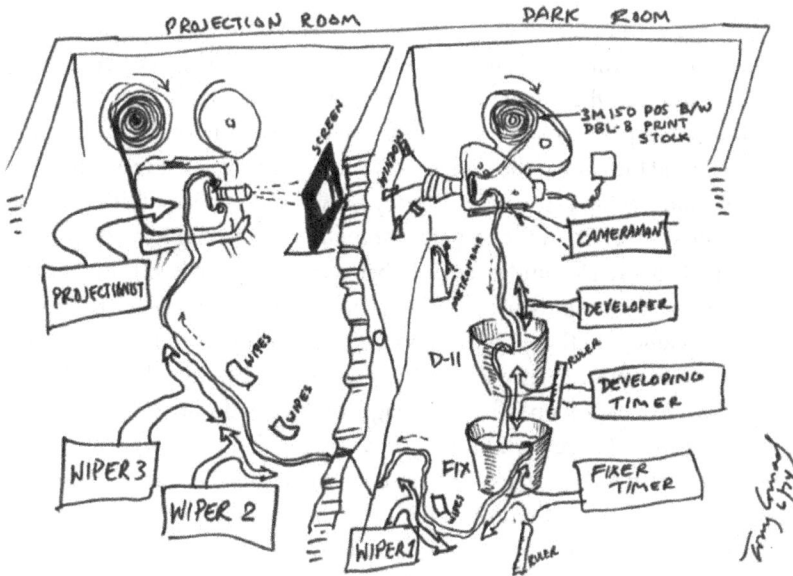

Fig. 2.23. Tony Conrad, diagram for production of *Film Feedback* (1974). Courtesy of Tony Conrad.

very same qualities said to define digital media: interactivity and the "social" (as in "social media"). For many avant-garde filmmakers and critics, the environment of the microcinema and the traits of expanded cinema reveal digital medias' prized sociality as a pernicious fiction. Brett Kashmere and Walter Forsberg contrast "the splintered, solitary, 'snacking-in-bed' viewing experience of YouTube," and "the age of so-called 'participatory' media, in which people connect virtually using avatars and aliases," with the genuinely social experience of an event at a microcinema.[87] The embod-iedness of microcinema events and expanded cinema works trumps, as it were, the disembodied, individuated experience typical of digital media. This is the reversal of digital's remediation of film: cinema as the original, true social medium. Call this "an-terograde remediation."

We find an intriguing precedent in Tony Conrad's *Film Feedback* (1974, at least two realizations), which Conrad produced with a team of film students while teaching at Antioch College (fig. 2.23). What remains of the work is a short 16mm film viewable in the standard way, but it originated as an expanded work that collapsed produc-tion, chemical processing, and projection in something like a private performance in which the team of filmmakers also constituted the event's only audience. The

---

[87] Brett Kashmere and Walter Forsberg, "Introduction," *INCITE Journal of Experimental Media*, no. 4 (Fall 2013), p. 11.

filmmakers placed an Arriflex 16mm camera in a projection booth, aiming it through the booth's window at a screen in the adjacent room. A 16mm projector was placed behind the screen, so that the screen was positioned between it and the camera in the booth. In front of the screen, in view of the camera, was a lighted candle. Under normal circumstances, the camera body would have been closed to prevent the film inside from being exposed to light; in this case, the projector booth was dark enough to prevent this, and the back of the camera was left off. Instead of being wound around a take-up reel after being exposed at the very slow camera speed of five frames per second, the film passed from the camera, through trays of chemical developer and fixer, was wiped off, then fed under the door between projection booth and screening room to be threaded into the rear-screen projector. As the images began to appear on the screen, the camera in the projection booth recorded them, in turn re-recording those images as they appeared on the screen, and so on until the roll of film ran out. The result was a feedback loop of nested images of the candle and screen alternating positive and negative (since the film was negative, the first images put through the rear-screen projector were negative, followed by the negative image of that negative image—a positive image, again reversed in the next round, and so on) (fig. 2.24). By Fred Camper's description, the feedback imagery looks "like the images reflected in two parallel mirrors ... as the film approaches cinema's limits of resolution, it ends."[88] The candle, aside from providing more interesting image content than a blank screen, also reveals, as Le Grice noted, "the unbroken continuity of the action," that the alternating nested images were made in the same recording instance rather than a series of rephotographing or optical printing runs.[89] The description should sound familiar; we have completed the historical loop, circling from William Raban's layered temporal images in *2'45"* to Conrad's. Both works have received renewed attention as contemporary expanded cinema responds to remediation and media convergence in much the same way that earlier works responded to synaesthesia and intermedia.

While the "parallel mirror" and "time corridor" metaphors are apt for both *2'45"* and *Film Feedback*, Conrad and his production team actually had a different point of reference in mind. They produced a filmic feedback loop, a continuous chain of film shot and projected simultaneously. Many video artists at the time considered feedback to be one of their art form's unique effects, a decidedly un-cinematic property. Many of these artists had explored this effect of video by the time Conrad and his students made *Film Feedback*, often experimenting with the different layers of time that resulted from the inclusion of video feedback or prerecorded images in live performance. Conrad's film feedback system explored this property in a medium other than video, even though doing so required much greater effort. This seems to have been part of the point. Compare Conrad's desire to build an almost ludicrously complicated and difficult system for producing feedback in film with video artist Loren Sears's

---

[88] Fred Camper, "Film Feedback," *Chicago Reader*, September 8, 1994, http://www.chicagoreader.com/chicago/film-feedback/Content?oid=885424.

[89] Le Grice, *Abstract Film and Beyond*, p. 150.

Fig. 2.24. Tony Conrad, *Film Feedback* (1974). Frame enlargements from 16mm film.
Courtesy of Tony Conrad.

statement that he sought a "way of using the medium effortlessly" (see chapter 1). Sears added that some of his work attempted "to go right through the medium using what it can do easily."[90] Where for Sears feedback was a feature that differentiated the mediums of film and video (and cinema from video art), for the members of Pulsa, as Youngblood's intermedia "ecologists" or "design scientists," feedback was a trait of video technology that enabled interactivity, creating a microcosmic version of the noosphere, the technological and natural environment in which spectators engaged with their own electronic images. In Pulsa's light-sound video feedback installation at the Automation House in April of 1971, video cameras positioned across the venue's three floors subjected real-time images of gallery visitors to degrees of delay and color manipulation; these images were subsequently projected on screens mounted

---

[90] Cited in Youngblood, *Expanded Cinema*, p. 291.

Fig. 2.25. Pulsa, Light-sound video feedback installation (1971). Installation view. Automation House, New York City. Video projectors, plants, loud speakers, analog digital control system, etc.
Courtesy of David Rumsey.

throughout the space (fig. 2.25). Spectators moving through the Automation House could simultaneously experience both real time and delayed video images of their trajectories.

Creating feedback in *film* was a deliberately perverse exercise. The difficulties *Film Feedback*'s makers had to confront, and the sheer effort required to make the project work, stemmed from their goal of bending their medium to an image-making process that was considered to be one of the fundamental properties of another, and to which the materials of film were poorly suited. The rest of this book is about this process of negotiation between what cinema is believed to be and what it is assumed *not* to be, and of the idea that what was thought to lie beyond cinema's limits is in fact within its realm of possibility. This dialectic has moved to the foreground in moments of significant technological and artistic change, with expanded cinema emerging in these moments as a means to work through their ramifications for cinema's identity and autonomy. Hence, expanded cinema proposes that cinema can be "sculptural," "painterly," "performative," "musical," "conceptual," all while retaining its sense of self. But also at stake in expanded cinema is the identity of avant-garde or experimental cinema in particular, as the shifting contours of art and media environments have special consequences for that cinematic tradition.

PART II
MODES OF EXPANSION

3
Cinema as Performance

[F]or most people performance is wishy-washy compared to the finality of film. In the can, every frame accounted for, decisions decisions decisions, and no less alive for that . . .

[A]fter the very earliest public screenings projectionists had been tamed and toying with direction and tempo gave way to uninterrupted absorption in subject matter. Film was relegated to straight-ahead fixed-speed carrier ("Tote that star! Deliver that story!"), mechanism was expected to remain humbly invisible and not interrupt the trance. Invisibility would be furthered by developments in synch-sound, wide-screen color and verisimilitudinous 3D . . . Somewhere there is *film*, sitting alongside the sunset, both wondering why hardly anyone comes around anymore to see them do their stuff.
— **Ken Jacobs (2005)**

Film projection exceeds the limits of its concept as a mere functional apparatus for the mechanical performance of cinematic works. A concept of "projection performance" is, therefore, inherent to the medium which *performs* not only the negation of its mediation and thus subordination to the celluloid material, but also its resistance as a passive carrier . . . the concept of projection performance becomes a tautological concept in which "performance" merely doubles and thus foregrounds the specific functioning of the projective apparatus.
— **Sandra Gibson and Luis Recoder (2012)**

Expanded Cinema Between Film, Theater, and Performance

The four chapters in this section examine the ways expanded cinema has negotiated between cinema's specificity and its areas of overlap with and analogies to the other arts. Works of expanded cinema that incorporate live performance are the ideal starting point. One could say that expanded cinema begins and ends with performance. The earliest moving image works designated as "expanded" almost always included a live element, either directly, as in Whitman's pieces or Warhol's *Exploding Plastic Inevitable*, or indirectly, in courting audience participation and chance, which opened up the possibility of unique, unpredictable moments that would distinguish

Cinema Expanded. Jonathan Walley, Oxford University Press (2020). © Oxford University Press.
DOI: 10.1093/oso/9780190938635.001.0001

one instantiation of the work from another. Recall from Part I that the first attempts to delineate categories in cinema's newly expanded field very often fell back on performance labels. Renan identified "film/dance," "film/theatre," "light shows," and "color instruments," the latter invoking musical performance. His potpourri category "variations on the theme of film" consisted entirely of performance works: by Ken Jacobs, Nam June Paik, Takehisa Kosugi, and Standish Lawder. Even "multiple projection" and "television" were primarily performative for Renan, the former including live pieces by the Eameses, Warhol, and USCO, the latter Whitman, Alex Hay, and Robert Rauschenberg. During its first wave, then, expanded cinema was intertwined with developments in avant-garde performance. The second wave of expanded cinema would attempt, among other things, to disentangle the two.

The dominant form of contemporary expanded cinema is undoubtedly projection performance, in which the live action—usually of the filmmaker—is relegated to the manipulation of the projector in real time in a denial of the projector's automaticity. Projection performance has become common practice among filmmakers, including those who do not typically produce expanded cinema, and is a regular sight at avant-garde film festivals and microcinemas. But this abundance of "live cinema" is quite different from the situation during the mid-to-late 1960s. Across the second and third waves of expanded cinema, a process has unfolded of more firmly distinguishing cinema from theater while retaining and clarifying cinema's own performative dimensions. The irony of a live expanded cinema that is not also "theatrical" is only apparent. Rather than an "other" form sharing the same stage with cinema, performance has been integrated into cinema's expanded ontology.

To invoke performance is also to invoke theater. Though they are not the same, they are undoubtedly connected, and for avant-garde filmmakers and critics the former comes with the unwanted baggage of the latter. What is this unwanted baggage? To answer that question, it is useful to consider perceptions of theater and theatricality in the avant-garde at the moment of cinema's initial expansion, and to analyze the discourses around expanded cinema's relationship to theater. Controversies over theater established the basis for performative cinematic work that followed, which reoriented live cinema away from the theatrical and toward the specifically cinematic. *Theatricality*, in short, hampered this aim in a way that *performativity* did not.

This chapter is not informed by any particular theory of performance or of the distinctions between performance and theater. It takes the origins of these two words as a starting point; "theater" originally meant a specific place for viewing spectacles, a "seeing place," somewhat later extending to the art of writing and performing plays. "Performance," on the other hand, has never been specific to theater, both predating that word and having a much more generalizable meaning: to carry out, enact, or accomplish, as in performing a task. Indeed, the less spectacular and more task-like conception of performance in Fluxus and the postmodern dance of Yvonne Rainer, Steve Paxton, and Trisha Brown seizes on these meanings of performance in part as a way to distance it from the conventionally theatrical. Along these lines, this chapter is also informed by my survey of the discourses relating to theater and performance within avant-garde film culture, mainly during the 1960s. It was then that the "confusion" of cinema and theater became a serious concern, often standing in for the "confusion of the arts" in general, something that troubled modernist critics like Michelson and, of course, Clement Greenberg. Distancing cinema from theater was also a way for avant-garde film to distance itself from commercial filmmaking, which was "theatrical" in the sense of requiring a theater—a seeing place almost indistinguishable from a playhouse—and of privileging mimetic performance and spectacle. During the third wave of expanded cinema, another "confusion" has emerged, that between cinema and moving image art in the gallery, and by extension between the film and art worlds. In this context, projection performance asserts avant-garde cinema's uniqueness from gallery work, which may be occluded by apparent formal similarities and historical affinities between the two.

The Problem of Theater

In chapter 1, I argued that the first wave of expanded cinema was defined by spectacle, and more to the point the spectacle of new image-making and communication technologies in and of themselves. This wave of expanded cinema also staged, as it were, the merging of these technologies and live action, even everyday life, as in pieces by Robert Whitman, Roberts Blossom, Ken Dewey, and Stan VanDerBeek. Hence, it was another variant of the "blurring of art and life" that was the ethos of the expanded arts. As so many of the original designations for the expanded arts and intermedia reveal, liveness and performance were central features of work in those areas. Renan provides one example, though recall that theater was also the master form for George Maciunas's "expanded arts diagram," with expanded cinema, Fluxus, intermedia, kinetic art, and happenings all represented as variants of theater. It comes as no surprise, then, that expanded cinema was almost as frequently categorized as expanded theater, or "the new theater," a term credited to the artist and critic Michael Kirby.[1] Kirby identified "two dominant facets of recent theatrical thought: manipulation of the audience-presentation relationship and use of film as one element of a performance composed of many elements."[2] We might slightly revise this so that film in live performance was often used precisely to "manipulate" the "audience-presentation relationship." Multiple projections replaced conventional theatrical mise-en-scène with an illusory, sense-overwhelming field of moving images. In some such works, most famously Whitman's, performers interacted with these images in ways that confounded spectators' ability to discern the real from the recorded. In *Prune Flat* (1965), shots of a performer in varying outfits are projected over that performer, so that she seems as if by magic to change clothes instantaneously (figs. 3.1 and 3.2). A second projector provides background images of other actors moving through disparate

[1] Michael Kirby, "The New Theatre," *The Tulane Drama Review* 10, no. 2 (Winter 1965), pp. 23–43.
[2] Kirby, "The Uses of Film in the New Theatre," *The Tulane Drama Review* 11, no. 1 (Autumn 1966), p. 54.

Fig. 3.1. Robert Whitman, *Prune Flat* (1965). Performance at Fridman Gallery, 287 Spring Street, New York City. December 15–17, 2016.
Courtesy of Robert Whitman and Julie Martin.

Fig. 3.2. Robert Whitman, *Prune Flat* (1965). Performance at Fridman Gallery, 287 Spring Street, New York City. December 15–17, 2016.
Courtesy of Robert Whitman and Julie Martin.

spaces—woods, a grassy field, a city street—so that the live actor's location also appears to change abruptly. *Prune Flat* thus superimposes two projected images, a smaller image "nested" inside a larger one for yet another degree of spatial disorientation, with a third layer of live action. The question, then, was whether it was cinema or theater that was expanding here, or, put another way, whether cinema was absorbing theater or vice-versa. Was cinema gaining a liveness not previously believed to be part of its ontology, or was film simply being utilized as an element of theatrical mise-en-scène as Kirby had suggested? A third option was to forget questions of *Prune Flat's* specific artistic identity as theater or film and take it as either a film-theater hybrid or something in the interstitial space between cinema and theater.

Even expanded cinema works that were not as explicitly theatrical as Whitman's could still be thought of as "performing" or "staging" the often unwieldy convergence and dissolution of multiple, sometimes indeterminate art forms. Or else they were "demonstrations," to use Roy Grundmann's characterization of works by John Whitney, Warhol, and VanDerBeek, of the new technology that made expanded cinema possible and the artist's use of it. Writing of Warhol's *Outer and Inner Space* (1965), Whitney's *Experiments in Motion Graphics* (1967), and VanDerBeek's *TV Interview* (1967), Grundmann alludes to a kind of showiness or demonstrative quality, even though the expansion on view in these works was limited (all were films intended for conventional projection, though Warhol's utilized two projectors).

> In Warhol's films, as in the other two, what issues forth from the encounter with new media is a performative stance, a specific persona—the master of ceremony—that the artist invents to insert himself into the text so as to articulate his own relation to the new artistic tools he is utilizing. Because the emcee role ... helped artists come to terms with processing and presenting the welter of new electronic devices they were confronting at this historical moment, it appears to have been essential in order for expanded cinema to actually expand.[3]

Outer and Inner Space is a dual-screen 16mm film in which Warhol superstar Edie Sedgewick interacts with an off-screen interviewer and videotaped images of herself playing on a television monitor placed next to her (fig. 3.3). Warhol shot the video images with a Norelco slant-track video recorder, one of the earliest portable video recorders available, which Warhol had received during the summer of 1965 at the height of his brief but prolific filmmaking career. The primitive video images, already flat, contrast-y, and otherwise distorted, were further manipulated as Edie and her video double were subsequently filmed; at times a hand enters the screen behind the real Edie to adjust the horizontal hold dial on the video monitor, causing the image to perpetually "roll" upward. While not nearly as ambitious or spectacular as later video works by the likes of VanDerBeek and Paik, Warhol's film nonetheless showcases,

---

[3] Roy Grundmann, "Masters of Ceremony: Media Demonstration as Performance in Three Instances of Expanded Cinema," *The Velvet Light Trap*, no. 54 (Fall 2014), pp. 48–49.

Fig. 3.3. Andy Warhol, *Outer and Inner Space*, 1965. 16mm film, black and white, sound, 66 minutes or 33 minutes in double screen.

subtly, a limited range of visual possibilities for a new medium, throwing these into relief by placing them against the backdrop of the older moving image medium of film. For Grundmann, the "stagey-ness" of these works was part of a strategy by which the artist could showcase the possibilities of new moving image technologies without becoming merely their operator or a shill for the corporations that produced those technologies.

All of this is to say that intermedia in and of itself was understood as a kind of theater, regardless of the myriad forms specific works took. The qualities inter-media artists privileged—action, duration, chance and indeterminacy, audience participation—all required liveness. Such works also tended to possess an air of the demonstrative; the new technologies and ideas had to be shown off for an audience. And during the initial wave of expanded cinema there was indeed a relatively large popular audience eager for technological spectacle, sensory overload, and newness qua newness. These qualities of spectacle, theatricality, and "event-ness" help explain the attention the first wave of expanded cinema received from the popular press, which also raised the eyebrows of avant-garde filmmakers and critics like Michelson, Mekas, and Vogel. Michelson's critique of expanded cinema is telling. The resurrec-tion of "the old dream of synaesthesia, the cross-fertilization of dance, theater, and film" was a reference to the *gesamtkunstwerk*, a kind of intermedia theater before the word.

Of course, the best-known and most sustained critique of intermedia's inherent theatricality came not from Michelson, nor from the provinces of avant-garde cinema, but from the art world, in the form of Michael Fried's 1967 essay "Art and Objecthood." "Art degenerates as it approaches the condition of theatre," Fried wrote then.[4] Indeed, though "Art and Objecthood" was an attack on minimalist art, it was

---

[4] Michael Fried, "Art and Objecthood," *Art and Objecthood: Essays and Reviews* (Chicago: University of Chicago Press, 1998), p. 164. Fried's essay was originally published in the Summer 1967 issue of *Artforum* (vol. 5, no. 10).

really an attack upon a sensibility of theatricality that Fried found permeating the arts, and which had less to do with performance per se than the conditions of presence, demonstrativeness, and duration that he believed were characteristic of minimalism, though not only of minimalism. On works by minimalist artists like Robert Morris and Donald Judd, Fried wrote:

> the literalist espousal of objecthood amounts to nothing other than a plea for a new genre of theatre; and theatre is now the negation of art. Literalist sensibility is theatrical because, to begin with, it is concerned with the actual circumstances in which the beholder encounters literalist work.[5]

Like theater in the conventional sense, minimalist work existed for an audience, and indeed relied upon one for its completion: "the presence of literalist art, which Greenberg was the first to analyze, is basically a theatrical effect or quality—a kind of *stage* presence"; and later: "the beholder knows himself to stand in an indeterminate, open-ended—and unexacting—relation as *subject* to the impassive object on the wall or floor."[6] A minimalist artwork's insistence upon its own objecthood was theatrical, and moreover connected minimalism to broader developments in the arts that were also "corrupted" by a theatrical sensibility. Though Fried did not use the word intermedia, he invoked it. "What lies between the arts is theatre," he wrote, criticizing artists like Cage and Rauschenberg because, like the minimalists, they muddied the boundaries not just between art forms but, more importantly, between art and everything else.[7] That is, minimalism was a variant of intermedia not in the sense that it employed multiple media in the way Whitman or Warhol often did, but because it perpetuated

> the illusion that the barriers between the arts are in the process of crumbling and that the arts themselves are at last sliding towards some kind of final, implosive, hugely desirable synthesis. Whereas in fact the individual arts have never been more explicitly concerned with the conventions that constitute their respective essences.[8]

The qualities of minimalist art, Cagean music and performance, Rauschenberg's combines and multimedia works, and so on, were on view in expanded cinema as well. Hence, the interchangeability of terms during the first wave—expanded cinema, intermedia or multimedia theater, "the theater of mixed means"—was not merely a matter of personal taste or semantic hair-splitting. Expanded cinema, existing between art forms, "between art and life," in duration, staged for an audience, and in fact

---

[5] Ibid., p. 153.
[6] Ibid., p. 155.
[7] Ibid., p. 164.
[8] Ibid.

insisting on these qualities, was precisely theatrical and thus antithetical to modernism's essentializing project.

There was, however, one art form whose "respective essence" was inherently nontheatrical according to Fried: cinema. While this explained cinema's popularity with modernist artists, it also meant that it was not, and could never be, a true modernist art per Fried. Because, in his words, "cinema escapes theatre—automatically, as it were," it could only ever be a "refuge" from theatre, not a willed escape from it achieved by choice and the artistry of filmmakers.[9] As Fried explained in a footnote: "in the movies the actors are not physically present, the film itself is projected away from us, the screen is not experienced as a kind of object existing, so to speak, in a specific physical relation to us, etc."[10] These were exactly the differences between cinema and theater that expanded cinema erased. Performers were physically present, projection might be multi-dimensional, and both screen and projected image itself were "experienced as a kind of object" in relation to the audience. This last point likely needs some elaboration. In a single-screen film exhibited in the conventional way, the dimensions of projected image and screen are, ideally, identical. The screen "is" the image, a feat achieved by careful attention to the dimensions of the theater, the space between projector and screen, and the selection of the projector's lens, and by masking the image to fit the bounds of the screen. In multi-screen or multi-projector works, the very presence of multiple images, whether on a single screen or each on its own screen (as in certain expanded works by the Charles and Ray Eames), ruptures this identity of image and screen so that each can be experienced as an independent object in physical relation to other independent objects. In Warhol's dual-projection films (e.g., *The Chelsea Girls, Outer and Inner Space*) two reels are projected side-by-side on a single screen such that image and screen size are not equivalent and all three—two projected images and one screen—are more readily viewed as objects, each with a shape of its own un-obscured by overlapping borders. The same effect occurred in many of Whitman's works, including *Prune Flat* and VanDerBeek's "Moviedrome" performances. The Eamses multi-screen films, such as *Glimpses of the USA* (1959) and *Think* (1964) worked somewhat differently, though with the same result. Those films were produced for specially designed exhibition spaces that dramatically emphasized the presence of multiple large screens, each with its own image competing for the attention of the audience. In *Think* (fig. 3.4), the audience was lifted en masse by the enormous "People Wall," 400 seats in a dynamically raked configuration that rose over 50 feet, into the "Ovoid Theatre" where viewers watched still and moving images flicker across 22 screens of different shapes and sizes.

Whether incorporating live performance in the conventional sense, as in *Prune Flat* or *Exploding Plastic Inevitable*, or partaking of the over-the-top fairground attraction demonstrativeness of *Think*, these expanded works all fall into the large category of art that Fried attacked. Conventional cinema, on the other hand, automatically and thus

---

[9]   Ibid.
[10]   Ibid., p. 171, n. 20.

Fig. 3.4. An audience seated on the "People Wall" in the Ovoid Theatre view Charles and Ray Eames, *Think* (1964), in the IBM Pavilion of the 1964 New York World's Fair. ©Eames Office LLC (eamesoffice.com).

effortlessly overcame that theatrical sensibility. But while Fried's sentiments aligned with those of critics like Michelson, who also found expanded cinema's theatricality problematic, only someone who was *not* a filmmaker or cinema historian could have asserted that film overcame the corrupting clutches of theater so easily. From the earliest efforts of filmmakers and theorists to define their art form, theater had been that art form's bad ontological other. The presumed similarity, even identity, of theater and cinema stood as one of the major obstacles to the recognition of the latter's specificity. Expanded cinema's theatricality was troubling for exactly this reason. It was a regression to an earlier, pre-modernist period when cinema was still yoked to theater, either seen as a diluted, ersatz form of theater or, perhaps even worse, only valuable as a recording medium for plays. The history of this "battle for the recognition of [cinema's] specificity" does not need to be rehashed here, but a few points are worth making. "Theater" and "theatricality" were part of a larger semantic field of all those things that modernist cinema was not: presence, mimesis, the confusion of art and reality, and the reliance on dialogue, text, the literary. Hence, though Rudolf Arnheim was primarily concerned to distinguish film from our perception of reality, in doing so he simultaneously distanced it from theater. Films were not in color, they were silent, they need not unfold in real (unedited) time, the performers were not present, and the view of each film spectator was determined by the camera rather than his or her seat in the theater. To loose film from reality was also to contrast it sharply with theater. Indeed, Arnheim's only optimistic comment about the coming of sound to cinema was that sound films could usefully preserve important plays.[11] Jumping ahead to the period of expanded cinema, Regina Cornwell, in "Some Formalist Tendencies in the Current American Avant-Garde Film," attacked popular journalistic critics for their praise of performance and literary content in contemporaneous American new wave films like *The Graduate*. "The avant-garde of past and present represents, in large part, attempts to shake off the very vestiges of film's nineteenth-century beginnings and its groundings in a nineteenth-century aesthetics," Cornwell wrote.[12] In other words, cinema's literary and theatrical origins were the enemies, and in the 1960s they were, at least to a critic like Cornwell, still at large even in allegedly groundbreaking contemporary youth cinema. Film's escape from theater was by no means guaranteed by its automaticity.

To complicate matters further, this automaticity was also perceived as a problem by avant-garde filmmakers. For one thing, it had been evidence in support of the argument *against* the idea that film was an art form: "film cannot be art, for it does nothing but reproduce reality mechanically," Arnheim wrote, summarizing this position before dismantling it in *Film as Art*.[13] Deren, Brakhage, and James Broughton, to name but a few avant-garde filmmakers, developed their widely varying aesthetics against the automatic, artless operations of the machine—the mechanical functions of the camera, the natural chemical activities of shooting and processing, the naturalistic function of lenses. This automaticity had "been a major obstacle to the definition and development of motion pictures as a creative fine art form capable of creative action in its own terms," Deren had written in 1960, as though channeling Arnheim.[14] This theme has re-played across the decades of avant-garde cinema history in a series of variations, recurring most recently in the comparisons between film and digital that highlight the former's difficulties and the latter's point-and-shoot design, as surveyed in Part I.

Avant-garde cinema—between theatricality and automaticity, between being subsumed by another art form and losing its identity as art altogether. If its automaticity was a refuge from theater, it also placed severe limitations upon the film artist, the limitations of both reality (film's raw material) and the narrow range of parameters designed into the machines by its manufacturers. Live cinematic performance offered a solution to the problems of automaticity, and could indeed be seen as simply extending the logic of avant-garde cinema's personal, artisanal, organic aesthetic discourses, and the more social and interactive forms its exhibition took, all of which mitigated against film's mechanical and industrial nature. But this solution posed problems of its own. The remainder of this chapter examines works from the second and third historical waves of expanded cinema, which staked out a position for live cinema between the corruption of theatricality and the stifling constraints of automaticity.

---

[11]   Arnheim, *Film as Art*. See especially pp. 8–34 and 154–156.

[12]   Regina Cornwell, "Some Formalist Tendencies in the Current American Avant-Garde Film," *Kansas Quarterly* 4, no. 2 (Spring 1972), p. 62.

[13]   Arnheim, *Film as Art*, p. 8.

[14]   Deren, "Cinematography," p. 60.

These works inserted real life into the cinema by way of performance while avoiding the theatricality, spectacularity, and confusion of the first wave of performance-based expanded cinema.

Cinematic Performance

Notes for a program of performances by Nam June Paik, Charlotte Moorman, and Takehisa Kosugi at the November 1965 New Cinema Festival at the Filmmakers' Cinematheque announced the following "leitmotiv":

> -How to make films without filming?
> -How to convert the film to live performing art
> from "canned" art to "cooked" food?[15]

An entry in Jonas Mekas's "Movie Journal" column in the *Village Voice*, penned a few months after the New Cinema Festival, may shed light on this. Mekas wrote of an exchange between himself and the organizers of the Cannes Film Festival, who had solicited recommendations of films from the "New American Cinema," of which Mekas was the lead proselytizer. Mekas had urged the organizers to show live multi-screen works like Warhol's, Harry Smith's, and Barbara Rubin's (especially Rubin's *Christmas on Earth*). The suggestion was ignored. "The film in the can isn't really the thing by itself," he wrote, adding that the best new work could not be "wrapped up, canned, and shipped."[16] Written shortly after the New Cinema Festival, which was alternately named the Festival of Expanded Cinema, the article indicates that Mekas, as co-organizer of that festival, was clearly feeling skeptical about the "canned" film, and found live performance a means to stage a resistance.

The "cooked food" reference surely had in mind Peter Kubelka, who was already making analogies between filmmaking and cooking by 1965, and in 1967 formally took up the study of cuisine and other cultural forms, famously integrating all of these in a long series of classes and lectures. The distinction Paik may have been making was between something industrial, "canned," not fresh, and something freshly prepared, made to order, and served up immediately for consumption. The idea, then, was that "converting the film to live performing art" produced a more immediate, personal, and unpredictable cinematic experience.

Paik, Moorman, and Kosugi screened films by VanDerBeek and Robert Breer with live musical accompaniment and, in one case, showed an unidentified film by VanDerBeek "where everything is changed by Moorman, Paik, & [assistant Linda] Sampson and Kosugi's 'Anima 7 no. 2' performed simultaneously by Kosugi." The

---

[15] Paik's program notes are in the collection of the San Francisco Museum of Modern Art, and accessible online: https://www.sfmoma.org/artwork/2015.80.

[16] Mekas, *Movie Journal*, pp. 249–250.

Fig. 3.5. Nam June Paik, *Zen for Film* (1965). Photograph by Peter Moore (1965), gelatin silver print. Paper size: 8 × 10 in. (20.3 × 25.4 cm). Image size: 6 × 8 in. (15.2 × 20.3 cm). ©2019 Barbara Moore/Artists Rights Society (ARS), New York. Courtesy of Paula Cooper Gallery, New York.

lack of detail here, and of documentation of this performance, leave much to the imagination, but it sounds like the kind of demonstrative, busy, and technologically complex expanded works discussed previously. Two other works on the program, however, offered a different take on the question of making film a performing art. One of these was Paik's legendary *Zen For Film*, performed in two different versions according to the program notes (fig. 3.5). The other was listed simply as "Takehisa Kosugi's Composition performed by composer." Though this is not entirely certain, in all likelihood this is Kosugi's rarely discussed *Film & Film #4* (1965).

Zen For Film and *Film & Film #4* are two early examples of an expanded cinema that "replaces the complexity of technology with the simplicity of shadow play" and "explores the old technology, expanding the possibilities and exigencies of cinema technology as it has existed for eighty years," to borrow Deke Dusinberre's description of later European expanded cinema.[17] That is, they ran against the grain of expanded cinema as chronicled by Youngblood and practiced by artists like VanDerBeek. In *Film & Film #4*, Kosugi, working very slowly and deliberately, made a series of rectangular cuts of steadily increasing size from a paper screen illuminated by the beam of an empty film projector (fig. 3.6). He began

---

[17] Dusinberre, "On Expanding Cinema," p. 220.

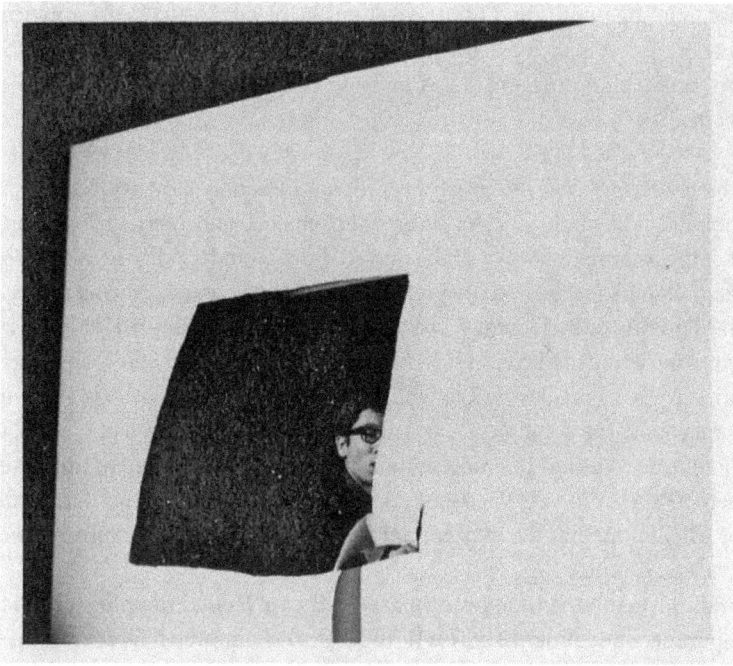

Fig. 3.6. Takehisa Kosugi, *Film & Film #4* (1965). Photograph by Peter Moore (1965).
©2019 Barbara Moore/Licensed by VAGA at Artists Rights Society (ARS), New York City. Courtesy of Paula Cooper Gallery, New York City.

in the center of the screen with a cut no bigger than an index card, and steadily worked his way out, making a void that expanded in a series of concentric rectangles until there was no screen left and the projector beam passed through the empty frame that had held the paper and struck the back wall of the space. Though it used no film and was a performance work also billed as a "composition," *Film & Film #4* was modeled upon material conditions specific to filmmaking. Its alternations of black and white (which extended to Kosugi's clothing) evoke black and white photography and positive and negative imagery, while the cuts made to the screen suggest actions of framing, editing, and the organization of change across duration. They also reverberate with one of the central preoccupations of modernist cinema: the tension between film's illusory depth and its actual flatness, a tension that also structured contemporaneous avant-garde films like *Wavelength*, *Serene Velocity*, *The Flicker*, and *T,O,U,C,H,I,N,G*. Like many other works of expanded cinema, *Film & Film #4* makes the illusionistic depth of film into literal depth, acknowledging the space of projection, the throw of the projector beam, the directionality of shadows.

Julian Ross, countering claims that *Film & Film #4* represents a pared-down, "cinema degree zero," argues instead that it "offers a platform to summon the impurities of cinema":

Rather than the purification of the mediums involved, Kosugi's performances of the period, including his expanded cinema, aimed at exposing its susceptibility to interaction with other mediums as an intrinsic component of the individual mediums.[18]

Undoubtedly *Film & Film #4* brings together forms normally associated with different media, introducing performance into cinema and, perhaps, standing as a variant of the intermedia works of the period. But I would modify Ross's claim, characterizing Kosugi's piece as an integration of performance into cinema rather than a haphazard mixing or incidental sharing of the same stage. *Film & Film #4* derives its form from the nature of film's physical medium (projected light, photochemistry) and the aesthetic effects made possible within these material parameters. These include the interplay of flatness and depth, or stillness and motion, as well as editing, understood not just as "cutting" but more importantly as the articulation of time and space on screen. As such, *Film & Film #4* meets the criteria for artistic cross-fertilization set forth by Michelson: that the merging art forms are clear in what constitutes each of their "respective ontologies."

A variation on this theme appears in the writings of Hollis Frampton, one of the few contemporaneous commentators on Kosugi's work. Frampton references *Film & Film #4* in two essays, his 1968 "A Lecture" and "For a Metahistory of Film: Commonplace Notes and Hypotheses." In the former, itself a cinematic performance, Frampton declares:

> The art of making films consists in devising things to put into our projector. The simplest thing to devise, though perhaps not the easiest, is nothing at all, which fits conveniently into the machine. Such is the film we are now watching. It was devised several years ago by the Japanese composer Takehisa Kosugi.[19]

Though Frampton's description simplifies Kosugi's work for rhetorical purposes, it nonetheless captures the way in which what Frampton called the "film machine" could structure unorthodox, expanded, or, in this case, filmless films, precisely because it could function as a structuring absence. Thus, Frampton recuperates *Film & Film #4*'s lack of film and its perfomativity into an expanded filmic ontology. And like Frampton's "Lecture," Kosugi's performance further uses the act of projection as an analogy for other stages of filmmaking activity, those completed before the film is "canned" and projected: editing, lighting, cinematography, and even writing—it's a paper film, after all. *Film & Film #4* thus provides an object lesson in the assimilation of performance by cinema. The live actions of the performer/filmmaker are analogous to the operations of the medium, the aesthetic traits of cinema as art form,

[18] Julian Ross, "Beyond the Frame: Intermedia and Expanded Cinema in 1960–1970s Japan" (PhD diss., University of Leeds, 2014), p. 106.
[19] Hollis Frampton, "A Lecture," in Sitney, ed., *The Avant-Garde Film*, p. 276.

or the work of the filmmaker in production. In this way, cinematic performance references the workings of the film medium while de-automatizing them, casting live performance not as an external, non-cinematic form, but as something inherently cinematic.

Two years earlier, Takahiko Iimura had produced a film performance very much like Kosugi's. Like *Film & Film #4*, Iimura's *Screen Play* (1963) molded live performance to the shape of film and filmmaking. Iimura projected his earlier film *Iro* (*Color*, 1963) onto another performer's back; that performer sat reading a newspaper, his back to Iimura, the film projector, and audience (fig. 3.7). Working in a manner similar to Kosugi in *Film & Film #4*, Iimura cut increasingly large squares out of the back of the other performer's jacket, revealing more and more skin until the cut out section of cloth was the same size as the projected image. Like Kosugi's work, *Screen Play*, even in its title, is based upon a series of cinematic analogies, the obvious ones being to framing and cutting. But a less overt analogy was to a sense of temporality and spatiality that was emerging in the discourses of avant-garde film at this moment, and which I introduced in chapter 1 with respect to the "time shape": the notion that cinema unified space and time and thus was not strictly a temporal art form. This idea was especially prominent in discussions of narrative structure and the analogs for that structure on view in structural film. Though the projected film in *Screen Play* was non-narrative, the performance, if not precisely narrative, took a kind of directionality or shape in time that many avant-garde filmmakers and critics also ascribed to structural films like *Wavelength*. Both *Film*

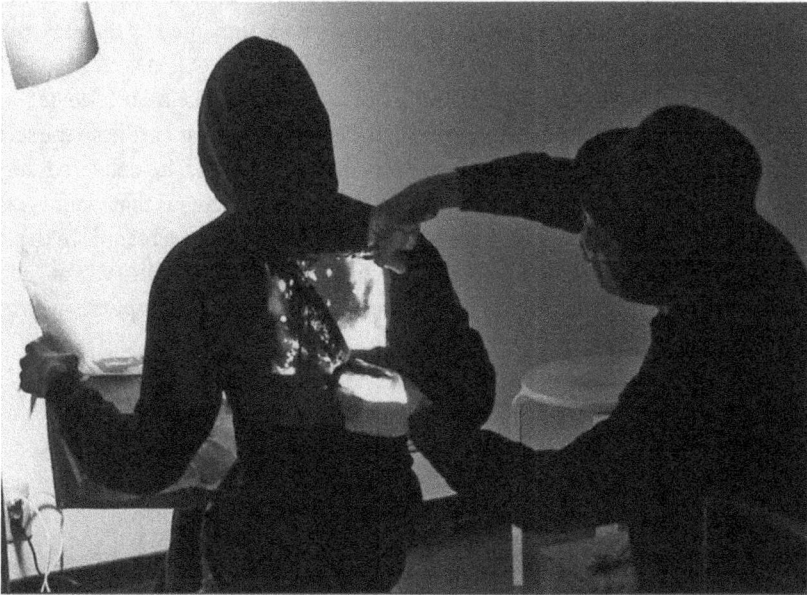

Fig. 3.7. Takahiko Iimura, *Screen Play* (1963). Re-creation 2012.
Courtesy of Takahiko Iimura.

& Film #4 and *Screen Play* were performed slowly, methodically, like the zoom in Snow's film. The forward or inward direction of these films and performances is almost immediately apparent to the viewer. The "drama," a trait Michelson ascribed to *Wavelength*, comes from the anticipation of the trajectory's completion. I raise this point because in their parallel cutting actions, *Film & Film #4* and *Screen Play* have in common with contemporaneous structural film a specific "time shape." Schematically, this shape is one of concentric squares or rectangles, not unlike Frank Stella's paintings (e.g., *Tomlinson Court Park* [1959] or *Double Concentric: Scramble* [1971]). If imagined in three dimensions, the concentric rectangle image is one of either recession or protrusion, of an image receding into deep space or emerging from the screen toward the spectator. It is also an analogy for the changes in scale resulting from different lenses, from close-up to wide shot, which produce the gradual expansion or contraction of space in films like *Wavelength* or Gehr's *Serene Velocity*. By extension, the shape also implies the similar dimensions of the projector beam, which inverts the lines of convergence in the illusory three-dimensional space of the photographed image—the projector's throw being widest at the surface of the screen and receding to a point inside the projector gate.

This latter shape, or vector, of the light beam was the subject of an early and obscure projector performance by Sharits, alternately titled *Unrolling Movie Screen* and *Unrolling Event* (1966). The performance centered around Sharits's 1965 film *Instructions*, one of the "official" program of Fluxus films assembled, numbered, and copyrighted in Fluxus's name by George Maciunas in 1966. In that film, which was also distributed by Maciunas as an 8mm loop, Sharits's characteristic flicker punctuates still images illustrating the proper use of toilet paper accompanied by text describing each step in that process: "PULL DOWN ROLL / FOLD INTO PAD / WIPE UNTIL CLEAN / DROP INTO TOILET / FLUSH AWAY PAPER." For *Unrolling Movie Screen* Sharits projected the film loop while affixing the ends of toilet paper rolls to the screen and slowly unrolling them toward the projector. As he did this, he delivered "an informal lecture on the logical necessity of developing movie screens that would realize the projected image at every point, from the projector lens to the screen."[20] In the lone extant description of *Unrolling Movie Screen*, which he re-created in 1977 at Galerie A in Amsterdam (fig. 3.8), Sharits makes the connection to the temporal and visual structure—the "time shape"—of *Wavelength*:

> Snow understood the vectorial implications of the projector light beam and this seems to account at least in part for *Wavelength*'s directional structure. Physically, the conical shape is directive toward the projector lens; yet, we sense the internal projectiveness of the beam directing itself toward the screen, as if magnitude was its target.[21]

---

[20] Sharits, "Words Per Page," p. 39.
[21] Ibid., p. 38.

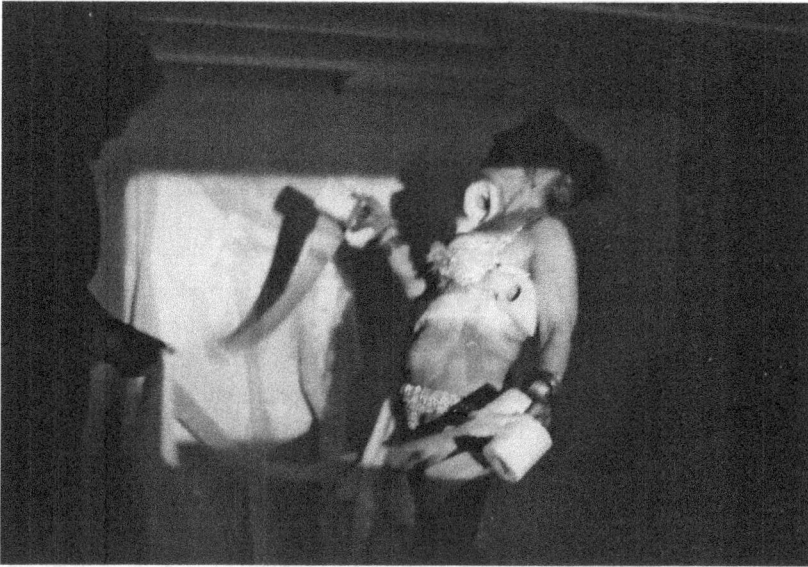

Fig. 3.8. Paul Sharits, *Unrolling Event/Unrolling Movie Screen* (1966), photographic documentation of a performance at Galerie A, Amsterdam, July 9, 1977 (Sharits stands to the left of the frame, in shadow).
Courtesy of Fondazione Bonotto.

I will take up the scatological associations of *Unrolling Movie Screen* later. For now, the interest of this obscure performance is in its numerous implications for the live expanded cinema of the period. Unlike later works of performative cinema, which primarily involve the manipulation of the projector behind the scenes, the primary field of performance action during expanded cinema's first and second waves was the space between projector(s) and screen, in the cone of light extending between the two. The screen, as both image and surface, in that modernist play of illusion and object, was the interface between the photographed profilmic space and the actual deep space of the theater, the space that included projector and audience. The conception of cinematic space in these terms, shared by so many avant-garde filmmakers of the time, helps explain the significance of the image structure of nested, concentric rectangles of *Film & Film #4, Screen Play*, and *Unrolling Movie Screen*.

William Raban's *2′45″*, discussed in chapter 2, also takes this form. In reference to that work, Raban has written, "Expanded cinema is, of course, cinema in the present tense where film production and film exhibition become conjoined within the same time frame."[22] This represents yet another perspective on such works. The multiple slices of time in the nested negative/positive images of *2′45″* stand for this collapsing

---

[22] Raban, "Reflexivity and Expanded Cinema," p. 103.

of different times into a single moment, an image of different chunks of duration and action laid out all at once for the viewer. The film is made as it is shown and vice-versa, the filmmaker appearing in the work both in person and as image, similarly standing for this conjoining of normally distinct phases of production. Much the same could be said of Tony Conrad's *Film Feedback* (1974), which he called a "private performance" simultaneously produced and viewed by Conrad and his team of filmmaking students at Antioch College (see chapter 2).[23] That is, Conrad's team produced the same kind of *mise-en-abyme* image that Raban had in *2′45″*. *Film Feedback* can only be viewed now as a 16mm film print, an artifact of shooting, processing, and projecting that the performance collapsed into a single event. It is a "film in the can" that is decidedly not "the thing by itself."

Writing about *Film Feedback* in 1974, Le Grice compared it to *2′45″*, noting that the "delay factor," the celluloid-specific version of video feedback that produced the nested images in both works, "caused the resulting perspective corridor of screen frames to be a most satisfactory space (illusion) for (relative) time analogue."[24] To understand what this means and what it can tell us about the role of live performance in contemporaneous expanded cinema, it is useful to consider Le Grice's own cinematic performance *Horror Film 1* (1971), another variation on the theme of temporally layered images (fig. 3.9). The work consists of three 16mm projectors arranged side-by-side, each projecting color field loops onto a single screen. Because one projector was fitted with a different-sized lens than the other two, the composite image produced by all three was of a smaller rectangle of light nested inside a larger one (a simpler variation of the corridor-like image of *2′45″* and *Film Feedback*).[25] The film loops cycled through variations of color and brightness, fading in and out of black, from one hue to another, in loose rhythms. At times the edges of the different frames would be distinct, standing out against one another in starkly contrasting colors, while at other moments these sharp divisions would fall away—only occasionally would it be evident that the image on screen was being produced by three separate light sources. Le Grice stood facing the screen, his nose almost brushing its surface, his shadows shifting and becoming more or less distinct as the loops ran through their cycles of changing color and degrees of brightness. With the same sort of deliberate action as Kosugi in *Film & Film #4*, Le Grice moved his arms and hands so that their shadows seemed to seek out, trace, and even caress the boundaries of the smaller frames nestled in the center of the screen. At certain moments Le Grice's shadow looks something like the comic stereotype image of the movie director making a "frame" with his hands as if looking for the perfect shot. His shadowy fingers measure the gap between their borders of the concentric frames, carefully marking out their dimensions until, in the next second, they change color or intensity and vanish into one another. Le Grice's shadowy hands appear to grasp the edges of one of the interior frames, as if

[23] Tony Conrad, personal interview, October 7, 2004.
[24] Malcolm Le Grice, "Vision," *Studio International* (July–August 1974), p. 75.
[25] An earlier version of the work utilized two 16mm projectors and a slide projector.

Fig. 3.9. Malcolm Le Grice, *Horror Film 1* (1971).
©Malcolm Le Grice. Image courtesy of the artist.

he is holding it up, which produces a curious mix of sensations; the frame seems to take on depth and weight even though it is obviously flat and, since it is made of light, undeniably immaterial. Because the projectors' beams overlap on screen, the viewer tends to forget that there are three images rather than one. This results in perhaps the most striking effect of *Horror Film 1*, which occurs when Le Grice stands in the path of one projector beam but not another, his shadow blocking only that beam while being partially "filled in" by the other. In these moments Le Grice's shadow appears to occupy an impossible interspace between the nested frames, as if in front of one but behind another, suddenly seeming to open up the flat screen space into an illusory depth. Because these effects are transitory, fading in and out as the on-screen colors shift, the viewer may feel a kind of vertiginous impression of the screen space expanding out and contracting back in like an accordion.

As the performance unfolds, Le Grice slowly backs away from the screen toward the projectors. His shadows grow, and by the end of the performance only Le Grice's shadow hands or head can fit into the screen, the culmination of a gradual shift in scale that mimics the impression of a zoom in or change in shot scale. We are reminded that, closest to the projector, the beam of light is at its narrowest, so objects there will cast unnaturally large shadows on screen, just as they would appear disproportionately magnified when held close to a camera lens. Though the light and shadow images cast on screen are manifestly flat, Le Grice's carefully choreographed movements produce a corresponding effect of recession or protrusion "within the screen," to use Snow's description of the apparent depth of the image in *Wavelength*. This is an analog of the literal depth of the projector beam, as if the throw of the projector and the receding space on screen are two pyramids placed base to base.

Le Grice wrote that his intention in *Horror Film 1* was "to build a complex visual experience out of the simple and readily available aspects of the projection situation."[26] He also described his performance as "a series of formal actions."[27] The "form" the actions take is that of the varying scale of images and shadow, the act of tracing these changing relations of size in ways that evoke filmmaking activities such as framing a shot, selecting shot scales, focusing an image, and staging elements of the profilmic event. That is, the work folds the temporally discrete stages of filmmaking into a single moment in time, albeit metaphorically or via analogy. This was one of several ways that Le Grice's film practice of the early 1970s reflected his commitment to what he called "the primacy of the projection event":

> The direction of my thinking, and the tendencies in my films, keep returning me to an affirmation of the projection event as the primary reality. In other words, the real TIME/SPACE event at projection, which is the current, tangible point of access for the audience, is to be considered as the experiential base through which any retrospective record, reference or process is to be dealt with by the audience. This reverses the situation common to the cinematic language where experience of the real TIME/SPACE at projection is subsumed by various aspects of manipulated retrospective "reality."[28]

Making films and works of expanded cinema that affirmed the reality of projection over the unreality of represented time and space, as in a narrative film, was more than an aesthetic choice for Le Grice. It was an ethic, a political principle that ran through much of the filmmaking activity in and around the London Filmmakers' Cooperative in the 1970s. Privileging the moment of projection was an anti-illusionist act, but not simply because it placed the projector in the audience's field of view. More importantly, it short-circuited conventional cinema's "pre-structured substitute and illusory reality," its abstract time, not of the here and now, which made the viewer a passive receiver rather than active participant.[29]

The "primacy of projection" was both spatial and temporal. The projector and film were there, in the same space as the viewer, and projection and audience shared the same real time while the image on screen was a record of a past time. Thus, it was in the

[26] Malcolm Le Grice, "Real TIME/SPACE," in Le Grice, *Experimental Cinema in the Digital Age*, p. 162.
[27] Ibid.
[28] Ibid., p. 156.
[29] Ibid.

projection event that cinema's merging of time and space was most palpable, which accounts for Le Grice's concept of "real TIME/SPACE," the slash indicating that these two dimensions of experience were conjoined in cinema. From this perspective, Le Grice's expanded cinema was the most complete realization of the aim established by Peter Gidal for more conventionally produced structural-materialist films: "Each film is a record (not a representation, not a reproduction) of its own making ... viewing such a film is at once viewing a film and viewing the 'coming into presence' of the film."[30] Gidal meant that even when a structural-materialist film contained recognizable photographic images, as Gidal's and others' almost always did, the film worked against the perception that those images referred to another time or place. The emerging formal system of the film took place in the real time of projection, and was what the film was "about." Returning to *Film Feedback* with this in mind, we can describe that film's "time corridor" image as an analog—in the sense of a trace—of the temporal layers of film production and reception. The existing 16mm print is, again, a trace of that moment in Conrad and his team's private performance of the film's "coming into presence," quite literally, before the eyes of its filmmaker-audience.

An even more literal-minded examination of the relations among viewer, space, and apparatus is Raban's *Take Measure* (1973) (fig. 3.10). Raban describes the film's genesis:

> The thing that strikes me going into a cinema, because it's such a strange space and it's organized to allow you to get enveloped by the whole illusion of film, when you try and think of it in terms of real dimensions it becomes very difficult. The idea of a sixty foot throw or a hundred foot throw from the projector to the screen just doesn't enter into the equation. So I thought the idea of making a piece that made the distance between the projector and the screen more tangible was quite an interesting thing to do.[31]

In *Take Measure*, once the film is threaded into the projector the front (or "feed") reel is removed and unwound outward toward the screen. The film is cut at the point where the reel reaches the screen, leaving a long line of celluloid extending back through the space from screen to projector. When projection starts, this naked strand of film is pulled back through the space, usually allowed to drag along the floor. The on-screen image is of a length of 16mm film being pulled though an editing device called a synchronizer, and indeed the pro-filmic film and real film move at the same speed: 24 frames per second or one foot (40 frames) every 1.6 seconds. That is, the screen image is precisely analogous to the real situation, the profilmic synchronizer counting the footage of the real filmstrip, thus measuring the distance between screen

[30] Gidal, "Theory and Definition of Structural/Materialist Film," p. 2.
[31] Mark Webber, "Interview with William Raban," in Webber, ed., *Shoot Shoot Shoot* (program notes accompanying the 2002 film exhibition "Shoot Shoot Shoot: The First Decade of the London Film-Makers' Cooperative and British Avant-Garde Film, 1966–76," which Webber curated), p. 1.

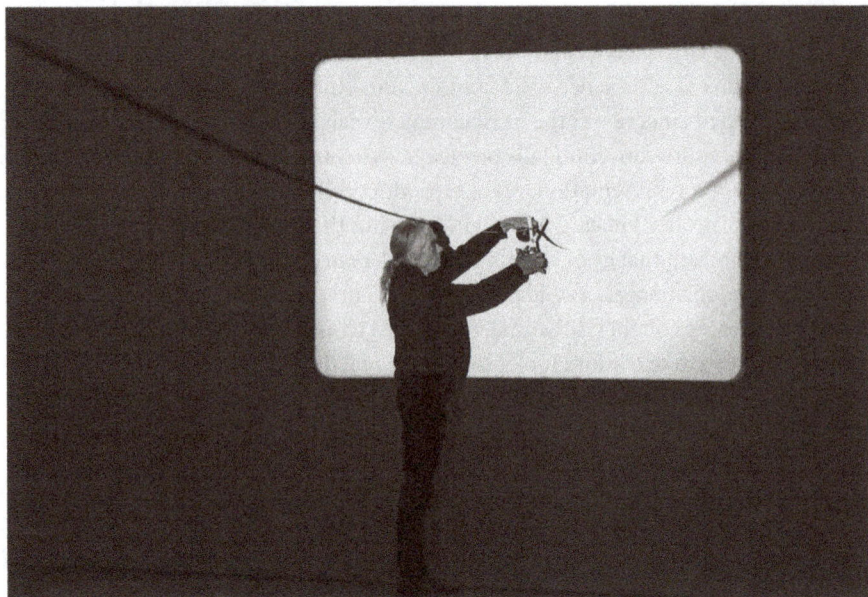

Fig. 3.10. William Raban, *Take Measure* (1972). Performance at Raven Row, London, March 4, 2017. Photo: Mark Blower.
Courtesy of William Raban.

and projector, which in turn determines the duration of the film. When the real film reaches the projector and is about to conclude its passage through the gate, the projector is turned off, so that the last number the audience sees on the counter before the screen goes dark indicates the precise length of the real space they occupy between screen and projector.

Variations on a Theme: External ("Excessive") References

Guy Sherwin's *Man With Mirror* (1976) and *Paper Landscape* (1975) take these formal concerns in a somewhat different direction. Both are live expanded cinema performances in which Sherwin interacts with a film of himself engaged in a simple task, what Le Grice might have called a "series of formal actions." The live Sherwin, facing the projector, repeats these actions, adhering as closely as possible to the movements and rhythms of his earlier, pro-filmic self. For *Man With Mirror*, Sherwin filmed himself standing in a medium shot in the midst of a wooded area, facing the camera and holding a rectangular mirror. In the film, which is about 10 minutes long, Sherwin turns and tilts the mirror, sometimes holding its reflective side toward the tripod-mounted camera, other times flipping it around so that its blank white reverse side catches the dappled shadows cast by sunlight passing through the surrounding trees (fig. 3.11). On its own, the film might have been a formal study of the interplay of on- and off-screen space, including the off-screen space occupied by the camera, with the movements of the mirror confounding this simple dichotomy by bringing off-screen space into the frame via its reflections. The mirror was cut to the same 4:3 dimensions as the filmed image, thus introducing another formal element, a series of relationships between profilmic event and the structure of the medium itself—camera aperture, film frame, projection screen. The same formal concerns appear in some of Sherwin's other, non-expanded films, including *Portrait With Parents* (1977), a three-minute, single take film of Sherwin's parents facing the camera with Sherwin (operating the camera) captured in a mirror on the wall behind them. But *Man With Mirror* is *not* a film on its own. In the performance, Sherwin faces the projector and holds the same mirror, precisely repeating the movements he had made in the film. As the real, live Sherwin tilts and turns the mirror, whose reverse side acts as a screen, the interplay of on- and off-screen space becomes an at times baffling display in which the live—and ever aging—Sherwin suddenly slips from view to be replaced by the filmed image of his younger self, standing in exactly the same position, "framed" identically

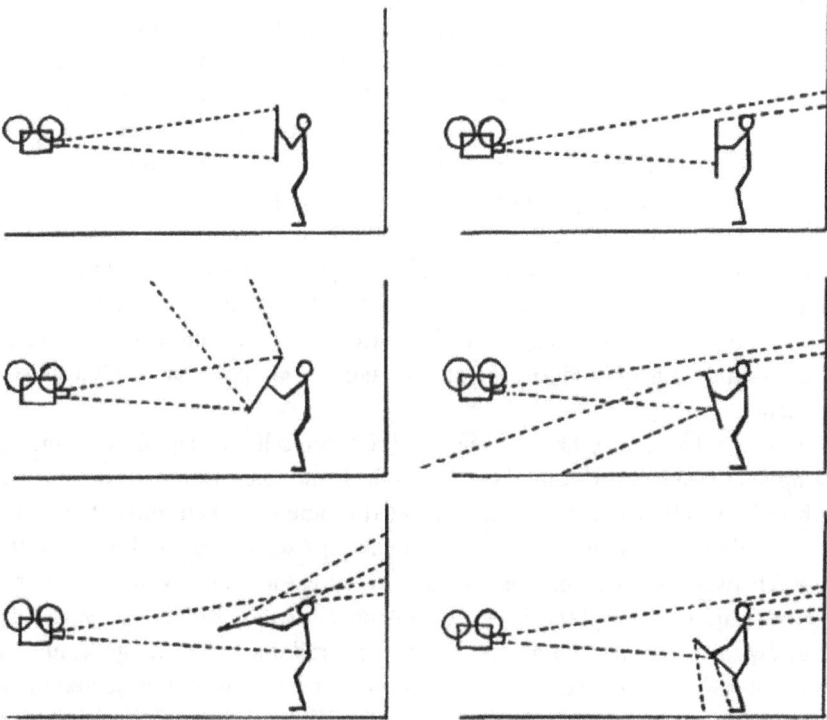

Fig. 3.11. Guy Sherwin, original drawing for *Man With Mirror* (1976). Courtesy of Guy Sherwin.

Fig. 3.12. Guy Sherwin, *Man With Mirror* (1976). Performance view, 2003.
Courtesy of Guy Sherwin.

(fig. 3.12). At several points in his performance Sherwin holds the mirror so that its white "screen" side faces out, tilting it up and down so that its surface is at one moment parallel to the floor, the next facing the audience and blocking their view of the real Sherwin. As this happens, his face is seamlessly replaced by that of his younger self, an effect akin to a wipe in a conventional film, and a live version of a temporal ellipsis from younger to older man. At another point, both filmed and live Sherwin rotate left and right, turning at the waist with feet planted, holding the back side of the mirror toward the projector. The live and profilmic Sherwins thus rotate in and out of view, appearing to dissolve into one another, again mimicking an editing device that expressively conveys the passage of time. The effect is startling, and indeed *Man With Mirror* plays out like a magic show, with video documentation of recent performances capturing gasps and laughs from the audience taking pleasure in the illusory experience.

For *Paper Landscape*, Sherwin again filmed himself in natural surroundings (Hampstead Heath) with a camera on a tripod. He mounted a large paper screen directly in front of the camera, cut once again to the same 4:3 dimensions as the camera aperture, about six feet wide by four feet high. This screen was positioned so that it stood between Sherwin and his camera, just filling the frame. As the camera ran, Sherwin, standing behind the screen, slowly tore away pieces of the paper, working in narrow rows from left to right, bottom to top, until the screen was gone, fully revealing Sherwin and the surrounding environment that had been obscured by the paper. In the performance, the film is projected through a transparent sheet mounted in a metal frame, cut to the same dimensions of the profilmic paper screen. Sherwin faces the projector from behind the plastic screen. Matching the direction and pace

Fig. 3.13. Guy Sherwin, *Paper Landscape* (1975). Performance view, 2003.
Courtesy of Guy Sherwin.

of his earlier, filmed self, the live Sherwin applies white paint to the plastic screen, converting it from transparent window to reflective surface. The live Sherwin is thus slowly obscured while the filmed Sherwin is slowly revealed as he tears away the profilmic paper screen. For most of the performance, the audience sees the lower portion of the recorded Sherwin haphazardly conjoined with the upper portion of the real Sherwin, in a kind of evolving exquisite corpse of past and present, real and filmed bodies (fig. 3.13). By the final few minutes of the performance, the plastic screen is completely covered with white paint, the live Sherwin thus totally obscured by the image of his younger self, now projected onto the paint (fig. 3.14). The filmed Sherwin steps carefully through the frame that had held the paper screen and walks first toward the camera, then away from it, making a long walk into the receding landscape of Hampstead Heath. When he is nothing more than a tiny dot in the far background, the real Sherwin repeats this action, cutting away the painted plastic screen and stepping through the supporting frame toward the projector. He turns it off, ending the performance.

Man With Mirror and *Paper Landscape* recall, if indirectly, the nested frame or "time corridor" structures of *2'45"*, *Horror Film 1*, and *Film Feedback*. Their shifting frames, expanding and contracting visual fields, and oscillations between past and present comprise an analog of cinematic time and space, giving form to temporality. Their increasing duration, characterized by Sherwin as ongoing since they were first

Fig. 3.14. Guy Sherwin, *Paper Landscape* (1975). Performance view, 2003.
Courtesy of Guy Sherwin.

filmed and performed, is a variation of Le Grice's "primacy of the projection event," as they essentially extend that event over an ever spreading swath of real time. In "Real TIME/SPACE," Le Grice wrote that his own work had "drawn me into an overriding concern with the projection event itself, and an increasing desire to limit retrospective input to that situation, or at least to have it clearly subservient to the current reality."[32] By "retrospective input" he meant any profilmic event, the projected image of a past time and place whether fictional or documentary. Making this "subservient" to the moment of projection meant somehow shaping the filmed action to the literal, live action of projecting the film for an audience. If that moment of projection also included a live performer, then that person's actions, too, would be structured accordingly. Every element—filmed action, projection, performance—was of one formal piece, that form determined by the contours of the medium and the defining qualities of cinematic experience as understood by each individual filmmaker.

In Sherwin's performances, however, we see something different. Certainly those works are cinematically structured, formal explorations of cinema's fundamental features. But Sherwin's works also introduce external references. *Man With Mirror* and *Paper Landscape* may be about framing, editing, the structuring of time, the materiality of projection, and such, but they are also about the passing of time on a human

[32] Le Grice, "Real TIME/SPACE," p. 161.

scale. As Lucas Ihlein and Louise Curham have put it, *Man With Mirror* is "a poetic reflection on change and mortality."[33] In a recent interview, Sherwin acknowledged the emotional power of the work in similar terms:

[P]eople always like that piece. And it's to do with ageing, I know it is, it's become something different from what it was originally. I still get people being completely blown away by it. It's always at the end of the show, because you can't do anything after that piece.[34]

Such meanings and responses ran against the grain of the formal asceticism of much avant-garde filmmaking of the time, especially in the British context. Contra the theorizations of Le Grice and Gidal, for example, Sherwin relies on the power of photographic representation and the emotional effects of photography's references to the past. The mimetic, or as Gidal and Le Grice would have it illusionistic, power of cinema is central to Sherwin's performances, which Sherwin confirmed in the same interview:

You know, film is an illusionistic device par excellence. Now Peter Gidal would only talk in terms of material. The material aspect of the film is only interesting in relation to the fact that film is an illusion as well. It's got two things at once; it's an illusion and it's material ... So, rather than deny the illusionary aspect of the film, which I think is sort of Peter's idea, I'm presenting that in all it's illusionary-ness and then I'm masking it and destroying it too—and so it's a kind of dialogue between the image and material.[35]

The performer then, is not strictly relegated to undertaking "formal actions" modeled upon those literal elements of the projection situation. The performer's status as living person, for whom time and space are not simply formal dimensions but affective phenomena loaded with poetic or philosophical associations, is central to the meanings of these works.

Much the same can be said of Sharits's *Unrolling Movie Screen*, which, while very much about the dimensions of projection and the relations of projector, screen, and exhibition space, in its choice of scatological imagery draws an analogy between these things and the functions of the human body. Elsewhere in his work, Sharits played upon analogies between film and the body, between the mechanics of the medium and the human neurological and physiological systems that medium engaged, most

[33] Lucas Ihlein and Louise Curham, "Re-enacting Expanded Cinema: Three Case Studies," a "research report" written as part of Ihlein and Curham's re-enactment of *Man With Mirror* (as *Woman With Mirror*) in 2009. See http://www.teachingandlearningcinema.org/wp-content/uploads/2012/03/TLC-Reenacting-expanded-cinema-three-case-studies.pdf.
[34] Duncan White and Lynn Loo, "Interview of Guy Sherwin by Duncan White & Lynn Loo" (2008) on Rewind: Artists' Film and Video in the 70s and 80s (http://www.rewind.ac.uk/ expanded/Narrative/Interviews_files/SherwinTS.pdf), p. 12.
[35] Ibid., p. 15.

famously in *Epileptic Seizure Comparison* (1976). Like Sherwin, Sharits not only acknowledged but relied upon the inherently representational or illusionistic nature of
film. The photographic image content of films like *Instructions, Peace Mandala End
War* (1966), and *T,O,U,C,H,I,N,G* (1968) carried all manner of associational baggage,
while the flicker structure of those films triggered automatic biological responses
in the spectator's perceptual apparatus that could be analogized to other extreme
physical conditions like seizures. Sherwin's imagery in *Man With Mirror* and *Paper
Landscape* is less loaded, but in the context of a performance with Sherwin himself
present, that imagery becomes expressive, as Ihlein, Curham, and Sherwin himself
point out.

Such works are disruptive to the standard account of structural and structural/
materialist filmmaking in the 1970s, which, to phrase it in Sharits's terms, sought a
"meaningless syntax" for cinema, a purely literal form not in the service of signification.[36] Narrative cinema was the bad object here, as the title of a 1977 debate between
Le Grice and P. Adams Sitney attested: "Narrative Illusion vs. Structural Realism."[37] In
the semiotic and psychoanalytic film theory produced around the same time, which
influenced European avant-garde filmmaking, narrative form came under scrutiny,
its ideological implications revealed, including those of its fictional temporality.
When Christian Metz wrote of the early filmmakers who had invented uniquely cinematic representations of different temporal modes, he contrasted the increasingly
complex temporality of their narratives with the primitive real time of the very first
films by the likes of Lumières. But he might just as well have been distinguishing between conventional narrative film and the materialist films of Le Grice, Gidal, and
others, whose work restored the literal continuousness of celluloid running through
the projector. Le Grice referred to this as "shallow time," a one-to-one correspondence between the duration of the profilmic event and that of projection, as in Warhol's
early silent films, for example.[38]

In his expanded cinema performances, Sherwin executed simple, formal tasks that
were circumscribed by the structure of filmmaking and projection and made reference to the material realities of film. And the films made for each performance consisted of single long takes, another assertion of real time, or of the equivalency of
profilmic and projection times. In these ways, they took place in Le Grice's "shallow
time." But they also rely for their visual *and emotional* effects on the representation of
time, specifically the viewer's ability to recognize the growing temporal distance between the live Sherwin and his younger, filmed self. As such, the performances gain
a layer of meaning from a more expressive form of temporal representation. From
this perspective, a mirror or a painting functions as more than just an analogy for
aspects of filmmaking or a device for producing specifically cinematic visual effects;

---

[36] Sharits, "Words Per Page," p. 32.
[37] The debate was held at the Millennium Film Workshop on December 19, 1977, and printed in
Millennium Film Journal No. 16/17/18 (Fall/Winter 1986), pp. 309–326.
[38] Le Grice, *Abstract Film and Beyond*, pp. 93–95.

they suggest parallels between cinema and other human activities, such as reflection, contemplation of one's self and one's mortality, and the preservation of the past through portraiture. The bodily presence of the filmmaker himself, as performer, amplifies these analogies and their non-literal, extra-cinematic meanings. Le Grice's actions in *Horror Film 1* were purely film-referential; Sherwin's performance actions in *Man With Mirror* were similarly cut to the measure of cinema's material and formal parameters, but they also transformed what would otherwise have been a purely aesthetic exercise in screen space into a meditation on a fundamental facet of the human condition.

Annabel Nicolson's *Reel Time* and Conrad's *7360 Sukiyaki* (both 1973) are two more examples of live expanded cinema in which the filmmaker performs a series of simple tasks in front of a screen. In these works, however, the tasks are those of a banal domestic activity to which cinema is being analogized: sewing in Nicolson's work, cooking in Conrad's. *Reel Time* took place in an open, non-theatrical space, allowing the audience more freedom of movement and a variety of perspectives (fig. 3.15). Nicolson sat at a table in the center of the room facing its rear wall, her back to the spectators, a Singer sewing machine in front of her on the table. To her right was a standing film screen positioned at a 45-degree angle to the rear wall. Two film projectors were placed behind Nicolson, one aimed at the wall she was facing, the other at the angled screen, both positioned in such a way that Nicolson would partially block their beams. A long loop of 16mm film ran from the first projector, over a series of rollers suspended from the ceiling, down and into the sewing machine, then back

Fig. 3.15. Annabel Nicolson, *Reel Time* (1973). Courtesy of British Artists' Film and Video Study Collection, Central Saint Martins, University of the Arts London.

to the projector; the filmic image was that of Nicolson seated at a sewing machine, taken from over her shoulder at a slightly elevated angle, as if from the perspective of the loop projector behind her. The second projector, placed to Nicolson's left, ran empty, casting a partial shadow of Nicolson and the sewing machine onto the angled screen to her right. As the enormous loop of film ran its course around the room, Nicolson fed it through the sewing machine between the needle and the bottom "throat plate," puncturing segments of the film on each pass. As the damaged sections of film passed through the projector, these punctures would subsequently appear on the screen as ragged spots of white light flickering through Nicolson's image. As this went on, volunteers from the audience read aloud the threading instructions from the operating manuals for both sewing machine and projector. The more passes the film made through this loop, the more damage would accrue, eventually causing the film to break. The projector and sewing machine would then be stopped, the split ends of celluloid picked up and spliced back together, and the performance resumed, the passage of the film around the room became more and more difficult. Felicity Sparrow, who attended *Reel Time*'s first performance, describes the audience lifting the film off the floor and helping it along its way, until, inevitably, it lost its integrity altogether and could no longer pass through the projector.[39] This ended the performance.

Reel Time's deliberate roughness belies a complex and even elegant structure of extra-cinematic allusions that re-frame the resolutely materialist, medium-specific practices of 1970s avant-garde cinema. The purely mechanical parallel between filmmaking and sewing opens onto other analogies, no less material but not strictly limited to the operations of projector and sewing machine. Filmmaking, at least as practiced within the avant-garde, is an individual activity, conceived as a form of artisanal, not industrial, labor, much like sewing (again, assuming home craft rather than industrial manufacturing). Both activities are tactile, and involve the stitching together of disparate pieces of material into a single object—a film, a garment—that nevertheless retains visible evidence of its manufacture. They are processes that are curiously at once productive and destructive. Film projectors and sewing machines can easily damage the materials passing through them, and when operated properly exercise a kind of controlled violence on those materials; the very same intermittent mechanism in those two machines is what allows machine guns to work. And finally, both sewing and avant-garde filmmaking are forms of occluded labor, the former as a traditionally feminine activity, the latter as a marginalized artistic tradition. It is upon this analogy that Sparrow builds a feminist interpretation of *Reel Time*:

> The Singer sewing machine (invented some 45 years before the Lumières' Cinematograph) is both a familiar household object and potent symbol of women's hidden labour in the home and in sweatshops; by contrast the film projector, traditionally hidden above and behind cinema spectators in a closed-off box and

---

[39] Felicity Sparrow, "Annabel Nicolson: The Art of Light and Shadow," commissioned essay for luxonline.org (http://www.luxonline.org.uk/artists/annabel_nicolson/essay(1).html), 2005, n.p.

operated by male projectionists, symbolises a vast male-dominated entertainment industry. That these two differently gendered machines could be thus linked was at the time revelatory, anticipating future ground-breaking work by feminist art practitioners.[40]

Sparrow's interpretation rightly traces lines of correspondence not just between two machines, but between the complimentary ideological functions of those machines vis-à-vis gender as well. Sparrow does not mention that editing, the filmmaking activity most easily analogized to sewing, was one area of commercial filmmaking in which women were able to find work even in the early years of cinema—from Blanche Sewell and Margaret Booth, who was supervising editor at MGM, to Dede Allen and multiple-Oscar-winner Thelma Schoonmaker. Of course, this stemmed from the gendered assumption that women had both sewing experience and smaller fingers than men, and thus had an advantage in the editing room, and further assured that women's labor in the film industry would be as "invisible" as the edits they made. The point to be made is that *Reel Time*, while as much a materialist work as *Horror Film 1* and *Take Measure*, differs from those works by placing that brute materialism into a larger historical and political context, commenting upon cinema's institutions and ideologies in addition to its mechanics.

With this in mind, *Reel Time* prefigures with uncanny precision the notion of the cinematic apparatus, the theorization of which developed mostly *after* 1973, the year Nicolson first performed the work. One of apparatus theory's central tenets was that the spectator's perceptual activity during a film both mirrored and was mirrored by the operations of camera and projector, which produced the ideological effect of interpolation whereby the spectator identified with both the human action on screen and the operations of the apparatuses that created these. In doing so, the viewer unconsciously believed s/he produced the spectacle on screen, which confirmed the unity of the viewer's ego and made her or him the "transcendental subject," cornerstone of the idealist worldview that apparatus theory critiqued. Consider Metz's analysis of the cinematic apparatus in action in *The Imaginary Signifier*. Referring to the tacit (and mistaken) belief that visual perception works both through emission of light rays from the eyes and the intromission of reflected light, Metz traces the ways in which film exhibition trades upon this fantasy:

> During the performance the spectator is the searchlight I have described, duplicating the projector, which itself duplicates the camera, and he is also the sensitive surface duplicating the screen, which itself duplicates the film-strip. There are two cones in the auditorium: one ending on the screen and starting both in the projection box and in the spectator's vision insofar as it is projective, and one starting from the screen and "deposited" in the spectator's perception insofar as

---

[40] Ibid.

it is introjective (on the retina, a second screen). When I say that "I see" the film, I mean thereby a unique mixture of two contrary currents: the film is what I receive, and it is also what I release ... Releasing it, I am the projector, receiving it, I am the screen; in both these figures together, I am the camera, which points and yet which records.[41]

Reel Time corresponds to this conception of cinema's structure in several ways. The filmed image of Nicolson at her sewing machine is from the same point of view as the projector behind her, which is projecting the image, creating it just as the camera did when it was shot, prior to the performance. Both projectors cast Nicolson's image in shadow—as viewer, seated in the screening space—onto the screen, where they join the other shadow image of her, on celluloid. Nicolson's role is both filmmaker, producing the images projected on screen, and spectator, seated before the screen, alluding to apparatus theory's assertion that film viewers unconsciously imagine themselves "producing" the film they are watching. The passage of the film along its giant loop traces the complimentary cones of light Metz describes, and which are implied by the nested rectangle structure of the other expanded cinema performances discussed earlier. My claim is not that *Reel Time* was simply a dogmatic enactment or "illustration" of apparatus theory, since, after all, it predated that theory. Rather, the comparison is intended to illuminate *Reel Time*'s sophisticated analysis of both cinema's machines and their ideological implications, an analysis built upon a series of analogies or correspondences, much like Metz's.

Conrad's *7360 Sukiyaki* similarly turns its view outward from the materials of filmmaking to the institutions of cinema, also via an analogy between filmmaking and a domestic and gendered activity. In the early 1970s, Conrad was married and raising a child, and found himself "frequently pinned down at home."[42] Home crafts thus became what Conrad called "algorithms" for producing films, including cooking, canning, and weaving.[43] In *7360 Sukiyaki*, Conrad prepared sukiyaki with Kodak EK 7360 film stock, mixing the celluloid in a bowl with tamari, vegetables, beef, and raw egg, stir-frying the mixture then hurling it onto a film screen—"projecting" it, in his words (fig. 3.16). Though *7360 Sukiyaki* was characteristically playful and irreverent, Conrad nonetheless recognized that it was still fairly easily explained according to the primary "critical contextualization of the day," as a materialist commentary on so and so many aspects of filmmaking and projection.[44] But

---

[41] Christian Metz, "The Imaginary Signifier," in *The Imaginary Signifier: Psychoanalysis and the Cinema* (Bloomington: Indiana University Press, 1982), pp. 50–51.

[42] Conrad, "Is This Penny Ante or a High Stakes Game?," p. 105.

[43] Tony Conrad, personal interview, October 7, 2004.

[44] Conrad, "Is This Penny Ante or a High Stakes Game?," p. 106.

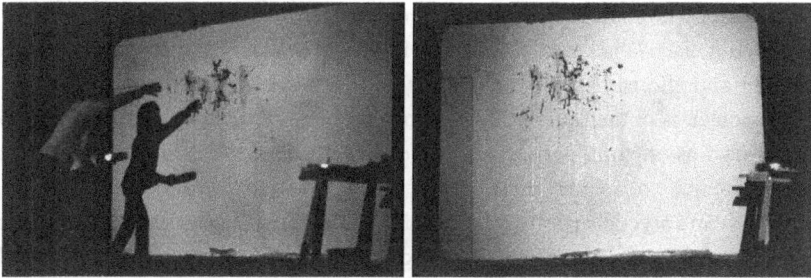

Fig. 3.16. Tony Conrad performing *7360 Sukiyaki* (1973).
Work ©The Estate of Tony Conrad. Photo courtesy of Tony Conrad Archives.

Conrad also points to something more, an "excess" that overflowed the bounds of materialist film criticism:

> The "excess" in this instance is not my overarching figural reference to Japan, but rather the ironic displacement of expectation, and the doubling of institutional channels, that come about through the splicing of *cuisine* and *cinema*. The displacement engenders audience laughter; the splicing produces embarrassed consternation. Together, these responses—laughter and consternation—effectively erased the critical capacity that the more serious aspects of the work intended.[45]

Conrad's "splicing of cuisine and cinema" analogizes an art form to an activity usually perceived either as part of the banal domestic sphere or as a form of service: as he put it, "the audience clientele is being waited upon."[46] The latter association stems in part from co-presence of filmmaker and viewer and the merging of production and exhibition, understood here as "serving clientele," characteristic of expanded cinema performances in this period. As Conrad put it, "*7360 Sukiyaki* brings the filmmaker and the audience together, collapsing the mediation that ordinarily habituates the activities of film making and viewing."[47] Citing Nicolas Bourriaud's *Relational Aesthetics*, Conrad reads his performance as making explicit the social exchange implicit in all artwork, which entails what Bourriaud calls "a certain ambiguity ... between the utilitarian function of the objects [the artist] is presenting, and their aesthetic function."[48] Thus, the "excess" in *7360 Sukiyaki* at once acknowledges the social dimensions of artmaking and "consumption" and analogizes art to something common and utilitarian. This, presumably, is why Conrad's performance produced embarrassed laughter and consternation,

---

[45] Ibid., p. 107.
[46] Ibid., pp. 107–108.
[47] Ibid., p. 107.
[48] Ibid., p. 109. See Nicolas Bourriaud, *Relational Aesthetics* (Dijon: Les presses du réel, 2002), p. 35.

which "erased the critical capacity" he intended for *7360 Sukiyaki*. It also speaks to the power of the materialist, medium-specific interpretive framework to close down other meanings and effects, in this case not only institutional critique, but also humor and the sensuousness of the performance's gooey physicality. Most importantly, what was framed out was any link between film and the outside world, as in the "overarching figural reference" to Japanese culture and cuisine. Misaligned as they were with the reductiveness and asceticism of materialist film, these excesses were treated like a kind of toxic industrial bi-product. Conrad's cooking metaphor (and Kubelka's, examined in the next chapter), along with Sharits's of anatomy and neurology, Sherwin's of biography and aging, and Nicolson's of marginalized female labor or the myths of cinema spectatorship, were shunted to the side if not pulled offstage entirely.

Reflecting on two decades of avant-garde film in 1978, Annette Michelson tracked an analytical, intellectual "critique of illusion" from the mature films of Brakhage to the structural films of Sharits, Snow, and Conrad:

Current work is increasingly concerned with an unpacking of analytical concerns and processes, so that the conditions of making, projection, and viewing are the substantive and formal axes around which recent work, beginning with the immense achievement of Brakhage, revolves. Brakhage's insistence upon the materiality of the filmic support, the filmic filtering of light, his revision of sound-image relation, his subversion of the space in which narrative takes place initiates the development of that detailed critique of illusionism which marks the passage from cinema to film.[49]

Michelson's curious phrase, "the passage from cinema to film," refers to the avant-garde's rejection of the illusionism that formed the basis of mainstream cinema in favor of a modernist analysis of filmic specificity. "Cinema," as critics and filmmakers of the time frequently reiterated, was derived from *kine*, the Greek word for movement. The appearance of movement in film was the founding illusion of the cinema, the basis for its representations of other times, places, and worlds, and the material ground for the ideological effects attributed to it by theorists like Metz. "Cinema," then, stood for all these things that the avant-garde's critique of illusionism was aimed against, while "film" was the material reality that avant-garde films concerned themselves with instead.

Works like *Reel Time* and *7360 Sukiyaki* reversed this trajectory, turning their gaze outward from the medium of film to the institutions and ideologies of cinema. They were no less anti-illusionist in doing so, but in this case they interrogated the "illusions"—the false beliefs, the myths—of cinema rather than its invisible material operations. By placing cinema in this social sphere, side-by-side with the myriad other human activities to which they analogized it, filmmakers like Nicolson and Conrad could analyze it as political phenomenon.

[49] Michelson, "Paul Sharits and the Critique of Illusionism," p. 86.

Another Anti-Illusionism: the Projection Performances of Ken Jacobs

Further complications of anti-illusionism can be found in Ken Jacobs's remarkable body of expanded cinema performance. Jacobs has engaged in two major forms of cinematic performance more or less continuously since 1965. This, and the fact that he has been a crucial figure in avant-garde film institutions since the late 1960s, including educational ones, makes him a key link between the second and third waves of expanded cinema. Indeed, Jacobs's performance work of the last five decades constitutes one of the most sustained and productive investigations of the nature of cinematic illusion and the dialectic of materiality and ephemerality characteristic of the art form. These have become the major preoccupations of recent expanded cinema, as well.

In the works surveyed thus far, performance takes place in the space between projector and screen, the filmmaker following at least a loose script or score, a predetermined set of "formal actions." Jacobs shifted the locus of cinematic performance to the projector, reconceiving projection as a form of live action rather than a purely automated activity, in essence using the projector as a creative instrument. Jacobs's refusal of the projector's perfect automaticity was critical; it was another way to collapse the phases of filmmaking and exhibition, and the precondition for his distinctive variant of anti-illusionism, which raises questions about cinema's ontology and the experience of film viewing.

By the time of his first expanded cinema performance in 1965, Jacobs had already begun to establish himself as an important figure in the world of avant-garde film, partly through his collaborations with Jack Smith. Jacobs had been making films on his own and with Smith since 1955. Between that year and the early 1960s, Jacobs made or at least started the films that are still considered his major achievements, including *Star Spangled to Death* (1957–1959, revised and completed 2004), *Little Stabs at Happiness* (with Smith, 1958–1960), *Blonde Cobra* (with Smith, 1959–1963), and *The Sky Socialist* (1964–1965, regularly revised as late as 2009). That so many of these major films remained incomplete for so long has often been attributed to Jacobs's restless artistic temperament and his suspicion of complete, formally cohesive art works. His 1969 found-footage film *Tom, Tom the Piper's Son* is perhaps the most frequently cited example of Jacobs's resistance to such closure. To make the film, Jacobs projected the 1905 Billy Bitzer short of the same name on an analytic projector and filmed the results directly off the screen. The analytic projector allowed him to stop and start the Bitzer film at will, run it forward and in reverse at varying projection speeds, and freeze frames. He thereby extended the short narrative film to nearly two hours, slowing, reversing, stopping, and repeating scenes and filming them from varying angles and distances from the screen. Figures in the frame become unrecognizable as Jacobs magnifies them in close-up, transforming them into purely optical objects while greatly magnifying the swirling film grains (fig. 3.17). The source film is

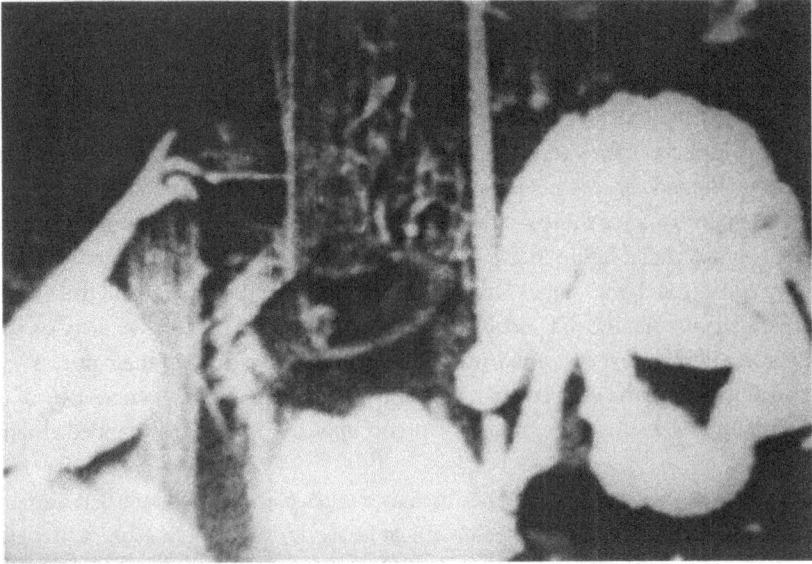

Fig. 3.17. Ken Jacobs, *Tom, Tom, the Piper's Son* (1969). Frame enlargement.
Courtesy of Ken Jacobs.

shown in its entirety at the beginning and end of Jacobs's version, suggesting a process in which the original is broken down, obsessively analyzed, and then reconstituted to reveal visual qualities that its conventional form obscured and that the mimetic power of the medium mitigated against.

In a 1974 interview in *Film Culture* Jacobs spoke of the "analytical" filmmaking process of *Tom, Tom the Piper's Son,* though it immediately becomes clear that his conception of analysis differs radically from the one of which Michelson wrote the same year with regard to Sharits. Jacobs described the experience of the film this way:

> I don't think there's any movement to grasp some underlying map or bones or the scheme, the system, the plot. I don't even think those things are there. I think just the opposite is happening ... I'm with what's there, but only to get lost, not to track something down, to say this is the scheme: a line over here and a line up there and now we've got it, you see. We've got the essential structure. I think I'm doing just the opposite. The film is going into smoke, vaporizing. It's really going so far away from that kind of schematics.[50]

Though referring to a 16mm film, Jacobs could just as easily be describing his expanded cinema, invoking his resistance to notions of good design and his acts of

[50] Lindley Halon, "Kenneth Jacobs, Interviewed by Lindley Hanlon [Jerry Sims Present], April 9, 1974," *Film Culture* nos. 67–69 (1979), p. 74.

de-structuring and dematerializing films, and implying a very different sort of spectatorial experience than the one contemporaneous structural films sought to produce.
Though early critical accounts of Jacobs's work, largely on the basis of *Tom, Tom the
Piper's Son*, placed him in the structural film camp, more recent critics have emphasized the deliberately unfinished quality of Jacobs's works even if they are not literally
incomplete. Paul Arthur argued, for instance:

> Part of [Jacobs's] cachet in the postmodernist artistic scene is due to an exem-
> plary refusal of mastery and aesthetic closure. Similarly, his insistence on sponta-
> neous, additive structures—the antithesis of traditional appeals to architectonic
> complexity—align him with those favoring openness and improvisation over tight
> design ... His repeated insight that there is already far too much extant film, that its
> onslaught demands some process of studied retardation, some slowing down or
> rupture that allows for more detailed consideration of even a few radiant frames,
> restates in practice certain familiar axioms of influential theorists Roland Barthes
> and Jacques Derrida.[51]

Like the previous passage, this one points to some of the major features of Jacobs's
expanded cinema: improvisation, the deconstruction of existing footage (implied in
the references to Barthes and Derrida), and the disruption and derailment of form. It
also sums up Jacobs's conception of analysis as a destructive act intended to subvert
structure rather than reveal it. For Michelson, the analytical mode of structural film
was quasi-scientific, a "refined exploration of the epistemology of filmic enterprise"
and a "systematic attempt to explore and objectify the dynamics of the recording process and the materiality of film."[52] Even Arthur implies a similar aim on the part of
Jacobs: the "studied retardation" and "detailed consideration" of found footage, as if
the intellect needs to catch up with the flood of images in the proliferation of "extant
film." Analysis here is conceived of as a sober, rigorous process that clarifies formal
structures, or subjects the materials of the medium to scientific scrutiny in an effort
to deprive them of their illusionistic power. But if we wish to call Jacobs an "analytical" filmmaker, it would have to be in the earliest sense of the term, as a release or
loosening, as in the unfastening of a sailing vessel from its moorings. This returns to
the liberatory claims of expanded cinema made by Renan, or the idea of liberated vision that runs through the history of avant-garde film and of which Brakhage is the
exemplar.

Jacobs's first foray into cinematic performance was *Naomi Is a Vision of Loveliness*
(1965). Jacobs screened a single roll of 8mm footage of underground luminary Naomi
Levine on an analytic projector, creating a live, improvisatory projection performance that extended the duration of the roll and transformed the action it recorded.

[51] Paul Arthur, "Creating Spectacle from Dross: The Chimeric Cinema of Ken Jacobs," *Film Comment* 33, no. 2 (March–April 1997), pp. 59–60.
[52] Michelson, "Paul Sharits and the Critique of Illusionism," pp. 84 and 87, respectively.

Alternating lenses on the projector also allowed Jacobs to distort the image and, according to Renan, caused "the image to spill off of the screen," illuminating the space surrounding it and breaking the image up into different planes—some on screen, some falling across the surfaces beyond the screen.[53] This simple work incorporated in nascent form many of the elements Jacobs would elaborate upon for the next five decades, including the creation of depth effects and the use of analytic projectors to manipulate filmic time.

Since 1965, Jacobs's expanded cinema has taken three distinct forms, all involving live performance. Two utilize projection systems that Jacobs invented himself: the "Nervous System" and "Nervous Magic Lantern." The former comprises two synchronized 16mm analytic projectors and a large, rotating external shutter; the latter employs no film technology at all, taking instead the form of a theatrical magic lantern operating on much the same principle as an analog overhead projector. The third form is shadow play, in which strategically illuminated performers cast shadows on a cloth screen between themselves and the audience. Jacobs's shadow plays, like the Nervous System and Nervous Magic Lantern works, produce striking depth effects, often with the aid of a special viewing filter given to audience members at the start of the performance. Here I will focus exclusively on the Nervous System film performances, returning to the Nervous Magic Lantern and shadow play works in the final chapter, which is about forms of expanded cinema that are entirely filmless, a branch of work that Jacobs christened "paracinema" in the 1970s. This bifurcation of Jacobs's oeuvre does come at the cost of separating works that obviously informed one another, all of which are variants of Jacobs's singular ideas about cinematic abstraction and illusion. But the "paracinematic" performances also link to a much broader tradition of filmmaking and theorizing that in many respects is much less relevant to the Nervous System works.

The Nervous System, which came into being in 1975, consisted of two synchronized analytic projectors mounted side-by-side, their beams overlapping on the screen to create a single image (fig. 3.18). A large propeller-like object in front of the two projectors acted as an external shutter, alternately blocking the left and right projector beams as it rotated. Two identical film prints were loaded into the projectors and cued up slightly out of phase with each other, often by as little as a single frame. During the performance, Jacobs controlled the direction and speed of both projectors with a single mechanism, improvisationally speeding up, slowing down, reversing, or stopping the action on screen, and increasing or decreasing the extent of asynchronization between the twin prints. The external shutter produced a pronounced flicker, punctuating the image with instants of complete darkness. The rapid alternation of two nearly identical, slightly out-of-phase frames triggered the illusion of apparent motion, making the contents of those frames appear to oscillate back and forth; even when Jacobs froze a single frame in each projector's gate, the image vibrated intensely, the tiny differences between the two alternating frames magnified by the

---

[53] Renan, *An Introduction to the American Underground Film*, p. 153.

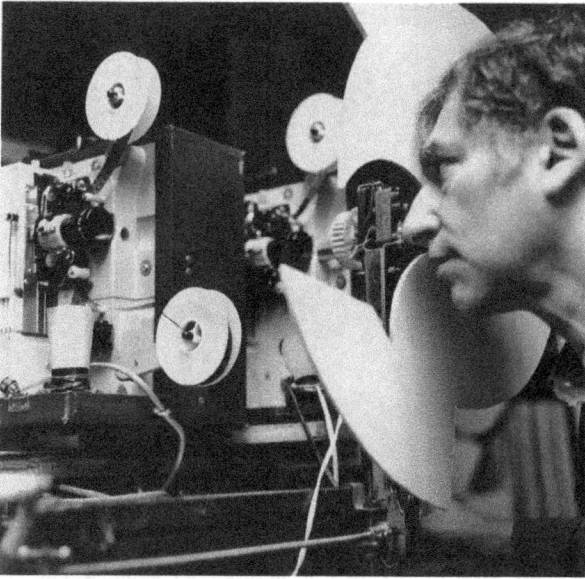

Fig. 3.18. Ken Jacobs and his Nervous System.
Photograph by Florence Jacobs, courtesy of Ken Jacobs.

Nervous System's process. This illusory movement was joined by another, even more remarkable illusion—that of depth, the appearance that the projected image suddenly opened up into deep space. This effect was most marked when the differences between two alternating frames was more substantial. In *New York Ghetto Fish Market 1903* (2006), for example, a brief sequence from the titular Edison film shows a wide, high-angle shot of the fish market. Lines of shoppers move up and down a long row of tables, and Jacobs exploits this pronounced sense of both depth and lateral movement in the shot to create some of the film's most striking visual illusions (fig. 3.19). In the foreground, a well-dressed man strolling through the market has stopped to look up toward the camera, while the merchants and shoppers around and behind him continue busily moving about. The camera in the source film pans slightly left at this moment. Jacobs freezes the Nervous System's projectors here, fluctuating between two sequential frames. Because the man in the foreground stands still while both the camera and the masses of people in the background move, the planes of depth in the image appear to separate, the background dropping away dizzyingly in a rapid blur as the well-dressed man remains still and in sharp focus. That is, the rapid alternation between frames in this moment grossly exaggerates the image's depth cues, an effect often called "quasi-3D" in critical accounts of the Nervous System performances.

The illusion of depth can be amplified even further when the audience views a Nervous System performance through a small filter held over one eye. Jacobs calls this the "Pulfrich filter," though he means that looking at movement through the filter creates the "Pulfrich effect," whereby an object moving side-to-side will appear instead to be advancing and receding. The filter itself is simply a neutral density filter, a slightly darkened piece of

Fig. 3.19. Ken Jacobs, *New York Ghetto Fish Market 1903* (2006). Documentation of Nervous System performance.
Courtesy of Ken Jacobs.

transparent plastic that reduces the brightness of light much like a sunglasses' lens. In an interview with Scott MacDonald, Jacobs explains the Pulfrich effect using a swinging pendulum as an example. Looking through the Pulfrich filter one sees the pendulum's lateral movement as a circular, advancing/retreating motion like an orbit.[54]

In early Nervous System works Jacobs mostly explored the ways he could exploit these illusory effects. One predominant technique was the sudden stopping and starting of the twin film prints, which produced the illusion of the spaces in Jacobs's archival films violently expanding and contracting. Michael Sicinski describes this effect in his account of *Bi-temporal Vision: The Sea* (1994): "A perfectly flat, black-and-white Jackson Pollock painting suddenly rotates on an off-center axis, becoming the Milky Way in receding perspective. A rural meadow, in turn, flattens into a Franz Kline composition."[55] This effect was particularly apparent in the multi-part performance *The Impossible* (1975–1980), based on the original version of *Tom, Tom, the Piper's Son*. In the source film, Tom steals a pig and is chased through the town by a growing mob of angry citizens, an event that culminates as the whole group bursts through a dead-bolted door toward the camera. The scene became the centerpiece

[54] MacDonald, "Ken and Flo Jacobs," in *A Critical Cinema 3: Interviews with Independent Filmmakers* (Berkeley, Los Angeles: University of California Press, 1998), p. 386. The generally accepted explanation of the apparent depth the filter produces is that the reduction of the image's brightness in one eye slows the transmission of that image to the brain via the optic nerve, thereby creating an apparent temporal lag between the image from the covered eye.

[55] Sicinski, "Motion Study/Motion Painting: Ken Jacobs's *Bi-temporal Vision: The Sea* [excerpt]," n.p. http://academichack.net/jacobs.htm.

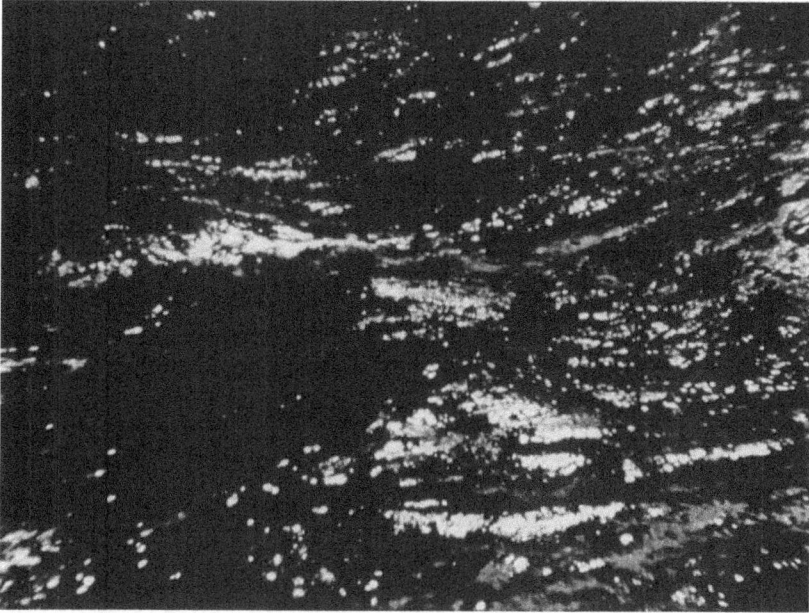

Fig. 3.20. Ken Jacobs, *Bi-temporal Vision: The Sea* (1994). Documentation of Nervous System performance.
Courtesy of Ken Jacobs.

of *The Impossible, Chapter Three: All Hell Breaks Loose* (1980). In a performance described by J. Hoberman, Jacobs simply allowed two sequential frames of the door shattering to alternate for over 15 minutes, limiting the impression of depth to a few splinters of the bursting door appearing to vibrate in space in front of the screen, before finally allowing the action to proceed and the characters to come spilling through the doorway in almost full 3D.[56] Jacobs pushed this effect further in many performances by gradually increasing the degree to which the twin prints were out of synchronization. A one or two frame difference simply registered as slight vibration of a character or object. When Jacobs coaxed the two prints further out of phase, by four, five, or more frames, the movement became more violent and the apparent depth more pronounced; as Hoberman put it, "the lockstep movements of the on-screen characters ranges [*sic*] from discrete twitching to a St. Vitus Frenzy."[57]

Bi-temporal Vision: The Sea was one of the most complex and accomplished Nervous System performances, and one of a very few to use contemporary footage made especially for the Nervous System. Eight seconds of high contrast 16mm film shot of ocean waves taken by Phil Solomon, a former student of Jacobs, was extended to approximately 70 minutes of improvisatory back and forth projection viewed through the Pulfrich filter (fig. 3.20). The two simultaneously projected

[56] J. Hoberman, untitled review of *The Impossible*, *Artforum* 18 (Summer 1980), p. 79.
[57] Ibid.

prints of Solomon's footage were kept out of phase by a single frame for the entire performance, with Jacobs altering the usual movement of the external shutter to allow brief instances in which the two images were visible at once and thus super-imposed. Solomon's imagery is, in and of itself, disorienting due to the high degree of contrast and lack of spatial cues like horizon or shoreline. The waves become an abstract field of morphing black and white shapes in 3D. Viewed through the filter, the undulating patches of black and white to which the advancing waves have been reduced were perceived as two distinct forms in different planes of depth and moving in opposite directions rather than as a single form rolling toward the camera. Moving the filter from one eye to the other instantaneously reversed the apparent direction of the waves, something Jacobs encouraged his audience to do in the accompanying program notes:

> The image is strongly 3-D even without the filter but the filter will strongly enhance the depth. It can also radically change arrangement in depth. Choice of eye determines which parts of the scene are in front of or in back of other parts, and in which direction movement flows. The more abstract and non-representational the scene—releasing the mind from its knowledge of phys-ical law and its expectations re: behavior of objects in space—the more it is that changes can be seen; that is, acknowledged by the mind. So I suggest using the filter most intensively when this depiction of water is least rec-ognizable as water . . . Try it, for instance, when the overall scene becomes lighter in tone following the first advancing wave. (A wave rumbling forward slightly below eye level that will transform to a massive cloud-form moving overhead . . .).[58]

At the moment Jacobs began producing expanded cinema, a changing of the guard was taking place in avant-garde film culture, a shifting of aesthetic dominants. A dis-tinction emerged between an aesthetic that privileged the transformation of vision, along with the excitement and disorientation such a transformation could produce, and one that appealed to the viewer's intellect and the capacity for analysis. Writing in 1973 for an exhibition that included a screening of *Tom, Tom, the Piper's Son*, Michelson argued:

> The cinema of *this* time . . . articulates an investigation of the terms of cinematic il-lusionism. It turns, from the fascinated consciousness of the eidetic, lyric mode, to precisely that "course of genuine investigation" which so preoccupied Eisenstein

---

[58] Jacobs, program notes for *Bi-temporal Vision: The Sea*, not paginated. On Mark Webber's web-site: http://markwebber.org.uk/archive/category/seasons/london-film-festival-2000/.

as he speculated upon the nature of "intellectual cinema" as a bodying forth of the processes of analytic consciousness . . .[59]

Michelson aligned sixties and seventies avant-garde film with that branch of the pre-WWII avant-garde (i.e., Eisenstein) that privileged the analytical, anti-illusionist mode of filmmaking rather than the graphic tradition that reached its apex in the "lyric, eidetic mode" represented by the films of Brakhage. In the structural film era, film had once more become the object of exhaustive, analytical investigation.

At first glance, the Nervous System performances seem open to the usual anti-illusionist interpretations applied to structural and related films since the 1960s. By altering projection speed and direction, Jacobs removed the images on the archival films he works with from the context of narrative and conventional photographic representation, laying film itself bare for our scrutiny. The very name of the projectors Jacobs uses—analytic—invites this interpretation; Jacobs's "analysis" of normal film via slowed time, freeze frames, and repetition subverts its illusionism, presenting its raw materials for detached intellectual contemplation. This has been the primary interpretation of *Tom, Tom, the Piper's Son*, an important source for the Nervous System works. Taking their cue from Jacobs himself, who dubbed *Tom, Tom* a "didactic film,"[60] critics have interpreted it as an analysis of the specific qualities of the medium such as film grain, the flatness of the screen, and the flickering light of the film projector, revealed when Jacobs reaches into the frame and lifts the screen. Because this revelation of filmic specificity is enacted directly on the surface of a more conventional narrative film, which Jacobs treats as a kind of illusionist foil, *Tom, Tom* has easily been read as exemplifying structural film's defining project: the "critique of illusionism." According to Regina Cornwell, "The materials of film, as used by Jacobs, paradoxically defeat the illusions they had served to create in the original."[61] Lois Mendelson and Bill Simon, writing in *Artforum* in 1971, followed the anti-illusionist line as well: "[Jacobs] is concerned with exposing, through the systematic reduction of images, the two major illusions upon which the filmic image depends."[62]

But clearly the Nervous System performances are not an anti-illusionist cinema in any conventional sense of that term, nor are they so easily incorporated into the project of intellectual, analytical cinema. If anything, Jacobs upends these related

[59] Annette Michelson, "Intellectual Cinema: A Reconsideration," in Alan Shestack, ed., *Options and Alternatives: Some Directions in Recent Art* (exhibition catalogue) (New Haven, CT: Yale University Art Gallery, 1973), p. 13.

[60] Jacobs, program notes for *Tom, Tom, the Piper's Son* at the Gallery of Modern Art in New York, April, 1969, cited by Lois Mendelson and Bill Simon in "*Tom, Tom, the Piper's Son*," *Artforum* (September 1971), reprinted in Gidal, ed., *Structural Film Anthology*, p. 78. Interestingly, Gidal included the essay in the anthology as an example of anti-materialist writing, in that the essay focused solely on the formal properties of the work and the materials of the film medium rather than the more broadly "materialist" context of the avant-garde film institution (a flaw Gidal also attributed to the film itself). See "editor's note" in *Structural Film Anthology*, p. 86.

[61] Cornwell, "Some Formalist Tendencies in the Current American Avant-Garde Film," p. 113.

[62] Mendelson and Simon, "*Tom, Tom, the Piper's Son*," p. 80.

concepts in his performances. As the aforementioned passage from the *Film Culture* interview attests, the breaking down of a whole into parts is aimed *against* orientation and clarity, according to Jacobs. Analysis should obliterate the source material to produce a radically new and utterly disorienting experience of it: "what you really find [through analysis] is mystery. You don't find a schematic."[63] This sentiment echoes a discourse of anti-intellectualism in avant-garde cinema reaching back to earlier generations. It is summed up by James Broughton's admonition, which embraces the ideals of direct perception and experience:

> Analytical theorizing is often felt to be "over one's head." It is nothing of the sort. In fact it is under one's feet. It is the mud one has to wade through: the bog of uncreative minds who build labyrinthine swamps of intellect to protect themselves from direct experience. What is truly over one's head is the realm of the poetic imagination.[64]

The passage is from Broughton's book *Making Light of It*, published in 1977, at a moment when avant-garde film was still oriented toward the intellectual and analytical. Broughton urged avant-garde filmmakers in the other direction, pitting experience against intellect. Similarly, Jacobs places analysis in the service of the decidedly anti-intellectual aims of transforming vision and disorientating the optical and cognitive processes of normal film viewing. Certainly the Nervous System was designed to produce a different kind of viewing experience than the one offered by commercial cinema, but many critics have also contrasted it with contemporaneous avant-garde film. In particular, they set it against structural film, seen by comparison as a dry, repetitive, overly restrictive mode, and moreover one whose dominance in the 1960s and 1970s obscured other forms and the respective kinds of viewing pleasure they offered. In so doing, such critics follow Jacobs's lead. Speaking of the Nervous System work *Disorient Express* (1995, also realized as a 35mm widescreen film), which repeats and exhaustively permutes a 1906 train travel film, Jacobs distinguishes it from the analytical forms of structural film: "where methods of ordering film materials often came to take on paramount value. (The viewer at some point grasped the method and that could pretty much be it)." Though Jacobs acknowledges that "method is always evident," his way of phrasing modernism's baring of the device, he asserts that the Nervous System's primary purpose is to "provide perceptual challenges to our understanding of reality" (fig. 3.21).[65] The Nervous System was Jacobs's antidote to the overly cerebral and well-ordered aesthetic of structural film, which he replaces with irrational space and time, unpredictability, and cognitive disorientation.

These qualities explain the poetic, sometimes ecstatic language in so many accounts of the Nervous System performances, which feels out of place in critical and

[63] Hanlon, "Kenneth Jacobs, Interviewed by Lindley Hanlon [Jerry Sims Present], April 9, 1974," p. 74.
[64] Broughton, *Making Light of It*, pp. 6–7.
[65] Jacobs, program notes for *Disorient Express*, not paginated. On Mark Webber's website: http://mark-webber.org.uk/archive/2000/11/10/ken-jacobs-nottingham/.

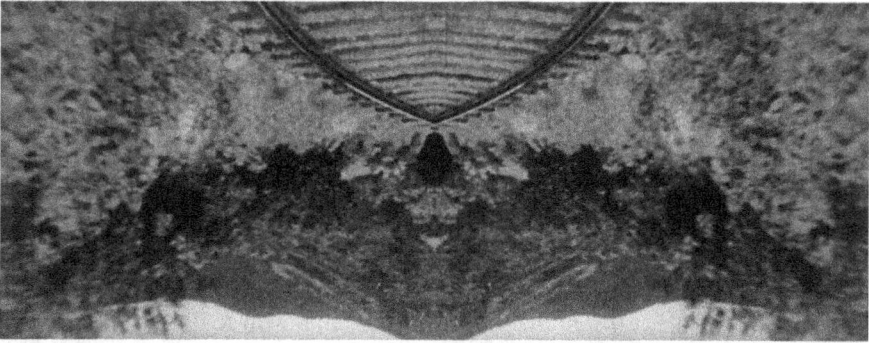

Fig. 3.21. Ken Jacobs, *Disorient Express* (1995). Frame enlargement from 35mm film version.

Courtesy of Ken Jacobs.

academic writing. It can be seen as a response to the quasi-scientific discourse of formalist film criticism, re-asserting a different set of aesthetic values, attempting to compensate for the under-valuation of lyricism, illusion, and pure physical sensation in the era of structural film. Paul Arthur wrote of the Nervous System causing "on-screen figures to leap into the space between eye and projection surface, defying all attempts to logically explain or control the throbbing apparitions," leading viewers "to discover in the ceaselessly reforming shapes spectral images of monsters and other horrors coming straight from their own subconscious storehouse of anxieties."[66] And while Sicinski makes a scholarly argument about the historical and aesthetic importance of the Nervous System performances, he also feels compelled to describe the experience of "getting lost in the piece":

> [Y]ou will be set adrift, with virtually no reference points, on a vast sea of light. You will have no concrete narrative events with which to locate yourself temporally in the piece ... You will embark on a perceptual journey marked by protracted time, and oscillating, vertiginous space. Occasionally, you will find a toehold. But it will be momentary, and you will then feel it slip away. Any sense of visual control over the spectacle is undercut by painterly effects, shifts in figure/ground relationships, and the resolute intangibility of the liquid expanse.[67]

Writing about *Chronometer* (1990), a variation on the Nervous Magic Lantern performances, Fred Worden claims that it allowed the viewer to escape time, an experience made more poignant by Jacobs's use of very old, deteriorating film footage (fig. 3.22). Worden calls this experience "transcendent": "It implies infinity. This is motion induced directly in perception. Familiar and strange at the same time. If angels really

---

[66] Paul Arthur, "Creating Spectacle From Dross," p. 62.
[67] Sicinski, "Motion Study/Motion Painting," n.p.

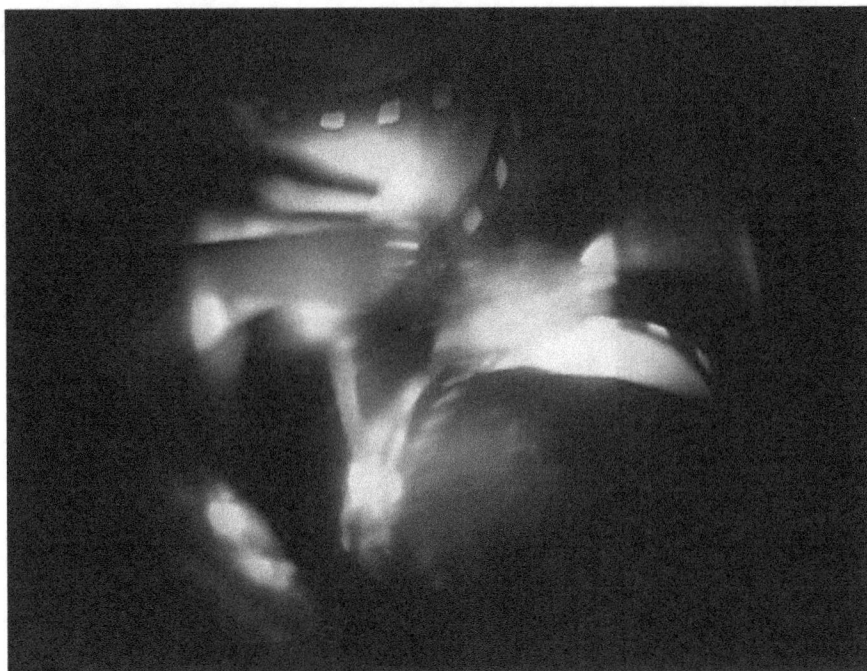

Fig. 3.22. Ken Jacobs, *Chronometer* (1990). Documentation of Nervous Magic Lantern performance.
Courtesy of Ken Jacobs.

did dance in foreverness it would have to look something like this."[68] Such expressive passages, appearing even in the context of academic texts, suggest that the coolly objective language of formalist film criticism is ill-suited to tracking the pleasurably disorienting experiences of the Nervous System performances.

Indeed, Jacobs's work points up the limitations and logical shortcomings of anti-illusionist film theory. The distinction between illusionist and anti-illusionist film practice really stands for a cluster of opposing concepts: narrative vs. non-narrative, referential vs. reflexive, analogous to other art forms vs. medium-specific, fictional vs. real, false vs. true—in short, "bad" and "good" aesthetic and political traits and values. Within this discursive nexus, illusionism became equated with narrative, which in turn was equated with mimesis: the use of the film medium to represent something other than itself. The ideological problems with narrative, which the continental film theory of the time so exhaustively explored, infected all the other concepts in the cluster. Le Grice's "Narrative Illusion vs. Structural Realism" debate with Sitney is one example of how this semantic field worked in practice.[69]

---

[68] Fred Worden, "Ken Jacobs' Chronometer," *Cinematograph* 5 (1993), p. 53.

[69] For elaboration on this point, see my essay "Experimental Cinema's Elusive Illusion," *Moving Image Review and Art Journal* 2, no. 2 (2013), pp. 239–250.

The assumption that illusion means narrative—recognizable action in the continuous time and space of the real physical world—which furthermore means mimesis, ignores other possible forms of cinematic illusion. These include illusions that some filmmakers have identified as inherently cinematic, aesthetically productive, and politically efficacious. And the assumption that anti-illusionism in cinema is limited to the revelation of the filmstrip's materiality loses sight of other filmic mechanisms that might be bared, with markedly different results. The Nervous System's external shutter does exactly this, producing illusions by making the flicker visible, but illusions that no viewer could mistake for reality. The Nervous System produces illusions that are unique to cinema, or at least inextricably associated with cinema, which it is designed to amplify rather than obscure. This form of illusionism cannot be equated with mimesis, realism, or narrative, as it disrupts all of these. Nor can these illusions be equated with "fiction" or "falsehood," in the sense of duping the viewer into believing that something is occurring on screen that is not. The intense illusions of the Nervous System cannot be overlooked; as Arthur and Sicinski suggest, they bring about an apperceptive state in which viewers experience their own visual and mental processes, scrutinizing and taking pleasure in them at the same time. It is this quality of the Nervous System works that led Sicinski to describe them as engendering "a mode of knowing both analytical and astonished."[70]

In his vivid account of *XCXHXEXRXRXIXEXSX* (1980), in which Jacobs treated archival pornographic footage to a Nervous System rendition, Solomon attempts something like a reconciliation of illusionism and anti-illusionism by invoking a major spokesperson of each position:

> Here, at last, is the happy union of Eisenstein and Bazin—one can explore the deep space of the frame at one's leisure, peruse underneath an oscillating armpit to a shimmering waterfall of movement behind, privately relish the vibrating illusion of depth ... and yet this "static" frame is virtually created by the "montage of attractions," the collision between one picture and the next—a dynamic, breathing, living frame. In the excitement of experiencing a really new cinema, I wonder for a moment: Can I ever watch a normal film again?[71]

For Solomon, the illusionistic deep space prized by Bazin offers the occasion for contemplation, including the analytical breaking down of the components of the image—armpit, waterfall, and so on. That illusion is heightened by the "vibrating" effect of the Nervous System, its distinct variant of stereoscopy, what Eisenstein would call the "collision" of two frames to produce an effect that either of the single frames alone could not. That effect might be purely optical; Eisenstein explained apparent motion in terms of collision, the dialectic of two static frames producing the synthesis

---

[70] Sicinski, "Motion Study/Motion Painting: Ken Jacobs's *Bi-temporal Vision: The Sea* [excerpt]."
[71] Phil Solomon, *XCXHXEXRXRXIXEXSX*, *Cinematograph* 5 (1993), p. 55.

of illusory motion.[72] But the effects Eisenstein privileged were emotional and intellectual, wherein ideas were given "emotional dynamization" that made them more compelling.[73] This was a facet of Eisenstein's film practice that Michelson overlooked when she traced the origins of structural film's project of intellectual cinema to him. By the same token, critical glosses on Bazin typically omit the importance of analysis in his deep-space, long-take aesthetic, and his belief that this realist aesthetic accomplished in a single shot what montage did in multiple shots, laying out the space of narrative action for the viewer's analytical eye.[74] The dialectic of illusionism and anti-illusionism that Solomon sees taking place in the Nervous System is at once a reconciliation of all the attending aesthetic values in that dyad: realism and modernism, visual pleasure and intellectual analysis, lyricism and literalism, entertainment and didacticism.

Jacobs is a crucial bridge between the second and third waves of expanded cinema, making expanded work continuously from the 1960s into the present, and playing foundational roles in some of avant-garde film's central institutions, including the Collective for Living Cinema, Millennium Film Workshop, and the film department at SUNY Binghamton. In reconceiving film projection as a creative act, making the previously passive projector into a locus of intervention by the filmmaker, Jacobs in effect incorporated live performance into cinema's ontology, and with it the possibility of chance and improvisation in the moment of exhibition. Put a different way, cinema was not simply exhibited in the projection space, but *made* there, the artistry of the filmmaker extended into a new dimension. Finally, Jacobs struck a balance between the set of opposing values staked out by anti-illusionism, re-admitting emotional response and sensory pleasure into materialist cinema. This revised conception of projection, and of modernist cinema itself, provided a model that subsequent generations of avant-garde filmmakers have enthusiastically taken up.

The Third Wave: Projection Performance

Since the early 1990s, "live cinema" has become "projection performance," which is undoubtedly the most common form of expanded cinema among contemporary experimental filmmakers. "Common" is putting it mildly, in fact; projection performance is no fringe practice but a mode of working shared even among filmmakers not known as makers of expanded cinema. It is ubiquitous in avant-garde film exhibition, frequently part of screenings not identified as expanded cinema events per se.

---

[72] Sergei Eisenstein, "A Dialectical Approach to Film Form," in *The Film Form: Essays in Film Theory* (San Diego: Harcourt Brace & Company, 1949), pp. 45–63. See especially pp. 49–50 and 55–56.
[73] Ibid., pp. 57–58.
[74] André Bazin, "The Evolution of the Language of Cinema," in *What Is Cinema?* vol. 1 (Berkeley: University of California Press, 1967), pp. 33–39.

What at first may sound like a narrow format, the live manipulation of film projectors by the filmmaker/performer, is in practice a surprisingly rich and varied cinematic form, continuing as it does avant-garde film's project of atomization and reconfiguration of its material and formal elements. The moment of projection is taken as a kind of amalgam for this project. Refusing the projector's automaticity, projection performers have discovered that it is a fertile field for intervention: focus, registration, aperture, projection speed, the film gate, the lens, the mechanisms of sound, and the beam of light itself are all subject to live machinations. Any one of these aspects of projection can become a long-term area of exploration, each providing the ground for a kind of subgenre of the form.

Projection performance shifts the locus of attention and meaning from the body of the filmmaker illuminated by the projector beam (as in *Horror Film I* or *Film and Film #4*) to the projector itself and the on-screen results of the filmmaker's live manipulations of its mechanics and optics. There are exceptions, of course. The duo Abject Leader's (Sally Golding and Joel Stern) *The Face of Another* (2008) features Golding acting as corporeal screen for superimposed images of "other" bodies onto her own. Images from horror and medical instruction films, of skulls and transparent bodies with their musculature or organs revealed, merge with Golding's own features, making her the interface between moving image and real space, spectacle and audience (fig. 3.23). In Alex MacKenzie's *Happiness* (2010), made in collaboration with dancer-choreographer Barbara Bourget, MacKenzie's mobile analytic projectors illuminate Bourget's live Butoh dance, at times obscuring the difference between live and on screen bodies. Dirk de Bruyn has made a remarkable series of projection performances on the subject of trauma. While remaining behind the audience to operate a bank of 16mm projectors, he interacts with the bewildering fields of overlapping images vocally, belting out guttural yells, obsessively repeated number series, and "seemingly involuntary fits of concrete poetry" through a megaphone while whipping the beam of a flashlight through the space.[75]

There is a sense, however, that performance of this sort is redundant, and that the filmmaker intervening in the machinery of the projector is itself the performance. The instrument has become the projector rather than the body or the screen, the live-produced images showing off not only the capacities of the projector but the technical skill of the projectionist/performer as well. The projector is normally viewed as a practical necessity rather than a creative tool, less variable than the camera, lens, filmstrip, or optical printer. But the discourses of filmmakers who engage in projection performance are replete with references to the liberation of the projector from its role as automatic reproduction machine and projectionist as merely passive operator or overseer. Both are removed from their place at the end of a long chain of filmmaking processes that they are expected only to reproduce automatically, consistently, and

[75] Sally Golding, "Expanded Cinema Unowned: Noise and Live-ness in the Contemporary," program notes for *Perpetual Motion*, a program of projection performance at the San Francisco Cinematheque, September 17–December 7, 2016.

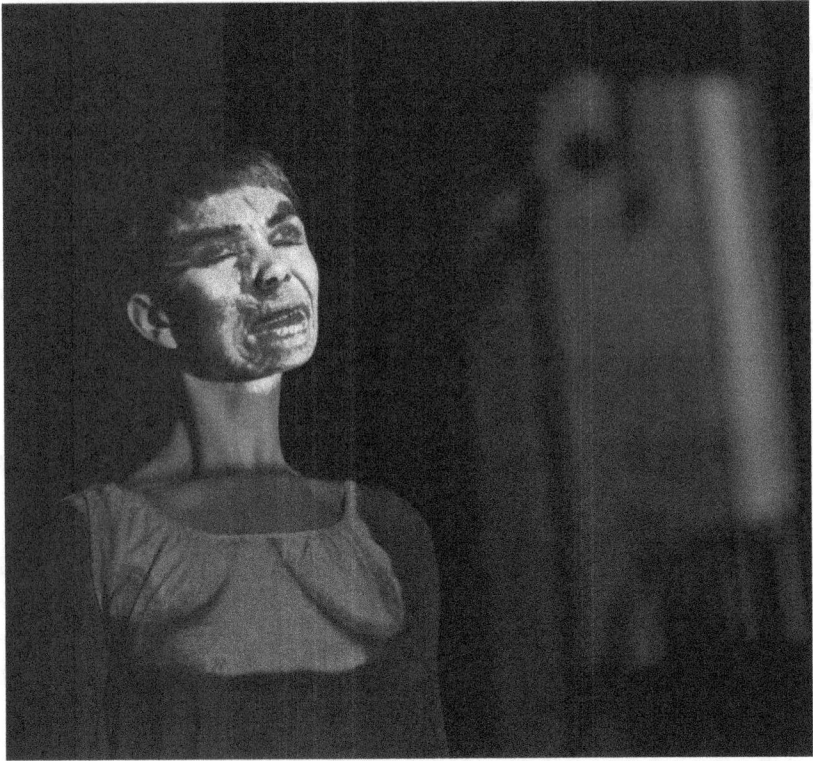

Fig. 3.23. Abject Leader (Sally Golding and Joel Stern), *The Face of Another* (2008). Performance documentation.

Photography by Steve Trigg. Image courtesy of Sally Golding.

predictably. Instead, they are made, in the words of Bruce McClure, "the star" rather than "cinema's silent and faithful servant "shunted to the wayside."[76]

In no other section of this book would the hope of comprehensively chronicling a form of contemporary expanded cinema be as forlorn as it is here. This is not just because of the sheer amount of it, nor the fact of its site-specificity and ephemerality—if one does not see it live, and adequate documentation does not exist, it is in effect gone forever. Beyond these factors, the challenge to the critic or historian addressing this kind of work is that it has become more than a "genre" or subtype of expanded cinema. It is as though the conditions of performance—liveness, interactivity, audience participation, and the courting of chance—have become those of contemporary avant-garde cinema itself. A performative approach to projection emerges organically from the personal, hands-on methodologies of filmmakers who continue to

[76] Bruce McClure, program notes for *Thwarted, Throttled, Thrown, and Then ... Thump ... !*, projection performance at Ocularis, Brooklyn, New York, March 13, 2006.

work with analog media, and extends logically from the technological, economic, and social conditions that obtain in the current experimental film world.

As I argued in chapter 2, the model of exhibition that defines contemporary avant-garde film, which is embodied in the microcinema though not limited to that space, is one of heightened sociality, participation and interaction, chance and improvisation, and a loose and heterogeneous approach to presentation. While these qualities have to a degree always marked this mode of film practice, contemporary experimental film has elevated them to the point that a difference of degree has become one of kind. The mobility of avant-garde filmmakers, their adaptability to so many different types of exhibition space, serves what could be called (without any negative connotation), opportunism: a willingness to work within whatever confines or parameters an open space presents, in the interest precisely of exhibiting in as many such spaces as possible. This demands an openness to improvisation, on-the-spot problem solving, and creativity with respect even to the often un-thought fundamentals of setting up seats, projectors, and screens. Those tasks hidden in commercial theatrical exhibition and the art world are by necessity visible in experimental film screenings, which might take place in "proper movie theaters, microcinemas, museums, galleries, classrooms, outdoor parks, a few planetariums, a Freemason's lodge, and more."[77] That is Roger Beebe's list of venues for his own work, which include multi-projector performances in tandem with single-channel films and videos. Beebe describes his initial foray into multiple projection, which led to performances for up to nine projectors, as the unintentional result of the accidental nature of the circumstances of exhibition. Traveling with two 16mm projectors to avoid lag time between films, Beebe decided on a whim to show his handmade film *TB/TX Dance* (2006), of which he had both a positive and negative print, in a dual projector, side-by-side, "poor man's cinemascope" version (fig. 3.24).[78]

During these shows, Beebe, presumably like other filmmakers, had to acclimate himself to the co-presence of viewer, filmmaker, and projectors in small, make-shift screening spaces. Taking an increasingly performative role as filmmaker-projectionist, Beebe essentially integrated this necessity of microcinema-type exhibition into his artistic method, eventually utilizing multiple projectors as the basis for new expanded work rather than simple expediency. This includes his best-known piece, *Last Light of a Dying Star* (2008/2011), performed with five 16mm, one 8mm, and, in some versions, three video projectors (fig. 3.25). *Last Light of a Dying Star* expands upon the faux-widescreen format Beebe created with *TB/TX Dance*, and can be seen as a deliberately ersatz Cinerama, using the battery of projectors to create a single, more or less seamless image. The imagery of *Last Light* comes from found 16mm and 8mm educational films on astronomy and Beebe's own handmade film loops, which include animated star images (produced by friend and fellow filmmaker

---

[77] Quoted in Kathryn Ramey, *Experimental Filmmaking: Break the Machine* (New York: Focal Press, 2016), p. 357.
[78] Ibid., p. 355.

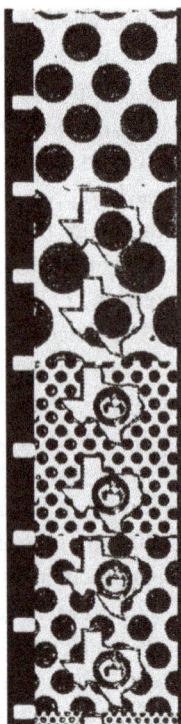

Fig. 3.24. Roger Beebe, *TB/TX Dance* (2006). Frame enlargement.
Image courtesy of Roger Beebe.

Jodie Mack), chemically treated bits of film, and a loop of opaque leader Beebe has punctured with a pin. The different film gauges and various lens lengths on the projectors produces a field of diverse aspect ratios, with frames often overlapping each other. Multiple prints of the same film allow Beebe to adjust the scale of his images and the overall shape of the composite compositions; for example, a high-contrast shot of solar flares from an educational film begins at the center of a triptych-style arrangement on screen, then suddenly flickers out to be replaced by two identical smaller images stacked one above the other. At the end of the performance, a small, lone image of Jupiter occupies the center of the screen as soft white blobs come into view, dancing around it. These blobs are the deliberately out of focus pinpricks of light shining through Beebe's hand-pierced black film loop, which he slowly brings into focus, evoking twinkling stars or meteor showers.

Last Light evokes the end of celluloid, a "dying star" referenced by Beebe's trashed and rescued educational films, displaced from classrooms long ago by videos and the internet. At least one of these films, however, would probably have informed us that the light of a dead star will continue to be visible on earth for centuries (the films are played without their soundtracks, the only sound is a prerecorded musical score and the clattering of the projectors). But *Last Light* also takes its formal structure from the

Fig. 3.25. Roger Beebe, *Last Light of a Dying Star* (2008/2011). Performance documentation.

Photograph by Nanci Unjung Lee, courtesy of Roger Beebe.

baseline decisions about projection made in the moment: the number of projectors, the lengths of their throws, lens types, positioning of images on screen, and so on. The interpersonal immediacy and ad hoc nature of avant-garde film exhibition endows it with what could be called muted or informal "liveness," which expanded works like Beebe's elevate into the truly performative.

Alex MacKenzie has traversed a similar arc from the quasi-liveness of micro-cinema exhibition to projection performance. Having founded and run two micro-cinemas between 1995 and 2003 (Edison Electric Gallery of Moving Images and Blinding Light!!! Cinema), MacKenzie amassed an enormous collection of found 16mm films. Following the format of many other microcinemas, which has its origins in Amos Vogel's Cinema 16, MacKenzie co-programmed avant-garde films with selections from his diverse collection of medical and instructional films, documentaries, PSAs, and the like. Becoming more appreciative of this type of filmic ephemera, MacKenzie began systematically working his way through his collection by viewing them on a Steenbeck editing machine, which also allowed him to scrutinize films frame-by-frame, in slow or fast motion, backward and forward, and in freeze frame. As he identified segments that particularly intrigued him, he began to rework them through optical printing or rephotography from the screen. Both processes enabled

Fig. 3.26. Alex MacKenzie performing *Parallax* (2005).
Image courtesy of Alex MacKenzie.

MacKenzie to recreate the experience of viewing films on the Steenbeck, an experience he extended further by projecting the resulting films live on dual analytic projectors. Like the Steenbeck, the analytic projectors gave MacKenzie precise control over the speed and direction of the films, in what he has called "a kind of spontaneous optical printing effect."[79] Added to these are other forms of manipulation, live or otherwise: chemical alteration of emulsion, movement of the projectors in mid-performance, and the use of external lenses, color gels, and hand masking.

In *Parallax* (2005), two reels of MacKenzie's painstakingly assembled and photochemically reworked found footage are projected side-by-side (fig. 3.26). MacKenzie then slowly angles the projectors inward, sliding their two projected frames together in superimposition, another effect normally achieved through optical printing but realized here in real time. The "poor man's version" of wide screen created by the diptych composition transforms into a low-tech, D-I-Y variant of 3D, as MacKenzie coaxes depth effects from the images by placing a gel over the lens of one of the projectors, or throwing one frame out of focus, producing the impression of distinct depth planes. A striking example appears in *Apparations* (2016), as superimposed images of train tracks, taken from the rear car of a moving train, are projected in opposite directions: forward on one projector, in reverse on the other (fig. 3.27). The image is a disorienting, impossible representation of the same space simultaneously advancing and receding, calling to mind Jacobs's Nervous System works.

[79] Mike Holboom, "Live and Letting: Alex Mackenzie Talks About Pictures," unpublished interview conducted for the 2005 Media City Film Festival, Windsor, Ontario, n.p.

Fig. 3.27. Alex MacKenzie, *Apparations* (2016). Performance documentation.
Image courtesy of Alex MacKenzie.

Note the give and take of contrasting values here. On one side are time-consuming processes: close viewing of hours of film on a Steenbeck, and laborious hand-processing methods, including burying film in the ground to await chemical change. On the other are strategies of immediacy: manipulations to the image performed live, in the moment, improvisationally. In an examination of the preponderance of hand-processing and long-term chemical manipulation of film in current experimental cinema, Kim Knowles identifies an "aesthetic and an ethic of slowness":

> On the one hand, the process involves a temporal investment on the part of the filmmaker that implies the art of waiting; on the other hand, the films register a deep geological or environmental time that presents an alternative to human notions of efficiency and instantaneity embedded within a society predicated on speed.[80]

Knowles contrasts this "slow cinema" with both earlier modernist films like Abel Gance's *La Roue* (1922) or Man Ray's *Emak Bakia* (1926), which celebrated speed and

---

[80] Kim Knowles, "Slow, Methodical, and Mulled Over: Analog Film Practice in the Age of the Digital," *Cinema Journal* 55, no. 2 (Winter 2016), p. 149.

dynamism, and modern digital technology, characterized by instantaneity and comparatively tiny lifespans.

In projection performances like MacKenzie's, handmade films carefully crafted over long periods of time, or found footage obsessively pored over, are brought into a format that restores a sense of immediacy to them. At the same time, however, manipulation of projectors creates analogs of time-honored avant-garde filmmaking devices like optical printing, repurposing found footage, or distressing the film surface by hand. Exhibition becomes a site where these things happen live. The operating distinction here, then, is not so much "fast vs. slow," but "slow vs. immediate," the time-consuming crafting of film objects (MacKenzie even crafts his own emulsion) versus the immediacy of liveness. And its ephemerality—the reels of *Parallax* or *Last Light of a Dying Star* are at least semi-permanent, but the on-the-fly machinations of the projector and the improvised responses to the specifics of screening space and audience only exist in the moment, and each performance is unique. MacKenzie acknowledges this tension, claiming to have been drawn to performance because "creating a store of work [finished films] was sucking me into commodity-like thinking . . . so I wondered how I could keep the development of these works alive, and performance seemed the obvious way. It also required my presence at screenings and enforced communication with audiences."[81]

"Immediacy" has two related meanings. There is temporal immediacy, wherein the effects produced by the filmmaker are perceptible immediately, and a physical or psychological sense of immediacy, when the distance between filmmaker, film object, and spectator is closed. The word "immediacy" literally means a lack of mediation, the removal of something standing between two other things. Projection performance encompasses both senses of the term, requiring the co-presence of filmmaker and audience and introducing live, which is to say immediate, variants of working methods that normally take place in the studio with the filmmaker in isolation. Thus, the experience of discovery in reviewing found footage finds its analog in the live projection of that footage on analytic projectors. The intimacy and laboriousness of hand processing is paralleled by the manual adjustments of focus, lens lengths, projection speed, projector position, or intensity and color of the beam.

A projection performance by the Crater Collective (Luis Macías and Adriana Vila Guevara), *3quinOx* (2013), offers an especially clear example of this. Four projectors are threaded with loops that flicker rapidly between black leader and a shot of a forest floor dappled by sunlight. Different loops contain different scales of this image, as if at different stages of a zoom in from a wide shot of the forest to a tighter shot of a brightly lit open space beyond the forest's edge (fig. 3.28). Taken together, they imply a movement out from the forest to an adjoining field via a slow zoom as in *Wavelength*. The composition suggests a corridor through the trees, which flank a rough path receding from the image plane and terminating at the edge of the

[81] Holboom, "Live and Letting."

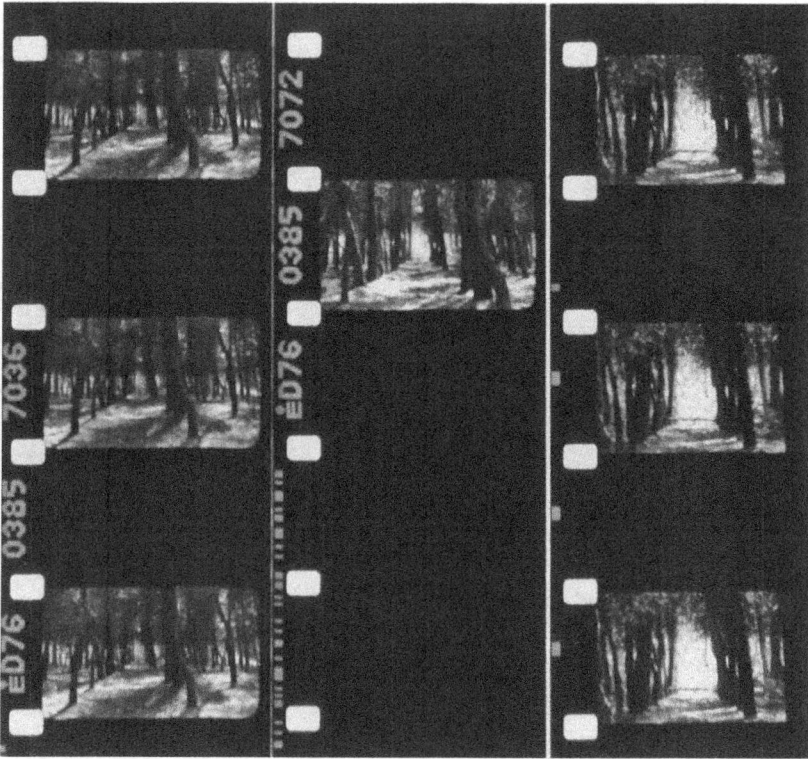

Fig. 3.28. Luis Macías and Adriana Vila Guevara (performing as Crater Collective), flicker loops for *3quinOx* (2013). Frame enlargements.
Courtesy of Luis Macías and Adriana Vila Guevara.

forest. In this way, it also recalls the lone image of Gehr's *Serene Velocity* (1970), a long hallway receding dramatically from the camera and ending in an exit door with a small window to the outside. Over the course of a single night, Gehr filmed this space one frame at a time, alternating the length of his zoom lens according to a predetermined metrical score. The resulting film is one of increasingly intense spatial expansion and contraction, what Sitney describes as a movement "from a vibrating pulse within an optical depth to an accordion-like slamming and stretching of the visual field."[82] There is no flicker in *Serene Velocity*, but the image scales alternate so rapidly, the lens length changing every four frames, that they trigger the same sorts of illusionistic effects as flicker. "Slamming and stretching" nicely captures the impression of violently advancing and receding depth in the film. An almost identical effect occurs in *3quinOx*, but is accomplished via projection. The different shot scales of the forest shown simultaneously on multiple projectors, each fitted with lenses of

---

[82] P. Adams Sitney, *Visionary Film: The American Avant-Garde, 1943–1978* (Oxford: Oxford University Press, 1979), p. 438.

Fig. 3.29. Luis Macías and Adriana Vila Guevara, *3quin0x* (2013). Performance documentation.

Courtesy of Luis Macías and Adriana Vila Guevara.

varying lengths, produce a composite, tunnel-like image of nested depth planes (fig. 3.29). Introducing flicker into each of these loops and adjusting focus during the performance results in a shimmering, ghostly image that never entirely coheres, in essence softening the percussive pounding of *Serene Velocity* without losing the strong impression of three-dimensionality. The filmmaker Lynn Loo achieves a similar effect with multiple overlapping projection in *Autumn Fog* (2010), in which identical color film prints—one negative, one positive—are projected one on top of the other. The footage is of foliage in Loo's garden in London, taken in early morning and late afternoon autumnal light; greens and oranges therefore predominate, inverted into oranges and greens in the negative footage, in an approximation of anaglyph stereoscopy (not unlike Le Grice's 1972 paracinematic performance *Horror Film 2*—see chapter 6). Leaves, branches, and a spider web stand out in striking bas relief, visible without special 3D glasses or filters.

Macías and Vila Guevara label *3quin0x* a "performance of Structural-Expanded Cinema," implying what is evident in the work itself: that projection performance is a means of recreating the familiar production techniques of avant-garde filmmaking in live form, restoring a sense of immediacy to them. The phrase "Structural-Expanded Cinema" suggests that slide from the customary methods of structural filmmakers done in production to analogs for these methods in projection. Luis Recoder has gone so far as to identify this facet of expanded cinema as the necessary step for anti-illusionist film practice. Reflecting on films by Owen Land and Paul Sharits that contain footage of filmstrips burning in a projector's gate, Recoder writes:

Land and Sharits' destructive efforts are in the end recuperated in the form of photographic reproductions, i.e., film prints ... all this is re-photographed by the camera, re-staged for its reproduction on light-sensitive film. And for this to be really real one would have to take it a step further, that is to take these burnt-frame films and put them through a kind of "second-degree burn" wherein the final product would in turn be destroyed during their projection before an audience.[83]

As Recoder points out, these films only appear to reveal the material beneath their photographic illusions. Hence, even as the most stridently anti-illusionist films purported to reveal film grain, sprocket holes, and framelines, they still required the illusions of apparent motion and flicker fusion. To overcome this impasse, Recoder shifts the burden of a genuinely anti-illusionistic film practice to the act of projection, an escape route from the recuperation by re-photography of putatively reflexive acts made upon film.

Sharits would have been aware of this, of course. His filmic objects and installations took the step Recoder urges, removing film from projection, and the projectors from their hiding places in booths, to display their materials and actions directly. He conceived of this act in terms of film's "object/projection duality," which, for him, severely complicated cinema's ontology.[84] Material objects so central to the kind of filmmaking Sharits practiced became something else in projection. Sharits's writings and expanded cinema exhaustively mapped out this object/projection dualism, mostly in the form of object-based works like the *Frozen Film Frames* series and film installations (see chapters 4 and 5). But his 1966 projection performance *Unrolling Movie Screen*, described earlier in this chapter, "actualized" the projector beam and thereby revealed its "projective and volumetric vectorial characteristics": in a word, its objecthood.[85] *Unrolling Movie Screen* thus performed the inextricability of space and time, and concomitantly of concrete objects and ephemeral experiences, central to the theory and practice of avant-garde cinema at the moment of cinema's first wave of expansion.

Unrolling Movie Screen also illustrated what Sharits called the "remarkable structural parallel, which is suggestive of new systems of filmic organization, between a piece of film and the projections of light through it; both are simultaneously corpuscular ('frames') and wave-like ('strip')."[86] This makes it an especially prescient work. It forecasts a "new system of filmic organization"—projection performance—for which the dualism of objecthood and ephemerality is the defining aesthetic preoccupation, and that further creates "structural parallels" linking the two sides of that dualism, as in works like *Parallax* and *3quin0x*. Projection performers seek to preserve

[83] Luis Recoder, "The Death of Structural Film: Notes Toward a Filmless Cinema," in a special supplement to *Spectator* 27 (Supplement 2007) on the occasion of "Deaths of Cinema," a conference organized by the Cinematic Arts graduate program of the University of Southern California, p. 27.

[84] Sharits, "Words Per Page," pp. 35–36.

[85] Ibid., p. 39.

[86] Ibid., p. 37.

something of the experience of working with the film object even as that object enters into the projector's mediation. The projector, then, has been reinvented not only as a new creative instrument but a powerful symbol of avant-garde cinema's ideals and aspirations, in contradistinction to the camera or film frame, for so long the principle visual signifiers of that film culture. The projector embodies cinema's essential dualism, its dialectical ontology, as those other objects cannot.

We can further specify the foregoing notions of "immediacy," and of bridging the ontological divide of object and projection, in terms of collapsing distinctions between production and exhibition. While the concept of modes of film practice distinguishes between the stages of production, distribution, and exhibition, each phase can nonetheless be taken as a microcosm of the entire mode, embodying its values in its own terms: as in the interactivity and "indecorousness" of the microcinema. It is only logical that, in a mode of film practice where the individual filmmaker retains control over every aspect of production and distribution, exhibition follows suit. Thus, though live expanded cinema is usually understood as cultivating chance and unpredictability within the usually automatic act of projection, it must also be seen as an extension of avant-garde filmmakers' desire to maintain control over their work, and to intervene in the machines and processes of cinema through the moment of exhibition.

Two of the earliest practitioners of projection performance envisioned their work in precisely these terms: the ensembles silt (Keith Evans, Christian Farrell, and Jeff Warrin) and La Cellule d'Intervention Metamkine (Jérôme Noetinger, Xavier Quérel, and Christophe Auger: Metamkine for short). Metamkine, who identify themselves as "researching the relationship between image and sound," find in live musical performance a model for breaking down the distinction between production and projection.[87] Live music combines these two phases much more seamlessly than cinema, where the object must be completed prior to screening. Metamkine's interventions in projection and creation of live sound, neither of which they regard as prior to or accompaniment for the other, are offered as instances of live filmmaking, where the processes of production unfold in real time before an audience. The interpenetration of pre-made object and improvisation, of "score" and "performance," is a consistent theme across their own writings and statements. By way of "ingenious live on-stage editing, Metamkine produces and directs a new film with each of their performances. Working around a core narrative, they spill eddies of impromptu vignettes."[88]

The three members of Metamkine set up in front of the audience, between screen and spectators, who are ideally on elevated, raked theater seats so they can see performers and projection alike (fig. 3.30). The intercession of bodies between audience and screen is of a different order here than in earlier instances of live cinema, of Le Grice, Nicolson, or Whitman. Metamkine's operations are not center stage; the visual effects of their actions rather than the actions themselves are the contents of

[87] From Metamkine's statement on their website, http://metamkine.free.fr/metamnotes.htm, n.p.
[88] Ibid.

Fig. 3.30. La Cellule d'Intervention Metamkine (Jérôme Noetinger, Xavier Quérel, and Christophe Auger) performing in Spike Island, Bristol, during Arika's 2008 Kill Your Timid Notion Tour.
Courtesy of Bryony MacEntyre.

the work, and they require the screening space to be as dark as possible. Quérel and Auger operate two banks of three 16mm projectors placed on either side of the floor and aimed toward the audience rather than the screen. Two large mirrors reflect the projected images onto the screen, an arrangement that increases the "throw," or distance between projector and screen, significantly magnifying the images. Additional projectors run from a table behind the spectators in a more conventional theatrical screening setup. Between the two mirrors, also on the floor, Noetinger produces sound from tape loops and long outdated synthesizers—all Metamkine's materials are analog.

The projected films are mostly of Metamkine's own making, hand processed at their lab Atelier MTK, a miniature version of the London Filmmakers' Cooperative and further evidence of the group's desire to consolidate and control all phases of production and post-production. Quérel and Auger adjust focus, insert gels, film reels, and their own hands and bodies into the projector beams, and the projectors themselves cast giant distorted shadows onto the screen as light bounces about the space unpredictably. The images shift suddenly from projected films to shadowplay; moving images abruptly halt as a film is held by force in the projector gate and begins to melt; projectors and mirrors are moved, sliding the projections off the screen and across the room. Because at least six projectors are in use, a nest of images fills and overflows the screen, the individual layers impossible to discern until one of the projectors is moved or thrown out of focus. What at first looks like a single image of abstract forms and blotches of color is revealed to be a composite of multiple projections as one element evaporates into soft focus or slips off the edge of the screen. This composite image expands or contracts in quasi-3D as each layer transforms. Each of these "moves" is analogizable to a corresponding cinematographic or editing choice—camera movements, focus pulls, cuts, dissolves, fades, and split screen effects.

The approach silt took to projection performance was similar to Metamkine's, consisting centrally of hand-made and hand-processed films on multiple projectors, with live adjustments of focus, image size and color, and manual interventions into the path of the beam by objects and bodies. But silt's model was not live music. What appears to have made silt's members, all filmmakers in their own right, turn to live projection was a related desire for immediacy and for muddying the distinction between making and projecting films. But this took form according to a much different source. A hint of this source is found in one of the many characteristically brief references to silt in experimental film literature. In a 1997 interview with Scott MacDonald, Brakhage interrupted a discussion of his film *Commingled Containers* (1997) to marvel at a film he watched Warrin make during a visit to Brakhage's home in Colorado:

> Jeff Warrin came to Boulder and got so excited about *Commingled Containers* that we went to Boulder Creek and upstaged me beautifully. He took just a Kodachrome Super-8mm cartridge, which has a little aperture that he covered with tape and then put a pinhole through it. He picked up a stick, something he could turn the film with, and stuck the whole thing under Boulder Creek and turned the film, exposing frames. Well, of course, with a pinhole camera he is getting infinite focus, so you see all the little bubbles in all directions and whatever little thing that is coming down that stream, every little piece of dirt and whatnot—it's a fabulous, fantastic, beautiful film.[89]

Brakhage's anecdote, and particularly his use of the word "upstaged," is revealing. To make *Commingled Containers* Brakhage had used a special device for microphotography attached to his camera and submerged into the waters of Boulder Creek. His description of the process emphasized his deliberate misuse of this device in the interest of a less mediated filmmaking process. Previously he had avoided using the microphotography device because it came with a complex manual and series of charts for determining proper exposure, exactly the kind of "proper" filmmaking Brakhage famously subverted across his career. Brakhage's improvisatory shooting methods, his willful violation of the rules of filmmaking, and his obsession with nature imagery are all facets of an aesthetic of immediacy, of an intimacy with both nature and Brakhage's own interior subjective world. To achieve this required Brakhage to overcome the technological, rule-laden mediation of his physical medium. Warrin's "upstaging" of

[89] Scott MacDonald, *A Critical Cinema 4: Interviews with Independent Filmmakers* (Berkeley: University of California Press, 2005), p. 115.

Brakhage was in his even more direct, de-mediated filming of the older filmmaker's home turf, without camera, lens, or the parameters of proper focus or exposure.

Thus, silt's performances translated Brakhagean filmmaking procedures to projection, and were insistent on de-mechanizing the medium and treating it almost as an object from the natural world. All silt's films were hand processed and subjected to organic post-processing chemical treatments: buried, left out in the environment (on the forest floor, for example), rusted, and affixed with organic debris (figs. 3.31 and 3.32). Live performance extended these acts of de-mechanization, both by resisting the automaticity of the projector and introducing natural objects like leaves, branches, and animal bones into projection. Filmed images gave way to empty projector light casting shadows of sticks and pine boughs placed into the path of the projector, or affixed to the projector to slowly rotate on a jerry-rigged takeup reel. In one of their *Field Studies* performances of the early 2000s, Evans, Farrell, and Warrin each operated one of three 8mm projectors whose images formed a triptych composition on screen. Films made without a camera and therefore frameless, dubbed "microfossilographs" by Evans (fig. 3.33), were projected through branches and fern fronds, their distorted shadows looming out from the screen or receding into its imagined depths.

silt referred to themselves as "paranaturalists," a term Evans still uses today as a solo artist. "Para" indicates more than an analogy, but a homological relationship between filmmaking and naturalist inquiry. "The dynamism of the landscape [silt's Bay Area home] is mirrored in the varied perspectives and improvised cinematic techniques they employ. silt's process-oriented approach to filmmaking results in performances that are uniquely organic."[90] This takes "experimental filmmaking" literally, extending the idea of naturalist observation into the moment of projection. This would become perhaps the central theme of the generation of projection performers that came after silt and Metamkine, the expansion of shooting and post-production activities into exhibition, even to the extent that film and camera became far less significant than the projector.

The Exploded View: Plumbing the Depths of Projection

While not the first projection performance, Hollis Frampton's "A Lecture" (sometimes known as "Hunter College Lecture") is nevertheless the ur-text of the form. While best known as a printed text, it was initially a performance that staged, among other things, the automaticity of film projection and audio playback. A recording of the lecture, written by Frampton but read by Michael Snow, played on a tape machine on a table beneath the screen at the front of the lecture space.

---

[90] Program notes for "silt: Field Studies," a performance at the Headlands Center for the Arts, October 23, 1998. https://archive.org/stream/sanfranciscocine98sanfrich/sanfranciscocine98sanfrich_djvu.txt, n.p.

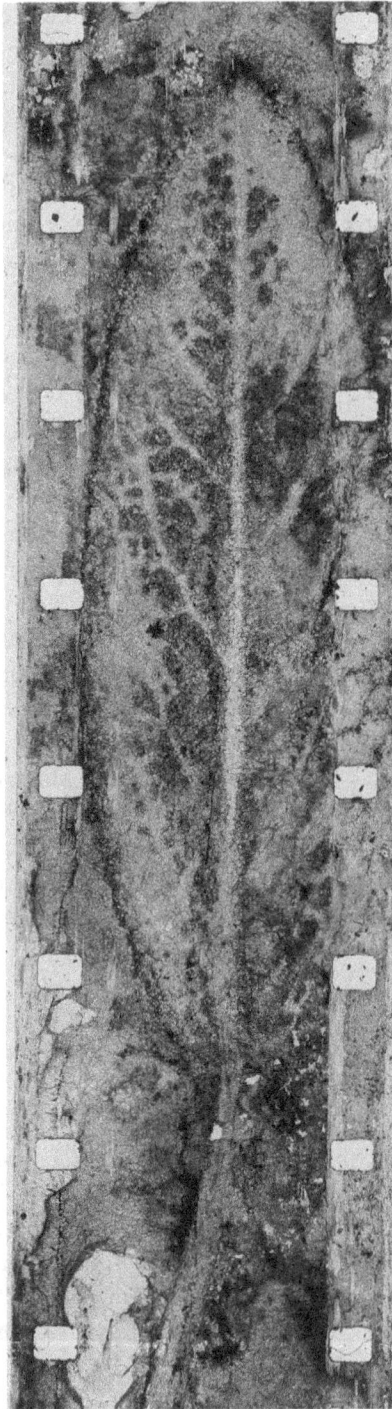

Fig. 3.31. silt (Keith Evans, Christian Farrell, and Jeff Warrin), 16mm filmstrip "sage."
Image courtesy of Keith Evans.

Fig. 3.32. silt (Keith Evans, Christian Farrell, and Jeff Warrin), 16mm filmstrip "snakeskin."
Image courtesy of Keith Evans.

Fig. 3.33. silt (Keith Evans, Christian Farrell, and Jeff Warrin), 16mm "microfossilograph."
Image courtesy of Christian Farrell.

A handful of instructions for the projectionist, operating a film-less projector at the back of the room, appear in the text but were not read by Snow. At points during the roughly 25-minute performance, the projectionist was instructed to turn the projector on, place a red gel over the lens, block the lens completely with a hand, and insert a pipe cleaner into the projector gate, casting its shadow onto the screen. According to Frampton, each tiny intervention in the beam counted as a film, including simply allowing the projector to run without film, making what Frampton called an "eternal" rectangle of light: "Only we come and go: we say 'This is where I came in.' The rectangle was here before we came, and it will be here after we're gone."[91] In the simultaneously expansive and reductive view typical of Frampton's writing, filmmaking is nothing more or less than "devising things to put into our projector," such as the red gel over the lens or the pipe cleaner pushed into the gate.[92] The implication is that the machine was built around the film, manufactured to its specifications, and thus subservient to it, its eternal rectangle always awaiting new films. The projector was

> a precision machine. It sits behind us, out of sight usually. Its range of action may be limited, but within that range it is, like an animal, infallible. It reads, so to speak, from a score that is both the notation and the substance of the piece.[93]

Frampton famously once spoke for three hours on the subject of film processing, exhaustively cataloging the "parameters of processing" and making a case for

---

[91] Frampton, "A Lecture," in Sitney, ed., *The Avant-Garde Film*, p. 276.
[92] Ibid.
[93] Ibid.

avant-garde filmmakers to regain control over a means of production that had been taken from them by the industry.[94] In other words, processing had been rendered automatic, removed from the sight of filmmakers who simply shipped their exposed films to the lab. Frampton cast processing as a final frontier for experimental filmmakers. Replace "processing" in "the parameters of processing" with "projection," and we get an idea of a new final frontier, a plumbing of the depths of projection, even to the extent of eliminating film, an act of de-centering celluloid in favor of the mechanics, optics, and the very institution of projection. Bruce McClure, one of the foremost projection performers, phrases this in direct response to Frampton's lecture. In "Know Thy Instrument," McClure inverts Frampton's conception of the relationship between film and projector:

Lit by the open gate of a projector, my reappraisal of cinematic heirlooms responds to the charge that "the art of making films consists in devising things to put into our projector." To me disclosing the projector gate is as plain as housework; an invitation to enjoy light's compass across a room free of clutter and film's distress … I fancy myself outlined as a renegade, a claim jumper, disregarding film's title and taking possession of the territory inside the projector … During my tenancy of a room, I measure it by a projector's metes and bounds and film is parceled to an administrative capacity like the timing belt of a reciprocating engine.[95]

McClure's statement suggests a process of externalization, of making the "invisible" tiny interiors and operations of the projector visible, a process that simultaneously diminishes the importance of film.

McClure performs with two to four 16mm projectors and flicker loops (fig. 3.34), occasionally incorporating found footage into his work as well (he has repeatedly denied being a "filmmaker," as he does not use a camera or make his own footage). He makes the flicker loops using black (opaque) leader, determining the ratio of black to clear film and using bleach to remove the emulsion from individual frames accordingly. The projector's optical sound head reads the clear frames as white noise, so a flicker loop produces both a visual and sonic pulse, though these are out of sync with one another given the 26-frame distance between the projector's aperture and sound head. Multiple projectors running loops with different ratios of black and clear frames produce overlapping rhythms that shift in and out of phase. McClure projects these images onto the same space on

[94] Hollis Frampton, "Processing Parameters," *Millennium Film Journal* 56 (Fall 2012), pp. 77–87. The lecture was delivered on May 1, 1976, at "The Materials of Film: A Conference on the Basic Elements of the Medium and Its Operations," held at the Center for Media Study at SUNY Buffalo. See Gerald O'Grady's introduction to the transcribed lecture in *Millennium Film Journal* 56 (Fall 2012), pp. 74–76.
[95] Bruce McClure, *Know Thy Instrument* (Milan: Atelier Impopulaire, 2014), p. 16. McClure's essay was published with Frampton's lecture in a "split" edition.

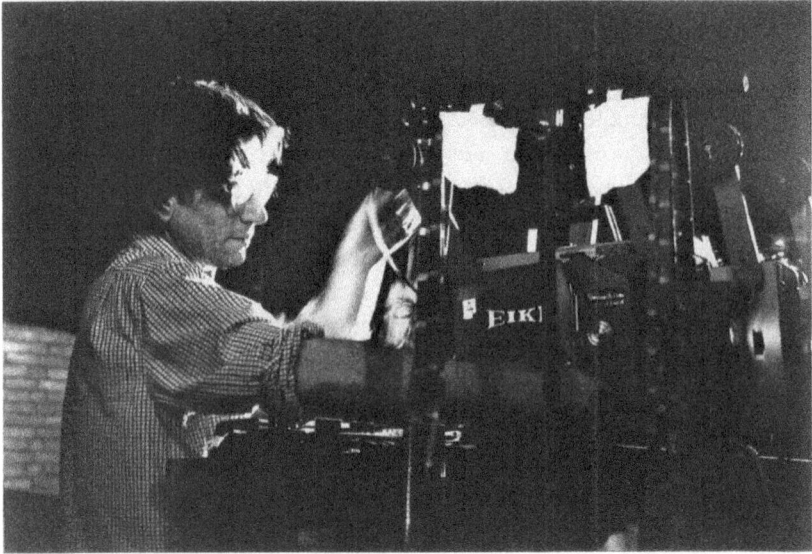

Fig. 3.34. Bruce McClure with projectors and flicker film loops (foreground right), at the 44th International Film Festival, Rotterdam, Netherlands. January 23, 2015.
Photo: Robin Martin, courtesy of Bruce McClure.

the screen, producing a composite image that slowly unfolds through permutations of superimposition, which are further adjusted—always quite slowly and methodically—as McClure manipulates the focus and brightness of the projectors. Having wired rheostats into his projectors, he has precise control over the intensity of each projector's light; when multiple projectors are running simultaneously, each with different loops and projecting through gels, McClure can make extraordinarily subtle adjustments to the brightness, color, size, and shape of the frame. McClure further alters the images from his projectors even further by soldering handcrafted metal plates into their gates, masking part of the familiar light rectangle or changing its shape (fig. 3.35). In *Christmas Tree Stand* (2004), he fitted the gates of four projectors with metal plates into which he had stamped circular holes and covered with thin metal mesh, resulting in a circle of light crisscrossed by an animated moiré pattern, a flickering orb within which squares of different hues throbbed and rotated kaleidoscopically (fig. 3.36).

In some performances, McClure "bi-packs" his loops, loading a flicker loop and a found footage loop together into a single projector, one loop inside the other. Because the opaque frames block the images and sounds of the found footage loops while the clear sections allow this information through, the found material is essentially molded to the pattern of the flicker loop, which acts as a kind of template or stencil through which the documentary's pictures and soundtrack intermittently burst. In the series *Pie Pelicane Jesu Domine* (2008–2010), for example, two short loops from a

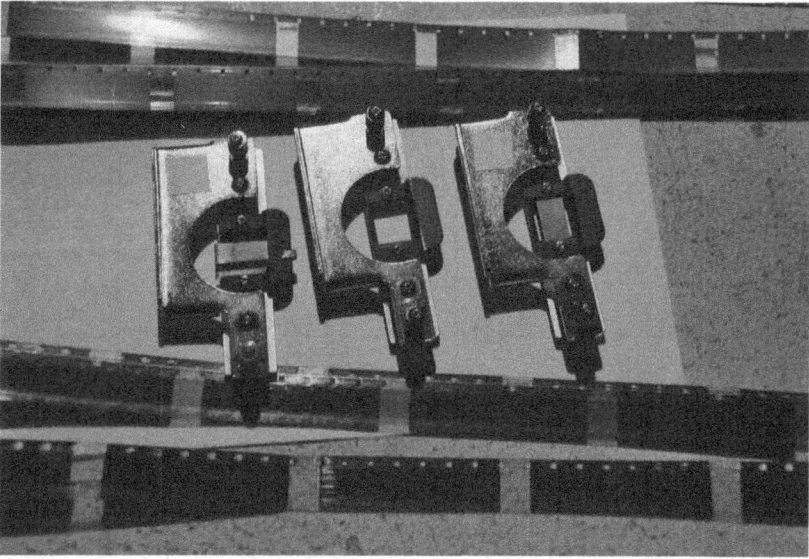

Fig. 3.35. Bruce McClure, flicker film loops and modified projector gate inserts for *Unnamed Complement* (2007).
Image courtesy of Bruce McClure.

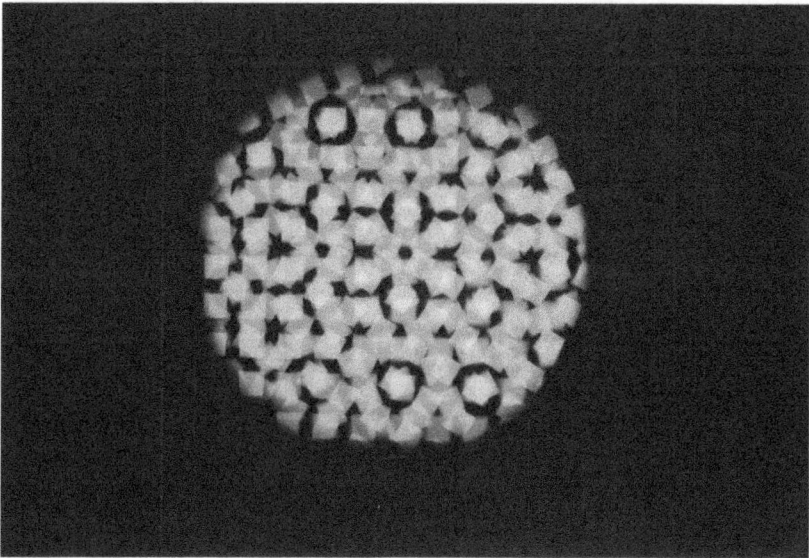

Fig. 3.36. Bruce McClure, *Christmas Tree Stand* (2004). Performance for four 16mm projectors, each fitted with hole-punched brass pressure plates covered by screens oriented at 45, 60, 75, and 90 degrees.
Photo: Robin Martin, courtesy of Bruce McClure.

Fig. 3.37. Bruce McClure, frames from positive and negative flicker loops used in *And Like Their Parents They Lift Their Heavy Bodies From Their Perches* (from the series *Pie Pelicane Jesu Domine*, 2008–2010).
Photo: Robin Martin, courtesy of Bruce McClure.

nature documentary about birds are nested inside flicker loops and projected in superimposition. The imagery barely changes, consisting of only a few seconds' worth of action (two pelicans in their nest, one suddenly lifting its wings and flying off), but McClure extends this into a nearly 50 minute process of variation on brightness, color, flicker rhythm, on screen movement, and sound (fig. 3.37).

Descriptions of McClure's performances almost always attribute a strong sense of physicality to them; they are "physically intense," "visceral," "vertiginous," "throbbing," "aggressive," and "violent." They are notorious for placing extreme demands on the senses. A typical account of McClure's performances describes the difficulties they pose: "A certain uneasiness usually accompanies the onset of one of Bruce's performances; sensory overload—both visual and aural—is par for the course … At some point … you either walk out, or give in."[96] In addition to subjecting viewers to intense flicker over long periods of time, McClure also patches the projector's sound through a battery of guitar effects pedals and sound synthesizers and massively amplifies them to levels of over 100 decibels.

Ventriloquent Agitators (2010) is a performance for four 16mm projectors, each threaded with one of four identical flicker loops that project a single frame of light four times per second (a ratio of one clear frame to five opaque ones). Though the loops are structured identically, they do not flicker in synchronization as they are threaded on four different machines, all unavoidably varying by tiny increments from a perfect 24-frame-per-second projection speed. Each projector is aimed at a different quadrant of the screen, producing a window pane–like grid of two upper and two lower frames, each only visible in the instant one of the lone transparent frames of film passes through the projector gate; otherwise, the opaque leader completely blocks the light from the projector's lamp.

---

[96] Che Chen, "Interview with Bruce McClure," *O Sirhan, O Sirhan* no. 2 (2007), p. 1.

McClure has soldered tiny metal squares into one corner of each projector's aperture, which leave a square notch of shadow in a different corner of each white frame. McClure strategically arranges the projectors so that these notches meet in the middle of the flickering grid; the impression on screen is of a single large flickering frame of light whose center is blocked by a square shadow that appears to hover just over the surface of the screen (fig. 3.38). That is, the shadows of the four metal notches "read" as a single shape, just as the four flashing frames tend to be perceived as a single square of flickering light. Looking at digital documentation of the performance frame by frame reveals that no more than two squares of light are visible at any one time, a result of the asynchronization of the four projectors. But in real time, the light flickers rapidly enough to trigger the illusion that all four white frames are simultaneously visible, or almost so, with the added illusion of a kind of spiraling motion, an apparent rotation of the frames around the central black square cast by the carefully aligned notches in each projector's gate.

As the piece unfolds, McClure adjusts focus on each projector, shifting focus from the edges of the projected frame to the metal plates soldered into the apertures. When the edges of the frames are in focus, the outline of the internal black square is soft, and vice-versa. During the central portion of the approximately 45-minute performance, McClure focuses on the aperture plates themselves, making their outline crisp against the much fuzzier-edged light frames. This makes for the striking visual effect

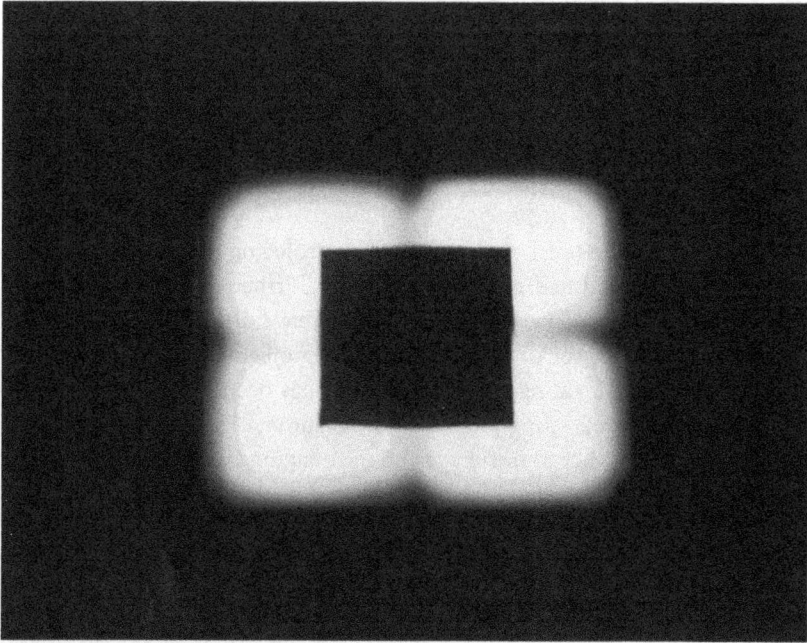

Fig. 3.38. Bruce McClure, *Ventriloquent Agitators* (2010). Performance documentation. Photo: Robin Martin, courtesy of Bruce McClure.

of a solid square object somehow floating in the air in front of the projectors. Shadow becomes almost tangible, as though one could grasp the dark object and remove it from the projector beams' path. Variations in focus also trigger depth illusions. When the black square is in focus, it appears to hover in front of the screen, but as McClure shifts the focus to the edges of the flashing frames the interior shadow seems to recede into illusory depth, as though the flickering frames are being sucked into a black void at the center of the screen.

The characteristic techniques of McClure's performances—dimming the projectors' lights, altering the shape of the beam, privileging the action of the projectors' sound heads, and mostly using films without photographic imagery—are strategies of resistance to "the hegemony of the film frame," against which McClure proposes "recognizing the integrated structures of projection."[97] Focus plays the key role in this. The metal objects McClure solders into the projector become added focal planes, what he calls "stops along the way" between film plane and screen.[98] McClure reminds us that when a movie is "out of focus," the projector is simply focused on another part of its own gate. For the image content to be in focus, the edges of the frame must be soft—these are the edges of the projector's own internal mechanism:

> One may focus on the frame, or on the film plane. When you focus on the film you often see a fuzzy boundary … Then you can focus on the gate or the aperture that's in the shoe, which gives you a crisp edge. The content of the film consequently becomes blurry … Then the pieces of metal, they are a third thing that you can focus on. So you have these different focal planes, any of which can be called "in focus." Ordinarily one looks at the grain of the film, or the image on the surface of the frame, or the surface of the film itself. And when these things are in focus, you say, "Oh, well the film is in focus." Anything other than that is out of focus. With these metal plates, you start to demarcate positions of focus that didn't exist before.[99]

In identifying multiple focal planes *within* the projector, and creating additional such planes in his modified machines, McClure further de-centers the filmstrip from its privileged place in cinema's ontology: "I have dislocated the homologous relationship between sprocketed frames and the projector's rotational timing," he writes, another way of stating that the projector has been built around the structure of the filmstrip, relegating projection to an automatic operation requiring no artistry, only subservience to the image and the imagined narrative world it usually projects.[100]

[97] Bruce McClure, program notes for "Live Cinema: Walls of Sound," presented by the San Francisco Cinematheque at the San Francisco Exploratorium, October 25, 2007.
[98] Bruce McClure, "Interview with Brian Frye," *Brooklyn Rail* (July 2006). http://www.brooklynrail.org/2006/07/film/bruce-mcclure-with-brian-frye, n.p.
[99] Ibid.
[100] McClure, program notes for *Live Cinema: Walls of Sound.*

The title *Ventriloquent Agitators* likens the projector to a liberated ventriloquist's dummy no longer being told by someone else what to say. McClure dubs the metal plates in this performance "salient agitators," which "intercede and emancipate the projector and its incandescence from servitude to film's foreground scenics."[101] The flickering image of the film plane in *Ventriloquent Agitators* is indeed displaced from the foreground by the hard-edged shadow of the intervening metal plates, which, when in sharp focus, hovers in front of the fuzzy blocks of projected light. The abstraction of McClure's work, then, is only apparent. It is more accurate to say that the visuals are indexes of the interior of the projector. Projection is externalized and amplified, hidden materials and mechanisms enlarged and given palpable form.

In making projection the seat of the essentially cinematic, McClure often makes anthropomorphic analogies between the projector and the audio-visual sensorium of the viewer. That other machine so often humanized by experimental filmmakers—the camera—is dead in McClure's idiosyncratic metaphorical universe:

> The movie camera engraves light traces on silver lockets. I prefer the giving company of a movie projector that can paradoxically transubstantiate still births reviving them in the minds of the living ... I am fortunate to share the reciprocity of this fascinating machine [the projector] and our senses ... This living hand—see, here it is—I hold it toward you.[102]

This variation of contemporary experimental cinema's organic analogies valorizes projector over camera, and projection and viewing over the making of films. For McClure, who routinely insists that he is not a "filmmaker," camera and film are dead objects. The projector, a "giving" presence whose inner workings are analogous to the audience's perceptual mechanisms, reanimates the dead past locked in the cold, inorganic chemistry of photographic emulsion. The experience of projection is, once again, immediate, compared to the indirect, illusory experience of seeing a fictional world preserved in the chemistry of the filmstrip.

Writing of his projection performances with Sandra Gibson, Luis Recoder places the projector squarely at the center of a cinematic ontology in which materiality and ephemerality commingle:

> What is simultaneously projected and thus superimposed in a kind of double-projection is the intermittent play of cinematic illusion and disillusion. However, the maintenance of this material-immaterial dialectic (perhaps embodied in the figure of the projectionist) quickly transpires in the dissolving forgetfulness of an audio-visual seduction.[103]

---

[101] Bruce McClure, program notes for *Ventriloquent Agitators*.

[102] Bruce McClure, program notes for *Locative Enigma, Frameshape of Hard Mettles, a Personal Problem* (2009). Performed at the Nightingale Cinema in Chicago on April 24, 2009, n.p.

[103] Luis Recoder, "Performative Contradictions," included in the program notes for a program of performances by Gibson and Recoder, with sound artist Olivia Block, presented at the Serralves Foundation in Portugal, October 1–2, 2011, n.p.

Recoder is referring to conventional projection in this passage, prior to any re-invention by avant-garde filmmakers. The ultimate illusion of cinema is not the occlusion of the medium's materials, but of the dialectic taking place in projection wherein machines and other objects produce insubstantial images. The "audio-visual seduction" is the on-screen world consumed by moviegoers, doubly immaterial: made of light, and fictional, what Robert Smithson called "a wilderness of elsewheres."[104] The hyphenate "audio-visual" speaks to the apparent unity of synchronized images and sounds, which in reality—the reality of projection—are separate objects and distinct mechanical processes.

Recoder wrote this of *Aberration of Light: Dark Chamber Disclosure* (2010–2011), a performance for two 35mm projectors linked by the "changeover system," which under normal exhibition circumstances allows the multiple reels of a feature-length film to be projected without interruption, alternating automatically and seamlessly between projectors. This is another illusion created by the projector, in which multiple reels of film are experienced as a continuous flow of light, time, space, and narrative. The irony of the word "disclosure" in the title is that in this and almost all their projection performances, Gibson and Recoder work in the projection booth, something they have expressed as a preference and in fact as critical to their work. Like traditional projectionists, Gibson and Recoder are invisible to the audience, secluded in darkness and sealed away (fig. 3.39). If their aim is to "disclose" some defining feature of projection, this purposeful invisibility seems an odd choice. But the contradiction is only apparent; Gibson and Recoder forego a simplistic baring of the device, which Recoder calls "meta-cinema's catastrophic attempts at medium-specific self-reflexivity," the same recuperation of filmic materialism by illusion for which Recoder critiqued Land and Sharits.[105] Gibson and Recoder's performances are precisely about projection, not simply the projector—the act not reduced to the machine. "*Aberration of Light* performs the concealed contradiction of the cinematic apparatus within the apparatus itself. For it cannot be pried open, teased-out, or unveiled in any other fashion."[106] That is, Gibson and Recoder begin with the projector in its standard context, the home territory of the movie theater and projection booth. They have called this "projecting projection," thereby characterizing projection performance as a redundant term, the "elevation" of the already performative work of projection to a "second degree awareness" (that of the spectator). In the statement that opens this chapter, Gibson and Recoder paint a picture of the projector itself as performing either its absence—the "negation of its mediation"—or its "resistance as a passive carrier."[107]

This is the ground against which Gibson and Recoder "pry open" projection, mostly through the sculpting of light and re-shaping of image by the lens, which is

[104] Robert Smithson, "A Cinematic Atopia," *Artforum* (September 1971), p. 53.
[105] Luis Recoder, "Performative Contradictions."
[106] Ibid.
[107] Sandra Gibson and Luis Recoder, "Projecting Projection," paper presented at the Society for Cinema and Media Studies Conference, March 2011, New Orleans, LA, p. 1.

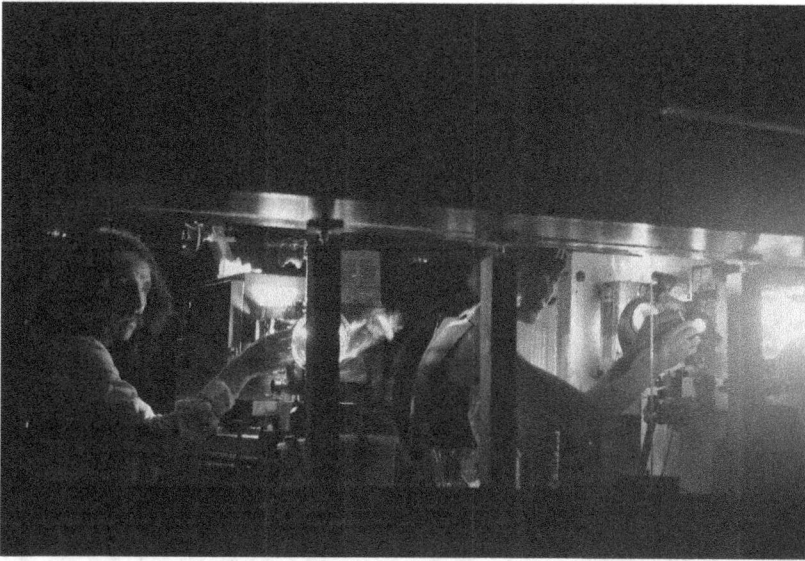

Fig. 3.39. Sandra Gibson and Luis Recoder performing *Aberration of Light: Dark Chamber Disclosure* (2010–2011). 35mm film, dual 35mm projection changeover performance, glassware, hardware, audio by Olivia Block, 50 minutes.
Photo: João Brites. Courtesy of the artists and Curtas.

doubled by an array of substitute "lenses" the duo employs: crystals, glasses, color gels, liquid and steam, their hands, and external irises that allow them to control the brightness of the projector's beam. The normally stable, seemingly solid and continuous rectangle of light on screen shimmers, undulates, drifts in and out of focus, fades in and out. Wavering, smoky light forms, barely taking shape, appear and disappear, rotate side to side, or in and out of the illusory depth of the screen (fig. 3.40). To heighten the impression of a liminal zone between objecthood and immateriality, Gibson and Recoder use found footage in *Aberration of Light*, a relative rarity in their performances. A vaguely recognizable image—someone walking through the frame, a figure seated at the wheel of a car—briefly materializes before dissolving into a field of light and color that moves like billowing smoke or rippling water. The imperfections on the hand-blown glass vases that slowly rotate on turntables in front of the projector lenses read on screen as waves passing through the indistinct images.

This use of found footage, the sources of which Gibson and Recoder do not reveal to their audience, throws into relief their material–immaterial dialectic. The film and its captured images serve as a foil for the operations of the projector, which, as in McClure's work, is no longer made to reproduce the images perfectly. The stability and clarity of these images in regular exhibition rests on a very narrow, specific use of the projector: consistent brightness, focus on the film plane, softening of the image's otherwise sharp edges, masking, and, of course, a lens built to reproduce both the camera's lens and normal human vision. Gibson and Recoder reverse this, varying

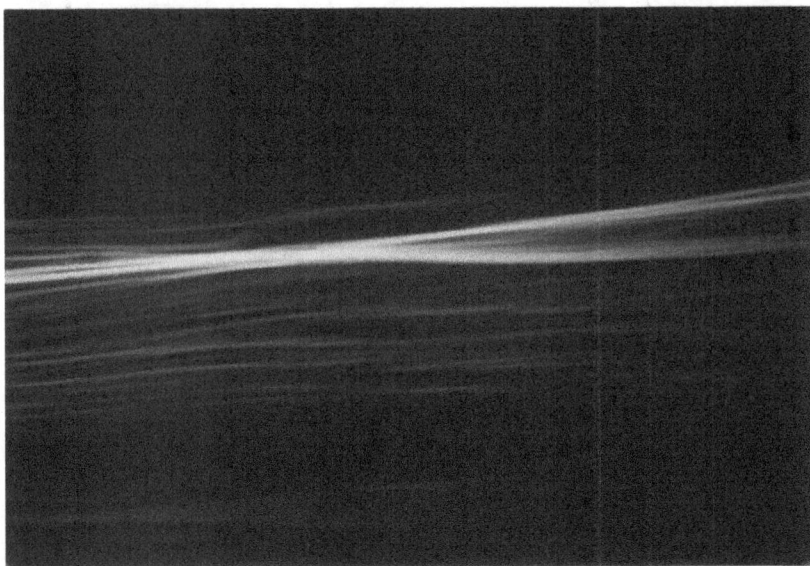

Fig. 3.40. Sandra Gibson and Luis Recoder, *Aberration of Light: Dark Chamber Disclosure* (2010–2011). 35mm film, dual 35mm projection changeover performance, glassware, hardware, audio by Olivia Block, 50 minutes.
Photograph by Gibson + Recoder. Courtesy of the artists.

the parameters of projection to produce an unstable and often unrecognizable image. The image of the film gives way to the "image" of projection itself, the modulation of light unbound by the dictates of photographic illusion and narrative designed into the machine.

In many of their other performances, Gibson and Recoder use handmade flicker loops similar to McClure's, substituting pure light and darkness for image content. *Untitled* (2008) begins with no film at all. Two filmless projectors are aimed at the same area of the screen, each affixed with a different length lens so that one frame of light is smaller, and nested in the other (fig. 3.41). Changes in focus on one or both projectors cause the frames to soften and expand, or to sharpen and contract, the effect being the occasional disappearance of one or both frames as their sharp edges go out of focus. Both projectors' beams pass through small panes of glass mounted over tiny humidifiers, which fog the glass and cause each image to shimmer, further destabilizing the rectangles of light. In the second half of the piece, Gibson and Recoder introduce loops of bleached black leader. Where the bleach has been sprayed, the opaque emulsion has been eaten away to varying degrees, blocking the light intermittently and unpredictably, creating a flickering, pock-marked image. These abstract loops are introduced in one projector first, which is completely out of focus and partially dimmed by an external iris. The flickering splotches of the bleached leader thus exceed the bounds of the other projector's frame and at first are not even recognizable.

Fig. 3.41. Sandra Gibson and Luis Recoder, *Untitled* (2008). 16mm film, dual 16mm projection performance, humidifiers, glass, hardware, audio by Olivia Block, 42 minutes. Limited edition DVD on SoS Editions.
Courtesy of the artists and SoS Editions.

As they are slowly brought into focus, they come to resemble sparkles of light dancing on the surface of the screen, an effect similar to the one Roger Beebe created for *Last Light of a Dying Star* by punching holes into black leader (fig. 3.42). Slowly this image is focused, the soft orbs of light contracting, pulling within the bounds of the other projector's frame, becoming lumpy monochromatic forms in a chaotic swirl. This is followed by the same procedure on the other projector, which adds another layer of abstract imagery over the first. The performance ends as both projectors are once again unfocused and the external irises are closed down in a slow fade to black. The duo has interpreted this structure as a "curve [that] is telling a story about the history of cinema: before there was film, magic lanterns just lit up the screen, and then slowly, after 15–20 minutes, the introduction of film, and what is film but movement and rhythm."[108] By this reading, the slow fade out harkens the end of cinema, or at least of filmic cinema. But given the imagined historical origins of cinema symbolized by the pre-filmic section of *Untitled*, this is not the death knell it might sound like. Gibson and Recoder's de-centering of film from the central position of cinema's history reflects a cinematic ontology from which film has vanished. "To ask about cinema is not the same thing as [to] ask about film," they have written, going on to displace a distinction between materiality and immateriality across a series of biological metaphors: film is "rotting flesh made up of bones" (in reference to the gelatinous nature

---

[108] In a recorded interview with Mario Kozina conducted during the 2012 25 FPS Festival in Zagreb. See https://vimeo.com/54849141.

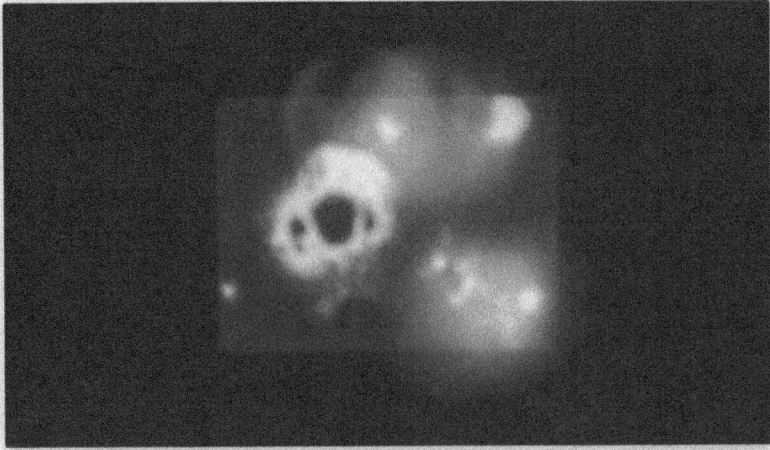

Fig. 3.42. Sandra Gibson and Luis Recoder, *Untitled* (2008). 16mm film, dual 16mm projection performance, humidifiers, glass, hardware, audio by Olivia Block, 42 minutes. Limited edition DVD on SoS Editions.
Courtesy of the artists and SoS Editions.

of emulsion); film is "the long intestine (umbilical/spinal chord [*sic*]) ... slithering silently behind our backs (our spines)"; the organic thing "dies" in projection as it is transformed from solid object into "dreamlike immateriality."[109] In this way, Gibson and Recoder recuperate the death of film into an essential ontological property of cinema, expressed through this chain of metaphors for cinema's simultaneously solid and evanescent nature. "Call it the immateriality of the material."[110]

It will be plain by now that projection performance entails the creative *misuse* of the projector, though predicated upon an intimate knowledge of how the machine works. The filmmakers who perform with projectors are at once deeply informed about the mechanics and history of projection and disruptive of these. The latter, in fact, necessarily proceeds from the former. A homely expression for this might be that projection performers are aware of what the projector is supposed to do, but more concerned with what it *can* do, especially when pushed to its limits. In chapter 2 we saw how a performance like Bradley Eros's *Burn* emerged from this attitude, originating as it did from a program at the Robert Beck Memorial Cinema entitled "Mistakes (everything you can do wrong)." The intensified scrutiny of the film medium, whether upon celluloid, projection, light, or the space of exhibition, incorporates acts of misuse, abuse, and destruction as means of fully understanding the

---

[109] Gibson and Recoder, "Cinema/Film," n.p.
[110] Sandra Gibson and Luis Recoder, "FILM IS ... NOT FILM," *INCITE! Journal of Experimental Media & Radical Aesthetics* no. 2 (2011). See http://www.incite-online.net/gibson-recoder2.html, n.p.

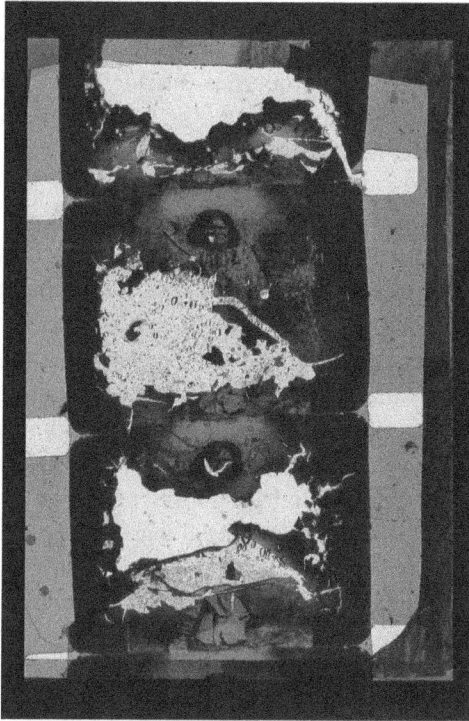

Fig. 3.43. Distressed filmstrip from Mediamystics (Jeanne Liotta and Bradley Eros),
Subverted Horseplay (performance series, 1994–1997).
Image courtesy of Jeanne Liotta.

possibilities of cinema. Eros began such work in the early 1990s, often working with
Jeanne Liotta. Performing under the moniker Mediamystics, Eros and Liotta showed
films in projectors that lacked shutters, pull down claws, and registration pins, their
lenses removed, interfered with, or replaced by alternative external lens-like objects.

Subverted Horseplay (1994–1997) prefigures works like *Aberration of Light*
and *Pie Pelicane Jesu Domine* in using commercial found footage as the familiar
ground that Eros and Liotta systematically destabilized, in this case Hollywood
and TV Westerns (fig. 3.43). Images were thrown out of focus, pulled through projectors by hand, and diffracted by glass, gels, hands, and bodies. While Eros has
framed this work in anthropomorphic and organic metaphors common among
his peers, he also casts it in the light of Gnosticism, by his own definition "recognition or self-knowledge through direct experience, to emphasize the material
to arrive at something beyond the physical; to overcome matter."[111] He quotes a
Christian Gnostic saying, "Split the stick, and there is Jesus," and echoes it with

---

[111] Eros, "There Will Be Projections in All Dimensions," p. 87.

his own cinematic Gnostic maxim, "Scratch the emulsion, and there is film."[112] This notion of the transcendence of film through an intensified "amplification" and even destruction of its material properties is made in answer to an earlier version of expanded cinema that abandoned film. Citing Gene Youngblood's claim, "when we say expanded cinema, we actually mean expanded consciousness," Eros offers in its place a view of expanded cinema that transcends film from the inside out as it were, rather than simply jettisoning it in favor of other, newer media. By "consciously magnifying a filmic element to emphasize the cinematic concrete," he writes, "a philosophical dialogue comes into play between existence and matter. Film becomes the lens of this metaphysical debate."[113] This is one more reference to cinema's dialectic of materiality and immateriality, with projection identified as the privileged place of synthesis.

One filmic element in particular has been the subject of "precise focus" and amplification among projection performers. This is the projector's optical sound head. This device converts the light impulses produced by the film's optical soundtrack—a wavelength of light running alongside the picture frames opposite the row of sprocket holes—into sound. The identity of light and sound designed into film's physical structure has been the basis for a reimagining of sound as a cinematic, and this has been on view most prominently in the work of projection performers like McClure, Golding, Sherwin, Lynn Loo, and Greg Pope, as it is in the moment of projection that light becomes sound. To make her films *Washi #1* and *Washi #2* (16mm double projection, 2014), Loo affixed decorative washi tape to clear 16mm film, covering the entire width of the filmstrip so that the designs on the tape extend into the area where the optical soundtrack would normally be (fig. 3.44). The lines and grids, all different colors, thicknesses, and degrees of opacity, produce rhythmic ticks, thuds, and bursts of white noise, which Loo alters in small increments using an audio mixer, projecting two lengths of treated film simultaneously on side-by-side projectors aimed at the same area of the screen (fig. 3.45).

The *Washi* films were inspired, according to Loo, by Mary Martin's drawings for *Expanding Permutation* (1969), in which a grid pattern composed of black and white squares is exhaustively varied—the squares vary in darkness (depending upon how thickly Martin applied the ink) and are filled in by horizontal, vertical, or diagonal lines. The resulting impression is one of implied movement as the grids vary in tiny increments from one drawing to the next, not unlike individual frames of an abstract film. Loo's films seize upon this permutational quality, extending it into the temporal dimension suggested by Martin's work, and further elaborating the permutational field by layering multiple films at once and adjusting the audio output live as she watches and responds to the patterns unfolding on screen. Loo thus grants, as it were, temporality and movement to Martin's static abstractions, in yet another

[112] Ibid.
[113] Ibid., pp. 86–87.

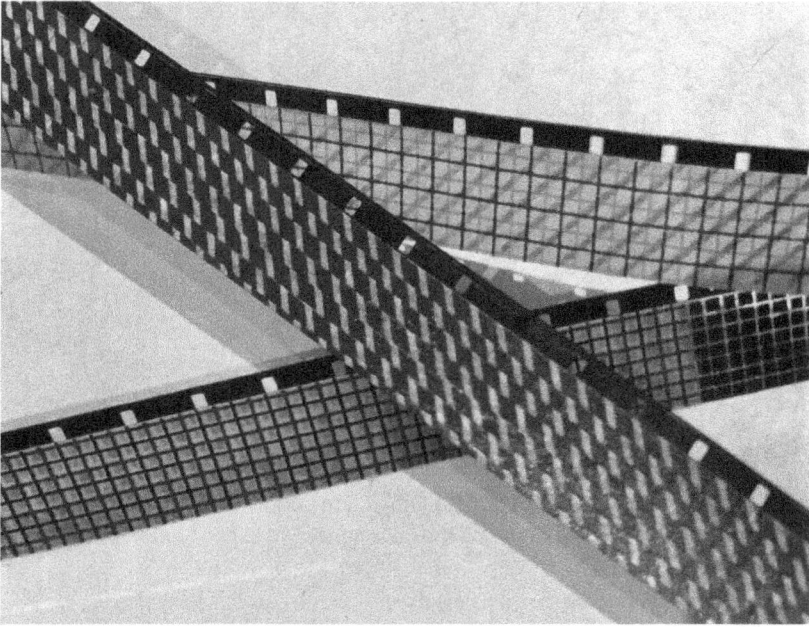

Fig. 3.44. Lynn Loo, treated filmstrips for *Washi #1* and *Washi #2* (2014).
Image courtesy of Lynn Loo.

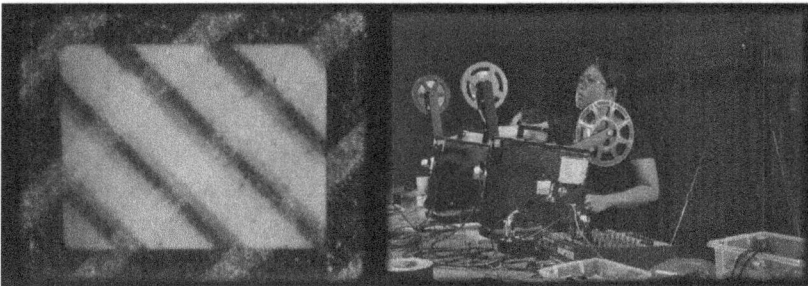

Fig. 3.45. Lynn Loo, *Washi #2* (2014). Performance documentation, He Xiangning Museum, Shenzhen, China, 2014. Left: screen image; right: Loo adjusting sound output and focus of film projectors.
Image courtesy of Lynn Loo.

variant of the notion of abstraction's inherently dynamic form—as in "gestural" and "action" interpretations of Abstract Expressionism, which we will see taken furthest in Ken Jacobs's Nervous Magic Lantern performances. Loo's methodical approach to live projection parallels the hidden labor behind Martin's work, making that labor, by necessity time-based, explicitly part of the work.

Fig. 3.46. Hangjun Lee, *Film Walk* (2011). Projection performance, co-presented by Lampo, the Smart Museum of Art, and the Reva and David Logan Center for the Arts, January 23, 2016.
Photo: Alex Inglizian. Image courtesy of Hangjun Lee.

Hangjun Lee's *Film Walk* (2011) is perhaps the *ne plus ultra* of this branch of projection performance, treating the projector literally as an instrument. In this work, which has varied in form across several years, and has been performed in collaboration with Metamkine's Jérôme Noetinger, Lee threads 16mm film through only the sound head of a projector tuned on its side, bypassing the projector's gate (fig. 3.46). This film is "double-perf," meaning a second row of sprocket holes runs along the side of the strip where that soundtrack would normally be. As these pass over the sound head, they produce an electronic purr, or, when amplified enough, an unpleasant metallic grinding comparable to the sound of a buzz saw. Lee pulls the film through the projector by hand, yanking it roughly through the sound head. The variations in speed that result from Lee's manual movement of the filmstrip cause abrupt changes in the frequency and timbre of the sprocket sound. Lee slowly works his way through the screening space, in some versions threading the film through additional projectors (a "quadrophonic version" passed the film through four of them), sometimes exiting the space and pulling the film along with him. Sally Golding, herself a key figure in projection performance, describes an iteration of *Film Walk* at Café Oto in London:

> The audience sat inside, listening to the squeals of the slippage of film against the spinning optical sound head, and surely marveling at the strength of the polyester film which held sway against the semi-closed door. The friction of the film within this newly constructed super-projector—the room with its cabaret style tables and chairs and its essential orifices acting as enlarged projector mechanics—tensely

focused the audience's awareness as to the possibilities of failure but also the extended abilities of the film strip.[114]

Note how Golding's language parallels Eros's: Lee's "tense focus" on a single, irreducible material element of the medium opens onto an expanded field of exhibition possibilities predicated upon the misuse and the "possibilities of failure" inherent in Lee's willfully abusive treatment of film and projector.[115] Like Eros, Lee himself describes his practice as beginning at the resolutely material but leading toward a much more expanded register of the cinematic, one with metaphysical implications.

> Each film has a specific weight, thickness and length that depends on its duration. To measure the mass and volume of film, we can use gallons (gal), kilograms (kg), milligrams (mg), grams (g), and litres (l). Measurements of filmic material are technological realities but do not necessarily define what we call the cinematic ... Filmmakers and archivists convert the thickness, length and weight of film into time. Through filmmaking and archiving a feeling for film's physical substance develops, time-conscious becomes tangible ...[116]

This fixation on the minutiae of film's material properties might cut filmmakers off from anything beyond a mechanical, techie conception of cinema, but time and again the reverse turns out to be the case. The material and the metaphysical become concomitants of one another in a filmmaking practice that sees in its medium a philosophical stuff, a set of analogs for ideas about time, nature, humanity, spirituality, and history.

One variant of cinematic purism, seen in Arnheim, for example, regarded the introduction of sound as an intrusion into cinema's essentially visual nature and therefore a betrayal of its autonomy and dilution of its aesthetic power. The preponderance of work with sound in projection performance points to the opposite line of thinking. Sound is an inevitability, simply another zone of the projector with which to experiment. And after all, in projection sound is in fact another form of light. McClure, for instance, humanizes the projector partly on the grounds that it mirrors the unified sensory experience of light and sound produced by our eyes and ears.

While embracing the label "expanded cinema" for her work, Golding has been critical of writing on the subject for over-emphasizing the 1960s and '70s and ignoring "contemporary concerns, for example how new work sits with related trends across diverse art forms such as sound art, live performance, or audiovisual and multimedia art."[117] Golding's work is as attentive to sound as projected light; she began her

---

[114] Golding, "Expanded Cinema Unowned," n.p.
[115] Ibid.
[116] Hangjun Lee, press release for "Hangjun Lee: Nebula Rising," at Christine Park Gallery, March 6–April 11, 2015, n.p.
[117] Cathy Rogers, "Issues in Contemporary Expanded Cinema: A Discussion with Sally Golding and James Holcombe," in a booklet published for the Contact Festival, May 2016, Apiary Studios, London, p. 25. See https://sallygolding.com/word#/issues-in-contemporary-expanded-cinema.

Fig. 3.47. Sally Golding and Spatial, *Light Begets Sound* (2017). Performance documentation (Golding at far right).
Photo: Melina Pafundi, LaborBerlin. Image courtesy of Sally Golding.

expanded cinema practice as part of the duo Abject Leader, whose other member was the sound artist Joel Stern (*The Face of Another* was a major early piece). In a series of performances with UK sound artist Spatial (Matt Spendlove) under the blanket moniker *Light Begets Sound* (2017–ongoing), external shutters fitted with multi-colored glass and gels rotate in front of two filmless 16mm projectors. The shifting hues of projected light scan in slow, intermittent waves across four photo-resistor microphones attached to the wall, which Golding/Spatial dub a "light sensitive prepared screen" (fig. 3.47).[118] The microphones convert light into sound; when the projector light hits them, they emit a soft static noise that Golding and Spatial further manipulate from behind the projectors. Another cluster of works, including *Ghost—Loud and Strong* (2012) and *Super Grotesquerie* (2009), Golding has named "darkroom compositions," made by manually contact printing images and sounds from Golding's personal collection of science films and Super 8mm horror movies onto 16mm film, or by converting "printed waveforms and made sound graphics" to optical tracks in a similar manner (fig. 3.48).[119] All are handmade, hand-processed, subjected to additional surface alterations, then projected live in the form of reels or loops. During the performance, Golding manipulates focus and uses refracting lenses and gels to expand

[118] See Golding's website, https://sallygolding.com/performance/#/light-begets-sound/.
[119] See Golding's website, https://sallygolding.com/performance#/ghost-loud-strong/ and https://sallygolding.com/performance#/super-grotesquerie.

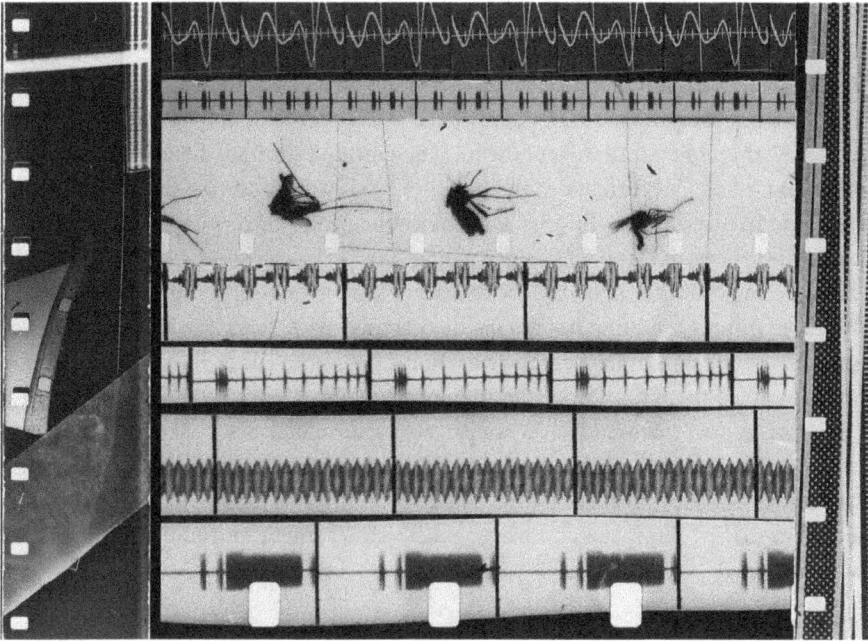

Fig. 3.48. Sally Golding, optical sound filmstrip collage produced for *Composted Memorial* (2009), dual 16mm projector performance for layered single screen. Film loops, original 9.5mm archival images, waveforms, insects, obstructions.
Image courtesy of Sally Golding.

and contract the image. It is not uncommon to see sound-centered projection performances like these at music and sound festivals or rock venues, and both Golding and McClure have released the sound from some of their performances as freestanding audio recordings. Projection performance ensembles are almost as numerous as individual performers, their names calling to mind indie rock bands: silt, Projexorcism, Wet Gate Ensemble, Crater; Gibson and Recoder performed for a short time as "The Presstapes." Golding has claimed a "punk aesthetic" for her work as well as Lee's, and avant-garde composer/performer Tom Cora wrote of Metamkine, "Of course, they do belong to the tradition of experimental cinema, a tradition that Metamkine has deepened by acting like a band."[120] Deepened, not turned away from, run against, or subverted. The "problem of theater," where the theatrical threatened to infect cinema, does not seem to have a correlating "problem of music." The link between image and sound and the play of fusing and decoupling audio and visual tracks in projection performance are the bases for a musical analogy that, unlike comparisons to theater, is not unwelcome in the experimental film world.

---

[120] Tom Cora, program notes for the Klangspuren Festival, Schwaz, Austria, September 1996: http://metamkine.free.fr/metamnotes.htm, n.p.

An important precedent, relatively obscure until the mid-2000s, is Tony Conrad's *Bowed Film* (1974). Conrad sat beside a screen lit by an empty film projector, with one end of a short film loop (a closeup of a violin bow in action) wrapped around his head, passing over his ears. Conrad fastened the other end of the loop to a clip a few feet away; this configuration kept the loop taut around Conrad's head and pulled the other end into a "V" formation, the two sides coming almost to a point where they were held in place by the clip (fig. 3.49). With the projector running, Conrad passed a violin bow over the loop while peering into the "V" at the other end of the loop. In the flickering projector light, the movement of the bow across the surface of the loop produced minute vibrating images inside this tiny space. Since the loop passed over his ears, Conrad could also hear the vibrations in stereo; a contact microphone on his head amplified these sounds for the audience, but only Conrad could see the images. Like *Film Feedback, Bowed Film* was a private performance that collapsed the categories of production activity (the bowing of the film) and resulting pictures (the miniscule moving images). It was experienced as a sound piece despite its title, made by a musician-turned-filmmaker, utilizing a musical instrument, and audible but invisible to spectators.

Fig. 3.49. Tony Conrad, *Bowed Film* (1974). Performance documentation. Berks Filmmakers, Reading, PA.
Photo: Linda Edelstein, courtesy of Tony Conrad.

Like so much of Conrad's expanded cinema of the 1970s, *Bowed Film* parodied avant-garde film's aesthetic of materialism and filmic purity. But in its sheer oddity it raises a serious point, especially when viewed in the light of contemporary projection performance. "What are the irreducible axioms of that part of thought we call the art of film," Eros asks, quoting Hollis Frampton.[121] One of these is optical sound, which *Bowed Film* makes "optical sound," a film-aesthetic figure based upon conceptual premises built into the mechanisms. He did much the same in *7360 Sukiyaki* when he transformed projection into "pro-jection," actually throwing film onto the screen. The premise of *Bowed Film* is the analogousness of image and sound in film, all understood as forms of vibration in air. Sound, of course, is vibration by definition, and when converted into an optical track becomes an image of vibration, of minute fluctuations of size and shape running along the side of the film. In *Bowed Film*, the sound comes from the passage of the film across another object, in this case the violin bow acting as a substitute for the projector's sound head. These vibrations generated the shimmering images Conrad could see in the "V" of his loop and were made audible by the contact microphone. Conrad's strange, utterly unique take on one of film's irreducible elements implies almost the opposite of irreducibility: that each part can be further atomized, to be opened up into an ever widening field of highly specific expanded forms. Concentrated attention to optical sound, lenses, shutters, aperture plates, or focus leads to seemingly endless variations, to the extent that McClure, for example, has built an entire apparatus and mode of working around the simple fact of film's transparency as the basis for sound in projection.

Projection Performance and Avant-Garde Cinema's Historical Turn

In the work of some projection performers the elaboration of filmic elements into expanded cinema practices takes on an historical vector. The preponderance of projection performances centered on optical sound speaks to this. The skepticism about sound expressed in one line of essentialist film theory is answered by another position that recognizes film's silence as an historical accident rather than cinema's ontological destiny. Frampton went so far as to identify organized sound—the songs of prehistoric insects, specifically—as film's metahistorical point of origin.[122] But one does not need to go that far, temporally or imaginatively, to find evidence of the arbitrariness of sound's exclusion from the province of the essentially cinematic.

It should also be easy to see the appeal of such an historical view for projection performance. In the very early years of the medium before film exhibition was

<hr/>

[121] Bradley Eros, "More Captivating Than Phosphorous," *Millennium Film Journal* 56 (Fall 2012), p. 43. Frampton originally asked the question in "A Pentagram for Conjuring the Narrative," p. 284.
[122] Hollis Frampton, "Hollis Frampton: Three Talks at Millennium," *Millennium Film Journal* 16/17/18 (Fall–Winter 1986–1987), p. 292.

standardized, projection was done on a dizzying array of machines and performed live on hand-cranked projectors. Even when hidden in a projection booth, the work of the projectionist was still very much on view to spectators and the industry itself. Tom Gunning has famously argued that the "radical heterogeneity" of cinema before about 1907 offered a model for avant-garde filmmakers, who turned "the earlier carnival" of cinema in its first decade into radical, oppositional forms.[123] Though Gunning was thinking of film form, precisely the same thing could be said of early cinema's graveyard of film machines and unconventional, or pre-conventional, projection practices.

MacKenzie's remarkable projection performance *The Wooden Lightbox* (2007–ongoing) exemplifies avant-garde cinema's historical turn both toward antiquated devices of projection and historical imagery going back to film's "primitive" period. The title names both the performance and the handmade 16mm projector MacKenzie built for it. The Lightbox was assembled from discarded parts of other 16mm projectors and contains only the absolute minimum of necessary parts for projection: a rudimentary shutter, sprocket wheels, lens, crank handle for manual projection, and a 50-watt bulb (much lower than the typical 200–700 or more watts in standard-issue 16mm projectors). All of this is enclosed in a makeshift wooden box that bears more than a passing resemblance to the Lumière Cinematographe (fig. 3.50). The dim bulb is necessary because MacKenzie cranks the machine slowly, often freezing a single frame or methodically moving the film backward and forward as though reviewing his footage on a Steenbeck. A brighter bulb would be hotter, risking damage to MacKenzie's fragile handmade emulsions. The trade-off of the Lightbox's more forgiving treatment of film is the dimmer image, but MacKenzie make this into a benefit—an aesthetic, in fact: "full darkness and a relatively small image size in the screening space is crucial. The piece is most effective in a small screening space or gallery, as this enhances the intimacy and places the projector and performer in amongst the audience."[124] In numerous interviews and statements, MacKenzie has referred to his device as harking back to the period of early cinema prior to the standardization of projection speed and the elimination of flicker, before the Latham loop, before automaticity, before the isolated and invisible projection booth. Each of its antiquated features allows the operator more precise control of the image, and each represents a road not taken in the technological history of cinema exhibition. But more than a reference to old technology, *The Wooden Lightbox* references the period before the full flowering of the film industry for which standardized projection was paramount.

The film *The Wooden Lightbox* incorporates found and original footage, all hand processed and chemically treated and further subjected to the improvisational and exploratory form of projection the Lightbox enables. It is a film historical palimpsest, at once referencing early cinema and the history of avant-garde film, as if

[123] Gunning, "The Cinema of Attractions," p. 70.
[124] Alex MacKenzie, one-sheet description of *The Wooden Lightbox: A Secret Art of Seeing*, n.d., n.p. Also see https://www.alexmackenzie.ca/lightbox.html.

Fig. 3.50. Alex MacKenzie's Wooden Lightbox.
Image courtesy of Alex MacKenzie.

operationalizing Gunning's association of the two in "The Cinema of Attractions." Two of the earliest images in the film are an illustrated bird and cage, seen separately at first, then in rapid alternation, a projected equivalent of the Thaumotrope, one of so many pre-cinematic optical devices. The bandit from Porter's *The Great Train Robbery* (1903) makes a brief, dim appearance, aiming his pistol and the audience and firing, then un-firing as the projector is run in reverse. MacKenzie scans back and forth over a closeup of a child's hands moving erratically over a black tabletop, an image from the remarkable pre-credit sequence of Ingmar Bergman's *Persona* (1966), itself about the act of projecting film (fig. 3.51). Across the other ten 100-foot reels that comprise the film—the machine cannot accommodate anything larger—runs a veritable hit parade of images from the history of avant-garde cinema: a crudely drawn lightbulb recalls an almost identical image from Sharits's *N:O:T:H:I:N:G* (1968); closeups of a cat echo Maya Deren and Alexander Hammid's *Private Life of a Cat* (1944); an eye chart comprised of blocky three-pronged shapes resembles the monogram with which Hollis Frampton signed his films; long shots of a little girl dozing outdoors on a blanket are reminiscent of Warhol's *Sleep*, while jittery and rapidly cut shots of nature suggest Brakhage (fig. 3.52). The implication is that avant-garde film realizes the *promesse du bonheur* of early cinema, activating

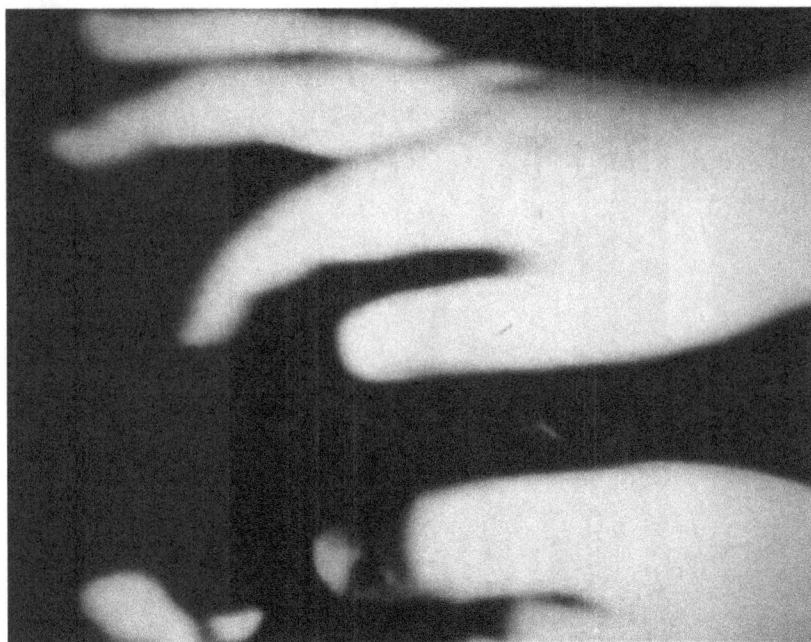

Fig. 3.51. Alex MacKenzie, *The Wooden Lightbox* (2007–ongoing). Frame enlargement: optically printed shot from *Persona* (Ingmar Bergman, 1966). Image courtesy of Alex MacKenzie.

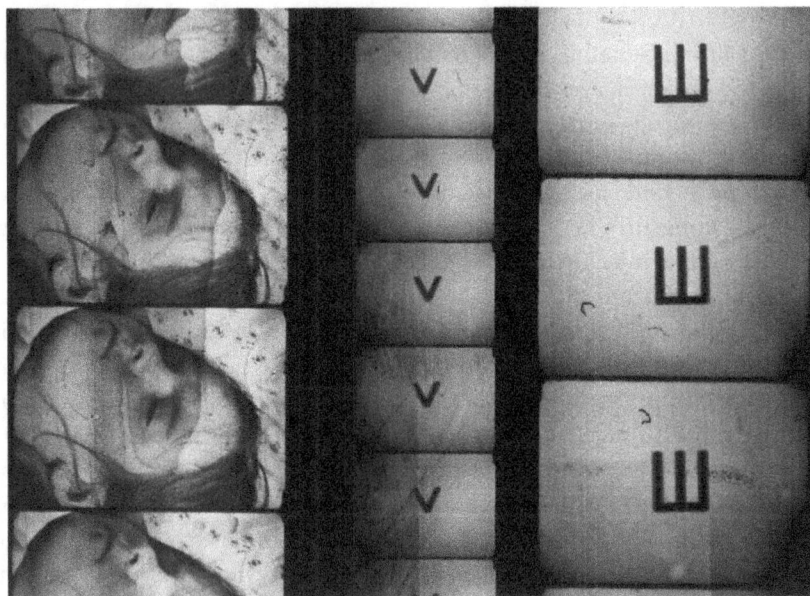

Fig. 3.52. Alex MacKenzie, *The Wooden Lightbox* (2007–ongoing). Frame enlargements. Image courtesy of Alex MacKenzie.

its radical potential in the face of the technological and institutional standardization that came afterward.

Other projection performers have played upon different historical connections, following cinema's genealogical lines into obscure corners where it intertwines with arcane practices and beliefs like magic, alchemy, and spiritualism. Each of these provides at once a set of generative ideas for expanded cinema and the basis for sematic fields used in critical accounts, including those written by the filmmakers themselves. Describing her 2004 projection performance *The Handcranked Muse of Cinema*, which utilized a 1921 ACME hand-operated 35mm projector, Kerry Laitala analogizes herself to the itinerant projectionist of early cinema. According to her, the co-presence of projector, projectionist, and audience was a hallmark of a more interactive and knowing relationship among the three.[125] Once more, early cinema is taken as an emblem of avant-garde film's ideals of active spectator and resistance to the commercial film industry. Citing Gunning, Laitala implies that the standardization and automaticization of projection parallels the dominance of commercial narrative cinema over the avant-garde. Both occlude an "other," potential cinema in the service of profit: "the projector being scurried out of sight, cinema quickly became manacled, enslaved by the traditional notions of narrative and theatre that would determine its function in society on a mass scale to be a storytelling apparatus."[126] *The Handcranked Muse of Cinema* attempts to revive the more direct, live relationship of projectionist to spectator.

Laitala made the film by contact printing 35mm slides of magic lantern images onto 35mm film. The images were mostly of signs guiding audience behavior: "Loud talking and whistling not allowed"; "Please don't spit on the floor—Remember the Johnstown flood!" These had been reduced to 35mm slide format in the 1940s by the Blackhawk Film Company, which also released 16mm and 8mm film versions for amateur exhibitors. Laitala restored them to 35mm film using a slide duplicator, then transferred them to 35mm motion picture film stock by laying the slides over the unexposed film and using a flashlight to make a clandestine contact print. She used the same process to transfer images of odd objects lying around her apartment; bits of star shaped confetti and Laitala's own hair, rescued from the bathtub drain, feature prominently in the film. The film shifts between images of the magic lantern slides, crudely animated via Laitala's D-I-Y contact printing process, and the jittery, abstract shadows produced by her collection of personal detritus. In one segment, whitish blobs on a blue background, which appear to be some sort of liquid (possibly bleach, which dissolves film emulsion) splattered onto the film, rapidly alternate with signs admonishing audience members against spitting: "If you expect to rate as a gentleman you will not expectorate on the floor" (fig. 3.53). Cylindrical objects, possibly beads or bits of jewelry, are intercut with a circular sign reading "Please applaud with hands only" ringed by images of clapping hands. Periodically, a contemporaneous

---

[125] Kerry Laitala, artist's statement, http://www.kerrylaitala.com/hand-crank-muse.html.
[126] Kerry Laitala, "Cinema as Material Presence."

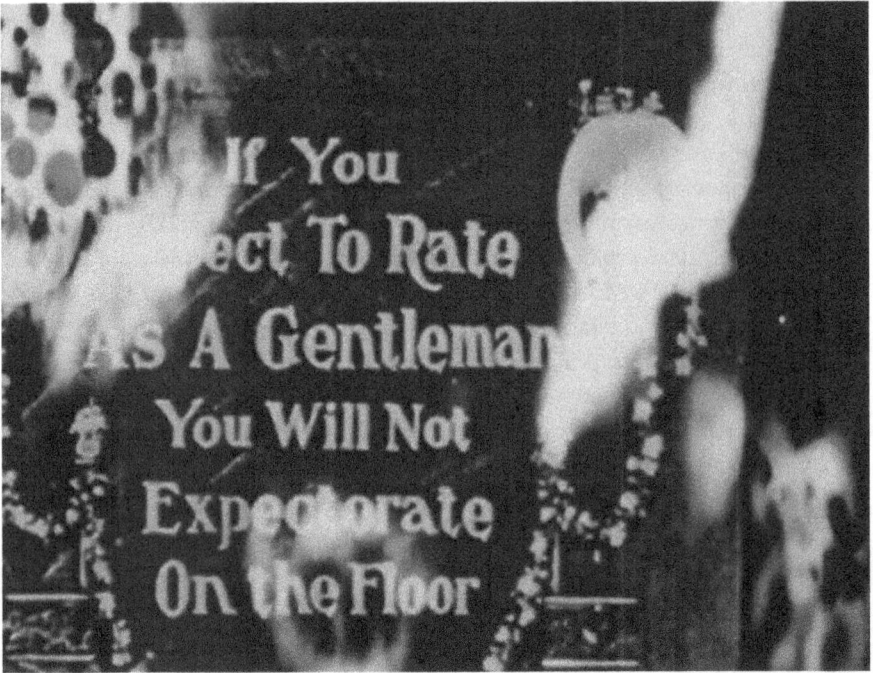

Fig. 3.53. Kerry Laitala, *Handcranked Muse of Cinema* (2006). Frame enlargement from 35mm film used in projection performance.
Image ©Kerry Laitala, courtesy of the artist.

image of a magic lantern flickers on the screen, superimposed over a field of trembling abstract forms. The film is accompanied by a mashup of Tin Pan Alley music, a sonic equivalent to the imagery Laitala produced in collaboration with Robert Fox.

The specific choices of magic lantern slides in *The Handcranked Muse of Cinema* points to the historical theme of audience decorum in the cinema, a concern that moral reformers and the film industry shared. The creation and maintenance of behavioral standards for audiences was as much a part of the standardization of exhibition as setting technical specifications for projection. It helped exhibitors draw women and children, the first step to legitimizing cinema in the eyes of the middle class—two slides read "Mashers! Watch Out: The Law is Watching You," and "Ladies Without Escorts Cordially Invited." Laitala's slides, then, look in both historical directions: to a more indecorous moviegoing past and the coming changes to exhibition intended to exert control on audiences and films alike. To a filmmaker like Laitala, long active in San Francisco's vibrant alternative cinema scene, the idea of a lost utopia of makeshift screening spaces populated by marginalized audiences actively participating in the spectacle would surely be appealing, a distant relative of the microcinema. Many of the slides in *Handcranked Muse* make direct reference to the projectionist: "One Moment Please: The Operator is Adjusting the Film," one reads,

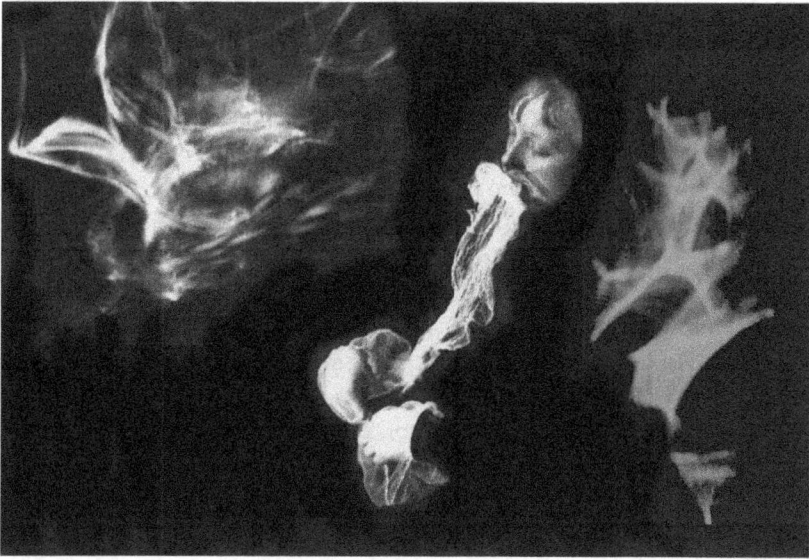

Fig. 3.54. Kerry Laitala, *Hocus Pocus...ABRACADABRA!!!* (2007).
Image ©Kerry Laitala, courtesy of the artist.

with an illustrated projectionist in tears over a malfunctioning projector spilling film onto the floor.

The magic lantern is also the link to another lost history, distinct from cinema but associated with it, which constitutes another field of meaning animating Laitala's work. Referring to the intensive hand-processing that *The Handcranked Muse of Cinema* underwent, Laitala writes that it "provide[s] a meditation on this medium of alchemy and magic."[127] While she has made this analogy frequently, and often uses it metaphorically, the connection she makes here is more literal and histori-cally grounded. The use of magic lanterns by spiritualists to prove the existence of ghosts or the afterlife (or at least to trick clients into believing in them) is well doc-umented. Placing the magic lantern in a privileged position in cinema's genealogy thereby brings necromancy and prestidigitation into film's history. Laitala dramatizes this in *Hocus Pocus ... ABRACADABRA!!!* (2007), an "expanded cinema séance" employing multiple screens and film, slide, and video projectors (fig. 3.54). Still and moving images of the paranormal appear on an elevated projection screen and an adjacent white sheet, loosely suspended from the ceiling and billowing in the breeze of an oscillating fan. The soundtrack combines playfully silly horror movie sound effects like thunder and creaking floorboards with what sound like genuine record-ings of a séance: "Hello, everybody on the other side. Can you break through?" A slide

---

[127] Kerry Laitala, artist's statement on *Muse of Cinema*, 2006.

projector casts an image of a disembodied hand, symbol of the ascent to heaven, while two film loops depict images that could be spirit energy or ectoplasm. Illustrations and photographs of faces dissolve in and out on the surface of the wafting sheet— Nicola Tesla, Athanasius Kircher, and Maya Deren, among others. It is a montage strategy similar to MacKenzie's in *The Wooden Lightbox*, associating avant-garde cinema with historical figures who stood somewhere between science and mysticism. And between the concrete and the ephemeral, as well. Deren, experimental film's representative in *Hocus Pocus*, translated this dualism into cinematic terms, fascinated as she was by both religious ritual and medium specificity.

Links to alchemy, magic, and spiritualism have a long history in avant-garde cinema, often deployed as signifiers of that cinema's cultural otherness, which envisions "the magic of the movies" in darker, more subterranean terms. The incorporation of such references as models for contemporary live cinema originate in the work of Jürgen Reble and the Bonn filmmaking and projection performance group *Schmelzdahin* ("melt away"). Reble, Jochen Lempert, and Jochen Müller formed the group in 1979, initially experimenting with hand processing and the effects of decomposition and chemical alteration of film. During a tour of mostly European filmmaking venues in 1988 and 1989, *Schmelzdahin* introduced live performance into the repertoire, bringing the chemical decomposition methods they had been refining for a decade into the act of projection. Reble continued to employ the group's specific performance methods in his work as a solo filmmaker after the group disbanded around 1989. A loop of found footage, approximately 15 to 20 feet in length, runs from the projector over a makeshift workspace where it is subject to forms of chemical and manual distress. The loop traverses the space immediately around the projector and group members, then back into the projector (fig. 3.55). *Schmelzdahin* experimented with several different trajectories for the loop, often dependent on the nature and dimensions of the performance space. A photograph of a 1988 performance in Frankfurt shows the loop passing over a hook on a coat stand that happened to be in the room; documentation of a 1987 performance in Bonn shows the loop threaded through a film spool attached to a wooden beam Reble holds in one hand as he abrades the loop with the other (fig. 3.56). For a 2017 performance in Stuttgart the film passed through a large metal loop suspended between projector and screen.[128] The film loop was large and loose enough that Reble, Lempert, and Müller could grab sections of it and hold them still as they passed from the projector to the adjacent table, scratching, puncturing, coloring, and chemically abusing them before releasing the loop to continue along its path. Pots of dye, dishes of chemicals, and an array of metal objects occupy the messy workspace beside the projector. The duration of each performance was determined by the resiliency of the film loop; eventually the emulsion was entirely scratched, rubbed, and chemically burned away, leaving the remaining base to melt in the heat of the projector lamp. The performances ended as

---

[128] See *Schmelzdahin*'s website for excellent photographic documentation of their performances and films: http://www.schmelzdahin.de/.

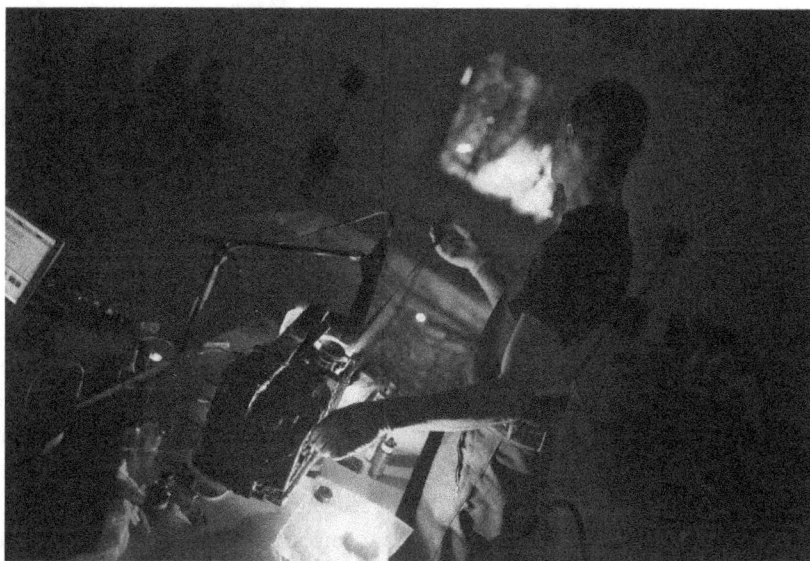

Fig. 3.55. Jürgen Reble, *ALCHEMY* (2010). Performance documentation. Kunsthalle Schirn, Frankfurt, Germany. August 8, 2010.

Photograph by Sascha Rheker, courtesy of Jürgen Reble.

Fig. 3.56. *Schmelzdahin*, unnamed projection performance. Bonn, Germany, 1987. Performance documentation.

Image courtesy of Jürgen Reble.

the white light of the lamp finally scorched through the film frame, leaving only the charred and ragged edges of the film's base. Prior to this, the found footage, usually from very early films, slowly accrued layers of scratches, increasingly vivid colors, and reticulated emulsion forms that pulled away from their diegetic referents to become abstract images on the surface of the frame, further obscuring the original content of the film as the performance wore on.

Film loops served a purpose in *Schmelzdahin*'s work that distinguishes it from the many other projection performances and film installations that utilize them. Each passage of the loop is unique, bearing new traces of manual and chemical damage with each pass, though simultaneously repeating the original narrative or documentary imagery of the source film. Like Nicolson's *Reel Time*, the repetition of the loop serves as a base against which the changes wrought on the filmstrip become markers of time passing, new physical processes being layered on with each cycle, and, more metaphorically, of concepts like flux, change, and ephemerality. The destruction of film in *Schmelzdahin*'s performances was indeed framed as a kind of ritual sacrifice of the material object in the name of cinema's impermanence (candles, which provided light for the group to work by, also further connoted ritual). In associating the physical impermanence of chemical destabilization and the temporariness of the performance event with alchemy and ritualism, *Schmelzdahin* and Reble rhetorically elevated the materials of filmmaking to the status of philosophical objects. Reble offers a narrative of his and *Schmelzdahin*'s process that leads in this way from material to idea, and to the larger realizations that film's decay might prompt:

> In the end, nothing is left but a dance of chemical elements—basic ingredients—and a dance of basic (philosophical) principles as well. The audience is present at a process of formation and decomposition that unfolds in actual, material time. Shapes and colors are born and disappear continually. What one sees seems to be stripped of meaning. One is left understanding that we participate only fugitively in the processes of chemical change, and that beyond a certain point one is little more than the spectator of these phenomena—that is to say—an onlooker, a bystander.[129]

The by now familiar features of projection performance were present in *Schmelzdahin*'s work quite early. Their performances collapsed production and exhibition into the same moment in an attempt to close the distance between filmmaker and audience. "Performance proceeds as a conspiracy between two basic elements, the public and myself," Reble has written.[130] Historical found footage served as signifier of the connection of past and present, of film's fragility and resiliency, and associated experimental cinema with arcane belief systems. Finally, *Schmelzdahin*'s performances

[129] Jürgen Reble, "Chemistry and the Alchemy of Colour," *Millennium Film Journal* 30/31 (Fall 1997), p. 17.
[130] Ibid.

celebrated a kind of temporally discrete, non-repeatable experience shared by film-makers and viewers, which ran counter to dominant presumptions of film production and preservation and implicitly critiqued the ideology of the art world. The sort of work *Schmelzdahin* produced, Reble writes, "proceeds from an emphatic (even categorical) rejection of the logic inherent to museums as well as the world of art, for which its quality as a precious object leaves a work of art to be surrounded, encircled, hemmed in by solicitude—something that is to be preserved."[131]

* * *

If we imagine an exploded view of the film projector, we see a map of the preoccupations of contemporary projection performers. McClure's zone is the aperture plate, the lamp, and the sound head—a zone also occupied by Golding, Lee, and Sherwin. Other filmmakers gravitate to different zones; Gibson and Recoder, Laitala, and Metamkine to the lens and light beam, for instance. Overlaying a family tree of projection's history onto this exploded view, we see historical lines explored by Laitala, MacKenzie, Eros and Liotta, and *Schmelzdahin*. Projection performance has played out a process David James identified at the heart of structural film, the elaboration of a "periodic table" of works "based upon an atomized model of the entire cinematic process."[132] This charting of projection, this plumbing of its depths, only begins at filmic specificity, as it simultaneously maps the values, historical associations, and thematic fields that form avant-garde cinema's universe.

---

[131] Ibid.
[132] James, *Allegories of Cinema*, pp. 242–243.

4

Cinema as Object I

Most critics and historians still regard the *tentative* experience of perceiving
a film as "more real," in their definitions of cinema, than holding in their
hand a non-tentative strip of celluloid that has a measurable length and
width and that has a measurable series of "frames" ... in normal cinema we
neither see the motion of the film strip nor are we aware of a succession of
frame units. The cameramen who shoot such "movies" utterly and disdainfully ignore the frame structure of their medium.

—Paul Sharits (1970)

I like making things. Objects that are distinct, take up space, have weight
and texture, can be given as gifts, are occasionally sold, contain the very
story of their making in the material of their being. And so it is with a stubborn adolescent fury that I refuse to believe that the work I do as a filmmaker
is being pushed so quickly and definitively from the three dimensional into
the digital and ultimately to the virtual world.

—Lynne Sachs (2014)

Cinema on Display

"I saw a film." What we really mean is that we saw the trace of a process wherein two
objects interface to produce an insubstantial image—an image made of light. The two
objects are the medium format in which "the film" is encoded (celluloid strip, videotape,
DVD, digital file) and the machine that decodes it to make "the film" visible (film projector, VHS or DVD player, digital projector or computer monitor). They are designed to
one another's specifications and are not intended by their manufacturers to be seen; their
invisibility is necessary for "the film" to be visible. Though we tend to think of cinema
as being manifestly about display, our typical experience of it depends as much upon
occlusion. Even those avant-garde films said to call attention to cinema's materials require those materials to be made invisible via the same processes at work in conventional
cinema. To see *The Flicker*, we must *not* see the flicker of the projector's shutter.

Reflecting on one such film, Brakhage's *Mothlight* (1963), Paul Arthur writes that
it causes the viewer to feel "an intuition that aspects of the perceived filmic organization can be clarified/contradicted by direct viewing of the strip."[1] Following

[1] Paul Arthur, "Structural Film: Revisions, New Versions, and the Artifact," *Millennium Film Journal* 2
(Spring/Summer 1978), pp. 7–8.

Cinema Expanded. Jonathan Walley, Oxford University Press (2020). © Oxford University Press.
DOI: 10.1093/oso/9780190938635.001.0001

this intuition and viewing *Mothlight* "off the reel," Arthur claims, "confirms its in-clusion in a class of films which direct the viewer from the projection experience 'back' to the source at the physical object."[2] This object is clear 16mm film to which Brakhage affixed leaves, blades of grass, moth wings, seeds, and the like—a came-raless and therefore frameless film that reads on screen as a dynamic fluttering of organic debris of varying recognizability (fig. 4.1). We could read Arthur's argu-ment as just one more explication of one more avant-garde film in terms of medium specificity and reflexivity, the familiar claim that such films "remind" viewers that they are watching a film and "call their attention to" any number of film-specific qualities. But Arthur does not simply claim that *Mothlight* produces this aware-ness. His scenario in which we walk into the projection booth and look at the film-strip itself, taking it off the projector and holding it up to the light to scrutinize its unique construction, implies a context in which such an act is not only possible but imaginable in the first place. A social situation in which viewers can do more than speculate about the physical structure of the film and actually engage with the material directly, something no cinematic culture other than avant-garde film accommodates. Arthur's interpretation further implies the separation of the film-strip from projection, as though the latter is not necessary to appreciate the former. In referring to "the condition of film as simultaneously artifact and performance," Arthur imagines two different modes of experience, equally viable, each with their own rewards.[3]

Arthur's imagined situation in which a curious viewer enters the projection booth to contemplate a filmstrip can stand as a model for this chapter and the next. This chapter is devoted to works of expanded cinema that directly display the celluloid strip or other parts of the film medium as objects. The next chapter is about works that put the entire cinematic situation into view—moving image medium interfaced with projection device operating in a particular exhibition context such as a theater or gallery space, the arrangement of objects and people such that we can at once "see a film" and *not* see it. The distinction elaborated in these two chapters is that between object and installation. The former stands alone, independent of its surroundings, in the same sense that a painting or sculpture is normally understood and experi-enced. The latter consists of multiple objects in a particular system of relations, where the function and meaning of each object is determined by the system. Returning to Arthur's example of *Mothlight*, the film on the reel, removed from the projector and appreciated for its own physical qualities, is an object in the sense I have in mind. The experience of the film in exhibition, which depends as much upon projector, screen, space, and screening conventions as the filmstrip itself, is produced by a system of relations that cinematic installations re-create in a variety of ways. I offer this not as a rigorous theoretical distinction between "art objects" and "art installations," only as a

Fig. 4.1. Stan Brakhage, *Mothlight* (1963). Frame enlargement.
Courtesy of the Estate of Stan Brakhage and Fred Camper (www.fredcamper.com).

working model that attempts to approximate distinctions at large in the discourses of avant-garde film culture.

Echoing that process of expansion and contraction described earlier, the works in the two chapters that follow split the cinematic apparatus. One group isolates the physical objects that constitute cinema's machines; the other meditates upon the context in which those machines are deployed—the institution of "going to the movies" or "viewing cinema." The theorist Jean-Louis Baudry introduced the term *dispositif*, usually translated as "apparatus," into film studies at the same time that avant-garde filmmakers made works in both expanded and non-expanded forms that brought the combination of technologies and social conventions of traditional cinematic exhibition into focus. According to Baudry, to view a film in the conventional format of theatrical exhibition is to be imbricated in a nexus of complimentary technological and institutional operations. "Cinema" by this definition is the totality of physical materials and routinized exhibition practices through which audiences "see a film." The arrangement of projector and screen, the mechanical process that animates still images into illusory movement, the impression of three-dimensionality designed into the lens of the camera that made those images, and the arrangement of the viewer in a passive, supine position in the dark between the image and its source—all these constitute cinema's specificity for Baudry:

> Cinematographic specificity (what distinguishes cinema from other systems of signification) thus refers to a *work*, that is, to a process of transformation. The question becomes, is the work made evident, does consumption of the product bring about a "knowledge effect" [Althusser], or is the work concealed?[4]

Baudry's use of the term "work" elides two meanings of that term: "a work" (i.e., a film) and "the work" of cinema (the technological and social mechanisms that hide the material realities of film production and exhibition). Each work of film does the work of the apparatus, which is to position real viewers as idealized "transcendental subjects," a process that serves the dominant ideology.[5] The illusion of cinema according to apparatus theory is not limited to that of an apparently moving three-dimensional image, but extends to the denial of the material realities that produced the image and that "produce" the subjects of ideology.

For our purposes we can leave aside the complicated and often befuddling psychoanalytic entailments of apparatus theory. These do not appear to have become significant to avant-garde filmmakers until the mid-1970s as filmmakers like Peter Wollen and Laura Mulvey, McCall and Tyndall, and Yvonne Rainer began making narrative avant-garde films said to abandon structural film's formalist project for a return to reality and its politics. But apparatus theory did parallel thinking within contemporaneous avant-garde filmmaking in taking the entire system of cinema production

---

[4] Baudry, "Ideological Effects of the Basic Cinematographic Apparatus," pp. 40–41.
[5] Ibid., pp. 43–44.

and exhibition as "the medium" of cinema. Baudry's model of cinema's specificity could just as easily have been the statement of any number of avant-garde filmmakers working at about the same time. His question, whether "the work" of the cinematic apparatus is acknowledged or hidden, suggests the kind of filmmaking practice he would endorse. Avant-garde films that put cinema's materials and processes on display disrupted the ideological operations of the apparatus, one of which was to render the spectator passive, taken in by illusion rather than being critically aware of it. In addition to expanding upon avant-garde cinema's increasingly sophisticated ontological ideas, apparatus theory was a variant of yet another of that cinema's defining concepts: the active spectator alert to the material realities of film and their own spectatorship.

Rosalind Krauss has made explicit the link between apparatus theory and the theorizations of film within the avant-garde. What she calls film's "aggregate condition," its component nature, which would become the focus of apparatus theory, productively problematized any simplistic conception of a medium.[6] Film could not be reduced to celluloid strip, or camera, or projector, or light beam and screen, but was all of these, including the positioning of the viewer amidst these elements. Krauss argues that this re-invigorated notion of medium specificity became a model for other artists, who still wished to work in a generally modernist tradition but did not want to promulgate a reductively materialist idea of the nature of their own media. Structural film provided "support for a newly conceived idea of an aesthetic medium, one that, like film's, could not be understood as reductive but again, like film's, was thoroughly Modernist."[7] This new idea broke from the overly restrictive, singular specificity of Greenberg (i.e., painting as ultimately about flatness) for a subtler idea of a medium as something heterogeneous, or "internally differentiated" in Krauss's words.[8] Having made this argument, Krauss offers an intriguing interpretation of structural film, that it "set itself the project of producing the unity of this diversified support in a single, sustained experience."[9] The task of structural film was to create "models" of the "utter interdependence" of the diverse materials and conventions that constituted cinema as understood within the avant-garde. Hence, structural films could be thought of as frameworks within which all the various technologies and conventions of cinema, reimagined under the rubric of "the apparatus," were unified. Snow's oft-cited statement about *Wavelength* indicates the extent to which apparatus theory coincided with avant-garde film's ontological conception of cinema. Snow writes of "trying to make a definitive statement of pure film space and time, a balancing of 'Illusion' and 'Fact,' all about seeing. The space starts at the camera's (spectator's) eye, is in the air, then is on the screen, then is within the screen (the mind)."[10] Snow's characterization of cinema

[6] Krauss, *A Voyage on the North Sea*, pp. 24–25.
[7] Ibid., p. 26.
[8] Ibid., p. 30.
[9] Ibid., p. 25.
[10] Michael Snow's statement is quoted in Michelson, "Toward Snow," p. 173.

as at once illusionist and literal ("illusion" and "fact"), wherein the illusory depth on/ in the screen image mirrors the real space between projector and screen—and further "within" the viewer's physical and mental space—would be echoed by apparatus theory within a few years. Snow's statement also supports Krauss's claim about structural films being works through which one could experience all of cinema's ontological diversity in a highly condensed, unified form.

Krauss's account is salutary in suggesting that avant-garde filmmakers did not merely adopt the ideas and forms of the more "advanced" arts but engaged instead in an even exchange with them. All too often critics have interpreted trends or movements in avant-garde cinema as re-treading territory pioneered by the other arts: structural film revisits minimalism, lyrical films like Brakhage's rehash the aesthetics of Abstract Expressionism, Deren's trance films are indebted to Surrealist films like *Un Chien Andalou*. It is refreshing to see an art scholar break from this copycat model and argue that avant-garde cinema's complex theorizations of its medium inspired artists like Richard Serra, Carl Andre, and Robert Smithson. What may be questionable about her argument, however, is the extent to which it posits the *unification* of cinema's ontological heterogeneity as the aim of avant-garde filmmakers during this period. This chapter and the next will show a broader spectrum of ideas about the cinema as apparatus or *dispositif* that inform avant-garde filmmaking, including a tendency within works of expanded cinema to *disrupt and fragment* the unity of that apparatus in order to propose new forms and new arrangements for cinema.

Apparatus theory offers a multi-layered cinematic ontology, by which I mean an ontology dispersed rather than limited to one specific material element of film like the filmstrip or projector. This dispersal is both spatial and temporal. Spatially, cinema's medium is at once in front of and behind the spectator, a collection of machines and actions with the spectator in its midst. Temporally, it extends back from the moment of projection to the production of the film, itself a temporally dispersed process. This link between space and time in the emerging cinematic ontologies of the 1960s will be a recurring theme as we encounter works of expanded cinema that engage cinema's many spatiotemporal complexities. What they have in common is that they make visible, and more to the point physically palpable, what conventional cinema masks. And in laying claim to spatiality as a cinematic trait rather than a sculptural one they manifest a nexus of concepts at large within avant-garde film culture and the art world, including the redefinition of what constitutes an art "object" in the first place. With the advent of digital technology and the increasing presence of moving image art in the gallery, these concepts return with new urgency.

Filmic Objects

One group of expanded works removes the filmstrip from the mediation of projection to put it on display directly. Peter Kubelka and Paul Sharits worked in this form in the 1960s and 1970s, and Kubelka revisited the practice in 2012 with the film *Antiphon* and the exhibition of that film and his earlier work *Arnulf Rainer* (1960) as filmstrips mounted on a wall. *Arnulf Rainer* consists of alternating lengths of black and clear 35mm film accompanied by alternations of silence (unrecorded magnetic tape) and loud, jarring white noise. At times, the alternations of black and white or silence and sound are rapid, producing an aggressive flicker on the screen and percussive, machine-gun-like rhythm on the soundtrack. In other passages, long strips of black or white, and of sound or silence, continue uninterrupted. In the first minute or so of the film, the pulsating soundtrack seems to follow the flickering pattern of the image, the white noise corresponding to the sections of white screen, the silences to those of black. But the film very quickly breaks this pattern so that the bursts of noise are unpredictable and all the more grating. In addition to exhibiting the film in the conventional way, Kubelka cut a print of it into 64 strips of equal length and mounted these in horizontal rows so that the film "ran," in order, from the top left to the bottom right of a large rectangular grid of black and white frames (fig. 4.2).

Antiphon, made 52 years later using the same materials, is a mirror image of *Arnulf Rainer*, each black frame in the former corresponding to a clear frame in the latter, each burst of sound in one met with silence from the other. "Antiphon" is a musical term for choral arrangements in which two choirs sing in a call-and-response pattern formed by carefully coordinated alternating musical phrases—the sonic equivalent of the mirror construction of *Arnulf Rainer* and *Antiphon*. Kubelka's 2012 *Monument Film* joined the twin works in both projected and unprojected forms. Ideally, when the two films are projected simultaneously (either side-by-side or superimposed) they produce visual and aural antiphony. For the installation version of *Monument Film*, Kubelka displayed the strips on facing walls of a gallery, while on the wall between them mounted both films superimposed. Because each clear frame of one film precisely correlated with a black frame in the other, the result of the superimposed installation version was a black rectangle, Kubelka's symbolic fading out of celluloid film in the digital age (figs. 4.3 and 4.4).

From 1971 to 1976 Sharits displayed several of his color flicker films in a similar manner under the heading "Frozen Film Frames" (fig. 4.5). Unlike Kubelka, who mounted his filmstrips directly to the wall, Sharits arranged his dissected films sandwiched between clear sheets of acrylic glass (and in vertical rather than horizontal rows). This allows light to pass through the strips onto the wall behind them, creating a kind of projection of the film simultaneous with its display as physical object. Sharits seems to have arrived at the idea for the *Frozen Film Frames* series by way of his practice of drawing "scores" of his flicker films in advance with colored ink and graph paper, producing a frame-by-frame equivalent to a storyboard (fig. 4.6). These scores map out all-at-once the monochromatic 16mm film frames we see sequentially in his films, bringing to light structural relationships between the individual frames and the total architecture of each film that a viewer likely misses when seeing the films projected. Each variant of the work—drawn score, Plexiglas-mounted

Fig. 4.2. Peter Kubelka standing in front of his film *Arnulf Rainer* (1960). Date and photographer unknown.
Courtesy of Peter Kubelka.

filmstrips, and projected film—represent one of film's "modes of being," from initial conceptualization through projection.[11] Indeed, Sharits frequently displayed score and film together, in both *Frozen Film Frames* exhibitions and his "locational" film

[11] Paul Sharits, "Statement Regarding Multiple Screen/Sound 'Locational' Film Environments—Installations," *Film Culture* 65–66 (1978), p. 79.

Fig. 4.3. Installation of *Monument Film* (Peter Kubelka, 2012) at BFI Southbank, London (October 2012). From left to right: *Arnulf Rainer* and *Antiphon* superimposed, *Antiphon*. Photograph ©2012 Mark Webber.

environments, Sharits's term for film installation before that form became an art world mainstay. The point was to de-hierarchize the different modes, reconceiving projection not as the ultimate aim of filmmaking but simply the final link in a chain of conceptual and material activities, all of equal value. Removing his films from the mechanisms and routines of the apparatus was not an act of isolating them as reified, fetishized objects, but of fragmenting the temporal and spatial unity of the apparatus the better to bring it to the attention of spectators.

This last point begins to respond to a possible objection to including such decidedly "filmic" works in the category of expanded cinema. It might seem counterintuitive to refer to such works as expanded when they seem so manifestly *contracted*, limiting cinema to a single medium and moreover to a solitary element of that medium. Isn't such a practice far too "limiting" to be called expanded cinema? Doesn't it play out an endgame of medium-specificity, a materialism *ad absurdum* that follows the logic of reflexive filmmaking to an inevitable dead end? We could easily interpret works like *Arnulf Rainer*, *Antiphon*, and the *Frozen Film Frames* according to the simplistic medium-specific schema that reduces so many avant-garde films to circular content-as-form/form-as-content materialism. This renders them literally dumb, speaking (meaning) nothing other than their emulsion grains, sprocket holes,

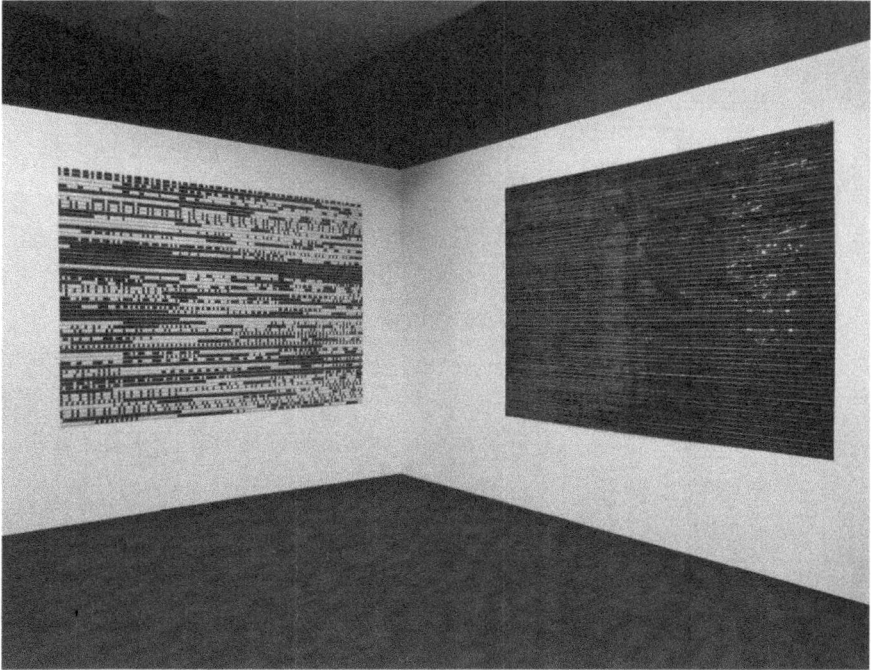

Fig. 4.4. Installation of *Monument Film* (Peter Kubelka, 2012) at BFI Southbank, London (October 2012). From left to right: *Arnulf Rainer, Arnulf Rainer* and *Antiphon* superimposed.
Photograph ©2012 Mark Webber.

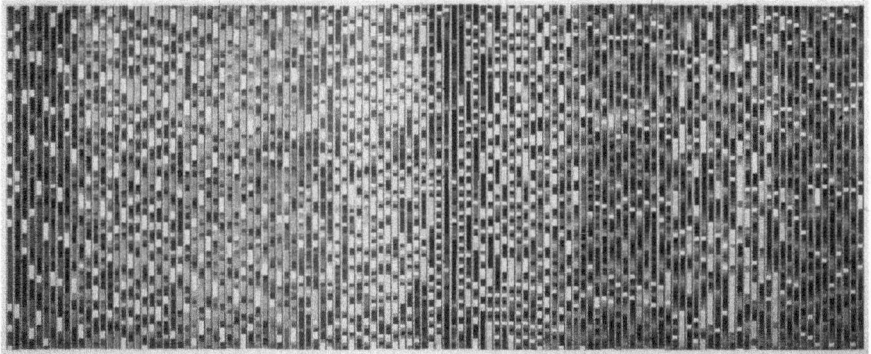

Fig. 4.5. Paul Sharits, *Frozen Film Frame Series*, ca. 1971–1976. 16mm filmstrips and Plexiglas. 30 × 75 in. Burchfield Penney Art Center. Gift of Christopher and Cheri Sharits, 1994.
Image courtesy of Burchfield Penney Art Center. Permission from Christopher and Cheri Sharits.

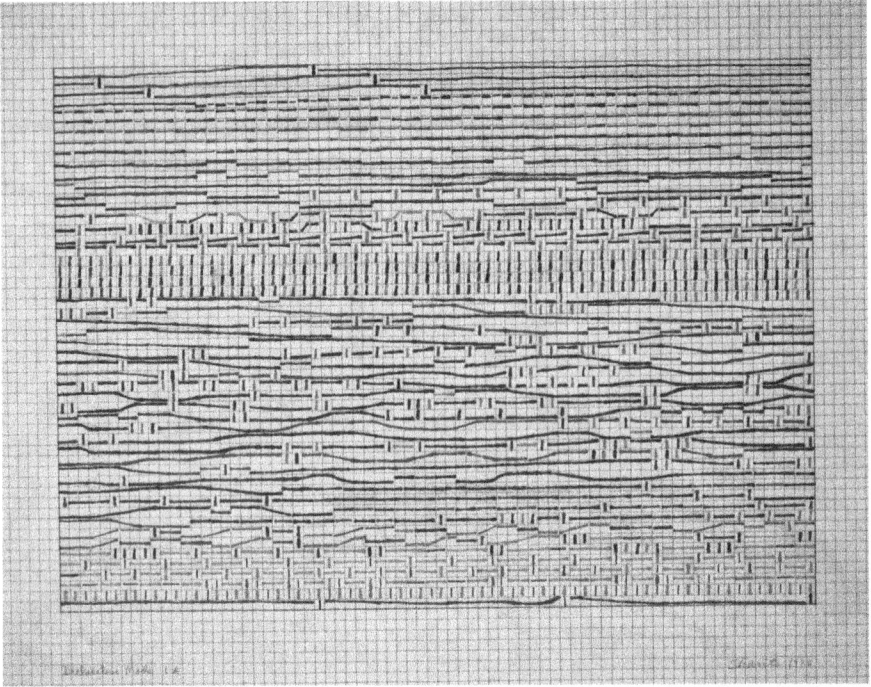

Fig. 4.6. Paul Sharits, score for *Declarative Mode 1A*, 1976–1977. Colored ink on graph paper. 14 × 21 in. Burchfield Penney Art Center. Gift of Sarah Hornbacher, 1988.
Image courtesy of Burchfield Penney Art Center. Permission from Christopher and Cheri Sharits.

and frame lines. And since they take the form of objects, as will the other expanded works in this chapter, we might further critique them as cynical attempts to make marketable artworks by reducing film to tangible physical stuff and associating it with painting and sculpture.

Looking more closely at the historical context from which such works emerged gives the lie to these simplistic readings, however. In a note on his *Frozen Film Frames* Sharits points us toward a richer understanding of these contracted works:

[T]his process of making, at the same time, both a temporal "score" and an all-at-once "drawing" oscillates consciousness at a rate of change which propels one into wholly unexpected tributaries of the "stream" of filmic consciousness (which is the specific perimeter-boundary conditions of the film's total structure); within these perimeters, the "scores" are recordings of co-existing maps of intersected layers of "pattern-consciousness" and maps of gestalted time zones.[12]

---

[12] Paul Sharits, "Exhibition/Frozen Frames," a statement for the 5th International Experimental Film Festival, Knokke, December 1974," *Film Culture* 65–66 (1978), p. 81.

Like many of Sharits's statements, this one requires some decoding. The multiple spatial metaphors here—"tributaries," "perimeter-boundary" relations, "maps," "gestalts," and "zones"—are appropriate to Sharits's task, which is to lay out diagrammatically the entire range of cinematic experiences, including spatial ones. That is, Sharits claims a spatial dimension in cinema to complement its temporal one. That putatively non-temporal art forms like painting and sculpture gained a temporal vector in the discourses of the expanded arts is a truism of art history. What has received much less acknowledgement is that the breakdown of the distinction between temporal and spatial art forms cut both ways, with cinema—and time itself—retheorized under the rubric of *shape*. While Sharits's prose style is often idiosyncratic, his project of re-mapping the spectrum of possible modalities of cinematic experience extended a long history of writing by avant-garde filmmakers about the "shapes" of temporality: in his words, "time shapes."[13]

"The structural film insists on its shape . . . ," Sitney had written in 1969; "that shape is the primal impression of the film"; he also wrote of the "outline" and "field" of structural films.[14] As avant-garde filmmakers searched for new ways to "orchestrate duration" (Sitney again) in structural films, they explored compositional modes that emphasized film's spatial or object properties, militating against its inherent temporality. Such filmmakers could find precedent for this project in Deren's writings on "horizontal" and "vertical" modes of cinematic time, the latter escaping the seemingly undeniable temporal linearity of film for de-temporalized concentration on "the ramifications of the moment."[15] Her 1946 book, *An Anagram of Ideas on Art, Form and Film*, was a temporal form (writing) structured as a grid that could be entered at any point, which is to say not necessarily read linearly (see chapter 6). Scanning the history of avant-garde cinema from Deren to Brakhage to Snow, Michelson traced out a tradition of negating temporality, "an attempt to situate film in a kind of perpetual Present," finding Snow's *Wavelength* to be a culmination of this endeavor that merged the temporal and spatial.[16] Snow described his film as a "time monument" existing as much in space as in time. As Michelson and other critics have pointed out in different ways, the film's relentless zoom is a metaphor for the inextricability of cinematic time and space: simultaneously a temporal event and spatialized object. In Europe, Le Grice explored the possibilities of a non-linear cinema, writing, "from our temporal perceptions we can model spatial relationships, or link temporal events to construct a hierarchy which is not itself linearly causal."[17] Le Grice's filmmaking and theorizing were aimed against narrative illusionism, as were Gidal's, and linearity and causality were the hallmarks of that illusionism. The question for such filmmakers

[13] Sharits, "Words Per Page," p. 38.

[14] Sitney, *Visionary Film*, pp. 369–370 and passim.

[15] Deren made this statement during a symposium on poetry and film held at Cinema 19 on October 28, 1953. The other participants were Willard Maas, Arthur Miller, Dylan Thomas, and Parker Tyler. See "Poetry and the Film: A Symposium," in Sitney, ed., *The Film Culture Reader*, p. 174.

[16] Michelson, "Toward Snow," p. 176.

[17] Malcolm Le Grice, "A Non-Linear Tradition—Experimental Film and Digital Cinema" [1997], in Le Grice, *Experimental Cinema in the Digital Age*, p. 292.

became: how can one organize cinematic works into non-linear, atemporal forms when the medium of film itself was inherently linear—a strip of material passing in a line through a projector, its frames and shots necessarily experienced in sequence? Continental film theory of the 1960s and '70s, which quickly aligned itself with avant-garde filmmaking, articulated the possibility of atemporality in cinema via a cluster of metaphors of grids, tableaux, friezes, and volumes.

Such was the expanded field of cinematic time that avant-garde filmmakers had been mapping out when Sharits turned his attention to the subject in the early 1970s. Outlining an ambitious cinema curriculum at SUNY Buffalo in 1974, one that brought together art history, psychology, linguistics, and philosophy, Sharits proposed a course on "non-temporal cinema."[18] Glossing a history of films that escaped linearity, including "those which poetically suggest *instantaneousness*," Sharits pointed to more recent experimental films that "do not even seem to confront the issue of temporality but exist simply as isotropic 'modulating durations.'"[19] Elsewhere he referred to such films as temporally "homogeneous," lacking a sense of temporal development or of possessing a beginning and end. Reflecting on Sitney's category of structural film, Sharits suggested that such films were perceivable as shapes, as all-at-once compositions, despite the obvious fact that they took time to view:

> [T]he edges of the temporal shape of some new films are highly emphasized; this is because a film's shape, its time-surface area is comprehensible as a discrete unit. The factor of "wholeness" is central to this discreteness. In time, this wholeness is sensed in homogeneous structured works as a constantly simultaneous gestalt.[20]

As examples, Sharits referenced films that appeared to him as fragments of extended processes without a strong sense of temporal development. In Snow and Joyce Weiland's *Dripping Water* (1969), water drips from an off-screen faucet into a white dish in a sink basin for ten minutes; the film begins and ends arbitrarily, as the titular event has no necessary start or end. Sharits also mentioned Warhol's notoriously long and apparently action-less early silent films like *Sleep* (1963) and *Empire* (1964), which also lacked prominent temporal vectors. The very word "vector," which Sharits used in reference to a time/arrow analogy, indicates the unity of temporality and spatiality in his writings and filmmaking practice, which would lead the way to expanded cinema works designed for the gallery space.[21] That expansion was not only into new moving image media, or new forms like performance or multi-screen projection, but into space and thus into the realm of objecthood. And this expansion was not simply the result of avant-garde filmmakers' obsession with the physical materials of their medium. While foregrounding these materials surely made filmmakers more

---

[18] Paul Sharits, "A Cinematics Model for Film Studies in Higher Education," *Film Culture* 65–66 (1978), p. 65.
[19] Ibid., pp. 65–66.
[20] Sharits, "Words Per Page," p. 38.
[21] Ibid., p. 39.

sensitive to the object properties of cinema, what ultimately led to works like *Frozen Film Frames* or the installation version of *Arnulf Rainer* was a reconceptualization of cinematic time that predated structural film and extended to films that were not "materialist" in any obvious ways.

Sharits's diverse output, from drawn scores and *Frozen Film Frames*, to conventionally projected films, to his "locational" film installations designed for galleries and museums, constitute points on a constellation of avant-garde cinema's temporal and physical modalities. We can triangulate each work's position between three modes of cinema's "objecthood": the physical materiality of the filmstrip itself, the formal contours of films as "time shapes," and the institutional space of the cinematic *dispositif* or apparatus. All three conceptions of cinema as object converged by the end of the 1960s, opening up new territory into which cinema expanded. Within this context, the meaning of the film medium was much more complex than standard medium-specific interpretations of films like Sharits's, Snow's, or Warhol's let on. Consider Sharits's claim that thinking of his works simultaneously as "temporal" scores and "all-at-once" drawings "oscillates consciousness at a rate of change which propels one into wholly unexpected tributaries of the 'stream' of filmic consciousness." In describing film's static and dynamic conditions in terms of "oscillation," he invokes the intermittent motion of a strip of film passing through a projector, shifting between the momentary immobility of the film frame in the gate and the smooth, continuous flow of that strip into and out of the projector. In short, by its very physical nature, the film medium was especially well suited as a metaphor for two interconnected ontological states of cinema: as non-temporal material object and temporal, immaterial event. Sharits's *Frozen Film Frames* invoked this expanded field of cinematic traits.

"Cinema is a Greek word that means 'movie,'" Frampton wrote with his tongue in his cheek in 1971:

The illusion of movement is certainly an accustomed adjunct of the film image, but that illusion rests upon the assumption that the rate of change between successive frames may vary only within rather narrow limits. There is nothing in the structural logic of the filmstrip that can justify such an assumption. Therefore we reject it. From now on we will call our art simply: film.[22]

According to Frampton, the film medium was a machine, the "film machine" his answer to Baudry's concept of the apparatus. Every film ever made was a "part" of that machine, designed to interface with it. But Frampton also posited that the "film machine" could run just as well without a film, that "nothing at all" in a running projector was just as much a film as any other.[23] The above passage inverts this principle; rather than removing the filmstrip, Frampton removes everything else, examining the "structural logic of the filmstrip" just as Arthur imagined doing with *Mothlight*.

[22] Frampton, "For a Metahistory of Film," p. 137.
[23] Frampton, "A Lecture," p. 276. See previous chapter.

But even so removed, the lone, naked filmstrip continues to resonate with all the other parts of the film machine, which remain present conceptually even if they are absent materially.

Sharits saw his filmmaking practice as one part of a much broader philosophical inquiry that extended to making objects, writing theoretical essays, and teaching. He referred to this whole body of work as a paradigm in the specific sense employed by structuralist linguists: a range of options whose individual meanings are at least in part defined by all the others, with each choice implicitly referencing the other possible choices *in absentia*. Sharits's tendency to display scores, strips, and film installations together is proof of this:

> In proximate spaces one can observe: scores which have generated a film; that film can be viewed as an object (seen as physical strips serially arranged and encased in plexiglass sheets); and, the projection of my analysis of that film object. There may also be follow-up diagrams and drawings concerning the findings of the inquiry.[24]

Thus, we cannot see this isolation of filmstrips from their normal context (projection) as an act of medium specificity taken to its absolute limits. Rather, the direct mode of display was one strategy among many Sharits employed to embody his expanded paradigm of cinematic qualities and forms.

Kubelka's filmstrips-on-display similarly resonate with other aspects of his filmmaking practice. His small but influential body of work tends to foreground the material of the filmstrip in ways akin to structural film, though most of his major films, including *Adebar*, *Schwechater*, and *Arnulf Rainer*, predate structural film. High-contrast images, rapid flickering of black and clear film, and mathematically precise editing certainly remind viewers of the objecthood of celluloid and the mechanics of projection. But it may be more difficult to draw a line between Kubelka's naked filmstrips and another of his major contributions to avant-garde film history. The "Invisible Cinema," conceived by Kubelka in 1958 and built as Anthology Film Archives' theater in 1970, was designed "to completely eliminate everything but the screen from the visual field" and prevent all environmental distractions—including the audience itself—from interfering with absolute and reverent attention to the screen.[25] The Invisible Cinema was entirely black, with the fire exit signs, a reluctant concession to the fire code, providing the only light other than of the projector. Concave hoods atop each seat surrounded the viewer's head, preventing any communication between spectators and minimizing the very sense of an audience in the first place (fig. 4.7). "There was a feeling," Kubelka has said, "of being in the dark mother's womb from which one would then be born into another world, the world of the film."[26]

---

[24] Paul Sharits, "Cinema as Cognition: Introductory Remarks," *Film Culture* 65–66 (1978), p. 78.
[25] Peter Kubelka, "The Invisible Cinema," *Design Quarterly* no. 93 (1974), p. 32.
[26] Ibid., p. 34.

Fig. 4.7. Inside at the Invisible Cinema at Anthology Film Archives, 1970. From left to right: P. Adams Sitney, Jonas Mekas, Peter Kubelka. Photographer not known. Courtesy of Peter Kubelka.

How can we reconcile Kubelka's materialist filmmaking practice, which disrupts the ideological operations of the cinematic apparatus, with his Invisible Cinema, which looks like the most perfect version of that apparatus ever built? Kubelka's womb metaphor echoes the psychoanalytically inflected descriptions of the apparatus put forth by theorists like Baudry; the passive spectator is absorbed into the fictional world of the film, which replays the formation of the spectator-subject's ego in infancy during what Jacques Lacan called "the mirror phase." Kubelka further claimed that the Invisible Cinema was designed precisely *not* to accommodate expanded cinema: "This kind of cinema is not for multimedia, multi-screen, multiple speakers or for action mixed with film."[27] He distances his project from expanded cinema, claiming, "There is nothing really radical in this project, this is a normal cinema."[28] As Noam Elcott has astutely observed, "*Invisible Cinema* was less an avant-garde reconfiguration of the classical cinema than a bulwark against its avant-garde corruption," further noting "the setting disappears so that the spectator can be more fully absorbed in the projected image."[29] This seems to confirm the Invisible Cinema as the cinematic apparatus par excellence. But if the physical space of the Invisible Cinema was built to be unnoticed—which, ironically, the more unconventional aspects of its

[27] Ibid.
[28] Ibid., p. 35.
[29] Noam Elcott, "Darkened Rooms: A Genealogy of Avant-Garde Filmstrips from Man Ray to the London Film-Makers' Co-op and Back Again," *Grey Room* 30 (Winter 2008), pp. 19 and 20.

design prevented—it was precisely so the physical palpability of the film could be felt all the more forcefully. "In a cinema, one shouldn't be aware of the architectural space so that the film can completely dictate the sensation of space," Kubelka wrote.[30] This suggests the minimizing of one kind of object to make way for a fuller experience of another—the film itself, and the screen. As Elcott reminds us, many of the films shown in the Invisible Cinema treated the screen as surface rather than window, an analog of the surface of the filmstrip itself. In the blackness of Kubelka's theater the screen, its edges unsoftened by curtains to further differentiate the cinema from a theatrical space, appeared as a radiating object rather than an opening onto an imaginary world, a solid instead of a hole. "One has to bring out the sensual taste of cinema"; indeed, Kubelka's conception of cinema was as something tangible not only to the eye and ear but the senses of touch and taste as well.[31] He famously analogized filmmaking to cooking, though his ideas about the latter are unconventional to say the least. For Kubelka, cooking and eating provide us with a more vivid physical experience of our world and our place within it. Consuming something we have cooked reminds us of the labor involved in the preparation, the distances traveled to acquire the ingredients, the struggles with nature to take its fruits and grains, milk and meat. Clearly this is a non-industrial sense of food preparation, a pre-industrial one. Kubelka jokingly compared buying packaged food in a grocery store to the "hunting and gathering" of prehistoric humans. Thus, his cooking analogy speaks of a more intimate relationship between food, preparer, and consumer, and is thus less an analogy to filmmaking in general than to the specific cinematic tradition of avant-garde film. Elsewhere in his writings are references to cinema's sensuousness and tactility. His theory of metrical filmmaking is based on a sense of rhythm and impact, of physical sensations beyond those experienced by the eye and ear:

> I heard this expression yesterday, "to hit the screen," that's fantastic, in English. Hit the screen—this is really what the frames do. The projected frames hit the screen. For example, when you let the projector run empty, you hear the rhythm.[32]

For Kubelka, then, the cinema is a universe of physical and sensual experiences, of real objects rather than illusory substitutions. His rejection of photographic realism is aimed at creating objects with palpable mass, volume, and weight. His hope for the Invisible Cinema was to imbue all the films in Anthology's Essential Cinema program with this sense of objecthood, which necessitated building a theater whose own architectural and spatial properties were pushed into the background. His filmstrips-on-display are simply another variant of this idea of cinema.

---

[30] Kubelka, "The Invisible Cinema," p. 32.
[31] Ibid., p. 35.
[32] Peter Kubelka, "Theory of Metrical Film," in Sitney, ed., *The Avant-Garde Film*, p. 139.

"Reductionism ad Absurdum"

Between 1972 and 1975, Tony Conrad engaged in a concentrated critique of the technologies and institutions of conventional cinema, one that additionally targeted avant-garde film. During this time he produced a series of cinematic objects, installations, and performances. Among these was a group of films Conrad made without a camera, working with the material directly in ways that rendered the results semi- or un-projectable and thus requiring a direct mode of display. *Deep Fried 4-X Negative* (1973) was made just as the title indicates; 400 feet of that stock on a core was fried in cooking oil, the result a mass of melted and warped film too brittle to remove from its film can (fig. 4.8). The process changed the warm brown of the original unexposed stock to a range of other colors, and the smell of the oil remained even after decades had passed. *Pickled 3M 150* (1974) consists of 12 glass jars containing twisted strips of film, vinegar, red peppers, and spices (fig. 4.9). Conrad had to "restore" the work in 2006 because chemical reactions inside the pickling jars had caused their metal lids to corrode. For *Roast Kalvar* (1974), Conrad twisted a length of vesicular film stock into a tight mass of curls, stapled the ends together, exposed it to sunlight for several

Fig. 4.8. Tony Conrad, *Deep Fried 4-X Negative* (1973). Fried 4-X negative 16mm film stock.

Photograph by Andrew Lampert.

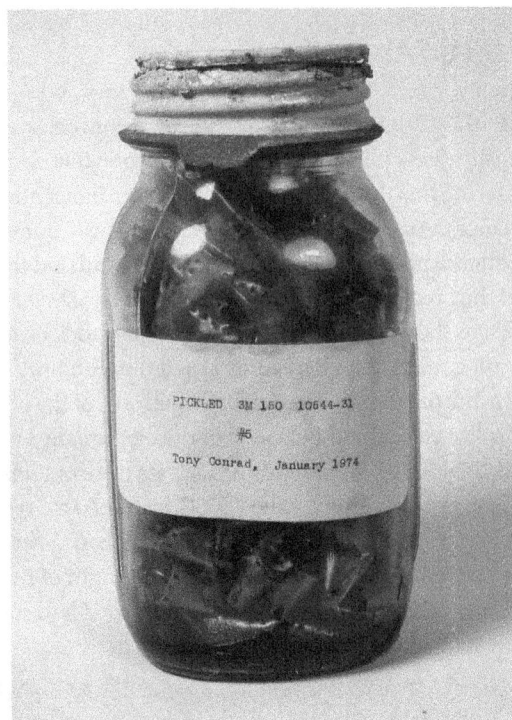

Fig. 4.9. Tony Conrad, *Pickled 3M 150* (1974). 16mm film stock in canning jars with vinegar, vegetables, sugar, salt, and spices.
Courtesy of the Tony Conrad Estate and Greene Naftali, New York.

minutes, then roasted the film in an oven at over 400 degrees. Kalvar was a brand of vesicular film, which is only sensitive to UV light and is processed by heating rather than the usual chemical methods, so Conrad's treatment of the stock was not so unusual. But roasting the stock rather than heating it at the recommended 200 degrees caused the mass of film to become brittle, crisping around the edges so that it can only be displayed in a hair net nestled inside a wooden box, gently passed from one audience member to another during "screenings." As an object, it is visually striking—cobalt blue with lighter shades of blue around its chipping edges, damage that Conrad has described as a "record of its own history of transport and exhibition."[33]

The first thing to note about these films is that they seem at once to fetishize the film medium and subvert it. Their direct modes of display are consequences of their unprojectability, which is to say that they are simultaneously more and less visible than conventionally produced films. It should be added that, until very recently, these works were historically invisible—practically unknown even among experimental

[33] Tony Conrad, program notes for *Roast Kalvar* for Exprmntl 5, Knokke-Heist, Belgium, 1974. From Conrad's personal files.

film scholars. Their highlighting of film stock obviates the other material elements of the medium such as cameras, projectors, and screens that materialist films made into their content at least as frequently as emulsion grains and sprocket holes. The links in the chain of production and exhibition are swapped out for alternative processes; rather than expose the films with a camera, Conrad subjected them to heat, direct sunlight, or cooking liquids; projection is abandoned for a more direct and tactile exhibition mode, in which "visuals" are accompanied by qualities perceived through senses of touch and smell. Chemical processing is replaced by other means of altering the physical structure of the emulsion.

To understand the peculiarities of these films and their apparent ambivalence toward the medium itself, we must understand that Conrad intended them as interventions in what he saw as a major obstacle for avant-garde cinema. He has playfully described this obstacle as "an apotheosis of avant-garde omphaloscopsis."[34] Conflating omphaloskepsis and omphaloscopy, both of which mean "navel-gazing," Conrad is referring to the intensive medium-specific reflexivity of avant-garde film during the period. In 1972 Conrad had spent time in Kassel, Germany, showing several of his films and assisting the avant-garde composer La Monte Young, with whom he was co-founder of the avant-garde musical ensemble the Theatre of Eternal Music. At Documenta Conrad saw for the first time structural-materialist films by Raban, Le Grice, and Gidal, all made in the London Filmmakers' Cooperative. These rigorously formal, reflexive "films about film" were dubbed "ascetic" by the critic Deke Dusinberre, meaning they denied any reference other than self-reference, reference to the materiality of film and filmmaking labor. Conrad was influenced by these films, but he also felt that the unprecedented extent to which they took filmic formalism was a liability, and an indication of a larger problem facing avant-garde filmmakers.

Conrad's experience at Kassel revealed a disparity between self-identified "avant-garde filmmakers" and artists from the gallery world who had recently taken up film to extend their interests in conceptual, performative, and process-based work. He recalls:

> When I arrived at [Documenta 5], I found that the work by filmmakers was shown at the local movie house, while the films by artists were displayed more generously *in the palace* [the Rotes Palais]. The filmmakers were—and for the most part still are—very obviously being sent to the back of the bus.[35]

It was during this time that the distinction emerged in the avant-garde between "filmmakers" and artists who made films among many other kinds of artworks, where the former were much more concerned with filmmaking materials and craft than the latter (a comparison can be made to Pearlman's distinction between "craft-" and

---

[34] Tony Conrad, untitled email to Fred Camper (March 14, 2001), posted on Frameworks Experimental Film Discussion List, http://www. frameworks.com/archives.htm.
[35] Conrad, "Is This Penny Ante or a High Stakes Game?," pp. 103–104.

"concept-based" artists discussed in chapter 2). For Conrad, the obsession with materiality characteristic of avant-garde filmmakers but not of "artists" who made films was both aesthetically exhausted and politically suspect. It was exhausted because the formalism of structural and structural-materialist films had played out in the other arts a decade earlier by Conrad's reckoning, which meant that avant-garde filmmakers were bringing up the rear in the modernist project of artistic progress. It was politically suspect because it bought into modernism's rhetoric of artistic "advancement," a term that appeared throughout Greenberg's writings. According to the dominant Greenbergian strain of modernist art history, art "advanced" through formalism, as each art form clarified and explored the formal territory unique to it. During an association with Fluxus in the early-to-mid-sixties Conrad had come to think of modernism as serving the needs of the art market by promoting, in his words, a "progressive and idealist sense of discovery and development."[36] He had turned to avant-garde film at that time because he had been attracted to its detachment from the art market and its alternative economic model in which film prints were not regarded as art objects and thus not marketable. But by the time he participated in Documenta 5 he had begun to feel that this ethic of progressivism had crept into avant-garde cinema, abetted by the formalist aesthetic of structural film.

Conrad wasn't alone in his suspicions of avant-garde film's materialism. Recall Dusinberre's criticisms of structural-materialist film's literalism outlined in chapter 2. Even Gidal, one of the targets of Dusinberre's critique, distanced himself from the kind of filmic purism typically attributed to structural-materialist film, warning against a merely "mechanistic materialism" and claiming that "the assertion of film as material" was nothing more than another mode of representation that by no means guaranteed anti-illusionist demystification of cinema.[37] In her introduction to the film and video exhibition catalogue for "A Survey of the Avant-Garde in Britain," presented in 1972 by the Gallery House in London (figs. 4.10 and 4.11), curator Rosetta Brooks urged filmmakers to move on, as it were:

> Much is spoken presently of the need to "explore the film medium" and there is a general appreciation of the necessity for changing the extant norms of filmmaking and redeveloping the practice upon newly acknowledged fundamentals ... However, a purely reductionistic tendency can rarely be sustained without reason, i.e. without acknowledgement of some "conclusion." This is to say that the logical objective of reductionistic filmmaking must be in the construction of new norms of action. A blind insistence upon reductionism as norm is ultimately self-defeating. A prescription at this point might be to make more explicit the speculative component of film works because to ignore this aspect, i.e. to leave it as an implicit component in the film work is to prescribe "reductionism ad absurdum."[38]

[36] Ibid., p. 103.

[37] Peter Gidal, "Theory and Definition of Structural/Materialist Film," p. 15 and pp. 2–3, respectively.

[38] Rosetta Brooks, "Introduction," from *A Survey of the Avant-Garde in Britain* exhibition catalogue (London: Gallery House, 1972), p. 1.

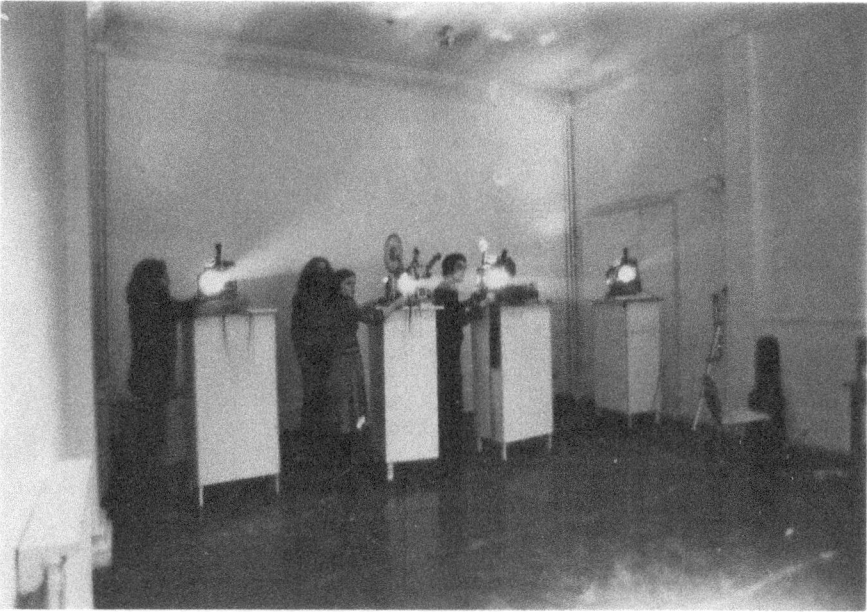

Fig. 4.10. The Filmaktion Group (left to right Malcolm Le Grice, Gill Eatherley, and William Raban) performing during "A Survey of the Avant-Garde in Britain" at the Gallery House in London, March 1973.
Image courtesy William Raban.

While acknowledging the necessity of materialist "reductionism" for the development of more heterogeneous and likely more progressive modes of filmmaking, Brooks also notes a drawback to such a practice. Implicit in her remarks is a critique of the structural-materialist aesthetic as leading to a dead end wherein filmmakers merely reiterated film's properties rather than revealing undiscovered possibilities for the medium—Dusinberre's "tautological" bind that reduced each work to a "film about film." That is, the foregrounding of the materials of film had become an end in itself rather than one step in a process of creating "new norms" of film production and spectatorship that challenged the assumptions about cinema underpinning the old norms. The question, then, was "what next?" How to escape this bind, how to exit the materialist cul-de-sac avant-garde film was circling?

Noël Carroll has argued that Frampton's concept of the "metahistorian of film" was a response to precisely this challenge. What Carroll calls cinematic "essentialism," his label for the medium-specific purism of structural film, eventually posed a serious problem for its practitioners: "once the essential destiny of an artform is reached, the form effectively dies (in the sense that there is no reason for anyone practicing in that artform to continue making work in it)."[39] Once a strategy for producing genuinely

[39] Noel Carroll, "A Brief Comment on Frampton's Notion of Metahistory," in Carroll, *Theorizing the Moving Image* (Cambridge: Cambridge University Press, 1996), p. 315.

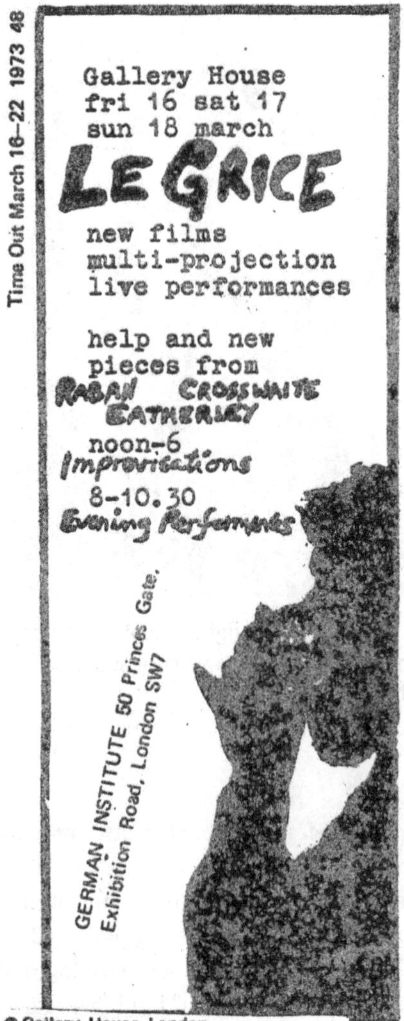

● Gallery House London
50 Princes Gate, SW7 (589 7207)
(South Ken tube)
Fri to Sun:
An exploration of projection and the relationship of pre-filmed material to current Time/Space by Malcolm Le Grice, David Crosswaite, William Raban and Gill Eatherley, plus spatial projection event by Annabel Nicolson. Entrance free, come any time during the day (noon to 6.00). From 8.00 to 10.30 there will be a more formal show of Multi Projection films and live event film pieces. Worth turning up at the start for this. See Film News for futher comment.

Fig. 4.11. Advertisement in *Time Out* (March 16–22, 1973) for film performances by Malcolm Le Grice, William Raban, David Crosswait, Gill Eatherley, and Annabel Nicolson during "A Survey of the Avant-Garde in Britain" at the Gallery House in London. Image courtesy Malcolm Le Grice.

new work, the essentialist approach quickly brought filmmakers to a dead end. As Carroll states it, the approach "promote[d] a situation in which the answer to the question 'What is to be done?' is 'Nothing.' This is scarcely a viable *modus operandi* for the working avant-gardist."[40] Frampton's metahistorian of film re-enters cinema's past to (re)discover possibilities that tautological assumptions about the art form's "destiny" or essence do not, and cannot, acknowledge. The historical turn prescribed by Frampton could provide the means for "the construction of new norms of action," to use Brooks's words. But while the metahistorian looked back upon cinema's mixed and decidedly essence-less past for new possibilities, Conrad did the opposite, imagining the near future of an essentialist cinema finally exhausting itself and thus freeing filmmakers to "get a move on." He has described his work of this period as initiating an endgame designed to "intervene by hastening the inevitable playing out of formalist exploration, in which waves of filmmakers would otherwise painfully and incrementally claim delusively novel territory, leading in the end to the already familiar depletion of new formal ideas and the 'dematerialization' of the medium."[41] In this statement, Conrad invokes the interplay between contraction and expansion whereby a concentrated materialist filmmaking practice ironically results in its opposite: the dematerialization of cinema. Pushing the reductionist project to its limits reaches a point of reversal where cinema is no longer closed down but opens up into a diverse domain of forms and materials. This is precisely what Conrad's work did. And while strips of film displayed in pickle jars, bound in hairnets, or smelling of cooking oil parody a materialist filmmaking practice that might be said to fetishize the medium, Conrad did not intend them solely as comic barbs. The films genuinely undermine the conventional means of production and exhibition, interrogating their underlying values and offering alternative possibilities.

These alternative possibilities do not just point the way out of a filmmaking style rapidly getting old. For Conrad, expanded cinema was a political necessity for moving past an aesthetic that reinforced the progressive rhetoric of modernism and placed filmmakers in a subsidiary position relative to other artists. But it was also a political necessity because structural film's medium-specific formalism reproduced the technological and economic determinism inherent in all filmmaking. Presenting several of his cameraless films at the Millennium Film Workshop in June 1974, Conrad explained it this way:

> I have a certain sense of disappointment about the fact that the filmmaker is expected to use a certain kind of material that he buys in a box ... He runs down to Kodak and he buys a box of this stuff ... and then he takes it home and he puts it into an instrument manufactured by somebody else, and then he's supposed to perform specific operations on it, like cutting the material, and then putting it back together ... and then running it on a projector, manufactured by somebody

---

[40] Ibid.
[41] Conrad, "Is This Penny Ante or a High Stakes Game?," p. 104.

else, and this inextricable bind to the commercial process infuriates me to some degree ... and in seeking an outlet for that, during last fall, I looked to alternative mechanisms to working with the material other than using the camera and that might allow me to express some sentiment about the material and the way I felt about it.[42]

The specific film of which he was speaking was *4X Attack* (1973). In very simplified terms, Conrad created the film imagery by exerting pressure on the emulsion rather than exposing it to light. Specifically, he hammered 50 feet of surplus machine-gun film into hundreds of tiny bits, which he then collected, flash-exposed with a strobe light to make the effects of the hammering evident in projection, and processed chemically in a cheesecloth sack. He then obsessively glued the tiny pieces back together, checking his work against the edge numbers. Having completed this painstaking editing task, Conrad printed the film onto positive stock (fig. 4.12). The imagery that results in projection is minimal, but knowledge of the process behind it allows one to recognize evidence of the hammering, exposing, and gluing. Light-gray scratches stand out against the darker gray background. The missing bits of emulsion that Conrad never found register as bright white holes in the film, and shadows of emulsion flecks flicker across the screen in varying shades of gray and degrees of focus depending on their relative position in the mass of film pieces at the moment they were exposed to light.

If Conrad was looking for filmmaking methods that would "express some sentiment about the material and the way I felt about it," *4X Attack* comically suggests that the sentiment he had in mind was rage. That is, Conrad was frustrated by the extent to which supposedly radical filmmakers were in fact limited by strictures imposed upon them by the corporations that owned the materials and processes of filmmaking: Kodak, Pageant, Fuji, and so on. An aesthetic that so heavily emphasized these inadvertently accepted the yoke of this determinism, for Conrad a kind of third strike against the already ponderous and arbitrarily constraining formalism of structural film. His statement about *4X Attack* situates his cameraless films within avant-garde cinema's tradition of seeking alternative means of production that rejected the values of industrial filmmaking. But, with a view toward the other meaning of "industrial film" described in chapter 2, Conrad extends the scope of the avant-garde's project to the entire institutional framework in which films are made, circulated, and seen. Conrad's work circumvents the entire chain along which a film moves through a mode of film practice, from the processes of production to the mechanics of projection and the conventions of exhibition.

This act of circumvention is expanded cinema's defining gesture. *4X Attack*'s title recalls Sheldon Renan's claim about the origins of expanded cinema, that "the artists have *attacked*" conventional filmmaking. Conrad's expression of frustration during

---

[42] Tony Conrad, partial transcription from a talk given at the Millennium Film Workshop, printed in "Montage of Voices," *Millennium Film Journal* 16/17/18, p. 257.

Fig. 4.12. Tony Conrad, stills from *4X Attack* (1973). 16mm film, black and white, silent. Running time 60 seconds.

Photograph by Branden W. Joseph.

the Millennium screening resonates with the liberatory rhetoric of expanded cinema's first wave, which saw tradition as a constraint to be thrown off. But there is a crucial difference between Conrad's attack and the one described by Renan. While Conrad indeed subverts the standard practices of filmmaking, he nonetheless maintains a link to those practices by way of analogies to normal modes of working with the medium. In this sense his cameraless films, along with other expanded cinema works to be discussed shortly, align with Dusinberre's critique of British structural-materialist film's literal meaninglessness. Conrad did precisely what Dusinberre claimed was necessary for materialist film to become meaningful, cultivating an analogy between his films and an external, non-filmic meaning system. Like Kubelka, Conrad chose cooking, as the titles of so many of his cameraless films attest: *Deep Fried 4X Negative, Pickled 3M 150, Roast Kalvar, 7360 Sukiyaki, Curried 7302* (1973), *Raw Film* (1973), *Pickle Wind* (1974), *Boiled Shadow* (1974). Conrad's analogic approach was somewhat more complex, however. Cooking was an "algorithm" rather than an analogy. While an analogy can be a loose connection, an algorithm is more systematic, providing a rigorous structure that directs each stage of the filmmaking process. Conrad, who had a degree in mathematics from Harvard, seems to have imagined this process as something like an algebraic equation whose variables could be filled by any specific material or action. For instance, the camera could be swapped out for any other mechanism that could produce images on film, such as hammering, roasting, pickling, or direct exposure to light.

Cooking was not Conrad's only algorithm. Domestic activities that we might call "home crafts" or domestic hobbies like sewing and knitting, collage, scrapbooking, or doing puzzles also provided the outline for alternative filmmaking modes. Conrad's *4X Attack* combined several of these. A late work in the series of cameraless films was *Flicker Matte* (1974), a play on the flicker films Conrad had made in the 1960s and early '70s, and would continue to make for another year: *The Flicker* (1966), *Straight and Narrow* (with Beverly Conrad, 1970), the performative work *Ten Years Alive on the Infinite Plane* (1972), *The Eye of Count Flickerstein*, 1967/75, and *Articulation of Boolean Algebra for Film Opticals* (1975). Conrad interwove strips of black and clear 16mm film leader into a square mat, the alternative spelling of "mat" possibly suggesting matte work in the production of special optical effects in conventionally made films (fig. 4.13). Another "alternative mechanism to working with the material other than using the camera" was what he dubbed the "pickle wind." There is one film that bears the name *Pickle Wind* from 1974, but that term refers to a method Conrad used in several cameraless works including *Roast Kalvar*. This method was something akin to knitting. Conrad removed the strip of film from its spool and wound it over and over again onto itself until it could not be twisted any further. He devised a mathematical formula that determined the number of twists possible for a given length of film: the square root of the quantity "s" (the length of the filmstrip) over multiplied by 0.004 (the thickness of the filmstrip in inches).[43] Once he reached the maximum

[43] Tony Conrad, personal interview, October 7, 2004.

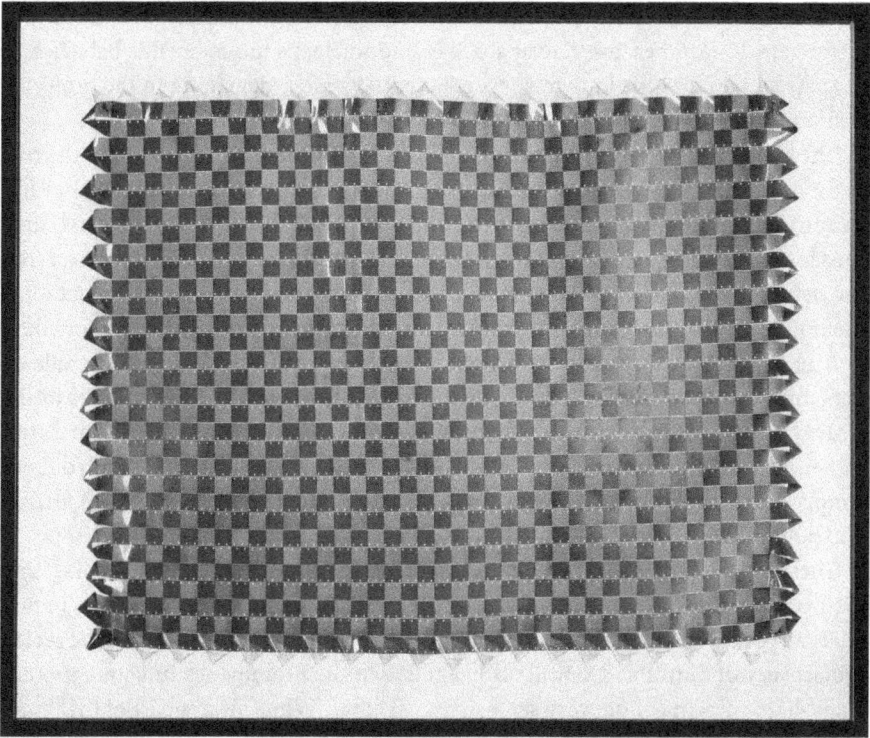

Fig. 4.13. Tony Conrad, *Flicker Matte* (1974). Kalvar 16mm film stock and microfilm, 21½ × 27¼ inches (54.5 × 69 cm).

©The Estate of Tony Conrad. Photo courtesy Galerie Buchholz, Berlin/Cologne.

number of possible twists, he stapled the ends of the filmstrip together so the tight helix form would hold. From there, the pickle wind could be processed and presented in several different ways. For the original *Pickle Wind* (536 twists, approximately four minutes long if projectable), Conrad again used Kalvar, as that stock's relative insensitivity to light allowed him to make the wind in normal room light without overexposing it. Once he had completed the twisting, he flash exposed the mass of twisted film to sunlight, heated it to 200 degrees in an oven, then untwisted it and reprinted it on regular film stock for projection.

Like *4-X Attack*, *Pickle Wind* reveals a record of its own making when projected. Black and white shadows of the different layers of the twisted helix flash across the screen in varying shades of gray and different degrees of focus dependent upon how distant each section of the film was from the outside edges of the wound mass. Thus, the film reflects, however obliquely, the structure of the wind, its three-dimensionality. Conrad made *Shadow* (1974) much the same way, only he did not reprint the Kalvar original but unstapled its ends, untwisted it, and re-spooled it onto a film reel for standard projection. The twisting and baking process rendered the film difficult to project, so it often lost its loops or intermittently slipped out of registration in the projector gate. In fact, because Kalvar stock is so durable, its unpredictable behavior in the gate and around the loop formers is potentially more damaging to the projector than to the strip itself.

The home crafts algorithm suggested itself when Conrad found himself in the role of "house husband" in the early 1970s, caring for a child and home he had with Beverly Grant when both were professors of film at Antioch College. His cameraless films thus interrogated this traditionally feminine social position as much as they explored the nature of the film medium, which is to say that his crafts algorithm linked filmmaking to an exploration of the political ramifications of gender roles, reconciling radical artistic practice and the constraints of domesticity in a manner that paralleled contemporaneous work by Annabel Nicholson, Gil Eatherly, and Lis Rhodes in the United Kingdom. Concomitantly, Conrad reclaimed filmmaking as an artisanal craft rather than an industrial process. Like EXPORT's expanded cinema, Conrad's did not simply reject traditional filmmaking out of hand but purged it of perceived artistic and political liabilities, realigning it with the avant-garde's values.

These works constitute an early, indeed prescient example of a filmmaker asserting his work as artisanal craft scaled to the level of individual labor rather than industrial, corporate, assembly-line production à la Hollywood studio products. The recent rediscovery of films like Conrad's is likely due to the prominence in contemporary avant-garde cinema of the very same artisanal ethos. While always part of that cinema's history, that ethos has found its most direct expression in recent work. Craft, in the specific sense elaborated thus far, has become a wellspring of meaning for a new generation of filmmakers. So too have analogies between film and the natural world, the human body, and scientific inquiry, envisioned as the work of individuals rather than R&D branches of corporations—amateur opposed to professional science. The direct display of film makes plain the physical traits of the medium that projection necessarily masks, opening the film object to bodily, organic, scientific, and craft analogies. For each of these there is a related set of emotional evocations, often based upon a perceived threat that resonates with the threat of obsolescence that film faces in the wake of digital media's remediation of it. Organic things decay, the body dies, experiments fail, craft at the individual level is both marginalized and vulnerable to the obsolescence of materials and practices enforced by profit-motivated industries. These dyads of positive value and accompanying danger are at once reflexive, in that they are metaphors for film's precarious position in the digital age, and externally referential, in that they relate the medium to another paradigm of materials, activities, and ideas.

One final observation to be made about the filmic objects of artists like Conrad, Sharits, and Kubelka is that they elaborate a wide range of unexplored formal possibility in a simple strip of film viewed by itself. They suggest something that later filmmakers have taken to heart: that viewing a strip of celluloid "off the reel" not only satisfies our curiosity about how its images are produced, but is a source of aesthetic pleasure in and of itself. Sharits's *Frozen Film Frames* and Kubelka's *Monument Film* favor the mathematical precision of frames, lines, and sprocket holes, taking these as the basis for their austere grid patterns. Conrad's tortured filmstrips, though frequently based upon algorithms, are messy and imprecise, showing off film's sinuousness and flexibility, offering the same kinds of pleasure we might take in looking at natural objects and phenomena. Even *Flicker Matte*, which is a grid, is constructed more like a loose braid of natural material. It is to the *Frozen Film Frames* or *Monument Film* what a child's needlepoint project is to a professionally stitched garment, a thatched hut compared to a modern house. Taken together, then, the displayed filmstrips of Conrad, Sharits, and Kubelka mapped out a terrain of visual possibilities and metaphoric associations in which contemporary avant-garde filmmakers continue to work.

"Materiality Made Expressive"

Conrad's cameraless filmmaking project was at once an extension of Brakhage's direct filmmaking techniques and a kind of joke on the conceit behind them. When Conrad spoke of wanting to "express some sentiment about the material [of film]," he comically invoked Brakhage's link to Abstract Expressionist painting and the mythic scale to which it raised the artist's work. Conrad's hammering of film stock aped the interpretations of Abstract Expressionism as "gestural" or "action" painting, interpretations that were extended to Brakhage's films and of which Michelson was critical; Conrad undoubtedly would have felt much the same way. An unrealized and unrealizable film "performance" outlined around 1969 by Sharits aims the same expressive fury at the materials of the medium and similarly generates grim humor at the expense of the Brakhage school of filmmaking. *Didactic Movie Event—Autological Suicide: scene for film artist at the end of his rope* is an illustrated "score," though in a much different spirit than the drawn and painted color grid scores Sharits produced in connection with his flicker films (fig. 4.14). *Didactic Movie Event* illustrates a figure lying on his back against a film screen spread out on the floor. The figure grasps the end of a cord connected via a system of suspended pulleys to a film projector dangling precariously over his head. A series of instructions accompanying the illustration explains the arrangement, the final instruction reading: "Let go of cord; brain imagery will be projected onto screen." Another section of text, separate from the instructions, makes terms for expressive cinematic devices into death metaphors, including "a stylish lap dissolve of death-into-life" and " 'self-projection' through 'image' un-focusing—a truly static, but deeply 'moving' picture." In addition to playing out many of Sharits's familiar preoccupations—physical violence, parallels between the film medium and the body, film's dual nature as static object and moving image—*Didactic Movie Event* parodies the lyrical, mythopoeic strain of filmmaking epitomized by Brakhage and

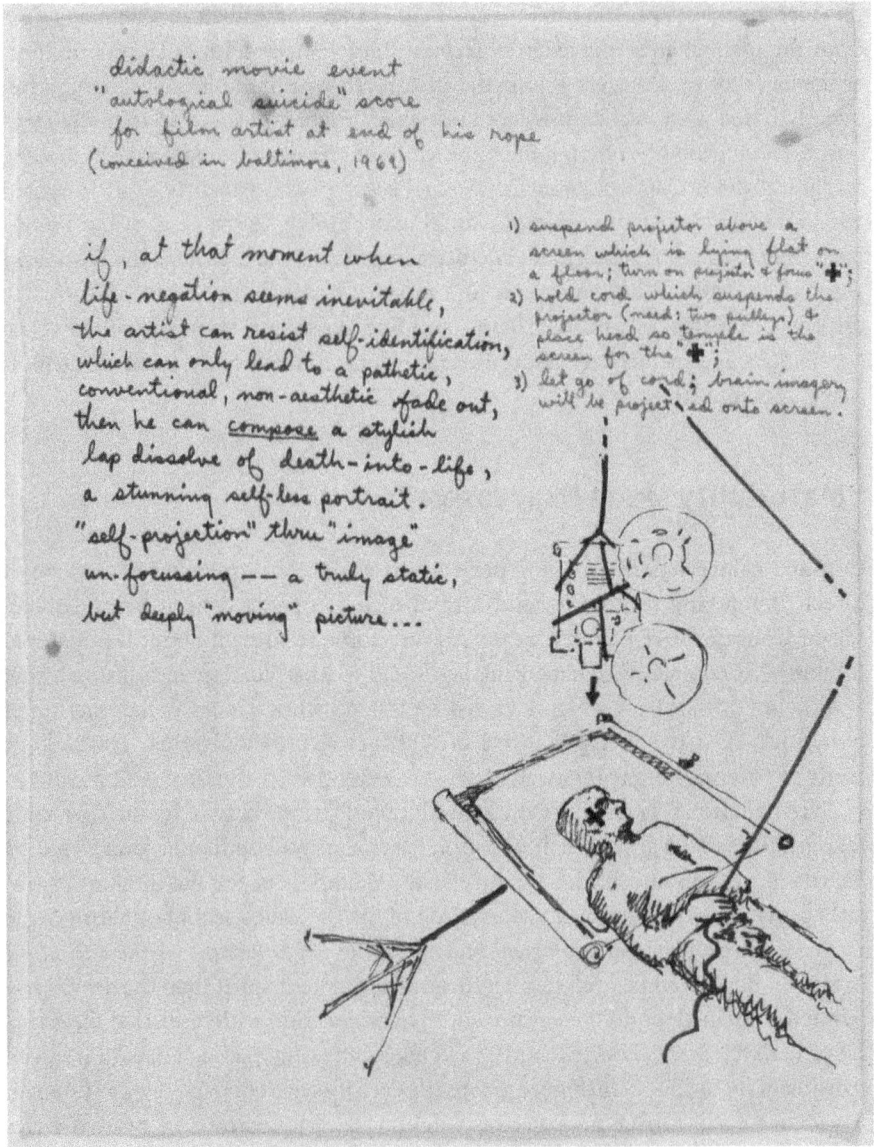

Fig. 4.14. Paul Sharits, *Didactic Movie Event—Autological Suicide: scene for film artist at the end of his rope* (1969).
Permission from Christopher and Cheri Sharits.

embodied in Abstract Expressionism's heroic rhetoric of individual expressivity. It grotesquely literalizes the projection of the filmmaker's mental world into the splattering of "brain imagery" onto the screen.[44]

---

[44] *Didactic Movie Event* is in the Paul Sharits file of the Museum of Modern Art.

We have seen how films and works of expanded cinema by structural filmmakers like Conrad and Sharits have frequently been taken as literally meaningless, signifying only the materiality of film itself and thus dangerously cut off from reality. That some of their works also mocked the notion of using film to convey psychological states seems to be further evidence of their cinematic literalism. But the terrain here is complicated. Analogies to homemaking and craft (Conrad) or to the human body and its frailties (Sharits) were links between materialist filmmaking and external meaning systems that endowed films with the potential for referencing something other than their own materials. And the translation of the expressionistic mode of filmmaking espoused by Brakhage into literal, physical terms entails a sense of tactility and, more to the point, fragility, heightened when film processing and projection are imagined as violent acts. In short, there is a sense of pathos in these works because of the ways they suggest the vulnerability and mortality of both film and the human body. In this way, the historical works of expanded cinema discussed thus far are important precursors to contemporary work not only in directly displaying the filmstrip, but also in making that material expressive. I use the word "expressive" in the simple, pre-theoretical sense of representing something, as in a film referring to something other than itself. Perhaps this seems too simple, but it is critical given the still widespread perception of materialist films as didactic primers on film as film without any other meanings.

Reflecting on recent developments in avant-garde cinema in 2003, Arthur took this criticism even further: "a varied cadre of American artisanal image-makers have [sic] embraced what is essentially a decorative ideal, color and texture without apparent overall shape, drained of subjective or expressive cues, immune to internal metaphor."[45] About Bruce McClure's early projection performance Indeterminate Focus (1999), which utilized film McClure had scratched with sandpaper of varying grit sizes and densities, Arthur claimed, "This technique produces swirling filigrees of color or line that build and recede, but there is no feeling that such developmental cues can be translated into non-literal meanings, allegories of emulsion grain or microcosmic worlds."[46] Arthur implies that such works make no meanings whatsoever, not even the tautological meaning of reflexivity: "films about film." "Decorative" here stands for meaningless, inexpressive abstraction. I hope to have made some headway already in showing the flaws in this position. The rest of this chapter will show the ways in which both literal and figurative meanings are not only present in contemporary works of expanded cinema, but more to the point are mutually sustaining. Interestingly, Conrad and Sharits worried over abstract film's "decorativeness" in 1975, on the occasion of the first screening of the former's Articulation of Boolean Algebra for Film Opticals. Conrad recalls a conversation he had with Sharits after the screening: "Whatever, [Sharits] wondered, was the answer to the problem of film,

[45] Paul Arthur, A Line of Sight: American Avant-Garde Film Since 1965 (Minneapolis: University of Minnesota Press, 2005), pp. 167–168.
[46] Ibid., p. 168.

which as it began to share in the values of other artists generally also began to share in the quandary of ultimately appearing decorative, to the extent that it assumed the personality of abstract art."[47]

By "expressive" I also mean the more art-specific sense of evoking ideas and emotional states by strategically utilizing a medium's materials. This is not necessarily to say that works of art should be interpreted as expressing the thoughts and feelings of their makers, though this is one possibility. "Expressive" here simply means that artworks can suggest or imply emotions and evoke them in a perceiver. This is often thought of as a matter of subsuming artistic media to referential meaning, as in Greenberg's claim that "[r]ealistic, naturalistic art had dissembled the medium, using art to conceal art; modernism used art to call attention to art."[48] This is especially significant for cinema. "Cinematic expressivity" usually means the expression or evocation of narrative content, which requires, if not complete concealment of specifically cinematic devices like continuity editing, at least their camouflage under the veil of narrative motivation. A certain camera angle, lighting pattern, editing choice, or strain of non-diegetic music conveys story information or amplifies the emotions of the scene. This way of thinking about cinema's expressivity may seem irrelevant to avant-garde film, which "calls attention to art" and by most accounts minimizes external reference and appeals to the intellect rather than the emotions, with aesthetic pleasure an especially suspect emotional response to a materialist film. Finally, expressivity in mainstream cinema is also conventional, relying on extrinsic norms rather than building unconventional, intrinsic norms, which is the innovation expected of avant-garde cinema. The common phrases "cinematic language" or "film grammar" speak to this conventionality in a linguistic sense. For all of these reasons, one might hesitate to attribute expressivity to works of expanded cinema. But this is exactly the quality that contemporary makers of expanded cinema have cultivated, and they have taken their cue, if sometimes indirectly, from the work of the previous generation, which turns out to be not so strictly materialist after all.

In addition to their projection performances, Sandra Gibson and Luis Recoder have also produced a large body of cinematic installations and objects. No other avant-garde filmmakers have explored the idea of "the death of cinema" as deeply, at once tapping into the pathos generated by the notion of film's obsolescence and questioning the veracity of that very notion. Indeed, one of the animating principles of their work seems to be that death, decay, and loss are essential qualities of the medium. While digital technology may have ushered in an era of "cinema without film," Gibson and Recoder have staked a claim for the opposite, underpinning a body of work made from "film without cinema." Recuperating death as an unavoidable, creatively generative feature of film rather than the result of external historical

---

[47] Tony Conrad, "Articulation of Boolean Algebra for Film Opticals," unpublished document from Conrad's personal files, dated November 2, 1975, p. 1. Available on the online Vasulka Archive: http://www.vasulka.org/archive/Artists1/Conrad,Tony/BooleanAlgebra.pdf.

[48] Clement Greenberg, "Modernist Painting," in Francis Frascina and Charles Harrison, eds., *Modern Art and Modernism: A Critical Anthology* (New York: Harper and Row, 1982), p. 6.

Fig. 4.15. Sandra Gibson and Luis Recoder, *Hand-Cranked* (2012). 35mm hand-painted film, 35mm film rewinds, dimensions variable. Installation view, *Cinematograph: Gibson + Recoder*, The Craddock-Terry Gallery, Lynchburg, VA, January 6–February 19, 2012. Photograph by Gibson + Recoder. Courtesy of the artists and The Craddock-Terry Gallery.

circumstances, Gibson and Recoder have made a group of filmic objects that oscillate between the poles of anxiety or sorrow over film's loss and pleasure in its resiliency and resurrection.

In Gibson and Recoder's 2013 gallery show *Cinematograph*, an array of objects placed about the space represented the fracturing of film and cinema. Pieces of filmic stuff removed from the system in which they typically operate and which, one could say, "gives them life," sat atop plinths, hung from the ceiling, or were mounted in frames on the walls. A multicolored strip of 35mm film dangled from two reels set up on a pair of rewinds—a long outdated mechanism for editing film (*Hand Cranked*, 2012) (fig. 4.15); a pile of variously colored lengths of 35mm film were stuffed in a glass display case (*Color Film Display*, 2012); short strips of film encased in plastic sleeves swayed in the breeze from a nearby electric fan, casting colored shadows against the white gallery walls (*Mobile Movies*, 2012); lengths of Gibson's hand-painted film *Outline* (2006 were strung in tight parallel lines between two wall mounts (fig. 4.16); a 16mm projector, still in its dust cover, rotated slowly on a turntable (*Dust Cover [Eiki Sound]*, 2016 (fig. 4.17). *Melt Film* (2012) was a 16mm projector whose film-advancing mechanisms had been dismantled, so that individual frames of film sat in its gate slowly melting and burning (fig. 4.18). A thin trail of smoke rose from the gate while the image of each frame's protracted destruction played out on a nearby screen.

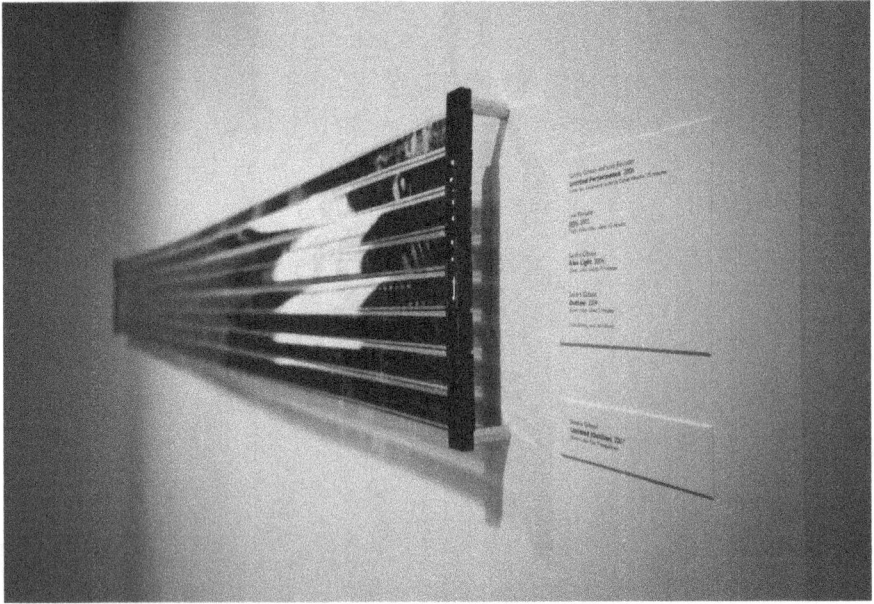

Fig. 4.16.   Sandra Gibson and Luis Recoder, *Outline* (2006). 35mm film, hardware, 96 ×
12 in. Installation view, *Light Works: Gibson + Recoder*, University of Virginia Museum,
Charlottesville, VA, February 20–March 19, 2007.
Photograph by Gibson + Recoder. Courtesy of the artists and University of Virginia Museum.

Once one frame was completely obliterated, a gallery attendant advanced the film by
hand to restart the spectacle.

"Cinematograph" is, of course, named for the *cinematographe*, invented in 1895 by
Auguste and Louis Lumière. This ingenious machine functioned as camera, printer,
and projector. A Lumière camera operator could shoot in the morning, process the
film in the afternoon, and project it at night for an audience who could reasonably
have expected to see themselves—or family, friends, and familiar local sights—in
the film. That is, in both name and function the *cinematographe* was not simply the
first camera, but in fact the first instantiation of the cinematic apparatus. Multiple
parts, each with its own function, were condensed into a single system, denying the
autonomy that Gibson and Recoder's show restored to film, camera, projector, and
screen.

The overall impression of "Cinematograph" was similar to that of *Machine Gut*: of
something gone awry, of infernal machines in revolt against the constraints that
held them in place for over a century. Having escaped from the cinematic apparatus,
the parts of the film machine take on simultaneously comic and melancholy tones,
depending upon whether one reads their newly gained autonomy as liberation from
convention or abandonment by the larger mechanism that allows them to function "correctly." (Gibson and Recoder once rebuked me for using the phrase "empty

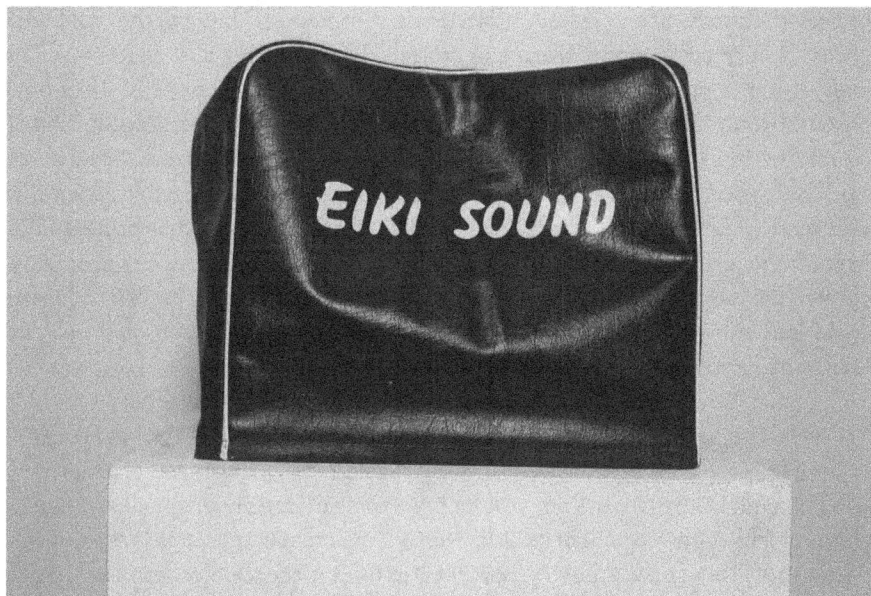

Fig. 4.17. Sandra Gibson and Luis Recoder, *Dust Cover (Eiki Sound)* (2016). Vinyl protective cover, motorized display unit, hardware, 12 in. × 15 in. × 11 in. Installation view, Gibson + Recoder Studio, Brooklyn, NY.

Photo: Rachel Hamburger. Courtesy of the artists.

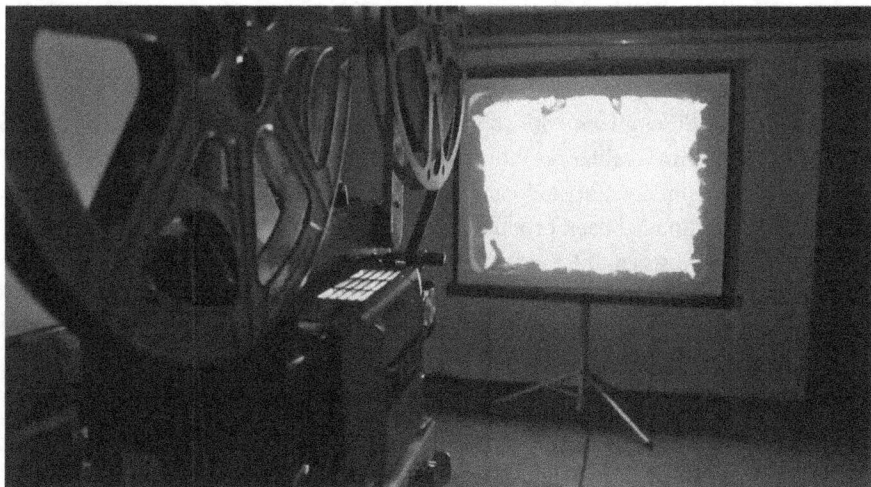

Fig. 4.18. Sandra Gibson and Luis Recoder, *Melt Film* (2012). 16mm film, modified 16mm film projector, screen, dimensions variable. Installation view, Courtisane Festival (Artists-In-Focus: Gibson + Recoder), Ghent, Belgium, March 21–25, 2012.

Photograph: Courtisane. Courtesy of the artists and Courtisane.

projector" in reference to certain projection performances. "Empty," they said, implicitly reaffirmed the normative use of projectors as animating film, suggesting that without film a projector was useless, or at least being used incorrectly. They proposed the term "film-less" instead.) The little projector constantly turning like a bit of cosmic detritus in space might evoke feelings of loneliness, uselessness, or waste, of a perfectly good machine abandoned by a culture that has moved on to a better one. This sense is bolstered by the fact that it is still in its cover, on which is printed "Eiki Sound," though the projector is perpetually silent. Detached from the apparatus, covered up, prevented from making either image or sound, *Dust Cover (Eiki Sound)* could indeed be a symbol of and sorrowful comment upon film's obsolescence. By Gibson and Recoder's lights, however:

> Film is obsolete. But if this is the case from an economic point of view, it has always been the case from an artistic one. Artistic obsolescence in the medium of film is a primordial fact that does not wait for the waning of its technological base; film is obsolete at the moment of its birth. Film is fundamentally obsolete in the same way that all art is obsolete at the moment of its birth. In the realm of aesthetics, the emergence of beauty is utterly precarious, unstable, decomposing before our very eyes.[49]

Referring to film's obsolescence as "primordial fact," Gibson and Recoder signal its immediate disappearance in projection, when both the technology of projection and the expectations institutionalized in the conventions of exhibition make film vanish in the service of an escape into illusion and narrative. This effect was present from the beginning, in the design of one of the earliest film cameras, the rapid standardization of projection and theatrical exhibition, and the swift rise to prominence of narrative and visual conventions that rendered the medium invisible. By Gibson and Recoder's logic, then, film differs from *both* conventional cinema and new digital media, and thereby varies from a familiar position within contemporary avant-garde film culture, which contrasts film's tactility favorably with digital media's presumed ephemerality. This contrast has indeed been productive for contemporary avant-garde filmmakers and critics. But Gibson and Recoder think of film projection in similar terms, as the moment in which film's tactility gives way to cinema's transience. Hence their distinction between film and cinema, the latter cast as the moment of projection and thus of film's illusory disappearance or false death:

> The death of film is not the death of cinema. Disembodied/disemboweled from an apparent (though not transparent) darkness, film is cut loose from its immaterial bond (its false disappearance, its fake death) and made to roam the world for the first time. Film can do without cinema once and for all.[50]

---

[49] Sandra Gibson and Luis Recoder, artists' statement accompanying "Cinematograph," n.p.
[50] Sandra Gibson and Luis Recoder, "Cinema/Film," n.p.

If Gibson and Recoder recuperate film's death on technological and historical grounds, they also do so in another way, making a leap from conditions specific to film to a quality of art in general: the precariousness of beauty, the fleetingness of aesthetic pleasure. In envisioning film as something organic, Gibson and Recoder, like many other avant-garde filmmakers, admit both life and death into their filmic ontology, resiliency *and* decay, persistence *and* loss. This counters the reigning notion of the death of film, as Elena Gorfinkle points out: "Gibson and Recoder posit cinema's much-mourned decay as coincident with the resolute, stubborn recalcitrance of the film object's materiality."[51] In addition to echoing the dual image of persistence and decay traceable across Gibson and Recoder's writings, Gorfinkle's description aligns these qualities of film with difficulty, its "stubborn recalcitrance" in contrast to digital media's ease-of-use. This same quality underlies avant-garde film culture's cultivation of mistakes, difficulty, and failure. What the Otherfilm Collective called "the very inconvenience of film," which demanded its users be disciplined, is further associated with those positive qualities so prominent in Gibson and Recoder's work: in Otherfilm's words, "whimsy, organicism, numinousness," as well as "fragility" and "evanescence."[52]

Two works that connote all these virtues are Gibson and Recoder's *Loop* and *Threadbare* (both 2013) featured in their 2013 gallery show *Transparency*. In *Loop*, an approximately six-foot loop of film dangles from a hook on the gallery wall, blown by a small electric fan directly beneath it (figs. 4.19 and 4.20). The loop's movements in the breeze are surprisingly graceful and fluid, suggestive of ripples on water or the lithe curves of a slithering snake. In some iterations a filmless 16mm projector illuminates the loop, which catches the light and throws dynamic luminous streaks across the white walls of the gallery. It is a sort of variant on traditional exhibition, with the film disarticulated from the projector but nonetheless modulating its light to create patterns of movement on the adjacent surfaces, casting a dancing shadow in the empty square of projected light on the wall. Film loops have been common sights in art galleries since the 1960s; the irony of *Loop* is that it by design fails to do what film loops are typically employed to do, which is repeat perfectly from one pass through the projector to the next. A film loop's literal circularity creates an image of temporal circularity, but only if it is exhibited under normal technical conditions, subject, that is, to the operations of the film projector, whose automaticity imposes a formal regularity on the film loop that it need not possess. Taken out of the projector, the strip of celluloid can be animated in new and unexpected ways, still shaping the projector's light but on its own terms, as it were. A problem familiar to any projectionist is the projector losing its loop, which happens when the film slips out of the Latham loop that reduces tension on the filmstrip and allows the intermittent

[51] Elena Gorfinkle, "At the End of Cinema, This Thing Called Film," catalogue essay for *Light Spill*, University of Wisconsin–Milwaukee Art History Gallery, January 27–February 10, 2011, n.p. See http://www.lolajournal.com/1/end_of_cinema.html.
[52] This statement is discussed in chapter 2.

Fig. 4.19. Sandra Gibson and Luis Recoder, *Loop* (2013). 35mm film, electric fan, tungsten lighting kit, hardware, dimension variable. Installation view, *Transparency: Gibson + Recoder*, Robischon Gallery, Denver, CO, November 14– December 28, 2013.
Photo: Robischon Gallery. Courtesy of the artists and Robischon Gallery.

mechanisms in the projector gate to function properly. *Loop* is an expanded variant of this technical failing, making a mechanical mishap into a new formal possibility. The pairing without coupling of film and projector represent expansion in the specifically chemical sense of a substance taking up more volume without increasing its mass via the weakening of molecular bonds and resultant increase of distance between elements. Thus, one possible mode of cinematic expansion is dilation—not necessarily the replacement of film with another medium, but the deployment of film's materials in

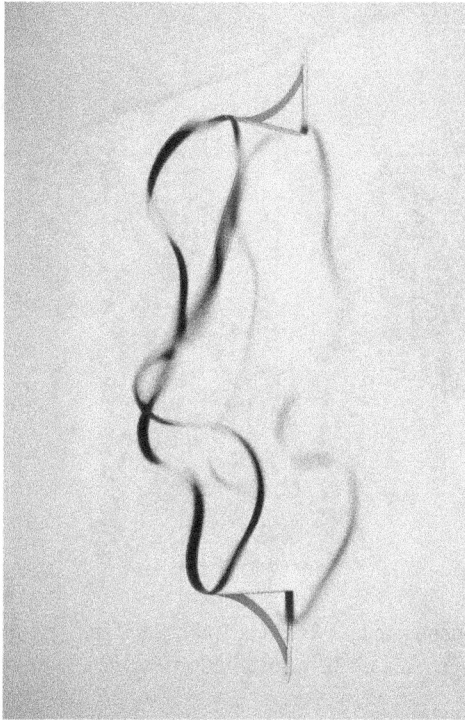

Fig. 4.20. Sandra Gibson and Luis Recoder, *Loop* (2013). Detail.

new spatial configurations. The version of *Loop* that utilizes a projector transforms the singular film object into an installation by making the space of the cinematic apparatus part of its form and meaning. This branch of expanded cinema will be the subject of the next chapter.

If *Loop* is lively, *Threadbare* once more raises the specter of the death of film. Masses of 16mm found footage, gone magenta from decades of neglect in whatever institution eventually de-accessioned it, encase a 16mm projector, reels and all (fig. 4.21). The piece obviously comments on film's obsolescence, portraying film and projector as a kind of mummy and taking a title that connotes something near the end of its utility, something wearing out and showing signs of its age. But, as with many of their other filmic objects, *Threadbare* also continues Gibson and Recoder's motif of film's liberation from the constraints of projection and by extension from cinema. It enacts a role reversal. While the projector normally obscures film, here film turns the tables, completely covering the projector, rendering it inoperable and mute, reduced to a supporting shape for the heaps of celluloid wrapped around it. Like the image of an abandoned house reclaimed by nature, *Threadbare* evokes a wealth of contrasting associations and emotions. If it is a gloomy symbol of film's obsolescence, it can also be taken as a sign of its persistence and fecundity.

Fig. 4.21. Sandra Gibson and Luis Recoder, *Threadbare* (2013). 16mm film projector, 16mm film, reels, 27 in. × 35 in. × 12 in. Installation view, Gibson + Recoder Studio, Brooklyn, NY.
Photograph by Rachel Hamburger. Courtesy of the artists.

Start Filmstrip (2012), another work in *Cinematograph*, signals this reorientation of the death of film into richer and ultimately more positive terms (). A small 35mm filmstrip projector, like those common in schools in the decades before VHS, projects the first frame of a filmstrip onto a nearby screen: "START" in bold white letters, a cue to begin an accompanying audio cassette, absent in this installation. In the context of *Cinematograph*'s return to film history's beginnings, and of Gibson and Recoder's organic conception of film, the image is of the medium's ongoing potential and promise despite claims to the contrary circulating in the zeitgeist. Freed from cinema and "made to roam the world for the first time" on its own, film, though pronounced dead, can "start" again, which is another way of articulating the multivalent emotional effects of their work. The melancholy of isolation, abandonment, and loss implied by their filmic objects, including their regular use of 16mm films de-accessioned by schools or libraries, alternates with the pleasure of their often supple, colorful, and visually dynamic forms, pleasurably soft and lightweight in some cases, reassuringly solid and weighty in others.

This last point is worth emphasizing. It is easy to look past the aesthetic appeal of works like *Loop* and *Threadbare* because they are so open to thematic interpretations, being such frank depictions of the popular narrative of film dying. *Threadbare* is indeed a symbol, but it is also an aesthetically pleasing object in the conventional sense.

Fig. 4.22. Sandra Gibson and Luis Recoder, *Start Filmstrip*. 35mm filmstrip projector, found filmstrip, gesso board panel (8 in. × 10 in.). Installation view, *Cinematograph: Gibson + Recoder*, The Craddock-Terry Gallery, Lynchburg, VA, January 6–February 19, 2012.
Photograph by Gibson + Recoder. Courtesy of the artists and The Craddock-Terry Gallery.

Light gleams on the smooth surface of the film, or passes through and illuminates the rich magenta, or is lost in the black depths of the multiple layers of celluloid. Such works simply show off the visual dynamism of film itself, and its capacity to transform light in pleasurable ways, whether projected or ambient. Gibson and Recoder take up a tradition wherein film is conceived as both an aesthetically and philosophically rich material, whose direct display needn't be reduced to a rote "film as film" reading. Film "by itself" as it were, "as [only] film," is full of other, non-literal, possibilities.

A Matter of Life and Death

If some of the preceding language has seemed ornate, it is only because we are not used to attributing sensuous properties and visual pleasure to materialist works. Materialist film theory, or *any* strictly reflexive interpretations of works like Gibson and Recoder's, proscribe the range of qualities and effects of their objects along with the range of appropriate responses to them. Pleasure and non-literal associations were not within this acceptable range. But the organic metaphors of the works I have surveyed give us the basis for a critical language with which we can more meaningfully describe them, allowing us to re-admit referential meaning and aesthetic fascination into the experience of viewing a materialist work, not to mention an array of emotions that non-literal meanings can evoke. This is not only the case with contemporary works of expanded cinema; from the vantage point offered by work like Gibson and Recoder's, we can recognize these other meanings and pleasures in work by Conrad or Sharits. Their (re)discovery is not only the result of historical revisionism in film criticism, but a condition of contemporary expanded cinema's willing embrace of the subterranean metaphoric associations in historical works.

While filmmakers have recuperated the idea of film's death into more positive conceptions of the medium, elsewhere the idea appears as yet another variant of the tautological critical mantra "film is film." In the hands of some critics, the millennial proclamation of the death of film has become a new totalizing semantic stamp with which to flatten out avant-garde cinema's formal variety into one constantly repeated statement: "this is another film about film." Akira Gottlieb's review of the 2012 Whitney Biennial is representative of this tendency: "A proposition, based on sampling three months of contemporary American cinema at the 2012 Whitney Biennial: from now until the final reel of celluloid is shot and projected, every film's primary subject will be film itself."[53] "Mournful" filmmakers "holding fast" (Gottlieb's words) to the medium even as digital technology makes it redundant continue to churn out works of "cinema *qua* cinema, as an analogue for nothing but itself."[54]

Such claims are usually found in museum publicity and journalistic reviews, which often must rely on soundbites given limitations of space, at worst to grab attention and at best to generalize about very large swaths of artmaking. But these characterizations of current avant-garde film practice are made at the expense of nuance, losing sight of the many other ways that the life-and-death metaphors of avant-garde cinema function. They overlook the expressive power of the myriad acts of destruction done upon celluloid in contemporary work. Undoubtedly the meaning of using film has changed now that digital is an option, just as it changed when analog video and other moving image technologies cropped up in the 1960s. But the death-of-film schema presently in vogue utterly overdetermines traditional filmmaking, not so much shining a new light on it as casting it into the shadow of the new medium that has putatively rendered it obsolete and made mere fetishists out of its users. The death of film implicitly affirms the notion that new media make older ones unnecessary. Once more the covertly progressive rhetoric of new media theory glosses over the more complex realities of what it means to work in a specific medium.

"What is it that lights up at the moment of a technology's death?" Hal Foster asked in a roundtable discussion on obsolescence in the journal *October*.[55] It is a recurrent theme in critical writing on obsolescence: that simultaneous with a medium's death is a sudden, albeit brief, flowering of new life, like a star going supernova. Frampton and Krauss both argued that moving image technologies could only become artistic media after they became unnecessary, when they were replaced by

[53] Akira Gottlieb, "Last Picture Shows: Film and Obsolescence," *The Nation*, October 8, 2012, p. 39.
[54] Ibid., p. 41.
[55] Malcolm Turvey, Hal Foster, Chrissie Iles, George Baker, Matthew Buckingham and Anthony McCall, "Round Table: The Projected Image in Contemporary Art," *October* 104 (Spring 2003), p. 74.

new technologies.[56] Art, that is, requires its technical base to be literally use-less. This goes some way to explaining the current appeal of organic metaphors for film, as these combine associations of life and death, integrating death and loss into the very ontology of the medium, countering the death of film with its resurrection. But contemporary announcements of film's obsolescence cannot be the determining historical factor. Long before digital, avant-garde filmmakers analogized film to the natural world, where life and death played out in the form of representations of violence or the fecundity of decay. Sharits's operating analogy for his filmmaking was the body, particularly the body under duress, in surgery, during epileptic seizures, or sliced by sharp objects. Conrad drew vegetal analogies, as in *Pickled 3M 150* and *Deep Fried 4-X Negative*, finding the layers of film on a core to be onion-like. The durations of these films were determined by the actions of decomposition, which eventually corroded the metal lids of the pickling jars and necessitated preservation.

Such analogies obviously were not generated by millennial announcements of the death of film. They are, rather, instances of a practice of envisioning the medium in organic and anthropomorphic terms, which extends far back into cinema's history. A pattern in this discourse has been to identify the moment of film's destruction as the moment in which its aesthetic potential—its "life"—is most visible. Filmmaking and exhibition are imagined as violent acts upon the medium, which traumatize it while simultaneously revealing its vitality most palpably. Writing in 2015, Catherine Elwes describes structural film and expanded cinema as engaging in

> forensic, though often tender, dissection of [film's] components and processes ... isolating mechanisms whose interdependence have [sic] defined mainstream cinema since the last century. This structural vivisection enables us to call on different manifestations of expanded cinema to draw up a provisional anatomy of film itself.[57]

Elwes's suggestion that violence against the medium is a necessary step toward fully understanding it recalls Dziga Vertov's image of a revolutionary avant-garde cinema born of brutality enacted upon the medium itself, penned in 1922:

> The innards,
> the guts of strong sensations
> are tumbling out
> of cinema's belly,
> ripped open by the reef of revolution.
> See them dragging along,
> leaving a bloody trail on the earth

---

[56] Frampton, "For a Metahistory of Film," pp. 135–136; Krauss, "And Then Turn Away?," pp. 5–33
[57] Catherine Elwes, *Installation and the Moving Image* (London: Wallflower Press, 2015), p. 187.

that quivers with horror and disgust.
It's all over.[58]

And, according to Vertov, along with the contemporary inheritors of his organic metaphors, begun anew. Vertov and Elwes, writing from opposite ends of avant-garde
cinema's history, also stand on either end of a continuum of biological associations.
Elwes's references to vivisection, anatomy, and forensics evoke an elegant scientific
conception marked by cleanliness and surgical precision, apt descriptors of Sharits
and Kubelka's mounted filmstrips and much of Gibson and Recoder's work. Vertov's
bloody shuddering intestines are much messier, calling to mind Conrad's cooked
and otherwise roughly treated film objects or Shartis's gruesome image of a projector
splattering the brains of an imagined filmmaker.

That film may be nearer to its death now than it was in the 1970s may amplify these
metaphors or make them newly relevant, but it is surely does not account for their
existence to begin with. Pointing out the long historical lineage of film's death and re-
birth in the language of avant-garde film culture is a corrective to critics who assume
that recent works of celluloid-based cinema are solely the product of nostalgia over a
material made obsolete by current historical conditions. Film has been dead before.

Unraveling Another Expressive Analogy

The most prominent instance of a contemporary experimental filmmaker's work
evoking bodily associations is Luther Price. Since the 1980s, Price has made a series
of 8mm and 16mm films, and, more recently, filmic objects (mostly 35mm slides collaged from pieces of found film footage) (fig. 4.23). Most of Price's work utilizes found
footage, and he often favors imagery of the body subject to violence, as in medical
films and sadomasochistic pornography. *Meat* (1990) and *Fancy* (2006), for example,
feature graphic images of surgery; *Sodom* (1989) is comprised of 8mm gay porn rescued from dumpsters after the adult home movie market abandoned film for video.
Even the films that are not frankly anatomical tend to reference the frailty, failings,
and destruction of the human body. The acclaimed *Biscotts* series (2005–2008) is
composed of 13 identical prints of a 1970s documentary about poor Southern blacks
in nursing homes. Numerous other films utilize home movie footage discovered by
Price and used semi-autobiographically, as stand-ins for his own troubled family history, which is part of a darkly tragic artistic persona that casts an extratextual shadow
over his films in much the same way Kenneth Anger's did, making the already violent
and disturbing images of Price's work all the more pointed.

But the referential images of tumors, sickly people, and explicit sadistic sex in
Price's films are complimented by his working methods, which subject the surface

[58] Dziga Vertov, "Kinoks: A Revolution," in Annette Michelson, ed., *Kino-Eye: The Writings of Dziga Vertov* (Berkeley: University of California Press, 1984), pp. 11–12.

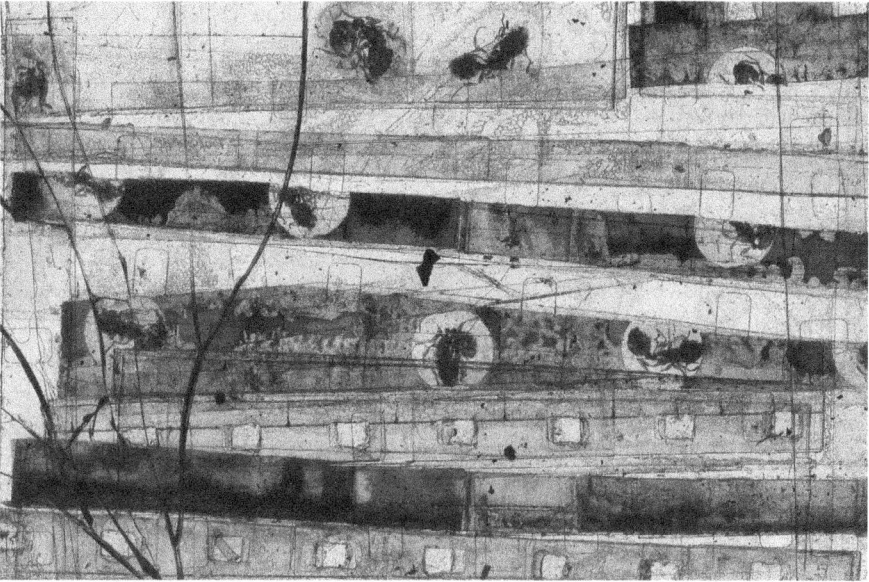

Fig. 4.23. Luther Price, *Number 9* (detail) (2012). 160 handmade slides in two slide carousel projectors, variable dimensions.
Courtesy of the artist and Callicoon Fine Arts, NY.

of his films to physical duress in the form of scratching, piercing, tearing, painting, and chemical changes brought about by burying and other purposefully destructive organic operations. Upping the destructive ante, Price notoriously refuses to make prints of these films, insisting instead that the originals be projected, which in many cases is difficult if not impossible. The films are frequently described as "struggling" through the projector, a condition of their material precariousness that in turn forms the basis for metaphorical leaps that endow Price's films and the medium itself with organic, bodily, and human traits. Price's refusal to make prints of his tortured film reels necessarily turns projection into a live spectacle of film's physicality, one tinged with the sense of impending disaster as barely cohering filmstrips thickened by tape, sprinkles, and organic matter or weakened by tears and punctures disrupt the easy automaticity of projection. Each screening is unique, as well as challenging and unpredictable for projectionist and projector alike.

If we wished to find Price on the continuum between Elwes's "tender vivisection" and Vertov's quivering intestines, it would doubtless be on the messier side. The surgical analogy becomes one of botched surgery, its scars prominently featured on the surface of the films as much as on the bodies of the people in them. Not since Sharits has a filmmaker created such a strong impression of violence by paralleling brutal imagery with destructive working methods. But, as though taking Recoder's advice to refuse to recuperate the destruction of the filmstrip through rephotography or making prints, Price escalates that impression by extending the act of filmic destruction into the real time of projection.

So much is the critical consensus about Price's work. Not surprisingly, the associations of surgery and other forms of violence committed upon the skin of film are deployed in a contested sematic field. Is Price's preoccupation with death and decay a symptom of anxiety or mournfulness over the death of his chosen medium, or an assertion of film's continued vitality even as it comes under attack? The surgical analogy is one more that accommodates both life and death, showcasing at once the vulnerability and resiliency of the body. Price himself has suggested this, steering interpretations of his upsetting medical imagery in more life-affirming directions. James Hansen explains the distinction quite neatly: "In film and performance, [Price] examines the body under duress as a mode of ritualistic, destructive healing ... For Price, surgery finds the body suspended between preservation and destruction, life and death."[59]

This has not prevented other critics, enamored of the mythic death of film, from seizing upon Price's degenerative aesthetic to once more proclaim the dramatic end of film at the turn of the millennium. Promotional copy for screenings of Price's work at the 2012 Whitney Biennial repeatedly rang this refrain: Price's work was about "the death drive," and constituted "studies of a dying technology."[60] The latter statement was made specifically in reference to Price's recent 35mm slide work, which he has claimed as an extension of his filmmaking rather than a departure from it, a "static" cinema rather than another art form that references film.[61] The arc of Price's filmmaking career vis-à-vis film as object could be described as a steady move away from integral temporal forms ("films" as we know them) through increasingly precarious and unstable objects that threaten to break apart into their constituent physical parts, leading eventually to unprojectable films and filmic objects. This begins with found footage films that imply the literal dis-integration of the source materials via distinctive editing strategies, and ends with film-based objects that literalize this process and produce its final result—the static cinematic work. Thus, even the more conventionally made found footage films imply works of expanded cinema in different temporal and spatial modalities than projection. The instability of his films in projection has led many commentators to take them as objects. Even those films intended for projection are insistent in their objecthood, chugging and rattling through the projector, coming loose from the gate, experienced more as "reels" than "films." Use of the word "reel" in place of "film" is common in critical writing on Price's work, a shift from a temporal experience

[59] James Hansen, "A Matter of Tape: Luther Price," in Bradford Nordeen, David Everett Howe, and Karl McCool, eds., *Dirty Looks at MoMA: Mining the Collection* (New York: Dirty Looks NYC, 2013), pp. 79–81.

[60] From program notes for screenings of Price's films during the 2012 Whitney Biennial, March 1–3, 2012.

[61] Aaron Cutler and Mariana Shellard, "The Hand Made Luther Price," *Idiom*, October 2, 2012, http://idiommag.com/2012/10/the-handmade-luther-price/, n.p.

unfolding on screen to the static piece of equipment mounted on the projector, frequently refusing to interface properly with it.[62]

As fertile a field for bodily analogies as Price's work is, the dominant narrative of the body in distress so common in discussions of his films occludes another association that is at least as illuminating. The analogy I have in mind is to sewing or weaving—that is, artisanal textile production. Looking at Price's work from this vantage point will place him in some unexpected company, including filmmakers whose imagery substantially differs from his. This includes a group of contemporary artists who make film weavings in the spirit of Conrad's *Flicker Matte*, paralleling their work with textiles much as Annabel Nicolson did in *Reel Time*.

The totality of Price's film work enacts a process wherein their material and formal unity unravels, individual shots coming apart at the splices, and the quasi-narrative integrity of the film's formal architecture dissolving, or at least threatening to. The emphasis in critical writing on Price's films has been on the former, on the celluloid literally breaking apart in projection, films slipping out of the projector and eventually becoming so damaged over multiple screenings as to be no longer viewable. But insofar as a shot is as much a formal building block as a material one, a length of physical stuff and a length of content, the loss of integrity in Price's films is not only material but aesthetic as well. Price's editing strategies imply the breaking up of the aesthetic object embodied in the material one, even if the latter manages to retain its integrity.

Consider Price's *Kittens Grow Up* (2007), a found footage film that interlaces an educational film about kittens, accompanied by a folksy song reminiscent of *Sesame Street* vignettes from the 1970s, with what appears to be a more or less contemporaneous film about the effects of domestic violence on children, possibly a public service advertisement. Images of frolicking and nursing kittens alternate unpredictably with a miniature narrative in which a housewife, already frazzled by the antics of her three children, confronts her late arriving, drunken husband, who eventually slaps her and storms out. Though jarring, the juxtaposition makes sense in a darkly comic, ironic way, not uncommon to found footage films. The two sets of images contrast each other, each undermining the tone of the other but ultimately complementing each other in a dialectical structure that meditates on the poignant vulnerability of children and the corruption of innocence as kids, if not kittens, grow up. But Price escalates the conflict between the two sets of images in an almost Eisensteinian manner, in the methods he uses to at once link and de-couple the disparate sources of footage. First, because he honored his commitment to the original and refused to copy the workprint, Price was not able to adjust the source footage's soundtracks. The optical soundtrack on a 16mm film is 26 frames behind the corresponding picture frame, as the sound head on the projector is that same distance from the picture

[62] See, for example, Chloë Penman, "Nine Films by Luther Price: Thomas Beard and Ed Halter at the LUX/ICA Biennial," *Real/Reel Journal*, June 7, 2012, https://realreeljournal.wordpress.com/2012/06/07/lutherprice/, n.p.

302 Modes of Expansion

gate. This means that a cut in the image from kittens to dysfunctional family, indeed any cut Price makes, is asynchronous with the sound cut, which comes just over one second later. For example, at one point the wife yells at her husband, "You've got no right to make it sound like I'm not doing my share! I'm doing *more* than my share! I'm doing more than *you*!" In the midst of that last sentence, the image cuts from a closeup of the couple's daughter, fearfully clutching her doll as she overhears her parents' arguing, to an image of the mother cat bathing one her kittens. The wife's voice continues across this cut, however, as the last 26 frames of optical sound from the PSA passes over the sound head *after* the cut in the picture. The shouted "more than *you*!" accompanies the first second of the much more pleasing shot of a cuddly kitten gently licked by its mother. The same thing happens in reverse when the shots of kittens give way once more to the PSA footage, which picks up exactly where it had left off earlier. A gentle voice intones "Hungry ... hungry ... " in a sing-song way as the PSA resumes (the fight takes place over dinner, so "hungry" in reference to nursing kittens neatly fits the image of upset children waiting out domestic discord for their meals). These moments of sonic lag could have been corrected had Price made an exhibition print of the film, making a new optical track and re-synching it to eliminate the jarring offset of sound and image cuts. His refusal to do so is both a commitment to the fragile original work print and an aesthetic of disintegration.

Price increases the impression of clunkiness in the editing by occasionally interpolating lengths of black leader between shots from his source footage. This "slug" footage lacks an optical soundtrack; in its place is another row of sprocket holes, which make a buzzing or purring sound as they pass over the sound head. The same sound/image lag occurs at cuts to and from black leader, though the effect is even more disruptive as the image unexpectedly flicks off and on again and the unpleasant electronic buzz of the sprockets cuts in and out asynchronously with the cuts in the picture. Accounts of Price's screenings often refer to this distinct filmic sound, which Price seems to prefer to be played as loud as possible.[63] At high enough decibels, it can sound like a woodchipper. Again, Price could have eliminated this by making a screening print of the original.

Finally, Price has also cut in footage from other sources that are much less easy to identify than the main source footage due to extreme decay of the emulsion, which also affects the quality of the optical sound. As the drunken husband stumbles in and his wife chides him for being late for dinner, Price cuts in closeups of a plate of food. The image is discolored and washed out, the sound practically inaudible—whether Price simply used footage that was already in an extreme state of decay or further damaged the emulsion manually is unknown.

The overall impression of *Kittens Grow Up* is that the source footage barely coheres into an integral whole. Thematically, the link between the kitten and PSA footage makes sense as a dark reflection on childhood and the failings of family units. But this

---

[63] See Andrew Lampert, "Luther Price," *BOMB* 120, July 1, 2012, https://bombmagazine.org/articles/luther-price/, n.p.

competes with the feeling of formal and material disunity, as through the film is ready to fall apart into the pieces of rescued celluloid Price haphazardly taped together. The canonical found footage films, by Bruce Conner, Craig Baldwin, and Abigail Child, for example, evince a dense and thoroughly integrated weave of thematic lines. Those filmmakers' editing strategies make disparate source images cohere, albeit in unexpected and radical ways. Graphic matches, rhythmic patterns, and variations of traditional analytical and continuity editing devices link previously unrelated pieces of footage into a new, unified aesthetic form, as in Sitney's "formal film": "a tight nexus of content."[64] Foregoing these methods, Price retains the impression of autonomous celluloid strips prior to editing:

> Most film-collagists attempt, in some form or another, to create new, integral contexts for the images they recycle, be they personal reverie (Cornell's *Rose Hobart*), social criticism (the films of Bruce Conner), rhythmic invention (Abigail Child and Julie Murray), or media jamming (Craig Baldwin). Price, in a sense, does the same thing, but in reverse. His films usually refuse to cohere, seeming to resist the clear meanings or interpretive semiosis that recognizable imagery seemingly should enable. But more than this, the physical filmstrip as Price assembles it frequently appears to be on the verge of snapping apart into its component parts, as though their coalescence into "a Luther Price film" were some sort of momentary aberrant clusterfuck of dirty celluloid.[65]

The passage expresses this quality of Price's work beautifully, but the contrast of Price with Joseph Cornell is misleading. Looking at the available output of collage films by Cornell, it is not clear that he attempted to create "new integral contexts" for his recycled footage. In fact, as unexpected as the connection might be between Cornell's gentle, sentimental cinema and Price's much darker and more brutal one might be, the two artists have in common an ethos of the incomplete, a conception of filmmaking that frustrates the expectations of formal unity and even baseline physical integrity in the singular object we call "a film." Both artists evoke the dissolution of that object in their films and related assemblages (Cornell's boxes and Price's slides). Not surprisingly, these manifest the same refusal of coherence characteristic of their films.

Cornell did not make expanded cinema, working before the invention of the term and never identifying his boxes as "cinematic." But Price has referred to his 35mm slides as films, specifically "static films," which are released from stasis when he projects them in rapidly turning slide carousels either during film screenings or as installations. Price makes these slides by collaging bits of 16mm found footage with bits

[64] Sitney, *Visionary Film*, p. 369.
[65] Michael Sicinsky, "NYFF Views 4," *Greencine Daily*, November 3, 2007: daily.greencine.com/archives/004851.html, n.p. Also see program notes for "*Nine Biscotts* and More: New Films by Luther Price," Yerba Buena Center for the Arts, San Francisco, November 9, 2007, http://www.sfcinematheque.org/wordpress/wp-content/uploads/2009/02/Price_2008.pdf, n.p.

of organic detritus, complementing the chemical degradation he has inflicted on the source material in his customary ways. The results are often ecstatically colorful and richly textured. Markers of filmic specificity like sprocket holes and edge lettering are overlaid with a record of surface alteration and natural objects like crushed flies, bits of hair, and flecks of dirt. In installation, multiple slide projectors arranged side-by-side on a line of plinths project a row of serial images on the opposite wall, evoking a group of "shots" at once autonomous and related in a sequence, much like Sharits's multi-projector installations (fig. 4.24). They evoke editing in both the sense of joining shots materially and orchestrating image content in time, realized here as a line in space.

These slide pieces are the logical outcome of a filmmaking practice that has increasingly loosed film from projection and thus from illusory movement; that has granted the shot more and more autonomy from an overarching form; that has pushed further and further a radical conception of film editing to the point that it needed an expanded form. Editing, constructive and temporal in conventional cinema, is made deconstructive and spatial in Price's work. Static assemblages or films falling apart in projection express an editing aesthetic that disrupts the seamlessness aimed for by conventional montage. Price's characterization of his work as having a sculptural quality is telling:

Fig. 4.24. Luther Price, *#9 A Study in Decay* (2012–2013). 400 handmade slides in five slide carousel projectors, variable dimensions. Installation view, Institute of Contemporary Art, Boston, MA, 2013.
Photograph Charles Mayer. Courtesy of the artist and Callicoon Fine Arts, NY.

I have a physical relationship with all of my films. I feel like although they are projected and they are considered in the medium of film, I still feel consider myself in
many ways … I'm not saying that I'm not a filmmaker, but I feel like I'm a sculptor.
I don't feel like I ever gave that up. I remember how freeing it was to shoot my first
roll of film and have a piece that I was working on in my pocket instead of having to
lug huge pieces of metal and fragments of stuff in the back. I was like, "Hm, wow.
I can actually shoot something, put it in my pocket, and walk down the street, and
wear something that doesn't smell like resin. And I'm not covered in sawdust." It
was really freeing.[66]

Price gives voice to a "freeing" editing aesthetic, which, in a sense, frees the individual
shot, endowing it with a greater sense of individuality and mobility, actually moving
with him as he walks down the street. This intimacy Price feels with his materials further indicates this respect for the autonomy of shots. The bit of film in Price's pocket
recalls another, quite famous mobile shot, of the bandit firing his gun into the camera
at the beginning and/or end of Porter's *The Great Train Robbery*. The comparison provides another link between Price and Cornell. Their filmic objects give their components a freedom of movement, including a semantic mobility that they can only
have figuratively in a film. If Price's work with film can be called "sculptural," it is an
acknowledgement of the objecthood of film in the analog editing process, which conceives of shots as objects in the formal, sematic sense as well.

Hence, the surgical analogy so many critics have made about Price's work is actually more apt if we turn away from the preoccupation with death or bodily trauma
and look instead to what the metaphor implies about such notions as structural integrity and formal wholeness. Price's fascination with "meat" aside, his films and expanded cinema are just as preoccupied with finding the threshold beyond which film
editing disarticulates its materials rather than unifying them. Surgery may find the
body hovering between life and death, recalling Hansen's words, but it also identifies
a liminal state between wholeness and atomization. The stitches and subsequent scars
are markers of this status, like the interruptive editing devices of films like *Kittens
Grow Up*. These, in turn, point the way to a further atomization whereby the joined
objects are deliberately prevented from cohering.

But there is more than a metaphor at play here. A real part of the filmmaking process, not a figurative stand-in, suggests expanded work. The process of editing, so
physical for Price, is lost in a conventionally made film when it is projected. In Price's
work, that process and the experience of it are retained. As if to underscore this, Price
has included a replica of his 16mm editing workspace in a recent installation called
Meat, Chapter 3: The Maggots Will Find You (2015) (fig. 4.25). Reels mounted on
rewinds are joined by a loosely dangling piece of altered film, stretched over a lightboard as though in mid–editing process. Around it are, among other more enigmatic

[66] Ed Halter, "Body of Work," *Mousse Magazine* 36, December 2012–January 2013, http://moussemaga-
zine.it/product/mousse-36/, p. 131. Also see http://www.edhalter.com/luther.pdf.

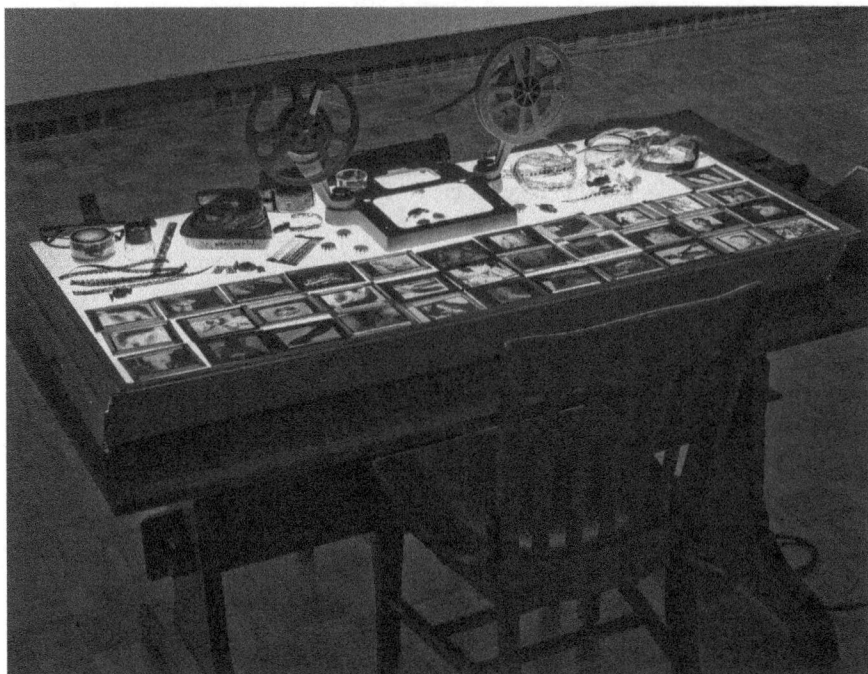

Fig. 4.25. Installation view, *Meat, Chapter 3: The Maggots Will Find You*. Usdan Gallery, Bennington College, Bennington, VT, 2015.
Courtesy of the artist and Callicoon Fine Arts, NY.

objects, additional lengths of hand-altered film, magnifying lenses used by editors to scrutinize film frames, and a warped, practically disintegrated roll of film on a plastic core, evidently buried for too long in Price's garden.

The expanded forms of works like this preserve certain qualities and experiences of filmmaking that are not accessible in projection. Rather than yet another instance of a materialist film reminding the viewer of film's materials qua materials, it seems that Price wishes to preserve subterranean formal traits and pleasures that are rendered invisible to the film viewer when the film is completed. Price thus stands in a line of experimental filmmakers who resisted completion and the attendant senses of ephemerality, seamlessness, and perfect repeatability that normal film exhibition presumes. Price's forms negotiate this divide between "a work" and "the work" that went into it, between integrity and dissolution, completeness and incompleteness. Eyed through this lens, Price suddenly aligns with another group of filmmakers producing a quite different sort of filmic object. That object is the film quilt or weaving. Though there are historical precedents to such objects, in recent years it has been revived and thoroughly reimagined by filmmakers like Sabrina Gschwandtner, Richard Kerr, Mary Stark, and Jennifer West.

Fig. 4.26. Sabrina Gschwandtner, *Elizabeth Keckley Diamond* (2014). 16 mm film, polyester thread, lithography ink, LEDs. 15 7/8 in. × 15 13/16 in. × 3 1/16 inches.
Collection Munson Williams Proctor Arts Institute. Photo: Tom Powel Imaging. Courtesy of the artist.

Film (as) Weaving

Unlike *Flicker Matte* and *Reel Time*, the sewn objects of these filmmakers utilize complex patterns of celluloid strips, frequently following traditional quilting patterns like log cabins, arts and crafts, or crazy quilts. Strips of film are either interwoven in over-under fashion or stitched together with thread, sometimes with the use of a sewing machine. They are intended for rear illumination, which allows their vibrant patterns of color and intricate designs to become visible along with the tiny serial images that comprise the source material on a micro level (fig. 4.26). Contemporary film weavings offer varied sorts of viewing experiences depending in part upon the distance between object and viewer, which has implications for the temporality of cinema spectatorship. But like Conrad's woven mat and Nicolson's projection performance with the Singer machine, the film weavings of Kerr, Gschwandtner, Stark, and West emerge from an experimental filmmaking practice in which the tactile experience of working with film is paramount. And like Price's work, these weavings reconfigure the temporal and other expressive tropes of editing into spatialized pictorial forms.

Though these filmmakers all maintain that their work is a direct extension of avant-garde film aesthetics, we should take note of the fact that the film/weaving analogy is of a different order than the other analogies surveyed thus far. This complicates the ontological issues attending a body of cinematic work that takes the shape of another art form. The filmic objects in, say, Gibson and Recoder's *Cinematograph* installation evoke emotional states like loneliness (the lone empty projector idly spinning in space), and the surface of celluloid may be comparable in some ways to human skin. But these are comparisons, expressive associations that shape both the working methods of artists and interpretations of critics. Film can, however, literally be woven or stitched. A quilt made from strips of film is a quilt in a way that a film with decaying emulsion is not identical to its epidermal referent. And film's technological base is part of a larger industrial history that is directly linked to sewing—not analogous to it but within it, a facet of it, of a history that is also one of women's roles in industrial labor. As Donna Harkavy and Flavia S. Zúñiga-West write, in relation to Gschwandtner's film quilts:

> [T]he artist likes to point out that in the era of early Hollywood, most film editors were actually women. Their sewing skills provided the expertise for the tasks required by film editing: Moving film through a projector (or Steenbeck) is similar to feeding fabric through a sewing machine. Moreover, cutting and splicing are integral to both filmmaking and quilting.[67]

There are several implications of the directness of the film/quilting analogy, which will be teased out here. Suffice to say for the moment that it is much more than a framework for materialist analyses of these works. While one cannot avoid attending to the reality of film when it is so directly displayed, film weavings in fact subsume their material into formal patterns that are not reducible to the physical appearance of film. This isn't to say that they use film in an illusionistic manner, exactly, but to be fully appreciated as aesthetic objects the fact of their celluloid base must be "seen though," so to speak. Their visual pleasure, that is, doesn't stem solely from the material, but from its arrangement into complex patterns that shift as one moves closer to or further from them in the gallery. This is very much after the model of structural-materialist film, central to which was the interplay of part and whole, and the process the spectator underwent in reconciling the moment-by-moment apperception of their micro-structures and the larger patterns in which these figured.

But "moment-by-moment," while apt for projected films, is perhaps better stated here as "piece-by-piece." That is, film weavings give spatial form, perceptible all at once, to the unfolding temporal experience of cinema viewing. In particular, the

---

[67] Donna Harkavy and Flavia S. Zúñiga-West, catalogue essay for "Assembling Narratives: Quilting Impulses in Contemporary Art," Dorsky Gallery Curatorial Programs, Long Island City, NY, April 11–June 27, 2010, n.p.

editing innovations of the avant-garde, in opposition to traditional continuity editing, are rendered schematically. But like any textile, they imply a temporal dimension to perception wherein the viewer traces the individual threads within the larger woven patterns; quilters, especially, see this in terms of narrative. But while this may be the case with any textile, the micro-level serial structures of film make this temporal viewing experience more concrete, as if giving a precise measurement in frames and sprocket holes of the object's "movement" and the spectator's tracking of it.

Filmmaking's historical and aesthetic resonances with textile arts are most prominent in the work of Kerr, Stark, and Gschwandtner. These artists take most seriously, and to its furthest reaches, the analogy between filmmaking and home craft explored by Conrad and Nicolson. In the case of Gschwandtner, the interrelations between the two become especially complicated, to the point that film and weaving become fused at the ontological level, which will require us to sort out where one form leaves off and the other begins. But for all three of these filmmakers, the link between film and weaving informs an intervention, at once formal and political, in much the same way that Conrad's landmark work of the 1970s did.

The long and distinguished career of Richard Kerr, one of the most prominent Canadian experimental filmmakers of his generation, took a troubled detour into feature filmmaking in the mid-1990s with *willing voyeur* (1996). To that point, Kerr had worked almost exclusively in 16mm film. Since *willing voyeur*, which was shot in 35mm, he has worked either in digital video (as original capture format or for post-production of films shot in 16mm) or with various types of filmic objects, most significantly a series weavings in 16mm, 35mm, and IMAX. His source footage is almost always popular commercial films or trailers, including the "front matter" of release prints—countdowns, "China girls," SMPTE leader and other color leader used to identify prints but not seen by audiences. Sifting through countless strips of this material, usually working with a single source film at a time, Kerr identifies patterns in color, form, and image content and arranges the strips in interlaced grids to produce weavings that, from a distance, are abstract. These are framed against custom made lightboards and mounted on walls like paintings. At times, Kerr inserts colored gels between the lightboard's surface and the filmstrips to further shape the color patterns that have been formed by his arrangement of the source material. In some weavings he treats the film chemically, usually misting it with bleach, which eats away at the emulsion to create splotches of color, like a textural overlay of visual interference. This further abstracts the otherwise recognizable photographic images in the film frames, which become at least semi-visible upon close inspection. From several feet away—the usual polite distance one stands from a painting in a museum—Kerr's weavings look like the geometrical abstractions of Mondrian or some of the more grid-like paintings of Kandinsky (e.g., *Square With Concentric Circles*, 1913) or Theo von Doesburg (e.g., *Neo-Plasticism: Composition VII*, 1917), or, more recently, Sarah Morris (e.g., *Banco Safra [Rio]*, 2012). The individual film frames are usually visible, even as they are taken up into the abstract patterns. That is, the size and shape of the filmstrips and their serial frame structure remain visible as the basic building blocks of the grids. It is upon closer viewing that the multiplicity of pictures, colors, and text within the frames become visible along with their sprocket holes and framelines.

Love and Anarchy (2016, 35mm), for example, is crafted entirely from leader material, the unseen film at the heads and tails of release print reels used to label them and provide markers for projectionists or for the video transfer process (fig. 4.27). At a distance, it calls to mind Mondrian's *Broadway Boogie Woogie* (1942–1943) and *Victory Boogie Woogie* (1944), though its grid is denser. Horizontal and vertical lengths of blue, red, and yellow predominate, punctuated by strips of black, transparent leader, and light greens. These lengths of color are dispersed more or less evenly across the 30 inch by 30 inch field; there are no areas in particular that draw the eye, unless one can begin from a distance to make out bits of text or recognizable imagery in specific frames of film. While the impression of a grid structure remains when the weavings are viewed more closely, that sense of regularity is threatened by the impression of visual busy-ness that emerges at closer range. One of the most intriguing aspects of Kerr's weavings is that he is able to produce such distinct and pronounced patterns from such dense and visually heterogeneous material. These latter qualities only come into view as one "zooms in." In *Love and Anarchy*, at least two different "China girls" are visible, facing the camera, flanked by blocks of color, smiling out from a field of letters, words, other images, framelines, symbols, and scrawls (fig. 4.28). Bart Testa has eloquently described the process of back-and-forth between the global patterns seen from a distance and the minute, frame-sized details of Kerr's weavings:

> The filmstrips accumulate large-scale abstract patterns to entice the viewer to enter the space of the image and then trace the succession of tiny images. Kerr restores the viewer to the material of film itself—to a substance one can pass through the palm of a hand, as well as a projector gate. Instead of a single imposing *mise-en-scene*, Kerr discerns in cinema a tactile art of the eye and the hand. The closer we approach these pieces, the more cinematic the film strips become.[68]

Testa also observes that, like the scale of our visual attention, "movies likewise oscillate between first-effect spectacle and narrow-range inspection."[69]

The notion of "oscillation" harks back to Sharits, who referred to the same process of shuttling between film as a still and moving thing, expressed in the language of film's intermittency. This material process of shooting and projecting film, both of which require intermittent movement, is elevated to a larger concept, a defining feature of both cinema and human perception at play in Sharits's *Frozen Film Frames* and visual film scores. Kerr has cited Shartis's projected films and Plexiglas-mounted

---

[68] Bart Testa, "Richard Kerr's Recuperation: *After Motion Pictures* and *Les Collages des Hollywood*," in Brett Kashmere, ed., *Industry: Recent Works by Richard Kerr* (exhibition catalogue) (Montreal: Telecine Editions, 2005), p. 35.
[69] Ibid., p. 32.

Fig. 4.27. Richard Kerr, *Love and Anarchy* (2016). 35mm celluloid film, Plexiglas, fluorescent light, artist's lightbox.
Courtesy of Richard Kerr.

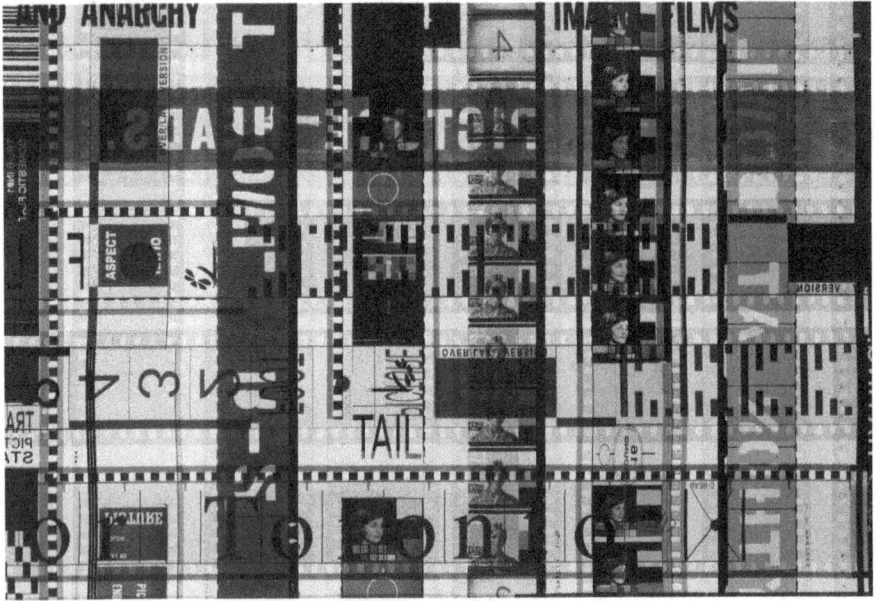

Fig. 4.28. Richard Kerr, *Love and Anarchy* (2016). Detail. 35mm celluloid film, Plexiglas, fluorescent light, artist's lightbox.
Courtesy of Richard Kerr.

strips as influential on his own work, as models for cinema's speed and dynamism and its static solidity as physical object.[70] Weaving, then, is a form that allows Kerr to create an experience marked by both rhythm and stasis with a much greater degree of tactility and weight than a projected film.

There is another link to be made between Kerr's work and Sharits's, signaled, albeit obliquely, by the Sharits quotation that began this chapter. There, Sharits contrasts his work with "normal cinema," in which the reality of the filmstrip is subsumed by illusion in the service of representation.[71] He does not just contrast two cinematic aesthetics, however. Sharits denigrates the "cameramen" who shoot these movies because they "disdainfully ignore the frame structure of their medium." "Cameramen" he writes, rather than "filmmakers," implying the division of labor in conventional filmmaking and suggesting that this mode of production in and of itself contributes to the illusionism of industrial cinema. It is as if the camera operators, who ought to know better, are simply cogs in a machine that forces film to do things that run contrary to its nature.

These are the very conditions in which Kerr found himself while making *willing voyeur*, on which he is listed in his own filmography as "Director and Producer,"

---

[70] See, for example, Randolph Jordan, "Industry: An Interview with Richard Kerr," *Synoptique*, November 1, 2004, http://www.synoptique.ca/core/en/articles/industry, n.p.
[71] Sharits, "Words Per Page," pp. 34–35.

working with a director of photography, co-editor, sound designer, and relatively large cast on an adaptation of a story by Alan Zweig. The film was provincially funded by the National Film Board of Canada and other agencies. The end credits scroll for three minutes. Pre- and post-production on the film occupied far more time than shooting, which lasted only 13 days in roughly four years of overall production time. In a deeply cynical account of this experience, Kerr describes this mode of film-making as overwhelming him. The multiple funding sources for the film are lumped into an Orwellian "Agency" that hilariously misunderstands Kerr's intentions and filmmaking pedigree, with dreams of "Antonioni/Godard-like innovation." "You sign up for the program," Kerr writes, "and enter the world of development hell for a thousand days."[72]

In the same piece, Kerr describes himself, in the second person, as a "*plein air* filmmaker":

You like to move about the landscape, light metre and camera in hand. You work from a feeling and not much of a plan, and certainly never with a script. You work like this from 1976 until 1990, never questioning the value of your practice, nor your view from the margins. After a dozen movies, you get your movie-making act down. You need time and light more than money and you realize that experience brings clarity, and clarity, in turn, removes doubt.[73]

In short, an experimental filmmaker, totally at odds with the mode of production Kerr entered with *willing voyeur*. As Testa and several other commentators on Kerr's work have noted, the film weavings were a response to the feeling of alienation from his materials brought about by industrial filmmaking's dispersal of labor, the displacement of "filmmaker" by director, screenwriter, director of photography, and so on. As Lee-Ann Martin puts it, Kerr missed "the direct involvement with materials" and "sought to affirm the essential physicality of the filmmaking process."[74]

Kerr's frustration with alienated labor was compounded by the increasing prevalence of digital postproduction taking place in the film industry at the time. These two problems intersected, as both distanced the filmmaker from his materials and the intimate mode of working those materials call for. What happens to the celluloid strip when it is digitized is akin to what happens to the "*plein air* filmmaker" absorbed into the industrial mode of film practice. Kerr merges these two—digital media and the structures of commercial production—into a larger conception of mainstream cinema in which the individual, with all the connotations of intimacy with materials and the world that word entails, is alienated. The weavings restore this intimate relationship, recalling Allison Perlman's definition of craft and the

[72] Richard Kerr, "The Making of the *willing voyeur . . .*" *Take One* (Fall 1996), pp. 15–16.
[73] Ibid. p. 14.
[74] Lee-Ann Martin, "The After Motion Picture Series" (exhibition brochure), Mackenzie Art Gallery, Regina, Canada, 1998, n.p.

importance of empathy therein. Discussing his work with the 35mm trailers that become the source material for his weavings, Kerr confirms this: "the first thing that you do is that you look at the trailers on a Steenbeck and you start to listen. I mean it's like that with any material, not just this. You just listen to your materials and you respond to it."[75] By "listen," Kerr does not mean attending to the audio of the trailers, but, more poetically, treating the materials as though they were communicating to him, hinting at paths through the process of working with them. At least as heuristics for making or interpreting this work, the concepts of intimacy and empathy suggest themselves. And as Gregory Zinman points out, one appeal of this direct method is "the element of chance that inheres in its creation, which includes the necessary trial and error that comes from making films by painting on tiny individual frames, or by submitting the emulsion to strange substances, or by purposefully decaying the film."[76] This is especially evident in Kerr's *Drill Blue (Woven)* (2016), a woven version of his 2014 film *Drill Blue*, made by drilling holes into a canister of unexposed 35mm film, which Kerr then left outside under moonlight so that the film was exposed directly through the holes. In the projected version, black holes of varying sizes flicker rhythmically across a mostly abstract blue-black background. Flashes and flecks of other colors occur unexpectedly, punctuated by sudden appearances of the ghostly outlines of sprocket holes, a slew of indiscernible shapes, and fingerprints, all the result of the messy aleatoric method of handmaking and hand processing the film.

In the digital version, made because the original is likely unprojectable, Kerr slowed down sections of the film in a manner akin to step printing, allowing the viewer to appreciate single frames and make out details, including the remarkable clarity of surface texture and color. The film is manifestly about the surface of the strip, transparent in conventional film, and at times takes on a quasi-three dimensionality. Magnified in this way, surface details appear in layers, like the stark, slightly ragged edges of the drill holes, rendered in such crisp focus that the viewer can actually see the depth of the punctured stock. These stand out in the sharpest focus as other layers of the image remain slightly soft. Bits of hair and dust also pop out from the softer focus background, as if this film, though made without a lens, nonetheless possesses image fields with multiple planes of depth.

While the digital reproduction of *Drill Blue* enables this degree of visual clarity, it works against another quality, which is the unmediated experience of handling the original. The woven version sees Kerr "yanking film back" from this mediation and the alienation it implies, to use Testa's words (fig. 4.29).[77] Directly displaying the object restores actual depth, most visible in the over-under weave pattern Kerr uses for all his woven films. It is another 30-by-30-inch grid, this time of blacks, blues, and greens. The almost metrical alternation between dark and light mark the varying

[75] Jordan, "Industry."
[76] Zinman, "Handmade," p. 10.
[77] Testa, "Richard Kerr's Recuperation," p. 34.

Fig. 4.29. Richard Kerr, *Drill Blue (Woven)* (2016). 35mm celluloid film, Plexiglas, fluorescent light, artist's lightbox.
Courtesy of Richard Kerr.

Fig. 4.30. Richard Kerr, *Drill Blue (Woven)* (2016). Detail. 35mm celluloid film, Plexiglas, fluorescent light, artist's lightbox.
Courtesy of Richard Kerr.

density of the stock and the weave, as in certain spots the lightboard behind the film-strips is more clearly visible while in others the blacks are entirely opaque (fig. 4.30).

It is surprising that no other author on Kerr's object-based film work has made the obvious historical connection for which the weaving analogy and Kerr's pugnacious attitude toward industrial cinema cry out. Kerr's move from a film like *willing voyeur* to these objects was precisely Luddite, an act of political resistance not to new technology as such, but to a mode of making films that said technology serves. While Kerr has used digital technology in his filmmaking since *willing voyeur*, he has assimilated it, to use Federico Windhausen's term, to his avant-garde, "*plein air*" practice rather than submitting to the working methods he believes it facilitates and the values these embody:

> [T]hat digital revolution stuff was a bust—it was the biggest con that ever happened to young practitioners. And the ones that were smart enough to hang on to their old cameras, and learn how to hand-process film … it's just that the 100% totally digital world, to me, has an evil aspect to it. It all backs up to M.I.T. somewhere and some sense of military R&D.[78]

---

[78] Jordan, "Industry."

Of course, this is a polemical position on digital media to say the least. The extent to which it is true, or fair, isn't important. It explains Kerr's preference for a certain working process above and beyond any specific media, simultaneously avoiding the extremes of either detaching methods from mediums entirely or reducing the former to the latter. These preferences are not merely fetishistic, obtusely contrarian, or nostalgic, as they are not absolutely determined by a specific technology.

More Film (as) Weaving: "Domain Shifts"

In their works and writings, Mary Stark and Sabrina Gschwandtner plumb the depths of the film/sewing analogy, cataloging the historical and formal dimensions of it and tracing deep structural parallels between the two forms to the point that their work could be said to make a case for ontological identity. Or at least ontological reciprocity, structural similarity that goes beyond loose associations or metaphorical leaps. The links between filmmaking and sewing, and between films and woven objects, are precise, forged by a series of point-to-point material, historical, and aesthetic correspondences whereby the formal language of one can be translated to that of the other. Stark and Gschwandtner thus exemplify the tendency among avant-garde filmmakers to develop unique and often idiosyncratic cinematic essentialisms that in turn sustain expanded work.

Stark's weavings are part of a larger constellation of textile-based film works, including installations, projection performances, and hand-processed cameraless films. All of these stem from Stark's treatment of film as thread, in both the literal sense—as a long, thin strand of pliable material—and a figurative one—as comprising "stands" of content, as in the multiple plotlines of a narrative film. It is by way of this specific comparison between one of cinema and sewing's fundamental objects that Stark, not unlike many British structural-materialist filmmakers, developed a conception of filmic duration as both temporal and spatial, a length of film material corresponding to a certain span of time. Weaving film is thus an analytical act for Stark, the projection of cinematic time into the spatial register as a means of discovering and creating visual patterns analogous to temporal ones. Stark mostly works with found footage, weaving entire feature-length films reel by reel, working more or less from head to tail rather than prearranging filmstrips into patterns as Kerr and Gschwandtner do. The feature films must be in the form of 8mm reduction prints, however, as a complete film of that length in 35mm would run over two miles in length, requiring a much larger studio space than experimental filmmakers customarily have access to. The almost comical idea of an 8mm print of a blockbuster epic like *Star Wars* also speaks to a radical shift in the relationship between film and spectator, from the movie theater to the living room, and the greater degree of intimacy that entails.

Fig. 4.31. Mary Stark, *That's Entertainment* (2012). Woven super 8mm feature film and unspooled film projector. Cornerhouse Micro Commission with support from the Paul Hamlyn Foundation.
Image courtesy of the artist.

But even in their reduced form, these films allow Stark to pursue her aim of translating time into physical form, a way of measuring the "thread" of film. Stark has woven reduction prints of *Star Wars* (1977) and *That's Entertainment* (1974) into large-scale tapestries, which are suspended from the ceiling some distance from any wall so that light, usually from a film projector, can pass through them (fig. 4.31). Filmless 8mm projectors illuminate the shimmering celluloid weavings and cast their shadows on the opposite wall, with Stark using special refracting lenses to further manipulate the projected light. Like Kerr, Stark redirects the viewer from the spectacle of

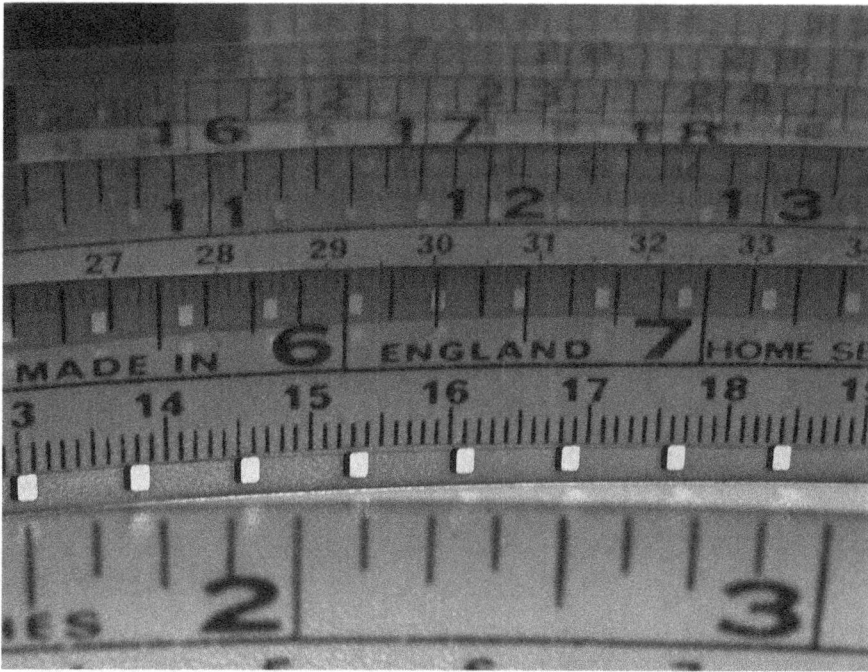

Fig. 4.32. Mary Stark, *Tape Measure Film* (2013). 16mm cameraless black and white film loop with optical sound. Produced at Mono No Aware VII, New York, December 2013. Image courtesy of the artist.

the source films to "the spectacle of the material and its presentation through an apparatus."[79] One way to read this is as a magnification of the space inside the projector and the exteriorization of those invisible mechanisms not unlike Bruce McClure's. Stark removes film from standard projection, but projects it nevertheless, placing it outside the machine where it continues to function as a template for projected light. This act of externalization is historically linked to the work of filmmakers within the London Filmmakers' Cooperative, particularly Le Grice and Raban, whose expanded works gave shape to the experience of cinematic time. In *Tape Measure Film* (2013), Stark contact printed the markings of a tape measure directly onto raw 16mm stock (figs. 4.32 and 4.33). In both its title and its precise measurement of running time when projected, *Tape Measure Film* rhymes with Raban's *Take Measure* (1973; see chapter 2). Writing of her cameraless films, Stark has claimed that such direct filmmaking methods "allow the filmstrip to be negotiated as surface area."[80] The same

[79] Samuel le France, "Heavy as a Thread: An Interview with Mary Stark," *Cleo: A Journal of Film and Feminism* 3, no. 3 (Winter 2015), http://cleojournal.com/2015/11/24/heavy-as-a-thread-an-interview-with-mary-stark/, n.p.

[80] Mary Stark, "Points of Translation and Transformation," blog entry on Stark's residency at La Escocesa, Barcelona, 2013, https://marystarkbarcelona.wordpress.com/2014/01/31/ points-of-translation-and-transformation/, n.p.

Fig. 4.33. Mary Stark, *Tape Measure Film* (2013). Installation view (loop runs until no longer projectable). 16mm cameraless black and white film loop with optical sound. Produced at Mono No Aware VII, New York, December 2013.
Image courtesy of the artist.

ambition animates the woven filmworks, bridging the gap between the filmmaker's experience with the film surface and the viewer's, for whom that surface is lost when it becomes a projected image. Making her film weavings both surface and screen, something simultaneously seen and seen through, fuses these impressions. The resulting projection looks nothing like the original, obviously. There is no mistaking Stark's *Star Wars* for the original, but as Stark points out, those familiar with the original might recognize it by picking out individual frames magnified against the adjacent wall, though these shimmer in and out of focus as the air circulating in the space makes the tapestry sway.

The expanded mode of exhibition does, however, approximate another original experience—that of the editor handling so and so many strands of film and lengths of story duration. And in its grid formation the work implies a range of options, of possible arrangements of patches or lines of color. That Stark describes this viewing experience as doing away "with the idea of invisible cuts, since the viewer can see one or two hundred and the splice tape that join and hold the whole thing together" confirms this analysis.[81] The original *Star Wars* is restored to an even more "original,"

---

[81] Le France, "Heavy as a Thread."

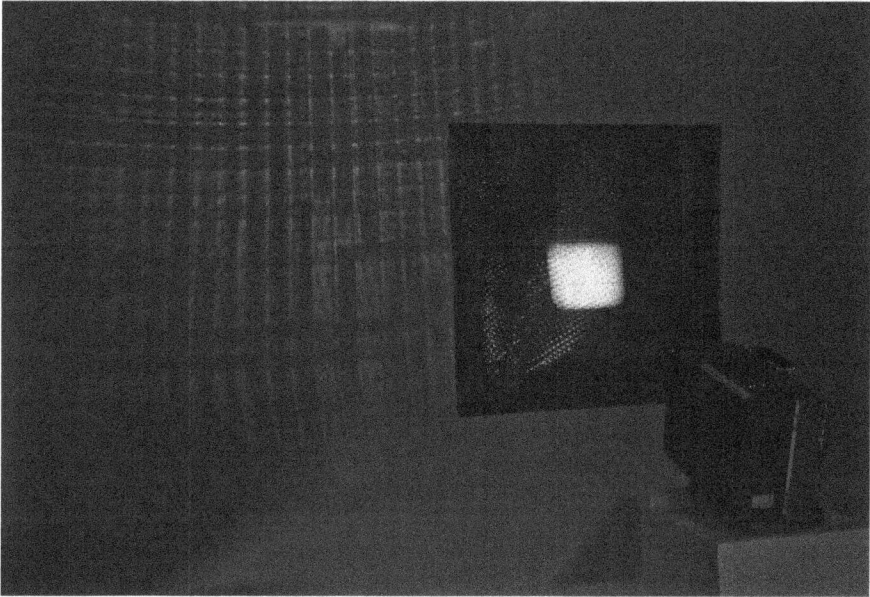

Fig. 4.34. Mary Stark, *Star Wars Super 8mm.* (2012). Installation view. Woven super 8mm feature film and unspooled film projector. Mono No Aware VI, New York, December 2012. Image courtesy of the artist.

primary version, before the invisible edits obscured the material realities of film and work behind the finished product (fig. 4.34).

Stark has explained her application of the working methods and craft language of sewing in terms of Richard Sennett's concept of the "domain shift." In *The Craftsman*, a sociological study of craft that extends the idea quite broadly, Sennett defines the domain shift as the process whereby "a tool initially used for one purpose can be applied to another task, or how the principle guiding one practice can be applied to quite another activity."[82] Stark cites Sennett's example of boat builders drawing upon the techniques of cloth weaving to construct stronger joints between pieces of wood (Sennett also argues that the same domain shift took place a second time, as the new notion of "weaving wood" was taken up by city planners crafting "an urban fabric").[83]

The domain shift from textile arts to filmmaking reaches its apex in the film quilts of Sabrina Gschwandtner, who is highly regarded as both an experimental filmmaker and a quiltmaker and proponent of knitting craft. Gschwandtner finds many of the same points of connection between textiles and film: the physical similarities of film and thread, the related practices of found footage filmmaking and the use of leftover

---

[82] Richard Sennett, *The Craftsman* (New Haven, CT: Yale University Press, 2008), p. 127.
[83] Ibid., p. 128. Stark's reference is in "Film, Textiles, Industry & Domestic Space," https://marystarkbar-celona.wordpress.com/2013/12/15/film-textiles-industry-domestic-space/, n.p.

industrial scraps used by artisanal weavers, formal similarities between sewing and editing, and historical parallels between the institutional conditions of filmmaking and textile work in both their mass market and independent forms. References to the creatively generative interpenetration of her two art forms are everywhere in her writings: "In conceiving of an approach to filmmaking that was in part defined by the craft ethos of mending and recycling but still devoted to the history of avant-garde cinema, I was able to expand on the potential for the projected image, but place it within the context of handcraft."[84] She writes of media as a "textile" and of knitting as the overarching model for all her work.

The subject matter, image content, and even the provenance of the films Gschwandtner works with are critical to her practice, becoming sources of form and meaning. Like Stark and Kerr, Gschwandtner uses found footage, though almost exclusively from documentaries and educational films on craft-related subjects, and always on 16mm. Her earliest quilts were crafted from a collection of reels dropped from the Fashion Institute of Technology's library and donated to Anthology Film Archives, who in turn passed them along to Gschwandtner (fig. 4.35). Included in the collection was Pat Ferreros's award-winning documentary *Quilts in Women's Lives: Six Portraits* (1980). In that film, six women from diverse backgrounds discuss and demonstrate their quilting, connecting it to their personal histories and political and artistic outlooks. A contemporaneous review of the film in a journal of oral history forecast with uncanny accuracy the approach Gschwandtner would take to the material nearly three decades later:

> Who can resist comparing the film to its subject? *Quilts* assembles some similar, some contrasting stories; each retains its individuality, yet patterns emerge from the finished work. Recognizing and interpreting these patterns, however, is largely left to the viewer. Each quilter speaks her piece . . . [85]

The intersection of formal ideas about narrative structure and the referential content of the stories is equally evident in Gschwandtner's quilts. The richness and extraordinary craftspersonship of her work is difficult to do justice to in language, but an attempt at a close analysis of a representative quilt will hopefully be revealing nonetheless.

Elizabeth Keckley Diamond (2014) pays tribute to a former slave of mixed race who befriended Mary Todd Lincoln and worked for the Lincolns in the White House. Her intimate friendship with the first lady became the subject of a controversial book by Keckley, who served as seamstress to Mrs. Lincoln and several other wives of major

---

[84] Sabrina Gschwandtner, "Statement of Craft: Knitting Is . . . ," *Journal of Modern Craft* 1, no. 2 (July 2008), p. 272.

[85] Anne R. Kaplan, "*Quilts in Women's Lives: Six Portraits*," *Oral History Review* 18, no. 1 (Spring 1990), p. 123.

Fig. 4.35. Sabrina Gschwandtner, *Quilts in Women's Lives IV* (2013). 16mm film, polyester thread, polyamide thread, cotton thread, lithography ink, permanent marker, LEDs. 23¼ in. × 23¼ in. × 3 in.

Photo: Tom Powel Imaging. Courtesy of the artist.

political figures in Washington, DC. Her sewing helped support her family, even paying for her freedom and that of her son ten years before the Civil War. *Elizabeth Keckley Diamond* at once references this story and exemplifies the multiple layers of the film/textiles analogy.

From a distance, this small piece (about 15 inches square) looks like simple geometric abstraction, ideal for visual works made entirely from rectilinear objects; Gschwandtner has cited Joseph Albers as an inspiration, though the vibrating, almost 3D effect of contrasting colors in many of her quilts are reminiscent of Hans Hoffman's paintings (figure 4.36). Even from a distance, its patchwork construction from multi-colored strips stands out. A gray-scale diamond shape is nested inside a reddish orange square; the former is actually just a smaller square rotated 45 degrees so that its corners bisect the lengths of the external square's sides. The "45-degree diamond" is a classic quilting pattern, usually consisting of multiple small squares set corner-to-corner within a rectangular quilt. The use of multiple fabrics, each with its own colors and patterns, makes for a dynamic visual effect of radiating hues and vibrating shapes. One can in effect choose to see the overall form as a cluster of

Fig. 4.36. Sabrina Gschwandtner, *Elizabeth Keckley Diamond* (2014). Detail.
Photo: Tom Powel Imaging. Courtesy of the artist.

squares, diamonds, or triangles, an effect enhanced in *Elizabeth Keckley Diamond* by the use of starkly contrasting colors.

Closer examination reveals that the diamond shape is in fact composed of four right triangles arranged so their right angles meet at a point in the exact center of the quilt. From that center point, four identical strips of black and white 16mm film extend in each direction—left, right, up, and down—ending where the points of the diamond meet the outer edges of the quilt. These four strips are all taken from one shot, a medium close-up photograph of Elizabeth Keckley presumably taken from a documentary about Keckley (or Gschwandtner may have filmed the oft-reproduced portrait herself). The series of images of Keckley—each strip is 18 frames long, or just under six inches—form the base of each gray-scale triangle; the rest of the triangle is filled out by strips of film that appear to contain a portrait of an African American family around the time of Reconstruction. These grow shorter as each triangle tapers to a point at the edge of the quilt. Looking closely at these adjacent strips reveals varying shot scales, some containing the entire group, others focusing in on one or two of its members. The impression is that the source footage utilized a visual trope familiar from Ken Burns documentaries—the camera panning across a still photographic image and zooming into details rather than shooting the photograph from a static vantage point. Each triangle follows the same pattern of images, the same order of strips along the axis from the long strip of Keckley's portrait to the point where the base and hypotenuse of the triangle meet at the edge of the quilt.

The "background," really another set of right triangles laid hypotenuse to hypotenuse with the gray triangles of the central diamond, is made mostly of orange, red, and yellow filmstrips. Many of these look like the light-struck ends of color film or the colored leader found at the heads and tails of reels, though Gschwandtner also applied lithography ink to some of them to achieve the remarkable degree of chromatic uniformity that marks the piece. Like the strips of the diamond, these are arranged in a pattern that repeats from top to bottom, though Gschwandtner inverts this pattern in two of the four background triangles. Ambiguous images, one of an ornate coffee pot one might have seen in the Lincoln White House, punctuate an otherwise abstract field of colors, washed out images, and chemical splotches.

Each quartet of triangles, orange and gray, is further composed of two complimentary pairs, which mirror each other in their arrangement of specific shots. For instance, the order of strips in the upper right orange triangle is inverted in the bottom right triangle, but mirrored exactly by the lower left one. Hence, while at first glance it may look haphazardly constructed, *Elizabeth Keckley Diamond* is a rigorously structured weave of echoing lines and rewards lengthy and concentrated examination. The precision of this arrangement is masked by the deliberate roughness of the stitching and resulting unevenness in the alignment of the strips. This roughness is unavoidable: incredibly, Gschwandtner sews the strips together using a sewing machine, an extremely time-consuming and difficult task that leaves imperfect angles and some give in the quilt. Loose crisscrosses of polyester sewing thread run through the ragged holes punched in the film by the sewing machine.

Elizabeth Keckley Diamond depicts Keckley and her historical milieu through its photographic imagery and form alike. Keckley and the unknown African American family are at once centered in the quilt's composition and isolated by it, contrasted starkly with the images of wealth and privilege that surround them in the more colorful external triangles. Keckley stands as a mediating figure between the two worlds, more upwardly mobile than a typical black woman but still severely restricted by the structure of the society in which she lived. Her place at the center of the quilt elevates her as subject but also emblematizes her distance from white society and power. The quilt can thus easily be read as a schematic visual narrative of Keckley's position between integration into the white world and deprivation of the power and privilege that should come with it. Her dress is markedly different from that of the African American family that flanks her image. She wears the clothes of a wealthy antebellum society woman but is clearly not one, a fact expressed through the work's form above and beyond its referential imagery.

A common theme in critical discussion of quilting is that quilts indeed tell stories, including those of the individuals who made them. Even the review of *Quilts in Women's Lives* makes this claim as it analogizes the interwoven narratives to the structure of a quilt. Moreover, the belief that quilts are narrative forms extends from the images in the fabric to the handiwork itself. Unlike their machine-made, mass-produced counterparts, handmade quilts bear the traces of the life of the person who made it. The unavoidable irregularities and imperfections are understood not as lapses in craft but narrative signifiers, traces of a real life as opposed to an automated machine process. As Zinman notes, "the handmade mark also carries psychic weight because it is often invoked with regard to notions of authenticity or the real."[86]

This "notion of the real" in relation to textile-based works of expanded cinema is worth pursuing a bit further. Gschwandtner, who studied with Valie EXPORT briefly in 1988 before taking a degree in art and semiotics at Brown University (also a telling connection), has invoked EXPORT's definition of expanded cinema in reference to her own expanded work:

> I remember something Valie EXPORT said about expanded cinema. She said that in expanded cinema, film is split up into its formal components and put back to-gether in a new way. What I think makes my work different from the Sharits work you're describing is that I'm splitting up the components of film by taking out the projection and replacing a traditional, physical kind of linearity, with a multilinear, three-dimensional quilt.[87]

EXPORT's definition of expanded cinema actually went further: the components of the medium were not just atomized but "partially replaced by reality in order to install new signs of the real" (see chapter 1). This included film being replaced by reality, photographic illusion switched out for direct experience of the real physical world, in *TAPP UND TAST KINO* for example. Gschwandtner's approach is somewhat different. Clearly, film remains in her work, and its images are critical to the meaning of the quilts, as in the representation of race and power in *Elizabeth Keckley Diamond*. But those strips of filmic representation are themselves "signs of the real" regardless of their image content. Removed from the mediation of projection, their material status is reaffirmed, and they become the signifiers of Gschwandtner's own hand and craft-work as both quilter and "editor." EXPORT's project was informed by a desire to liberate filmmaking from the ideological constraints at work in normal film production and exhibition such as illusionism and industrial determination. Aspects of the medium that were regarded as liabilities were jettisoned in favor of expanded forms that restored reality to the cinema.

While Gschwandtner does not abandon photographic representation, she dramatically alters the terms of our engagement with images by placing them in a form that is not a representation but a real object. The work does not allegorize quilting, it is literally woven. It is not just about a seamstress, but the work of one as well. This makes the intermediality of her film quilts the most complicated relative to other filmmakers

---

[86] Zinman, "Handmade," p. 9.
[87] Andrew Lampert, "Sabrina Gschwandtner," *BOMB Magazine*, December 19, 2013, https://bombmag-azine.org/articles/sabrina-gschwandtner/, n.p.

who weave film. It also further parallels her with EXPORT, whose expanded work at once maintained a sense of cinema's specificity crucial for her intervention while simultaneously forging links between film and the other arts. Gschwandtner has written, "although I had been rigorously devoted to experimental and avant-garde film during all four years of college [where she discovered knitting], handcraft had become my guiding creative format."[88] In making quilts from celluloid, Gschwandtner makes aspects of each art form resonate with one another, including historical themes like the occlusion of female labor in a patriarchal society and of artisanal labor in an industrial one.

Gschwandtner, Stark, and Kerr also reimagine montage in spatial forms, lending them a concreteness they lose otherwise and throwing into relief the tropes of editing made invisible by narrative action. Gschwandtner suggests this when she states that her quilts replace the "traditional, physical kind of linearity" of film in projection "with a multi-linear, three-dimensional form."[89] The disarticulation and reassemblage of component parts is not just an act upon the medium of film, but more to the point upon cinema's formal trait. Editing is not just an assembly of pieces but an aesthetic feature of a film as well, the creation of time, space, and meaning by a process of coordinating shots, which the editor experiences but the viewer does not. Unless, of course, that process is given a spatial analog. As Testa explains, "Kerr's woven light boxes also bring us into an intimacy with cinema that, *unless we happen to make films,* we never would have known about."[90] In a way, these works are the underground precursors to the infographic images currently enjoying a vogue online, which diagram temporally complex Hollywood films like *Pulp Fiction* and *Inception.* But while those images act as maps to orient curious viewers to the complicated temporal contours of those kinds of movies, the weavings of Gschwandtner, Stark, and Kerr are not designed to make some original object cohere. Rather than providing a line through, they are, in Gschwandtner's words, "multi-linear," an open field the spectator's eye is invited to move through in any order.

That idea, and the very act of weaving strands of film, calls up one last film-historical context that bears upon these works. "Film is a textile," Gschwandtner writes. As practiced by critics like Raymond Bellour and Thierry Kuntzel, following Roland Barthes's model, textual analysis imagined films as dense tapestries of interwoven lines of action and meaning—as textiles. The analogy signaled those theorists' resistance to film's narrative linearity, the seemingly natural and seamless flow of cause-and-effect leading to resolution. This relentless forward movement closed down the film text's semiotic plurality. In *S/Z,* Barthes explained this in terms of the inherently open, tabular nature of the text getting "vectorized," channeled into a "logico-temporal order."[91] Kuntzel adopted this characterization of literature in his

---

[88] Gschwandtner, "Statement of Craft," p. 272.
[89] Lampert, "Sabrina Gschwandtner."
[90] Testa, "Richard Kerr's Recuperation," p. 36.
[91] Roland Barthes, *S/Z* (Oxford: Blackwell Publishing Ltd., 1990), p. 30.

analyses of classical films like *The Most Dangerous Game*, which were intended to return tabularity and polysemic openness to the highly vectorized, causally driven classical Hollywood cinema.[92] Stopping the relentless forward thrust of a narrative and regarding the text not as a unidirectional line but a constellation, field, or *tableau* (all Kuntzel's terms), revealed the text's buried polysemiousness, opening it to subversive readings.

Without being technologically deterministic, it is fair to say that the flatbed editing machine was central to the development of the textualists' methodology. The flatbed allowed analysts to work directly with film prints, where previous generations of theorists had been forced to rely on their memories of viewings in the theater. This shift surely helps account for the object-oriented critical language of textual analysis. In defining the terms of their analytical methods, Bellour and Kuntzel indirectly described the experience of working with a film print on a flatbed: viewing it in slow motion, entering it from either end, running it in reverse, holding it still. Barthes wrote that "the step-by-step method, through its very slowness and dispersion ... is never anything but the decomposition (in the cinematographic sense) of the work of reading: a slow motion, so to speak, a way of observing the reversibility of the structures from which the text is woven."[93] Bellour and Kuntzel's near-obsessive subdivision of films into smaller and smaller units, shuttling from macroscopic to microscopic patterns in a kind of fractal zoom from large-scale narrative segment to single frame, grew out of this newly available analytical tool. The reconfiguration of narrative form implied by the language of weaving, of "decomposition" and "reversibility," begins, then, with the direct handling of the film on a machine that could produce those very experiences at the material level. This must have informed the textualists' superimposition of film's formal and material linearity, at once a narrative form and a strip of celluloid.

The will to decompose form, especially comfortably familiar forms, is a defining feature of avant-garde cinema. This is the appeal of the weaving analogy as a generative model for expanded cinema. The weaving is easily unwoven, and retains the trace of the individual threads composing it, which in turn recall the artist's hand, the filmmaker's labor. It frees the viewer from linear experience of the film in projection, making film legible as an object to begin with and re-projecting cinematic time into spatial forms. The tightly woven, seamless film is dispersed as it is made into a textile, endowing cinema's temporal forms with the solidity of objects.

---

[92] Thierry Kuntzel, "The Film Work, 2," *Camera Obscura* 2, no. 2 (Spring 1980), pp. 6–70.
[93] Barthes, *S/Z*, pp. 12–13.

5

Cinema as Object II

Films have to be made which amplify cinema's general infrastructures. The task is curious since, on the one hand, we have to rebuild cinema in order to analyze it but, on the other hand, we have to (speculatively) analyze it—build micromorphological structure-function models—in order to rebuild it.

—**Paul Sharits (1975)**

[E]xpanded cinema is the spatial aspect of the moving image … I want to incorporate past within a present moment—that kind of complex relationship with time that is either conceptual or formal subject matter. Then there is the physical expansion, in that it expands outside of just one screen, taking on the specificity of its context, whether a neutral space, an underground car park, an auditorium, or a museum or gallery. The work becomes a reading of the work itself. It's not simply a form of display. The spatial or architectural element is an integral part of the meaning that the work explores. It expands in relationship to a temporal, or filmic, cinematic moment.

—**Noor Afshan Mirza (2007)**

Black & White/Boxes & Cubes: Variations on a Theme

A tiny 16mm film loop, 24 frames of unexposed emulsion or "black leader," its ends joined by a tape splice, set inside a clear plastic cube measuring three inches high, three inches wide, one inch deep. A razor thin clear line has been etched through it, running along the middle of the strip, a loop within a loop. Engraved on the bottom of the cube: "TAKA '08." This is Takahiko Iimura's *ONE SECOND LOOP = INFINITY: A White Line in Black* (fig. 5.1). Almost comic in its smallness, unprojectable (one imagines an impossibly minute film projector), hence the joke of the title: a loop is "infinite" in that it can be projected indefinitely, but this particular loop's necessarily static condition as filmic object renders it literally timeless.

Somewhere *A White Line in Black* has a corresponding object, *ONE SECOND LOOP = INFINITY: A Black Line in Clear*. It is identical to *A White Line in Black* except that the little loop inside the clear plastic cube is clear film with a black line printed along its length. Two black (opaque) and white (transparent) loops in a white

Cinema Expanded. Jonathan Walley, Oxford University Press (2020). © Oxford University Press.
DOI: 10.1093/oso/9780190938635.001.0001

Fig. 5.1. Takahiko Iimura, *ONE SECOND LOOP = INFINITY: A White Line in Black* (2007). One-second-long 16mm film loop, 3 in. × 3 in. × 1 in. Edition of 20.
Image courtesy of the artist.

(clear) cube. These filmic objects are relics, what Sharits might have called "ontological documents of [film's] objects-processes."[1] They memorialize Iimura's film installations of the 1970s, all of which were based upon alternations of opaque and clear film running in large loops through a gallery space, their parallel projections—a white frame bisected by a black line or a black frame by a white line—cast against the white gallery wall. Loops, projectors, plinths, images, space, were all visible in a brightly lit gallery. The open display of what Iimura named "the film system," which these installations were designed to reveal, was to be visible to the spectator, and so the illuminated space of a gallery was required rather than the darkened movie theater and the veil of the projection booth:[2]

> To expose the system, so that it no longer hides in darkness or behind the projection booth, every facility and material must be "visible," including non-visible light. To achieve this, I use, rather than a theater with seats, an open space like

---

[1] Sharits, "Statement Regarding Multiple Screen/Sound 'Locational' Film Environments," p. 79.
[2] Takahiko Iimura, "On Film-Installation," *Millennium Film Journal* no. 2 (Spring–Summer 1978), p. 74.

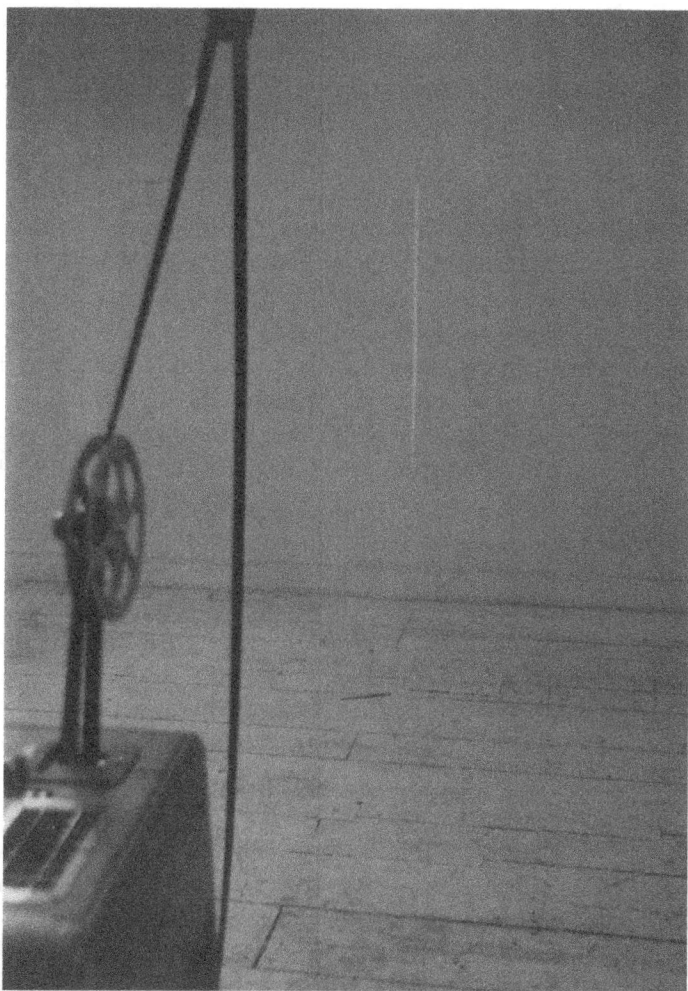

Fig. 5.2. Takahiko Iimura, *Loop Seen as a Line* (1972). Installation view. Two 16mm film loops (black and clear) and two 16mm projectors.
Image courtesy of the artist.

that of a gallery, where people can come and go at any time, and walk around the installation.[3]

The corresponding boxed loops come from Iimura's 1972 film installation *Loop Seen as a Line* (fig. 5.2). Two film loops, much longer versions of the diminutive specimens in the boxes, were threaded through side-by-side 16mm projectors on plinths, both

---

[3] Ibid.

aimed at a space on the opposite wall. Each loop was over 30 feet long, and passed along spools mounted from the ceiling—two directly above the projectors, two more near the wall where the images were projected. Iimura used older model projectors whose feed and takeup reels were both at the front of the machine, one above the other (in contrast to the usual orientation, in which film passes from the feed reel at the front of the machine to the takeup reel at the back). The long, loosely hung, almost graceful loops passed downward into their respective projectors, through the gates, out over the lower reels, then angled upward toward the opposite wall, then back toward the projectors once more.

Iimura's entire body of film installation work was based on a series of contrasts and correspondences, resolutely dualistic. He used only black and clear film; imagery, if any, was restricted to lines or holes punched through the frames. The projector light passed through the clear film and was blocked by the opaque emulsion, the latter constituting the "non-visible" light to which Iimura alludes in the above passage. Projectors were either threaded with a variation of Iimura's basic loop or left running filmless, often lighting up another projector or the loops themselves. In all but one installation, the gallery wall functioned as screen. The exception was *Film Installation* (1974), which used no projectors, only two contrasting loops following the same parallel paths, unprojected (fig. 5.3). For that work, Iimura installed two white paper screens side by side on the wall where the image would have appeared had there been projectors. He did not regard the installation as "lacking" projectors or "projectorless." Rather, in the context of the entire series, in which each installation referred to the totality of the "film system," the missing projectors were a structuring absence, not physically present in the room but there by implication. They were the reverse, or negative image, of other installations in the series in which the projectors were threaded. In *Projection Piece* (1972, initially *Dead Movie*, 1968), a filmless projector cast the shadow of another projector, this one running film, against the back wall (figs. 5.4 and 5.5). In *Film as a Line* (1995), 20 loops hung from the ceiling into a field of projectors, through which they could be threaded or not. Some were simply left to dangle in the space and shimmer in the light of the projector beams.

Black and white, opaque and clear, loop and projector, circle and line, light and shadow, empty wall and paper screen—all components of a web of corresponding filmic elements over which sat the duality of positive and negative. For example, the lack of image produced by black film contrasted with the positive rectangle of light passing through clear film. But Iimura complicated this dualism: black film was both positive, as it possessed a layer of emulsion that clear film lacked, and negative, in that it completely blocked light and therefore cast no image. A presence in terms of "*film* as material" was an absence in terms of "*light* as material."[4] The play of presence and absence, positive and negative, film and light, constituted the film system for Iimura: "what one sees on the screen is not the sole object to be seen in the

---

[4] Ibid.

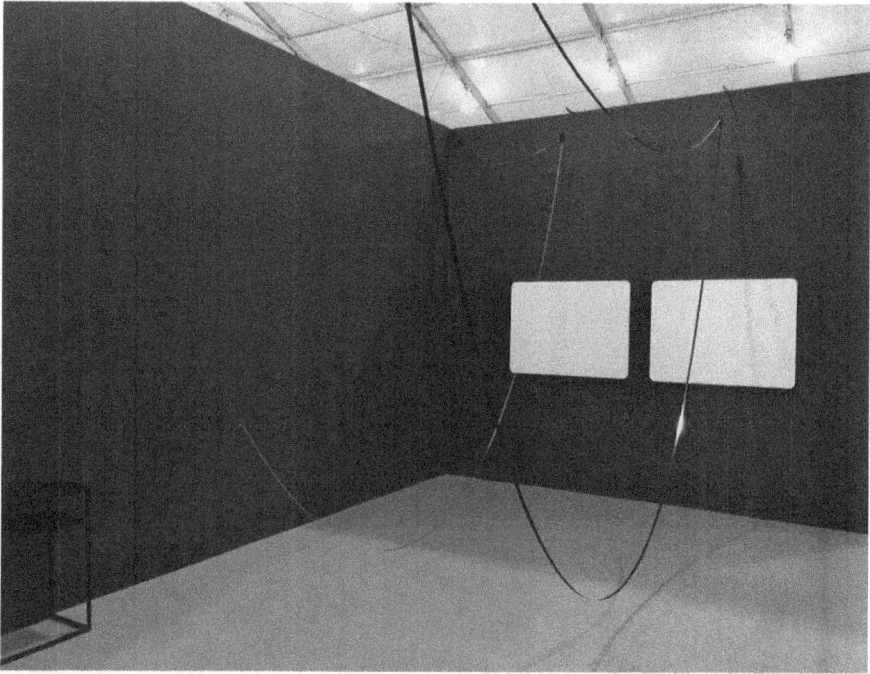

Fig. 5.3. Takahiko Iimura, *Film Installation* (1974). Installation view. Two 16mm film loops and white paper screens. Frieze, New York, May 2–5, 2019.
Image courtesy of the artist and Microscope Gallery.

film-installations, but simply one object that refers to the system."[5] By this logic, even negations were presences, as in *Film Installation*'s missing but conceptually present projectors. In this way, what at first blush might have seemed like a simplistic either/ or duality was in fact a multi-layered permutational set of film's fundamental materials and their possibilities. Iimura exhaustively explored this set from 1968 on, a process realized most recently in the revival of his installations and performances from the 1970s and the release of the memorializing boxed loops in 2007.

Beginning as it did in 1968, Iimura's installation work is an early instance of an avant-garde filmmaker's foray into the gallery. As if recognizing the potential confusion this move might cause, and the questions about its medium-belonging or artistic identity it could raise, Iimura wrote:

The film installations should not be seen in term [*sic*] of Expanded Cinema (as formats other than regular single screen projection have been called). Expanded Cinema still refers, more or less, to the image on the screen as the main

[5] Ibid.

Fig. 5.4. Takahiko Iimura, *Projection Piece* (1972, initially *Dead Movie*, 1968). Installation view. Two facing 16mm projectors, one 16mm film loop.
Image courtesy of the artist.

object—though there may be multiple screens; nor should the installations be seen as movie-sculpture consisting of the machines.[6]

Iimura's notion of expanded cinema seems curiously contracted, limited to multiple-screen films that, unlike his installations, did not acknowledge or engage the space of exhibition or the materials of the moving image system. But he was not alone in distancing his work from expanded cinema. Other experimental filmmakers who made installation or other space-based cinematic work in the 1970s either explicitly distinguished their work from expanded cinema or simply did not employ the term— we will see this in the cases of Sharits and Anthony McCall, for example. Including Iimura's installations in a book about expanded cinema obviously signals that I want to take issue with the distinction he makes between the two. When he made this work, a particular version of expanded cinema, more or less synonymous with Youngblood's model, was dominant, and came with associations that many avant-garde filmmakers wished to avoid. This was especially the case in the United States, where expanded

[6] Ibid., pp. 74–75.

Fig. 5.5. Takahiko Iimura, *Projection Piece* (1972, initially *Dead Movie*, 1968). Detail.
Image courtesy of the artist and Microscope Gallery.

cinema was synonymous with new media technology, visual spectacle, and the rejection of medium specificity. Quite a different situation obtained in Europe, particularly in the United Kingdom, the implications of which will become apparent later in this chapter. For now, the point to be made is that Iimura distanced his film installations from both expanded cinema and what he called "movie-sculpture," by which he presumably meant gallery-based moving image works by artists like Robert Morris and Dan Graham, which employed film but did not make "apparent what the film system is." In other words, like expanded cinema, the film installations were cinematic, meditations on film rather than sculpture or any other art form. But unlike expanded cinema in its earliest American incarnation, the film installations were not limited to their projected images, decidedly unspectacular, and were committed to a version of medium specificity, albeit one that was as much about forms, concepts, and experiences as physical materials like celluloid. This is what distinguished them from other types of moving image installation despite the fact that they occupied the same space as such works.

Writing around the same time about his own film installations, which he called "locational film environments-installations," Sharits also acknowledged the ontological questions raised by film's entry into the gallery:

> Despite the fact that my more philosophically focused work of 1971 onwards . . . has been generally better received in the museum-gallery art context than in the theatrical art ("film-making") context, I do not regard myself as either a "film-maker" or

an "artist who makes films"; rather, I view my activity as prototheoretical and I view myself as an artisan of infrastructural cinema.[7]

Though Sharits appeared unwilling to explicitly self-identify either as artist or film-maker in this statement, his language undoubtedly places him squarely within the tradition of avant-garde cinema. He defines his work as cinematic rather than sculptural or intermedial, invokes experimental film's artisanal mode of production, and describes his work as film-ontological research. He concludes this statement by making clear that his locational works, like Iimura's, were about the film system:

> In a museum-gallery space I can display together not just the outcome of an investigation (i.e., a film or a film piece composed of several ongoing, recycling, variational-permutational films-in-relation-to-each-other) but the whole thought and making process which has formed the film(s) (the infrastructural "Blow up"). In proximate spaces one can observe: scores which have generated a film; that film can be viewed as an object (seen as physical strips serially arranged and encased in plexiglass sheets); and, the projection of my analysis of that film object. There may also be follow-up diagrams and drawings concerning the findings of the inquiry ... I am interested in the questions they might suggest—not questions such as "what constitutes a shot?" or "what codes are implied in the 'zoom function'?" but deeper questions concerning the grain particle, the frame and its duration, the shutter and its rotation, and other infra-structural units of information, signification and meaning.[8]

This is one of many statements in Sharits's body of theoretical writing that signals another dualistic ontology of cinema. Here, his locational environments range from such basic "infrastructural" elements as film grain and shutter to cinematic signification, running the same gamut from material to meaning seen in contemporaneous writings of post-structuralist film theorists like Metz, whose work Sharits knew. Sharits's project of an exhaustive analysis of cinema was better suited to the installation format and thus the gallery context, or, at least the gallery *space* if not the larger art world context in which it existed. The installations, all using film loops, could run indefinitely, allowing for prolonged attention and analysis. The open space of the gallery accommodated the display of all manner of other cinematic objects: projectors, the *Frozen Film Frames* series, diagrams and film scores, and written texts could "form the conjunctions and punctuations between the projected works," collectively constituting what Sharits called "the infrastructural blow-up."[9] In short, the well-lit, open, multi-purpose space of the gallery was preferable to the theater, accommodating the

---

[7] Sharits, "Cinema as Cognition," p. 77.
[8] Ibid., p. 78.
[9] Ibid.

Fig. 5.6. Paul Sharits, *Soundstrip/Filmstrip* (1972). Installation view. Restored by Bill Brand in 2007 for the General Council of the Territory of Belfort, France for the Espace Multimédia Gantner.
Photograph by Bill Brand. Permission from Christopher and Cheri Sharits.

radically alternative modality of exhibition Sharits needed to model his prototheoretical infrastructural cinema.

Soundstrip/Filmstrip (1972) was the first of these models and one of the most technologically complicated (fig. 5.6). Four cartridge-format Super-8mm projectors, each installed in a specially designed box, projected images of a pinkish strip of film moving laterally, from right to left, a movement made visible by the passage of sprocket holes at the top of each projection and vertically oriented framelines through the middle. The four projected images were lined up in an even row, abutting each other in an approximation of a single giant filmstrip turned sideways, oriented horizontally rather than vertically, its row of sprocket holes at the top of the composite image. The filmstrips in each of the four projected frames moved at different speeds, increasing and decreasing velocity arbitrarily, at times moving rapidly enough that the sprocket holes and framelines became blurs of lateral motion.

The projectors Sharits used for *Soundstrip/Filmstrip*, Fairchild Seventy-07s, were housed in suitcases. According to Bill Brand, who assisted Sharits with the installation and produced 16mm and digital restorations of it in 2007, the Fairchild

Seventy-07s were used by traveling salesmen as portable visual aids.[10] When the suit-case was opened, a screen unfolded from its confines. The film in the Super-8mm cartridge ran through the projector gate sideways rather than vertically, but its image was reoriented by a compact system of mirrors seated behind the pop-up screen. Sharits, however, wanted to restore the sideways orientation of the image, so Brand built yet another set of mirrors into the projectors to "re-re-orient" the image and cast it out from the small projection screen to the wall of the gallery. The four projected loops, each ten minutes long, were 8mm reduction prints of 16mm films Sharits had pains-takingly shot, hand altered, and re-photographed from the screen. Sharits began by shooting a single sheet of pink paper at various exposures, producing gradations of brightness and saturation. Once the films were processed, Sharits scratched each one along its entire length, the scratch running diagonally from left to right for the first half of the roll, then right to left for the second; in projection, this line would appear to move slowly down the frame for one half of the film, then reverse its direction for the second.[11] Sharits then projected the scratched films on a projector that lacked a shutter, claw, and registration pin, through which the film would therefore run con-tinuously rather than intermittently. He re-filmed this image from a rear projection screen, running the projector at varying speeds as he did, then reduced the resulting 16mm prints to 8mm, etching the same long diagonal line on those films that he had on the originals.

As this description of Sharits's working method will hopefully suggest, the result-ing loops collapse multiple temporal and material layers of image. An illusionistic scratch—that is, its filmed image—is paralleled by a real scratch etched into the Super-8mm loops. Additional scratches that accrued during the installation's three-month run overlaid the real and photographic scratches on the originals with another layer of time and material distress, an added record of the entire work's filmic pro-cesses. Brand notes the interpenetration of real and illusory movement, and of flow and intermittency, in the work: "When projected, the illusionary scratch speeds up and slows down with the illusion of the moving filmstrip but the real scratch on the super-8 prints is steady because it is on the real film passing through the super-8 pro-jector with intermittent motion at 24 frames per second."[12]

The loops also contained magnetic soundtracks. One syllable of the word "miscel-laneous" was looped onto each film's soundtrack and patched through to four speak-ers, one for each projector, placed in different locations in the space. That is, meaning was atomized phonetically, materially, and spatially, broken into its component pho-netic elements and then further dispersed across the four film loops and individual speakers. The viewer was required to move through the space from speaker to speaker to discern the divided word from the cacophony of overlapping voices.

---

[10] Bill Brand, "The Artist as Archivist," in Andrew Lampert, ed., *Results You Can't Refuse: Celebrating 30 Years of BB Optics* (New York: Anthology Film Archives, 2006), p. 73.

[11] Brand is also responsible for creating the device that allowed Sharits to make such a precise diagonal etching across the entire 100-foot length of film. See Brand, "The Artist as Archivist," pp. 72–73.

[12] Ibid., p. 73.

Marveling at the formal complexity of *Soundstrip/Filmstrip*, Rosalind Krauss neatly encapsulated the multiple material and aesthetic dualisms it put into play. These were not limited to the work itself, but were shared by the viewer, who "physically traverses the space of the room of the film."

> Time, then, is the subject of *Soundstrip/Filmstrip*; time, in relation to what might be called the analytic mode of consciousness. The experience of film is normally about being caught up in the flow of time, of being so enmeshed in the process of duration that one suspends all sense of the fusion of past and present occurring within that experience. The analytic act—the standing back from the experience in order to ask what it is and how it is made—obviously rends the fabric of duration. In tearing it apart in order to examine it, one has not duration but stasis; one has an analytic movement and an inert object or reflection.[13]

Here Krauss recognizes the filmmaker's obsession with film's oscillations between static object and temporal event, between reality and illusion, and, for the viewer, between two kinds of cinematic experience: "caught up in the flow of time" and "standing back from" it analytically. Or, as Krauss phrased it, "Sharits's will in *Soundstrip/Filmstrip* is to give us that moment of reflection without destroying its object; to give us at one and the same time the abstract components of film and the reality of its experience."[14] Krauss's description of the nested space of the installation— "the *space* of the *room* of the *film*"—is another expression of the oscillatory cinematic ontology that informed it.

This oscillation between formal and perceptual modes embodied what was perhaps Sharits's overarching concern in the early and mid-1970s: that film, or what Sharits called "the filmic enterprise," possessed "characteristics which suggest processes of human knowing."[15] Its varying material states, that is, were analogizable to complimentary perceptual and cognitive experiences that defined consciousness. These comments came from a short statement entitled "Cinema as Cognition: Introductory Remarks," written in 1975. In addition to claiming a homological relationship between cinema and consciousness, Sharits asserted that the locational mode was the best means of modeling this idea. In her analysis of the locational works, Annette Michelson, who had made much the same analogy between film and consciousness in her phenomenological reading of *Wavelength*, also noted the necessity of a gallery-type space for the realization of Sharits's ambitions:

> Moving his work recently out of the theater situation and into the gallery is, of course, a first step, not only into a different space, but toward the clarification and redefinition of a filmic temporality. Its consequence is the obvious cancellation of

13 Rosalind Krauss, "Paul Sharits," *Film Culture* no. 65–66 (1978), pp. 93–94.
14 Ibid., p. 94.
15 Sharits, "Cinema as Cognition," p. 76.

the beginning-middle-end structure of theatrical projection and the distension of viewing time.[16]

And though Michelson acknowledged the apparent hybridity of the installations and compared them to minimalist sculptural works of the same period, she at once reiterated their filmic specificity and left the question of their identity open. Sharits had passed "through an objectification of a filmic ontology, into a hyper-space whose nature and limits remain to be defined."[17]

So began speculation and debate about the categorical belonging of artists like Iimura and Sharits and installations like *Loop Seen as a Line* and *Soundstrip/Filmstrip*. Certainly the involvement of the filmmakers in other art forms and movements contributed to this. Iimura linked his work with intermedia and was an active participant in major exhibitions of such work in New York and his native Japan. Sharits painted, illustrated, sculpted, performed, and made videos in addition to his single-screen films and multi-projector installations. He had been affiliated with Fluxus in the mid-1960s, and not infrequently analogized his filmmaking to painting and music. But the artistic identity of film installations in particular has been subject to more rhetorical wrangling than any other form of expanded cinema in this book. From the beginning, critics like Krauss and Michelson noted the sculptural qualities of film installations, especially their affinity with minimalist sculpture, for which the implications of the co-presence of viewer and object were paramount. But installations like *Soundstrip/Filmstrip* don't seem any more or less formally hybrid than cinematic performances like those of Sally Golding and Bruce McClure, or filmic objects like Richard Kerr's and Sabrina Gschwandtner's. Yet film installation has been the subject of much more discussion and controversy than these other forms of expanded cinema with respect to their categorical status.

The reason for this has much less to do with the intrinsic formal traits of film installations, as in their apparent sculptural-ness, than with the extrinsic institutional and discursive contexts in which their meanings and historical lineages are ultimately determined. This is a process that begins at the first moment of cinema's expansion in the 1960s and continues today as moving image installation has become ubiquitous in museums and galleries, what Hal Foster has derisively called the "default category" of the contemporary art world.[18]

Simultaneous with the first wave of expanded cinema was the appearance of film and video installations made by artists, as distinct from "filmmakers," made in studio spaces and designed for the gallery rather than the types of exhibition spaces in which expanded cinema debuted. Robert Morris, Bruce Nauman, Dan Graham, and Dennis Oppenheim were among the many visual artists who produced such installations.

[16] Michelson, "Paul Sharits and the Critique of Illusionism: An Introduction," p. 87.
[17] Ibid.
[18] Malcolm Turvey, Hal Foster, Chrissie Iles, George Baker, Matthew Buckingham, and Anthony McCall, "Round Table: The Projected Image in Contemporary Art," *October* 104 (Spring 2003), p. 93.

But as widespread as this practice was, it was never included under the heading of expanded cinema. Neither Renan nor Youngblood wrote about such work, despite the fact that it employed moving images in unconventional ways and seemed obviously poised between media. Other commentators, including VanDerBeek and Mekas, left it out of their accounts of expanded cinema as well, and none of the artists who made film and video installations made the association either.

Why is it that expanded cinema, which included so much that was not intuitively "cinematic," did not apparently include moving image installations by such major visual artists as Morris and Graham? The explanation has to do with the unique conditions under which the ontological status of moving image work in the gallery was determined. As I have argued, "expanded cinema" was a handy designation for the parade of new moving image technologies and forms of the 1960s and '70s. "Cinema" indicated that they involved moving images, or projection, or light, or spectacle, while the "expanded" qualified the work as novel, intermedial, unconventional. Moving image art in the gallery, however, did not require explication by way of a cinematic metaphor even though it too was an emerging form. The use of film or video by artists who had already established themselves as painters or sculptors, and who used film and video to extend their studio practices, was not so easily absorbed under the rubric of "cinema," or even "expanded cinema." Moving image installations such as those by Morris or Graham were designed for the gallery not just in the material sense (i.e., they required a very different kind of space than that of the cinema) but in a discursive one as well. Any ontological indeterminacy of moving image installation, then, was resolved in the terms of the art world under the blanket concept of "the sculptural." The conceptual categories of the art world could be applied to materials that might otherwise be considered cinematic, transforming them discursively into sculpture, itself radically expanding at the same moment.

Reflecting on and to an extent reproducing this phenomenon during the Whitney Museum's 2001 exhibition *Into the Light*, curator Chrissie Iles wrote that moving image installation art of the 1960s and '70s "played a critical role in creating a new language of representation, as artists used film, slides, video, and holographic and photographic projection to measure, document, abstract, reflect, and transform the parameters of physical space."[19] The physical space Iles refers to was the gallery, wherein the spatial relationships between art objects, viewers, and the architecture of the gallery became the center of artists' attention. Iles invokes the distinction between the "black box" of cinema and the "white cube" of the gallery; the illusory image dominates in the former, transporting viewers from their actual physical surroundings, while in the latter, the power of the image is undermined in an effort to return viewers to those surroundings.[20] Iles identifies the very same new media that others included

[19] Chrissie Iles, "Between the Still and Moving Image," in Iles, ed., *Into the Light: The Projected Image in American Art, 1964–1977* (exhibition catalogue) (New York: Whitney Museum of American Art, 2001), p. 34.
[20] Ibid.

in the category of expanded cinema, such as video, slide projection, and holography, but reorients them under a non-cinematic interpretation grounded in a similarly expanded notion of the sculptural. One direction this expansion took was to incorporate temporality as a condition of viewing sculpture, which informed phenomenological interpretations of minimalism and the language of process art. Having thus construed the experience of viewing art in the gallery as temporal, artists who used moving image media did not need the category of the cinematic to support or explicate their move. In fact, it would have been a liability for these artists, the "black box" anathema to the apperceptive experience of real objects and environments so central to them.

Iles's interpretation of Morris's film installation *Finch College Project* (1969) is instructive. To make that piece, Morris had the cinematographer Robert Fiore film a group of workers installing a large photograph of a film audience on one wall and a mirror of equal size on the opposite wall of a white gallery space (figs. 5.7 and 5.8). Both objects had been divided into squares of uniform size, which the workers glued to the walls one by one until each object was reassembled. They then reversed the process, de-installing the photograph and mirror one square at a time until nothing remained but a grid of dried patches of the adhesive substance used to affix mirror and photograph to the walls. While shooting, Fiore slowly rotated his camera, producing a constantly turning 360-degree view of the gallery and the work going on

Fig. 5.7. Robert Morris, *Finch College Project* (1969). Installation view.
Courtesy Castelli Gallery, New York.

Fig. 5.8. Robert Morris, *Finch College Project* (1969). Installation view.
Courtesy Castelli Gallery, New York.

within. The resulting film was projected as a loop in an identical space—complete with splotches of dried glue—by a projector rotating at the same slow pace as Fiore's camera. Fiore appears in the film when the camera's field of view crosses the plane of the mirror on the facing wall.

According to Iles, both the mirror and the illusory projected image moving across the gallery walls "dematerialize" the space even as they reveal it, continuing a theme Morris had first explored in his more traditional sculptural work, such as *Four Mirrored Cubes* (1965). While Morris's mirrors "incorporated the viewer and the surrounding gallery space," thus heightening the apperceptive experience minimalist sculpture was said to produce, the film images introduce "illusory" space into the work, by Iles's interpretation.[21] In short, Morris's use of film projection and reference to cinematic viewing via the audience photograph were emblematic of the very type of viewing experience that works like Morris's undermined. Thus, the gallery is the symbol of the literal, the here and now, and of viewer self-awareness; the cinema is that of illusion, where real space vanishes and the viewer is disembodied.

Two kinds of aesthetic experience literally face each other in *Finch College Project* and figuratively face off in art world discourse on the moving image. In Morris's audience photograph, spectators in rows of comfy movie theater seats face the camera, which is positioned where the screen would be. Already disconnected from one another physically, they look into the camera/at the screen waiting to be removed even farther from their surroundings. This conception of cinema, understood as illusionist, escapist, and therefore ideologically dangerous, is based upon mass-market filmmaking and does not take into account other, much more radical cinematic forms. Hence, "the black box of the cinema" is an abstraction against which moving image art in the gallery has contrasted itself. Of course, that contrast rests upon the occlusion of other models of cinematic experience that similarly resisted the transported mode of viewing represented by mainstream film. This point is critical: the black box of the cinema stands for one particular kind of cinema, the effects of which artists like Morris aimed to thwart. This is not intended as a criticism of Iles, as her explication of *Finch College Project* in these terms is both insightful and consistent with how such works were discussed by their makers and contemporaneous art critics. But Iles also extends this approach to works that, until they appeared in *Into the Light*, were generally considered cinematic rather than sculptural or intermedial. This stoked a controversy that continues into the present.

Later sections of this chapter will return to this controversy. The point here is that the distinction between the black box of cinema and the white cube of the gallery is underpinned by the presumption that the latter is the realm of the literal, and of the direct, self-aware experience of space, objects, and perception itself. Hence, if these

---

[21] Ibid., pp. 39–40.

were the primary concerns of filmmakers like Iimura and Sharits, their work *cannot* be cinematic, and must have entailed the abandonment of any essentialist notion of cinema for something else, a different set of aesthetic values than those for which the black box stands.

In a recent study, Andrew Uroskie locates early expanded cinema "somewhere between the immersive tradition of the movie theater's black box and the more distanced perception characteristic of the gallery's white cube."[22] Of course, this statement still assumes specific kinds of experience inherent to the gallery or movie theater, and on this assumption Uroskie argues that the first generation of expanded cinema artists had to abandon both. Displacing themselves from Hollywood cinema's mode of exhibition and viewing was not enough; artists like Stan VanDerBeek, Robert Whitman, and Ken Dewey, by Uroskie's account, also worked "outside the framework of the European art cinema" and were "equally distant from the expressive, personal, and 'visionary' experimental film."[23] It was within these two modes that the assertion of cinema's autonomy and thus parity with the other arts was made most forcefully, just as cinema was expanding. Hence, the escape from the black box of the theater was, more importantly, a liberation from any version of artistic specificity:

> Not content to restrict cinema to an autonomous and isolated purity, these artists sought to mobilize the idea of cinema in order to intervene within a diverse array of exhibitionary situations. By destabilizing accepted conventions of exhibition and spectatorship, these artists did not seek to bolster a modern art of cinema, but rather to leverage the aesthetic, historical, and even ontological hybridity of cinema to initiate an interdisciplinary transformation of postwar art and its institutions.[24]

Uroskie is describing what I have called the first wave of expanded cinema, and so his mapping of the conceptual terrain in which artists like VanDerBeek and Whitman intervened is enlightening. But the presuppositions underlying his characterizations of the cinema theater/art gallery dyad is monolithic, even if his historical and ontological positioning of specific artists and works is more nuanced than in previous accounts like Youngblood's and Renan's. The nature and meaning of the movie theater and the gallery space remain more or less intact. More importantly, work that genuinely critiques embedded assumptions about spectatorial experience is deemed impossible in the cinema theater. Any expanded cinematic form must, by this account, showcase cinema's "ontological hybridity," and any critique such work makes must be addressed to the institutions of the art world rather

[22] Uroskie, *Between the Black Box and the White Cube*, p. 15.
[23] Ibid., p. 14.
[24] Ibid., p. 52.

than those of cinema. I interrogate and ultimately contest these assumptions in this chapter.

Cinema's Expansion Into "Real TIME/SPACE"

When filmmakers like Sharits and Iimura began making installations, they were said to have "moved into the gallery." But what were the origins of this movement? Where did the filmmaking arc that had its end point in the gallery begin?

A theme that will play out across this chapter is that film installations like those of Iimura and Sharits, along with related multi-screen films designed for the conventional theatrical exhibition format, were about the inextricability of time and space in cinema. This condition is what the word "duration" meant in the language of avant-garde cinema during the late sixties and seventies. Space here does not mean the illusionistic fictional space represented on screen. Space is the actual space occupied by projectors, screen, and audience, in which that audience collectively experiences the unfolding of time. The subtitle of the Tate Modern's 2009 expanded cinema conference neatly sums this up: "activating the space of reception." This was also the activation of the viewer, particularly in works like *Soundstrip/Filmstrip* that encouraged movement and interaction, though not limited to such overtly participatory works, as we shall see.

Of course, in conventional narrative cinema, time and space are also inseparable, whether we think of this in terms of the filmstrip as literally a length of time, or in more formal terms, as in "the sculpting of time" or "orchestration of duration," in the simultaneously temporal and structural architecture of a film's plot, for example.[25] Thus, from one point of view many expanded cinema works threw into relief a condition of all cinema. The point is offered as a corrective to the black box/white cube distinction, which would see Iimura's or Sharits's entry into the gallery as a complete break from conventional cinema. While the move did indeed result in unconventional forms, we must recognize this line of continuity. Sharits and Iimura, among others, claimed that the installation format was revelatory of the deliberately veiled aspects of cinema as we know it. Iimura intended his installations to reveal the "film system" rather than abandon it. Sharits's rendering of filmmaking and viewing schematically was an attempt to reveal cinema's

---

[25] Variations on the phrases "sculpting time" and "orchestrating duration" appear throughout writings and statements by filmmakers and critics, including those outside the precinct of the avant-garde. Sitney argued that the challenge Warhol's early silent films posed to a new generation of experimental filmmakers was "how to orchestrate duration; how to permit the wandering of attention that triggered ontological awareness while watching Warhol films and at the same time guide that attention to a goal." Sitney, *Visionary Film*, p. 352. Probably the best known instance of the idea of "sculpting time" comes from Andrey Tarkovsky's book *Sculpting in Time: Tarkovsky the Great Russian Filmmaker Discusses His Art* (New York: Knopf, 1987). Also see Justin Remes, "Sculpting Time: An Interview with Michael Snow," *Millennium Film Journal* 56 (Fall 2012), pp. 16–21.

infrastructures—presumably *all* cinema was meant by this. The loop, film installation's most common feature, is the perfect sign of the notion of cinematic duration at work here, as it unifies temporal process (loop as a verb) and the contours of a physical object (as a noun), and implies both movement and stasis. But another common device provides an ideal starting point for cinema's expansion into real space and the objectification of film's temporal tropes that was a hallmark of this expansion. This is the use of multiple projectors.

In a reappraisal of expanded cinema written in 2003, Peter Weibel identified experiments in multiple projection as one of the major branches of the form. The screen was "exploded and multiplied, either through division into multiple images using split screen techniques or by placing screens on several different walls."[26] Notably, Weibel makes a distinction between multi-screen environments designed to overwhelm the senses ("an invasion of space by the visual image") and the use of multiple screens as an experimental narrative technique.[27] He cites Charles and Ray Eames's *Glimpses of the USA* (1959), shown on as many as fourteen screens, as an example of the diffusion of action into a fragmentary experience rather than the familiar linear form of the standard narrative film. Weibel's distinction is curious, as it splits temporal and spatial experiments with multiple screens into two different sets of works: sense-invading visual environments like VanDerBeek's *Movie Drome* and USCO's ten projector *We Are All One* (1965) create a virtual image space; multi-screen films like *Glimpses of the USA* or Roman Kroitor's *In the Labyrinth* (1967) spatialized unfolding action, breaking a linear plot line into its component elements in a new form of narration. In fact, most multi-screen works did both, though "time" should not be understood solely as narrative time but as encompassing other kinds of temporal experience as well. Multiple projector films, that is, followed both impulses: representing cinematic time spatially and, in doing so, re-inventing temporal devices originally invented for the single-screen narrative film.

Andy Warhol's dual-screen films offer a case in point. In 1965 and 1966, Warhol made a number of films intended for side-by-side projection, including *Outer and Inner Space* (1965), *Lupe* (1965), and *The Chelsea Girls* (1966). In Warhol's *Exploding Plastic Inevitable* concerts (1966, sometimes billed as *Up-tight*), multiple films were projected over the Velvet Underground and various members of Warhol's entourage and stable of superstars, who danced and engaged in quasi-performances of BDSM (figs 5.9 and 5.10). An April 1966 advertisement for an iteration of the *EPI* at the Dom in New York City promises:

Live music, dancing, ultra sounds, visions, lightworks by Daniel Williams, color slides by Jackie Cassen, Discotheque, Refreshments, Ingrid Superstar, Food,

---

[26] Peter Weibel, "Expanded Cinema: Video and Virtual Environments," in Jeffrey Shaw and Peter Weibel, eds., *Future Cinema: The Cinematic Imaginary after Film* (Cambridge, MA: MIT Press, 2003), p. 112.
[27] Ibid., p. 116.

Fig. 5.9. Ronald Nameth, *Andy Warhol's Exploding Plastic Inevitable* (1966). Frame enlargement.

Fig. 5.10. Ronald Nameth, *Andy Warhol's Exploding Plastic Inevitable* (1966). Frame enlargement.

Celebrities and Movies including: *Vinyl, Sleep, Eat, Kiss, Empire, Whips, Faces, Harlot, Heddy, Couch, Banana*, etc., etc., etc. All in the same place at the same time.[28]

The last line of this breathless list hints at the chaotic and sense-overpowering experience of the *EPI*, an environment of light-based and moving image media squarely in line with expanded cinema as defined by Youngblood—multi-media, multi-sensory, and environmental (fig. 5.11).

By contrast, Warhol's dual-screen films were more refined, like cinematic chamber pieces each organized around a much more limited number of formal parameters. Indeed, this can be said of all Warhol's filmmaking between 1963 and 1968. And while the results, numbering in the hundreds, were mixed, Warhol's process during this period seems to have followed a consistent pattern, each film taking a few formal elements as a permutational set to be obsessively and minutely worked through. The apparent sloppiness of technique for which Warhol's films were infamous belie a working method that could at times be quite rigorous. The standard story of Warhol's filmmaking for many years was that it was utterly unconcerned with cinematic technique. As P. Adams Sitney put it, "Warhol ... advertised his indifference to direction, photography, and lighting. He simply turned on the camera and walked away."[29] More recent scholarship has revealed the care Warhol actually took with elements of composition, lighting, editing, and camerawork, even if the outrageousness of the film's contents upstaged these nuances.[30]

Each of Warhol's single-screen films establishes a narrow range of formal devices and engages these in a pattern of theme and variation. For instance, the second reel of *My Hustler* (1965) consists of a single 35-minute-long take of the title character (Paul America) and Joe Campbell (credited as "the Sugar Plum Fairy"), both shirtless, showering and grooming themselves in a cramped bathroom as Ed Hood moves in and out of the frame periodically joining the conversation between the two men (fig. 5.12). The action is shot from just outside the bathroom door, the left and right edges of that door acting as a frame within a frame, as does a bathroom mirror visible in the upper right quadrant of the film frame. For most of the shot, America and Campbell occupy the middle ground of the relatively deep composition, while Hood, hovering in the doorway, occupies the foreground. In the background is a shower, which Campbell uses at one point during the scene. The opening and closing of the shower curtain, like the coming and going of Hood in the foreground, alternately opens up or closes down the sense of deep space. This is further complicated by the

---

[28] Advertisement from the *Village Voice*, April 7, 1966.

[29] Sitney, *Visionary Film*, p. 409.

[30] See especially Callie Angell, *Andy Warhol Screen Tests: The Films of Andy Warhol Catalogue Raisonné* (New York: Abrams/Whitney Museum of American Art, 2006); *The Films of Andy Warhol Part II* (New York: Whitney Museum of American Art, 1994); and "Andy Warhol: Filmmaker," in Callie Angell, et al., *The Andy Warhol Museum* (New York: Powerhouse Books, 1994), pp. 121–145.

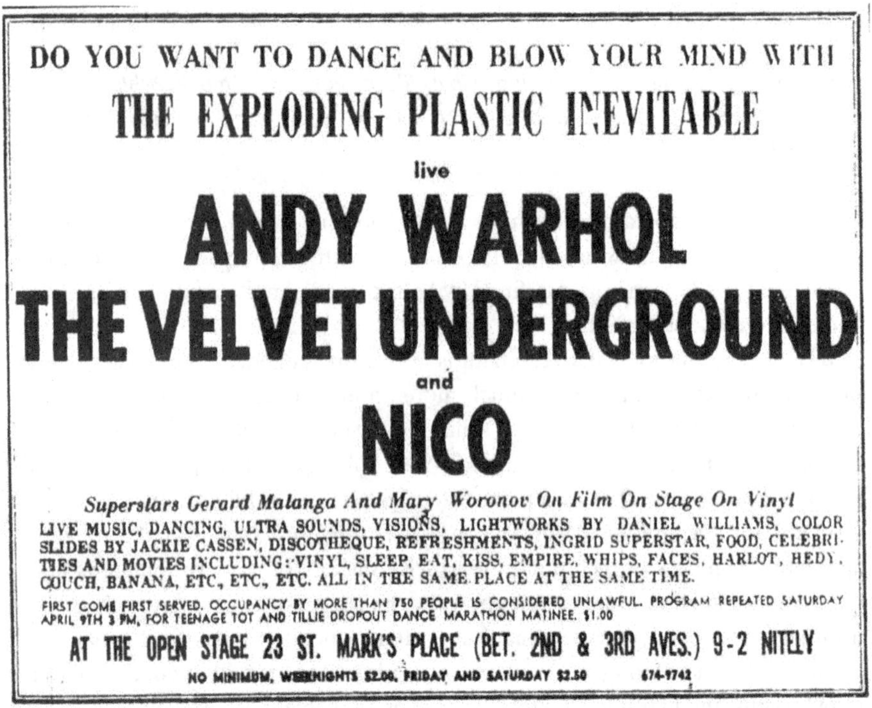

Fig. 5.11. Advertisement for Andy Warhol's *The Exploding Plastic Inevitable*. *Village Voice*, March 31, 1966.

Fig. 5.12. Andy Warhol, *My Hustler* (1965). Frame enlargement. 16mm film, black and white, sound, 67 minutes.

mirror, in which viewers can occasionally see Campbell's face even when he is off screen. The shot's arrangement produces some *tour de force* moments of staging and composition, both laterally and in depth. At one point Hood stands in the doorway, flanked by America on screen left and his reflection in the mirror screen right, with the off-screen Campbell's face strategically positioned just behind and to the left of American's reflected head and shoulders.

These are the formal parameters that unfold within the film's variations on planes of depth and the action occurring in them, the interplay of on and off screen space, real and reflected image, and character positions measured in both width and depth. America is behind Hood relative to the camera, while his real and reflected images flank him relative to the lateral dimensions of the screen. *Haircut #1* (1963) similarly played with compositions in depth and lateral screen space across its six 100-foot reels, as did *Restaurant* (1965), which adds a variation in the form of the zoom lens, which expands and compresses the depth planes through a series of meticulously layered compositions of Edie Sedgwick and friends gathered tightly around a table at a café.

Dual-screen projection seems to have been a way for Warhol to expand the range of visual effects and compositional devices to explore, enriching the play of stylistic elements being put through their paces by doubling the visual field. The final moments of the dual-screen *Lupe*, also starring Sedgwick, loosely re-enact Lupe Velez's suicide by drug overdose in 1944. The roughly three-minute sequence begins with two nearly identical compositions of Sedgwick slouched on a bathroom floor against a toilet, her head hanging in the bowl (fig. 5.13). This is reflected in a large mirror opposite Sedgwick on the right side of the screen, as though two Edies are facing one another. One of the side-by-side reels holds this composition for the entire length of the scene, while the other varies it through a series of in-camera edits and adjustments of the zoom lens, at times cutting between closeups of Sedgwick's real and reflected faces (fig. 5.14). One could read this as contrasting two historical filmmaking styles, one favoring the long take, the other analytically breaking the time and space of the action into discrete components (Velez's head, her reflection, the harshly lit white bathroom tile, Velez's body slumped against the toilet). The use of dual-screen composition allowed Warhol to present two stylistic options for scene coverage simultaneously, contrasting them as variations of each other while also increasing the range of formal options the scene presented.

In *The Chelsea Girls* (1966), the side-by-side images represent action taking place in different rooms of the Chelsea Hotel (see Introduction). This simple conceit is complicated by the fact that, at least initially, the reels could be shown in any order and thus any pairing. While the film now has a standardized order and left-screen/right-screen arrangement, the temporal complexities remain. Reels five and six are variations on the same series of events in the same room; reels nine and ten both feature Eric Emerson at different stages of an LSD trip; reels one and

Fig. 5.13. Andy Warhol, *Lupe* (1965). Frame enlargement. 16mm film, color, sound, 72 minutes or 36 minutes in double screen.

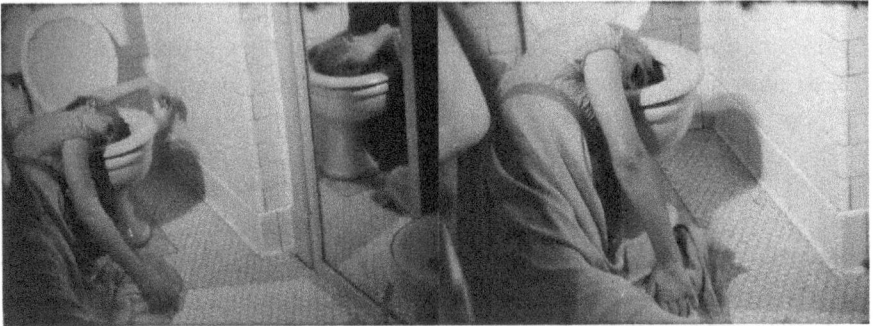

Fig. 5.14. Andy Warhol, *Lupe* (1965). Frame enlargement. 16mm film, color, sound, 72 minutes or 36 minutes in double screen.

twelve, which bracket the film, both show Warhol superstar Ondine (Robert Olivo) as "Pope Ondine," seated on a sofa in a darkened room taking confession. Thus, in addition to representing different hotel rooms in a sprawling quasi-narrative, the varying configurations of the action on the two screens translates editing devices into diptych form: crosscutting, flashbacks and flashforwards, temporal ellipses, analytical editing, and so on. It is worth noting that after 1966 Warhol returned to the single-screen format exclusively, but retained the greater degree of temporal complexity dual-screen projection had allowed, condensing it into more straight-forward representational strategies. Variations of crosscutting, shot/reverse-shot, and other montage devices appear in these later films, which also tend toward more conventional narrative structures. In *Bike Boy* (1967), for example, a scene in a clothing store crosscuts between shots of two different men, one of them the title character (played by Joe Spencer) trying on clothes. Both men appear to be in the same corner of the shop, which suggests that each is there at a different time, though the editing implies temporal simultaneity. Each segment alternates, through a series of in-camera edits, between a master shot of the mens' full bodies and closeups of crotches, stomachs, and buttocks in various states of undress. Compositional similarities between shots of the hyper-masculine title character and the other customer, who is stereotypically effeminate, are either intended to contrast two diametrically opposed sexualities or imply something about the main character's overplayed machismo. This impression of compared and contrasted spaces, characters, and characterizations came directly from Warhol's earlier use of dual-screen projection, as though that format opened up possibilities for spatio-temporal, compositional, and narrative representations that were not present in most of Warhol's earlier films.

With the example of Warhol in mind, Weibel's distinction between spatial and nar-rative experiments with dual screen seems at once too absolute and too limited in its view of the temporal effects made possible by multiple screens, restricting these to the domain of narrative. Thus, in place of that distinction, we can substitute a more accommodating model that combines both. Warhol's dual-screen films adapted the diptych or multi-panel compositional structure of many of his silkscreen paintings (e.g., *Marilyn Diptych* [1962] and *Elvis I and II* [1964]). As in these paintings, com-position in dual projection multiplied the possibilities of subtle variation and nuance characteristic of the early films, doubling the permutational set constituted by com-positional elements available in a single screen work. This idea of multi-screen projec-tion expanding the limited formal possibilities of a minimalist art work surely reaches its peak in Sharits's *SYNCHRONOUSSOUNDTRACKS* (1974), a three-screen loca-tional work featuring sliding horizontal frame imagery similar to that of *Soundstrip/Filmstrip* (fig. 5.15). In a letter to Michelson, Sharits wrote of a mistake he had made in estimating the number of "variational relationships" amongst the three screens, and therefore the length of time the piece could run before all permutations of frame-to-frame combinations were exhausted. "I guessed at one month ... but what is actually

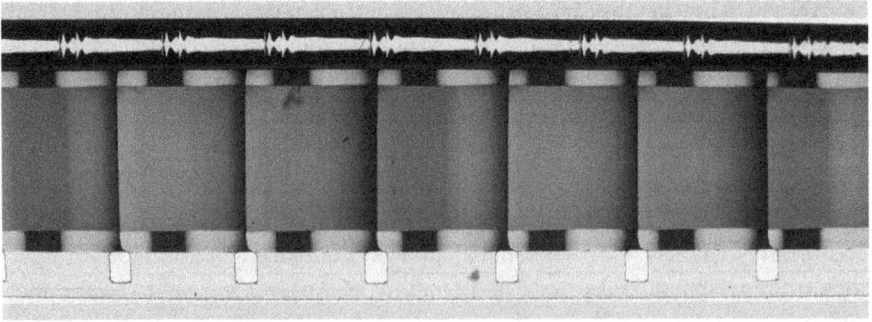

Fig. 5.15. Paul Sharits, *SYNCHRONOUSSOUNDTRACKS* (1974). Filmstrip.
Permission from Christopher and Cheri Sharits.

possible, unless my math is off, is 7,784,722 days 5 hours."[31] In other words, the duration of the piece, conceived as one round of a massive loop measured in terms of the
time required for a complete playing out of all possible frame combinations, was over
21,000 years.

Dual screens multiplied to three, four, five, and more (fig. 5.16). But even the addition of just one screen by necessity augments the impression that the film frame
is an object, and thus initiates, if tentatively, the expansion of cinema into space.
Commenting on his own multi-screen films and performances, Nicky Hamlyn
explains this: "The intention is to steer the focus away from image per se towards a
mutually reinforcing interplay between screen, image, and projector configuration,"
and to "question the teleology of film production from camera to screen, as well as
the hierarchies of projector-image."[32] Multi-screen works, by this interpretation, "engage the rectangle of the frame as a form in its own right."[33] I take Hamlyn to mean
that multiple projection breaks the identity of image and screen, a fusion that conventional movie theaters labor to produce by masking the image, its edges already in
soft focus and thus deemphasized. The individual objecthood of screen and image
are fused in this way, in service of the illusion that the screen is, in effect, not there
and that the projected image is not a surface but an aperture into illusionistic space.
Even multiple projection systems like Cinerama or Abel Gance's "Polyvision" tried
to achieve this effect, though unsuccessfully, as the seams between the three abutting
projections always remained visible. But the multiple projection films of the avant-
garde do not aim for this seamlessness, either among the projected images or between
the surfaces of image and screen. Both image and screen, then, regain autonomy and

---

[31] Quoted in Michelson, "Paul Sharits and the Critique of Illusionism," pp. 87–88.
[32] Nicky Hamlyn, "Mutable Screens: The Expanded Films of Guy Sherwin, Lis Rhodes, Steve Farrer, and
Nicky Hamlyn," in Rees et al., eds., *Expanded Cinema: Art, Performance, Film*, p. 220.
[33] Ibid.

ENGLISH AVANT GARDE

EXPERIMENTAL FILMS

DOUBLE AND TRIPLE SCREEN
BY

GILL EATHERLEY FROM LONDON

A SERIES OF SHORT SINGLE, DOUBLE, AND THREE SCREEN WORK - TREATING FILM
AS FILM - EXPLORING SPACE AND TIME.THE FILMS FALL INTO THREE CATEGORIES
- THOSE THAT ARE PURELY EXPERIMENTAL IN TECHNIQUE, COLOURS, WITH SOUND
AND RE-FILMING. THEN THOSE THAT ARE MORE STRUCTURED AND OBSERVATIONAL-
PLAYING WITH LIGHT , SINGLE FRAME SHOOTING AND CAMERA MOVEMENTS - AND
THIRDLY THE "LIGHT OCCUPATIONS" SERIES, WHICH ARE SIMPLE, SILENT
STATEMENTS, COMMENTS ON FILM PROCESS,PROJECTION,LENSES AND A GREY
CONVERSATION BETWEEN TWO CAMERAS!!

PREVIOUS SCREENINGS THROUGHOUT EUROPE AND U.K. AT FESTIVALS,COLLEGES,
NATIONAL FILM THEATRE,ART MUSEUMS-STEDELIJK,TATE.KUNSTHALLE COLOGNE ETC.

the filmmaker will be present and participate in all the
screenings

Fig. 5.16. Promotional flier for a program of Gill Eatherley's multi-screen films. 1973
or 1974.

Image courtesy of British Artists' Film and Video Study Collection, Central Saint Martins, University of
the Arts London.

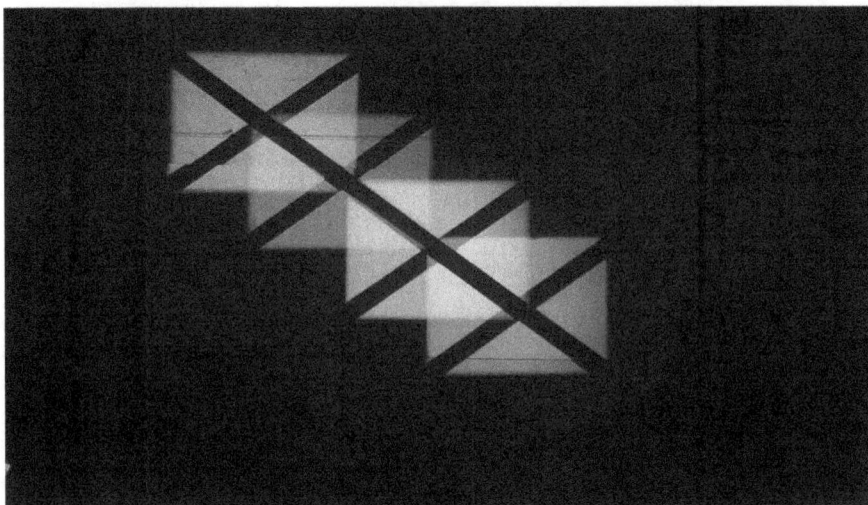

Fig. 5.17. Nicky Hamlyn, *4 x Loops* (1974). Performance documentation.
Image courtesy of Nicky Hamlyn.

are both more readily experienced as objects, a perception that extends to the sources of the images—the projectors.

Hamlyn's multi-screen work took the implications of the dual-screen films of filmmakers like Warhol and Le Grice further, using four projectors, their positions shifted during performances, to multiply the image field's elements to an even greater extent. His *4 x Loops* (1974) is a projection performance consisting of four clear 16mm film loops whose empty visual fields are punctuated by a black "X" twice per second, for six frames (1/4 of a second) each time. The crisscrossing diagonal lines of the "X" reach all the way into the four corners of the frame and provide the only image content of the piece. During the roughly 20-minute performance, Hamlyn repositions the projectors to make different configurations of the four frames on screen. At one point they are arranged in an overlapping descent from the upper left to the lower right of the screen, like stairs, such that the corresponding lines of the "X" (those running from top left to bottom right of each frame), align into one long black bar traversing the screen (fig. 5.17). Another adjustment of the projectors arranges the projected frames into a diamond formation, the corners of each frame touching the adjacent ones, leaving an empty space in the middle (fig. 5.18). Slowly, Hamlyn brings the four frames together, overlapping them in the center of the screen in a composite image. The flashing "X"s on each loop slip in and out of sync with one another, their otherwise predictable flickering rhythms lost as the loops drift in and out of phase.

Hamlyn's *4 x Loops* is decidedly non-narrative; but the regular pulse of the flashing "X" establishes a simple rhythm, which Hamlyn transforms by adjusting

Fig. 5.18. Nicky Hamlyn, *4 x Loops* (1974). Performance documentation.
Image courtesy of Nicky Hamlyn.

and superimposing the four screens. The constant slide of the Xs in and out of synchronization with each other recalls contemporaneous musical compositions based on phasing by Steve Reich, or, to take a more proximate example, Brian Eno. Both composers worked with short musical phrases performed over and over, such as Reich's *Violin Phase* (1967), or played on multiple tape loops in varying degrees of synchronization, as in Reich's *It's Gonna Rain* (1965) or Eno's *Discrete Music* (1975). The introduction of small variations in melodic lines or of delay into the tape loop playback—the defining feature of the tape playback system Eno used—led the repeating segments of sound to slide in and out of phase, generating minute changes across long durations. Hamlyn's work does the same visually, generating an ever-changing permutational structure of blinking imagery paralleled by the constant incremental adjustments to the positions of the screen images. This amplifies even further the sense of their physical autonomy, their status as discrete objects independent of the screen surface. Differentiating, then, between purely temporal or purely spatial effects of multi-screen projection is not tenable, as the viewer's perceptions of the rhythmic patterns change as the frames are moved, and the discreteness of those frames, even when superimposed, is a necessary condition of the experience of the work's temporality.

Hamlyn made *4 x Loops* during a period of intensive experimentation with multiple projection in the United Kingdom, the leading figure of which was Le Grice. Most of Le Grice's films of the 1960s and '70s were for at least two projectors or else existed in both single- and multi-screen versions. Le Grice was a central figure in the London Filmmakers' Cooperative (LFMC) after it moved from a bookstore to its own location in a former dairy in Price of Wales Crescent in northern London in 1971. Le Grice and David Curtis were instrumental in developing the Coop's filmmaking resources, including film processing equipment and an optical printer. The history and major formal preoccupations of the LFMC in this period are fairly well established, as is the materialist bent of Le Grice's filmmaking and writing at the time. In his seminal 1972 essay "Real TIME/SPACE," Le Grice announced the major thrust of his work: "the affirmation of the projection event as the primary reality. This reverses the situation common to the cinematic language where experience of the real TIME/SPACE at projection is subsumed by various aspects of manipulated 'retrospective reality.'"[34] What Le Grice meant was that the conventions of narrative cinema and normal film exhibition denied the reality of the "projection event" in favor of producing another "reality," the spatiotemporal elsewhere on screen. Le Grice's neologism "TIME/SPACE," always written in that way, was another expression of the belief in the inseparability of the temporal and spatial in film. For Le Grice, the emphasis of the filmstrip's material properties was not an end in itself, but a means to redirect viewer attention to the moment of projection, to the reality of a length of material passing through a machine and modulating actual, not fictive, time and space. Most of Le Grice's films of the period, single screen or otherwise, were heavily optically printed, a process of re-photography that tends to bring out emulsion grain and that Le Grice used to reproduce images within the frame and to reveal the source material's framelines and sprocket holes.

But perhaps his most favored optical printing effect was superimposition. A common technique of Le Grice's was to superimpose two identical images, altering the color values or lateral orientation of one or both superimposed layers. The process either implied dual-screen projection, the "splitting" of overlaid images into a side-by-side composition, or was simply another variation of it. Both enabled Le Grice to exhaustively permute the usually simple formal elements of very short lengths of film he used into long loop structures. *Berlin Horse* (1970), for instance, was made using two short strips of film, each containing images of horses. One was a circular panning shot Le Grice had taken of a horse being exercised in a courtyard in a village near Hamburg, the other a piece from a found Edison newsreel of horses being rescued from a burning stable. Though the multiple layers of visual effects Le Grice created with the optical printer make this difficult to determine for sure, neither piece of footage can have been much more than 30 seconds long; the same source images, especially of the exercising horse trotting in a circle, repeat over and over

---

[34] Le Grice, "Real TIME/SPACE," p. 156.

Fig. 5.19. Malcolm Le Grice, *Berlin Horse* (1970). Dual-screen version. Left: color positive image; right: black and white negative image.
Image courtesy of Malcolm Le Grice.

with variations of color, contrast, speed, direction of movement, and framing for nine minutes. The film's soundtrack was composed by Eno, and consisted of a sort of sonic analog of the looped imagery made using the process that would become known as "Frippertronics." Brief segments of melodies played on a toy piano are looped and overlaid, their playback subject to slight delays. They pile up, falling into and out of rhythm with one another, echoing the same pattern of theme and minute variation produced by Le Grice's printing processes. Both film and soundtrack, then, showcase the generative possibilities of repetition and variation. As if to underscore this further, Le Grice originally projected *Berlin Horse* as a two-screen film, re-printing the film in black and white and projecting it next to the highly saturated color original (fig. 5.19).

Writing in 1972 about avant-garde film's "strategies of resistance" to conventional linear narrative and its ideological power, Le Grice once more emphasized the primacy of projection and the autonomy of the image vis-à-vis both screen and photographic referent. Films like *Berlin Horse* and Peter Kubelka's *Adebar* (1957) affirmed "the separate identity of the image—as a pattern of light and color on a screen—from its object reference. Transforming or manipulating the image itself . . . shifts the experience of the viewer away from a passage through the image to its denotation towards an experience of the image construction and transformation itself."[35] Again, the discreteness of the projected image, and by implication the projector, as objects not in fee to the representation of "other" times, places, and meanings, was paramount for Le Grice. Multi-screen projection was one means of asserting this discreteness, and of returning the viewer to the apperceptive experience of real TIME/SPACE, wherein "time can be thought of as a dimension almost in a sculptural sense, and the distribution of projectors and sound sources can be specified as part of the work."[36] But,

[35] Le Grice, "A Non-Linear Tradition," p. 294.
[36] Le Grice, "Real TIME/SPACE," p. 161.

LONDON FILMAKTION GROUP PRESENT
NEW CONCEPTS & TECHNIQUES IN
CINEMA INCLUDING MULTI-PROJECTION
& LIVE PIECES

20th to 27th JUNE 1973

Walker Art Gallery Liverpool

NEW DIRECTIONS IN FILM-ART

FILMAKTION FILMAKTION FILMAKTION

A continuous programme of recent work by young, independent film makers. Emphasis will be on film installations, live action pieces, expanded events and multi-screen work with opportunities for informal discussion. There will be children's workshops on three mornings.

From a broad base of using film as film, materially and formally, a concern has developed to treat the projection situation as an immediate reality in time and space. This exploration of film and perception is a mainspring of all the work.

Each film maker works individually within a co-operative framework, sharing equipment, facilities, distribution and a cinema.

New pieces will include :

Roger Hammond's "Polaroid Installation" "Audition Phonation"

Gill Eatherley's "Light Occupations"

Annabel Nicolson's "Sweeping Changes" and "Frames"

Malcolm Le Grice's "Pre-production", "Four wall duration"

David Crosswaite's "Thames Studio Installation"

Mike Dunford's "Logical Propositions"

William Raban's "two minutes, forty-five seconds"

PROGRAM

	10am - 5pm INSTALLATIONS	7 - 9pm FILMSHOWS
20 Wed	ROGER HAMMOND ANNABEL NICOLSON	MIKE DUNFORD ROGER HAMMOND
21 Thurs	ANNABEL NICOLSON DAVID CROSSWAITE KIDS WORKSHOP	GILL EATHERLEY DAVID CROSSWAITE
22 Fri	DAVID CROSSWAITE GILL EATHERLEY	ANNABEL NICOLSON WILLIAM RABAN
23 Sat	GILL EATHERLEY MALCOLM LE GRICE	MALCOLM LE GRICE & OTHERS 5 FM FORUM
24 Sun	MALCOLM LE GRICE ROGER HAMMOND	PETER GIDAL & OTHERS
25 Mon	ROGER HAMMOND PAUL BOTHAM KIDS WORKSHOP	PETER GIDAL STUART POUND JOHN DU CANE MIKE LEGGETT
26 Tue	PAUL BOTHAM WILLIAM RABAN KIDS WORKSHOP	TICKETS SHOW FOR MEMBERS OF WALKER ART GALLERY & MUSEUMS
27 Wed	GRAND FINALE	

FREE ADMISSION TO EVENING EVENTS BY TICKET AVAILABLE FROM WALKER ART GALLERY & MERSEYSIDE ARTS ASSOCIATION.

Further information from Walker Art Gallery 051-207 1371

Promoted by Merseyside Arts Association & Walker Art Gallery

designed by david crosswaite

Fig. 5.20. Promotional brochure for Filmaktion program at the Walker Art Gallery, Liverpool, June 20–27, 1973.
Image courtesy of William Raban.

as Le Grice also noted several times in his landmark essay, the standard film theater was not ideally suited to these ambitions. "The most suitable existing possibility must lie in performance or installation in the art gallery situation."[37] The following year, 1973, Le Grice and a group of fellow LFMC filmmakers put these ideas to their most vigorous test to date, in a series of expanded cinema works exhibited under the name "Filmaktion."

The core members of Filmaktion, insofar as it was ever a group rather than a name for shared film-aesthetic interests, are usually identified as Le Grice, Raban, Nicolson, and Eatherley, though many other LFMC filmmakers participated in Filmaktion events, including Roger Hammond, David Crosswaite, Mike Dunford, and Peter Gidal. According to Lucy Reynolds, Raban claimed that the name Filmaktion was used only once, for a week-long series of installations and performances at the Walker Art Gallery in Liverpool in June 1973, and that it was applied retroactively to smaller group shows that had taken place earlier (fig. 5.20).[38] But the name also appears in the program for expanded cinema events at the International Festival of Independent

---

[37] Ibid., p. 163.
[38] Lucy Reynolds, "Defining Filmaktion," essay for an online exhibition by Luxonline, http://www.studycollection.co.uk/filmaktion/.

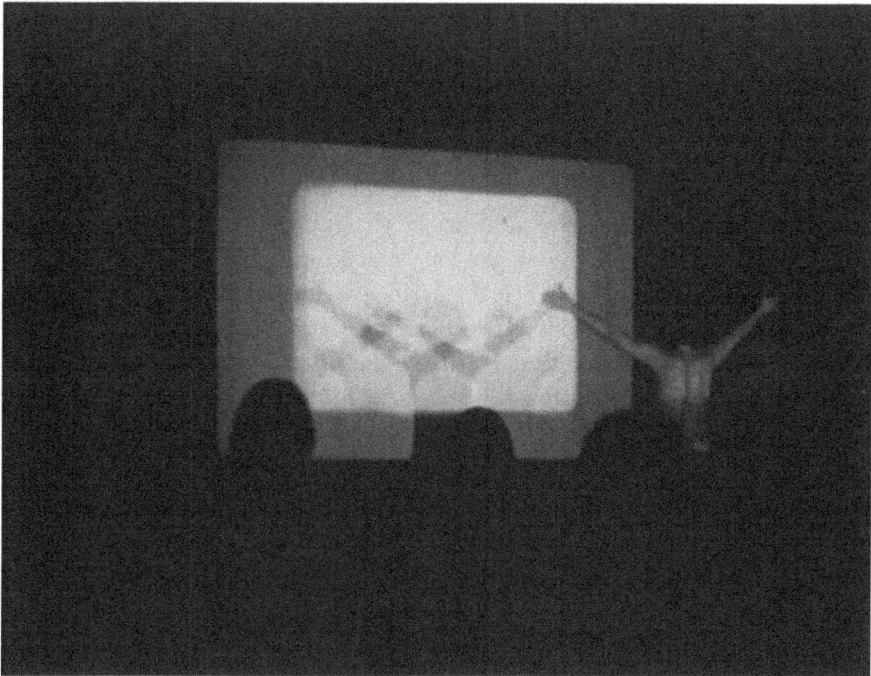

Fig. 5.21. Malcolm Le Grice performing *Horror Film 1* (1971) at the Walker Art Gallery Filmaktion program, Liverpool, June 20–27, 1973. Frame enlargement from William Raban, time-lapse 16mm film documentation of Walker Art Gallery program. Courtesy of William Raban.

Avant-Garde Film at London's National Film Theatre in September of that year (at which Tony Conrad, Ken Jacobs, Peter Weibel, and Valie EXPORT also performed). Few records of the Walker or National Film Theatre events exist, and more recent scholarship by Reynolds suggests that the name "Filmaktion" is best thought of as identifying a filmmaking ethos rather than a specific group of people.[39]

One Filmaktion document that does remain is a time-lapse film of the entire Walker Art Gallery program shot by Raban. Because it condenses dozens of works across eight days into seven minutes of grainy, underexposed black and white film, Raban's document can only offer tantalizing glimpses of performances, installations, and screenings, many of them lost to history, some of them prototypes of works that would become more well known in later versions (fig. 5.21).[40] However, the film does reveal quite clearly the appeal of the gallery for the kind of expanded cinema Le Grice and others were making. For one thing, the space was mutable. The screenings usually required rows of seats, but the installations, performances, and workshops called for

---

[39] Ibid.
[40] Raban's film can be seen at https://lux.org.uk/work/timelapse-of-filmaktion.

tables, chairs, makeshift stages and platforms, microphones and speakers, and other objects in arrangements unique to each work. It was also large, especially compared to the screening space in the Coop at the time. A high and wide screen stood at one end of the gallery crossing nearly the entire width of the space. Even for those spectators seated farther from it, the screen must have come close to exceeding the horizontal field of vision, and many of the multi-screen films, some for as many as eight projectors, made use of its entire width and height. The depth of the space accommodated long projector beam throws and thus large images, the entire setup enabling filmmakers to produce an image field that seemed to engulf one end of the gallery and dwarf individual performers or spectators coming near it. The Filmaktion event at the Walker show thus lent support to Le Grice's claim that a more open and accommodating space like that of a gallery was better suited to work intended to emphasize the primacy of the projection event's "real TIME/SPACE."

Cinema's expansion into multiple screens was not only a lateral move, however. It was also an expansion in depth, as many works opened up into the space of the viewer along the "z" axis running from projector to screen. Le Grice's *Castle One* (1966, also known as "The Light Bulb Film"), a single-screen film designed for projection in a traditional theatrical setting, is an early example of the attempt to make the depth of real space a formal dimension of an expanded cinema work. *Castle One* is a chaotic jumble of found images and sounds from newsreels periodically interrupted by shots of a flashing light bulb dangling from a cord against a white wall. A real light bulb hangs a few inches in front of the screen, switched on and off by the projectionist with a switch installed next to the projector (fig. 5.22). When illuminated, the bulb floods the space with light and obliterates the projected image, exposing the empty screen previously shrouded in darkness. The visual effect created by its flickering is of space radically expanding and contracting, opening up as the bulb flashes on to reveal the theater and its occupants, rapidly receding into the small, gray rectangle of the projected film when the bulb goes dark. The stark contrast between the fully illuminated theater and the screen image, isolated against an abstract darkness, makes for an almost tactile experience of throbbing space, accentuated by the discomfort the excessively bright light bulb causes for the viewer and the sense of suspense generated by the unpredictability of the flashing.

Le Grice had written of the "distribution of projectors" as a formal dimension of expanded work. The side-by-side arrangement of projectors for films like *Berlin Horse* was followed almost immediately by a multitude of other layouts. The aesthetic of rigorous permutation of limited formal elements characteristic of structural and structural-materialist film—described in the latter as an "ascetic" sensibility—extended to the elements of exhibition. This was less a matter of asserting the objecthood of the film medium than of drawing out the implications of the spatial arrangement of that medium's parts. Each work, in its own way, articulated the space and time of projection, as if each were a machine designed at once to measure and modulate duration and create a perceptual experience that dramatized the indivisibility of cinematic time and space. Whether made for standard theatrical screening

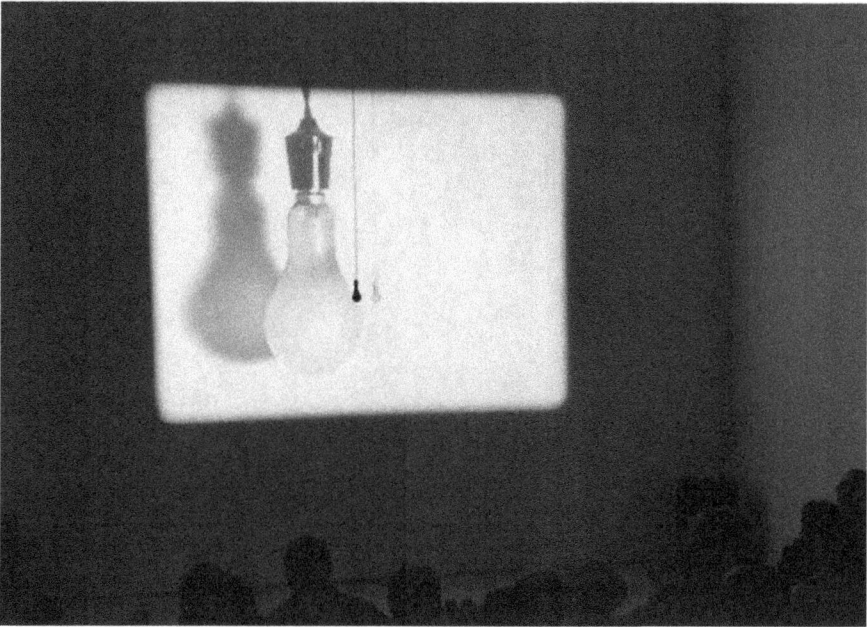

Fig. 5.22. Malcolm Le Grice, *Castle One* (1966). Performance view.
Image courtesy of Malcolm Le Grice.

or the gallery, expanded cinema works charted the axes of real space: width, height, and depth of the room, the throw of the projectors, trajectories of light, and relative dimensions of image and screen.

Lis Rhodes's *Light Music* (1975) creates a visual field oriented both vertically and horizontally. Two 16mm projectors face each other from either end of a long open space, each projecting images of horizontal black and white bars constantly widening and narrowing along the vertical axis in an accordion-like fashion. These images appear on two enormous screens, one behind each projector (fig. 5.23). A hazing machine thickens the air in the space between projectors, making the crisscrossing projector beams visible and almost physically palpable (we will see this again in McCall's "solid light" films). Elongated into three dimensions in the hazed air, the black and white imagery resembles light filtering through venetian blinds. The distance between the projectors, which constitutes the horizontal field of *Light Music*, naturally varies with the screening venue, but ideally the distance between the two projectors is at least 30 or 40 feet. This leaves ample space for viewers to move through as they inspect the screen images on either side of the room and interact with the ever-shifting bands of light emanating from the projectors.

The patterns formed by the black and white bars in the frame are reproduced in the area of the optical soundtrack, where the projectors' optical sound heads read the bars as a sine wave, its pitch rising when the bars become thinner (thus increasing

Fig. 5.23. Lis Rhodes, *Light Music* (1975). Installation view at Tate Modern Tanks (2012). Image courtesy of Lis Rhodes.

sonic frequency) and falling as they expand.[41] Rhodes's images, in fact, look exactly like variable-density optical soundtracks, which consist of blocks of varying degrees of opacity and transparency stacked vertically alongside the picture frame, in contrast to the more commonly used variable-area optical track with which most people are familiar (fig. 5.24). The average spectator may not be aware of this aspect of film technology, especially in the digital era, but the structure of the work at least enables the recognition of identity between image and sound. It does not take long to pick up on the pattern—that visual elongation is matched by a decrease in pitch, compression by an increase. That sound and light are analogous in *Light Music* is also meaningful in another way. The rising and falling sound, usually substantially amplified, gives a sense of mass and weight to the modulated projector beams. The correspondence of changes in sound and image evoke sensations of rising and falling in space, or of stretching outward and receding inward. Even the projector beams themselves acquire something like tactility as they take shape in the haze. As the imagery

[41] Some accounts of *Light Music* claim that the bars extend beyond the frame edge into the space usually occupied by the optical soundtrack, so that the image simultaneously produces the sound. This is not the case, however. Though the soundtrack indeed reproduces the same patterns in the film's visual field, Rhodes made the film's optical soundtrack separately. This allowed her to synchronize the shifts in sonic frequency with the corresponding changes of the bars' thickness in the film frame. This synchronization would not have been possible had the drawn bars simply extended into the optical soundtrack space, because the 26-frame distance between the projector's aperture and sound head would have resulted in a lag between image and sound.

Fig. 5.24. Lis Rhodes, *Light Music* (1975). Filmstrips with variable-density optical soundtracks visible, left.

Image courtesy of Lis Rhodes.

Fig. 5.25. Lis Rhodes, *Light Music* (1975). Installation view at Tate Modern Tanks (2012). Image courtesy of Lis Rhodes.

on the filmstrip changes, the slatted beams appear to rise or drop, or to suddenly grow thicker or thinner, denser or sparser.

Spectators' interventions in the paths of the beams, usually in the form of improvisatory, sometimes goofy shadow play, create on-screen forms that mimic the expanding and contracting movement of the projected bars, as their cast shadows increase in size on one screen and decrease on the other depending upon the direction of their movement (fig. 5.25). Rhodes has claimed that every projection of the film calls forth different audience responses and actions in its horizontal field—dancing, lying down beneath the beams, slowly moving through the piece and experimenting with shadows.[42] *Light Music* thus makes a virtue of interfering with projector beam, something that usually elicits angry shouts from audience members.

Light Music's annexation of three-dimensional space, its invitation to spectators to enter the projector beams, and the palpability it lends to projected light and the virtual image, are distinctive responses to the project of "activating the space of reception," of making the real space of film exhibition a formal dimension of cinematic work. What is more, temporal progression is bound to movement in space, in the

---

[42] See "The Tanks: Lis Rhodes," https://www.tate.org.uk/context-comment/video/tanks-lis-rhodes, documentation for an exhibition of *Light Music* at Tate Modern, July 19–October 28, 2012.

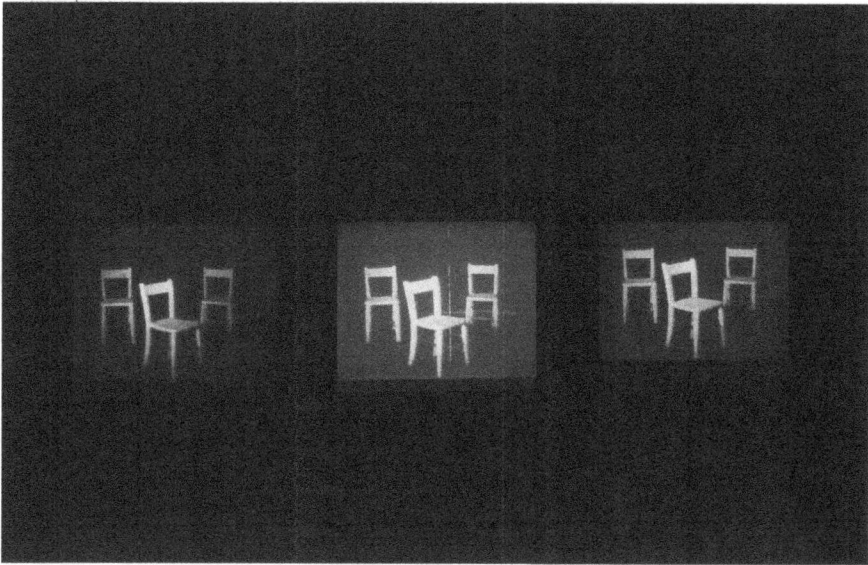

Fig. 5.26. Gill Eatherley, *Chair Film* (1971). Three-screen version.
Image courtesy of Gill Eatherley.

form of the visible vibration of the projector beams as the on-screen lines grow and shrink and the changes to the scales of viewers' shadows as they move to and fro in the film's spatiotemporal field. Rhodes's comparison of the film to music speaks to the film's dual status as object and temporal process, score and performance, wherein the film is "played" both by the projectors and spectators.

Gill Eatherley's *Chair Film* (1971) and *Chair Installation* (1973) exemplify this con-current expansion across the width of the screen and into the space of exhibition, and the use of that latter space as a compositional element in and of itself. The earlier work, *Chair Film*, has been identified as a two-, three-, and four-screen film, suggesting that it existed in multiple iterations (figs. 5.26 and 5.27). For recent screenings at the Tate Modern Tanks in 2012 and BFI Southbank in 2016, it was shown as a three-screen film with its projected images arranged as a triptych. Earlier versions, including one screened at the Walker Gallery Filmaktion event, stacked four projected images in a two-by-two-screen grid. The images consist entirely of white wooden chairs against a black backdrop, as though hovering in an abstract space. Some shots contain multiple chairs clustered together, while others isolate a single chair. This rudimentary content is put through a series of compositional variations not unlike Le Grice's films of the same period. The camera zooms in and out on the chairs, and a single chair appears to hurtle back and forth through space. In a series of optical printing runs, Eatherley added or subtracted color, rendered some images in negative, allowed the film to slip in the printer gate to produce a jittery de-registered image, and added crudely ani-mated chair forms, arrows, and squiggly lines. This combination of images increases the sense of depth in the film, as the animations and shifting color fields made in the

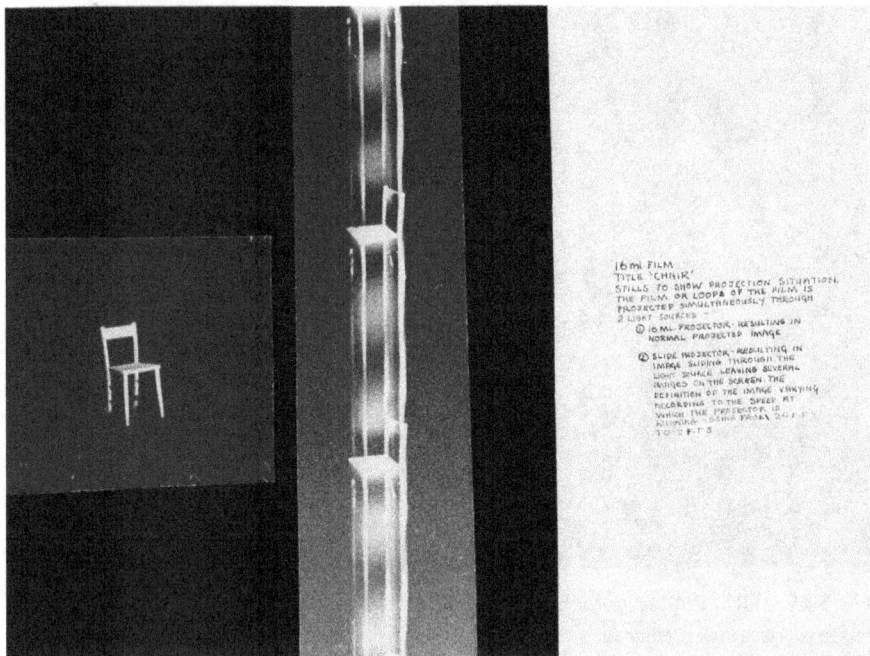

Fig. 5.27. Program notes for *Chair Film* indicating two-screen version with one film loop passed through a slide projector.
Courtesy of Gill Eatherley.

optical printer look flat relative to the photographed chairs, which retain a sense of three-dimensionality and weight. These varying visual elements establish a play of materialist surface and illusionistic depth, a quality of the film that Eatherley would expand upon in the installation version.

Chair Installation brings the imagery from the film into the screening space. A group of wooden chairs coated in fluorescent white paint are placed on the floor several feet in front of the screen (fig. 5.28). Over these are projected three 16mm film loops and three 35mm slide projections, all shots of white chairs arranged similarly to the real chairs. An ultraviolet light source bathes the room, in which the real chairs glow much like their filmic counterparts. The film loops, which Eatherley made specifically for a Filmaktion exhibition at London's Gallery house in March 1973, include a figure in black moving among the chairs, an element that was not part of the original *Chair Film* (fig. 5.29). The high degree of contrast in the image prevents the figure from being visible until it moves between one of the chairs and the camera, momentarily blocking the chair "so that it looks like [the chairs] are being scrubbed out with a rubber as they are being projected," as Eatherley has described it.[43] Eatherley also added a corresponding

---

[43] Gill Eatherley, artist's statement for *Chair Installation* on Luxonline, http://www.luxonline.org.uk/artists/gill_eatherley/chair_installation.html.

Fig. 5.28. Gill Eatherley, *Chair Installation* (1973). Detail. Re-creation by the artist, Raven Row, London. March 4, 2017.
Image courtesy of Gill Eatherley.

live performance element; dressed in black, she moved through the space, passing between the chairs and the audience, mimicking the actions of the figure in the film loops and creating a "curious sensation of chairs floating in space."[44] In conversation with Annabel Nicolson, Eatherley articulated a vision of building the screen imagery out into the viewing space, as though extracting it from virtual screen space toward the viewer, a process she imagined in steps or stages: "The interesting thing there for me was the idea of building up something, starting from loops and bringing it off the screen down into the actual gallery situation and working with objects and movement."[45]

In many ways a work like *Chair Installation* was typical of British avant-garde film of the time. Like so many other films and installations made in that context, *Chair Film* and *Chair Installation* radically reduce visual content the better to more rigorously explore the medium-specific parameters of filmmaking, the asceticism of the content clearing the way for the formal and material operations of the film

---

[44] Quoted in Reynolds, "Defining Filmaktion," http://www.studycollection.co.uk/filmaktion/Frameset24.html.
[45] Ibid.

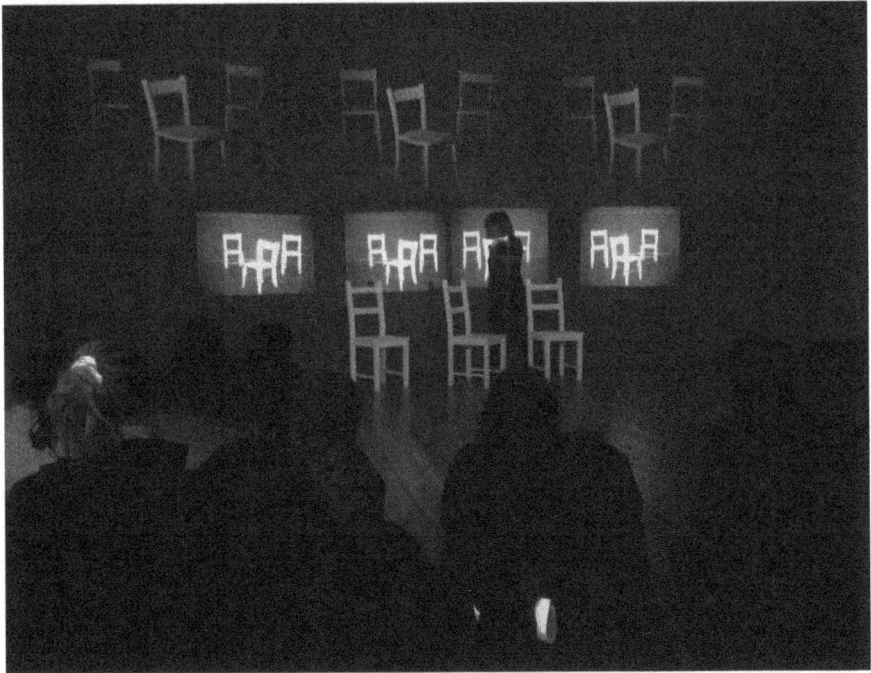

Fig. 5.29. Gill Eatherley, *Chair Installation* (1973).
Image courtesy of Gill Eatherley.

to be more visible. In this case, the field of formal experimentation was determined in large part by the LFMC's printer and the spatial effects created by Eatherley's choice of subject matter and variations in camera distance. Much has been made of the austerity of 1970s UK avant-garde film, of its drastic reduction of image content, stubborn refusal of visual pleasure, and jettisoning of anything that might rise to the level of event or even state of affairs, much less narrative action. All this, of course, was in the service of perhaps the most extreme version of anti-illusionism in the history of cinema.

But can we really call *Chair Film* and *Chair Installation* anti-illusionist? For all their attention to the processes of filming and printing, the autonomous projected frame, and the "real TIME/SPACE" of projection, they are also playful, at times ecstatically colorful, and, most of all, illusionistic. The chairs hover in a mysterious, impossible space, an effect that the large scale of projection at the Walker event and recent screening at Tate Modern increased. *Chair Installation*, though taking place in literal space, nonetheless transforms that space into a theater of illusionistic operations. Real and projected chairs appear and disappear, a figure emerges as if magically amidst the real chairs, repeating a similar illusion occurring in the loops. The ultraviolet light makes the chairs and surrounding space glow unnaturally, imbuing these everyday object with the quality of the uncanny. From this perspective, *Chair Installation* is a precursor to works like Laitala's "cinema séance" *Hocus Pocus ... ABRACADABRA!!!* (see chapter 3). Le Grice writes of one moment in *Chair Film* in which a chair "appears to hang and dance as an insubstantial ghost—an ectoplasm chair appearing, like those old fake photos, at a séance."[46]

Chair Film and *Chair Installation* embody a different attitude toward illusionism than the one usually attributed to the LFMC milieu, and in so doing parallel Ken Jacobs's Nervous System performances. Eatherley would likely have seen Jacobs's work at the International Festival of Independent Avant-Garde Film at the National Film Theatre the same year she made *Chair Installation*. Like the Nervous System performances, Eatherley's film and installation reveal the extent to which the illusionist/anti-illusionist semantic field was, in practice, much muddier terrain. This will have implications for the distinction between black box and white cube as well, and so is worth closer examination in the context of spatial works of expanded cinema.

In Anti-Illusionism's Shadow: Illusion, Meaning, and Beauty

In chapter 3, I argued that Jacobs's Nervous System performances did not sit comfortably on either side of a perceived split in 1970s avant-garde film culture between an anti-illusionist, analytical, "intellectual" cinema and a "fascinated," lyrical, experiential one. In Michelson's words, structural and structural-materialist film engaged in "an investigation of the terms of cinematic illusionism" and "a bodying forth of the processes of analytic consciousness."[47] Concomitant with this distinction was one between two different modes of film viewing: an emotional, poetic, even spiritual one and an analytical one that was cooler, emotionally detached, apperceptive. Jacobs's work troubled these distinctions. It was analytical, but understood analysis as disorganizing and liberating, ultimately an expressive and poetic act. The Nervous System works certainly investigated cinema's primary illusions, but often blurred the boundary between baring the devices of those illusions and using them to produce even more spectacular variants of them in the service of an anti-intellectual experience.

Jacobs was not the only filmmaker whose expanded cinema practices refused the neat categorizations of the illusionist/anti-illusionist split and the sorting of related values into "good" and "bad," with visual pleasure, spectacle, wonder, and emotion all on the "bad" side. In a 1978 essay on Sharits, Stuart Liebman rejected the distinction between "analytical" and "experiential" cinema whereby the former was believed to best represent the modernist impulse "to determine and use only the basic features of the medium":

---

[46] Malcolm Le Grice, "Gill Eatherly," https://www.luxonline.org.uk/artists/gill_eatherley/essay(1).html.
[47] Michelson, "Intellectual Cinema," p. 13. See chapter 3.

Fig. 5.30. Paul Sharits, *Shutter Interface* (1976). Installation view.
Courtesy of the Estate of Paul Sharits and Greene Naftali, New York. Permission from Christopher and Cheri Sharits.

Despite Sharits's dedication to Modernist principles, however, his films are never bluntly didactic … his films cannot be reduced to a mere rendering of the formal procedures constituting the work. Experiencing their sensual complexity remains an integral part of the films' statements. His cinema is ultimately less committed to an analytic reflection on the materials, filmic processes and psychological conditions of the medium than they are to celebrating the intricacy and variety of their combinations and consequences.[48]

Liebman's counter-intuitive reading of Sharits's films as sensual links that filmmaker with the aesthetic of lyrical cinema usually taken to be structural film's foil. Liebman argued that these qualities were most apparent in Sharits's locational works, such as *Shutter Interface* (1975) (fig. 5.30):

No marks of beginning, middle or end punctuate the undulating vibrations of color and sound. No protocols of the conventional projection situation help to orient the spectator in the work's dynamic process. Chronology and sequence are abandoned; time seems suspended. All reference is swallowed by the hypnotic, glowing profusion of colored lights animated by skeins of objectless

[48] Stuart Liebman, "Apparent Motion and Film Structure: Paul Sharits' *Shutter Interface*," *Millennium Film Journal* 1–2 (Spring–Summer 1978), p. 105.

motion. One is transported to some visionary source of cinema at the farthest possible remove from the narrative, illusionist modes dominating conventional films. Watching *Shutter Interface* evolve within an elemental continuity becomes—in an analogy Sharits himself has proposed—"like watching fireflies or water flowing over a dam—something that's moving." Like these simple, natural objects, *Shutter Interface* cultivates an infinite chain of changing hypnagogic imagery continually renewed by the work's splendid indirection and its fascinating, almost erotic elaboration of the perceptual conditions of its appearance.[49]

Though careful to distinguish Sharits's work from the illusionism of conventional cinema, Liebman finds other qualities in that work against which anti-illusionism writ large was also oriented, including, most surprisingly, an allusion to "hypnagogic imagery." This reference places Sharits in the company of Brakhage, of the visionary artist's quest to translate intensified emotional experience onto film.

An instructive example of the jostling of concepts within the discursive field of anti-illusionism is Conrad's *The Flicker* (1966). From one point of view, that film occupies a space between traditional and expanded cinema precisely because it occupies space when projected, in a way other single-screen films do not. Branden Joseph has observed that "*The Flicker*'s particular use of cinema's material components produces an environmental transformation not simply of the screen, but of the entire space of the theater."[50] In its flooding of the screening space with flickering light and throbbing sound, *The Flicker* makes the space and act of spectatorship palpable, as photographs of its first major audience (at the 4th New York Film Festival in September 1966) dramatically attest.

In a 1972 interview (conducted, notably, when Conrad was in Europe seeing structural-materialist films from the United Kingdom, Austria, and Germany), Conrad spoke very much in the language of Le Grice:

[C]inema is an extraordinary medium because it directly creates a total environment, the atmosphere that is in the room, by the combination of its elements (sound and light) ... People, however, never ask themselves what makes the atmosphere that surrounds them when they find themselves in a cinema, preferring to project themselves into the story being told. That's why I had the idea of making *The Flicker*, to confront them directly with the elements that make up this atmosphere.[51]

---

[49] Ibid., pp. 107–108. The Sharits quote to which Liebman refers is from Linda Cathcart, "An Interview with Paul Sharits," in *Film Culture* 65–66 (1978), p. 108.

[50] Branden W. Joseph, *Beyond the Dream Syndicate: Tony Conrad and the Arts After Cage* (New York: Zone Books, 2008), p. 300.

[51] In Gérard Langlois, "Les soirées underground du C.J.C.: Entrentien avec Tony Conrad," *Cinéma* 171 (December 1972), p. 11. The translation is Joseph's and is quoted in *Beyond the Dream Syndicate*, p. 300.

But alongside this filmic literalism was a form of filmic illusionism at its height. Conrad concluded that he believed "that the strangeness of this new environment could become, in its turn, a new form of spectacle."[52] Viewers of *The Flicker* experience optical and aural illusions, including colors on the screen and in space that are not present in the black and white film, and movements both on and off screen that the film triggers inside their own perceptual mechanisms.

Conrad's initial intention in making *The Flicker* was not to produce what he would later call "a recuperative exercise in structural minimalism along the lines of the formalist work of Le Witt, Morris, Smith, Olitski, et al."[53] That is, he did not want to make another film about film meant to "recuperate" film by aligning it with preexisting and widely lauded trends in the more established arts. Rather than an act of validating cinema as the newest terrain for minimalism or process art, Conrad saw his film as "an assault upon that estheticism, and as a sometime assault upon the expectations of the viewer."[54] Though, as Joseph has pointed out, "Conrad would come to embrace *The Flicker*'s reception as a structural film as one of several legitimate misreadings," his own emphasis was always on the environmental and illusionistic effects of the film.[55] But if it was a spatial work and thus a precursor to expanded cinema, that space was both real *and* illusionistic. The flicker illuminated the theater space but also set off perceptual illusions of "other" spaces, objects, and movements. In the same 1972 interview, Conrad traced an arc across which the spectator "gradually and inevitably develops away from the purely 'real' situation of the theatre simply lit from the screen," and into the virtual vortex of optical illusions generated by the stroboscopic projector beam.[56]

Elaborating on this notion of a temporal arc through real and illusionistic space, Conrad and his wife Beverly (*née* Grant) made *Four Square* (1971), a film installation for four screens (fig. 5.31). These are arranged along the four walls of an open space, each facing the center, analogous to the positions of players in the children's game of the same name. Four projectors are distributed among the screens, each one placed under one screen and aimed upward toward the opposite screen. The four reels of film each begin with a reddish field of light, which eventually becomes a red and white flicker, with yellow and orange introduced briefly and apparently randomly across the four films. The filmmakers' notes and projection instructions for *Four Square* describe the work as an environment, with audience members seated, preferably in such a way that each one could see as many screens at once as possible.[57] This enables viewers to undergo the intended process of the environment, which alters their perception of light and color over time according to a "script" in the projection diagram.

---

[52] Ibid., quoted in Joseph, *Beyond the Dream Syndicate*, p. 300.
[53] Conrad, "Is This Penny Ante or a High Stakes Game?," p. 101.
[54] Ibid.
[55] Joseph, *Beyond the Dream Syndicate*, p. 300.
[56] Langlois, "Les soirées underground du C.J.C.," quoted in ibid.
[57] Tony and Beverley Conrad, notes for *Four Square* accompanying the films reels. See http://filmmakerscoop.com/catalogue/tony-conrad-four-square, n.p.

Fig. 5.31. Tony and Beverley Conrad, *Four Square* (1971). Projection at PhoenixHalle, Dortmund during "Expanded Cinema: Film als Spektakel, Ereignis und Performance," September 2004.

Photograph ©2004 Christoph Kniel. Image courtesy of Mark Webber.

This film extends the viewer-film relationship out into the space of the environment. Colors are introduced in such a way that they unbalance the normal receptivity of the viewer's eye to color. Then, throughout the simultaneity of very short events in different areas of the viewing area, relationships are developed around the varying speed of perception in different areas of the viewer's visual field.[58]

The implication here is of a journey, and indeed the projection diagram, "*Four Square*: Operator Domains Landscape," suggests spectators moving through this flickering environment from processes of "adaptation" (i.e., to red), "re-adaptation" to normal ambient light, and "acceleration" and "deceleration," passing through fields of illusion and afterimage as along this imagined path while red, green, white, and yellow are introduced (fig. 5.32). By spatializing Conrad's work with flicker in *Four Square*, Conrad and Grant envisioned a trajectory through illusion, endowing the enclosed space created by the four screens with connotations of a journey even though spectators were advised to sit for the screening.

[58] Ibid.

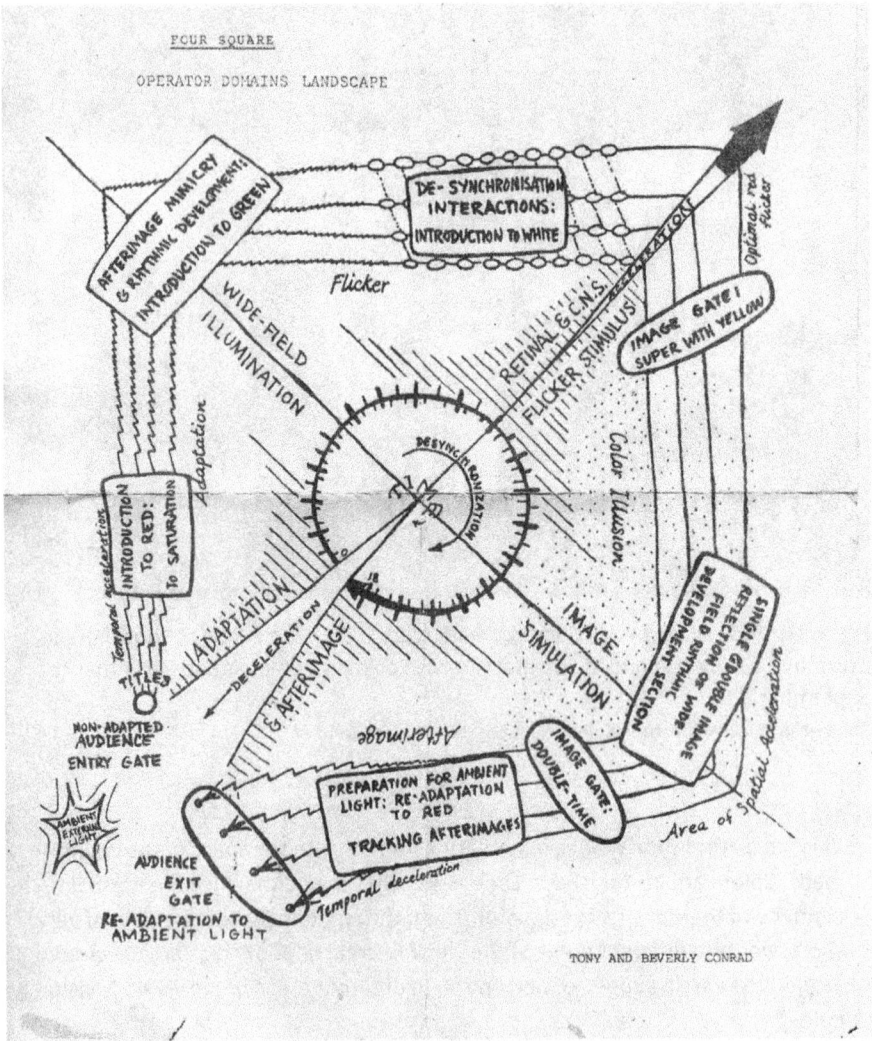

Fig. 5.32. Tony and Beverley Conrad, "Operator Domains Landscape" diagram of *Four Square* (1971).
Image courtesy of Tony Conrad.

William Raban's *Wave Formations* (1977) also represents an imagined, non-literal space, though, like *Four Square*, it is abstract and its imagery was made by entirely film-specific methods. The work employs three 16mm projectors placed side-by-side at the back of the theater and two additional projectors positioned at the lower left and right corners of the screen, both angled upward (fig. 5.33). All five reels of film contain pure color fields made using the LFMC's optical printer, fading in and out of black in a wave pattern as the title implies. On the filmstrips, these color fields extend into the area that normally contains the optical soundtrack, so the slow washing

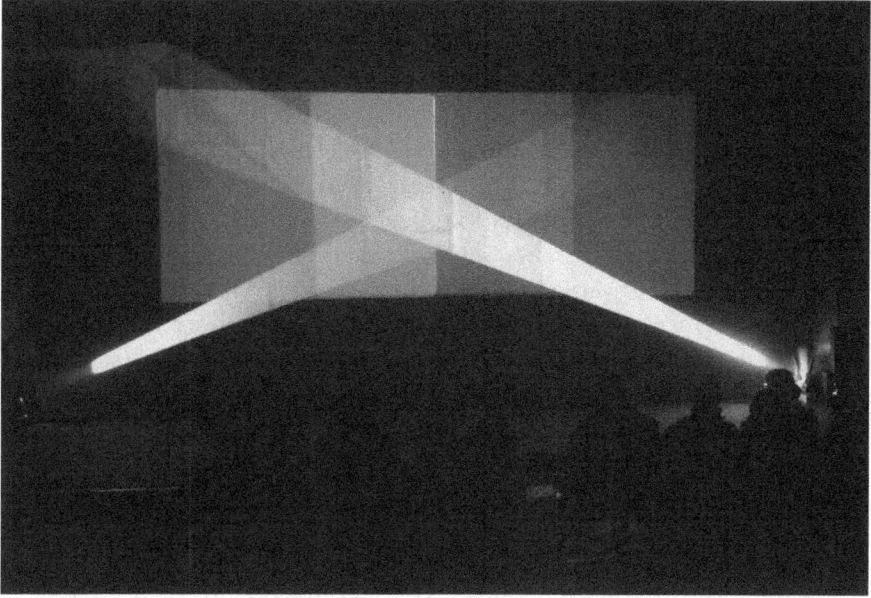

Fig. 5.33. William Raban, *Wave Formations* (1977).
Image courtesy of William Raban.

in and out of colors on screen generates a corresponding sound of rising and falling white noise. In most documented iterations of *Wave Formations*, the blocks of color coming from the projectors at the back of the space overlap, producing narrow vertical bands of mixed colors; a white frame projected over the abutting edges of red and blue frames creates two vertical pastel stripes of orange and aqua in the middle of the composition, for example. The two projectors at the lower corners of the screen are aimed at oblique angles toward the opposite upper corners, casting white bands of light that cross in the middle to form a wide "X" shape. This is usually accompanied by an additional visual phenomenon; if the fabric of the screen is not completely flat, which is not uncommon in makeshift experimental film venues, any ripples in that fabric cast shadows across the entire length of the screen. Thus, the otherwise solid, continuous bands of obliquely projected angular light are broken up by the shadows of the screen's surface irregularities. The "wave formations" of the title, then, are at once light waves, sound waves, and the waves of the screen's rippled fabric. The wave is also an apt metaphor for the combined spatial and temporal experience of cinema, both object and energy, an observation Sharits had made about both celluloid and light: "both are simultaneously corpuscular ('frames') and wave-like ('strip')."

But the materialist articulation of screen and exhibition space in *Wave Formations*, and its medium-specific take on the link between light and sound in film, are only half the story. Seen solely as an expanded instance of structural-materialist cinema, the film is abstract and non-referential, which is to say referential only to cinema itself.

But seen in the larger context of Raban's career, now about to enter its sixth decade, *Wave Formations* becomes something much different. By the time Raban made the film he had gained a reputation as one of the United Kingdom's finest practitioners of the landscape film, a sub-genre of English avant-garde cinema that many contemporaneous critics highlighted as the source of some of the most significant cinematic artworks of the period. Raban and Chris Welsby, who collaborated on the dual-screen film *River Yar* (1972), have been consistently singled out as the most accomplished landscape filmmakers. *River Yar* was shot over two three-week periods, during which Raban and Welsby took single-frame exposures of a riverbank from a fixed camera position at a rate of one frame per minute. At either end of the two reels—the first 14 minutes of the right screen, the final 14 minutes of the left—are shots of a sunrise and sunset, respectively, in real time. One reel, then, begins in real time before accelerating into the compression of frame-by-frame shooting while the other reel inverts this process (fig. 5.34). This facet of *River Yar*'s structure reflects, on a larger scale, the formal idea that generated the entire work: that it would combine unpredictable, natural events like changing weather conditions with systems and rhythms both natural and artificial, such as the rising and setting of the sun and the organization of real time into film-specific temporal patterns. Michael O'Pray has attributed this tension between the natural and formal to all Raban's landscape films, identifying it as the source of their aesthetic power:

Fig. 5.34. William Raban and Chris Welsby, *River Yar* (1972). Dual-screen 16mm film. Image courtesy of William Raban.

Raban's films often express an aggressive conflict between a conventional beauty, often of composition, and its mediation through formal properties of the film process ... Landscape, on such an account, is never the contingent imagery of a formal exercise, rather than landscape imagery absorbs the filmic work through which it is constructed as and in the film, ensuring that formal experimentation is invested with emotional and aesthetic affect.[59]

Deke Dusinberre, who had programmed several of Raban's landscape films at a Tate Gallery exhibition in 1975, expressed much the same sentiment as O'Pray, reconciling such qualities as mimesis and visual beauty with the filmic materialism normally positioned as anathema to those qualities: "The significance of the landscape films arises from the fact that they assert the illusionism of cinema through the sensuality of landscape imagery, and simultaneously assert the material nature of the representational process which sustains the illusionism."[60]

Statements like these might read as attempts to recuperate beauty, emotional effects, or aesthetic pleasure by making them ultimately subordinate to materialist reflexivity. The skepticism, even outright hostility, toward illusionism and sensuality in Gidal, for instance, may have made writers like O'Pray and Dunsinberre feel obligated to make such moves. But in fact, *both* the aesthetic and emotional richness of these films *and* their rigorous formalism are being recuperated here, each one by the other. The systematic materialist investigations of film prevent Raban's landscape films from being merely "insipid" or "picturesque" (O'Pray), while the sensuous beauty of the natural imagery qua imagery elevates the work from mere materialism.[61] It is not surprising to see Dusinberre making this critical maneuver, since at the same time he cautioned English avant-garde filmmakers against a purely reductive, self-referential film practice (see chapter 2).

If landscape, or more broadly nature itself, was reconcilable in this way with the materialism of filmmakers like Raban and Welsby, then one logical conclusion might be that an apparently abstract film could evoke the natural world solely through its use of film-specific devices. Dusinberre implied this, writing that landscape films like Raban's had moved "away from a sensual intuition of the landscape," and had instead sought to "evoke that landscape through an expanded cinema format toward a confrontation with the formal problematic of that representation."[62] That is, "format" itself, particularly that of multi-screen, could stand in for actual images of the natural world, as an analog of these. Even without a sophisticated theoretical model behind it, the idea makes sense intuitively. Landscape painting tends toward horizontal orientation, approximating the lateral span of the horizon and implying the experience

[59] Michael O'Pray, "William Raban's Landscape Films: The Formalist Imagination," in Nina Danino and Michael Maziére, eds., *The Undercut Reader: Critical Writings on Artists' Film and Video* (London: Wallflower Press, 2003). p. 108.
[60] Dusinberre, "St. George in the Forest," p. 11.
[61] O'Pray, "William Raban's Landscape Films," p. 111.
[62] Dusinberre, "St. George in the Forest," p. 14.

of being enveloped by the landscape. Diptych and triptych projections in works like *River Yar* or Raban's three-screen *Thames Barrier* (1977) similarly utilized expansive horizontality (as did Eatherley's *Chair Film*) the better to articulate—in essence take over—the space of the screen and auditorium.

Though Dusinberre made these remarks before Raban made *Wave Formations*, they fit that work precisely. The five reels of film that compose it were made entirely in the optical printer and contain no representational imagery. "Nevertheless," Raban wrote, "the rhythms produced by the counterpoint between screens evoke a very strong impression of a seascape."[63] The lack of photographed nature images did not preclude the film from denoting the natural world. The seeming abstraction of *Wave Formations* is referential; its washes of color, ripples of light and shadow, and white noise soundtrack are meaningful beyond literalism, eliciting emotion in addition to an analytical mindset. The white noise made by the alternating color fields is, in fact, so similar to the sounds of ocean waves that some accounts of the film identify it as such.

Works like Raban's, Conrad's, and Eatherley's traded in visual pleasure, non-reflexive meaning, and illusionism within a film culture that has usually been characterized as completely hostile to them. While the films' aesthetic and connotative richness and their illusionism could be reconciled with the strident materialism in certain quarters of the avant-garde, it may have required the passing of time and the changing of priorities in the experimental film world before these qualities could be fully recognized and appreciated. Liebman's reappraisal of Sharits was written in 1978 and published in the same issue of *Millennium Film Journal* as Paul Arthur's seminal revisionist account of structural film, as was an essay by Daryl Chin arguing that the modernist project of structural film was in decline.[64] That same year, Sharits had written of a shift in his own interests from ontology to "concerns with behavioral psychology and medical pathology," and that "human images, given up for images of various film-strips in 1968, returned to my work in 1976, a reflection of the new concerns."[65]

The initial impulse of multi-screen, multi-projector expanded cinema was to articulate cinematic space, to claim the third dimension as cinematic rather than exclusively the province of sculpture, and to map this space with the same degree of rigor as structural film's charting of filmic elements. Eventually, however, filmmakers like Sharits, Conrad, Eatherley, and Raban discovered in that space the potential for sensuousness and expressivity. This happened, however, as expanded cinema activity began to decline, with most of its major figures returning to single-screen filmmaking by the end of the 1970s. From 1977 to 1984, however, the San Francisco–based

---

[63] Federico Windhausen, "Minimalist Principles: An Exchange with William Raban," *Lux*, July 3, 2016, https://lux.org.uk/writing/minimalist-principles, n.p.

[64] Daryl Chin, "The Future of an Illusion(ism): Notes on the New Japanese Avant-Garde Film," *Millennium Film Journal* no. 2 (Spring/Summer 1978), pp. 86–94.

[65] Sharits, "Statement Regarding Multiple Screen/Sound 'Locational' Film Environments-Installations," p. 80.

filmmaker Al Wong produced a singular body of film installations that took seriously the illusionistic and expressive potential of the installation format. Wong's installations of this period play upon the same confusions between real and projected seen in *Chair Installation*, building upon the connotations of the ghostly, the magical, and the dreamlike.

Wong began his artistic career as a painter and started making films around 1965, one of which was screened at Expo '67 in Montreal. Wong became a faculty member of the film department at the San Francisco Art Institute in 1977, having received an MFA from the school in 1972. That year he curated a film program titled *Four and Seven: 26 Artists/26 Days*, which was intended, in his words, "to take film out of the 'movie theater' format with its entertainment associations, preconceived barriers, and its limited audience—to become simply an equal medium used in the aesthetics of art."[66] On the roster was a veritable who's-who of San Francisco's avant-garde film community, including George and Mike Kuchar, Janis Crystal Lipzin, Larry Jordan, James Broughton, and Gunvor Nelson, joined by major expanded cinema figures like Le Grice and McCall. Wong's first work of expanded cinema, *Corner Film* (alternately dated 1976, 1976–1977, and 1978, and sometimes titled *Corner*), screened at this event (fig. 5.35). Two 16mm projectors are set at right angles to one another, projecting into a corner of a gallery-type space, their frames abutting each other in the very spot where the two walls meet. In the two projected films, two men in a window-lit studio space (Wong's own studio in an abandoned newspaper building on Mina Street in San Francisco) amble back and forth, crossing the divide between the two screens, sometimes passing objects to each other across the corner boundary. At times, the two images are synchronized; a man on the right screen walks off screen left and appears instantaneously on the left screen, an apparently seamless movement across time and space and a momentary erasure of the visible boundary between screens. Later in the film, the two reels are no longer synchronized, creating the illusion of one or both men vanishing as they pass across the corner where the projections meet. In the final moments of the film, the cameras pan back and forth so that the space created by the side-by-side projections appears to fold in on itself and re-open, impossibly expanding and contracting the pro-filmic space. The panning also reveals that the action on screen had not, in fact, been shot in a corner, a further level of disorientation created solely by the strategic placement of the projectors, and amplified by the temporal disjunctions between the two screens and spatial illusions created by the contrasting camera movements.

Screen, Projector, Film (1977) is a catalogue of what Bob Cowan referred to as "perceptual riddles," carefully orchestrated moments of ambiguity between the real and the projected, all made possible by a simple structural device.[67] The

[66] Al Wong, from the exhibition catalogue for *Four and Seven: 26 Artists/26 Days*, San Francisco Art Institute, September 1–October 7, 1977.

[67] Bob Cowan, entry for *Screen Projector, Film* from exhibition catalogue for "Film Installations: Anthony McCall, Paul Sharits, Bill Lundberg, Al Wong" (Akron: Emily H. Davis Art Gallery, University of Ohio, 1987), n.p.

Fig. 5.35. Al Wong, *Corner* (1978). Installation view. Two 16mm projectors on two corners, black/white, silent, 16 minutes.
Photograph by Al Wong.

image of a small film screen is projected onto an almost identical screen suspended in the midst of a completely darkened gallery space (figs. 5.36 and 5.37). The diegetic screen is blown by an off-screen fan, doused with water and then paint, and finally burned. Because both screens—real and projected—are identical, the filmed actions appear to be taking place in real time and space: that is, to actually be taking place. The fact that there is no visible performer pouring water or lighting the screen on fire is not enough to dispel this powerful illusion. Once the diegetic screen has burned away, the film seems to end and the real screen appears empty, illuminated only by the light of a projector now running only clear leader. This light seems to reveal the silhouette of a support beam behind the screen. But all this is an illusion as well. The projector light fades to black briefly, and when it reappears the silhouette of the support beam is no longer visible, revealing it, too, had been a projected image rather than a feature of the real screen.

Corner and *Screen, Projector, Film* in some ways replicate the pro-filmic arrangement of cameras and objects. The dual perpendicular projectors in the former correlate to the cameras that made the footage, and the placements of projector and suspended screen in the latter more or less match those of camera and diegetic

Fig. 5.36. Al Wong, *Screen, Projector, Film* (1977). Performance documentation.
Projector and film, color, sound, 14 minutes.
Photograph by Al Wong.

screen. Wong took this structural principle further in *Shadow and Chair* (1980), which shares both subject matter and an element of technique with Eatherley's *Chair Installation*: 16mm footage of a chair coated in luminous paint is projected over a real chair given the same treatment. As Michael Jones notes, the film "hinges on the ambiguity of the filmic surface and the actual three-dimensional object."[68] The film portion of the installation is 10 minutes long. It was shot on high-contrast black and white film so that all colors, which were already minimized by Wong's choice of mise-en-scène, are reduced to either black or white with no intermediate grays. The film begins with a folding metal chair placed in the center of the frame against a brightly lit white screen. Wong, in silhouette, enters the frame and sits on the chair for a few moments, facing the camera. He then rises, walks to one side of the chair, kneels by it, and turns away from the camera and toward the illuminated screen. After waving his hand back and forth over the screen's surface, he reaches out and pulls it down, blanketing the entire frame in black. For several minutes the

---

[68] Michael Jones, entry for *Shadow and Chair* from exhibition catalogue for "Film Installations: Anthony McCall, Paul Sharits, Bill Lundberg, Al Wong," n.p.

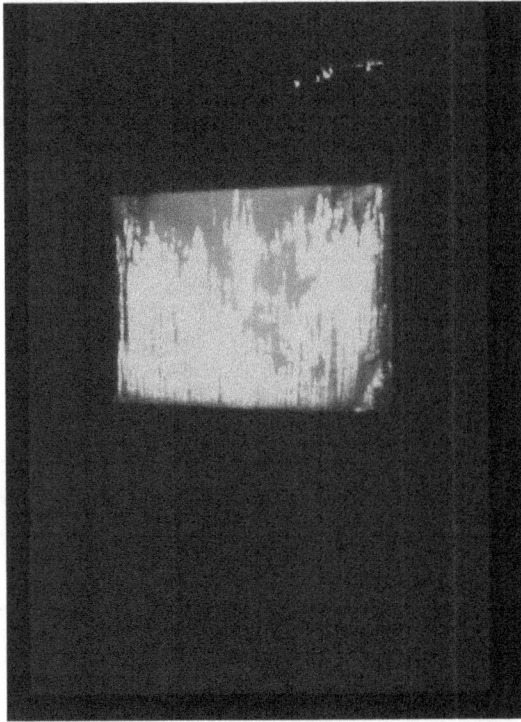

Fig. 5.37. Al Wong, *Screen, Projector, Film* (1977). Performance documentation. Projector and film, color, sound, 14 minutes.
Photograph by Al Wong.

screen remains almost completely dark, save for a point light source just visible at the top of the frame, which catches some sort of reflective metal surface beneath it. Wong is in the frame, but dressed entirely in black (including a black ski mask covering his head) and thus invisible. He angles the metal surface in his hand up and down to catch the light source above it and reflect it into the camera lens. Several more minutes of black screen follow, after which Wong reappears in a white t-shirt and once more sits in the chair. Only the t-shirt is visible, but Wong almost immediately begins slicing it with a blade, eventually tearing it from his body and tossing it aside, leaving the frame in total darkness once more. A few moments later, a small white form appears, moving back and forth in small circular motions, leaving a trail of white in its wake. It quickly becomes clear that Wong is painting the chair, previously invisible against the black background, with luminous paint, which picks up an off-screen light source and glows. Wong returns the metallic surface to the frame, again tilting it up and down to catch the light, then rises and walks directly toward the camera, blocking its view of the chair and casting the frame in blackness a final time. The film ends.

Fig. 5.38. Al Wong, *Shadow and Chair* (1980). Installation view. Black and white, silent film, 10½ minutes.
Photograph by Al Wong.

    In the installation, the film is projected over the same chair coated with the same luminous paint (fig. 5.38). Those portions of the celluloid frame that contain white— the lit up screen, the flashing light from the metal plate, Wong's shirt, and the glowing chair—are completely transparent, allowing the light of the projector to pass through the filmstrip to land on the chair, casting its shadow onto the screen over the projected image of its pro-filmic mate. The early images of Wong interacting with the chair and white screen read as shadows, as though an invisible figure has entered the installation space and is casting a shadow on the back wall. As the film continues, the white light projected onto the chair eventually causes it to glow, a state of affairs that continues after the film ends, extending the work's time into the real time of an illuminated object in real space. The glowing white chair against a black field inverts the film's opening image of the pro-filmic chair in silhouette against the bright background of projection screen (fig. 5.39).
    Wong would elaborate this interplay of real objects and projected shadows in later film installations, including *Moon Stand* (1980) (fig. 5.40) and *Shadow and Sheet* (1982). *Moon Stand* introduces the element of performance, with the real Wong interacting with projected shadow figures singing into a microphone on a stand, shot

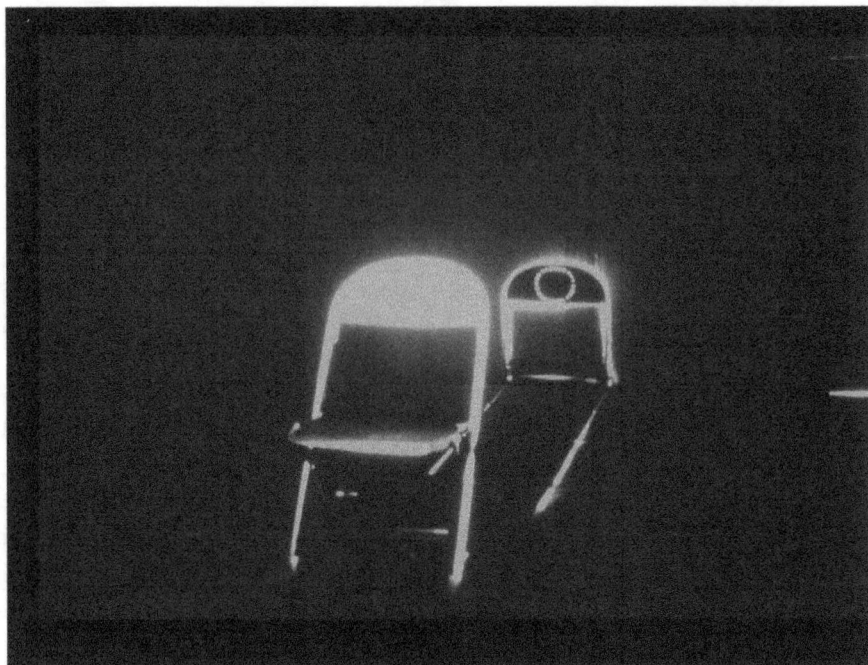

Fig. 5.39. Al Wong, *Shadow and Chair* (1980). Installation view. Black and white, silent film, 10½ minutes.
Photograph by Al Wong.

using the same high-contrast film and lighting techniques employed in *Shadow and Chair*. For most of the performance, the projected image of a woman silhouetted against a white background lip syncs to Billie Holiday's "Don't Explain," a characteristically dark love song whose repeated lyric, "don't explain, don't explain," in this context implies Wong's embrace of illusionism, an unwillingness to "explain" it away by baring the device.

The shadow effects in Wong's installations could be called ghostly, and the doubling of real and shadow figures in certain of his works evoke the doppelgänger, the central figure of Freud's uncanny, "that class of the frightening which leads back to what is known of old and long familiar."[69] In conversation Wong has alluded to a ghostly presence in his Mina Street studio, analogizing old movie stars like Lana Turner to dream figures whose elusiveness, at once powerfully present on screen but materially absent, he sought to re-create in his installations.[70] This may be an origin myth, though Wong's earlier single-screen films evince a fascination with surrealist

[69] Sigmund Freud, "The Uncanny," in James Strachey, ed., *The Standard Edition of the Complete Psychological Works of Sigmund Freud* (London: The Hogarth Press, 1948), p. 220.
[70] Al Wong, personal interview, April 12, 2013.

Fig. 5.40. Al Wong, *Moon Stand* (1980). Performance view. Black and white, sound, 13 minutes.
Photograph by Al Wong.

narratives, horror film, and psychodrama (*Moving Still* [1975], in particular, recalls Maya Deren refracted through a more contemporary psycho-dramatic horror film sensibility).

Wong's work occupies a curious place both historically and ontologically, coming between the golden age of expanded cinema in the 1970s and its renewed popularity after the mid-1990s, and meditating upon cinema's primary material elements while also employing those elements in playful illusionistic prestidigitation. As a film faculty member at the San Francisco Art Institute, he worked with some of the city's key avant-garde film figures and would likely have taught or at least made contact with many students who would become major experimental filmmakers and practitioners of expanded cinema themselves: Scott Stark, Kerry Laitala, Luis Recoder, and Bryan Frye, among others. Perhaps his unusual position between two major historical phases of expanded cinema helps explain the dearth of writing on his work. Its frank illusionism may also go some way toward accounting for this lack, but as I hope to have shown that that facet of Wong's installations does not distinguish him from putatively materialist filmmakers like Raban, Welsby, Conrad, Sharits, and Eatherley, though he may have gone the furthest in openly trading in illusionism and extra-filmic reference.

Behind the Screens: Isomorphism in Expanded Cinema Installations

The often eerie and disconcerting illusions of Wong's installations work in part be-cause Wong carefully constructed the films and the spaces in which they were installed to match one another. The material and dimensions of the pro-filmic screen in *Screen, Projector, Film* are identical to the real one suspended in the gallery. The real and diegetic chairs in *Shadow and Chair* are one and the same, the placement of the former relative to the projector mirroring that of the latter relative to the camera. This strategy is not uncommon in cinematic installations by experimental filmmak-ers. Their matching of real and pro-filmic spaces molds the installation space to cin-ematic form, even if it is a gallery, making it embody some quality of the filmmaking process, which is itself on display as part of the work. This is more than a matter of incorporating the materials of the medium into the installation, as all moving image installations do to some extent. Rather, the form these kinds of film installations take is intended as an analog of the aggregate of machines, processes, and decisions that define the act of filmmaking. This act takes place in space, of course. As I argued in the last two chapters, expanded cinema performance and filmic objects frequently aimed to preserve some quality of filmmaking itself within the completed work, closing the distance between production and exhibition. Much the same ambition is behind the expanded cinema installations I consider in this section. Filmmaking, understood as a series of decisions and processes related to space, is replayed in the physical arrange-ment and imagery of the installation.

Michael Snow's film installation *Two Sides to Every Story* (1974) is an important early example. Two 16mm projectors on pedestals face each other in the gallery across a space of 40 feet. They project onto either side of a screen suspended midway between them; the arrangement makes it impossible for viewers to see both images simultaneously, prompting them to move back and forth from one side of the screen to the other to follow the actions on either side (fig. 5.41). The two films, each eight minutes long and running on continuous loops, depict their own making processes. Snow reads a set of simple instructions to a woman standing halfway between two facing 16mm cameras on tripods, arranged in exactly the same way as the projectors, each camera operator visible in the background of the shot made by the other camera. Snow is seated in the background, next to one of the camera operators, hence visible in one shot and absent in the other (fig. 5.42). His instructions, along with the am-bient sounds of the cameras running, the woman moving in the space, and off-screen rain, compose the soundtrack. The woman walks back and forth between the two cameras at Snow's direction. She eventually reveals that a transparent sheet of plastic has been placed in the pro-filmic space in precisely the same spot as the installation screen. She first raises her hand toward the camera and presses it against this previ-ously invisible material, then sprays swirls of green paint onto it (fig. 5.43). Following this, a man walks into the frame and slices the painted plastic sheet down the middle.

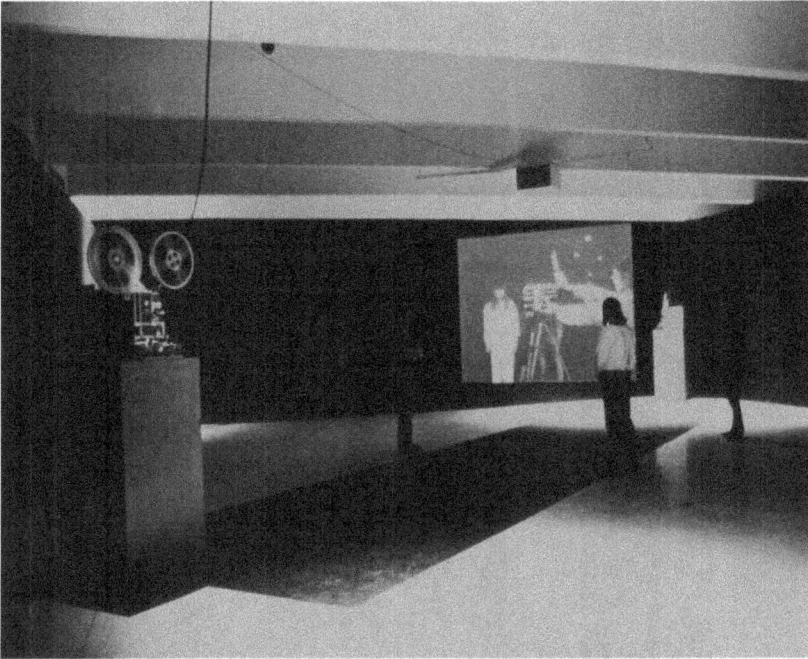

Fig. 5.41. Michael Snow, *Two Sides to Every Story* (1974). Installation view. Two 16mm color film loops, two 16mm projectors, aluminum screen, switching device. Installation space 300.0 × 600.0 × 1250.0 cm (approximate). Installation space 118.1 × 236.2 × 492.1 in. (approximate). National Gallery of Canada, Ottawa (Purchased, 1977). Courtesy of Michael Snow.

He and the woman walk through this opening, the sheet is taken down, and for the remainder of the film Snow instructs the woman to carry colored boards back and forth between the two cameras, and the operators to place similarly colored gels over the camera lenses. Finally, the woman returns to the middle of the space and raises her hand to the camera, miming the action of pressing her palm against the now absent transparent plastic sheet and, analogously, the surface of the installation screen she appears to be facing.

As Kate Mondloch sharply observes, *Two Sides to Every Story*'s act of "transposing" pro-filmic event into installation space extends to the spectatorial activity the work prompts: "One the one hand, the viewer's movements echo the protagonist's methodical pacing, so that the spectator is symbolically remade into the film's subject."[71] At the same time, viewers also "perform the same function as the film cameras, their role as mediators or translators of the work's meaning echoing the camera's mediation."[72]

---

[71] Kate Mondloch, *Screens: Viewing Media and Installation Art* (Minneapolis: University of Minnesota Press, 2010), p. 15.

[72] Ibid.

Fig. 5.42. Michael Snow, *Two Sides to Every Story* (1974). Installation view. Courtesy of Michael Snow.

That is, the transposition of pro-filmic activity preserved on opposite sides of the screen to the gallery space is not limited to the presence of the projectors as stand-ins for the cameras, or the arrangement of objects in both virtual and real spaces. In necessitating a specific kind of movement and activity on the part of the viewer, Snow's installation also reproduces the films' diegetic actions, "placing" the viewer in multiple positions. Indeed, these are the very same identificatory positions mapped out in contemporaneous film theory: identification with the camera and projector as well as with the characters in the film's fictional world. This admits the terrain of illusionism and narrative into *Two Sides to Every Story*, as Mondloch points out: "Snow's installation implicitly reintroduces precisely the virtual, illusionist space" that contemporaneous film and art theory attacked, "without, however, abandoning critical reflexivity."[73]

The play of illusionistic and real space, virtual depth and actual flatness, and of camera, projector, and spectator, replays the animating cinematic concerns Snow attributed to *Wavelength* seven years earlier: "I was thinking of ... trying to make a

[73] Ibid., pp. 16–17.

Fig. 5.43. Michael Snow, *Two Sides to Every Story* (1974). Frame enlargement.
Courtesy of Michael Snow.

definitive statement of pure Film space and time, a balancing of 'illusion' and 'fact,' all about seeing. The space starts at the camera's (spectator's) eye, is in the air, then is on the screen, then is within the screen (the mind)."[74] Though *Wavelength* was not a work of expanded cinema, it implies that the virtual spatial field of the loft and the movement through that space via the zoom extend beyond the screen surface into the exhibition space, where the spectators figuratively reproduce the projective actions of camera and projector. *Two Sides to Every Story* makes that virtual expansion of film space actual.

Describing *Two Sides to Every Story* in an interview with Snow in 1982, R. Bruce Elder referred to work's echoing of filming event and installation space as "isomorphic."[75] But after enumerating the isomorphic qualities of the work—the positioning of the projectors and screen, for instance—Elder qualified his statement:

The event we see on screen is projected onto a two-dimensional surface, while the event the camera recorded took place in three-dimensional space. This means that

---

[74] See chapter 1.
[75] Bruce Elder and Michael Snow, "On Sound, Sound Recording, Making Music of Recorded Sound, the Duality of Consciousness and Its Alienation from Language, Paradoxes Arising from These and Related Matters," in Michael Snow, ed., *The Michael Snow Project: Music/Sound 1948–1993: The Performed and Recorded Music/Sound of Michael Snow* (Toronto: Art Gallery of Ontario, 1994), p. 52. Accessible at http://www.fondation-langlois.org/digital-snow/media/pdf/14192_En.pdf.

if one had been present when the film had been made, one could have walked into the space of the performance, or one could have walked around and taken in different aspects of the objects in the space. If we situate ourselves in different positions in relation to the film screen, however, we do not see different aspects of the event but simply see the same flat surface from different angles.[76]

Elder adds that the film stock necessarily alters the colors we would have perceived had we been present for the filming, concluding, "The isomorphism thus suggests the identity but insists on the difference between the two circumstances."[77] But while this "difference" may be literal—the installation is not the pro-filmic event—what seems more important about *Two Sides to Every Story* is the chain of analogies is creates between filming, display, and viewing. It cannot recreate the act of production, of course, but it can produce a kind of spectatorial experience analogous to it, and, most significantly, analogous to the processes of spatial articulation that face every filmmaker, experimental or otherwise, as they translate three-dimensional space into two-dimensional image. Decisions about camera position, lenses, framing, and staging find their corollaries in decisions about projector throw, the arrangement of the viewing space, screen dimensions, and so on. These are the qualities of cinematic space Snow seems concerned to examine with *Two Sides to Every Story*, and, in another way, in *Wavelength*.

Like several of his other installations, Wong's *Puddle* (1982) takes an isomorphic structure, transposing the filmmaking process to the space of the gallery. The limits of this isomorphism—the fact that installation and pro-filmic event are not literally identical—are used to Wong's advantage, as his presence in the projected image but absence from the space once more connotes the paranormal or uncanny, as in *Shadow and Chair*. Wong filmed puddles in different locations and seasons, always placing the camera just a few inches from the water and aiming it obliquely across the puddle's surface. In each shot, Wong's reflection is visible in the puddle as he floats objects through it, makes ripples across it, or otherwise alters its surface. This specific, systematically employed shooting process and the interplay of puddle as both (reflected) image and surface are translated into the installation. Wong poured a mixture of water and white paint into a corner of the gallery and placed the projector in the same position relative to that puddle that the camera had occupied relative to the puddles he had filmed (fig. 5.44). The near identity of projected image and projection surface produces an effect similar to the one in *Screen, Projector, Film*, an ambiguity between real and filmed surface heightened by the presence of Wong's face in the pro-filmic puddle despite his absence from the gallery. The projected image also reflects off the surface of the real puddle onto the abutting wall, roughly analogous to the space Wong would have occupied as he stood over the puddles during shooting (fig. 5.45).

---

[76] Ibid., p. 53.
[77] Ibid.

Fig. 5.44. Al Wong, *Puddle* (1982). 9 minutes, color, silent. Installation view.
Photograph by Laura Wong.

The isomorphic form of such installations at once references and reveals what Bill Brand has called "the circular and reciprocating nature of the film medium," the fact that the acts of shooting and projecting are structurally similar, inversions of one another.[78] Brand's recently restored installation *Pong Ping Pong* (1971), which he describes as a "film and sound environment," throws this reciprocity into relief. The pro-filmic event was a ping pong game, which Brand filmed with a 16mm camera mounted on a dolly, repeatedly circling the table and players. What the camera

[78] Bill Brand, notes for *Pong Ping Pong*, https://www.billbrand.net/other-works-index/#/pong-ping-pong/.

Fig. 5.45. Al Wong pouring paint and water for *Puddle* (1982). 9 minutes, color, silent. Photograph by Al Wong.

actually filmed, however, was the reflection of the game in a circular mirror fitted in front of the camera's lens, which slowly rotated and tilted up and down, producing a spatially disorienting record of the pro-filmic event. The installation inverts the spatial arrangement of camera and event, placing the projector, sitting atop a turntable, at the center of the viewing space, whose outer boundaries are marked by a circle of 24 standing white screens (fig. 5.46). The same mirror mechanism is mounted in front of the projector lens, and slowly casts the projected image around the space, from one screen to the next, and up and down. Viewers, seated on the floor, attempt to follow the projected image across this unpredictable trajectory, which at times passes over their own bodies, or appears to slip outward into the dark space beyond the standing

Fig. 5.46. Bill Brand, *Pong Ping Pong* (1971). Screening at Oxford College (now Miami University). Oxford, Ohio, 1971.
Photograph by Bill Brand.

screens—indeed, *Pong Ping Pong*'s "reciprocal" structure entails a give and take between the centripetal arrangement of the shooting process and the centrifugal one of the installation. Brand refers to the latter as "turning the space inside out," yet another way of describing the spatial inversion implied by isomorphic form, and by the mirroring—literalized in this work by Brand's ingenious apparatus—of space and directionality in the dialectic of filming/projection.[79]

Robert Smithson's *Artforum* essay "A Cinematic Atopia," written the same year Brand made *Pong Ping Pong*, offers a model of the isomorphic installation format. In this text, Smithson describes himself as overwhelmed by the images of films in his memory, which overlap into "stagnant pools of images that cancel each other out."[80] Claiming that he is unable to remember a single film he liked or disliked—in other words, any particular film at all—Smithson instead can only call to mind "a pure film of light and darkness," as though he is seeing all these films projected on top of one another at once, the particulars of story, characters, and imagery lost in the glare.[81] An analogy would be Hiroshi Sugimoto's series of movie theater photographs, begun

---

[79] Ibid. *Pong Ping Pong* was shot in a gymnasium at Antioch College in Yellow Spring, Ohio (where Brand met Paul Sharits) in 1971, and premiered in the same location. Later the same year it screened at Oxford College, now Miami University, in Oxford, Ohio, also in a gymnasium. This added another layer of reciprocity, heightening the sense that the very space of the installation was being "turned inside out" (an inversion that the title itself mimics).

[80] Smithson, "A Cinematic Atopia," p. 53.

[81] Ibid.

a few years after the publication of Smithson's essay. To make these, Sugimoto placed a large-format camera near the back rows of movie palaces and made a single exposure lasting the entire length of the film. A blinding white screen glows in the center of various illuminated movie theater interiors, the composite image of every single projected frame. Smithson was undoubtedly referencing the eternal rectangle of light from Frampton's "A Lecture," reimagining it as a nightmarish limbo that represented the disorientation Smithson claimed to feel as he tried to recall the "wilderness of elsewheres" of all the films ever made.[82]

"A Cinematic Atopia" was published in the landmark September 1971 issue of *Artforum* guest edited by Michelson and devoted entirely to avant-garde film. That issue included Frampton's "For a Metahistory of Film: Commonplace Notes and Hypotheses," in which Frampton claimed that the historian of film confronted the "appalling problem" of being "responsible for every frame of film in existence."[83] Frampton's way out of this impossible situation was to propose a metahistory of cinema (see chapter 1). Smithson's escape route from the "vast mud field of images forever motionless" was his cinematic atopia:

> What I would like to do is build a cinema in a cave or an abandoned mine, and film the process of its construction. That film would be the only film shown in the cave. The projection booth would be made out of crude timbers, the screen carved out of a rock wall and painted white, the seats could be boulders. It would be a truly "underground" cinema.[84]

Smithson recalls visiting a tunnel carved into a mountainside and peering back toward the light visible at the tunnel's end. "One shot I had in mind was to move slowly from the interior of the tunnel toward the entrance and end outside."[85] Smithson incorporated a magazine photograph approximating this view in his collage *Towards the Development of a "Cinema Cavern,"* produced the same year he published "A Cinematic Atopia." "Moviegoer as spelunker" is scrawled next to the photograph, which is taped to a piece of paper on which Smithson has provided two rough sketches of his "cinema cavern," which he has labelled "truly underground," following his description of the unrealized project in his *Artforum* essay (fig. 5.47).

Bruce McClure adapted Smithson's idea into a film installation-cum-performance entitled, respectively, *A Cinematic Atopia: The Process of Its Construction* and *Build My Gallows High* (2014). The installation converted a large multi-purpose space in the Baltic Center for Contemporary Art in Newcastle into an unconventional screening space bisected diagonally by a thin sheet of transparent fabric. Spectators

---

[82] Ibid.

[83] Hollis Frampton, "For a Metahistory of Film: Commonplace Notes and Hypotheses," *Artforum* 10, no. 1 (September 1971), p. 35.

[84] Smithson, "A Cinematic Atopia," p. 55.

[85] Ibid.

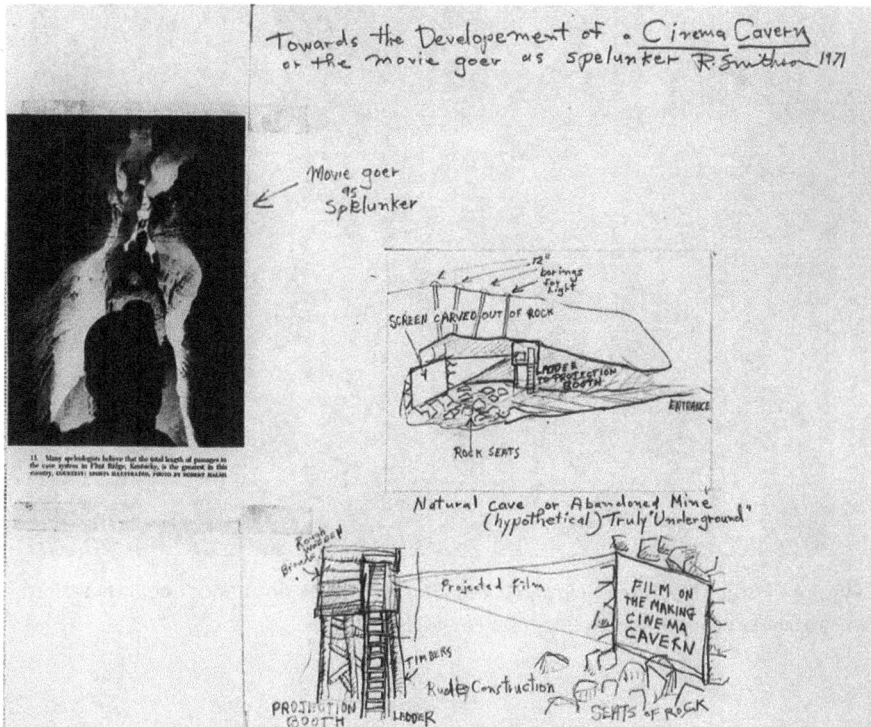

Fig. 5.47. Robert Smithson, *Towards the Development of a "Cinema Cavern" or the movie goer as a spelunker* (1971). Collage, pencil and tape on paper. 12 5/8 × 15 5/8 in. (32 × 39.7 cm).
©Holt/Smithson Foundation/VAGA at Artists Rights Society (ARS), NY.

were invited to watch this conversion, which bore the title *A Cinematic Atopia: The Process of Its Construction*, take place, and afterward to sit in casually arranged chairs and wooden benches on either side of this see-through screen. The two clusters of viewers on either side of the screen faced each other and were visible to one another during the installation process and ensuing performance, entitled *Build My Gallows High*. McClure's distinctive setup, this time utilizing only two film projectors, was arranged in one corner of the room, the projectors aimed toward the central screen, their beams casting images onto that screen but also passing through it to land on the opposite wall (fig. 5.48). Both projectors were threaded with McClure's characteristic black-and-white flicker loops and aimed at the same spot on the screen to form a composite image. One projector's aperture was fitted with a metal plate with a circular hole stamped through the middle. The projected image alternated through three variations: the white rectangle of the unaltered projector, the white circle of the adapted one, or both images at once, a white circle inside the white rectangle (fig. 5.49). This simple series could be further varied as McClure altered the brightness of each projector's lamp using rheostats, thus adjusting the hue of each. The aggressive flicker of the

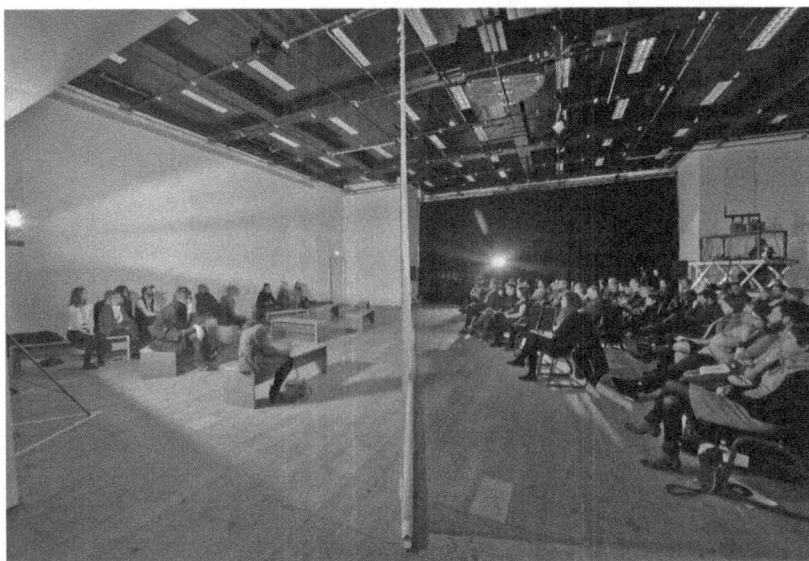

Fig. 5.48. Bruce McClure, *Build My Gallows High* (2014). Performance documentation. Photograph by Colin Davison, courtesy of AV Festival 14.

Fig. 5.49. Bruce McClure, *Build My Gallows High* (2014). Performance documentation. Photograph by Colin Davison, courtesy of AV Festival 14.

projectors was complimented by two strobe lights, one on each side of the transparent screen, whose flicker rhythms McClure could also control. The strobes were much brighter than the projector lamps, their light all but obliterating the projected images and lighting up the entire space, enabling spectators to see each other through the screen. Like most of McClure's performances, *Build My Gallows High* followed a pattern of crescendo-decrescendo, McClure giving his audience time to acclimate to the flicker, whose effect is greatly softened when the brightness of the projectors is low, and to the sound, which begins as an almost pleasing metallic warble before reaching dangerous decibel levels at the midpoint. A slow reduction of volume, brightness, and strobe flicker begins after this point, and the piece ends in complete darkness and relative quiet.

The back and forth between interiority and exteriority in "A Cinematic Atopia" would have appealed to McClure as an analogy of his own method of externalizing the mechanics of projection; the converted room of *A Cinematic Atopia: The Process of Its Construction* is a microcosm of the projector's interior. The *Wavelength*-like shot Smithson imagined, a zoom toward the point of light at the end of the long tunnel, evokes the same pattern of advance/recede in that film and suggested by the central image of McClure's performance: the circle inside the rectangle, a schematic representation of a zoom or iris in (or out) (fig. 5.50). That image also resonates with Smithson's and Frampton's eternal rectangle of all films ever made, and the reduction of these—and of all cinema—to that rectangle, which McClure takes as the image of cinema's essence.

McClure's exteriorization and enlargement of the projector gate finds a precursor in Raban's three-screen film *Diagonal* (1973), which has been projected in the customary theatrical format and configured as a looped installation. The three projected frames are arranged diagonally across the screen or gallery wall, stepping down from the upper left corner to the bottom right, in some iterations overlapping if limitations of space require it (fig. 5.51). The images on each reel are the same. Two superimposed flickering rectangles of varying colors move across the frame diagonally, sliding up and down against a black background. Their movements create the impression that the projected frame itself is throbbing and subtly shifting shape and on-screen position, when in fact the projectors remain still. Raban made the film on an optical printer, simply shooting the empty gate of the printer's projector through colored gels. Raban kept the focus on the projector's gate and the rotating shutter rather than on a filmed image inside that gate, in much the same way McClure's performances de-center the filmic image in favor of the crisply focused rectangle of the projector aperture. "This film is 'about' the projector gate," Raban writes, "the plane where the film frame is caught by the projected light beam."[86] He corrects the temptation to describe the film's imagery as abstract:

---

[86] William Raban, program notes for "William Raban: Independent Filmmaker," Carnegie Museum of Art, November 9, 1976, n.p. See http://www.luxonline.org.uk/articles/carnegie_institute(1).html.

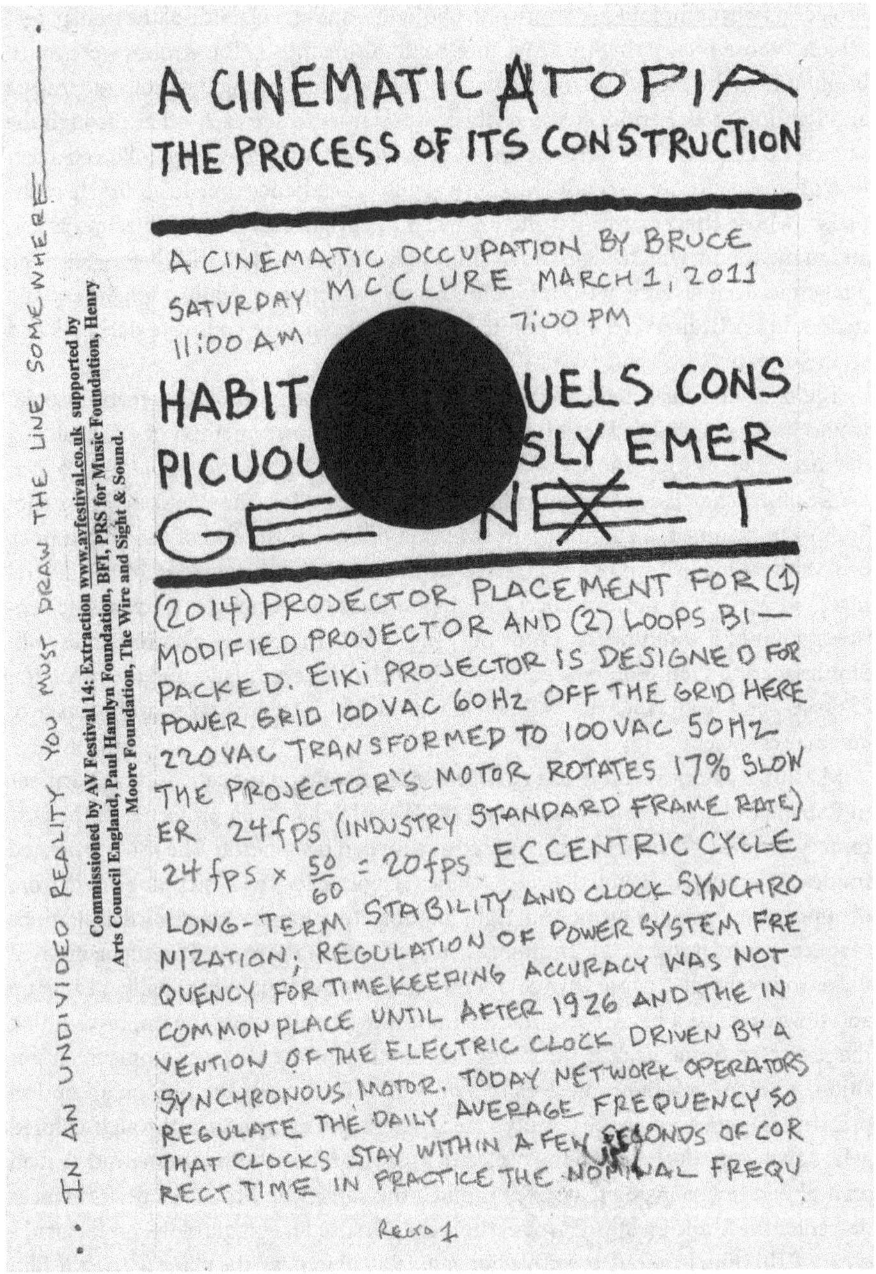

A CINEMATIC ATOPIA
THE PROCESS OF ITS CONSTRUCTION

A CINEMATIC OCCUPATION BY BRUCE
SATURDAY MCCLURE MARCH 1, 2011
11:00 AM   7:00 PM

HABIT   UELS CONS
PICUOU   SLY EMER
GE   NEXT

(2014) PROJECTOR PLACEMENT FOR (1)
MODIFIED PROJECTOR AND (2) LOOPS BI—
PACKED. EIKI PROJECTOR IS DESIGNED FOR
POWER GRID 100VAC 60Hz OFF THE GRID HERE
220VAC TRANSFORMED TO 100VAC 50Hz
THE PROJECTOR'S MOTOR ROTATES 17% SLOW
ER 24fps (INDUSTRY STANDARD FRAME RATE)
24 fps × 50/60 = 20 fps ECCENTRIC CYCLE
LONG-TERM STABILITY AND CLOCK SYNCHRO
NIZATION; REGULATION OF POWER SYSTEM FRE
QUENCY FOR TIMEKEEPING ACCURACY WAS NOT
COMMONPLACE UNTIL AFTER 1926 AND THE IN
VENTION OF THE ELECTRIC CLOCK DRIVEN BY A
SYNCHRONOUS MOTOR. TODAY NETWORK OPERATORS
REGULATE THE DAILY AVERAGE FREQUENCY SO
THAT CLOCKS STAY WITHIN A FEW SECONDS OF COR
RECT TIME IN PRACTICE THE NOMINAL FREQU

REEL 1

IN AN UNDIVIDED REALITY YOU MUST DRAW THE LINE SOMEWHERE

Commissioned by AV Festival 14: Extraction www.avfestival.co.uk supported by
Arts Council England, Paul Hamlyn Foundation, BFI, PRS for Music Foundation, Henry
Moore Foundation, The Wire and Sight & Sound.

Fig. 5.50. Bruce McClure, handmade program notes for *A Cinematic Atopia: The Process of its Construction* and *Build My Gallows High*. McClure's program notes are always handwritten and hand-drawn, with each photocopy individually stamped and signed (lower right).
Image courtesy of Bruce McClure.

Fig. 5.51. William Raban, *Diagonal* (1973).
Image courtesy of William Raban.

I was looking for a pure image, an image which was intrinsic to the medium of film. This film is not an abstract film; the subject is the projector gate, the plane where the film frame is arrested in the projected light beam, and the frame whose edges contain and divide the projected illusion from the blacked-out present of the movie theatre.[87]

Diagonal, then, takes an isomorphic form in that the space it creates on screen is an index of the space inside the projector. As in McClure's projection performances, *Diagonal* is a projecting out of a space designed *not* to be perceived as a space. Projection, here, is literally the "throwing" or "casting" out of a space of filmmaking, albeit a tiny one, into the space of exhibition. *Build My Gallows High* takes this further, literally converting the gallery where it was performed into a model of McClure's conception of the multiple focal points running along the projector's "z" axis, but *inside* its gate. The centrally located transparent screen parallels both aperture and film plane in the projector gate assembly.

---

[87] William Raban, statement on *Diagonal* for Luxonline, http://www.luxonline.org.uk/artists/william_raban/diagonal.html, n.p.

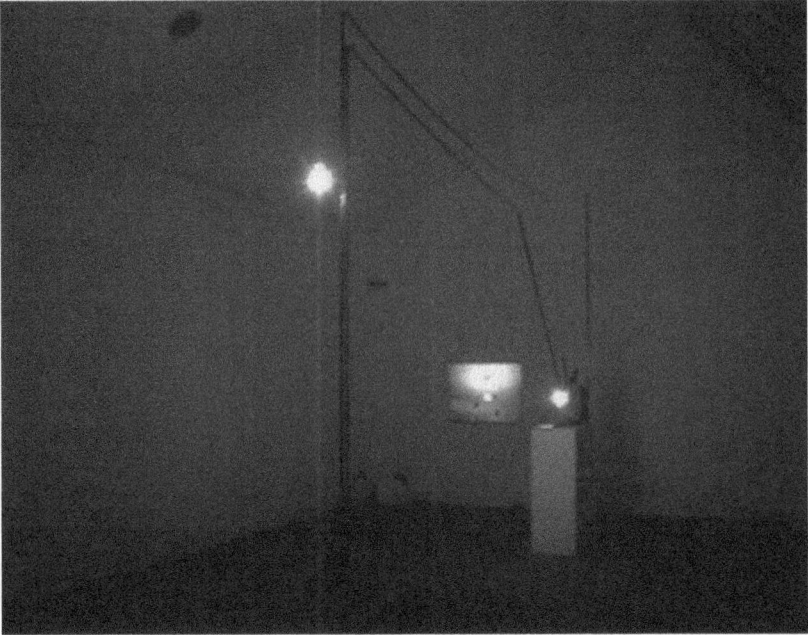

Fig. 5.52. Noor Afshan Mirza and Brad Butler, *Filmische Wahrheiten* (*Cinematic Truths*, 2007). Installation view. Heidelberger Kuntsverein, Heidelberg, Germany, 2007.

Filmische Wahrheiten (*Cinematic Truths*, 2007), by Noor Afshan (formerly Karen) Mirza and Brad Butler, is another contemporary example of isomorphic form in film installation, this one aimed quite pointedly at contemporaneous moving image work in the gallery. Describing the "site specificity" in moving image installation in an implicitly derogatory way, as a "loose fit between work and site implied by the notion of a work's 'responding' to a space," Mirza and Butler envision a site-specific film installation that makes "the space/site a rigorous determinant of the work's entire structure, up to and seamlessly including its space. The work thus breaks down the distinction between work and its space of presentation."[88] *Filmische Wahrheiten* does exactly this. A long 16mm film loop traces the contours of the gallery space over a system of rollers (similar to the looping system of Nicolson's *Reel Time*) and through a projector whose beam passes through a transparent photograph mounted in a suspended frame (fig. 5.52). The projected image, which strikes the opposite wall, thus superimposes the image on the film and the shadow cast by the transparent photograph. The beam also casts the shadow of the film loop, which drops from the ceiling in front of the projector, between the photograph and the opposite wall, then rises to the ceiling again before returning to the projector. The filmed image is a rapidly flickering closeup of a

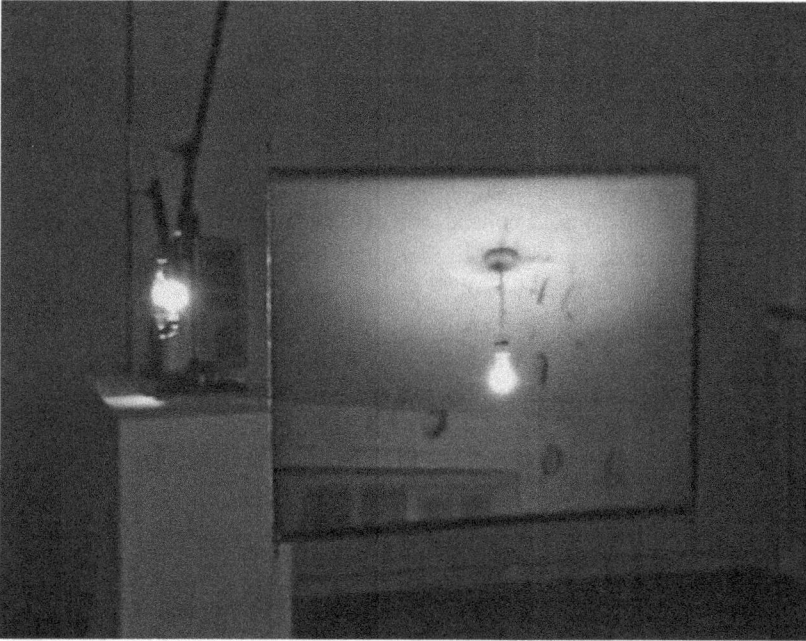

Fig. 5.53. Noor Afshan Mirza and Brad Butler, *Filmische Wahrheiten* (*Cinematic Truths,* 2007). Detail.

light bulb, alternating between positive and negative. The still photograph is a more distant view of the same light bulb, which reveals it to be the very same light bulb that hangs from the gallery ceiling (fig. 5.53). Mirza and Butler's program notes for *Filmische Wahrheiten* point to its isomorphic structure:

> The physical film strip defines the shape/volume of the actual space in which it is displayed. The planes are clearly defined and mapped out in both space and time, from the film plane as the filmstrip passes by the projector gate to the image bearing light resting on the surface of the photograph which stands in as the screen, to the surface of the filmstrip as it passes in front of the light bulb hanging in the space to the double projection of the shadow of the illuminated screen hitting the back wall.[89]

The installation's austerity, tautological filmic structure, and marked anti-illusionism, not to mention its nod to Le Grice's *Castle One* (in the form of its juxtaposition of real and filmed light bulbs), connect it to the previous generation of UK avant-garde cinema. The link is more than aesthetic; Mirza and Butler are co-founders of London's

---

[89] Ibid.

no.w.here lab, which was built on the model of the LFMC and rescued some of its film equipment. But the implied critique of site specificity in *Filmische Wahrheiten*, and Mirza and Butler's insistence that it be "more than site specific," is very much in response to the contemporary situation of the moving image in the gallery. Mirza's statement on the relationship between work and site, which opened this chapter, hints at the nature and circumstances of this response: expanded cinema is conceived of as "taking on the specificity of its context, whether a neutral space, an underground car park, an auditorium, or a museum or gallery. The work becomes a reading of the work itself. It's not simply a form of display."[90]

The proliferation of moving image art in the gallery and museum since the 1990s has been chronicled in detail, and so does not need to be rehearsed here. The Whitney's *Into the Light* exhibition was, among other things, an attempt to place this phenomenon in historical context. Given the amount of critical discourse the show engendered, the attempt seems to have been successful; since 2001 the subject has been at the center of cinema and art historical scholarship. In a 2003 roundtable discussion in the journal *October*, Hal Foster dubbed moving images "the default category" of the contemporary art world, and not without a note of concern.[91] During the 1960s and '70s, Foster claimed, the use of film and video by artists was "treated as a way out from other mediums or conditions," which is to say means of liberation from the constraints of traditional art forms and the strictures of the gallery.[92] By the time of *Into the Light*, however, the moving image had become "the dominant," which entailed its re-entry into the museum or gallery and, to Foster's way of thinking, its recuperation, as well as the diffusion of the radical potential the previous generation of artists had seen in film and video. The specific terms of this criticism had to do with the relationship between gallery-based moving image works and their space, and the extent to which such works still represented meaningful alternatives to traditional forms like painting. Foster was skeptical, to say the least. Responding to Chrissie Iles's comments on the relationship between moving image art and painting, Foster argued instead that contemporary work was marked less by a relation to painting than by

> a rampant pictorialism, which is to say a rampant virtualism . . . The pictorialism of projected images today often doesn't seem to care much about the actual space. Sometimes it doesn't matter when you walk in, or even whether you do. It's as if the work doesn't care whether you're there or not.[93]

Iles concurred, stating that the interrogation of the specificity of space in projected image works was a characteristic of earlier rather than contemporary moving image art.

[90] Karen Mirza and Brad Butler, "On Expanded Cinema," in Rees, et al., eds., *Expanded Cinema: Art, Performance, Film*, p. 258.
[91] Turvey et al., "Round Table," p. 93.
[92] Ibid.
[93] Ibid., p. 75.

Filmmakers and critics in the experimental film world have tended to share Foster's exasperation at the "rampant virtualism" of such work, at its illusionism, narrative absorption, and apparent disengagement from real space. One of many criticisms they have leveled against current moving image art in the gallery context is that it is so in thrall to popular cinema that it reproduces that cinema's aesthetic and ideological effects. While the "black box/white cube" distinction implies that the former occludes while the latter reveals, from this critical perspective the gallery is no more revelatory that the cinema. Site specificity is meaningless, as the "real" site of these works is the illusionistic diegetic space within the four corners of the projected image. In a recent review of two exhibitions of moving image work, by Philippe Parreno and Douglas Gordon, Nicky Hamlyn articulated this position:

[T]he environment [of the gallery] is closer, conceptually and physically, to a conventional cinema, which is where the films really belong. They are not installations ... The films take the spectator out of the gallery space and into the absorbingly illusionistic one of the film, in that nothing in the latter causes the spectator to reflect on the relationship between the space in the film and that in which it is being shown, and, concomitantly, their own bodily relationship with the space of the gallery.[94]

What's more, as an experimental filmmaker who has made multi-screen and installation work since the 1970s, Hamlyn comes from a cinematic tradition that sees even the "conventional cinema" as potentially receptive to space-based work—films that meaningfully address and engage the space of the theater and overcome the cinema's built-in resistance to anti-illusionism. This is a reversal of the values encoded in the black box/white cube distinction: the black box can house genuinely anti-illusionist and site-specific work, while the white cube is no guarantee against absorption, virtualism, and a kind of spatial abstraction that transports viewers in the same way conventional moviemaking does. As Hamlyn and many others have pointed out, the white cube in most contemporary moving image installations is rarely white, but darkened to make the projected image visible. And at the center of such work, more often than not, is another "black box," a mechanism of invisibility par excellence: the digital projector.

For filmmakers like Hamlyn, Mirza, and Butler, then, the conceit of the white cube is false. It is, as Mirza puts it, merely "a form of display." The isomorphic installation structure in which work and display space are co-determined is an antidote to a mode of installation in which the specificity of location is as meaningless as the specificity of media. Thus, while the entrance into the gallery by filmmakers like Mirza and Butler, Sharits, Iimura, Wong, and Snow, while taking advantage of the spatial options on

---

[94] Nicky Hamlyn, "What's Wrong with Cinema in the Gallery," *Moving Image Review and Art Journal* 1, no. 2 (September 2012), p. 265.

offer there, also resists the effects and discourses of that space, carrying the formal and political values of experimental cinema into new territory.

This last statement admittedly puts the process in pure, perhaps idealistic terms. In actual practice, it has always been a process of negotiation between different sets of ideas and aims, with costs and benefits weighed, concessions made, and balances struck. For Sharits, one of the primary attractions of the gallery was that it allowed what he termed a "democratic" mode of spectatorship, or "a new non-exclusive, non-theatric mode of presentation."[95] "Democratic" and "non-exclusive" meant, in essence, a viewing experience that was spatially and temporally non-hierarchical. The locational works refused to prescribe particular viewing positions or durations, freeing the audience—reconceived now as individual spectators rather than a group—from the spatial and temporal strictures of the cinema theater (scheduled screenings, arranged seating). The gallery space also allowed viewers to "share with me a respect and enthusiasm for the primary structures of cinema."[96] Reflecting on his earliest locational installation, *Sound Strip/Film Strip*, which first showed at The Contemporary Arts Museum in Houston in March of 1972, Sharits wrote of museum visitors who "enjoyed the piece to the extent of coming-going-coming back-leaving again-returning (like the looped films themselves), bringing with them other persons, some of whom grasped the primary conception, appreciated it and left quietly."[97] Le Grice has called this spectatorial mode "transient," and, like a number of other experimental filmmakers who have weighed the benefits and drawbacks of entry into the gallery, finds it too much of a liability, a hedge against the formal integrity of space-based expanded cinema: "I have largely rejected this form," Le Grice wrote in 2001, "because of the transience of the viewers' engagement and consequent lack of depth in time-based art in the gallery."[98]

Another problem with experimental film's forays into the gallery space is that the theorizing and historicizing of such work has tended to minimize or even ignore the context of its mode of film practice. Bringing avant-garde film and expanded cinema into the gallery, that is, comes with the risk of its identity being lost, its history cut off, and its aesthetic power diminished. For both an example of this problem and an opportunity to intervene in it, I turn to the "solid light" films of Anthony McCall.

Anthony McCall: "Artists" and "Filmmakers"

With the possible exception of Sharits, Anthony McCall has received more attention within the art world, as a "moving image artist," than any other figure in experimental cinema. Two qualifications need to be made immediately, however. The first is that

[95] Sharits, "Statement Regarding Multiple Screen/Sound 'Locational' Film Environments-Installations," p. 79.
[96] Ibid.
[97] Ibid., p. 80.
[98] Malcolm Le Grice, "Improvising Time and Image," *Filmwaves*, 14, no. 1 (2001), p. 18.

McCall has not always self-defined as an experimental filmmaker. His relationship to that artistic culture has been complicated; Branden Joseph has shown that McCall distanced himself from it, or at least from the dominant formalist tendencies within it, almost as soon as he had completed his cycle of solid light films in 1975.[99] In this respect, the arc of his filmmaking career in the 1970s recalls Tony Conrad's. Conrad, in his own words, "had been drawn to [experimental] film because of its hopelessly shabby integrity, and also because of its restive and anarchic aspects, which implicitly challenged the progressivism of the art market." But he became disillusioned as "'structural film' became a kind of fashionable doxology, within which younger filmmakers felt compelled to revisit many of the formalist issues that had been run ragged in painting and sculpture a decade earlier."[100] By 1976, McCall believed that the radical potential of structural and structural-materialist film had been lessened by its institutionalization as an international style validated by its entrance into the gallery and museum world. We will return to this point in the next chapter, as McCall's ideas about this situation become clearest in relation to his filmless paracinematic work *Long Film for Ambient Light* (1975).

The second qualification to be made about McCall as experimental filmmaker is that his notoriety in the art world, particularly after 2001, hinged on the marginalization of the experimental film context by that world through its curatorial practices and critical discourses. Nonetheless, this context played a crucial role in McCall's work in the 1970s, both in London and New York, and continues to shape its reception in the present. From 1973 to 1975, McCall made a series of "solid light" films, culminating in *Long Film for Ambient Light*. With the exception of that last work, the solid light films were made on 16mm film. Simply animated white lines on a black background, when projected into an environment made thick with smoke or haze, mold the projector's beam into moving three-dimensional forms. Lines, cones, and trapezoidal bars of light are the focus of viewer attention rather than the two-dimensional screen image. Screening the solid light films places special demands on exhibitors. The room must be utterly dark, as even the ambient light from an exit sign or spilling from the projector itself diffuses the effect. The room must also be filled with smoke. McCall has joked that the films were easier to screen in the 1970s, when art spaces were often housed in dirty and dusty industrial spaces and smoking was permitted everywhere.[101] For screenings in the cleaner, slicker spaces of the contemporary art world, theatrical hazers are usually employed.

Most commentators on the solid light films note their obvious sculptural characteristics, including McCall himself. From the beginning, the seeming ambiguity of their medium-belonging underwrote all sorts of critical equivocations about the films. P. Adams Sitney called *Line Describing a Cone* (fig. 5.54) "the

---

[99] Branden W. Joseph, "Sparring with the Spectacle," in Christopher Eamon, ed., *Anthony McCall: The Solid Light Films and Related Works* (Evanston, IL: Northwestern University Press, 2005), pp. 39–40.

[100] Conrad, "Is This Penny Ante or a High Stakes Game?," p. 103.

[101] Anthony McCall, personal interview, March 12, 2003.

Fig. 5.54. Anthony McCall, *Line Describing a Cone* (1973), during the twenty-fourth minute. Installation view, Whitney Museum of American Art, *Into the Light: The Projected Image in American Art 1964–1977*, 2001.
Photograph by Hank Graber. Courtesy of Anthony McCall.

most brilliant case of an observation on the essentially sculptural quality of every cinematic situation."[102] This paradoxically implies that a work could be understood as essentially cinematic even if it took the shape and traded in the aesthetic effects of another art form, and that the cinema was, in some way, fundamentally sculptural. In a more recent essay on McCall's films, George Baker couches the same theoretical equivocation in more sophisticated language. McCall's films, Baker argues,

> proclaimed that it was the essence of cinema to have no essence. Cinema could only be particularized as the movement of form into becoming, multiplicity, and difference. The basis of film form would be its undoing of a fixed basis; the "content" of its abstract transitivity, the paradoxical revelation of its inherent embodiment of becoming, a movement that thus is always, logically, a becoming other ... Cinema would be cinema, and it would become sculpture.[103]

---

[102] Annette Michelson and P. Adams Sitney, "A Conversation on Knokke and the Independent Filmmaker," *Artforum* 13 (May 1976), p. 65.
[103] Baker, "Film Beyond Its Limits," pp. 22–23.

Baker's interpretation leaves McCall's films hovering between the aesthetic territory of sculpture and film, and, by extension, the worlds of the art gallery and the cinema. Such ambiguities and paradoxes would mostly come to the fore long after the 1970s, however, once McCall's work garnered new attention when *Line Describing a Cone* was included in *Into the Light*. But the fact that McCall worked in multiple media and art forms, and that his solid light films resonated with artistic practices outside of avant-garde cinema, has always been an important factor in any examination of his work.

Recent texts on the solid light films duly frame them in the context of his larger artistic career, which has included sculpture, photography, illustration, performance, and conceptual forms. While his films certainly cannot be isolated from that context, they also cannot simply be taken as representatives of a post-medium, post-minimal artmaking ethos in which distinctions among media are irrelevant. And in pursuit of the laudable goal of situating the solid light films in McCall's diverse oeuvre, many contemporary writers have lost sight of the specifically cinematic context that was unquestionably the most proximate influence on his filmmaking during the 1970s. The London and New York film avant-gardes not only shaped McCall's thinking about film (the medium) and cinema (the art form and institution), but also helped make his work legible as cinema in the first place. That the same films have been increasingly legible as sculpture since *Into the Light* is a condition of a shift in the art world's attitude toward moving image art and its ability to accommodate such work.

All of McCall's work of the 1970s problematized the distinctions between mediums and the broader aesthetic categories underpinning these. A special target for McCall was the difference between temporal and non-temporal art, which he rejected. At the same time, however, one especially prominent variety of modernist art theory, committed to qualities of absorption and instantaneousness found in painting and sculpture, denigrated temporal art forms. McCall has cited Mel Bochner's claim in a 1974 *Artforum* essay: "when you're interested in art, you're interested in the exchange that occurs when you stand in front of a work alone, and look at it. It is atemporal. That's not what happens when you see a film, or a dance or video, or any of the other performance arts."[104] Contrast this sentiment, and those of Michael Fried discussed in chapter 3, with McCall's own take on sculpture:

> Looking at sculpture takes time. The viewer has to walk round a sculptural object to discover what is hidden, and to come to an understanding of its complexities. This necessity is implicit in all sculpture. Most works of sculpture are immobile and unchanging; it is the viewer who acts in duration. Time-based art such as mine, on the other hand, is an art not of immobile form, but an art of disclosure and transformation. The "medium" is actually a process: the reciprocity between form and duration.[105]

---

[104] Anthony McCall, "*Line Describing a Cone* and Related Films," *October* 103 (Winter 2003), p. 56.
[105] From "Duration," a summary of the formal concerns relevant to McCall's time-based art, written by McCall in response to a question about the nature of duration, personal interview, March 13, 2003.

McCall coined the term "condition" in 1971 for a group of works he made that enacted his notion of "the reciprocity between form and duration." A number of performative, sculptural, drawn, and photographic works of this period bear that name. As McCall used it, "condition" denoted several related qualities. First, it implied that a work with that name was conditional, a temporally finite arrangement or situation that formed and dissolved. But this did not apply only to works that were explicitly time-based, like performances or films, but to object-based art as well, including drawings and photographic series. One consequence of McCall's belief that all art forms possessed a temporal dimension was a distinct conception of the relationship between artwork and spectator, one that reversed the value system in Fried's "Art and Objecthood." This leads to the another defining feature of the "condition," that the work of art and the viewer's experience of it were both conditional, as in shaped by an array of external factors that formed a broader context for both the formal properties of the work and the activity of viewers. At its simplest level, McCall's identification of certain works as conditions suggested that they should not be thought of as art objects per se, but rather as contexts in which both artist and viewer operated. This is especially true of the spatially and temporally large-scale condition *Landscape for Fire* (1972), perhaps the defining work of McCall's pre-cinematic career.

Landscape for Fire was performed three times in England in the summer and autumn of 1972, and also exists as a short 16mm sound film whose production was incorporated into one of the performances (fig. 5.55). It was one of several pieces that involved performers operating over large outdoor spaces and working with materials like fire, smoke, fog, and sound. Thirty-six pans of gasoline were arranged in a

Fig. 5.55. Anthony McCall, *Landscape for Fire II* (1972). Performance view.
Photograph by Carolee Schneemann. Courtesy of Anthony McCall.

rectangular grid and ignited and doused according to a complex score divided into three movements, taking place over a period ranging from 15 to 90 minutes depending on the performance (fig. 5.56). While the lighting process took place, a smoke generator blew white smoke across the grid and three distant foghorns sounded at an interval of once per minute. McCall also issued instructions to the performers over a megaphone. The performers, all in white boiler suites, moved across the grid lighting the fires, and though some of McCall's notes for *Landscape for Fire* suggest a pattern of diagonal movement across the grid from the center to the edges, it is not clear from available accounts of the performances whether each instance of the work followed the same score or if the pattern was even evident to spectators. Indeed, spectators may have been frustrated by *Landscape for Fire*'s impenetrable structure and McCall's resolute indifference to their ability to comprehend the piece in its entirety. "They stayed in clusters shifting only slightly to adapt to changing configurations in the pattern of fires," McCall stated in a contemporaneous essay on his conditions:

> when all the fires were out they shifted again and stood in the smoke belching from the smoke generator. When everything was out, and the shadowy figures [the performers] could just be detected in the darkness preparing a new alignment, they became impatient, finding themselves in a huge open field, without a focus, and with nothing to watch that was in proportion to what they had just watched. By the traditional standards of theater, television, film, concert hall or firework displays,

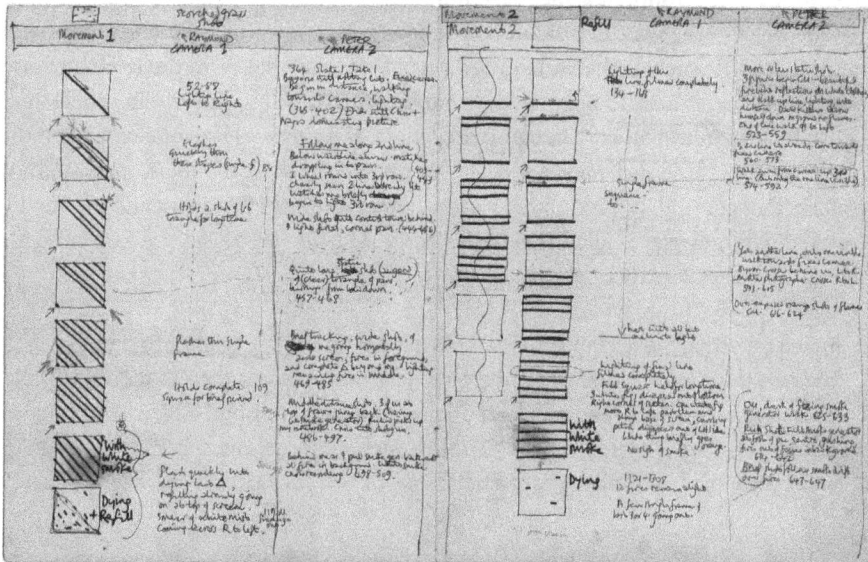

Fig. 5.56. Anthony McCall, *Landscape for Fire II* (1972). Performance score and editing schema. Notebook Sept. 5–Sept. 20, 1972.
Courtesy of Anthony McCall.

there seemed to be nothing happening (though surely it was obvious that some-thing was happening).[106]

Though I have called *Landscape for Fire* a "performance," McCall objected to that term. In contrasting the piece with "the traditional standards of theater, television, film, concert hall, and firework display," he differentiates conditions from performances in terms of their relationship to an audience. By "performance," McCall had in mind a work that was not only time-based but also temporally and spatially discrete, organized as a display for an audience who could comprehend the entirety of the performance from beginning to end and recognize a complete, unfolding structure. A condition, on the other hand, overwhelmed this discreteness, becoming too temporally and/or spatially large-scale to grasp as a single unified shape in time or space. And while a performance, according to McCall, was organized around the perspective of an audience for ease of comprehension, a condition was indifferent to these factors, as the impatience of the audiences for *Landscape for Fire* showed. The "performers," moreover, engaged less in performances than in simple tasks, lighting and extinguishing the fires, operating the cameras and sound equipment used to make the film version, and issuing instructions over the megaphones. Audience members were unlikely to be able to make out these actions given the work's spatial expanse and the encroaching darkness, all three variations of *Landscape for Fire* having been performed at dusk. McCall, in fact, did not refer to them as performers, or else did so only for the sake of convenience; "I want to get away from the notion of the performance ... I am moving far more towards prolonged and continuous conditions—in live works, in environmental pieces, in film."[107]

One effect of the scale of McCall's conditions was to introduce variables into spectatorial activity, such as the varied positions of viewers relative to the work—whose boundaries were fuzzy to begin with—and the differing amounts of time spectators chose to remain watching. Changing the length and physical size of a condition directly affected these variables. As McCall increased the scale of *Landscape for Fire*, a process that continued through the various incarnations of that work and eventually resulted in a new piece called *Fire Cycles I and II* (1973–1974) (fig. 5.57), he also altered the audience's experience:

Taken together, these changes created a quieter, lower-key relationship between the execution of the event and the watching of it. I wrote then that "the work ceased to be a 'performance' with a perceivable beginning and end, with boundaries like an art object, but became rather a condition of the space, as is a high wind, a building, or the activity of a building site."[108]

[106] Felipe Ehrenberg, "On Conditions (Felipe Ehrenberg Discusses the Work of Anthony McCall)," *Art and Artists 7* (June 1973), p. 41.
[107] Ibid., p. 42.
[108] McCall, "*Line Describing a Cone* and Related Films," p. 51.

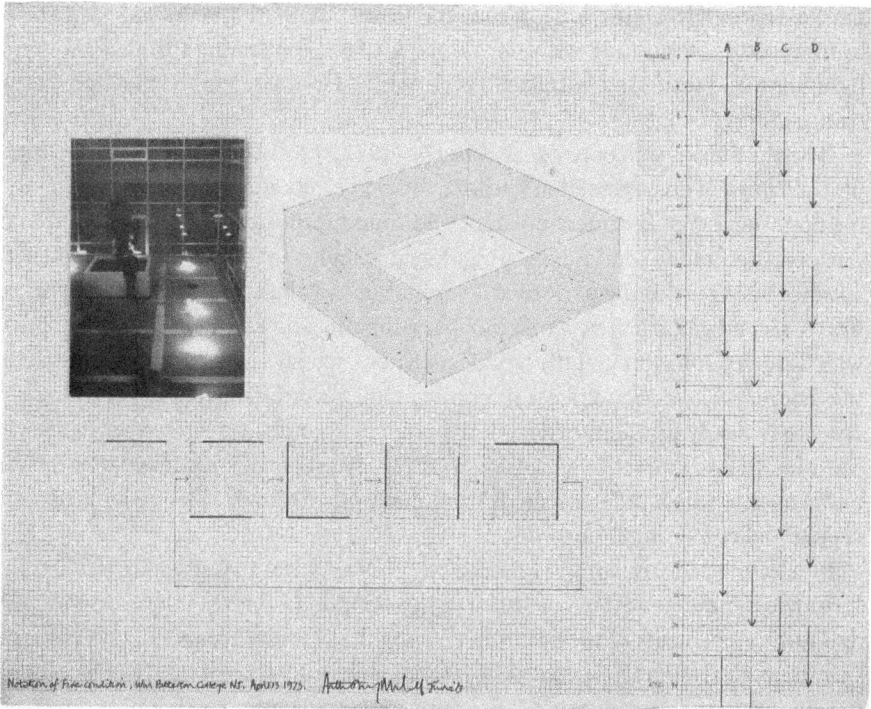

Fig. 5.57. Anthony McCall, *Fire Cycles I* (1973). Performance score. 44.5 cm × 56.5 cm, 17½ in × 22 in.
Courtesy of Anthony McCall.

Though McCall was pleased with these developments, his description of the later fire conditions as nearly boundless, lacking any formal edges to grasp, and as practically disappearing from view, signal a key problem. The objectlessness of the conditions was a liability for an artist seeking entrance to the gallery. McCall has often spoken of the difficulties of producing and gaining acceptance for time-based art during the early '70s, as galleries were either uninterested or, in some instances, willing to arrange "one-night stands" but offering "no proposals of marriage."[109] Much of the resistance was to the manner of attention required of time-based works relative to painting and sculpture, something McCall's solid light films would investigate much further. While McCall's works were not discrete performances that could, say, be viewed in a gallery according to a schedule, their temporality was nonetheless critical, and the gallery's mode of spectatorship militated against the perception of their slow and subtle unfolding. Of course, art works that could not be perceived or grasped as objects were also much more difficult to

[109] Walley, "An Interview with Anthony McCall," p. 69.

market (though this situation has changed in the intervening years). McCall's turn to filmmaking, beginning with *Landscape for Fire*, continuing through the solid light films, and resuming in 2003 after a lengthy hiatus, confronted these concerns from a different angle.

With the film version of *Landscape for Fire* (1972), McCall moved away from using film as a form of documentation toward a focused exploration of the possibilities the medium suggested. A camera operator and sound recorder were incorporated into one execution of the condition bearing the same name, their movements scripted in advance like those of the performers, whom the crew followed through the grid of fire. A second camera crew worked outside the fire field taking much wider shots, which convey something of the work's enormous spatial scale. *Landscape for Fire* is the first instance in McCall's use of photographic recording media in which the recording is clearly distinguished from the original event by its own formal structure. The film, that is, cannot be mistaken for a merely pragmatic documentation of the performance, which differentiates it from many other film or video records of conceptual and post-minimal art works.

In selecting and arranging the shots of the performance, McCall condensed it from forty-five minutes to seven. One effect of this temporal compression is that the back and forth movements of the performers along the rows are organized into patterns that did not exist in the original performance and, if they had, would not have been perceptible to the spectators because they were spread over a much longer duration. McCall emphasized this further by flipping the horizontal or vertical orientation of some shots, juxtaposing correctly and incorrectly oriented images (fig. 5.58). Thus, a single movement of the performers along a row will suddenly reverse its orientation and direction in the frame, the editing strategy generating a new form for that movement. The soundtrack similarly organizes the sounds of the event into patterns and includes sounds that likely would not have been heard by spectators attending the pro-filmic event, such as the explosive noises of the gasoline pans being lit, the shuffling of the performers' movements through the grass, and the sounds of the film equipment itself.

McCall has said that the film was originally intended as pure documentation but that he became interested in precisely the kinds of formal relationships and patterns he could create entirely through editing, and in the ways he could effectively reorganize the action of a preexisting event. This seems to have suggested to McCall that one of cinema's distinctive possibilities was the organization of movement. Thinking about this through the expansive framework of post-minimal art and expanded cinema in Europe suggested other forms of organization outside the contents of the film images. This would become the defining interest behind the solid light films: the organization of spectatorial activity and experience in relation to the space and time of the work. This emerged from the logic of film editing itself, as a means to structure duration and affect perception, and from the increased attention paid within the London Filmmakers' Cooperative to the literal space of cinematic exhibition. McCall began attending LFMC screenings in 1970, and found his interests being directed

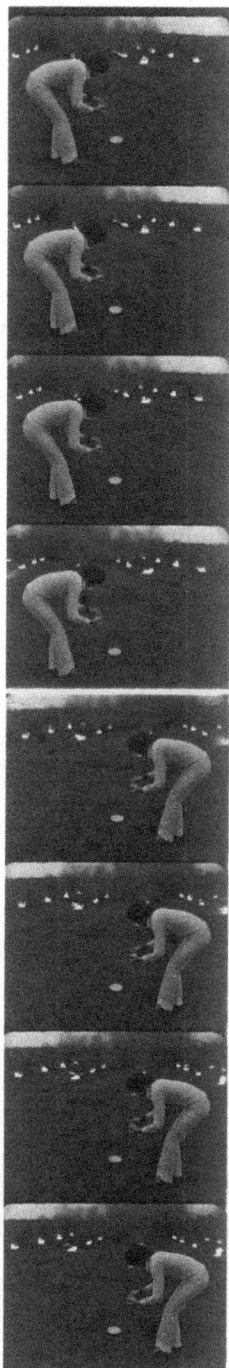

Fig. 5.58. Anthony McCall, *Landscape for Fire* (1972). Film frames revealing portion of shot flipped left to right.
Courtesy of Anthony McCall.

away from documentation of his conditions and toward the kind of tautological film aesthetic so prominent among LFMC filmmakers at the time:[110]

> I began to think about the possibility if a film that was only a film. What were the ir-reducible elements for a film ... The specific question that interested me was, how does an audience look at a film? How does an audience relate to a film? Was sitting and looking at a conventional narrative film a passive or active experience?[111]

McCall's interest in film's "irreducible elements" focused specifically on the codes of film viewing and the ways film exhibition molded the activities of spectators. This version of "materialism," which was more concerned with the reality of exhibition (Le Grice's "primacy of the projection event") than the raw materials of the film medium, was at the heart of the LFMC. Filmmaking in this context, then, conjoined McCall's two central preoccupations and focused them in a concentrated period of filmmaking activity: working with ephemeral materials like light, sound, smoke, and environment; and exploring the forms of spectatorial engagement that were possible within various types of time-based work. And in the LFMC, McCall found an idea of duration that paralleled his own and an artistic community that could accommodate and appreciate his work. Though McCall did not begin making his solid light films until he left England for New York in 1973, the seeds of the series were sown in this ground.

McCall made all of his solid light films on a Richmark Bell & Howell animation stand, photographing a series of drawings of simple shapes onto 16mm film one frame at a time (fig. 5.59). The camera was mounted on a vertical bar above a flat workspace, where McCall placed a black sheet of paper that provided the background for the abstract line drawings to be animated. The paper was lit from either side, resulting in even illumination across the surface and increasing the contrast between the white shapes and their black backgrounds. For *Line Describing a Cone*, McCall began with a white point at the bottom of the paper, slowly extending it into an arc and, finally, a complete circle.[112] The individual stages of the drawing process are animated into a smooth progression, the point of light tracing a white circle over the course of 30 minutes. In projection, the filmstrip acts as a sort of light stencil, sculpting the projector beam, which extends the two-dimensional image into a three-dimensional form following the arc stated in the film's title: a line of light that traces out a hollow cone in space.

McCall subsequently put this cone shape through three additional permutations. In *Partial Cone* (1974, 15 minutes), the image on the filmstrip does not change over

---

[110] McCall discusses his relationship to the LFMC in MacDonald, "Anthony McCall," pp. 160–161, and in Walley, "An Interview with Anthony McCall," p. 68.

[111] MacDonald, "Anthony McCall," p. 160.

[112] It should be noted, however, that the circle is imperfect. Due to an error in the drawing process a slight gap is left in the circle as the point of light completes its 360-degree trajectory. This was corrected when McCall remade *Line Describing a Cone* digitally in 2010, as *Line Describing a Cone 2.0*.

Fig. 5.59. Anthony McCall shooting *Cone of Variable Volume* on a Richmark Bell & Howell animation camera (1974).

Photograph by George Griffin. Courtesy of Anthony McCall.

time as it does in the previous film. The sole image in *Partial Cone* is a half-circle, which creates a half cone, or arc, in space. This image alternates with black frames, beginning with a rapid flicker—one illustrated frame to one black frame—that slows according to a metrical score that determined the entire film's rhythms (fig. 5.60). Each minute, McCall adjusted the ratio of illustrated to black frames, 1:1, 2:2, 3:3, and so on, until the midpoint, when the half cone blinks at an interval of one second, or 24 frames. At this point the pattern changes; the cone appears for bursts of 24 frames interrupted by a single frame of blackness. Over each subsequent minute, the interruptions increase by one frame at a time, 23:1, 22:2, 21:3, and so on, until the original 1:1 frame ratio of cone to black frame is restored and the film has come full circle. In *Conical Solid* (1974, 10 minutes), McCall did not use a circular form but a straight line, which appears in projection as a trapezoidal blade of light, its width increasing along the "z" axis of the projector lens. This line rotates in the center of the frame, its circular movement tracing out a virtual conical shape in space. The film is divided into eight parts, each part one minute and 15 seconds long, and each slowing the rotation of the line from a rapid four-frame rotation in part one to a 120-frame rotation in part eight (fig. 5.61). The rapid rotation of the projector beam in the early parts of the film registers as a flickering "X" shape in space, as the diagonal orientation of the blade of light alternates every frame between left-to-right and right-to-left. As the rotation of the beam slows down, however, the hallucinatory cone it carves out becomes increasingly apparent, the beam taking on a more discernible circular shape rather

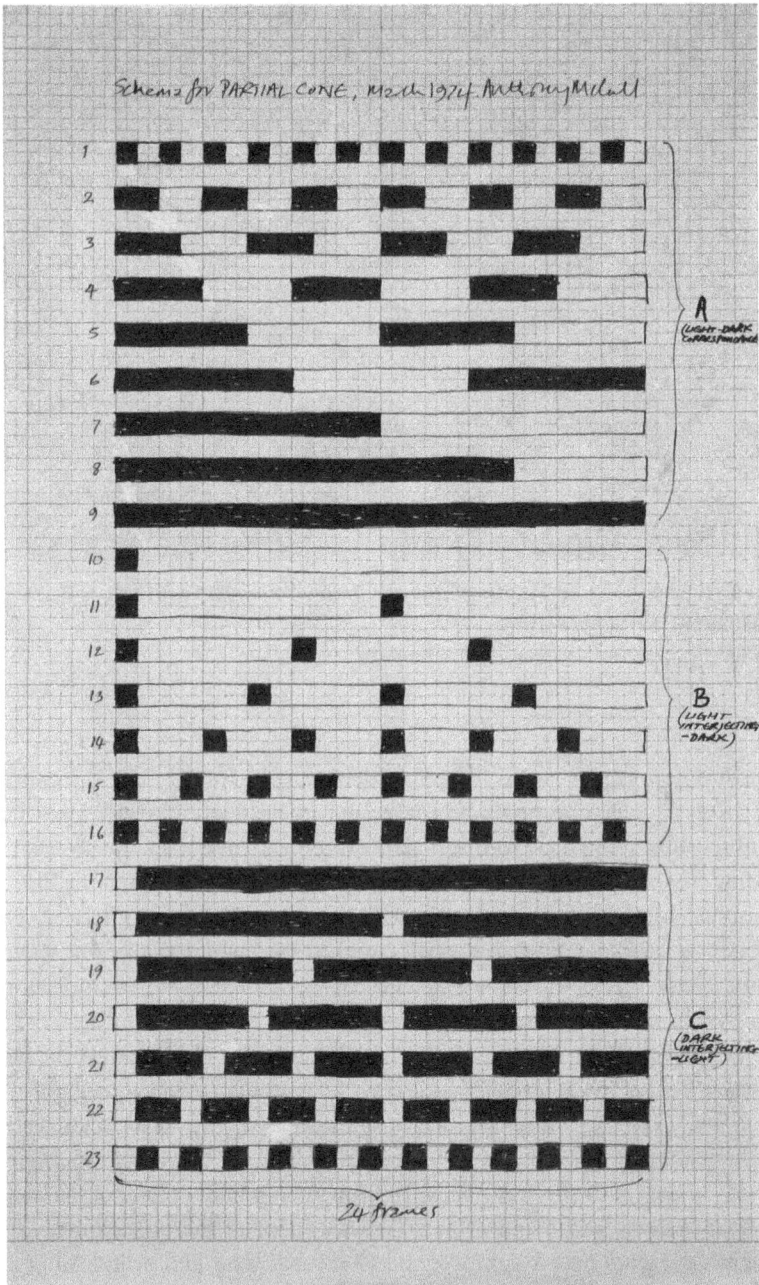

Fig. 5.60. Anthony McCall, *Partial Cone* (1974). Schematic drawing. Ink on graph paper, 35.5 cm × 21.6 cm, 14 in × 8½ in.
Courtesy of Anthony McCall.

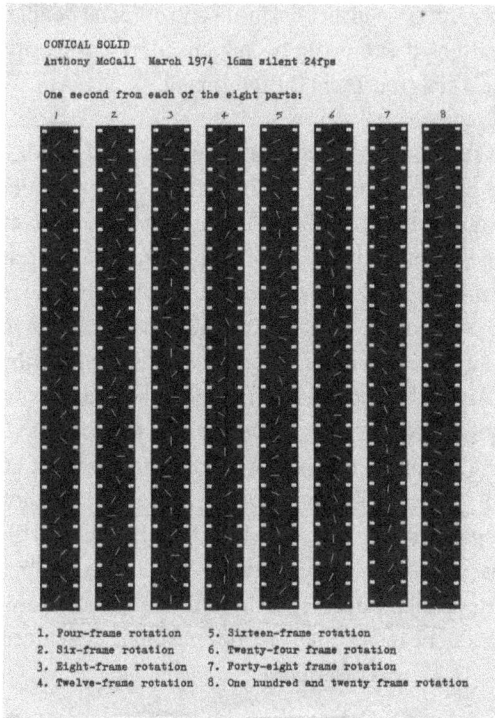

Fig. 5.61. Anthony McCall, *Conical Solid* (1974). Twenty-four frames (one second) from each of the film's eight parts. Photocopy and Wite-Out on paper, 27.9 cm × 21.6 cm, 11 in × 8½ in.
Courtesy of Anthony McCall.

than the more angular diagonal "X" of the earlier sections. Finally, in *Cone of Variable Volume* (1974), a complete circle, again forming a cone in space, expands and contracts in varying rhythms across the film's 10-minute duration. McCall achieved the effect simply by raising and lowering the camera on the animation stand so that the circle grows or shrinks relative to the frame. Expanded into three dimensions, the movement suggests breathing, a connotation to which McCall would return in his second iteration of solid light films beginning in 2004.

The specific historical circumstances of the LFMC, in dialogue with North American avant-garde cinema but distanced from it geographically, mediated the experimental film world's influence on McCall in a curious way. McCall has said that films like *Wavelength* and *The Flicker* influenced him indirectly, through descriptions he read in David Curtis's book *Experimental Cinema*, years before he was finally able to see them:

It was a surprise to me when I finally saw *Wavelength*, because it didn't have anything like the precision and cleanliness I had assumed from Curtis's description. It stopped and started; it jumped; light came in and out; and people arrived and left. It's quite funny to think that one can be influenced by a description of something which doesn't accurately represent the thing itself.[113]

This is a theme that runs through historical accounts of the LFMC and British avant-garde cinema more generally, of British filmmakers creatively misinterpreting landmark films based on discursive models of them rather than direct encounters. A. L. Rees, for example, has argued that several English avant-garde filmmakers made "interestingly creative misreadings of Warhol as film-maker," having read about Warhol's films but not having seen them.[114] Given the combination of exaggeration, selection, and reduction in so many contemporaneous accounts of those films (a phenomenon exacerbated when Warhol removed the films from circulation in the early 1970s), British filmmakers were left with a simplified model of Warhol's cinema upon which they could build a new filmmaking practice. According to Rees, Le Grice found confirmation in Warhol's cinema of his own idea of materialist "shallow" cinematic time, a one-to-one correspondence between the length of the film and that of the pro-filmic event. Le Grice was apparently unaware that Warhol's silent films were meant to be projected at 16 frames per second, creating a "one-and-a half to one" correspondence, and in many cases were heavily edited. Working from this inadvertently refined idea of Warhol's films, Le Grice was inspired

to take an independent route on which he and others had already embarked. Duration became a hallmark of British Structural film, a "road not taken" by mainstream cinema or by the lyric direction in avant-garde film, but which linked it to the advanced arts in Europe and—by way of Snow and Frampton—back to the post-Warholian film avant-garde in North America.[115]

Thus, while inaccurate or at least limited, the discursive versions of structural film in North America possessed a neat, schematic quality that helped account for the formal reductiveness of British work. This quality nicely characterizes the apparent simplicity and abstraction of McCall's films, which extract and thereby make more readily apparent what McCall would call "presuppositions behind film as an art form" in reference to *Long Film for Ambient Light*. McCall himself has alluded to this: "What I ultimately admired about [*Wavelength* and *Empire*] was their conceptual clarity," an impression he had formed from reading about those films, and which would be dramatically altered when he saw them in New York some time later.[116]

That McCall and other English avant-garde filmmakers were influenced, albeit in this mediated way, by Snow, Conrad, and Warhol will come as no surprise.

[113] MacDonald, "Anthony McCall," p. 163.
[114] Rees, *A History of Experimental Film and Video*, p. 77.
[115] Ibid.
[116] McCall, "*Line Describing a Cone* and Related Films," p. 59.

But Brakhage must also be mentioned here as a major influence. While the metaphysical flights in many of Brakhage's writings ran entirely against the grain of the more literal-minded materialism of British filmmakers, and his self-identification with Abstract Expressionist painting would have been seen by them as a capitulation, other aspects of his film practice were appealing. A better way to put this is that Brakhage's body of work and his writings, particularly his seminal 1963 text *Metaphors on Vision*, were subject to competing interpretations across the late 1960s and 1970s, taken alternatively as foil and important precedent for materialist filmmaking. Between 1966 and 1974, for example, Michelson's critical assessments of Brakhage's work were both positive and negative: skeptical of Brakhage's appeal to Abstract Expressionism, appreciative of his redefinition of filmic time and assault upon narrative. Michelson cited Brakhage as the major figure of the lyrical mode that anti-illusionist "intellectual" cinema turned away from, and, later, as one of the initiators of that anti-illusionist cinema.[117] Rees similarly conceives of Brakhage's importance for the LFMC in terms of anti-illusionism, though situating his work specifically in relation to British avant-garde cinema's intensive interrogation of literal space:

> The LFMC—in the spirit of Deren and Brakhage as it happens—was committed to film as an independent art form. The conditions of making and projecting film were taken to be internal aspects of the art form, to be investigated as its major content ... New roles were explored for maker, for viewer, and for the space—the viewing space, be it cinema or installation, live performance or film projection—which stands between them.[118]

This move is unusual, as Brakhage did not make expanded cinema and pursued a rather different form of spectatorial engagement than the one implied by Rees. But a passage from *Metaphors on Vision*, one that surely would have grabbed McCall's attention, is suggestive. In one of many diatribes against Hollywood's illusionistic duping of the passive audience, Brakhage turns his attention to the projector beam itself, hoping viewers will follow his lead. For the viewer no longer taken in by film's deceptions,

> the very comet of its overhead throw from projector to screen will intrigue you so deeply that its fingering play will move integrally with what's reflected, a comet-tail integrity which would lead back finally to the film's creator. I am meaning, simply, that the rhythms of change in the beam of illumination which now goes

---

[117] For elaboration on this pattern in Michelson's writings on Brakhage, see Walley, "Experimental Cinema's Elusive Illusion," pp. 244–245.

[118] A. L. Rees, "Locating the LFMC: The First Decade in Context," in Webber, ed., *Shoot Shoot Shoot: The First Decade of the London Filmmakers' Cooperative and British Avant-Garde Film, 1966–76* (London: Lux, 2002), p. 8.

entirely over the heads of the audience would, in the work of art, contain in itself some quality of a spiritual experience.[119]

Here Brakhage's anti-illusionism leads to the possibility of a three-dimensional cinema. Following this line of reasoning, Brakhage spoke of a new form that he believed was "appearing possible": utilizing "the projector as creative instrument with the film show a kind of performance."[120] This variant of anti-illusionism forecasts the solid light films and, more to the point, the activation of the exhibition space by expanded cinema.

More systematic theorizations of Brakhage's newly alert film viewer would follow on both sides of the Atlantic. The major account of a strain of filmmaking that engages the cognitive faculties of the spectator is Gidal's essay "Theory and Definition of Structural/Materialist Film." In the introduction, Gidal sets forth the central project, as he saw it, of structural-materialist film:

> In Structural/Materialist film, the in/film (not in/frame) and film/viewer material relations, and the relations of the film's structure, are primary to any representational content. The structuring aspects and the attempt to decipher the structure and anticipate/recorrect it, to clarify and analyse the production-process of the specific image at any specific moment, are the root concern of Structural/Materialist film.[121]

For Gidal, viewing such a film was a matter of apprehending the procedures of its production and, at the same time, the very cognitive processes through which that apprehension took place. References to this apperceptive experience appear throughout the writings of British filmmakers. Roger Hammond's notes on Mike Legget's film *Shepard's Bush* (1971) in the LFMC distribution catalogue speak of a "unique correspondence" between film and viewer, "one that calls for real attention, interaction, and anticipation/correction, a change for the audience from being a voyeur to that of being a participant."[122] In his program notes for a 1973 screening, Mike Dunford wrote, "My films are not about ideas, or aesthetics, or systems, or mathematics, but are about film, film-making, and film-viewing, and the interaction and intervention of intentive self-conscious reasoning in that context."[123]

Elaborating on his category of structural film, Sitney posited a subgenre of sorts, which he called the "participatory film." "Several filmmakers extended their aspirations for an unmediated cinema which would directly reflect or induce states of mind which first generated the Structural film, into a participatory form which addressed

---

[119] Stan Brakhage, *Metaphors on Vision*, extract reprinted in Sitney, ed., *The Avant-Garde Film*, pp. 125–126.

[120] Ibid., p. 126.

[121] Gidal, "Theory and Definition of Structural/Materialist Film," p. 1.

[122] In Webber, ed., *Shoot Shoot Shoot*, p. 3.

[123] Ibid.

itself to the decision-making and logical faculties of the viewer."[124] For Sitney, however, and indeed for most critics and filmmakers who invoked this kind of film/viewer exchange, "participation" referred to mental rather than physical activity. But the leap to an expanded sense of this concept, wherein the film organized viewer activity in space and prompted physical participation, would have been easy to make. This was the leap McCall took, in the spirit of Brakhage's paean to the projector beam though honed by his own distinctive conceptions of viewer activity in duration and the materialist bent of the LFMC. The solid light films make the temporal forms of structural film a feature of the exhibition space itself, creating spatial analogs for the cognitive activity that in Gidal's and Sitney's models operates solely in time. The films produce correspondences between the transformations of the projector beam and the actions of the spectator. As *Line Describing a Cone* evolves into an arc and then a cone, the possible spatial arrangements of the audience around or within the beam also change. At the beginning of the film the beam is only a thin line of light, limiting viewers more or less to the choice of which side to stand on. As the film continues, the changes in the beam's shape increase the range of options. The viewer may stand outside the arc or within it, and choices of distance become more meaningful. Closer to the projector, the cone is very small, limiting viewers' interaction with it to passing their hands through it, which the seeming solidity and tangibility of the light makes very tempting. Farther from the projector the diameter of the cone's circular base is much wider, and interaction is no longer limited to touch but can engage the entire body. Where the beam hits a wall the projected circle delimits a space within which several viewers can stand simultaneously, looking back toward the projector and observing other spectators passing in and out of the cone's interior. As these descriptions should make clear, the solid light films do not disclose themselves fully to the immobile spectator. The unfolding of each film is as much a function of the viewer's movements as the projector beam's.

After the four variations of the cone films in 1973 and 1974, McCall turned to new solid light forms and new permutations of viewer activity, which in turn entailed moving further away from standard cinematic exhibition. As in the fire performances, McCall began greatly extending duration to see how this move varied the kinds of experiences spectators had. *Long Film for Four Projectors* (1974) replaced the cones and arcs of the earlier films with a single trapezoidal blade, seen on the film frame as a diagonal white line and experienced in projection as a moving wall of light (fig. 5.62). *Long Film for Four Projectors* consists of four 45-minute reels of 16mm film, each reel loaded onto one of four projectors arranged in a wide square on the floor of a long rectangular space. The projectors face into the room, their beams crossing one another as they sweep through the space. The image on each film is the same, a thin white line extending diagonally from the bottom of the black frame to the top, moving slowly from one side of the

---

[124] Sitney, *Visionary Film*, p. 392.

Fig. 5.62. Anthony McCall, *Long Film for Four Projectors* (1974). Installation view (2003). Photograph by Hank Graber. Courtesy of Anthony McCall.

frame to the other, traversing the frame over the course of the film. Each reel is run through the projector in four ways: from head (the beginning of the reel) to tail (the end), from tail to head, from head to tail with the film twisted (which flips the image left to right), and from tail to head with the film twisted (fig. 5.63). Each variation changes the horizontal and vertical orientation and direction of the line, and every reel is put through each of these four permutations twice in different orders, a complete cycle of the film lasting six hours. The projected walls of light slowly carve out wedges of space from their respective corners of the room, intersecting one another and articulating the space in different ways as they idly sweep back and forth. McCall describes these four movements as causing viewers to "feel pushed in different directions ... This experience is paradoxical, since light—even 'solid' light like this—is, of course, insubstantial."[125] As in all the solid light films, the spectators are mobile and interact with the projected forms, but in this case their mode of attention is affected considerably by the film's extreme duration. *Long Film for Four Projectors* was designed not for traditional cinematic screenings with scheduled start and end times, but as an ongoing gallery installation that spectators could enter and exit at will, a return to the significantly expanded temporal scale of the conditions. McCall specified that the film could run for an

[125] McCall, "*Line Describing a Cone* and Related Films," p. 55.

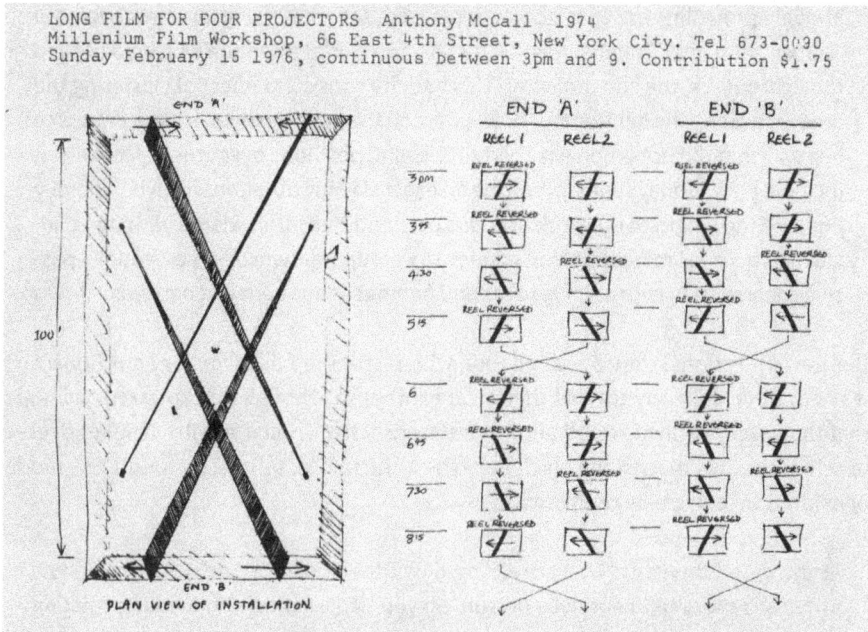

```
LONG FILM FOR FOUR PROJECTORS  Anthony McCall  1974
Millenium Film Workshop, 66 East 4th Street, New York City. Tel 673-0090
Sunday February 15 1976, continuous between 3pm and 9. Contribution $1.75
```

Fig. 5.63. Anthony McCall, *Long Film for Four Projectors* (1974). Announcement for the Millennium Film Workshop showing (1976).
Courtesy of Anthony McCall.

indeterminate length, extending well past the six hours of a single cycle into days or weeks. Each spectator's experience of the film's temporal and spatial unfolding is therefore unique and subject to their own choices of where to stand and how long to remain. In the longer versions of *Landscape for Fire*, the duration and physical size of the work prevented it from being comprehended as an object with sharply drawn temporal or spatial boundaries. The long duration, slow and subtle image variations, and relatively large expanse of *Long Film for Four Projectors* function similarly. The work also lacks the predictable, quasi-narrative event structure of *Line Describing a Cone*, whose arc the viewer can recognize quite early even if the title did not alert them to it in advance, and whose movement toward a completed cone generates anticipation, even something like suspense, and eventually closure. These qualities are deliberately jettisoned in *Long Film for Four Projectors*.

Though designed for a gallery space, *Long Film for Four Projectors* was devised specifically in relation to notions of cinematic exhibition and spectatorship that were elaborated within the context of avant-garde cinema, and as such envisioned as a critical intervention in the ideologies of *both* theater *and* gallery. In a production notebook, McCall articulated a desire to create a film-viewing situation that militated against a particular audience formation that he found ideologically suspect at the time, one that had obtained even in his earlier solid light films:

Though providing an enormously increased set of viewing options over the "screen" film, the "Cone" series still dictated an axis of attention which pointed to the light source, the film projector. This had the consistent effect of clustering the audience along the light-beam. Now, I wanted the light-beam to occupy the space in a way that did not emphasize certain viewing positions over others. Most films, including the "Cone" series, prescribe an exact viewing duration which is generally equal to the length of the work. It is this conventional form, shared with other social and political structures that creates the group "audience," an essentially passive congregation with a single focus and homogeneous behavior patterns.[126]

But the oppositional stance McCall took with respect to *Long Film for Four Projectors* was not directed solely toward theatrical exhibition. Though he expressed the hope that the gallery context would allow for a more active spectator with a higher degree of self-awareness than in the black box of the cinema, he ultimately found this mode of exhibition "extremely problematic":

At the time I thought that by breaking down the audience one would somehow arrive at a more self-conscious person. So you had a series of individuals relating to the work as they came in, separated from one another in both time and space. And it is probably true that people alone can give a different kind of concentration; this concentration relates to yourself and your own ideas in relation to the work. But that is precisely what every art gallery does—it separates people in time and space.[127]

McCall was thus as skeptical of the gallery's routines of spectatorship as he was of the film theater's. His ambivalence toward the former would resurface when *Line Describing a Cone* was reconfigured as a looped installation of indeterminate duration during *Into the Light*.

In the meantime, however, McCall's experiences with *Long Film for Four Projectors* and *Long Film for Ambient Light*, the last of the solid light films, led him to rethink his stance on the reception structures of traditional performance. In a 1976 interview on the political possibilities of formalist film, McCall spoke of "an important social function fulfilled by people meeting together in a group to confront a work, even as an audience."[128] This group, which McCall had only two years before called an "essentially passive congregation" might, after all, be redeemable. In an artistic environment in which political theory played an increasingly central role, the idea of the audience resonated with that of collective action, compared to the dispersal of individuals that McCall had seen happen in *Long Film for Four Projectors*. The audience

---

[126] Excerpted in Gautam Dasgupta, "Interview: Anthony McCall (Formalist Cinema and Politics)," *PAJ* 1, no. 3 (Winter 1977), p. 52.

[127] Ibid., pp. 55–56.

[128] Ibid., p. 56.

he most had in mind at the time was other artists, whom he believed needed to critically engage their place in society and interface with other kinds of professional communities (McCall specifically mentioned medicine and mental health). His next two films, *Argument* (in collaboration with Andrew Tyndall) and *Sigmund Freud's Dora* (1979, in collaboration with Tyndall, Jane Weinstock, and Claire Pajaczkowska) were densely theoretical film-texts designed to be screened in small workshops attended by other artists. Both were single-screen films shot and edited in 16mm and projected in the conventional manner. The conception of the audience, however, was quite different, and represented the last vestige of McCall's work in expanded cinematic forms. In an introduction to the published version of the script of *Sigmund Freud's Dora*, Pajaczkowska wrote that its project was to undermine the tripartite institution of filmmaker/critic/audience in a film's deployment. "We speak directly to an audience; not as an audience (in the sense of auditors), but addressing them as speakers, as actively engaged in 'speaking' the film and its politics."[129] The films, in other words, were vehicles for political discussion in which McCall and his collaborators participated with their audiences. The situation was analogous to the often collaborative participation of viewers of *Line Describing a Cone*, who invariably speak to each other during the film, sharing recommendations of good viewing positions and collectively enjoying the novel experience of light the film creates. *Argument* and *Sigmund Freud's Dora* transposed this group activity from the formal register to post-screening meetings in which the film was used as a catalyst for political discussion in the manner of a book group.

From 1980 to 2003, McCall made no films, and though he worked as a graphic designer for galleries, museums, and other artists, he did not exhibit any of his own work. The inclusion of *Line Describing a Cone* in the Whitney's Museum's exhibition *Into the Light* in 2002 brought new attention to his films and energized him to revisit the solid light film cycle, beginning with *Doubling Back* (2003), which would be the last solid light film made in 16mm (fig. 5.64). Additional works, including *Turning Under, Turning Round*, and *Breath* (all 2005) were made digitally, and have been sold in limited editions by galleries rather than distributed by film cooperatives. McCall has also tended to frame his recent work in terms of sculpture, a move that its exhibition in galleries in the form of looped installations supports (fig. 5.65). *Line Describing a Cone*, on the other hand, remains a canonical work of avant-garde cinema, commonly shown in experimental film exhibitions and university film courses, its circulation in this context made possible by the fact that it can be rented from co-ops like Canyon Cinema, the Filmmakers' Cooperative, and Light Cone (along with the lesser-known *Conical Solid*). McCall's career in the moving image, then, and his identity as an artist, is marked by a curious bifurcation, at once historical and institutional.

---

[129] In Claire Pajaczkowska, Anthony McCall, Andrew Tyndall, Jane Weinstock, and Jay St. Collective, "*Dora* Script: (A Case of Mistaken Identity)," *Framework: The Journal of Cinema and Media*, 15/17 (Summer 1981), p. 75.

Fig. 5.64. Anthony McCall, *Doubling Back* (2003). Installation view, LAC, Lugano, 2015.
Photograph by Stefania Beretta. Courtesy of Anthony McCall.

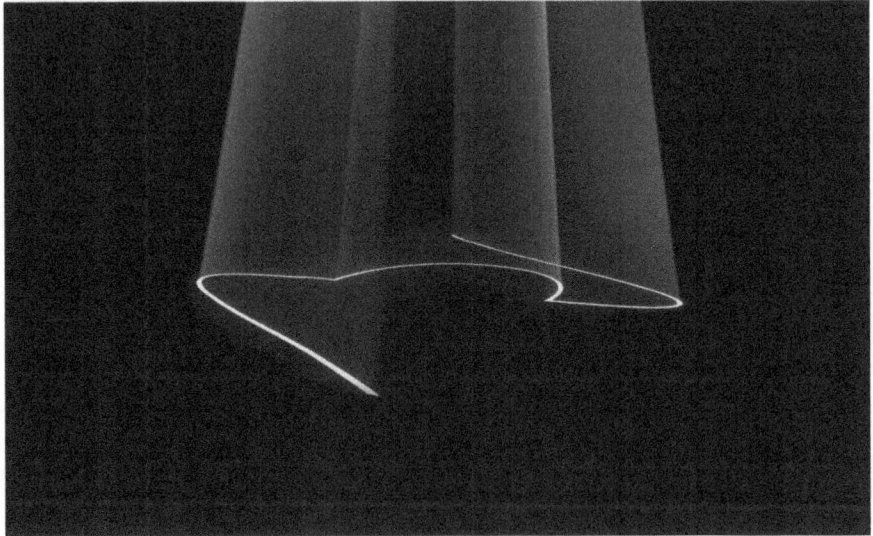

Fig. 5.65. Anthony McCall, *Breath III* (2005). Installation view at Hangar Bicocca, Milan, 2009.
Photograph by Giulio Buono. Courtesy of Anthony McCall.

That strange phrase "artist and filmmaker," commonly used to describe McCall, signals the split, which McCall himself has addressed:

> In recent years, the art world has paid a lot of attention to work in film and video, yet the dichotomy between avant-garde film (and video) makers, and artists "working in film/video," still seems to be with us. Despite the important role being played by the museums like the Whitney in bridging this divide, the two worlds sometimes seem like Crick and Watson's double helix, spiraling closely around one another without ever quite meeting.[130]

The reference to DNA is apt, implying that McCall himself, "artist and filmmaker," is a hybrid being with both the art and film worlds in his blood. But indeed, the Anthony McCall of the art world and the Anthony McCall of the film world don't quite meet, and that fact is indicative of a larger phenomenon, which can be traced to the period that McCall began his artistic career but which has become much more significant in the last two decades.

Black & White/Boxes & Cubes: Variations on a Theme II

Into the Light brought new attention to the very subjects at the core of this chapter: the ontological and historical place of film installations, and the relationship between avant-garde film and the art world, cinema and sculpture, the black box and the white cube. Though McCall had made *Line Describing a Cone* to be viewed from start to finish as in a conventional film screening, for *Into the Light* it was reconfigured as a looped installation that spectators could enter and exit on their own time, so to speak. While he approved of this change, McCall expressed concern that it would mute the film's temporal dimension. As visitors cycled in and out of the gallery where the film was installed they were at least as likely to take it as a static light sculpture as an evolving cinematic form. Iles's interpretation of the film further shifted its reception toward broadly sculptural terms: "*Line Describing a Cone* combined the phenomenological reductivism of Minimalism with the participatory inclusiveness of Happenings to create an ephemeral projection event."[131] And because the film was three-dimensional, it was "a complete reversal of conventional cinematic viewing."[132] Invoking conventional cinema rather than the avant-garde film culture of the 1970s with which McCall's film was in dialogue, Iles reads it as sculptural rather than cinematic. This suggests that certain aesthetic qualities or effects—say,

---

[130] McCall, "*Line Describing a Cone* and Related Films," p. 48.
[131] Iles, "Between the Still and Moving Image," p. 45.
[132] Ibid.

three-dimensionality, or the acknowledgement of the actual screening space—belonged to one art form and not the other.

Iles made a similar move with Sharits's *Shutter Interface*. In that locational work, four projectors in a row (reduced to three for *Into the Light*) face a long gallery wall, each projecting film loops made entirely of single frames of pure color (see fig. 5.30). The projectors are arranged so that their frames overlap on the opposite wall, the projected fields of flickering color merging at their edges to make still more colors, the entire spectacle accompanied by a throbbing, high-pitched soundtrack that matches the 24-frame-per-second rhythm of the visuals. Though Iles acknowledged that Sharits intended his locational films as models of the essentially cinematic, her reading of *Shutter Interface* skews much more toward the realm of the other arts. The linked frames of color recall both Minimalism (à la Donald Judd) and color field painting, and even the obvious preoccupation with filmic materiality and cinematic infrastructure are expressed, according to Iles, in "the structure of music"; she takes the flickering colors, percussive soundtrack, and lateral arrangement of the screens as signs of cinema's inherent musicality.[133]

It was around *Into the Light* that the specter of a divide between the gallery and experimental film worlds, or between "artists" and "filmmakers," was raised, mostly by filmmakers and film critics. At stake was—and is—the visibility of avant-garde film in the history of "the projected image in American art," which was the subtitle of *Into the Light*. A major exhibition of moving image art covering the years 1964–1977, a period almost exactly coterminous with the first two waves of expanded cinema, made little mention of avant-garde film. Those films by artists who had explicitly situated their work within that context and explicitly couched it in film-ontological language—for example Sharits and McCall—were re-oriented into a history of the moving image as sculptural, post-minimal, or intermedial, since they did not adhere to the aesthetic and exhibition norms of conventional cinema. George Baker's claim that McCall's solid light films "proclaimed that it was the essence of cinema to have no essence" gave voice to this very idea. The cinematic-ness of such work was illegible to this viewpoint, a problem made most evident in the rigidity of the categories of black box and white cube, which implied that cinematic work occupying spaces other than the theater was not, in fact, cinema. It was not clear what place there was in this framework for a film culture built upon the belief in cinema as a specific art form with its own histories, institutions, and aesthetics.

Into the Light was intended to provide historical context for the proliferation of moving image work in the gallery and museum, background to the work of artists like Matthew Barney, Douglas Gordon, Shirin Neshat, or Pierre Huyghe, who already enjoyed a much higher profile and commanded much higher fees than any experimental filmmaker could ever have hoped for. Many filmmakers and critics in the experimental film world already felt that their own work, along with the history to

---

[133] Ibid., pp. 46–47.

which it belonged, was occluded by the phenomenon of "artists' film and video." The international attention *Into the Light* received exacerbated the relative lack of attention historically granted to experimental film even in academia. The implicit alignment of all forms of cinema under the heading of the black box rendered critical differences between the ideals of exhibition among cinematic modes invisible. This invisibility was most pronounced for the already marginalized film culture of experimental cinema. Pointing to a series of major exhibitions that revisited the question of film's relationship to the other arts, all around the turn of the millennium, Barry Schwabsky called attention to a troubling irony:

> What has been peculiar in about this recuperation of art's relationship to film is that, in terms of the "film" or "cinema" part of the equation, it has consistently sidelined the kinds of film that would on the face of it appear most relevant to late-modern and contemporary artistic practice—that is, the various forms of avant-garde, experimental, poetic, materialist and structuralist cinema that have eschewed the conventions of the narrative feature. Instead, the focus has been precisely on narrative features, primarily of the Hollywood variety, secondarily those that arose in the wake of Godard, Antonioni, Fassbinder, and so on.[134]

By this view, artists' film and video's framing out of avant-garde cinema simultaneously elevates commercial filmmaking, if inadvertently. The increased spectacularity of major moving image installations, works of "high gloss and bombast" in Erika Balsom's words, is the sign of the contemporary art world's orientation toward mainstream cinema as both subject matter and institutional model.[135]

Elsewhere I have identified gallery-based moving image art and experimental cinema as two different modes of film practice in the avant-garde.[136] This distinction is not perceived neutrally, as simply a difference, but as a set of contrasting and even opposed value systems. "'Artists' films' ... you know what that means? That means painters who dabble in filmmaking and their films are 'art' because they're artists."[137] This was Ken Jacobs's opinion of the split between "artists" and "filmmakers" in 1986. Finding similar judgments against the art world within the provinces of avant-garde cinema is easy. Many filmmakers and critics in that world have taken umbrage at the high profile and economic success of "artists who make films" relative to experimental cinema's marginal status. They have rejected the economic model of the art world, in which films, videos, and moving image installations are made into marketable objects through enforcement of an arbitrary scarcity—limiting editions of works that are in fact endlessly reproducible. Some have claimed that moving image art

---

[134] Barry Schwabsky, "Art, Film, Video: Separation or Synthesis?," in Danino and Maziére, eds., *The Undercut Reader*, p. 2.

[135] Balsom, *Exhibiting Cinema in Contemporary Art*, p. 11.

[136] Walley, "Modes of Film Practice in the Avant-Garde," pp. 182–199.

[137] Lindley Hanlon and Tony Pipolo, "Interview with Ken and Flo Jacobs," *Millennium Film Journal* 16/17/18 (Fall–Winter 1986–1987), p. 51.

merely re-treads the innovations of earlier avant-garde filmmakers, or, like Hamlyn, that film and digital installations do not meaningfully utilize the space of the gallery, much less interrogate it.

My distinction between these two modes of film practice was meant as a framework for historical and theoretical work on the relationship between cinema and the other arts. It traces out institutional contours that, while fairly broad, sharpen the blunt instruments of black box/white cube. It should be needless to say that there are finer grained points to be made about the relationship between the two modes, and exceptions to the split between them. Critics of my argument are quick to point these out. In her exceptional study of cinema's entrance into the gallery, Erika Balsom argued against too clean a break between modes:

> Though Walley's distinctions serve an important heuristic value, they are lacking in historical specificity ... there is considerable evidence to suggest that the institutional boundaries between these two modes of production are in the process of breaking down as increasing numbers of experimental filmmakers move into the structures of distribution and exhibition proper to the gallery.[138]

Balsom adds that a number of experimental filmmakers have made film and video installations, naming Peggy Ahwesh, Jonas Mekas, and Martin Arnold. Balsom's corrective is well taken, and she is right to muddy both the contemporary and historical distinctions I made. But some qualifications are in order. The first is that the movement of individual artists between two different "structures of distribution and exhibition" does not necessarily entail that those structures are any less stable, only that some individuals have found ways to work between them. And it must be kept in mind that experimental filmmakers like Le Grice, Eatherley, Raban, Sharits, and McCall made installations or space-based film works outside the gallery context, challenging the idea that these were "proper" only to the structures of the art world.

The second qualification is that many contemporary experimental film venues, attuned to the history I have outlined in this chapter, are as accommodating of installation and other spatial cinematic work as they are of traditional single-screen projection. By the same token, traditional art galleries, especially some more recently established ones, showcase experimental film works qua experimental film works (not as "moving image art" or "artists' film"), in the context of avant-garde film history, with which many gallerists are increasingly aware. Brooklyn's Microscope Gallery, co-founded by artists and curators Elle Burchill and Andrea Monti, is a case in point, and one of the epicenters of contemporary East Coast expanded cinema work (Mirza and Butler's no.w.here lab in London and Artists' Television Access in San Francisco are similar venues.) Two of the filmmakers Balsom mentions, Ahwesh and Mekas, exhibited installations at Microscope, which represents and has presented work by

---

[138] Balsom, *Exhibiting Cinema in Contemporary Art*, p. 21.

filmmakers like Eros, Schlemowitz, Liotta, and Bauer, and hosted numerous installations and performances by Iimura. Founded in 2010 because Burchill and Monti
were "frustrated at the underrepresentation of time-based arts—film, video and digital art, sound, performance, among others—in art contexts, especially in commercial galleries," Microscope has shown moving image work side by side with work in
painting and sculpture, and has been particularly dedicated to expanded cinema.[139]
Its 2016–2017 series *Dreamlands: Expanded* was an adjunct of the Whitney Museum's
massive exhibition *Dreamlands: Immersive Cinema & Art, 1905–2016."* The purview of "Dreamlands" was at least as expansive as that of the earliest writers on expanded cinema like Renan and Youngblood, extending the history of "immersive
cinema" to 1905, and incorporating "works in installation, drawing, 3-D environments, sculpture, performance, painting, and online space."[140] Most of the artists
represented in the Whitney's exhibition did not self-identify as filmmakers, and in
many cases had never made films—the rider "and Art" communicating the idea that
cinema was but one small part of the history *Dreamlands* envisioned. Microscope's
Dreamlands: Expanded, on the other hand, ironically (and no doubt knowingly) *contracted* the range of moving image work on view, privileging more film- and cine-
centric expanded pieces by Iimura, Schlemowitz, Le Grice, Jacobs, Eros and Liotta
(reuniting as the Mediamystics), Barbara Hammer, and the expanded cinema ensemble Optipus (whose fluctuating membership has included Eros, Schlemowitz,
Bauer, and the artist-filmmakers Sarah Halpern, Lary 7, Simon Liu, Rachael Guma,
Kenneth Zoran Curwood, Tim Geraghty, Alison Nguyen, and several others). All of
this is simply to say that a filmmaker making installations need not leave the film
world to find audiences and accommodating exhibition venues for their work.

Finally, while there is no doubt that some filmmakers have been able to operate
successfully in both the film and art worlds, the idea that experimental cinema is not
only different from but more to the point oppositional to the ideology of the art world
persists, one of many discourses through which avant-garde film culture continues to
define itself. In her important ethnographic study of experimental film published in
2010, Kathryn Ramey outlined the major themes of this discourse:

> Presenting your work in a gallery takes away the power of the filmmaker to con-
> trol the viewer's experience because gallery work, like artwork, is treated like an
> object that can be scanned or read quickly and passed by. Filmmakers' work is
> about duration and experience of that duration. Thus art world presentation of
> film or video is often less than satisfactory. When a film is identified as an art ob-
> ject, viewed in a gallery or museum setting, the experience of viewing it changes

---

[139] Interview with Elle Burchill and Andrea Monti, on the Collecteurs website, https://www.collecteurs.
com/interview/elle-burchill-and-andrea-monti-of-microscope-gallery.
[140] From the Whitney Museum of American Art website: https://whitney.org/Exhibitions/ Dreamlands
(accessed Sept. 4, 2017).

temporally and experientially. It is removed from the discursive space of the avant-garde community.[141]

The last point is worth lingering on. What matters more than the physical location of a work in either an art or cinema institution is the discursive space it occupies. The individual filmmaker has some control over the situation of a film installation within certain discourses and not others, though a major art institution like the Whitney has the power to shift the discursive terrain, as in the case of the re-reading of *Line Describing a Cone* and *Shutter Interface* during *Into the Light*. But the "discursive space of the avant-garde film community" can be brought into the gallery, laid atop the physical space of that venue. The question is, to what extent can the discursive spaces of art world and experimental cinema cohabitate? This strikes me as prerequisite to a genuine breaking down of the institutional boundaries between the gallery and experimental film worlds.

With all this in mind, and by way of a conclusion, consider two recent film installations by artists who identify with the avant-garde film community but have also found success working in the gallery. In Mirza and Butler's installation *The Glass Stare* (2005), two side-by-side 16mm projectors on pedestals project black and white close-ups of faces onto two small screens suspended a few feet away. One film is negative, the other positive, and both images are projected upside down. The screen images are also caught by two circular mirrors mounted on a third pedestal facing the projectors. The mirrors invert the images and reflect them back onto a third screen that hangs in the center of the space, equidistant from the mirrors and projectors. Here the negative and positive images are superimposed into an odd composite of different faces and hues fading in and out (fig. 5.66). Though *The Glass Stare* does not possess the isomorphic form of *Filmische Wahrheiten*, the logic of its spatial arrangement must be puzzled out by the viewer, especially because the space must be completely dark for installation to work. Tracing the sources of the unusual images on the central screen—from that screen, to the mirrors, to the other two screens, to the projectors—takes time and movement through the installation's architecture, recalling the extension of a "participatory" cinema into physical activity in three dimensions.

The Glass Stare references the historical intersection of painting, photography, and cinema; its mirror inversion of upside-down images stands for the *camera obscura*, particularly its use by painters to create more naturalistic imagery. This is envisioned as the starting point for an art-historical trajectory running through painting and photography toward the moving image, "the move towards photo-realism within painting (Vermeer and Caravaggio) and paintings relationship to cinema (Andy Warhol's screen tests)."[142] This teleological metahistory recalls Bazin and, in

[141] Kathryn Ramey, "Economics of the Film Avant-Garde: Networks and Strategies in the Circulation of Films, Ideas, and People," *Jump Cut: A Review of Contemporary Media*, no. 52 (Summer 2010), https://www.ejumpcut.org/archive/jc52.2010/rameyExperimentalFilm/index.html, n.p.

[142] Karen Mirza and Brad Butler, artists' statement accompanying *The Glass Stare*, "Lumen," Leeds City Museum, 2006, n.p.

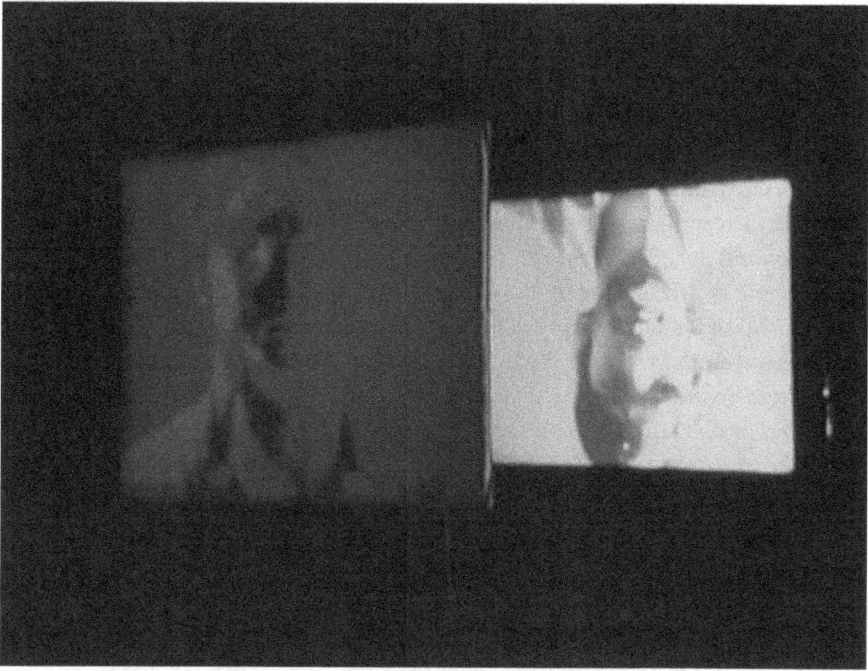

Fig. 5.66. Noor Afshan Mirza and Brad Butler, *The Glass Stare* (2005). Detail. Lumen, Leeds City Museum, 2005.

a different way, Hollis Frampton: "I venture to suggest that a time may come when the whole history of art will become no more than a footnote to the history of film"[143] This statement is from Frampton's infamous 1973 letter to then–Museum of Modern Art film curator Donald Richie, in response to Richie's proposal of a retrospective of Frampton's films for which the MOMA would not pay. Frampton's response, in the form of a savage critique of the implications behind Richie's offer, included this reversal of art history. By implication (and *only* by implication) it was also a reversal of the power differential between the art world and the experimental film community. As such, Frampton's letter stands as a minor landmark in the history of the relationship between filmmakers and the gallery, upon which *The Glass Stare* is a meditation. Mirza's own comments on the work go some way towards confirming this:

> It's almost an undoing of photography, of the photographic moments of fixing or embalming a moment in time. My interest in this got me excited about making a dematerialized art object, how to fuck up the system of commodification by making a dematerialized art object. And that's why expanded cinema is still in that

---

[143] Hollis Frampton, "Letter to Donald Richie," in Jenkins, ed., *On the Camera Arts and Consecutive Matters*, p. 160.

awkward space and causes the same headache for museums, trusts, foundations, collectors.[144]

While the physical space of a gallery is necessary for *The Glass Stare*, the discourses and routines of that space are cast by Mirza as anathema to the values the installation embodies. Expanded cinema, by Mirza's account, "fucks up" this system as it projects the ideals of avant-garde cinema into the world of art economics.

Gibson and Recoder's *Light Spill* (2005) enacts a similar reversal of the logic of film in the house of art, fucking up the gallery space in another, quite literal, way. *Light Spill* consists of a lone 16mm projector without a takeup reel, into which gallery attendants feed reel after reel of junked, de-accessioned film for the length of the installation. A sign on one wall instructs visitors to notify an attendant if the projector needs a new reel of film. The reels upon reels of film pile up in long, graceful loops around the base of the pedestal where the projector sits (fig. 5.67). If the installation runs long enough, the pile of film coils its way closer and closer to the projector and floods the room. Though the projector's lamp is turned on, the mechanisms in its gate that keep each film frame still in the instant it is projected are removed, resulting in an illegible cascade of blurred framelines and blobs of light. Any chance that a keen-eyed visitor might pick out a familiar frame and identify one of the films passing through the projector is even further diminished by the fact that *Light Spill* is intended for display in a well-lit gallery space, the rare example of a moving image installation actually requiring a truly white cube.

Light Spill plays out the nightmare of the conscientious film projectionist, charged not only with maintaining a clear image and acceptable sound levels but with preserving the filmstrip, protecting it from scratches and keeping it free of dirt. As such, it has prompted readings that see the work staging the death of film, or highlighting film's precariousness and resilience at the same time. As film gives way to digital, a work like *Light Spill*, according to Elena Gorfinkel, "posit[s] cinema's much-mourned decay as coincident with the resolute, stubborn recalcitrance of the film object's materiality."[145] The rising pile of celluloid suddenly resembles a living thing, according to Gorfinkel, who channels the organic metaphors of contemporary experimental cinema (and Gibson and Recoder specifically), "a vibrant refuse that refuses to remain dead."[146] Genevieve Yue offers a variation on this theme, seeing *Light Spill* as "sacrificing" film "with the purpose of liberating the idea of cinema."[147] Again, this speaks to an act of preservation, only by this reading of the idea of cinema rather than the material of film. Whether it is film's or cinema's life, or death, that *Light Spill* performs, there is another historical arc in which it intervenes. This is the history not of a medium but of institutions, of the entrance by experimental filmmakers into the

[144] Mirza and Butler, "On Expanded Cinema," p. 259.
[145] Gorfinkel, "At the End of Cinema, This Thing Called Film," n.p.
[146] Ibid.
[147] Genevieve Yue, "What Was Cinema," *La Furia Umana* 8 (2015), p. 69.

Fig. 5.67. Sandra Gibson and Luis Recoder, *Light Spill* (2005). 16mm film, modified 16mm projector, screen, dimensions variable. Installation view, *Celluloid: Tacita Dean, João Maria Gusmão & Pedro Paiva, Rosa Barba, Sandra Gibson & Luis Recoder*. EYE Film Museum, Amsterdam, The Netherlands, September 17, 2016–January 8, 2017. Photograph by Studio Hans Wilschut. Courtesy of the artists and EYE Film Museum.

gallery. That gallery is made into the staging ground for film's and cinema's continued existence, imagined in this work as an invasive species. This is less in reference to the installation's kudzu-like material overflow than to what *Light Spill* was intended to bring into the gallery conceptually, historically, and technologically. Gibson and Recoder's statement about the work inverts the values implied in the distinction between black box and white cube. The move from screening space to gallery, which has so often obscured the cinematic points of reference of installations by experimental filmmakers, is redefined. The white lights of the gallery illuminate cinema:

Film projectors and celluloid ... are deeply imbued with a history of viewership in the dark of the theater. To remove it from darkness is to flood this history and cast a certain illumination upon it. A certain exposure. Light spills in the shifting of film from its native darkness in enclosed chambers (*camera obscura*) to the uncanny openness and defamiliarized illumination of installation. We are exploring the shift, elaborating the displacement, recasting the light mechanics of a peculiar

estrangement of the medium. The art of cinema, yes. But more timely: the becoming cinema of art. That is the coming attraction for us.[148]

The phrase "the becoming cinema of art" replays Frampton's theme of art history
being absorbed by film. And in their punning use of the movie world argot "coming
attractions" for an installation, Gibson and Recoder re-cast the gallery space as a theater of operations into which cinema can expand without sacrificing its identity as
such. Gallery workers are required to become projectionists, and to re-spool the film
dumped on the floor when the installation ends; the room lights wash out the virtual
images projected against the wall in a reversal of the usual situation of moving image
installations in art spaces; the film projector, its internal mechanisms illuminated if
not actually externalized, can be examined as the black box of the digital projector
cannot.

These readings are admittedly partisan, though there is good evidence that *The
Glass Stare* and *Light Spill* are themselves partisan, each asserting the autonomy of
avant-garde cinema in a context that has at times been unable or unwilling to recognize it. Mirza and Butler's installation makes the gallery space into a black box, but
one completely re-articulated in the terms of experimental film by years of expanded
cinematic practices that cut the screening space to the measure of the film medium
rather than using it to make that medium vanish. Gibson and Recoder's piece brings
that process into the gallery, hijacking the white cube for the purposes of illuminating
cinema's distinctive forms of space and objecthood. The defamiliarization the artists
attribute to it finds its origins in the history of expanded cinema's various acts of re-
making the black box—multiplying and repositioning projectors and screens, tracing
out new trajectories of projection and movement, taking over and reshaping the space
of reception and the viewer's activities within it, and shifting cinematic space from the
representational to the real.

---

[148] Sandra Gibson and Luis Recoder, artists' statement, *Light Spill* (2005), n.p.

6

Cinema as Idea

> The *idea* of cinema, as much as or perhaps more than its concrete man-
> ifestations, has always pervaded the meaning we ascribe to the notion
> of *medium*. As an idea, cinema is a slippery, phantasmatic term, unteth-
> ered to the forms it temporarily inhabits. In the contemporary terrain of
> the *post*—post-medium, post-cinema—the idea of the cinematic medium
> becomes all the more ghostly, a spectral vision of the past in the present.
> Cinema no longer means film, its former material substrate, nor does it
> convincingly mean *something else*. This is not because film has been
> replaced by the digital, but because the medium never was completely
> film in the first place.
>
> **—Genevieve Yue (2015)**

> Movies always happen, and take place, in your imagination.
>
> **—Tony Conrad (2008)**

Cinema as Idea as Idea

The May 8, 1969, entry in Jonas Mekas's regular *Village Voice* column "Movie Journal"
was one sentence long: "Not to make films is as important as to make films," in quotes,
the statement attributed to Buddha.[1] Nothing in Mekas's previous or subsequent
entries—lambasting the underground press for ignoring experimental cinema and
a note on structural film, respectively—provided any context for this remark, though
looking a little further back we find clues. In the June 23, 1966, entry, entitled "On the
Tactile Interactions in Cinema, Or Creation with Your Total Body," Mekas recounted
an exchange with the organizers of that year's Cannes Film Festival, who had solicited
Mekas's recommendations of American experimental films they could screen as part
of the festival's recently established "International Critics' Week" program. According
to Mekas, the Cannes organizers had asked him to "ship to them some films." His response, at least as he paraphrased it in his column, was as follows:

> No—I wrote them—your thinking is all wrong. You are still thinking that all that's
> good and new and exciting in cinema can be wrapped up, canned, and shipped to

---

[1] Reprinted in Jonas Mekas and Gregory Smulewicz-Zucker, ed., *Movie Journal: The Rise of The New
American Cinema, 1959–1971*, 2nd ed. (New York: Columbia University Press, 2016), p. 351.

Cinema Expanded. Jonathan Walley, Oxford University Press (2020). © Oxford University Press.
DOI: 10.1093/oso/9780190938635.001.0001

you for "previewing": those days are come and gone. Some of us are making "film evenings," not "films," and you have to take to Cannes not only the "film" but the filmmaker and the equipment and, perhaps, technicians.[2]

Unfortunately, Mekas lamented, his recommendation was ignored, "and Cannes had another of their 'worst' years."

The "films" or "film evenings" Mekas had in mind were multi-screen and performative works by Andy Warhol, Robert Whitman, Harry Smith, and Barbara Rubin, all of whom had appeared in earlier "Movie Journal" entries on expanded cinema. "The film in the can isn't really the thing by itself," Mekas wrote on this occasion.[3] Perhaps his most striking assertion of this idea came in an entry dated June 25, 1964, entitled "Spiritualization of the Image." Recalling a series of screenings and performances of multi-screen films, film-less films, and works of pure light, Mekas concluded:

[W]e are only one step from the absolute cinema, cinema of our mind. For what is cinema really, if not images, dreams, and visions? We take one more step, and we give up all movies and we become movies: We sit on a Persian or Chinese rug smoking one dream matter or another and we watch the smoke and we watch the images and dreams and fantasies that are taking place right there in our eye's mind.[4]

Such proclamations about the possibilities of an expanded cinema were not uncharacteristic of Mekas, though as we saw in chapter 1 his enthusiasm was sometimes tempered by feelings that expanded cinema placed spectacle over craft, and by an apparent desire to reconcile so much heterogeneous new work with a more traditional conception of cinema. But his paean to a cinema of "dreams and visions" (what Vincent Canby had rather derisively called "eyeball cinema" in a tongue-in-cheek 1966 article on modern film trends) goes some way to explaining Mekas's "quotation" of Buddha a few years later. There was promise in "not" making films.

We can take Mekas one of two ways here. "Not to make films" could mean making something else, something other than celluloid that was still cinematic, somehow, a practice that might extend to taking mind-expanding drugs or staring into flickering lights. Or, it could mean making *nothing*, which, in the context of Mekas's disappointment in Cannes, could be seen as a political act of refusal, a complete withdrawal from the world of commercial narrative cinema and traditional theatrical—"canned"—screenings. The avant-garde film world's equivalent to "turn on, tune in, and drop out."

The works of expanded cinema in this chapter range across a space between these two options. Certainly they are not films in that they do not use any film medium. Nor

[2] Ibid., p. 256.
[3] Ibid.
[4] Ibid., p. 152.

do they utilize any other conventional moving image medium (i.e., video), though some of the filmmakers discussed in this chapter have invented their own utterly unique moving image machines. None of the works are "nothing," as in embodied only in a dreaming, drug-altered, or otherwise expanded mind or someone's rubbed eyeballs. But some are unquestionably negations: rejections—sometimes disillusioned, bitter, or violent—of the materials of a medium, and at times the values invested in that medium by the experimental film world.

The subject of this chapter is "paracinema," works identified by their makers as cinematic, and legible as such within the avant-garde film world, that are not made in film. The abandonment of the medium by paracinema is total. Unlike some of the works described in other chapters, which did away with projectors (Iimura's *Film Installation* or the film quilts of Sabrina Gschwandtner and Richard Kerr), or film (Kosugi's *Film & Film #4*, or Gibson and Recoder's filmless projector installations), paracinematic works jettison the physical medium of film completely. But they retain aesthetic traits and perceptual experiences deemed "cinematic" not just by the individual artists who make them, but at least implicitly according to the wider theoretical discourses of experimental film culture as well. Paracinema could be said to abstract these from the specific moving image medium in which they usually take shape, in so doing amplifying them, clarifying the essentially cinematic by re-invigorating it in a previously unfamiliar, unstandardized form. "Notes in Duration," the statement accompanying McCall's *Long Film for Ambient Light*, expresses this ambition succinctly: making a "film" without the film medium enabled McCall "to concentrate less on the physical process of production and more on the presuppositions behind film as an art activity" (see introduction).[5] Like Mekas, McCall put "films" in scare quotes, signaling that certain works of expanded cinema were "films" in a manner of speaking, and that a "film" could be made in something other than the medium of that name yet retain its connection to the art form that bears the same name.

Clearly this sort of language runs the risk of vagueness. A brief genealogy of paracinema is in order and will help elucidate its meaning. "Paracinema" (sometimes written "para-cinema"), as a label for completely filmless cinematic art, seems to have been used first by Ken Jacobs. He first mentioned it in print in a 1974 interview with Lindley Hanlon published in a 1979 issue of *Film Culture*.[6] This reference was specifically to a form of shadow play that Jacobs had been performing since 1965, and continued to produce until the early 1980s. He would soon extend the label paracinema to his Nervous System performances (see chapter 3) and, decades later, to a filmless version dubbed the "Nervous Magic Lantern." "[A]n equivalent cinema created by other than filmic means or by using film in any other than standard ways; equivalent, or *parallel to*, is what I had meant to convey," Jacobs wrote in 2005, by which time the word was less obscure than it had been at the time.[7]

[5] Anthony McCall, "Notes in Duration," in Sitney, ed., *The Avant-Garde Film*, p. 253.
[6] Halon, "Kenneth Jacobs, Interviewed by Lindley," p. 74.
[7] Ken Jacobs, "Painted Air: The Joys and Sorrows of Evanescent Cinema," *Millennium Film Journal*, nos. 43/44 (Summer/Fall 2005), p. 40.

The first use of "para-cinematic," distinct from "paracinema," in print to identify objects or phenomena that were not filmic but nonetheless intuited as cinematic was in Hollis Frampton's production notes for his 1970 film *Zorns Lemma*. The long central section of that film repeats a 24-letter alphabet over and over in the form of one-second long shots of words on streetsigns, in print, and in shop windows. One iteration begins with "About," "Baggage," "Calorie," and "Dance," for example. After several rounds of this, wordless images begin to replace the letters, one letter at a time; a shot of fire replaces "X," another of waves replaces "Y," and so on, until the entire alphabet has been replaced. Frampton's notes for the film set out three criteria for selecting the replacement images, one of which is "cinematic or para-cinematic reference, however oblique. To my mind, any phenomenon is para-cinematic if it shares one element with cinema, e.g. modularity with respect to space or time."[8] While this appears to be the only time Frampton invoked paracinema, or the "para-cinematic," he often made similarly expansive claims about the nature of cinema. Even though he did not make paracinema, then, his writings and statements frequently follow the same logic as those filmmakers who did. At times Frampton seems to have been intent on projecting his art form onto as many things as possible: other art forms, the natural world, human perception. This thinking extended into the historical dimension as well, with Frampton's idiosyncratic metahistory of cinema reaching further and further back into pre-cinema history, and finally into prehistory. In a series of talks at the Millennium Film Workshop between 1971 and 1976, he located cinema's origins not only in the very distant past, but in another art form as well:

> We feel that the visual cinema came first and sound was added to it with *The Virginian* or *The Jazz Singer*. What I'm about to suggest is that the aural cinema came first and then later pictures were added to it. By which I mean definitely to imply that there's a cinema of the ear. That cinema is a whole universe of sound ordered to aesthetic ends which subsumed music, among many other things. And music, of course, has a considerable history. If you are willing to entertain that conceit, then of course, cinema is not the youngest of the arts, but the oldest.[9]

In a later talk, Frampton made music's history even more "considerable" than it already was by claiming it to have originated in the sounds of prehistoric insects. Only later would come "wistful prefigurations of the addition to that sound track, of an image-track, the beginnings of a cinema for the eye."[10] Such leaps elaborated Frampton's metahistory, first introduced in 1971, which proposed "an infinite cinema," made by a "polymorphous camera" that had, from the beginnings of time, filmed everything, producing only black "film" before the invention of photography. Thus, by yet another art historical reversal, film predates still photography, which is

[8] Quoted in Sitney, *Visionary Film*, p. 396.
[9] Frampton, "Hollis Frampton," p. 277.
[10] Ibid., p. 292.

reimagined by Frampton as a cinema waiting to be animated. This is Bazin's "myth of total cinema" refracted through the radical cinematic ontology of the avant-garde film world, which took its furthest leaps during this period—the same period that produced *Long Film for Ambient Light* and many other seminal paracinematic works. For Bazin, the visual arts—painting, sculpture, and eventually photography—converged teleologically in the cinema, which Bazin saw as the ultimate realization of the realist representational ambitions of the earliest humans.[11] For Frampton, much more than other visual art forms converged in cinema; his metahistory exemplifies a process Pavle Levi has called "the general cinefication," in which reality is "increasingly understood as a sort of 'spontaneous' cinema."[12] Given the swath of historical and categorical territory of Frampton's cinema history, the parallel breadth of his conception of the "para-cinematic" as *anything* spatially or temporally changing is not surprising. "Para-" exponentially expands the range of an already radically expanded ontology of cinema.

The idea of paracinema was in the air by the mid-1970s, the word perhaps co-discovered or co-invented by several filmmakers and critics even though it is usually "officially" attributed to Jacobs.[13] Alan Berliner has credited Larry Gottheim with introducing him to paracinema, while acknowledging Jacobs's work and use of the term.[14] Gottheim and Jacobs were co-founders of SUNY Binghamton's Department of Cinema, where Berliner studied as an undergraduate beginning in 1973. Gottheim and a group of Binghamton students, including Berliner, produced a paracinematic performance entitled *The Perils of Space* at the Collective for Living Cinema in 1975.[15] No documentation of this work survives, though a few brief written reminiscences exist. Morgan Fisher, recalling a visit to Binghamton at this time, provides one of the only existing accounts:

> Larry Gottheim was doing a project with students on what he called "para-cinema . . ." There were wooden constructions scattered around the campus that in various ways enacted references to film. The one I remember was made of what must have been two-by-fours. It looked like a free-standing vertical ladder; that is, parallel uprights between which were evenly spaced horizontal members—a

[11] Bazin, "The Ontology of the Photographic Image," especially pp. 9–12.

[12] Levi, *Cinema by Other Means*, p. 77.

[13] Gerald O'Grady uses the term "paracinema" in a short statement that introduced "A Seminar in Teaching Making," which took place at SUNY Buffalo Center for Media Study in December of 1973. Participants in the seminar included Jacobs and Larry Gottheim, though it is not clear whether O'Grady was aware of their own use of the term. The event was reported, belatedly, in the *Village Voice*. See Gerald O'Grady, "When Visual Anarchists Convene," *Village Voice*, July 4, 1974, p. 57. The original statement is contained in a dossier of documents relating to the Media Study Program at Buffalo in the 1970s, accessible on the Vasulka Archive: http://www.vasulka.org/archive/RightsIntrvwInstitMediaPolicies/MediaPoliciesBinder/policies.pdf. Finally, Annette Michelson used the word "paracinematic" in a 1979 essay on Rene Clair's *The Crazy Ray* (*Paris Qui Dort*, 1924), to describe photocollages and illustrated novels by artists like Max Ernst. See "Dr. Crase and Mr. Clair," *October* 11 (Winter 1979), p. 41.

[14] Scott MacDonald, *A Critical Cinema 5: Interviews with Independent Filmmakers* (Berkeley: University of California Press, 2006), p. 152.

[15] Berliner mistakenly dates the performance 1976 in his interview with MacDonald.

diagram of a strip of film. It was maybe five feet across and its height was in proportion for a length of maybe five or six "frames."[16]

As should be clear by now, paracinema works by way of analogies to cinema as we know it, in this case through formal similarities between a filmstrip and the wooden construction Fisher recollects. Most paracinematic works are legible as cinema on the strength of this sort of analogy to elements of the film medium, though others are modeled on formal elements like projected light and shadow—Jacobs's shadow plays, for instance—or the articulation of duration by the modulation of light, as in *Long Film for Ambient Light*. In most instances, paracinematic works play upon multiple analogies between both materials and aesthetic traits of films made in more traditional ways (bearing in mind that the "traditional" filmmaking methods of avant-garde cinema are of a different order than those of commercial cinema). The link between paracinema and the film medium is important and complicated, at once an evocation of medium specificity and a denial of it. Because the invention of cinema as we know it was more or less coincident with the invention of the film medium, that medium occupies a place of privilege in the expanded ontologies of paracinematic works. At the same time, however, those ontologies posit a cinema beyond film, sometimes before it, and like all other works of expanded cinema deliberately trouble the concept of medium specificity and challenge its presumed dominance in experimental film practice.

This leads us to the other ontological side of paracinema, which is that, by most accounts, it embodies an "idea of cinema" not completely determined by the "material of film." "Cinema" is characterized here as a conceptual phenomenon, for how else could so many formally and materially varied forms be consolidated if not according to an abstract, idealized model? This idea, that cinema was itself an idea, has a long history both in and out of the avant-garde. Frampton's metahistory, like Bazin's myth of total cinema, was an invention of the imagination, "meant to inseminate resonant consistency into the growing body of [the metahistorian's] art." It provided a conceptual model for filmmaking, and was further articulated and specified by the films that model generated. One of the reigning ideas for Frampton was seriality, measured, according to him, in increasingly "infinitesimal" terms by mathematicians like Newton, who theorized the division of movement into discrete moments like the frames on a strip of film.[17] A mathematical model—essentially a concept—becomes cinematic by this reading, notwithstanding the fact that cinema was invented over 150 years after Newton's death. Readings of structural films and installations like Sharits's as models of consciousness by critics like Sitney and Krauss (and Sharits himself), paralleling the material traits of the medium to the operations of human knowledge, was

[16] Quoted in Scott MacDonald, *Binghamton Babylon: Voices from the Cinema Department, 1967–1977* (Albany: SUNY Press, 2015), p. 158. Fisher, like Berliner, is mistaken on the date, recalling his visit to Binghamton taking place in 1974 rather than 1975.

[17] Frampton, "For a Metahistory of Film," in Jenkins, ed., *On the Camera Arts*, p. 132.

a variation on this theme. The "film as consciousness" argument, like Frampton's discovery of the cinematic in theories of Newton and Zeno, posits a relationship of structural identity between cinema and decidedly non-filmic things. The origins of that
interpretation, furthermore, are to be found in Sergei Eisenstein's analogy of film and
human cognition, specifically montage and dialectical reasoning. Cinema's potential
as a medium of communication, and more to the point of persuasion, lay in the ways
its defining aesthetic feature—juxtaposition—so precisely mirrored the elemental
processes of thinking. Montage, he wrote,

> is not in the least a circumstance peculiar to the cinema, but is a phenomenon in-
> variably met with in all cases where we have to deal with juxtaposition of two facts,
> two phenomena, two objects. We are accustomed to make, almost automatically,
> a definite and obvious deductive generalization when any separate objects are
> placed before us side by side.[18]

Variations on this theme appear across the writings of experimental filmmakers
and critics in the 1970s. One relatively common claim was that certain works of expanded cinema conceptualized not "film" or "cinema" as a whole (as in "the idea of
cinema"), but specific material elements. In a 1975 essay, Dusinberre argued that one
branch of expanded cinema was distinguishable by its complete abandonment of the
film medium, a reversal of a tendency within expanded cinema toward more complex
technological arrangements. Such work

> replaces the complexity of technology with the simplicity of shadowplay; it
> explores old technology, expanding the *possibilities* and *exigencies* of cinema
> technology as it has existed for eighty years. Since this ultimately involves "first
> principles," some artists . . . have taken the principles out of their specifically filmic
> context and dealt with them conceptually (e.g., the idea of "projection").[19]

Sharits had made a related claim that even the apparently physical elements of film
could also be understood as concepts. The much commented-upon dualism of his
cinematic ontology did not entail an absolute, "either/or" break between the two, but
rather a permeable barrier. His enumeration of essential filmic "elements," frequently
in scare quotes as if to emphasize their uncertain material status, conflated objects,
processes, and intentions:

> There are at least: processes of intending to make a film; processes of recording
> light patterns on raw stock (films can be made which by-pass this mode); processes
> of processing; processes of editing; processes of printing; processes of projecting;

---

[18] Sergei Eisenstein, "Word and Image," in *The Film Sense*, translated by Jay Leyda (San Diego: Harcourt
Brace Jovanovich, 1947), p. 4.
[19] Dusinberre, "On Expanding Cinema," p. 220.

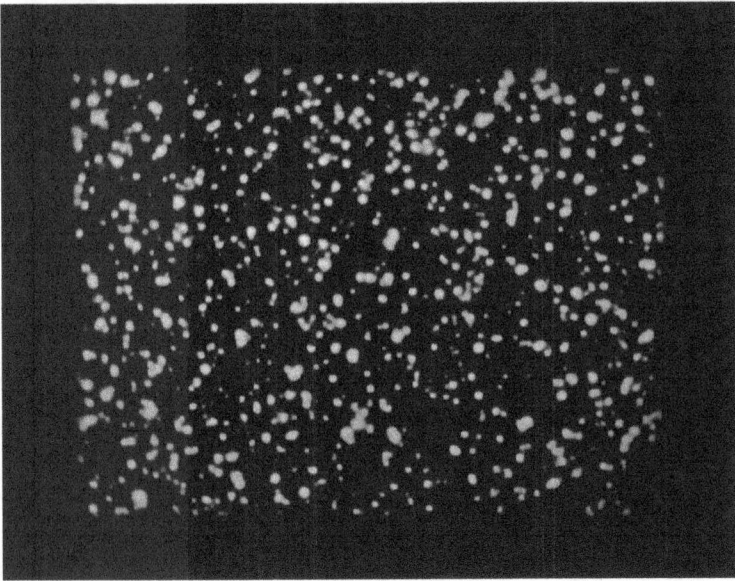

Fig. 6.1. Paul Sharits, *Apparent Motion* (1975). Frame enlargement.
Courtesy of the Estate of Paul Sharits and Greene Naftali, New York. Permission from Christopher and Cheri Sharits.

processes of experiencing. The problem of whether or not "concepts" like "intention" are "elements" complicates the issue; that is to say, even those "things" which are observable, such as "emulsion grains," can be shown to be essentially "concepts."[20]

The assertion that emulsion grains are concepts calls out for explanation. Program notes Sharits wrote for his locational film environment *Apparent Motion* (1975) may clarify. That work subjected a strip of underexposed black and white film to multiple blow-ups on an optical printer, which brought out the already prominent grain structure of each frame. Slowing down the footage, also on an optical printer, made the grains even more apparent, enabling viewers to discern what appeared to be patterns of movement among individual grains from one frame to the next (figs. 6.1 and 6.2). As Sharits pointed out, no such movement actually existed; the appearance of a single film grain vibrating on screen was, of course, an illusion produced as individual grains across adjacent frames seemed to merge into a single moving object in projection, which Sharits saw as a pure form of animation. That is, as *Apparent Motion*'s title indicates, the movement of grains is an illusion, a cognitive event rather than a real one, and thus, by Sharits's thinking at least, a concept.[21] The movement patterns

[20] Sharits, "Word Per Page," p. 37.
[21] Paul Sharits, notes for *Apparent Motion*, reproduced in the "Filmography" section of the special *Film Culture* issue on Sharits (nos. 65–66, 1978), pp. 119–120.

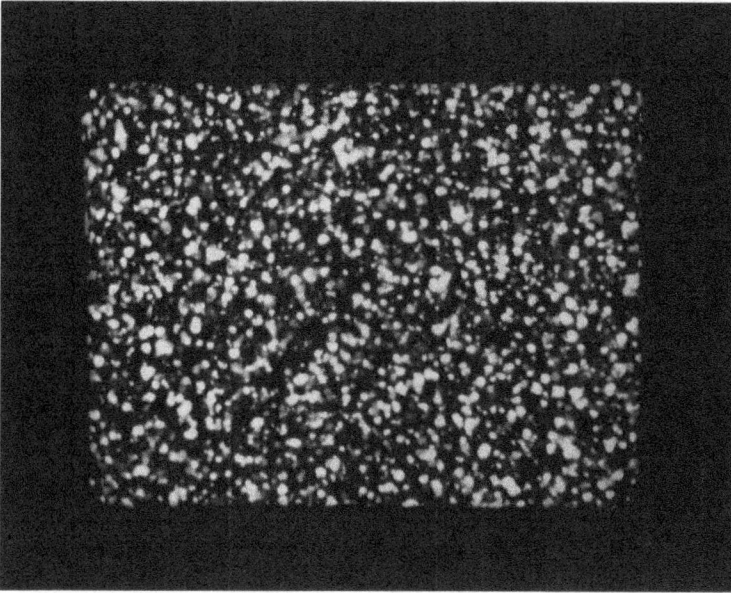

Fig. 6.2. Paul Sharits, *Apparent Motion* (1975). Frame enlargement.
Courtesy of the Estate of Paul Sharits and Greene Naftali, New York. Permission from Christopher and Cheri Sharits.

spectators believed they saw among the grains is an example of what perceptual psychologists call "objectless motion," another way of stating not only the illusionism of that movement but its immateriality, its status as purely mental action.

What this suggests is that the most staunchly medium-specific filmmaking practice could produce its opposite: a conceptual, non-filmic cinema. Plumbing of the depths of film as physical object, down to emulsion grains and "processes of [film] processing," often seemed to pass through irreducible materiality to open up onto a field of ephemeral forms divorced from the film machine. Interviewing McCall about his transition from the film-based "solid light" films to the film-less *Long Film for Ambient Light*, Scott MacDonald noted, "It's a though filmmaking had led you out of film."[22] Genevieve Yue's reading of Gibson and Recoder's *Light Spill* as playing out a release of cinema from film follows the same line of reasoning: "For Gibson and Recoder, the nature of cinema might be grasped by shedding the 'thingness' of film."[23] Yue and others have extended the distinction between the material of film and the idea of cinema into the contemporary moment, in which it has become especially prominent. The rise of digital technology and corresponding obsolescence of film has brought new attention to the topic of cinematic specificity, and the widespread presence of moving images in art and daily life has raised questions about the

[22] MacDonald, "Anthony McCall," p. 165.
[23] Yue, "What Was Cinema," p. 69.

medium-belonging of those images. The connection of cinema to film has been loosened, so to speak, with film historicized as one material stage in the history of cinema rather than its determining medium. Before this historical situation arose, however—before it was forced into being by technological change and economic imperative—the makers of paracinema had already made it happen of their own will. Rather than being imposed from the outside, such work emerged organically from the ontological ideas of experimental film culture. And filmmakers who continue to work with and value film, while making that commitment under different historical circumstances to be sure, elaborate upon the original models offered by artists like Jacobs, McCall, and Berliner. These models of a particular relationship between film and cinema can thus be useful tools for thinking through a process in which an art form becomes "post-medium." Yue's argument, a representative passage from which opens this chapter, is knowingly ambivalent: cinema is neither film nor "something else," at once embodied in that medium but not fully defined or accommodated by it. "Without this material apparatus," Yue writes, "the concept of cinema, or Bazin's 'idealistic phenomenon,' is shifty, elusive, and unstable."[24]

Pavle Levi has brilliantly reconceived this ambivalent, unstable relationship between film and cinema as a historical dialectic of artistic ideals and technological realizations, between an art form as conceptual—what Levi calls "an imagined cluster of (desired, projected, assumed) functions"—and as a "concrete material-technological support."[25] Levi argues that this process occurs in all the arts, and eventually leads to a state wherein artists are compelled to wrest their artistic medium from the physical one:

> Eventually, operational technology is declared normative. At that point, however, the Idea of the medium is substantially transformed: its immaterial conceptual design acquires a thus far unprecedented degree of specificity by being forever related to the structural-material dynamics of the standardized apparatus. What is more, at the point when the concept and the technology fully coincide, when the new medium has successfully been turned into a working artifact—*the medium would, in some sense, also have been excessively reified (and commodified)*. It is, therefore, only by repeatedly evoking, by enacting, the discrepancy between the idea and its technological implementation that the essential qualities and the radical, noninstrumentalist creative potential contained in any new medium are maintained.[26]

It is a remarkable argument, not least of all for reconciling elements of Bazin's idealist theories of the "myth of total cinema" and "evolution" of film language with the quite different theoretical perspectives of filmmakers like Frampton and Sharits—as well as

---

[24] Ibid.
[25] Levi, *Cinema by Other Means*, p. 44.
[26] Ibid., p. 45. Italics in original.

Rosalind Krauss's writings on the "post-medium condition." Though Levi is writing here about the interwar period, his characterization of this dialectic is equally apt of expanded cinema, and paracinema in particular. Paracinema does not cast off the film medium altogether, as the liberatory rhetoric of expanded cinema's first wave would have had it, but works in the interstices between a fully formed, standardized phys-ical medium and the ideas of which that medium is an artifact. Paracinema *creates* these interstices in a continuation of the dialectic Levi describes. To some extent, ex-panded cinema casts the film medium as an obstacle to the ambitions it was designed to fulfill. Reconfiguring that medium, deploying it in different spaces, and commit-ting destructive acts against it (as Conrad did in his cooked, electrocuted, and ham-mered films) is one way around the impasse presented by the medium in its standard form. Paracinema does not use the medium at all, but the forms it takes are meant to more directly realize the effects and experiences that were first observed once that medium was invented. A common claim about avant-garde cinema in general is that it rejuvenates perception, whether of reality, conventional cinema, or perception it-self. Paracinematic works may accomplish these aims, but the primary object of their reinvigoration is the medium itself, which at once suggests paracinema's forms and constrains them.

Claiming that paracinematic works represent an idea of cinema might invite comparisons to conceptual art. The possible connection requires brief clarification. The territory of conceptual art is contested, to say the least, and staking it out once again is not within the purview of this chapter. Two characteristics of conceptual art are worth mentioning in connection with paracinema, however. The first was a tendency to de-center the privileged object of art—the painting, the sculpture, the photograph—either by dispensing with these kinds of objects completely or making more apparent their position in a network of institutional and discursive relations. Lucy R. Lippard and John Chandler identified this historical development as one of "the dematerialization of art," which immediately drew criticism from conceptual art-ists on the grounds that it implicitly privileged traditional art forms over conceptual ones (Lippard would later adjust the phrase to "the dematerialization of the art ob-ject").[27] In an unpublished letter to Lippard and Chandler written in March of 1968, the members of the English conceptual art group Art & Language wrote that the term "dematerialized" reflected a bias against nontraditional art objects and reaffirmed for-malist aesthetic criticism as the norm: "All the examples of art-works (ideas) you refer to in your article are, with few exceptions, art-objects. They may not be an art-object as we know it in its traditional matter-state, but they are nevertheless matter in one of its traditional forms."[28] The group argued that a sheet of paper on which was written

---

[27] Lucy R. Lippard and John Chandler, "The Dematerialization of Art," in Alexander Alberro and Blake Stimson, eds., *Conceptual Art: A Critical Anthology* (Cambridge, MA: MIT Press, 1999), pp. 46–50. Also see Lippard, *Six Years: The Dematerialization of the Art Object From 1966 to 1972* (New York: Praeger Publishers, 1973).

[28] Art & Language, unpublished letter to Lucy Lippard and John Chandler, March 23, 1968. Reproduced in Lippard, *Six Years*, p. 43.

an artistic idea was as much a "matter-state entity" as a painting, and should not be thought of as dematerialized simply because formalism had nothing to say about the sheet ("the idea is 'read about' rather than 'looked at' "). "That some art should be directly material and that other art should produce a material entity only as a necessary by-product of the need to record the idea is not at all to say that the latter is connected by any process of dematerialization to the former."[29] The same objection could be made to any claims that paracinema is a "dematerialized" version of traditional cinema, as it has, like conceptual art, produced plenty of objects in a variety of physical media. That is, we want to avoid conflating "ephemeral" or "nontraditional" with "conceptual." Perhaps "re-materialization" is the better term, the realization of what Sheldon Renan called "the effect of film" in other physical forms that were often transient and less tangible than the materials of film. But like the work of Art & Language and the American conceptual artist Joseph Kosuth, paracinema displaces the film medium from its privileged place as the defining object of cinematic art while at the same time maintaining a link to the aesthetic forms and experiences developed within that medium.

The reference to Kosuth leads to the second point of comparison between paracinema and conceptual art. Kosuth referred to his works as "models," which were "approximations" of the ideas that constituted the actual work of art. The objects he made, then, were visual representations of conceptual models, and while these might have been models "of a particular art object I have in mind," what was more important for Kosuth was the modeling of the idea of art itself as opposed to making specific art objects.[30] Elsewhere, Kossuth elaborated:

> At its most strict and radical extreme the art I call conceptual is such because it is based on an inquiry into the nature of art. Thus, it is not just the activity of constructing art propositions, but a working out, a thinking out, of all the implications of all aspects of the concept "art."[31]

There is an analogy to be made here with paracinema. If cinema, insofar as it is envisioned by avant-garde film culture, is ultimately a conceptual phenomenon, then individual works of paracinema could be thought of as propositional models of particular aspects of that concept. Certain paracinematic works fit this description to some degree. Conrad's *Yellow Movies* series (1972–1975), which consisted of painted frames on paper, were instantiations of a particular model of cinematic form and experience. They were not viewable in their entirety, as Conrad conceived their "running time" to be as long as the pieces of paper they were painted on continued to exist.

[29] Ibid., p. 44.
[30] Joseph Kosuth, unpublished statement from *Nonanthropomorphic Art by Four Young Artists: Joseph Kosuth, Christine Kozlov, Michael Rinaldi, Ernest Rossi*, at the Lannis Gallery, New York, February 1967. Quoted in ibid., p. 25.
[31] Joseph Kosuth, "Introductory Note by the American Editor," *Art-Language* 2 (February 1970), n.p. Reprinted in Lippard, *Six Years*, p. 148.

Nor was each individual instantiation any more significant than the others—none of them possessed the aura of the singular art object (though more recently they have been recuperated as art objects by the gallery world). *Long Film for Ambient Light*, by McCall's description, was about the "presuppositions behind film as an art activity." In this respect, it resembles Kosuth's models, being a temporary, provisional condition that asserts fundamental principles of the idea of film, partly through written language. Furthermore, *Long Film for Ambient Light* could be, and has been, executed by others without McCall's presence.

But this analogy can only go so far. Kosuth rejected the idea of medium specificity not only in the limited "Greenbergian" sense, but in the broader sense of distinguishing among art forms in the first place:

> If one is questioning the nature of painting, one cannot be questioning the nature of art ... That's because the word "art" is general and the word "painting" is specific. Painting is a *kind* of art. If you make paintings you are already accepting (not questioning) the nature of art.[32]

While obviously inviting analogies to other art forms even more than other modes of expanded cinema, works of paracinema are unashamedly about cinematic specificity, however that concept may be construed by individual filmmakers. And many of them invite formalist analysis; such analysis reveals the distinct ways they translate cinematic forms into non-filmic materials, and thus is not so much a tool of appreciation as a necessary step to understanding paracinema's philosophical underpinnings and interventions in cinema history. This takes paracinema rather far from the realm of conceptual art, which, in so many of its variants, was fundamentally opposed to formalist theory and criticism. By contrast, the use of ephemeral materials in many works of paracinema is often a source of their aesthetic and emotional power as much as their meaning or theoretical import.

A Shadow of Its Former/Future Self: Paracinema as "Pre-Cinema"

In "The Myth of Total Cinema," Bazin posed a question that many other filmmakers and historians have also asked: why did it take so long for the cinema to be invented? "We must here explain," he wrote, "how it was that the invention took so long to emerge, since all the prerequisites had been assembled and the persistence of the image on the retina had been known for a long time."[33] Though film was a medium of

---

[32] Kosuth, "Art After Philosophy," p. 18. "Art After Philosophy" originally appeared in *Studio International* (October 1969), and Kosuth first made this statement in Arthur R. Rose, "Four Interviews," *Arts Magazine* 43 (February 1969), p. 23.
[33] Bazin, "The Myth of Total Cinema," p. 19.

the industrial age, utilizing some of the same technology as machine guns and sewing machines, this was not a historical inevitability according to Bazin. "Nothing had stood in the way" of the invention of a moving image medium before the industrial age; "the photographic cinema could just as well have grafted itself onto a phenakisto-scope foreseen as long ago as the sixteenth century."[34]

Seventy years later, Ken Jacobs repeated this claim in reference to his Nervous Magic Lantern, a filmless projection device of his own invention with which he has performed since the early 1990s:

> A mystery is that The Nervous Magic Lantern wasn't invented centuries ago, way before movies, as soon as a lamp could safely contain fire as light-source and there existed a glass lens for focusing on a surface. Decorative patterns on glass could've been projected or any small object that could take the heat. The spinning shutter before the lens could've been cranked by hand. The projected image would have immediately shown continuous motion while remaining in place … moving but not moving anywhere (it can't be imagined) in unquestionable deep space. It would've been terrifying. It would've made the history books.[35]

The Nervous Magic Lantern was built on the same principle as the original magic lantern, with some key modifications (fig. 6.3). While traditional magic lanterns were usually made to project slides, Jacobs's "nervous" version can accommodate both flat objects like photographs and three-dimensional ones, which are illuminated by a bright theatrical lamp. The heat of this lamp, to which Jacobs alludes in the quoted passage, is lessened by small electric fans housed inside the large makeshift box that houses the apparatus. Dual lenses inside the device project the image of whatever is inside it onto the screen (a point of reference might be the analog overhead projector). The slight difference in position of the two lenses relative to whatever object Jacobs has placed in his device results in two nearly identical images, like those viewed in a stereopticon. Were they viewed at the same time, one through each eye, they would produce a static three-dimensional image, as in stereo slide viewers. The Nervous Magic Lantern, however, projects the images in rapidly alternating sequence, allow-ing moments of overlap between the two images so that one appears to dissolve into the other, over and over, in a two-frame loop (fig. 6.4). It could thus be described as a temporalized stereopticon. An external shutter adapted from Jacobs's film-based Nervous System introduces what Jacobs refers to, with a hint of the cosmic, as "the black interval."[36] He recalls discovering how this momentary interruption of the projected light beam "cycled and melded the slightly out-of-sync and superimposed screen-images," producing "a molten 3D happen that could not only be seen without

---

[34] Ibid., pp. 18–19.
[35] Ken Jacobs, notes for "Abstract Expressionist Cinema: Ken Jacobs/Nervous Magic Lantern Festival," Anthology Film Archives, New York, January 2016.
[36] Ibid.

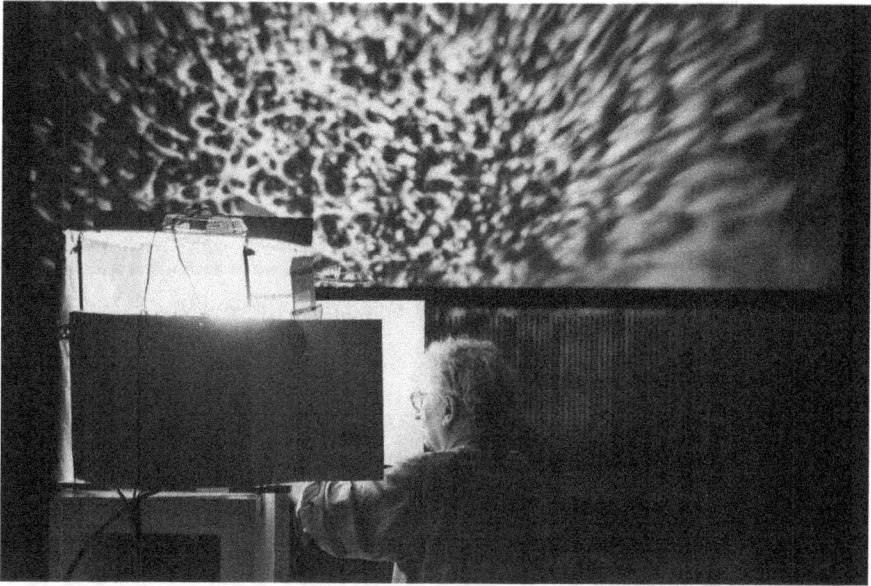

Fig. 6.3. Ken Jacobs performing with the Nervous Magic Lantern during the premier of *New Paintings by Ken Jacobs* (2015) at the (S8) Mostra de Cinema Periférico.
Photograph ©María Meseguer. Courtesy of (S8) Mostra de Cinema Periférico.

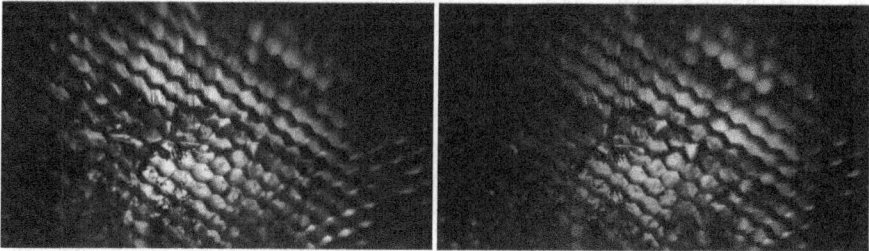

Fig. 6.4. Ken Jacobs, two frames from a Nervous Magic Lantern performance with Tom Chiu. Performance documentation. From Abstract Expressionist Cinema: Ken Jacobs/Nervous Magic Lantern Festival, January 22–24, 2016. Anthology Film Archives, New York.
Courtesy of Ken Jacobs.

spectacles but could be seen by one eye."[37] This "molten" quality is heightened by the amorphous shape of the projected images. Because they do not pass through a rectangular aperture, the images retain the soft, almost indiscernible edges created by the lenses (fig. 6.5). As if to emphasize the seeming boundlessness of the Nervous Magic Lantern's images, Jacobs often projects onto a conventional rectangular screen

[37] Ibid.

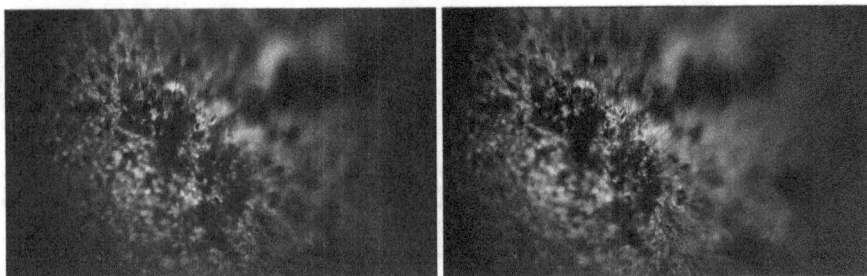

Fig. 6.5. Ken Jacobs, two frames from *Granular* (undated). Nervous Magic Lantern performance documentation.
Courtesy of Ken Jacobs.

Fig. 6.6. Ken Jacobs, two frames from *Brontosaurus* (undated). "Eternalism": 10-frame animated GIF file alternating positive and negative.
Courtesy of Ken Jacobs.

but positions the device close enough to it that the images exceed its borders and spill onto the surrounding walls and ceiling. The overall effect is one of disorientation, experienced first as physical discomfort at the dizzying rotational effect generated by the flickering stereo images. Even when Jacobs is not moving the objects in his machine, the impression of motion is marked, despite the fact that the difference between the two images is minimal. This effect is also on view in Jacobs's "Eternalisms," animated GIF files comprising six nearly identical photographic images taken from slightly different perspectives, flickering between positive and negative (fig. 6.6). Viewing the individual frames that compose the "Eternalisms" reveals only tiny intervals of distance or change between one image and the next, but when animated those images suddenly appear to rotate in depth as previously imperceptible planes in the image are thrown into relief.[38]

Descriptions of Nervous Magic Lantern performances typically concede that description is almost impossible, and that even when one sees the effects directly they

---

[38] See https://kenjacobsgallery.com/eternalisms. "Eternalism" is capitalized because it is a patented editing process belonging to Jacobs.

exceed comprehension and, by implication, language. This is a function of one of several tensions at work in Jacobs's device and the performances he creates with it. Jacobs himself has cast this tension in terms of the twin pleasures of magic shows— joyous astonishment and wonder at the tricks, followed by the satisfaction the magician's explanations provide. Though at one point Jacobs was evasive about the inner workings of the Nervous Magic Lantern, more recently he has allowed spectators to watch him dismantle it after performances and taken questions about its construction and operation. Re-thought through the framework of avant-garde film history, the Nervous Magic Lantern can be read as embodying two contrasting aesthetics. The first is a purely optical aesthetic, if not exactly anti-intellectual at least designed to prompt the spectator to hold intellect in abeyance while taking pleasure in the performance's astonishing, lyrical, and powerfully illusionistic effects. The second is the aesthetic of structural and structural-materialist film, committed to the breakdown of cinema's illusionistic hold by drawing the mechanisms behind those illusions to the filmic surface for analytical contemplation by the viewer. While these two aesthetics are usually set in direct opposition to each other, and even further isolated as temporally separate historical modes, as I argued in chapter 3 they are better thought of as both conceptually and historically intertwined. And in Jacobs's work, especially, they are reconciled. The Nervous Magic Lantern's illusionism is, in his words, a kind of "Modernist deception, stating itself as such in the same way Houdini attacked priestly miracle-makers and spiritualist con-artists by performing tricks and saying so."[39]

Most of the Nervous Magic Lantern performances employ imagery that would normally be called abstract, though spectators are naturally curious about the nature of the objects that produce these images, which are inserted into the apparatus and manipulated by hand. Hence, like the abstractions in films like David Gatten's *What the Water Said*, Brakhage's *Mothlight*, or by Schmelzdahin's live chemical abuses of film loops, the images in the Nervous Magic Lantern performances are indexically tied to concrete objects and processes, the nature of which viewers are prompted to puzzle out. In a series of 2016 performances, for example, Jacobs used a group of objects that appeared organic, covered with dirt and hair, pockmarked and oddly textured in ways that called to mind diseased or decomposed flesh (fig. 6.7). The ambiguity of the images is compounded by their extremely shallow depth of field, which enhances the impression of depth but obscures most of the objects' surfaces (a similar effect results from the deliberate misuse of anamorphic lenses, as in Sidney Peterson's *The Lead Shoes* [1949], Tony Hill's *Expanded Movie* [1990] or Alexandr Sokurov's *Mother and Son* [1997]). The images of the Nervous Magic Lantern thus constantly oscillate between strikingly realistic and frustratingly unrecognizable. The exaggerated representation of depth conveys a sense of an object's contours, weight, and mass, the markers of the image's indexicality. But at the same time the limitations of

---

[39] Ken Jacobs, program notes for *Celestial Subway Lines 3*, a Nervous Magic Lantern performance in collaboration with John Zorn, Anthology Film Archives, New York, January 2, 2004.

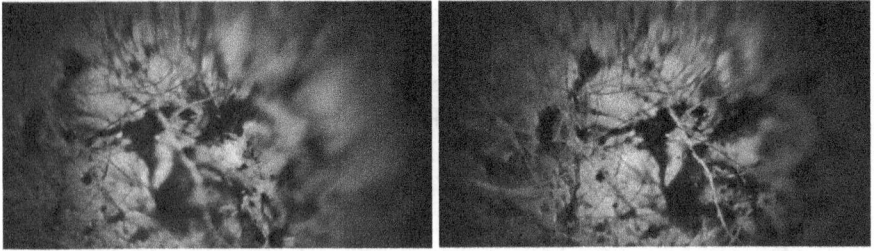

Fig. 6.7. Ken Jacobs, two frames from a Nervous Magic Lantern performance with Victoria Keddie. Performance documentation. From Abstract Expressionist Cinema: Ken Jacobs/Nervous Magic Lantern Festival, January 22–24, 2016. Anthology Film Archives, New York.
Courtesy of Ken Jacobs.

the lenses and the throbbing, liquid quality of the persistently shifting images render these objects abstract.

This oddly hybrid experience of abstraction and realism, where the impression of the latter is related to the indexical nature of all the Nervous Magic Lantern's images, may shed some light upon Jacobs's association of his work with Abstract Expressionist painting. On the occasion of a three-day series of Nervous Magic Lantern performances entitled "Abstract Expressionist Cinema," Jacobs analogized his work to Abstract Expressionism while distancing himself from its mythic heroes ("Would the genius-drunks have invited us into The Artists Club?").[40] Speculating further on the inexplicable delay of cinema's invention, Jacobs suggests that the deformation and abstraction of space by Modernist painting, from Picasso to Pollock, was necessary before viewers could accept the Nervous Magic Lantern's imagery. For Jacobs, reading Pollock and others through the lens of the "gestural" by which paint splatters are the traces of the artist's action in space, abstraction and indexicality merge. By this interpretation, Jacobs's performances are "Abstract Expressionist" not because they are abstract per se, but because they transform concrete objects into abstract images that nonetheless retain a sense of the gravity, shape, and texture of those objects in the same way "gestural" paintings were indexical images of the act of painting. Painting is performative on this account, a conceit that Jacobs's work literalizes. Furthermore, Jacobs reads the art historical line from Cubism to Abstract Expressionism as the opening up of depth in abstract space. Prior to becoming a filmmaker, Jacobs studied painting with Hans Hoffman, who elaborated a theory of three-dimensionality in abstract painting he often referred to using the colloquial expression "Push and Pull," which Jacobs has referenced frequently over the years.[41]

[40] Ken Jacobs, screening notes for "Abstract Expressionist Cinema: Ken Jacobs/Nervous Magic Lantern Festival."
[41] For the definitive account of Jacobs's debt to Hoffman, see Federico Windhausen, "Theories of Moving Pictures: Ken Jacobs After Hans Hoffman," in Michelle Pierson, David E. James, and Paul Arthur, eds., *Optic Antics: The Cinema of Ken Jacobs* (Oxford: Oxford University Press, 2011), pp. 232–244.

Though he has consistently noted this connection, especially in reference to his work with the Nervous System and Nervous Magic Lantern performances, more recently Jacobs has taken up painting with renewed vigor, in doing so reasserting his Hoffman-inspired conception of abstract painting as being unavoidably about the experience of depth. "Paintings, in their lack of dimensionality, long for depth," he has recently written:

> A flat painted surface, a texture at most, reaches out to limiting borders on a skin held taut ... If we have modern expectations, we look at a painted surface for what it can *do*. We look at applications of viscous substances allowed to harden and then look on to see what it—the complete painting, the *composition* if you will—can do, teasing out *perceptual or conceptual contradiction*. Will it enter the dimension of time by going through changes? ... Contradiction creates change, violent and instantaneous. Such contradictions must be planted, imbedded by the painter. Systems of depth signals evolve so that people of such cultures (with an interest in painting, in pictorialism to be specific) learn without realizing they learn. And so a painting will be *read*, or so it seems.[42]

Jacobs's account recalls not only Hoffman, but Eisenstein, for whom contradiction—"collision," in his words—was the essential feature of montage, and thus of cinema (see my discussion of Eisenstein later in this chapter). Collision was the condition even of the most basic cinematic effects such as apparent motion (one frame "colliding" into the next, resolved dialectically in the spectator's mind into the illusion of movement). In his film *Joan Mitchell: Departures* (2018), Jacobs seeks to enact the process whereby a viewer of abstract painting "reads" the work into depth, change, movement. Lengthy detail shots of Mitchell's characteristically loose, gestural brushwork suddenly appear to take on a kind of liquid motion in depth as Jacobs subjects the images to the uncannily contradictory rotational movement of expansion and contraction on view in the Eternalisms and Nervous Magic Lantern performances (fig. 6.8). The opening credits of the film explain that Mitchell's paintings "invite imagining in depth," an invitation that Jacobs's process of "Eternalizing" accepts. As if to further dramatize the spatial potential locked in Mitchell's work, Jacobs at times introduces barely visible images—taken by him on video—in superimposition during the moments of flicker. A blob of paint morphs almost imperceptibly into the outline of a building or some other fragment of architecture. About midway through the film, an awning materializes out of a streak of dark paint, the words "ENVIOS LLAMADAS" ("send calls") emblazoned on the front. Beneath the awning, one can barely make out the familiar horizontal lines of a closed city storefront gate tagged by graffiti.

Jacobs's appeal to Modernist painting as a historical reference point for the Nervous Magic Lantern is curious considering his other historicizing move, wherein he claims

---

[42] Ken Jacobs, "The Subject of Painting Is Depth," https://www.kenjacobsgallery.com/the-subject-of-painting-is-depth, n.p., n.d.

Fig. 6.8. Ken Jacobs, sequential frames from *Joan Mitchell: Departures* (2018). Frame enlargements from digital file. Left: negative image; right: positive image. Color, silent, 22 minutes.
Courtesy of Ken Jacobs.

that the device could have existed hundreds of years earlier. By this interpretation, if there were no technological obstacles to the device's invention centuries ago, there were cultural ones, which modernism removed. The Nervous Magic Lantern thus has both a long and short history. Jacobs's metahistorical thinking reverses the trajectory: modernism, including Modernist cinema, prompted artists like Jacobs to imagine properties of his art form outside their realization in a specific medium and then to project these properties backward into history, to "see" them existing long before the invention of the medium in which they were first encountered. This hints at the complications of paracinema's turn to pre-cinema history for some of its forms. In her study of Jacobs's Nervous System and shadow play performances, Michele Pierson rightly points out that the metahistorical thinking of filmmakers like Jacobs is in some respects at odds with the thinking of traditional film historians, who seek "to excavate the limits as much as the possibilities for drawing connections between one field of scientific, artistic, or industrial practice and another."[43] In other words, cinema historians would avoid the moves of retrograde remediation made by Jacobs, who re-invents the magic lantern and the shadow play as essentially cinematic, making over one cultural form in the image of another, later one. Pierson cites Tom Gunning's admonition that so-called "pre-" or "proto-cinematic" forms were "not simply waiting for cinema to appear and perfect" them.[44] The very terms pre-cinema and proto-cinema are teleological, reclaimed as moments in cinema's evolution toward its essentialist destiny. But Pierson also notes the utility for artists and critics to think in precisely this way. For filmmakers like Jacobs, it was creatively generative. For critics like Mekas, it was a rhetorical tool for stabilizing cinema's ambiguous identity during a moment when it was rapidly expanding. Mekas's responses to shadow

---

[43] Michele Pierson, "Where Shadow Play Is Cinema: The Exhibition and Critical Reception of Ken Jacobs's Shadow Plays in the 1960s and 1970s," *Film History* 29, no. 3 (Fall 2017), p. 34.
[44] Ibid. The Gunning essay Pierson cites is his introduction to Laurent Mannoni, *The Great Art of Light and Shadow*, translated and edited by Richard Crangle (Exeter, UK: University of Exeter Press, 2000), p. xx.

plays Jacobs performed in 1965 and 1968 work through the question of whether such works were genuinely cinema and, if so, on what historical and ontological grounds.

Jacobs took up shadow play in 1965, initially as a way to make "films" cheaply (mentions of Jacobs in Mekas's "Movie Journal" column repeatedly refer to his growing body of unfinished films and need for money). From then until 1975, when he built the Nervous System apparatus, his sole paracinematic work was in shadow play. His early shadow performances, up until 1970, did not employ 3D, and alternated between a traditional arrangement of backlit performers behind a translucent screen and a variation in which he used projected light to illuminate portions of the performance spaces and create shadow effects. His major work of this period was *The Big Blackout of '65* series, which unfolded from 1965 to 1968, starting at the Festival of Expanded Cinema held at the Filmmakers' Cinematheque in December of 1965. In *Apparition Theatre of New York: Evoking the Mystery: Chapter Four of the Big Blackout of '65* (1967–1968), Jacobs and his assistants (including Michael Snow on the organ) performed in the Washington Square Methodist Church on Fourth Street in Greenwich Village. As the audience sat in complete darkness, Jacobs lit up portions of the church's ornate interior with adjustable lights placed around the space. Movements of the lights caused corresponding changes in the dimensions of the shadows, and Jacobs discovered that such changes created the illusion that the lit object itself was moving or changing shape rather than its shadow.

Mekas's "Movie Journal" entries on Jacobs's shadow plays are a microcosm of his responses to expanded cinema in general. Mekas struggled with whether the welter of new moving image and light-based art forms were instances of cinema or of something else, and, if the latter, what the future of his art form would be. Ultimately Mekas reconciled Jacobs's work with the tradition of avant-garde cinema and distinguished it from intermedia and psychedelia, two terms that became codes in Mekas's writing for mere spectacle in contrast to genuine (cinematic) art. This reconciliation took two forms. The first was the rhetorical strategy of implying cinema's disappearance amid the explosion of new and expanded forms, immediately countered by the reassurance that, in fact, many of these forms weren't so new after all. Reporting on Jacobs's performance of the first chapter of *The Big Blackout of '65* series, Mekas wrote that "this art of shadow play that will become, during these few coming years, the controversial challenger of cinema as we know it today ... The ground is shaking and the cinema we knew is collapsing, the screen, the projector, the camera, and all." The very next sentence, however, refutes this dire note: "Suddenly, and without any bang (I am the only bang) the entire so-called underground, avant-garde cinema has shifted in time and space and has become part of the classical cinema, for our own and children's enjoyment."[45] Mekas's abrupt turnaround and his characterization of avant-garde film as "classical" are less startling when read in the larger context of his writings on expanded cinema during this period. The challenge shadow play posed to cinema's

---

[45] Jonas Mekas, from the entry "On the Art and Shadows of Ken Jacobs," originally in *The Village Voice*, December 2, 1965, reprinted in *Movie Journal: The Rise of the New American Cinema*, p. 225.

identity was averted by an act of retrograde remediation, which absorbed shadow play into the history of cinema, a move that also recuperated its illusionism and pleasurable spectacle, made palatable here by a kind of anthropomorphism of cinema, youthfully innocent in its classical phase.

That Jacobs was by this time establishing himself as an avant-garde filmmaker, partly through his work with Jack Smith on films like *Blonde Cobra* (1959–1963) and *Little Stabs at Happiness* (1958–1960), likely made it easier for Mekas to admit the shadow plays into the house of cinema. This leads to the second form of Mekas's reconciliation of Jacobs's paracinema with the narrower tradition of avant-garde film. Mekas's descriptions of the shadow plays drew on the interpretive framework of the revitalization of vision, which he had employed in passionate defenses of other filmmakers, especially Brakhage. From this point of view, Jacobs forced viewers to see reality in new and unfamiliar ways. *Apparition Theatre of New York, Evoking the Mystery*, for instance,

> uplifted the spirituality of the church. For the first time the sad, cold building was touched, explored, looked at with loving attention. Still resistant and frozen, it started coming to life, for thirty-five minutes ... when the pale light strikes fragilely the church ceiling, as the rest of the church remains in darkness—it's a breathtaking moment of meditative beauty; the church becomes a live thing and you identify with it, as if you were this church, alone at night, listening to the city noises with the car lights caressing your ceiling.[46]

The poetry with which Jacobs imbued the church was analogous to that which Brakhage's films revealed in the banal objects and spaces of everyday life. Renan followed a similar line of thought a few years later in his account of *Thirties Man*. Jacobs's shadow plays produced "the effect of film" without using film at all: "It is possible to have 'close-ups' and 'long shots.' And by manipulating the light sources in certain ways, it is possible to have cuts, and dissolves, and even multiple-imposition."[47] More specifically, the filmic effect in the shadow plays was that of the lyrical cinema of Brakhage. Renan did not mention Brakhage, or any other filmmakers, by name. But his claim that Jacobs's act of abstracting the distinct qualities of cinema from the film medium was in pursuit of a greater "sense of immediacy in his film work" clearly has a lyrical, first-person aesthetic in mind.[48] The directness of experience Brakhage sought was realized more powerfully by Jacobs's act of de-mediation, the removal of film from cinema: "The movie image is a shadow of an image photographed from life, while the shadow itself is a step nearer to life, being a shadow of life itself."[49]

[46] Jonas Mekas, from the entry "On Churches and the Shadow Metaphors of Ken Jacobs," originally in *The Village Voice*, February 1, 1968, reprinted in *Movie Journal: The Rise of the New American Cinema*, p. 314.
[47] Renan, *An Introduction to the American Underground Film*, p. 247.
[48] Ibid., p. 246.
[49] Ibid., pp. 246–247.

In 1970, Jacobs began to experiment with 3D, establishing the basis for later work with the Nervous System and the Nervous Magic Lantern. His shadow plays between 1970 and the early 1980s employed multiple light sources to produce both the on-screen shadows and the effect of 3D (fig. 6.9). Among these light sources were two bright bulbs mounted side-by-side on a beam, each covered by a different type of po-larizing filter. Viewers wore glasses with the same filters in the same orientation, one over each eye, so that each set of shadows cast by the side-by-side lights could only be seen by one eye, resulting in the illusion of 3D. Rotating the twin bulbs' mount and thereby reversing their left-to-right orientation made the shadows appear to advance or recede through the surface of the screen. The major shadow play of this period is "*Slow Is Beauty*"—*Rodin* (1974), performed in the fall of 1974 at the Idea Warehouse in New York; the same venue would house McCall's *Long Film for Ambient Light* less than a year later. An anniversary performance of sorts, titled *Febrile Fiber Phantoms*, took place in 1995 at the Cleveland Institute of Art. "*Slow Is Beauty*"—*Rodin* was an anthology show, bringing together several of the shadow play and light display forms in which Jacobs had worked since 1965, each engaging different perceptual mechanics of film viewing like depth perception, afterimage, and apparent motion. Each performance could be thought of as akin to a structural film, isolating a formal element of the medium for investigation and contemplation. The difference, aside from the fact that the performances were filmless, was Jacobs's characteristic insist-ence on disorientation, illusion, and obstacles to comprehension—on "analysis" as a

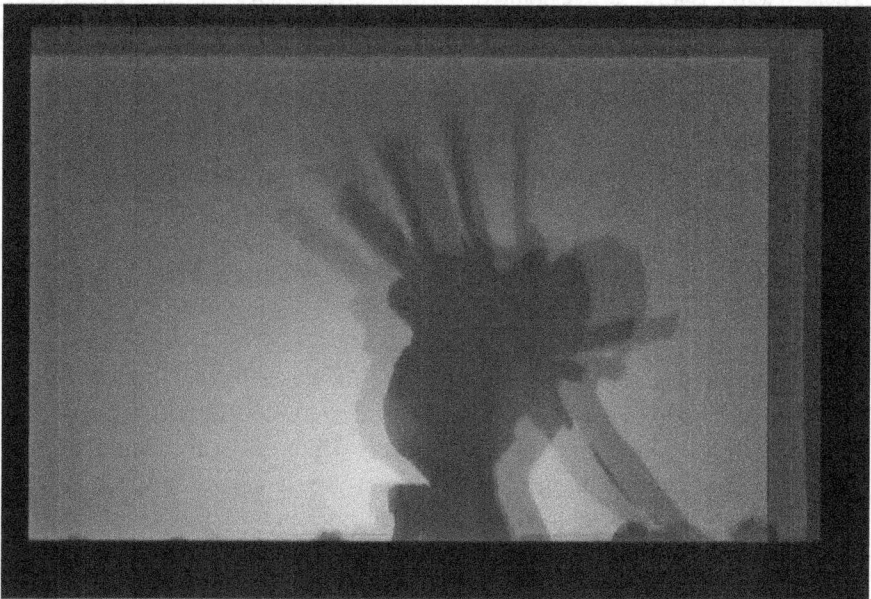

Fig. 6.9. Ken Jacobs, *Man and Wood*, from "*Slow Is Beauty*"—*Rodin* (1974). Performance documentation.
Courtesy of Ken Jacobs.

perplexing and destabilizing experience. Jacobs's commitment to this was such that the process of disorienting the spectators of *"Slow Is Beauty"—Rodin* began before the performance was even underway. Spectators were kept outside the Idea Warehouse and led inside in small groups by a guide. As they ascended to the performance space in a darkened elevator, the guide flashed a strobe light into each visitor's eyes, then led them from the elevator, onto a narrow plank that tilted like a seesaw as each dazzled viewer walked across it, and into the dim performance space. Having made it through this rite of passage, which Jacobs referred to as "committing oneself to disorientation,"[50] spectators were handed polarized glasses.

Several of the performances that followed returned to the forms of light play with which Jacobs had experimented in the mid-1960s, making the direct presentation of light the sole content of the piece. In *Light Under the Door* an intense point light source was shone underneath a closed door and slowly moved so that the oblong shape it cast scanned the floor of the space. For several minutes, the door was edged open further, allowing the operator to slide the light from the floor, into corners, up walls, and around the ceiling. The piece recalled *Apparition Theatre of New York: Evoking the Mystery*, in which the movements of the light created ambiguities of movement and shape. In a detailed chronicle of *"Slow Is Beauty"—Rodin*, Dorothy Pam described a moment when the light's passage over a textured section of the ceiling made it appear to ripple. The light's shaping of objects and surfaces created what Pam called "transitory sculptures."[51] In *Retinal Writing*, Jacobs stood in front of the translucent screen and, after issuing the instruction "look ahead, don't try to follow the movements," drew shapes in the air with a lighted wand. With all spatial points of reference in the room lost in the utter darkness, the afterimages on spectators' retinas seemed to move through the air independently, as though loosed from the virtual surface on which they had been drawn.

When the performance shifted to 3D works, Jacobs's voice prompted audience members to put on their 3-D glasses, or, in *Febrile Fiber Phantoms*, to hold a "Pulfrich filter" over one eye while keeping both eyes open (fig. 6.10). This square of transparent gray plastic alters the way the eye registers depth, increasing the contrast between light and dark areas of the frame and cueing the visual system to read these areas as occupying different planes. Lighter areas of the frame appear to recede and darker areas to move forward, the illusory orientation of depth planes changing as the filter is moved from one eye to the other. These effects were compounded by another perceptual ambiguity, this one a function of the positioning of the lights relative to the performers, screen, and audience. The backlighting of the performers vis-à-vis the spectators reverses the depth cue of size diminution. As performers move toward the *light*, their shadows grow larger and so appear to move toward the *audience*. The opposite illusion results when the performers change direction, their shadows shrinking as they approach the spectators. Viewers were in

[50] Quoted in Dorothy Pam, "The N.Y. Apparition Theatre of Ken Jacobs," *The Drama Review* 19, no. 1 (March 1975), p. 97.
[51] Pam, "The N.Y. Apparition Theatre of Ken Jacobs," p. 103.

Fig. 6.10. Audience (including Ken and Flo Jacobs, right) watching *Globe* (1969, originally titled *Excerpts From the Russian Revolution*), using Pulfrich filters. Centro Galego de Artes da Imaxe, June 4, 2015.

Photograph ©María Meseguer. Courtesy of (S8) Mostra de Cinema Periférico.

all likelihood conscious of this, but the depth cues nonetheless automatically triggered hard-wired responses that contradicted this conscious knowledge. This break between what the viewers knew and what they saw was one of the work's primary disorienting effects. In his account of *Febrile Fiber Phantoms*, Charles Bergengren explained this effect as a result of the audience's "identification" with the light. Because objects that got closer to the light actually appeared, in shadow form, to move closer to the viewer, the viewer's perception was re-oriented to the position of the light as if they were sharing the light's "point of view." Especially susceptible spectators could momentarily experience the sensation of movement when the light was moved: "the audience identifies with the light (objects moving toward the light seem to be moving toward us instead. When the 3-D light source moves, the audience feels like it moves with it!)."[52] Pam had described then same effect occurring in *Chair Piece*, in which a wooden chair was swung back and forth and eventually pulled apart by multiple strings: "When the chair seemed to be swinging at and over the heads of the audience, it was, in fact, swinging away from them" (fig. 6.11).[53] In

[52] Charles Bergenren, "*Febrile Fiber Phamtoms*: Ken Jacobs at the CIA," *The Drama Review* 41, no. 1 (Spring 1997), p. 73.
[53] Pam, "The N.Y. Apparition Theatre of Ken Jacobs," p. 104.

Fig. 6.11. Ken Jacobs, *Chair Piece*, from *"Slow Is Beauty"—Rodin* (1974). Performance documentation.
Courtesy of Ken Jacobs.

Hyperspace, whose title gestures toward this feeling of virtual motion, a light was passed over and through the contours of long coatrack. The already disorienting effects of 3D and the reversed depth cues of size were intensified by the sudden movement of the light toward the coat rack. Bergengren wrote: "as the light source actually moves into the coatrack, threading its way down the centers of the wag-gling hangers, the audience—still identifying with the now moving light source— leans into it, traveling with the light, impossibly, into the center of the jangling tangle ... The audience, wild, roars with disbelief."[54]

Commentators on Jacobs's shadow plays of this period repeatedly attributed to them qualities like fascination, wonder, and pleasurable stupefaction. Bergengren describes the finale of *Febrile Fiber Phantoms*, in which performers bounced balloons into the air, as practically unraveling in chaos as spectators and performers alike, their vision dazzled by afterimages and sense of balance completely thrown off by the illu-sion of 3D, were unable to discern real objects from their shadows (fig. 6.12).[55] Signs of the shift in avant-garde film's dominant critical discourses from the lyrical to the intellectual are evident in some of these accounts. For Pam, Jacobs's analytical act of isolating specific perceptual mechanisms in each sequence of *"Slow Is Beauty"—Rodin*

---

[54] Ibid., p. 75.
[55] Ibid., p. 84.

Fig. 6.12. Ken Jacobs, *Balloons*, from *"Slow Is Beauty"—Rodin* (1974). Performance documentation.
Courtesy of Ken Jacobs.

made room for detached contemplation quite at odds with the disorientation and awe she remarks upon elsewhere in her review. The predominant response, however, was one of wonder analogized by multiple critics to the emotions felt by the earliest moviegoers. This idea of regaining cinema's pre-classical, pre-industrial youth also manifested in another way. Jacobs regularly performed shadow plays made specifically for audiences of children, at one point remarking to Mekas that he had been happier with a special performance of *Apparition Theatre of New York* for children than he had been with a similar performance for adults initiated in avant-garde film: "He thought that the children understood everything he did immediately and had no problems of getting along with it."[56] There is an implicit appeal here to lyrical filmmaking's recurring theme of visual perception liberated from intellect, for which the "untutored eye" of the child is a central symbol.

The children's show Mekas referred to was performed during the expanded cinema program of the 1973 Festival of Independent Avant-Garde Film in London, probably the first major expanded cinema exhibition in which European and North American filmmakers were equally represented. Jacobs's performances, on Friday and Saturday, September 14 and 15, were preceded by Tony Hill's "floor films" (fig. 6.13) which may have included Hill's first performance of *Point Source* (1973). For decades Hill's work

[56] Quoted in Jonas Mekas, "Movie Journal," *Village Voice*, October 25, 1973. Reprinted in Mekas, "Expanded Cinema: Extracts from *Village Voice* 'Movie Journal,'" in Rees et al., *Expanded Cinema*, p. 79.

Fig. 6.13. Tony Hill, *2nd Floor Film* (1975). Frame enlargement. Super 8mm film, silent, 8 minutes. Designed for installation, to be projected back up onto a screen on the glass floor on which it was made.
Courtesy of Tony Hill.

has been preoccupied with the novel perceptual effects generated by strategic camera or projector placement and the manipulation of anamorphic and extreme wide-angle lenses. Hill has designed special camera rigs that produce some of these effects, including a bicycle-mounted apparatus on which the camera rotates synchronously with a rolling wheel (e.g., on a moving wheelbarrow or car), producing in the illusion that the wheel is still and the world is spinning around it (in *A Short History of the Wheel*, 1992). The floor films were designed for vertical under-screen projection onto a specially designed floor where spectators stood. Images of people walking on a glass floor above the camera, when projected as though they were below the viewers, invert assumptions about gravity and relative location in a multi-floored space. The paracinematic *Point Source* extended Hall's interest in spatial disorientation into shadow play, in a variation of the 3D effects Jacobs had been using in his own work. Hill's concise description of *Point Source* is as follows: "A small bright light is the projector, several objects are the film and the whole room is the screen. A spatial exploration of the objects with the light projects [*sic*] them as big as the room encompassing the audience" (fig. 6.14). Like many other paracinematic works, *Point Source* substitutes nonfilmic objects for elements of the film medium, in this case analogizing naked lamp to projector and a handful of everyday objects to "the film." Holding an extremely bright point source light in one hand, Hill moves a wicker basket, tea strainer, and a small, cubic metal grid around the light with the other. Unlike a projector bulb, Hill's light is not focused by a lens and emanates omni-directionally, bathing the entire space in

Fig. 6.14. Tony Hill, *Point Source* (1973). Performance documentation.
Courtesy of Tony Hill.

hard light and immersing the audience in the shadows the objects cast onto the walls and ceiling. This sense of immersion is indeed palpable, the audience experiencing the optical and tactile illusion that they are inside the projected objects, an effect similar to the one Bergrengren described in *Febrile Fiber Phantoms* yet achieved without filters or special glasses.

As I have argued, such pleasurably illusionistic work might have been perceived as being at odds with the ideals of British experimental filmmaking in the 1970s. Though Hill has performed *Point Source* numerous times in the last decade and the work is frequently cited in writings on expanded cinema, little, in fact, has been said about it. In the abstract, it can be easily reconciled with anti-illusionist film practice. But experienced, it is so powerfully illusionistic that the idea of detached contemplation of cinematic materialism seems entirely beside the point. The work's electronic soundtrack confirms this impression. A series of echoing electronic drones evokes the scores of science fiction films like *2001: A Space Odyssey* and *The Andromeda Strain* or the space rock of Tangerine Dream. The music acts to connote the purely perceptual experiences of 3D and bodily movement *Point Source* creates as a journey through space, and the shadows of Hill's objects as dread-inducing alien forms (the passage of the light through metal grid, for instance, recalls in miniature the star corridor scene of *2001*, released five years earlier).

A related cluster of popular references informs Le Grice's *Horror Film 2* (1972), a 3D shadow play performance that narrativized the abstractions of his projection

Fig. 6.15. Malcolm Le Grice, *Horror Film 2* (1972). Performance documentation (1972 performance).
Courtesy of Malcolm Le Grice.

performance *Horror Film 1*. Eatherley, Nicolson, and Roger Hammond enacted a series of tableaus behind a translucent sheet, including interactions with a life-sized plastic skeleton (fig. 6.15). Lit by red and green lights, the image approximated an anaglyph stereoscopic image, taking on a quasi–three dimensionality when viewed through spectacles with red and green lenses. As Lucy Reynolds has written, "rather than bringing an illusion of concrete form to the immaterial film image, the shadowy projections of the performers ... created shifting discrepancies of scale and perceptual ambiguity."[57] While it may have lacked realistic 3D, its unsettling perceptual games and direct references to horror cinema—Le Grice back-projected footage from black-and-white horror films onto the screen—prevent an easy fit between *Horror Film 2* and the project of "Real TIME/SPACE" articulated by Le Grice the very same year. As Reynolds notes, the performance cannot be reduced to "a structuralist stripping away of the illusory tactics of 'dominant' cinema," but instead can "be seen as a theatrical evocation of the uncanny and the spectral" (Reynolds makes a similar claim about Eatherley's 1973 film performance *Aperture Sweep*, in which Eatherley interacts with filmed images of her own shadow).[58] Like Jacobs, Le Grice at least partially reconciled the illusionism of his shadow works with his commitment to structural-materialist

---

[57] Lucy Reynolds, "Magic Tricks? Shadow Play in British Expanded Cinema," *Afterall: A Journal of Art, Context and Enquiry*, no. 23 (Spring 2010), p. 23.
[58] Ibid., p. 29.

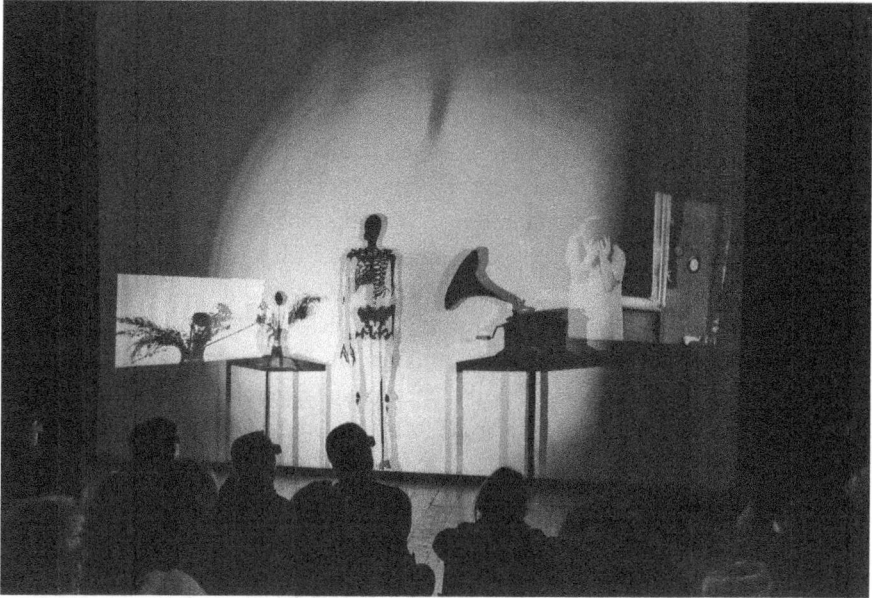

Fig. 6.16. Malcolm Le Grice, *Horror Film 2* (1972). Performance documentation. Frame from *Nosferatu* (F. W. Murnau, 1922) right. From "FILMAKTION: Expanded Cinema and Film Performance," Raven Row, London. March 4, 2017.
Courtesy of Malcolm Le Grice.

filmmaking by casting himself as a kind of modernist magician. *Horror Film 2* was "an illusionistic piece; in much the same way that the tricks of a magician are illusionistic, all the components for the illusion are concretely available."[59] Whether or not one is convinced that any spectator, even one accustomed to the avant-garde, could work out the mechanics of the performance's illusions without lifting the screen, Le Grice's squaring of illusion and materialism does not address the prominence of referential material in *Horror Film 2*. The evocative image of the skeleton, at one point standing under its own power with a flower clutched in its teeth, and those of the rear-projected horror movies, far exceed the status of mere props (fig. 6.16). While Le Grice rarely eliminated image content completely, the connotations of that content were never as pronounced in his other works as in this one. And along with these connotations of the supernatural, Le Grice alluded to two others: the grand guignol theatre and a vaudeville performance titled *Would You Believe It?*, a favorite entertainment of his own childhood. The latter was a 3D shadow play with similarly lurid and spectacular imagery Le Grice recalls seeing as a boy in Plymouth.[60]

[59] Le Grice, "Real TIME/SPACE," p. 162.
[60] Cited in Reynolds, "Magic Tricks?," p. 29.

Reynolds argues that this imagery is ultimately a foil for the anti-illusionistic aesthetic of filmmakers like Le Grice and Eatherley: "their revisitations of the ghost of an earlier pre-cinematic history were intended to investigate the ways in which the projection apparatus and performance might become revelatory tools for a renewed and radicalized form of perception and spectatorship."[61] While undoubtedly true, that both Reynolds and Le Grice must clarify this point speaks to the fact that works like *Horror Film 2* raise specters quite apart from the ones on stage or screen. The return to pre-cinema history by Le Grice and Jacobs, which is to say their re-invention of that history as pre-cinematic, entails a risk to cinema's legibility. Their remediative gestures open cinema up to other art forms ontologically and historically, and avant-garde cinema to the demons of mainstream film: illusion, spectacle, magic, and populism. This explains the moves made by experimental film critics and the filmmakers themselves, which acknowledge their art form's mixed pedigree while attempting—metahistorically, at least—to rein it in retroactively under the umbrella of cinematic essentialism and autonomy.

Industrial Interventions: Paracinema as "Pre-Cinema" II

Paracinematic works that take the form of shadow play or magic lantern performance reach back into pre-industrial history for their points of reference. This gesture decouples cinema from modern machine technology and by implication the standardization of filmmaking and viewing and the ideology of that process. This return to the pre-industrial, and in the case of shadow play the prehistoric, rediscovers qualities and potentials in cinema that were quashed by industrialization, where that term refers both to cinema's presumed basis in late-19th-century technological inventions and the formation of cinema into a commercial industry, organized like any other in pursuit of the same capitalist goals. "Industrial cinema" is a foil against which works like Jacobs's Nervous Magic Lantern performances and shadow plays posit their own kind of cinematic experiences. The persistent associations of youthfulness, joy, wonder, and childlike innocence in discussions of these works attest to this.

Another group of paracinematic objects, on the other hand, *re*-couple cinema and industry, revisiting the historical moment when the two fused. Where the works discussed above are concerned primarily with projected light, shadow, and lens optics—all available to pre-industrial artists—these "industrial" paracinematic works turn their attention to photography, electric light, and the mechanics of intermittency. In doing so, they discover long buried bonds between cinema and a host of other inventions, cultural forms, and popular discourses about perception, technology, and society. Or perhaps it is better to say that they forge, rather than discover, these bonds.

---

[61] Ibid., p. 34.

Like their pre-industrial counterparts, the works I examine in this section are un-abashedly instances of media archaeology, of metahistorical interventions in cine-ma's mechanical and industrial histories. Their explorations of cinema's technological bases open up options for the art form that existed during the process of cinema's technologicization: after industry, but before standardization. That is, before patent wars were won, and before the consolidation of the film industry yielded decisions about standard gauges, mechanisms, and exhibition formats.

Kerry Laitala's *Retrospectroscope* (1996, reconfigured 2000) is a veritable palimp-sest of the turn-of-the-century forces at work in the invention of the film medium. Laitala herself dubbed it "a paracinematic device" that "traces an evolutionary trajec-tory, encircling the viewer in a procession of flickering fantasies of fragmented lyri-cism."[62] Though she is referring mostly to the work's imagery, in the form of backlit transparent photographs, Laitala could just as easily be describing the entire tech-nological and visual form of the work. The *Retrospectroscope* consists of a vertically mounted Plexiglas disk, about five feet in diameter, lined with concentric rings of four by five transparent photographs radiating out from the disc's center (fig. 6.17). Each ring depicts a simple event in serial form, in approximation of a filmstrip: a woman enfolded by sheer white fabric slowly turning, a pointed finger waggling back and forth, the moon passing through its phases, a trio of dancing nymphs from a 1920s stag film, and footage of the Hindenburg disaster (the central and smallest image circle). A motor seated behind the disk and linked to it by a drive shaft rapidly rotates it, while a strobe light produces an ersatz intermittency, crudely animating the image for a viewer with their eyes fixed on one point within one of the rings of photographs. Though Laitala and others have likened the *Retrospectroscope* to a phenakistiscope or zoetrope, both of which employed spinning serial images, its inspiration was Ottomar Anschütz's much more obscure electrotachyscope (1887). That device was almost identical to the *Retrospectroscope*, creating a rudimentary illusion of movement with transparent photographs on a spinning, vertically mounted glass disk. The electrot-achyscope was viewed by a small group of spectators peering through an opening in an intervening wall or panel, a precursor to the aperture plate in a film projector. A Geissler tube illuminated each image as it passed by this opening, and a series of pins on the rotating wheel opened and closed the tube's electrical circuit, generating a rapid flicker in synchronization with the passage of the images past the aperture. Laitala's updating of this system of illumination with the more modern strobe light counterintuitively inverts the technological "progress" her choice implies; since the *Retrospectroscope* is viewed all at once, in its entirety, its intermittency is muted, its images blurry relative to those of its Victorian Era progenitor. In order to experience the illusion that the electrotachyscope produced so seamlessly, viewers of Laitala's de-vice must affix their eyes to one point in space, resisting the visual system's tendency to follow movement. The implications of the different modes of spectatorial address

---

[62] Kerry Laitala, unpublished statement for *Retrospectroscope*, 1997, n.p.

Fig. 6.17. Kerry Laitala, *Retrospectroscope* (1996). Installation view. From *Timeless Motion*, SOMArts Gallery, San Francisco, 2016.

Photograph ©Kerry Laitala, courtesy of the artist.

are clear: the electrotachyscope is part of a history of making moving images easier to consume; the *Retrospectroscope* is part of a cinematic tradition that has troubled that easy consumption.

The "evolutionary trajectory" Laitala attributes to the images is obscure, though each series represents one way new moving image technology was put to use from the beginning: documentation (the Hindenburg), titillating displays of the body (the stag film), scientific study (the moon), and education or instruction (the image of the pointing hand was inspired by Georges Demenÿ, who hoped to use chronophotography as a means of teaching lip reading to the deaf).[63] The photographs of the woman in white fabric, which constitute the largest circle of images, were also double-exposed. After the photoshoot with her model, Laitala used the same roll of film to shoot electrical discharges from the Van de Graff generator at the Boston Museum of Science. Viewed very closely, then, the figure in these photographs appears to loose lightning bolts from her fingers, which are mimicked by crude lightning bolt

---

[63] Walley, "Interview with Kerry Laitala," pp. 94–95.

shapes Laitala etched into the disk itself, intermittently visible in the flickering light. The associations are mystical—a godlike figure controlling the elements—but also associated with the history of moving image photography, as lightning was frequently referenced in scientific explanations of motion photography. An article in *Scientific American* on Anschütz's invention began with this very comparison (fig. 6.18):

> Moving objects when viewed by an instantaneous flash of light appear stationary. Examples of this phenomenon may be seen during every thunder storm occurring at night. The wheels of a carriage, a moving animal, or any moving object seen by the light of the lightning appears perfectly stationary.[64]

This explains both the clarity of the images in Anschütz's device, examples of what *Scientific American* frequently referred to as "lightning photography," and the effects of the electrotachyscope's ingenious flicker system.

Laitala's images also consolidate different cinematic forms and modes. Narrative and non-narrative, fiction and documentary, commercial and avant-garde commingle in the play of denotative and connotative meanings in the photographs. The machine itself references the histories of photographic motion analysis, pre-cinematic optical illusion devices, scientific studies of visual perception, technologies of intermittency, and electrical illumination. As a single object, the *Retrospectroscope* draws these historical lines together, though only to a degree. In its deliberately primitive, D-I-Y mechanical clunkiness, the device also disarticulates these trajectories, leaving them visible as traces running through a hybrid vision machine. It is, then, a thoroughly industrial object. But like the inventions it references, so many of them practically lost to history, the *Retrospectroscope* is a sign of technological invention before standardization, recapturing the thrill of scientific discovery before the subsequent processes of consolidation that formed the industrial cinema as we know it. This also makes the work an emblem of experimental film itself, which, for Laitala, is made into an unwilling source of formal research and development for mainstream media. Avant-garde film is

> part of an 80+ year history that is seldom written about and almost completely disavowed by the Hollywood monolithic industry, although its influences can be seen in the work of many popular directors. This trickle down effect is also rampant in advertising allowing corporations to reap huge financial gain. As this history is largely unknown, people see these mainstream imitators as being innovative without knowing in the slightest the origins of this overlooked history.[65]

[64] "The Electric Tachyscope," *Scientific American* 61, no. 20 (November 16, 1889), p. 301. No author identified.
[65] Kerry Laitala, "Cinema as a Material Presence," *Otherzine* 7 (Fall 2004), http://othercinema.com/otherzine/archives/index.php?issueid=1&article_id=8, n.p.

SCIENTIFIC AMERICAN

[Entered at the Post Office of New York, N. Y., as Second Class Matter. Copyrighted, 1889, by Munn & Co.]

A WEEKLY JOURNAL OF PRACTICAL INFORMATION, ART, SCIENCE, MECHANICS, CHEMISTRY, AND MANUFACTURES.

Vol, LXI.—No, 20.]
Established 1845.]

NEW YORK, NOVEMBER 16, 1889.

[$3.00 A YEAR.
Weekly.

THE ELECTRIC TACHYSCOPE.

Moving objects when viewed by an instantaneous flash of light appear stationary. Examples of this phenomenon may be seen during every thunder storm occuring at night. The wheels of a carriage, a moving animal, or any moving object seen by the light of the lightning appears perfectly stationary. The duration of the light flash in these cases is so brief as to admit of only an inappreciable movement of the object while the illumination lasts. If a moving object is viewed during a succession of light flashes, it will be seen in as many different positions as there are flashes. The stroboscope or zoetrope is based upon this principle, and depends further for its effectiveness upon the persistence of vision. As is well known, these instruments show a succession of images in different positions which are blended in the eye into one continuous image having the appearance of constant movement.

Up to the time when photography arrived at that perfection which would permit of taking an impression in a very small fraction of a second, the stroboscopic or zoetropic pictures were produced by drawing and engraving, and were very crude. The exceedingly sensitive plates have rendered it possible to take a succession of images of moving objects which could be blended together by a stroboscopic action so as to produce all the appearance of life and action.

We have recently on several occasions published the results of experiments of this kind made in our own country. We have now to present some examples of the same class of work produced by Mr. Ottamar Anschuetz, of Lissa, Prussia. This artist has been very successful in taking instantaneous pictures of flying birds, running horses, jumping men, etc., all of which compare favorably with pictures taken under more advantageous conditions. These fine results are due principally to the artistic tact and scientific skill of the operator, but the camera with which these pictures have been taken is an important factor. The principal feature of the camera is its shutter, which is arranged immediately in front of the sensitive plate. It consists of a curtain having a narrow slit which is as long as the plate, the width of the slot being made variable to adapt it to different conditions. This slitted curtain passes quickly over the face of the sensitive plate, exposing successive portions of the sensitive surface to the action of the light. By virtue of this ar-

(Continued on page 310.)

ANSCHUETZ'S ELECTRICAL TACHYSCOPE.

Fig. 6.18. Cover article on "The Electric Tachyscope." *Scientific American* 61, no. 20 (November 16, 1889), p. 301. No author identified.

By this logic, commercial media's unacknowledged exploitation of experimental film's innovations are analogous to the ruthless theft by figures like Edison of the technological inventions of others as the film medium was standardized and the foundation for a fully formed capitalist film industry were laid. A variation of this theme plays out in the enforced obsolescence of film by the manufacturers of digital technology, according to Laitala (giving voice to so many other independent filmmakers). In an essay entitled "Cinema as a Material Presence," Laitala describes the efforts of "businessmen" to "eradicate" film as a threat to the vitality of experimental cinema itself.[66] The *Retrospectroscope* is a model of this historical cycle of invention, co-optation, and standardization that the current technological situation facing avant-garde filmmaking continues.

Laitala's historical turn is toward machines and technological processes that have long been thought of as "pre-" or "proto-cinematic." Bill Brand's *Masstransiscope* (1980, restored 2008 and 2013), while taking the form of one of those pre-cinematic devices, also draws upon a very different technological history: that of train travel. Brand's work is justly famous as an instance of both expanded cinema and public art. It is unquestionably the most frequently seen work of expanded cinema in history, viewed on a daily basis by thousands of people and the subject of scores of YouTube videos. The *Masstransiscope* is installed in the long defunct Myrtle Avenue subway station on the Manhattan-bound side of the B, D, and Q lines. Its 228 paintings line the back wall of the platform, lit by an equal number of fluorescent lights affixed to a second wall that runs between the row of paintings and passing trains (fig. 6.19). As a train speeds through the station, commuters can see the paintings one at a time through a corresponding series of 228 slits in the wall nearer to them. The arrangement approximates the intermittency of film projection—though it is the audience that is in motion rather than the film—and animates the paintings. Simple, brightly colored abstract forms bounce about the "frame," become entangled in slithering lines, change color, and twice morph into vaguely human shapes. The brief animation culminates with the transformation of a red circle into the cone of a rocket that blasts off into illusory depth, finally disappearing "off screen."

Brand's paracinematic installation is, in essence, a greatly enlarged zoetrope. But more interesting than this reference is the *Masstransiscope*'s implication that rail travel is itself a paracinematic form. The perceptual similarities between train travel and film viewing—understood in essentialist terms—have been pointed out many times before. Brand's idea had, in fact, already been thought of over 70 years earlier by an unnamed inventor who proposed to install a series of backlit photographic panels along subway lines in 1909, "to relieve the monotony of subway travel."[67] An article on this proposal in *Scientific American* noted that the effect of intermittent motion in film projection "could be obtained if the pictures were stationary and the audience itself were in motion, so as

---

[66] Ibid.

[67] From the "Oddities in Invention" section of the "Patent Department" feature in *Scientific American*, October 30, 1909, p. 319. No author identified.

Fig. 6.19. Bill Brand installing *Masstransicope* (1980).
Photograph by Martha Cooper, courtesy of Bill Brand.

to view the pictures successively" (fig. 6.20).[68] Most people who have ridden subways have likely experienced the illusory effects caused by the intermittent view through the car's windows as the train passes pillars or other regularly spaced architectural features in the tunnel. In her study of the interconnected technological and social histories of cinema and train travel, Lynne Kirby recounts an anecdote first reported by Terry Ramsaye in which this very effect led to the idea of an improved motion picture shutter:

> Albert E. Smith, founder with J. Stuart Blackman of Vitagraph, is said to have solved the problem of flicker in film images while riding a train. Peering out the window while riding through the New Jersey landscape, Smith saw an analogy to screen flicker in the repetition of telegraph poles the train swept past. He remarked a similar effect in that produced by looking through a picket fence as the train passed through a station. "This gave him the notion of dividing up the flicker by adding blades to the then single-bladed shutter. He tried this out and found that by multiplying the flicker he in fact eliminated it in effect."[69]

Kirby takes train travel as "an important *protocinematic* phenomenon," and claims that the railroad was " 'first of all, a social, perceptual, and ideological paradigm

---

[68] Ibid.
[69] Lynne Kirby, *Parallel Tracks: The Railroad and Silent Cinema* (Durham, NC: Duke University Press, 1997), p. 47. The original reference is from Terry Ramsaye, *A Million and One Nights* (New York: Simon and Schuster, 1926), pp. 351–352.

ODDITIES IN INVENTION.

MOVING PICTURES FOR SUBWAYS.—Moving pictures are produced, as is well known, by a film traveling with intermittent motion before a projector or lantern which throws successive views on the screen. The same result could be obtained if the pictures were stationary and the audience itself were in motion, so as to view the pictures successively. An ingenious inventor has

ARTIFICIAL LIVE SCENERY FOR SUBWAYS.

hit upon this scheme to relieve the monotony of subway travel. He proposes to mount a continuous band of pictures at each side of the subway, and have these pictures successively illuminated, by means of lamps placed behind them. The circuits of the lamps would be successively closed, by means of a shoe upon the subway car engaging contact plates at each side of the track. The accompanying illustration indicates the method of accomplishing this result.

Fluid Siccative.—60 parts of old linseed oil are boiled with 3 parts of carbonate of manganese until viscid. The temperature required is about 536 deg. F. (280 deg. C.). The mass should then be dissolved in 120 parts or more of oil of turpentine.

Fig. 6.20. "Artificial Live Scenery for Subways." From the "Oddities in Invention" section of the "Patent Department" feature in *Scientific American*, October 30, 1909, p. 319. No author identified.

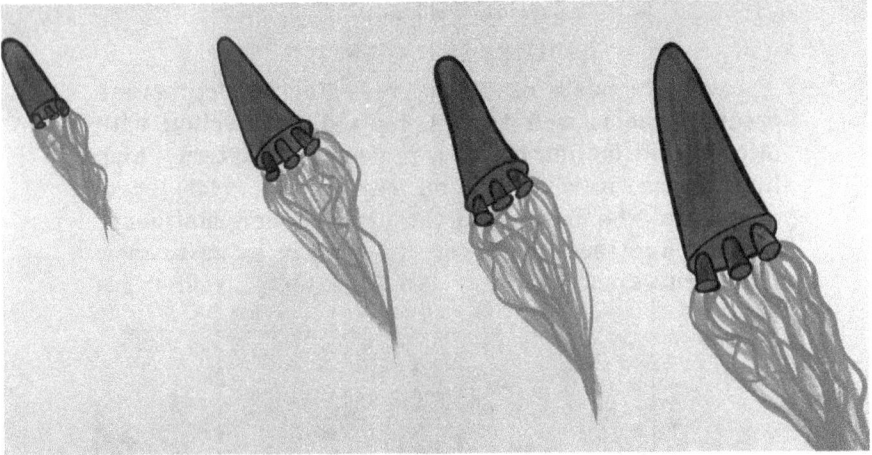

Fig. 6.21. Rocketship panels from *Masstransicope*.
Courtesy of Bill Brand.

providing early film spectators with a familiar experience and familiar stories, with an established mode of perception that assisted in instituting the new medium and in constituting its public and its subjects."[70] By this view train travel is an aggregate of the same technological and social histories as cinema. This allows the re-envisioning of one through the framework of the other, as in the *Masstransiscope* or, to return to the period of which Ramsaye and Kirby write, cinematic novelties like Hale's Tours or the plan to produce "artificial live scenery for subways" reported by *Scientific American* in 1909.

Given the *Masstransiscope*'s simplicity, its playfully cartoonish imagery, and accessibility, reading the work as a remediation of cinema in terms of modernity's transformation of vision might feel like overreach (fig. 6.21). Perhaps those qualities that have made it a beloved and frequently reported on work of public art undermine the *Masstransiscope*'s heady philosophical ambitions. This is the position taken by a review of the work on the occasion of its 2008 restoration. "After watching the installation a few times," Sophia Powers wrote:

> I was no less delighted by its apparition but increasingly put off by its actual appearance. While I am duly impressed by the piece's conceptual underpinnings, its execution leaves me unmoved. The idea could have lent itself to so much—both visually and narratively, but in my eyes it ended up looking a bit too much like a toddler's cartoon from 1970s public television.[71]

---

[70] Kirby, *Parallel Tracks*, pp. 2–3. Italics in original.
[71] Sophia Powers, "*Masstransiscope*: Restored and Reconsidered," *Millennium Film Journal* 52 (Winter 2009), p. 6.

After likening some of the imagery to pasta (without explaining why this counts against Brand's work) and criticizing the primitiveness of its animation, Powers concludes that the *Masstransiscope* does not measure up to its many imitators, created by advertisers in response to the pomp and circumstance that surrounded the restored work's unveiling: "Considering the corporate renditions against the *independent artist's*, however, I can't help feeling like perhaps the former have produced art works comparable to, if not more interesting than, Brand's."[72] While trifling, Powers's review raises specters that are worth addressing. The suspicion that the work is simplistic and merely gimmicky is likely one shared by others, and the review's publication (bafflingly) in *Millennium Film Journal* raises the stakes involved in tackling those views. What follows is offered less in the interest of defending the *Masstransiscope* than in restoring it to the proximate historical contexts from which Powers abstracts it. My discussion of these contexts will be brief, meant primarily to bring to light the specific stakes for an expanded cinema work's installment in a public space in the early 1980s.

During the late 1970s and early 1980s, expanded cinema followed the wider trend in experimental film toward more expressive, referential, and often humorous or playful forms, as in the expanded and paracinematic work of Al Wong and Alan Berliner. The *Masstransiscope*, while at times situated in relation to Brand's earlier formalistic films (including *Moment* [1972] and *Acts of Light* [1972–1974]), is an example of this turn, particularly in its nod to the tradition of experimental animation, through which those qualities of humor and playfulness have always run. As has often been noted, the generation of filmmakers emerging during this period distinguished their work from structural and materialist cinema and theory-saturated "New Talkies" like McCall and Tyndall's *Argument*, Yvonne Rainer's *Film About a Woman Who . . .* (1974), and Laura Mulvey and Peter Wollen's *Riddles of the Sphinx* (1977). Some filmmakers did this quite pointedly. In his 1985 "Cinema of Transgression Manifesto," Nick Zedd, writing under the pen name Orion Jeriko, declared war on the older generation of avant-garde film culture: "We openly renounce and reject the entrenched academic snobbery which erected a monument to laziness known as structuralism and proceeded to lock out those filmmakers who possessed the vision to see through this charade."[73] Among the values Zedd championed—shock, sexual explicitness, the assault on good taste—was humor: "We propose that a sense of humor is an essential element discarded by the doddering academics."[74] Other filmmakers were less polemical, but their work was no less distinct from structural film or the New Talkies. And while not necessarily seeking popular audiences or a greater degree of accessibility, generally speaking experimental filmmakers re-admitted non-academic humor into their films, represented political themes in much less rarified intellectual terms, and often modeled their work on the products of mainstream media. Many

[72] Ibid., pp. 6–7. Italics in original.
[73] Nick Zedd, "The Cinema of Transgression Manifesto," retrieved from UbuWeb, http://www.ubu.com/film/transgression.html, n.p.
[74] Ibid.

filmmakers began working with video across the 1980s, quite against the grain of the cinematic purism of the 1970s, all the more so for their gravitation toward television genres like commercials, PSAs, and music video. Similar developments took place in the wider world of the arts, evident, for example, in the resurgence of interest in craft, work by many artists in early music video, and, of particular relevance to the *Masstransiscope*, the popularity of graffiti art.

Here we come to the intersection of urban revitalization and a surge in public art support during the 1970s, with graffiti seen as both sign of urban blight and potential tool of renewal in the form of public art. Miwon Kwon has identified three models of public art running from the late 1960s into the new millennium: "art-in-public-places," "art-as-public-spaces," and "art-in-the-public-interest."[75] These run roughly chronologically, though with overlap temporally and in some respects philosophically (between the latter two models, in particular). Across the arc of transition from one model to the next, public art increasingly "abandoned its distinctive look of 'art' to seamlessly assimilate to the site," with artists and funders alike paying more attention to public art's relationship with its "community."[76] Though Kwon does not make this point explicitly, the word "community" in this context seems to be code for an audience uninitiated in avant-garde art, often in areas of the city outside the downtown arts precinct. This shift was in response to the physical and psychological inaccessibility of the initial "art-in-public-places" model, exemplified by large-scale abstract sculptural works by artists like Alexander Calder and Henry Moore. Kwon outlines the perceived problems with such works and signals the ideals toward which subsequent models of public art would shift:

> Many critics and artists argued that autonomous signature-style art works sited in public places functioned more like extensions of the museum, advertising individual artists and their accomplishments (and by extension their patrons' status) rather than making any genuine gestures toward public engagement. It was further argued that despite the physical accessibility, public art remained resolutely inaccessible insofar as the prevalent style of modernist abstraction remained indecipherable, uninteresting, and meaningless to a general audience. The art work's seeming indifference to the particular conditions of the site and/or its proximate audience was reciprocated by the public's indifference, even hostility toward the foreignness of abstract art's visual language and toward its aloof and haughty physical presence in public places. Instead of a welcome reprieve in the flow of everyday urban life, public art seemed to be an unwanted imposition completely disengaged from it.[77]

The extent to which public art did *not* look like minimal or post-minimal sculpture, and was thus thought to be better integrated into its community surroundings, was a

[75] Miwon Kwon, *One Place After Another: Site Specificity and Locational Identity* (Cambridge, MA: MIT Press, 2002), p. 60.
[76] Ibid., p. 72.
[77] Ibid., p. 65.

Fig. 6.22. Photograph of the United Graffiti Artists workshop. From the United Graffiti Artists 1975 exhibition catalog. Photograph by SJK 171, one of the first graffiti artists to document graffiti in New York City (SJK 171 tag visible on mural wall, upper left). Image © SJK 171, courtesy of the artist.

mark of its accessibility and thus its progressivism. The final stage of this evolution is the "art-in-the-public-interest" model, "distinguished for foregrounding social issues and political activism, and/or for engaging 'community' collaborations."[78] Kwon's paradigm case is the figurative sculptor and portraitist John Ahearn, creator of public artworks like *Homage to the People of the Bronx* (1981–1982), *Back to School* (1985), and a controversial trio of sculptures facing the 44th Street Precinct Police Station in the Bronx (1991, removed and relocated the same year).

Amid these changes in public art ideas and funding policies, graffiti came to the wider attention of the art world. This was due in large part to graffiti artists themselves documenting their work and organizing. SJK 171 (also known as "King of the A Trains"), one of the first graffiti artists to document his own work and that of fellow artists, was also a founding member of United Graffiti Artists. He recalls, "when we joined UGA in 1972 we became Graffiti Artists, without knowing that we were," capitalizing the term to indicate the sudden shift of perceptions of graffiti, and its entrance into the art world, in the early seventies.[79] Commenting on the first significant exhibition of graffiti art, United Graffiti Artists 1975 at Artists Space in Soho (fig. 6.22), Lawrence Alloway invoked the values of the "art-in-the-public-interest" model:

[78] Ibid., p. 60.
[79] Email to the author, October 7, 2019.

One of the visual pleasures of this work was its brilliant adaptation to the environment. Though the writing amounted technically to vandalism, it was hard to object to the brilliant floralization of complete trains. To see these ebullient logos compete at the scale of architecture and billboards was to enjoy the marks of individualism and a kind of primitive energy. The interaction of the rotund, zigzagging, bulging letters with the irregular geometrics of the urban environment was a great if unlegislated pleasure.[80]

Graffiti's "adaptation" to its surrounding architectural space, with which it was able to "compete," was a sign of its vitality and potential political value, to which Alloway alludes when he acknowledges that graffiti "hard to object to" even if it is illegal. For further evidence of graffiti's political efficacy, Alloway cited Hugo Martinez's catalogue essay for United Graffiti Artists 1975, which spoke of the "vast potential of Puerto Rican adolescents and what they might achieve by rechanneling their energies."[81] For Alloway, this "rechanneling" process meant "diverting the artists toward the manufacture of commodities. Thus social service (keeping them out of the train yards) converges with career protection (earning money and squeezing out the competition)."[82] Alloway recognizes that this is a kind of compromise that both diffuses the power of the work, "now packaged for the market" and re-made as "an ethnic craft for a sophisticated audience," and potentially takes the art form from those who invented it.[83] Though Alloway's tone here becomes skeptical, the process he imagines attending graffiti's attainment of the status of "art" makes it the ultimate "community" public art form by the standards of the art-in-the-public-interest model.

The *Masstransiscope* lies somewhere between Kwon's latter two paradigms, as legislatively endorsed graffiti made by an outsider to that art form's social context, but that nonetheless shed the look of museum art and celebrated an outsider artistic heritage to which graffiti was historically linked. Speaking of the work in a *New York Times* interview, Brand said that he "wanted to get an effect of epic scale, like a mural by Diego Rivera that was off and running ... What I produced in the end seems to me to be like a kind of cosmic history of public mural art ... "[84] The *Masstransiscope* was also funded by an organization committed to art-in-the-public-interest. That organization was Creative Time, Inc., founded in 1974 and, according to its mission statement, "committed to presenting important art for our times and engaging broad audiences that transcend geographic, racial, and socioeconomic barriers."[85] Two years prior to the *Masstransiscope*, Creative

---

[80] Lawrence Alloway, "Art," *The Nation*, September 27, 1975, pp. 285–286.
[81] Ibid., p. 286.
[82] Ibid.
[83] Ibid.
[84] John Russell, "Art People: The Ride-By Subway Mural," *New York Times*, January 16, 1981, p. C20.
[85] From the Creative Time, Inc., website, http://creativetime.org/about/. The descriptions of works funded by Creative Time that follow also come from this site.

Time, Inc., had organized "Downtown Drive-In" (1978), in which experimental and documentary films showcasing New York City were projected in the Edison Parking Lot in the Wall Street district (these included Paul Strand's *Manhatta* [1921], Marie Menken's *Go-Go-Go* [1964], and Red Grooms's *Fat Feet* [1966]). The project's aim was "cultivating a neighborhood atmosphere in the otherwise alienating environment," converting "the shuttered Wall Street area into a vibrant cultural nighttime destination."[86] One of Creative Time, Inc's earliest public art projects was Red and Mimi Grooms's *Ruckus Manhattan* (1975), "a multimedia, three-dimensional representation of Manhattan on display on the ground level of 88 Pine Street," also in the Wall Street district.[87] *Ruckus Manhattan* was in Grooms's characteristic cartoonish style, integrating high and low art references and built to "psychic" rather than physical scale, caricaturally magnifying major Manhattan landmarks as a child's drawing might. In this respect, it has in common with Brand's work a naïve or childish look, like "a toddler's cartoon from 1970s public television," to quote Powers's review of the *Masstransiscope*.

Powers is not necessarily far off in attributing this quality to Brand's imagery, but blunders in counting it as a debit against the work; again, her naïveté about historical context is a strike against her criticism. One avenue of economic and social revitalization in the late sixties and throughout the seventies was children's art programming, including television and film programming. These were seen as forms of educational outreach in terms parallel to the art-in-the-public-interest model. The defining example is the Children's Television Workshop, created in 1968 and understood by its founders from the beginning as a major intervention in both education and television programming policies. The CTW was avowedly experimental, drawing on experimental research in psychology and education conducted in house and dedicated to "experimental"—as in innovative—television production techniques, an indirect link to the first wave of expanded cinema.[88] The CTW's inaugural shows, *Sesame Street* and *The Electric Company*, featured work by an impressive roster of groundbreaking artists, including Philip Glass, Keith Haring, Herbie Hancock, and animators Sally Cruikshank and Carmen D'Avino. This sort of artistic outreach to young audiences was a sign of art's increased accessibility to a larger public as well as its investment in the public good. A related development was the growing number of avant-garde filmmakers and programs aimed at children, a development in which Brand was a key figure. As Children's Film Programmer at the Collective for Living Cinema from 1987 to 1990, he authored "Programming Experimental Films for Children," collected in a handbook assembled by the

---

[86] http://creativetime.org/projects/downtown-drive-in/.

[87] http://creativetime.org/projects/ruckus-manhattan/.

[88] See Edward L. Palmer and Shalom M. Fisch, "The Beginnings of Sesame Street Research," in Shalom M. Fisch and Rosemarie T. Truglio, eds., *"G" is for Growing: Thirty Years of Research on Children and Sesame Street* (New York: Routledge, 2011), pp. 3–24. The book was originally published in 2001 by Lawrence Erlbaum Associates, Mahwah, NJ.

Fig. 6.23. Experimenting with shadow play during the children's workshop of Filmaktion's Walker Art Gallery program (1973). Frame enlargement from William Raban's time-lapse 16mm film documentation of the event (1973).
Courtesy of William Raban.

Gallery Association of New York State, another public arts organization funded partially by the New York State Council on the Arts.[89] Ken Jacobs had performed shadow plays for children during the ICA expanded cinema event in London, and Filmaktion had held children's workshops during its Walker Art Center exhibition (fig. 6.23). While the *Masstransiscope* was not designed for children specifically, the quality of its imagery can in part be explained by the public arts and educational context of the period, and Brand's investment specifically in popular experimental film programming for young people. Setting aside the fact that producing over 200 large paintings would likely militate against Brand opting for a more refined painterly style, ideas about public art in the late 1970s validated the deliberate abandonment of a high art look aimed at an elite, narrow audience of adult art initiates.

The exodus of expanded cinema from the traditional film theater is usually described as an itinerary from black box to white cube (which ignores avant-garde cinema's multiple solutions to the perceived problems of the conventional film

[89] Also see Elizabeth Forbes, "Working the Crowd: Filmmaker Bill Brand Is Trying to Make Independent Films More Accessible to the Public," *Times-Union* (Rochester, NY), October 19, 1989.

theater—in the form of the microcinema, for example). But if expanded cinema wished to expand beyond these limits, one destination could be public space. As the most prominent notions of public art during the height of expanded cinema's second wave called for the integration of artworks and their architectural surroundings, it follows that filmmakers would seek out public spaces with "cinematic" traits, in which case trains and train stations would have suggested themselves immediately. The paracinematic parallel between trains and cinema rests on a cluster of concepts that are applicable to both—intermittency, flicker, and distended temporality, for example—and flexible enough to take shape in two entirely different things. To call trains cinematic is to identify perceptual phenomena, and concomitant cultural and social ones that, while embodied in the cinematic medium, are not contained by it. When filmmakers sought to escape these constraints in the form of expanded cinema, their work took shape according to ideas about whatever new spaces they took to.

"The Obstinate Resistance of Matter to Ideas"

"The cinema is an idealistic phenomenon," Bazin wrote in "The Myth of Total Cinema." "The concept men had of it existed so to speak fully armed in their minds, as if in some platonic heaven, and what strikes us most of all is the obstinate resistance of matter to ideas rather than of any help offered by techniques to the imagination of the researchers."[90] For the realist Bazin, cinema was hampered en route to its destiny by the very materials that brought it into being. The film medium was an inadequate vehicle for cinema's lofty aspirations. In this respect, Bazin has something in common with modernist theorizations of film from which he otherwise radically departs. Like Arnheim, for example, Bazin emphasized the limitations of the film medium. In *Film as Art* Arnheim had written, "The limitations of the [filmic] picture are felt immediately. It is a mistake to deplore this restriction as a drawback … on the contrary it is just such restrictions which give film its right to be called art."[91] The embrace of the "limitation" is characteristic of Arnheim's modernism, and was echoed by Clement Greenberg: "Purity in art consists in the acceptance, willing acceptance, of the limitations of the medium of the specific art … the history of avant-garde painting is that of a surrender to the resistance of its medium."[92] In the same essay, Greenberg called upon the modernist artist to "emphasize the medium *and its difficulties*."[93] The difference is that Bazin saw these limitations as obstacles to the perfection of cinema's capacity for mimesis, while Arnheim and Greenberg embraced those limitations as necessary conditions for artmaking.

---

[90] Bazin, "The Myth of Total Cinema," p. 17.
[91] Arnheim, *Film as Art*, p. 17.
[92] Clement Greenberg, "Towards a Newer Laocoön," in John O'Brian, ed., *Clement Greenberg: The Collected Essays and Criticism*, vol. 1: *Perceptions and Judgments, 1939–1944* (Chicago: University of Chicago Press, 1986), p. 32.
[93] Ibid., p. 34, italics mine.

These intersecting lines of thinking, by which a medium was an obstacle to an art form's ideals, extend through avant-garde cinema as well. In that cinema we find a history of theorizing the film medium as limited, difficult, obstinate. In most cases, the filmmakers themselves characterize film in this way, implying something like a love/hate relationship with their medium. While embracing and heralding the qualities of film, filmmakers have nonetheless often painted a picture of that medium as problematic and resistant to their visionary aims. The emergence of digital video and concomitant claims of film's obsolescence add a new layer to this rhetoric of limitation, one that counter-intuitively favors the recalcitrant old medium over the new and improved cinematic medium of digital video, which one-ups "you push the button, we do the rest" with "point-and-shoot." But these celebratory assertions of film's difficulty contra new media are not the product of the film-digital divide, but expansions upon a set of beliefs that reach back across decades of experimental film history. Recall Broughton's poetic depiction of editing as a process in which the artist struggled against obstinate material that resisted the ambitions of the film artist. Deren and Brakhage took a more Arnheimian view, seeing film's recalcitrance in terms of its automaticity and easy realism. For Deren, the camera and film stock's "infinite receptivity and indiscriminate fidelity" were "the major obstacle to the definition and development of motion pictures as a creative fine-art form."[94] For Brakhage, the film machine was "grinding" the spectator "out of existence," and the solution was nothing less than an assault on that machine and its normative operation.[95] That is, the medium had to be made *more difficult* to use.

Tony Conrad upped the aggressive ante over a decade later, expressing his fury at the "inextricable bind to the commercial process" of shooting, processing, and projecting film by hammering, burning, electrocuting, and cooking film stocks in a search for "alternative mechanisms to working with the material other than using the camera" (see chapter 4). Tossing aside the camera and projector, and torturing the film in non-traditional chemical processes, led to expanded exhibition modes, as in *7360 Sukiyaki* and *Bowed Film*. In another group of works made around the same time, Conrad abandoned film completely, leaving intact the shadow of an ontological structure, or what Conrad the mathematician referred to as an "algorithm," from which he evacuated the medium. Into that structure, Conrad inserted new materials that he felt were better suited to his particular film-aesthetic aims. He thus overcame film's obstinate resistance to his ideas by projecting a completely different set of physical materials into his cinematic ontology.

The *Yellow Movies* are large rectangular sheets of paper on which Conrad, in some cases with the assistance of Jerry Tartaglia, applied varieties of white or off-white household paint to sheets of paper (usually seamless photographic paper) inside a roughly painted frame of black paint (fig. 6.24). Most of the frames measure 72.5 inches wide by 54 inches high, an approximation of the pre-widescreen "Academy" aspect ratio of 1.33

[94] Deren, "Cinematography," p. 60.
[95] Brakhage, "Metaphors on Vision," p. 125.

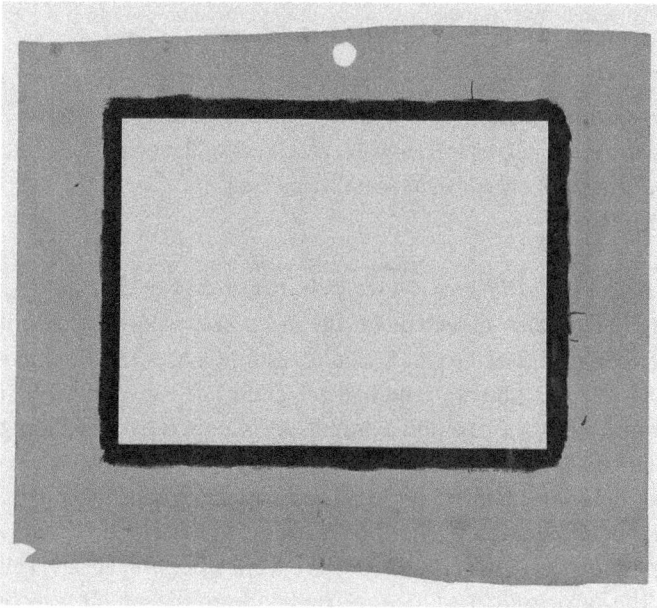

Fig. 6.24. Tony Conrad, *Yellow Movie 2/23–2/24/73* (1973). Emulsion: Sterling gray low luster enamel (water based, thick textured). Base: Dusty rose seamless paper sheet: 92 × 107 in. (233.68 × 271.78 cm). Collection Albright-Knox Art Gallery, Buffalo, New York. Courtesy the Tony Conrad Estate and Greene Naftali, New York.

to 1. As the sheets of paper are exposed to light over time, the paint yellows, a long-term process that according to Conrad defined the running time of each movie in the series. Each *Yellow Movie* is inscribed at the bottom of the frame with the exact date of its execution, conceived as the start time of the film, which is said to "run" indefinitely until the paper deteriorates completely or is destroyed. A *Yellow Movie* stolen from a van in New York in the 1980s was declared no longer running.[96] The movies "premiered" at the Millennium Film Workshop on March 10, 1973. Arranged in rows, they evoked the individual frames of a strip of film and thus encouraged a mode of viewing that clarified their status as cinematic objects. The accompanying program notes documented the materials and procedures involved in the making of each sheet, identifying these in the technical vocabulary of normal film production—for instance:

Yellow Movie 12/14 – 15/72
    Emulsion: Citron tinted low luster enamel, Speedflex Latex Colorizer, Brooklyn
    Paint and Varnish Co.

---

[96] Tony Conrad, personal interview, October 7, 2004. What's more, Conrad describes the ending of this particular *Yellow Movie* as a "sad ending," jokingly extending the criteria of normal film criticism to his paracinematic work.

Base: White seamless paper.
54 by 72.5 inches.

Yellow Movie 1/23 – 25/73
Emulsion: Honey beige flat Speedflex Latex, Interior flat finish midtone base.
Base: Uncut sheet of Avon representative memos.
41 by 55 inches.[97]

Conrad began the *Yellow Movies* series in November 1972 as he was returning
to the United States after an extended stay in Europe, where he had shown films
at Documenta 5 in Kassel, Germany, and assisted La Monte Young in a series of
performances. At Documenta 5 he had seen and been influenced by a number
of films produced at the London Filmmakers' Cooperative, including work by
Raban, Le Grice, Gidal, and Stuart Pound. According to Le Grice, Conrad "stayed
on [in Europe] for an extended period. He became more involved than most visiting American filmmakers in the problems of European work. He returned to the
USA to produce in 1973 his most innovative work since *The Flicker*, called *Yellow
Movies*."[98] The "problems" Le Grice referred to were the attempts to rethink the
nature of the film medium and especially the relationship between film and viewer
that was most extensively theorized in English experimental film. But Conrad's
taking on of this task was initially informed by a somewhat different problem—
that of the dominance of medium specificity in avant-garde cinema and the consequences of this aesthetic predilection for that cinema's institutional situation.
Conrad's experience in Kassel threw this problem into relief (see chapter 4). The
problem, in Conrad's view, was the program of formalism that characterized
avant-garde filmmaking in Europe and the United States, particularly its focus on
the materials of the medium and investigation of the unique signifying capacities
of cinema given these materials. Conrad found that medium-specific formalism
had become and end in itself, simply another new style in which filmmakers could
work to produce films that would be considered "advanced." The very notion of
"advanced art," a term that appears repeatedly in Greenberg's writings, suggested a
constant need for art to move forward, to produce novel works in an ongoing pattern of product differentiation that could sustain the art market.[99] Once admiring
of experimental film's independence from the art market, by the early seventies
Conrad had become suspicious of structural film's formalism (Conrad used the
terms "formalist film" and "structural film" interchangeably, just as he tended to

---

[97] Reproduced in Jonas Mekas, "Movie Journal," *The Village Voice*, March 22, 1973, p. 74.
[98] Le Grice, "Vision," pp. 74–75.
[99] Greenberg most famously used the terms "advanced painting" and "advanced sculpture" to describe the abstract art he championed. Indeed, his entire argument about the emergence of abstract art is a narra-tive of advancement, whereby a series of artistic discoveries brings each art form ever closer to its ultimate purpose, a purpose defined by the materials of each art form's home medium. See especially "Avant-Garde and Kitsch," "Towards a Newer Laocoon," and "Abstract Art," all in O'Brian, ed., *Clement Greenberg*, vol. 1.

elide the terms "formalism" and "medium-specificity"). In this sense, he antici-
pated David James's contention that structural film's appeal to the aesthetics of
Minimalism constituted an attempt to make films marketable in the art world. But
James errs in attributing this desire to Conrad, arguing that the *Yellow Movies* were
an example of how "the duration of projection was reduced into the timelessness
of painting by making more or less extensive selections from the film simultaneously visible."[100] By reading works like *Yellow Movies* in terms of their surface
formal affinities with art objects like paintings, James ignores the fact that they
were meant specifically to *disrupt* the practices of avant-garde film rather than
fit within the practices of the gallery world. In the former context, *Yellow Movies*
risked losing legibility. Thus, rather than seeing Conrad's paracinema as an art
market gambit, I would acknowledge this element of risk in his actions, especially
since that work received little recognition in either context.

Until around 2005, that is, when James's critical attitude toward the *Yellow Movies*
was belatedly borne out as Conrad successfully pursued gallery representation and
re-invented some of his expanded cinema works as art objects in a more traditional
sense (fig. 6.25). A statement Conrad wrote for 2006 exhibitions of the *Yellow Movies*
at Galerie Daniel Buchholz and Greene Naftali, and which was published in the exhibition catalogue co-published by the two galleries in 2008, is telling. It begins by
re-stating the initial objective of the series as intervening in 1970s film culture, dismantling the medium that stood in the way of an avant-garde filmmaker's goals:

> If "a movie" is a system of industrial entertainment production, then it is a studio, a
> camera, a sprocketed strip of transparent plastic, the projection apparatus, and a the-
> ater. On the other hand, if "a movie" is the starting point, on a screen, for the viewer's ex-
> perience, then it is not intrinsically any of the above ... Only by assaulting and occupying
> the arena of industrial film-material manufacturing (occupied by Kodak, Fuji, Orwo,
> etc.) could a movie experience be generated that would change almost imperceptibly
> slowly—"a movie" that would be very slightly, yet measurably sensitive to light.[101]

This is familiar, parallel to Conrad's language of "alternative mechanisms" and his assault upon film's industrial basis and the material and ideological obstacles it posed.
But, in light of history, Conrad in 2006 saw them differently: "the *Yellow Movies* were
not legible in the time of their own making, and so now invite a double reading. The
transitive reading that we are entitled to expect of art works today, announces the
Yellow Movies as a system of engagement between cinema and painting."[102] Once
again bearing in mind Conrad's training as a mathematician and his fondness for
using mathematical analogies for artmaking processes, his use of the term "transitive"

[100] James, *Allegories of Cinema*, pp. 272–273.
[101] Tony Conrad, "*Yellow Movies*," in Christopher Müller and Jay Sanders, eds., *Tony Conrad: Yellow Movies* (Cologne and New York: Galerie Daniel Buchholz and Greene Naftali Gallery, 2008), p. 22.
[102] Ibid.

Fig. 6.25. Four *Yellow Movies* among other works by Tony Conrad, including *Deep-Fried 4X Negative* (on plinth, right) original and restored versions of *Pickled 3M 150* (jars, center), and *Roast Kalvar* (center, on stand). From "Introducing Tony Conrad: A Retrospective." Institute of Contemporary Art, Philadelphia, PA, February 1–August 11, 2019.
Courtesy the Tony Conrad Estate and Greene Naftali, New York.

here suggests a relationship of parity between cinema and painting, which is quite different from an assertion that these works were essentially cinematic in spite of appearing painterly. This new take on the identity of the *Yellow Movies* suddenly validates them as the very sort of art objects of which Conrad had earlier been skeptical. And following this statement are pages upon pages in the exhibition catalogue of the *Yellow Movies* installed in the typically sleek spaces of an art gallery, followed in turn by the standard *catalogue raisonné* format that lays out individual works one per page, meticulously observing their materials, dimensions, and dates of origin. It is arguable that Conrad's original intention in providing such data was to parody art world conventions. Here, it is recuperated as straightforward documentation, guaranteeing the uniqueness of each (art) object.

I make this point about the contemporary historical situation of the *Yellow Movies* in part to clarify my own discussion of them here, where I will take seriously the claim that they were distinctly cinematic works made in response to circumstances unique to the avant-garde film world. In this context, the question of the relationship of the *Yellow Movies* to painting is still important, but takes on quite a different meaning. Even more than other kinds of expanded cinema, paracinema strains the logic of medium specificity and medium belonging to the extent of pointing out their limitations and internal contradictions. In his introduction to the catalogue for a program of avant-garde films organized by the American Federation of Arts in 1976, Whitney Museum film curator John Hanhardt had placed works like *Line Describing a Cone* and *7360 Sukiyaki* in in a strange, liminal state, implying that they at once engaged *and denied* the physical materials of film. His remarks about these films struggle to reconcile them with the model of medium-specific filmmaking:

> The avant-garde continues to explore the physical properties of film, and the nature of the perceptual transaction which takes place between viewer and film. It challenges theories of film which posit as its basis its photographic/illusionistic/representational properties. The traditional coordinates of film/screen/projection are being questioned by "artists who have denied the material and analytical basis of this judgment, not by ideology, but by materiality itself."[103]

Hanhardt's attempt to understand these works according to medium specificity placed him in a curious position, arguing that they at once used and did not use the materials of film. He did not explain how this paradoxical situation worked in practice, wherein a preoccupation with materiality led to its denial. This apparent contradiction appears often in theorizations of paracinema (whether or not the individual author uses that term). As Deke Dusinberre wrote, "the very material emphasis on the material nature of the cinema and of cinematic representation leads to immateriality."[104] McCall also recognized the paradox of the formalist endgame—"I am aware of the dangers of backtracking, that behind every 'first principle' lurks another." But, like Conrad, McCall described his paradoxical filmless *Long Film for Ambient Light* in similar terms, as a shift in emphasis from "the physical processes of production" to "the presuppositions behind film as an art activity." Dispensing with the medium was seen as a way into another dimension of cinematic practice.

The *Yellow Movies* enacted this paradox in order to force a confrontation with it and, perhaps, a resolution. The resolution Conrad imagined would be an end to the tautological bind of formalist filmmaking and the release of avant-garde filmmakers from the reflexive dead end they were circling, merely rehashing developments already exhausted by the "advanced" arts. In referring to the alternative non-filmic materials of *Yellow Movies* in the technical jargon of film production, Conrad extended formalism to its logical conclusion—the "dematerialization" of film, where medium specificity paradoxically contradicted itself. He did this in part by examining often unacknowledged assumptions about cinema's photographic nature, which medium-specific ontologies of cinema tended to take as given. By rethinking photography as the recording of light patterns on a surface, Conrad radically relativized

---

[103] John Hanhardt, "The Medium Viewed: The American Avant-Garde Film," in Marilyn Singer, ed., *A History of the American Avant-Garde Cinema* (New York: The American Federation of the Arts, 1976), p. 44. The quote Hanhardt uses is from Maria Tucker and James Monte, *Anti-Illusion: Procedures and Materials* (New York: Whitney Museum of American Art, 1969), pp. 36–37.

[104] Dusinberre, "On Expanding Cinema," p. 224.

the film medium within a diversified paradigm of emulsions, bases, and screens that could be substituted for one another to produce essentially photographic forms. The crux of this material shift was the radical extension of filmic duration it enabled. The reconceptualization of temporality in art that was the hallmark of the avant-garde at the time intersected with Conrad's jettisoning of filmic materials in *Yellow Movies*, radically opening up cinema's durational possibilities. Thus, to claim that the *Yellow Movies* sought to attain the "timelessness" of modern painting for film is to ignore the fact that the series was created to oppose that timelessness, adopting instead the logic of artistic expansion in which the limits of medium and temporality alike were tested. Incorporating the slow processes of photochemical change into his cinematic ontology effectively made the *Yellow Movies* temporal works—films. The move was perfectly legible within the culture of avant-garde cinema in the seventies. As Mekas wrote about the works when they were shown at Millennium:

> What [Conrad] likes about them, he stated, is that he has the maximum control of image, and that they "are always going." He likes, he stated, long durations in sound and image. Actually, the change of "image" on each canvas or "movie" is very very slow. The action is still slower, Conrad stated, when the canvases or "movies" are rolled into rolls. When unrolled, they are going faster. No actual change can be noticed during the time of one brief exhibition … Changes in image and speed of running could be noticed only after long intervals.[105]

The substitution of photographic materials according to a conceptualized model of film that paradoxically made that medium unnecessary, and the unprecedentedly long duration this allowed, constitute the core of Conrad's challenge to medium specificity. The *Yellow Movies* reveal the degree to which an adherence to medium specificity arbitrarily limited the range of meanings and effects a film could have. Medium specificity is conceived here as a form of technological determinism abetted by economic limits on duration, especially in the case of avant-garde filmmakers who lacked the economic resources of their Hollywood counterparts. But even the most heavily funded filmmaker could not produce a film that ran indefinitely. Warhol's longest films, such as the eight-hour *Empire* (1964) or the 25-hour *Four Stars* (1967), provided early models, as films of such lengths pushed toward the thresholds of spectatorial engagement and standard film exhibition alike, being physically very difficult and expensive to transport and increasing the degree of wear on projection equipment. In 1964, Mekas previewed *Warhol Bible*, a version of the Old and New Testaments with a planned running time of 30 days.[106] Not surprisingly, that film was never made. Though these films only reached the conceptual stage, they suggest that

---

[105] Mekas, "Movie Journal," p. 74.
[106] Jonas Mekas, "An Interview with Andy Warhol," in *Movie Journal: The Rise of a New American Cinema*, p. 153.

avant-garde cinema's predilection for duration had met the very limits of its medium and the strictures imposed by conventional film exhibition. As Conrad has explained:

> In time-based media the issue of duration was an armature for formal elaboration that had not been fully explored, in spite of Warhol and the Structuralists' long and notoriously tedious films. Scaling film to the duration of a human lifetime was the first problem I took up. Since no projector or film would run for fifty years or more, I turned to the underlying question of how to manufacture an image that could involve recorded light, but whose gradual change would articulately implicate the scale of a lifetime.[107]

Following developments within European and American avant-garde cinema to their logical conclusions, then, Conrad encountered the limitations of the material that, in his view, formalism fetishized. This mitigated avant-garde film's oppositionality, since all modes of film practice were ultimately organized around more or less the same filmic technology and routines of exhibition.

Conrad made this very point in the program notes for the "video versions" of *Yellow Movies*, which were exhibited at The Kitchen on May 7, 1973 (fig. 6.26). The video *Yellow Movies* consisted of two different "realizations" of the series, named *Yellow Movie 2/1/73* and *Yellow Movie 2/2/73*. Each realization was composed of 20 sheets, all silkscreened with seragraphic lacquer in the then-familiar video monitor shape of a rounded rectangle. These were arranged in stacked rows of four like televisions on display at an electronics store. The two video *Yellow Movies* were placed side by side at one end of the exhibition space facing a row of four black light fluorescent lamps on the opposite wall. The screens reacted to the excitation of the fluorescent lights by emitting their own light, which would gradually fade over the course of several months, had the exhibition lasted that long. In his program notes for the exhibition at The Kitchen, Conrad wrote:

> A large corporation manufactures a monitor. Another manufactures the energy that comes out of the wall. Plug it in. Inefficiently, it pumps a stream of electrons onto a phosphor plate, and you sit and watch it. Somebody who works in video can then use a complex hardware-software system for gating and modulating the pumping stream of electrons. He has worked with a lot of manufactured equipment, way out at the end of a string of electronic transfer processes, which by a miraculous string of logical identities becomes something you can call watching his tape … The meditative experience of slow change is hard to reach for when creation happens out at the end of the long string of electronic identities. Then it is time to take the manufacturing process out of the hands of big corporations and to sit inside of the monitor that the creator builds himself.[108]

---

[107] Conrad, "Is This Penny Ante or a High Stakes Game?," p. 104.
[108] Tony Conrad, unpublished program notes for *Video Yellow Movies*, 1973.

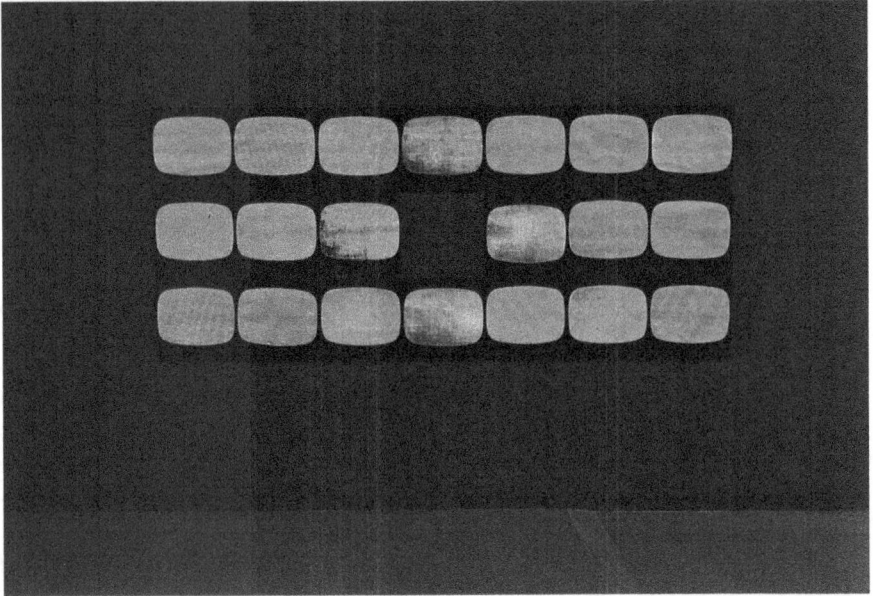

Fig. 6.26. Tony Conrad, *Yellow Movies (video)* (1973). Undone, Greene Naftali, New York, 2016. Citron Yellow Daylight Fluorescent Naz-Dar Screen Process Ink, Naz-Dar No. 5594, and Scrink Transparent Base, Craftint No. 493, applied over Super White Process Color, Art-Brite No. 700 on Black cards; GE F40BL Black Lights; contact microphones; speakers. Twenty 20 × 20 × 1/8 inches (51 × 51 × 0.3 cm) each.
Courtesy the Tony Conrad Estate and Greene Naftali, New York.

As in the case of the "film" versions of the *Yellow Movies*, the video versions were designed to facilitate the experience of extreme duration in a way standard video technology could not. Medium specificity is again implicated as a form of technological and economic determinism enforced on artists from the outside: making films and videos required the maker to follow a strictly delineated chain of production, post-production, and exhibition processes designed into technologies manufactured and controlled by large corporations like Kodak and Sony. If the film or video maker did not use the customary technology of the medium and did not work within the chain of technological production processes, the resulting work would *not* be a film or video by the logic of medium specificity. The aesthetic properties or effects that the film or video maker could explore were limited in the same way; though film and video artists were preoccupied with duration, as in the "meditative experience" mentioned in this passage, this was undermined by the technology they employed.

The *Yellow Movies'* substitution of new materials for camera, film stock, and screen simultaneously necessitated the reconsideration of exhibition. Conrad turned to the installation format in 1975 to further explore this, and especially to revisit questions raised by the *Yellow Movies* and video *Yellow Movies*, which their temporally limited exhibitions at Millennium and The Kitchen had been ill suited to answer. In *Shadow File*, exhibited for 11 days at the Wright State University Art Gallery in Dayton, Ohio,

Fig. 6.27. Tony Conrad, *Shadow File* (1975). Recto-verso installation view of lamps and photochromic panel. From *Luminous Realities: Projection and Video Art*, Wright State University Art Gallery, Dayton, Ohio. October 14–24, 1975.
Courtesy the Tony Conrad Estate and Greene Naftali, New York.

Conrad used photosensitive lacquer and fluorescent light sources as he had in the video versions of *Yellow Movies*. The longer duration of the exhibition, compared to the one-night stand at The Kitchen, allowed for the slow changes in the installation's imagery to become visible. Like the *Yellow Movies*, *Shadow File* was designed to run for an indeterminate period of time, potentially several months, though this running time was limited by the specific chemical composition of its materials. A large sheet of translucent diffusion material coated with photochromic lacquer was suspended in the center of a gallery space, allowing visitors to move around it and stand on either side, not unlike the arrangement of Snow's *Two Sides to Every Story*. The light-sensitive screen, which Conrad referred to as the "photochromic panel," changed color when it was exposed to different wavelengths of light. In ultraviolet light it would darken, passing from light pink to a darker red; in normal, visible light it would bleach. Two intense light sources, one ultraviolet, one visible, were placed on either side of the photochromic panel, thus maintaining a state of equilibrium wherein the panel neither darkened nor bleached (fig. 6.27). When a spectator blocked one of the light sources, the area of their shadow on the panel would be exposed to only one wavelength of light and would react accordingly. Hence, if a spectator stood in front of the ultraviolet light, the area of the shadow would only be exposed to normal light and would slowly lighten. If the spectator stood in the same spot for a minute or more, their shadow would remain on the panel even after they moved, "filed away" on the panel (fig. 6.28). Over a period of several months, the sensitivity of the photochromic panel diminished, causing the stored shadow images to become less and less distinct. Conrad also suggests in his program notes that eventually the various layers of shadow content stored on the panel would become indistinguishable from one another. *Shadow File* could therefore be said to exhibit a "double layer of temporal organization," in Conrad's words.[109] Within the relatively brief span of time that a

[109] Tony Conrad, program notes for *Shadow File*, in William H. Spurlock, ed., *Luminous Realities: Projection and Video Art* exhibition catalogue, Wright State University Art Gallery, Dayton, Ohio, October 14–24, 1975, n.p.

Fig. 6.28. Tony Conrad, *Shadow File* (1975). Installation view.
Courtesy the Tony Conrad Estate and Greene Naftali, New York.

spectator could be expected to interact with the work, that person could observe the
formation of shadow images within a minute or two, and the slow fading out of those
images as the panel returned to its state of equilibrium within a span of roughly 15
minutes. The second temporal layer, which would likely be less obvious to the spectator, was the steady deterioration of the photochromic panel and eventual blurring
together of all its stored shadows.

It was this longer-term temporal layer Conrad emphasized in his program notes
for *Shadow File*, the slow fading and blurring of shadow content and the panel's eventual loss of light sensitivity, which occurred over a much longer period than a viewer
could give to the work. The duration of *Shadow File*, then, was defined by the total
time of its installation at Wright State, a duration that no spectator could possibly
experience in its entirety. Thus, the gallery installation format was viewed as a solution to a problem wherein the typical cinematic exhibition format obscured a major
element of a paracinematic work—its radical extension of filmic duration. Conrad
explained this in his program notes:

> I would guess that the trigger for the inception of my interest in this piece was
> a responsiveness to questions that people had asked me about *Yellow Movie*.
> Comprising in fact a whole family of hundreds of works, the series *Yellow Movie* was
> an exploration of questions of film duration, making, and presentation ... Many of

the misconstruals of my work in the *Yellow Movie* series had to do with their resemblance to painting and the tremendous time scale of the films, which could "run" without perceptible change for weeks, months, or longer at a time.[110]

The "miscontruals" Conrad refers to involved the inability of many spectators at the *Yellow Movies* exhibition at Millennium to understand the work as time-based, a result of its "resemblance to painting" bolstered in part because the work was only presented in a single evening, which militated against the possibility of recognizing its temporality. Creating a piece for long-term gallery installation that could force viewers to recognize a mode of temporal organization that outlasted their presence in the gallery was Conrad's solution to the problems he had encountered with *Yellow Movies*. The use of the gallery became another technique in Conrad's repertoire for subverting the normal processes and materials of film-making and exhibition. His use of the gallery space was a strategy formulated in the terms of avant-garde cinema's radical re-conception of duration in film, itself part of the broader project of varying the modalities of the film/viewer relationship and offering alternatives to the kind of filmmaking and viewing delineated by medium-specificity theory.

Paul Arthur has provided one of the most significant theorizations of avant-garde cinema's search for these new modalities. In his seminal essay "Structural Film: Revisions, New Versions, and the Artifact," Arthur argues that structural film manifested a wider-ranging project in avant-garde film history of exploring alternative conceptions of film/spectator relationships, which Arthur implies is at the center of its opposition to mainstream cinema.[111] The essay's title notwithstanding, Arthur focuses on a small group of films never identified as structural film proper: Warhol's *Empire* (a "major precursor of the structural film" according to Sitney), Brakhage's *Mothlight*, and Conrad's expanded cinema, particularly *Yellow Movies* and camera-less films like *Deep-Fried 4X Negative* and *Pickle Wind*. According to Arthur, these films mark out the range of possible relations between film and viewer *other* than the normal exhibition context involving projection.

Arthur's discussion of *Mothlight* and some of Brakhage's other handmade films aligns with Sharits's model of filmic ontology as divided between object and projection event, at the same time positing Brakhage's work—rather unexpectedly—as an important precedent to Conrad's. Looking at *Mothlight* "off the reel," Arthur claims, "confirms its inclusion in a class of films which direct the viewer from the projection experience 'back' to the source at the physical object." The film, in projection, causes the viewer to feel "an intuition that aspects of the perceived filmic organization can be clarified/contradicted by direct viewing of the strip."[112] This awareness suggests

---

[110] Ibid.
[111] Arthur, "Structural Film," pp. 5–13.
[112] Ibid., p. 7.

the separation of the filmstrip itself from the act of projection, two different modes of experience each with their own rewards. According to Arthur, this implies a resistance on Brakhage's part to the mechanical limitations imposed by the industries of film technology. He sees this as a link between structural film and expanded cinema, concluding:

> What is important to state here is that the examination of the condition of film as simultaneously artifact and performance and the relations between that dynamic and the determining industrial-economic structures are not the exclusive domain of Structural and post-Structural filmmaking but find highly elaborated expression in works that pre-date and in certain ways anticipate this period as well as in films which otherwise have little in common with the Structural aesthetic.[113]

It is from this perspective that Arthur reads the *Yellow Movies* and Conrad's unprojectable or semi-projectable handmade films. Their discarding of some or all of film's materials was at once a refusal of technological and economic determinism built into them and a liberation of filmmaker and viewer from the restrictive positions necessitated by their conventional use. "The importance of these films," for Arthur,

> resides in their postulating a diversity of modalities that the film artifact can assume in relation to its viewer, from the object as sole mediator of the viewing experience to the object subsumed in theatrical performance. By short-circuiting specific agencies of the production system and exploding the fixed boundaries of image-duration, Conrad performs a kind of meta-commentary on current theoretical concerns.[114]

Arthur's phrase "exploding the fixed boundaries of image-duration," in reference to Conrad's position that the *Yellow Movies* were always running, suggests the most radical variation of the conventional film-viewer relationship in Conrad's work, one that Arthur does not directly examine. He begins his essay with a discussion of *Empire*, claiming it as a landmark in the avant-garde's reconception of film-viewer relations. Not only did its extreme duration encourage only "fragmentary contact" of film and viewer, who in this scenario comes and goes while the film remains present on screen; more to the point, the austerity of its image content and uniformity of visual style made more attentive viewing unnecessary. "[T]he form and image-content of the film are so immediately open to paraphrastic statement that one can construct a distinct impression of what its experience entails" without even seeing it.[115] By the time Arthur wrote his essay, Warhol had removed all of his films from circulation, making them accessible only at a level of remove, through descriptions, analyses, and

---

[113] Ibid., p. 10.
[114] Ibid., p. 12.
[115] Ibid., p. 5.

interpretations. Indeed, according to Arthur, the film's "existence as an imagined object in consciousness has become its essential condition, its locus of meaning and influence."[116] The well-documented importance of Warhol's unseen films for English structural-materialist filmmakers is evidence of this. Hence, Arthur refers to *Empire*'s "de-centering and emptying not only of image-content and means but of projection as the ontological requirement for film's status as artifact," and concludes, "at last, the first conceptual film."[117] As Conrad would later put it, "movies always happen, and take place, in your imagination."[118] This points to a final irony. The *Yellow Movies* could easily be "wrapped up, canned, and shipped," to return to Mekas's derisive characterization of his exchange with the Cannes Film Festival organizers in 1966, but they are clearly *not* the cinema they had in mind. Easily distributed and displayed (no projectionist, no theater, minimal technology required), but, though physically palpable as paper objects, essentially invisible as cinema. They assert cinema's essential invisibility, its status as ultimately *conceptual*. Conrad's dismantling of the medium in the *Yellow Movies* answered the call "not to make films" Mekas had made nearly a decade earlier. At last, the first "un-made" films.

Cinema on Paper

Conrad chose paper as the "base," literally and figuratively, for his initial foray into paracinema, in the interest of avoiding a merely arbitrary substitution of alternative materials for those of the film medium. He would do the same for his cooked films, introducing cooking processes on the grounds that film was materially similar to onions and that cooking was analogous to film processing because it involved heat, time, and chemical change. Paper and paint were photosensitive materials that changed color over time in response to exposure, preserving the images of objects that blocked or slowed this process, as when a picture frame removed from a wall reveals a rectangle of unweathered paint underneath. Paper, of course, was also usually rectangular, sometimes acted as screen substitute in underfunded or fly-by-night underground film venues, and, like film, could be cut. It implied actions like framing and composition, and frequently came on rolls.

These material parallels speak to a special relationship between cinema and paper beyond that imagined by Conrad in the *Yellow Movies* specifically. In addition to the obvious connection—that many films begin their lives on paper in the form of a script or storyboards—deeper structural and historical relationships can be found in "paper films," one of the earliest forms of film copyrighting, and in the long and complicated history of the analogy between cinema and written language. Even screenplays

---

[116] Ibid.

[117] Ibid., p. 6.

[118] Tony Conrad, recorded statement on *Yellow Movie 2/16–26/73* (1973), MoMA Audio: Special Exhibitions: *Here Is Every. Four Decades of Contemporary Art*, Museum of Modern Art, New York, September 10, 2008–March 23, 2009, https://www.moma.org/audio/playlist/220/2854.

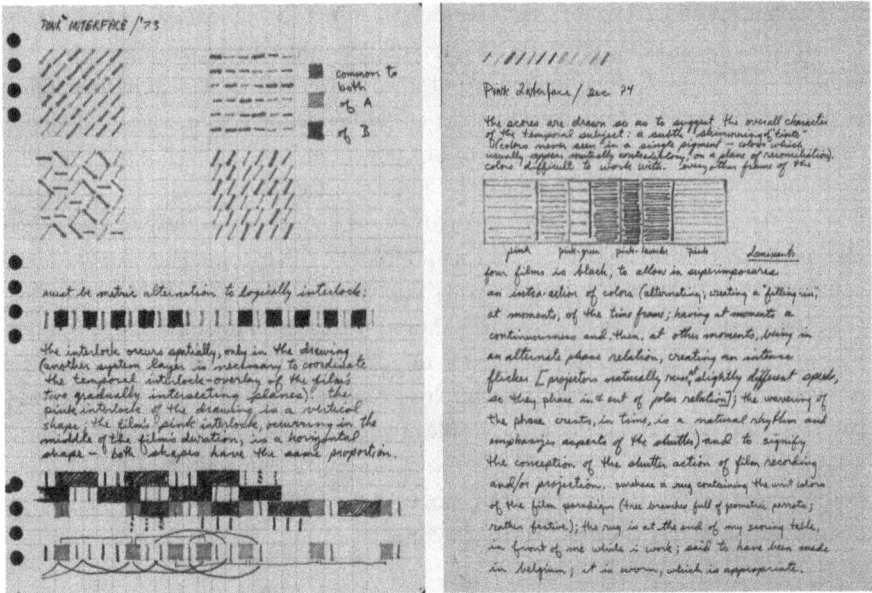

Fig. 6.29. Paul Sharits, illustrations for *Pink Interface*. Left: colored ink on graph paper. 8½ × 6 in. Circa 1974–1976. Right: colored ink on graph paper. 11 × 8½ in. December 1974. From the Paul Sharits Archive at the Burchfield Penney Art Center. Gift of Christopher and Cheri Sharits, 2006.
Permission of Christopher and Cheri Sharits.

and storyboards have been used to plumb the depths of the ontological identity of filmmaking and writing or graphic design in the hands of avant-garde filmmakers. "Cinematic" objects on or in paper include Sharits's illustrated and painted film scores and McCall's schematic designs for his solid light films and the quasi-narrative *Argument*.

The former's drawings and notes for *Pink Interface* (eventually renamed *Shutter Interface*, 1975; see chapter 5), show the filmmaker not merely using paper and ink to plan out a complex work, but thinking in terms of translation between media—of finding corollaries between the formal effects available in one medium (paper) and those available in another (film) (fig. 6.29). Referring to the metrical alternation of hues in the overlapping screens of the installation as an "interlock" (fig. 6.30) Sharits wrote:

the interlock occurs spatially, only in the drawing (another system is necessary to coordinate the temporal interlock-overlay of the film's two gradually intersecting planes). The pink interlock of the drawing is a vertical shape; the film's pink interlock, occurring in the middle of the film's duration, is a horizontal shape—both shapes have the same proportion.

Fig. 6.30. Paul Sharits, *Shutter Interface* (1975). Installation view.
Courtesy of the Estate of Paul Sharits and Greene Naftali, New York.

Once again, Sharits is speaking in the language of temporal "shapes," and thus is able to trace out an equivalent in the medium of paper, which is not intuitively temporal. Other notes for *Pink Interface/Shutter Interface* indicate that "the scores are drawn to suggest the overall character of the temporal subject: a subtle 'shimmering' of tints."

Eisenstein used print and illustrations on paper in much the same way, to approximate cinematic form in another medium, and to imply a non-temporal structure present, at least conceptually, the his film's interplay of filmic and musical composition—most famously in his notes on "audio-visual correspondences" in *Alexander Nevsky* (1938) (fig. 6.31).[119] Maya Deren's *An Anagram of Ideas on Art, Form, and Film* (1946). Published as a pamphlet by Oscar Baradinsky's (later Oscar Baron's) Alicat Book Shop Press in Yonkers, *An Anagram* was, according to Deren, "an organization of ideas in an anagrammatic complex instead of the linear logic to which we are accustomed."[120] For Deren, an anagram was not simply a word formed by re-ordering the letters of another word (e.g., Duchamp's *Anemic Cinema*), but a multi-directionally read structure, an open field of interrelated ideas rather than a linearly ordered sequence with a single point of entry. A hypothetical analogy might be

[119] Eisenstein, "Form and Content: Practice," in *The Film Sense*, pp. 157–216.
[120] Maya Deren, *An Anagram of Ideas on Art, Form, and Film* (Yonkers, NY: The Alicat Book Shop Press, 1946), p. 5.

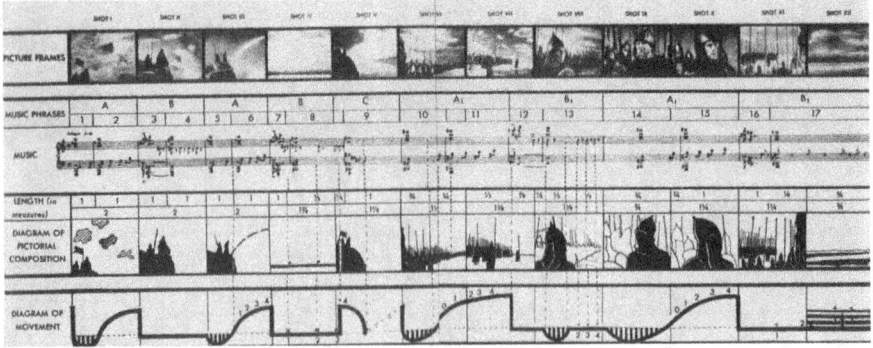

Fig. 6.31. Sergei Eisenstein, illustration of "audio-visual correspondences" in a sequence from *Alexander Nevsky*.

From *The Film Sense*, edited and translated by Jay Leyda (San Diego: Harcourt Brace & Company, 1947).

a sentence whose words could be read in any order and still make meaning. As Deren explained in the preface:

> An anagram is a combination of letters in such a relationship that each and every one is simultaneously an element in more than one linear series. This simultaneity is real, and independent of the fact that it is usually perceived in succession. Each element of an anagram is so related to the whole that no one of them may be changed without effecting [*sic*] its series and so effecting [*sic*] the whole. And, conversely, the whole is so related to every part that whether one reads horizontally, vertically, diagonally or even in reverse, the logic of the whole is not disrupted, but remains intact.[121]

Rather than a table of contents, Deren's pamphlet began with a three-by-three grid, each square sitting at the juncture of X and Y axes, labeled "A," "B," and "C," and "1," "2," and "3," respectively (fig. 6.32). Each of these was given a theme: "A" was "The Nature of Forms;" "1" was "The State of Nature and the Character of Man," so that section A1 addressed science and human nature and the difference between natural forms and those invented by humans. The superimposition, so to speak, of the horizontal and vertical implicit in *An Anagram* not only evoked Deren's own theories of horizontal and vertical composition in poetry and film, but implied a cyclical structure in the alternation of X and Y axes, as in a circular trajectory around the outer points of these intersecting axes, and thus the cyclical forms characteristic of Deren's films. That formal traits of her films was the equivalent of the structure of *An Anagram*. Though it might be read linearly, just as a film is necessarily viewed

[121] Ibid.

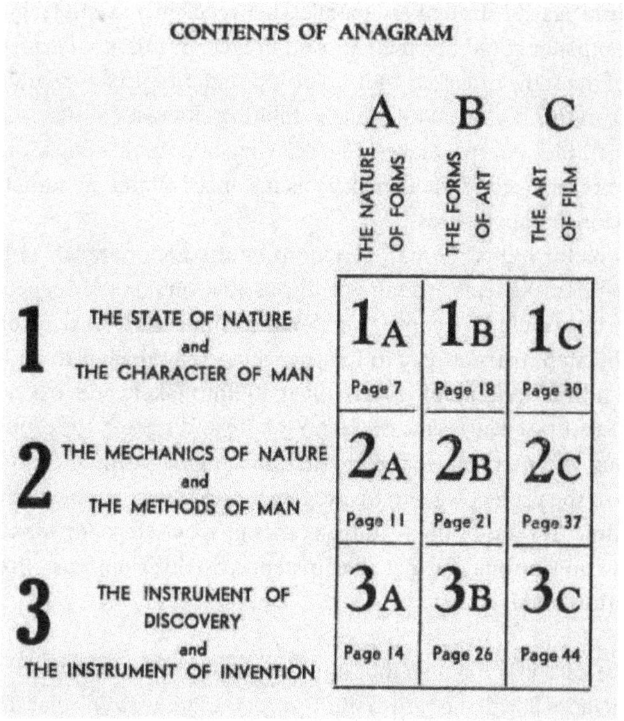

CONTENTS OF ANAGRAM

	A THE NATURE OF FORMS	B THE FORMS OF ART	C THE ART OF FILM
1 THE STATE OF NATURE and THE CHARACTER OF MAN	1A Page 7	1B Page 18	1C Page 30
2 THE MECHANICS OF NATURE and THE METHODS OF MAN	2A Page 11	2B Page 21	2C Page 37
3 THE INSTRUMENT OF DISCOVERY and THE INSTRUMENT OF INVENTION	3A Page 14	3B Page 26	3C Page 44

Fig. 6.32. Maya Deren, table of contents grid for *An Anagram of Ideas on Art, Form, and Film* (Yonkers, NY: The Alicat Book Shop Press, 1946).

from start to finish, it could actually be entered from any point and moved through in any order:

> In an anagram all the elements exist in a simultaneous relationship. Consequently, within it, nothing is first and nothing is last; nothing is future and nothing is past; nothing is old and nothing is new... except, perhaps, the anagram itself.[122]

We will return to this notion of composition with Alan Berliner's paracinematic *Cine-Matrix* (1978), drawing on the principles of post-structuralist textual analysis as a point of reference. For now, it is worth pausing to note Deren's prescience, producing a text in the mid-1940s that articulated ideas that would not be fully elaborated by artists and scholars for nearly three decades.

The theoretical texts of Eisenstein or Deren were not meant as films in the way the *Yellow Movies* were, but as expressions of a homologous relationship between cinematic structure and writing or illustrating on paper. To the expansive film-ontological

[122] Ibid., p. 6.

thinking of avant-garde filmmakers, parallels between cinema and language implied that a work on paper could be cinematic, or, in fact, an *instance of cinema*—a cinematic work of the same order as "a film." It is this latter type of paracinematic object that I address in this section. More than exhibiting cinematic traits or finding ways to schematize filmic concepts via writing, drawing, or graphic design, the works surveyed here were asserted by their makers as instances of cinema rather than paper substitutions for cinematic ideas.

"Instructions for Films" (2007), produced by the no.w.here lab in London and curated by William Rose, is a catalogue of possible versions of "paper films," ranging from scripts (including some that would be impossible to realize), to specific sets of step-by-step instructions, to images whose relationship to an imagined or hypothetical film is at best ambiguous. Over 40 filmmakers and artists were sent a blank white five-by-seven-inch card by no.w.here and invited to "propose instructions for a film. You may render the instructions by any means and appendages."[123] The purpose of the project was "to investigate how a film could be made using only the idea of film." Several of the resulting cards propose steps for making a film in more or less conventional format. For instance, Nicky Hamlyn's "Proposal for a Film Installation" reads:

> Position the card in a room so that it reflects sunlight into an area of shadows. Make a timelapse film of the card in situ. Project the film onto an adjacent wall.

Similarly, Yoko Ono's "Omnibus Film" (a revision of Ono's 1964 *Film Score #6*) instructs the card's reader to:

1. Give a print of the same film to many directors.
2. Ask each one to re-edit the print without leaving out any of the material.
3. Show all the versions together omnibus style.

Some of the cards in this vein provide instructions that would be difficult or impossible to follow. Gill Eatherley's card directed the reader to "assemble all parts of the camera; insert 8mm film; shoot"; on the reverse was Eatherley's illustration of a bewildering pile of camera parts, including tiny springs, screws, and gears—a total atomization of a camera. More to the point, these were only drawings. Even someone with the mechanical wherewithal to assemble a real camera from scratch would not be able to do so using Eatherley's card. Thorsten Fleisch's instructions called for a similarly impossible act of construction: a 16mm film loop that passed from the projector into the mouth of a "human subject" from whom it exited rectally on its way back to the projector (fig. 6.33). The imagery resulted from the

---

[123] See http://www.no-w-here.org.uk/index.php?cat=9&subCat=docdetail&&id=91.

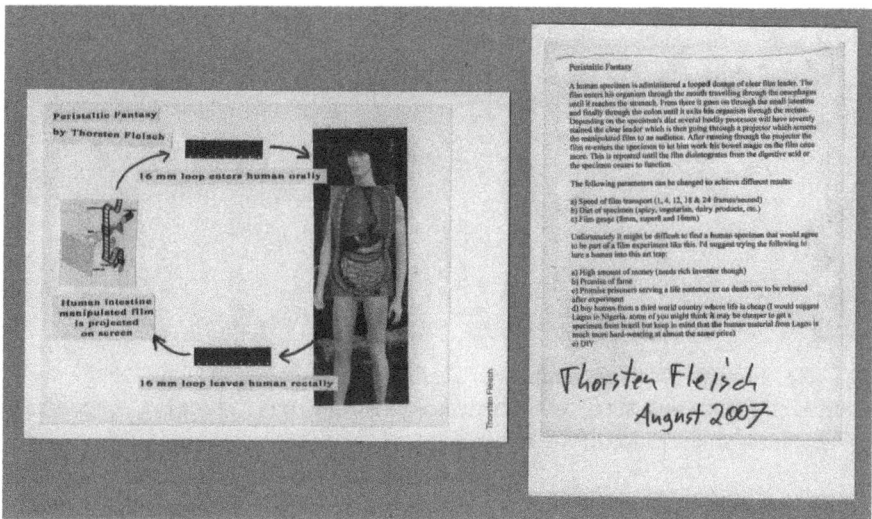

Fig. 6.33. Thorsten Fleisch, *Peristaltic Fantasy*, card for "Instructions for Films." 2007. Limited edition (of 400) set of boxed postcards published by no.w.here lab, London. Image courtesy of no.w.here and Thorsten Fleisch.

human subject's "bowel magic," and the film lasted until it was disintegrated by digestive acid or the subject died.

This latter type of "impossible" instructions imply a kind of conceptual film, one that can only exist in the imagination. As paradoxical thought experiments, in which one must entertain the idea of doing something that cannot be done, they once more invoke the recalcitrance of physical media to artistic ambitions while also bringing to the fore those dimensions of filmmaking that are imaginary, conceptual, or philosophical. A precursor would be Sharits's *Didactic Movie Event—Autological Suicide: scene for film artist at the end of his rope*, which instructed the filmmaker to drop a projector onto his or her head to cast "brain imagery" onto a floor-mounted screen.

Several of the "Instructions for Films," however, propose the card itself as the film. Or, more accurately, they propose an interaction between card and reader, or "user," that produces a film in the instant of that exchange rather than a film that could be made after the fact by following a list of steps. These are to be taken *as films* rather than scripts or stand-ins, and as such are examples of a paper-based paracinema. Benedict Drew and Emma Hart's card reads THE END on both sides (the words are inverted on one side, as though seen in a mirror) with the instructions "to be held in front of a projector" (fig. 6.34). The words, in all caps, appear embossed, which might suggest that they are to be cut out, making the card into a template for projector light, though this is not indicated on the card. Thus, the card could be illuminated by the projector like a tiny screen, or, if held close to the projector, could block its light entirely—a quite different sort of film. Pat O'Neill's contribution offers a grid of nine

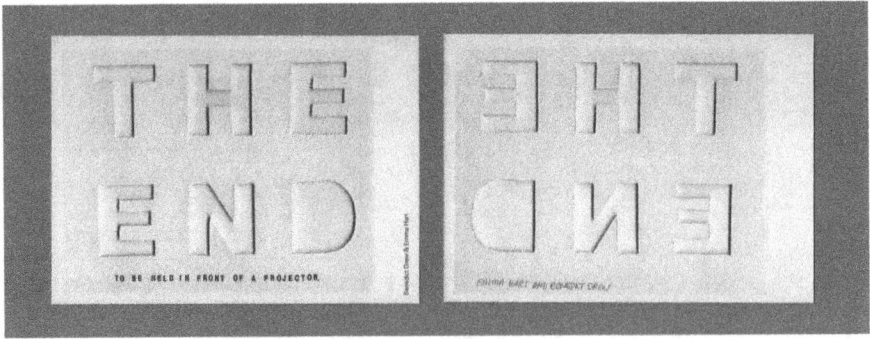

Fig. 6.34. Benedict Drew and Emma Hart, card for "Instructions for Films." 2007. Limited edition (of 400) set of boxed postcards published by no.w.here lab, London.
Image courtesy of no.w.here and Benedict Drew and Emma Hart.

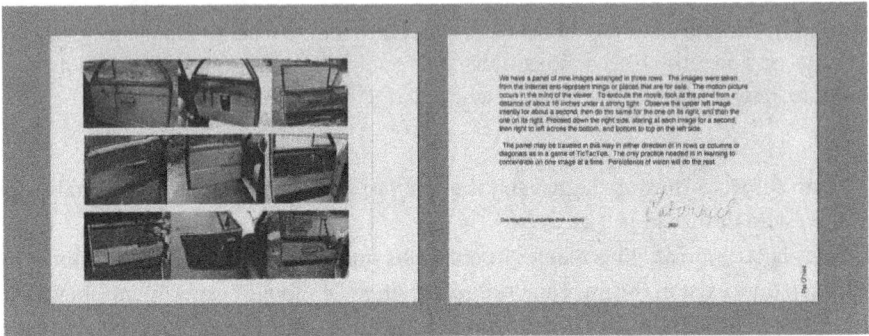

Fig. 6.35. Pat O'Neill, card for "Instructions for Films." 2007. Limited edition (of 400) set of boxed postcards published by no.w.here lab, London.
Image courtesy of no.w.here and Pat O'Neill.

color photographs of open car doors, which O'Neill explains "were taken from the internet and represent things or places that are for sale" (fig. 6.35). Presumably these images were intended to show the condition of the interior of a car for sale online. O'Neill's instructions read:

> The motion picture occurs in the mind of the viewer. To execute the movie, look at a panel from a distance of about 16 inches under a strong light. Observe the upper left image intently for about a second, then do the same for the one on its right, and then the one on its right … The panel may be traveled in this way in either direction or in rows or columns or diagonals as in a game of TicTacToe. The only practice needed is in learning to concentrate on one image at a time. Persistence of vision will do the rest.

O'Neill posits film viewing as defined by a certain kind of attention to serial imagery under intense light, and, like Deren, has sketched out a film with a non-linear, multi-directional structure, created in part by the purposeful visual and cognitive action of an attentive viewer.

The instruction cards Simon Payne and Bradley Eros contributed vary this theme. Rather than asserting the card itself as the material of the film, they use the card to reproduce an image of other paracinematic paper objects. Payne's card features two rectangles of thick paper or cardboard, one on either side (one green, the other orange), each with a smaller rectangular hole cut out of the center. These are presented without comment, but might be used in the same way as Drew and Hart's card, as a kind of light stencil or mask. Or, the viewer might shift her attention rapidly between the two pictured objects to produce a flicker of complimentary colors, an empty white space hovering in the center. Eros's card presents the image of a black zero or letter "O" printed on an off-white paper background. On the reverse, the same paper is seen from the other side, revealed to contain braille writing (untranslated), a high and narrow oval hole cut out in the same spot where the opening of the "O" would be on the reverse side. Next to his signature, Eros has penciled "open your apertures." The analogy of eyes to lens or camera aperture links to experimental cinema's trope of anthropomorphizing the film medium, while the oblique reference to blindness in the braille lettering is either an ironic commentary on "visionary film" or an intimation of alternative ways of seeing and reading the world. The analogy of film and paper here is paralleled by that between reading language visually and tactilely, with cinema represented as a multi-sensory form of comprehension available to multiple physical media.

Duncan White has referred to such works as "text-based paracinema," citing Dieter Meier's 1969 *Paperfilm* as an early instance.[124] *Paperfilm* was "screened" at the Institute of Contemporary Art in London on September 16, 1969 (fig. 6.36). Upon entering the theater, each audience member received a blank sheet of white paper and a small instruction card, reading "Paperfilm by Dieter Meier" on one side, "Instructions: hold the sheet of paper close to your eyes" on the other. A projected 16mm film, 20 minutes long, contained only a title card that repeated these instructions. The paper film "ran" for the same duration as the projected film, a playful inversion of the idea of screening notes, normally read prior to the screening and meant to instruct the viewer on how to "read" the film. Here, the projected film served as the instructions, more or less ignored once the real film began, occurring on the sheet of paper before each viewer's eyes.

An alternate version of *Paperfilm* appeared as a loose leaf page in the second issue of no.w.here's journal *Sequence*, and contained more specific instructions. This

---

[124] Duncan White, "Printology: Film Exercises on Paper," *Sequence* 2 (2011), p. 15.

Fig. 6.36. Dieter Meier, *Paper Film* (1969). Performance documentation. Institute of Contemporary Art in London. September 16, 1969.
Photograph courtesy Dieter Meier Archive.

version directs the viewer to turn the 8.5×11″ sheet of paper over and hold it close to their eyes, opening and closing them "in a certain rythm" [*sic*]. The sheet suggests a pattern this activity can take in the form of two identical columns of the words "open" and "close," one column for each eye, with each word representing a duration of half a second:

open	open
open	open
open	open
close	close
open	open
open	open
open	open
close	close
open	open
close	close
open	open
close	close

open	open
open	open
open	open
close	close
open	open
open	open
open	open
close	close
open	open
close	close
open	open
close	close

Each column consists of 24 words, or imagined frames, following a metric rhythm not unlike the verse-chorus-verse structure of a pop song (an idiom for which Meier, as one of the founding members of the electronic music group Yello, is better known). Thus, the instructional format of screening notes or any other kind of explanatory critical text gives way to another form of organizing language that invokes the cinematic. As White explains, this paracinematic form is "a film for the animated page; or for the animating reader who, through a particular set of actions, becomes a viewer, lighting the 'brain-screen', animating the printed page as a site for the re-patterning of perception."[125] White points out that such paper-based works often employ a simple dual structure; specifically, complementary or contrasting columns of words that parallel the oscil-lating or flickering structure of a film. White proposes that a third, invisible term could emerge from this process, making reference to Eisenstein's concept of dialectical mon-tage: in White's words, "the third or invisible image of hieroglyphs in combination."[126]

For Eisenstein, montage was the defining property of cinema, and he elaborated his conception of this property in his films and extensive theoretical writings throughout his career. Montage was not limited to editing, the joining of one shot to another, but extended into the composition of a single shot prior to any editing process and the relationships between sound and image or between sounds. Any two elements in dynamic juxtaposition—in "conflict," according to Eisenstein's dialectical language—resolved in the viewer's perception into a third element not present in either of the original two. On the basis of this expansive definition, Eisenstein saw montage as a basic metaphysical principle that could be found everywhere outside film. In a sense, then, film was only a recent technological embodiment of a phenomenon that pre-dated its invention by centuries. The simplest expression of this view is found in "The

---

[125] Ibid.
[126] Ibid., p. 17.

Cinematographic Principle and the Ideogram," in which Eisenstein draws an analogy between montage and Japanese pictographic writing. In an afterword to a 1929 Soviet publication on Japanese cinema where this essay first appeared, Eisenstein points to montage occurring "outside the Japanese cinema," in Japanese culture itself:

> Cinematography is, first and foremost, montage. The Japanese cinema is excellently equipped with corporations, actors, and stories. But the Japanese cinema is completely unaware of montage. Nevertheless the principle of montage can be identified as the basic element of Japanese representational culture.[127]

Eisenstein's argument here is that in pictographic writing, two or more adjacent symbols produce through their dialectical collision a new meaning not present in either of them. The symbol for "eye" combined with the symbol for "water" produces the more abstract meaning "to weep," for instance. In other writings, Eisenstein argued that montage could be found not only in cultural forms like pictographic writing but in natural phenomena as well, including human perception itself:

> This [associational montage] is not in the least a circumstance peculiar to the cinema, but is a phenomenon invariably met with in all cases where we have to deal with juxtaposition of two facts, two phenomena, two objects. We are accustomed to make, almost automatically, a definite and obvious deductive generalization when any separate objects are placed before us side by side.[128]

Eisenstein's claims about the ubiquity of montage suggest that film embodied something that existed before its invention. This inverts a kind of medium-specific thinking that locates an art form's essence in its materials; instead, the structure of those materials are conditions of an idea of the art form that preexists them.

The tour-de-force of paper paracinema is Alan Berliner's *Cine-Matrix*, one of numerous works in paper and corrugated cardboard Berliner made between 1977 and 1983. Having been introduced to the possibility of working "with cinematic ideas and concepts without actually making films" by Larry Gottheim and Ken Jacobs at Binghamton, Berliner continued in this mode as a graduate student at the University of Oklahoma in Norman.[129] This was not entirely by choice, however. As the only film student at a university that had no film department, Berliner encountered limited filmmaking resources, and for his entire two year career there made no films, but an assortment of videos and sculptures along with paracinematic works. In a statement on these works he refers to them "representing a range of cinematic 'ideas,' outside the conventional cinematic grammar."[130] The term

[127] Eisenstein, "The Cinematographic Principle and the Ideogram," p. 28.

[128] Eisenstein, *The Film Sense*, p. 4.

[129] Scott MacDonald, "Interview with Alan Berliner," in *A Critical Cinema 5: Interviews with Independent Filmmakers* (Berkeley: University of California Press, 2006), p. 152.

[130] Alan Berliner, unpublished statement on *Cine-Matrix* (1978), http://www.alanberliner.com/paracinema.php.

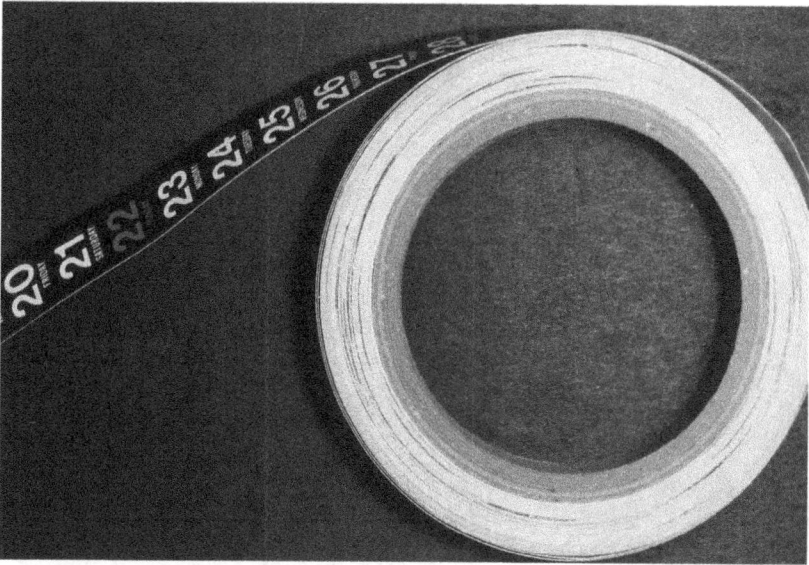

Fig. 6.37. Alan Berliner, *Paper Calendar* (1980).
Photograph by Alan Berliner. Courtesy the artist.

"grammar" here signifies the formal devices of filmmaking rather than, or in addition to, its raw materials: editing, for example, as both a physical process as cutting and joining filmstrips and a cinematically specific means of articulating time, space, narrative, and meaning. His body of paracinema includes "paper films—some of them found objects reimagined—photographic collages, assemblages of cardboard and other materials, and a wide range of other conceptual works, all in search of alternative ways of expressing my love of cinema without necessarily making (actual) films."[131] Some of these, including *Paper Calendar* (1980) and *Intersection* (1978) are modelled after physical elements of the film medium. The former is a roll of calendar dates, one day at time, with a "running time" of three years (fig. 6.37). The latter takes the form of a reel of film run manually through a viewer, mimicking the editing of a film on a Moviola and set of hand-cranked rewinds, a form of film editing that predates the flatbed (fig. 6.38). Fifty-two feet of single-faced corrugated cardboard, three inches wide, passes between two cardboard reels—"feed" and "takeup"—through a wooden viewer that isolates ten lines of corrugation at a time, demarcating a "frame" slightly wider than it is high, as in the typical pre-widescreen aspect ratio of 1.33:1. Berliner affixed lengths of black and white paper tape, masking tape, and strapping tape across these frames, which, when animated as it were by the cardboard's movement through the viewer's aperture, play out a series of permutations of the colors,

[131] Ibid.

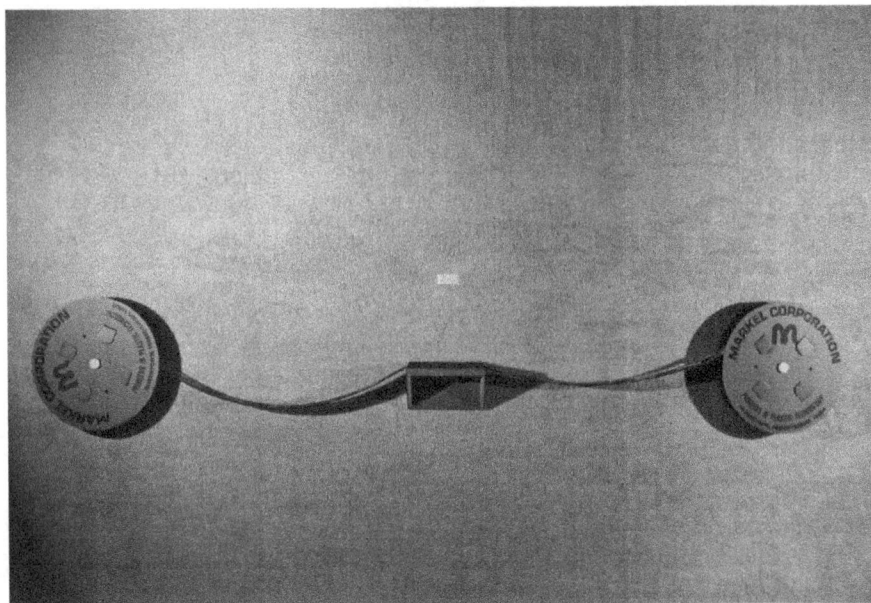

Fig. 6.38. Alan Berliner, *Intersection* (1978). Single-faced corrugated cardboard (52 ft. × 3 in.); four kinds of tape: ¾ in. black, ½ in. white, ½ in. masking and ½ in. strapping; two found cardboard reels (15 in. diameter); wood.
Photograph by Alan Berliner. Courtesy the artist.

widths, orientations, and types of tape. Berliner provides more detail about *Intersection*'s complex form:

> Every frame has a black arc. • Every second frame has either part of a sine wave crest-like arc. • Every third frame has one of three parts of a long sine wave crest-like arc with a straight line connecting the two outer arcs at the crest. • Every fourth frame has one of four parts of a complete sine wave shape—crest and trough. These sequences repeat themselves so that their intersection provides for all the possible combinations of consonant and dissonant orientations of the overlapping tape sequence. In addition, the procedural act of layering the tapes in order—black, white, masking and then striped), is belied by its apparent randomness.[132]

Like many of Berliner's paracinematic creations, *Intersection*'s construction follows a rigorously predetermined permutational structure "belied by [the] apparent

---

[132] Alan Berliner, unpublished statement on *Intersection*, http://www.alanberliner.com/paracinema. php?pag_id=164.

Fig. 6.39. Alan Berliner, *Intersection* (1978). Detail.
Photograph by Alan Berliner. Courtesy the artist.

randomness" of its imagery. Like serial music, the experience of the work does not tend to reveal the staggering formal complexity of the composition.

Nowhere is this more the case than in *Cine-Matrix* (fig. 6.40), Berliner's earliest paracinematic work and perhaps the fullest realization of Deren's ambitions in *An Anagram of Ideas on Art, Form, and Film*. It is also the most perfect expression of a desire to reimagine films as grids, tableaus, or matrices among contemporaneous textual analysts like Raymond Bellour and Thierry Kuntzel. Rather than modelling itself upon the materials of filmmaking—reels, rolls, tape, frames, viewers, and so on—*Cine-Matrix* represents a conception of editing as an organizational rather than a strictly material process. Unlike *Paper Film* and *Intersection*, it does not look like film, but instead embodies the structural possibilities of montage when that process is not conceived of as necessarily linear. As its title indicates, *Cine-Matrix* spatializes editing into a non-linear field of elements whose relations to one another may be traced in any direction, according to multiple overlapping numerical, textual, and color patterns, many of which demand careful teasing out. It is a monument to editing as the privileged form of cinematic signification.

Cine-Matrix consists of 156 frames cut out from pieces of found cardboard, each measuring three by four inches. The frames are arranged in a wide grid formation of 26 vertical columns and six horizontal rows. Though not identified as such in the work itself, each column corresponds to a letter (A–Z), and each row to a number

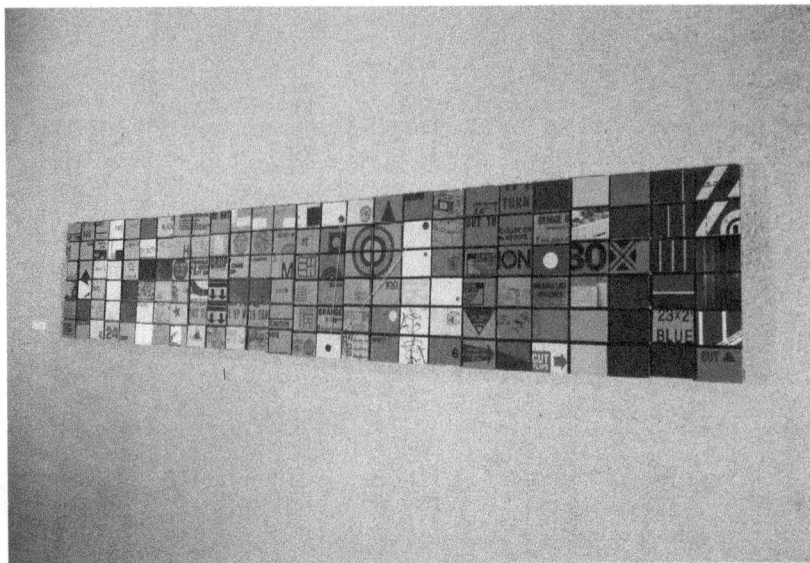

Fig. 6.40. Alan Berliner, *Cine-Matrix* (1977). 156 3 in. × 4 in. cardboard rectangles. Grid: 26 rows × 6 rectangles per row. 118.5 in. × 20.5 in.
Photograph by Alan Berliner. Courtesy the artist.

(1–6); hence, each frame in the grid can be thought of as occupying a unique place—A5, M1, S6, for example. This system provides the basis for a rigorous approach to composition that accounts for each cardboard frame and the relationship of one frame to another.[133] That the rows and columns are not labelled with their corresponding numbers and letters means the viewers must determine this serial compositional logic on their own, something that the large scale of the work makes all the more difficult. At first glance, from a distance, some simple patterns are immediately visible. The frames at P2, P3, Q2, and Q3 were cut from the same piece of cardboard, and together form a bright red circle whose center point is at the intersection of the four frames (fig. 6.41). In columns V through Z, there are far fewer text elements (letters, numbers, words) than in the other columns; colors predominate instead, shifting through the primary colors from orange in column V, yellow in column W, to blue in column Y. The six frames in column J all represent downward movement: J1 includes the words "DO NOT," J3 reads "DROP," J4 and J5 each contain pairs of arrows pointing down, and on J6 is a comic illustration of an anthropomorphized box being dropped on the ground with a grimace on its cartoon face (fig. 6.42). If the viewer discerns the alphanumerical structure of the grid and takes a closer look at individual frames, they can begin to make out the range of organizational principles playing out in each

---

[133] My description and analysis of *Cine-Matrix* are partly informed by Berliner's unpublished notes on the work and a personal interview conducted on May 21, 2013.

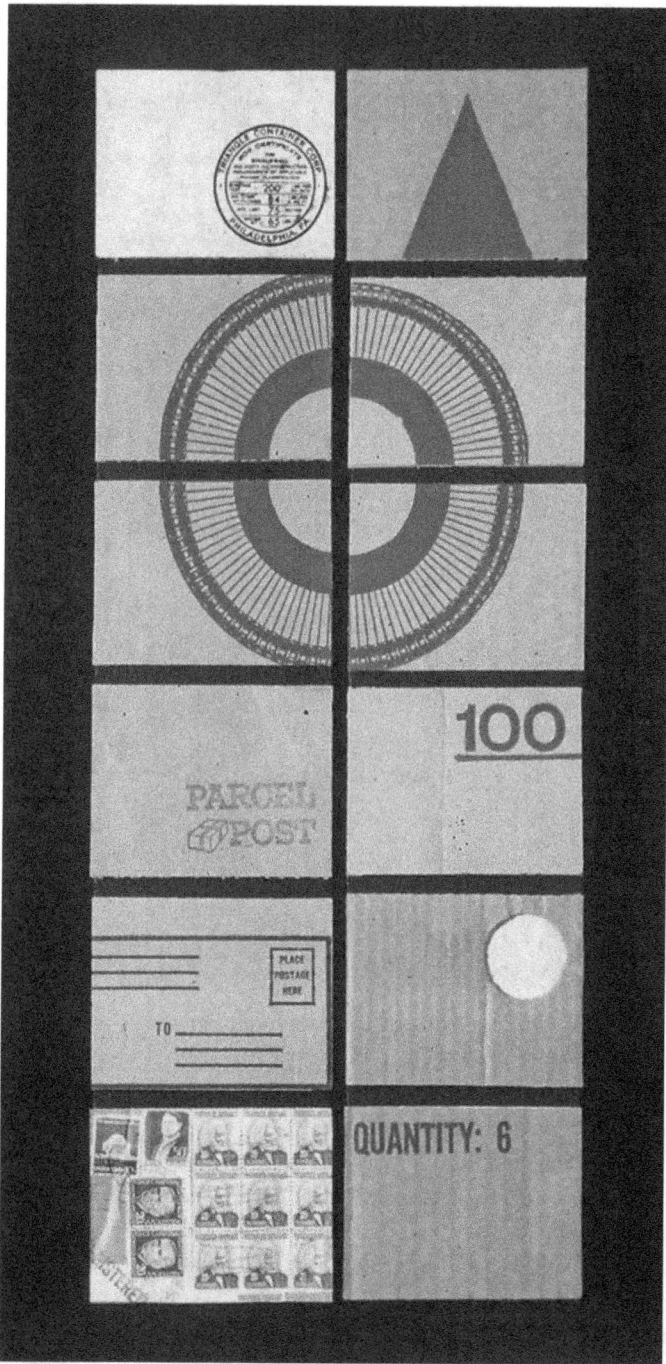

Fig. 6.41. Alan Berliner, *Cine-Matrix* (1977). Detail, frames from positions P2, P3, Q2, and Q3.

Photograph by Alan Berliner. Courtesy the artist.

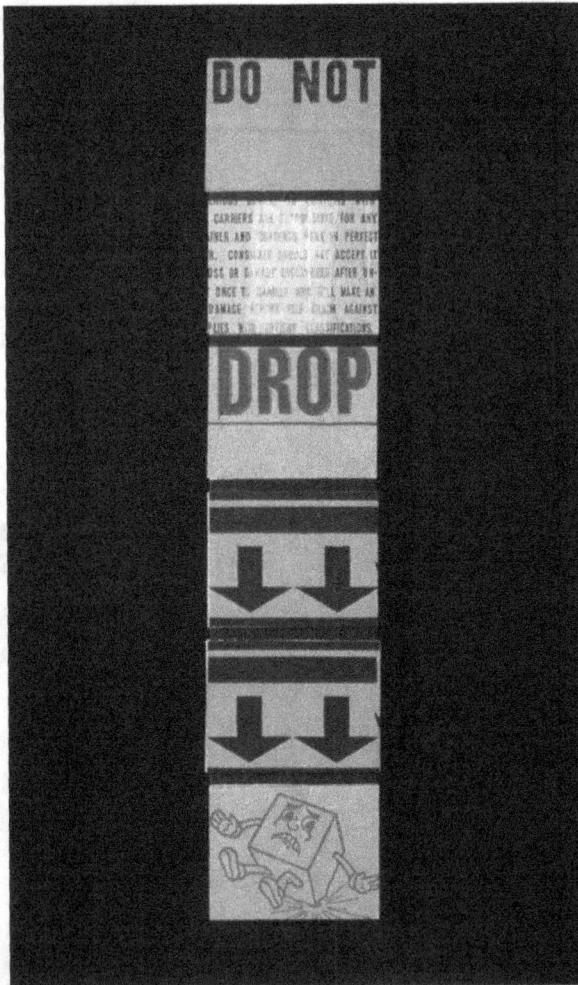

Fig. 6.42. Alan Berliner, *Cine-Matrix* (1977). Detail, column J.
Photograph by Alan Berliner. Courtesy the artist.

direction, and the way that Berliner has precisely structured each frame according to a language of numbers, letters, words, shapes, colors, "emphasis indicators" (arrows, pointing fingers), and "transitional clauses" (any mark that might lead a viewer's eye from one frame to another and indicate a relation). For example, frame D3 contains the image of a grid of four horizontal and three vertical squares (fig. 6.43). In addition to mirroring the overall shape of *Cine-Matrix*, the frame reflexively references its own position in column 4, row D. Frame D3 can be thought of as a "key" to the work, as the referential content in each frame—diagrams, words, colored forms—also reflexively refers to that frame's position in the alphanumerical grid. The number 24 appears on frame D6, the product of multiplying four (D being the fourth letter of the alphabet) and six. Other numbers indicate the same: 20 at D2, the 20th frame in the grid if one

Fig. 6.43. Alan Berliner, *Cine-Matrix* (1977). Detail, column D.
Photograph by Alan Berliner. Courtesy the artist.

counts down and across; the date 1/21/76 at M4 (the 76th frame counting the same way); "Carton #3" at C3; the word "FOUR" at F4, and so forth. Frames A1 and A2 juxtapose two illustrated hands, pointing across in the first, down in the second, offering another clue to the structure of the grid: that it can be read in either direction, each frame referencing its place in both column and row.

The analysis could continue, accounting for the position of each frame and tracing every relationship in all directions across groupings of frames, some adjacent, others quite far from each other. Suffice to say that the remarkable rigor and systematicity of *Cine-Matrix* models editing as much more than a process of building a timeline, of arranging shots one after the other in linear sequence. A reference to Eisenstein's own ideas about montage is unavoidable here. Contrasting his own conception of

montage with those of Lev Kuleshov and Vsevolod Pudovkin, Eisenstein rejected the
idea of editing as being akin to laying down rows of bricks, each functioning as a link
in a chain. He insisted instead on his much less linear model of shots in "collision,"
which implies multi-directionality rather than linearity, shots moving toward each
other to "collide" dialectically, the dialectic itself a simultaneously horizontal and vertical process.[134] Eisenstein imagined montage as occurring in a field or arena of action rather than along a line, as in his famous comparison of montage to an engine:

> If montage is to be compared with something, then a phalanx of montage pieces,
> of shots, should be compared to the series of explosions of an internal combus-
> tion engine, driving forward its automobile or tractor: for, similarly, the dynamics
> of montage serve as impulses driving forward the total film.[135]

Berliner offers a similar idea of the montage effects in *Cine-Matrix*, one that, like
Eisenstein's, evokes a field of dynamic activity in multiple dimensions as well as a
much more complex conception of internal relationships:

> A particularly crucial tension exists between its legibility as a fixed constellation
> and its inherent flexibility in that as the accretion in/through time of found bits of
> information, it is continually subject to reappraisal and shift. It has prescriptions
> that hinge so broad as to accommodate a wide range of interior landscape/vocab-
> ulary combinations.[136]

Berliner's language of matrices and constellations links his work directly to contemporaneous textual analysis, wherein filmic signifiers were loosed from their position in the linear
flow of classical cinema's chronology and causality and were seen to shift through a series of
transient significatory structures. Kuntzel referred to these as "constellations," writing just
two years after Berliner made *Cine-Matrix*. In his analysis of *The Most Dangerous Game*
(1932), Kuntzel read the opening image, an ornate door knocker depicting a wounded cen-
taur carrying the limp body of a young woman, as a "matrix" of signifiers that would "float"
through the rest of the film to be taken up into thematic motifs: "Constellation: group of
neighboring fixed stars forming a determined conventional figure," Kuntzel began. "By extension: a group of things scattered over a limited space":

> The camera frames the doorknocker. Repeated knocks. Something insists on
> being seen. Something—half-naked bodies, animality, a wound—in which desire
> and death are immediately intertwined. A floating figure which the narrative will
> take up again, vary, displace, transform. A floating figure, in its meaning, which the
> filmic discourse is going to insert into different signifying chains.[137]

---

[134] Eisenstein, "The Cinematographic Principle and the Ideogram," p. 36.
[135] Ibid., p. 38.
[136] Alan Berliner, unpublished notes on *Cine-Matrix*, p. 5.
[137] Kuntzel, "The Film Work, 2," p. 13.

That is, like the frames in *Cine-Matrix*, the elements of a narrative film, though customarily read linearly, were disarticulated from the causal chain within which their significatory potential was limited, and thus re-read across multiple non-linear structures in varied combinations determined by logics other than the sequentiality of the plot. The film is reimagined as a matrix, constellation, tableau, field, or, to return to the woven filmic objects of chapter 4, a tapestry or textile. In textual analysis, this thinking surely reached its apotheosis in Raymond Bellour's stunning aerial-view diagram of all 133 shots of the "crop duster" sequence from Hitchcock's *North by Northwest*, in his essay "Symbolic Blockage" (fig. 6.44).

Berliner makes this very point in unpublished notes for *Cine-Matrix*: "Literature is read horizontally left to right but no one ever investigates the matrix qualities of words as they rebound and resonate vertically."[138] The "reading" process for which *Cine-Matrix* calls out is that of the analyst for whom analysis is an activity of opening up a text in multiple dimensions, "loosening" it, to return to the conception of analysis we saw in Ken Jacobs's work. Kuntzel cites Barthes's model of reading in "The Film Work 2":

> [F]or those of us who are trying to establish a plural, we cannot stop this plural at the gates of reading: the reading must also be plural, that is, without order of entrance: the 'first' version of a reading must be able to be its last, as though the text were reconstituted in order to achieve its artifice of continuity, the signifier then being provided with an additional feature: shifting.[139]

Berliner acknowledged the question of medium belonging that paracinematic works like *Cine-Matrix* raised, not only in their use of physical media like paper, which other art forms employed, but in their likening of cinema to language: "Where and when can sculptural and two dimensional form assume cinematic context without being considered models of or models toward a projected film?"[140] That is, can a work on paper be an instance of cinema in and of itself rather than an "instruction for [a] film?" Does the fact that it utilizes printed language necessarily render it a non-cinematic work? Berliner navigated this ontological terrain by claiming certain terms and concepts as inherently cinematic, in much the same way McCall claimed the space of the Idea Warehouse as "a film" for a certain period of time under specific conditions. Berliner expresses this in linguistic terms:

> As a filmmaker I am trained in a certain vocabulary. On both the conversational communitive level and regulating my unconscious implicit assumptions regarding filmmaking is a foundation or core of cinematic conceptual frameworks, a repository of cinema's aesthetic issues, a vocabulary for thinking in terms of film. Words

---

[138] Berliner, unpublished notes on *Cine-Matrix*, p. 1.
[139] Kuntzel, "The Film Work, 2," p. 8.
[140] Berliner, unpublished notes on *Cine-Matrix*, p. 8.

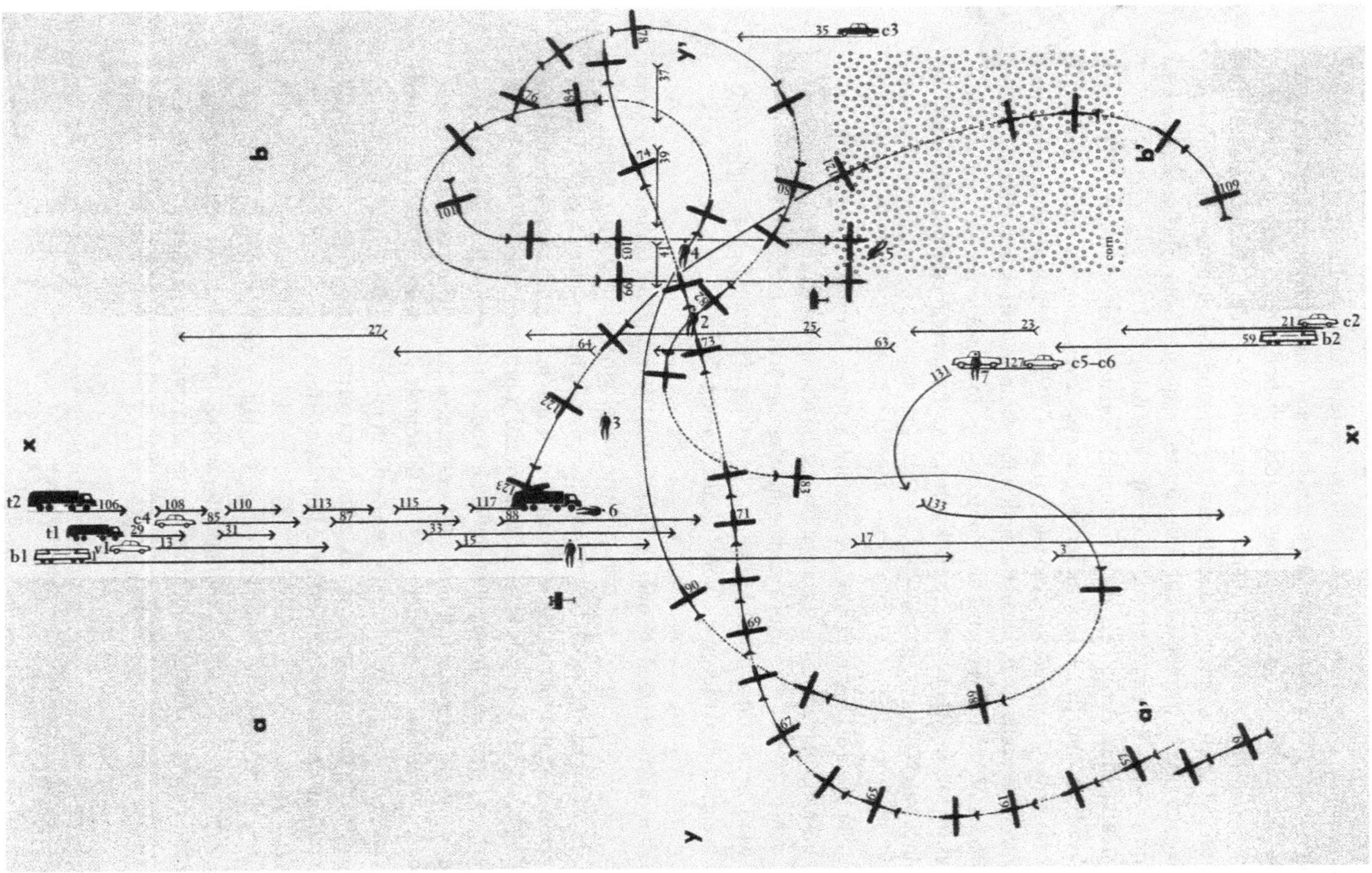

Fig. 6.44. Raymond Bellour, diagram of "Segment 14" of *North by Northwest* (Alfred Hitchcock, 1959).
From "Symbolic Blockage," in Constance Penley, ed., *The Analysis of Film* (Bloomington: Indiana University Press, 2000), p. 106.

like splice, shot, frame, cut are rooted in conventional cinema theory. I propose *Cine-Matrix* as a film.[141]

The project of a paper-based paracinema is not the same as that of analogizing cinema to language, a preoccupation that runs through both classical and contemporary film theory. More than analogizing cinema and language, these paracinematic works on paper reimagine both, reconfiguring each from linear to non-linear form, from unidirectional sequence to multi-directional fields of semi-autonomous units of signification. In cinema, this has extended beyond the linearity of the filmstrip, rendered viewable all at once by filmmakers like Sharits, Iimura, Gschwandtner, and Kerr. Expanded works like *2'45"*, *Film Feedback*, and *Reel Time* trouble the linearity of film production and exhibition, the chain of events from shooting, to editing, through projection. Certain forms of poetry and theoretical writing alike have treated written language similarly, offering models of a textual paracinema for which the printed page is the ideal medium.

What I have shown in this chapter is that a "conceptual cinema" does not rely on the facile notion of a simply "imagined" movie, or the "eyeball cinema" Vincent Canby proposed in 1966 in mockery of the far-out-ness of the first wave of expanded cinema (see chapter 1). It is as material as the most resolutely materialist film, while bearing in mind that some materials are more ephemeral than others. Furthermore, the material substitutions made by the filmmakers viewed in this chapter are not arbitrary. The claim is not that one can simply declare anything to be "cinematic." Paracinema, whether on paper, in light, in paint, in mechanical or ephemeral forms, is asserted and legible as cinema within a context that is, in essence, a shared language within a cinematic culture. Occupying the outer limits of cinema's expansion, paracinema offers an answer to the question with which we began: What *isn't* cinema? Are there any necessary conditions of cinema once the category has been expanded to include so many other things? Cinema, paracinematic work declares, is a bundle of aesthetic traits, effects, and practices, embodying a conceptual array shared by filmmakers and critics, and further specified within historically bound modes of cinematic practice. In the final analysis, the analogy of cinema and language characterizes the former as something collectively invented over time by a community of users. And so, slightly adjusting Tony Conrad's statement, we can say that movies always take place, and are defined, in the *collective* imagination of this community.

[141] Ibid.

Conclusion

Reframing Expanded Cinema

Most of my films accept the traditional theatre situation. Audience here, screen there. It makes concentration and contemplation possible ... My work is classical in the sense that it involves a definite directing of one's concentration. The single rectangle can contain a lot ... It can seem sad that in order to exist a form must have bounds, limits, set and setting. The rectangle's content can be precisely that.

—Michael Snow (1971)

The limitations of the picture are felt immediately. The pictured space is visible to a certain extent, but then comes the edge which cuts off what lies beyond. It is a mistake to deplore this restriction as a drawback ... on the contrary it is just such restrictions which give film its right to be called an art.

—Rudolf Arnheim (1957)

Un film comme les autres

This book has attempted to delimit expanded cinema, to re-frame it. Frames derive their meaning in part from what they frame out. And while the liberatory rhetoric of expanded cinema's first wave decried almost any limits, subsequent waves accepted the necessity of narrowing and specification. The practitioners of expanded cinema in its second and third waves have not always explicitly invoked the language of limits, but their work has nevertheless evinced a shift in thinking about the idea of cinematic specificity and the relationship of expanded cinema to tradition. This elaborates a theme that has been sounded throughout the history of avant-garde cinema, summed up in the statements that open this chapter: a negotiation by filmmakers between their art form's necessary limitations and the radical aesthetic ambitions that sometimes strained against these. "Resources limited, content almost unlimited," Sidney Peterson wrote of the production of *The Cage* (1947), in which whatever objects and ideas his Workshop 20 students at the California School for Fine Arts (later the San Francisco Art Institute) brought to the production were thrown into the mix. "It is precisely the universal 'gravitation' that makes the skills of the acrobat or aerialist both possible and meaningful," Hollis Frampton wrote. "The levitation of our dreams confirms the gravity of our wakefulness."[1]

---

[1] Frampton, "A Pentagram for Conjuring the Narrative," p. 285.

Cinema Expanded. Jonathan Walley, Oxford University Press (2020). © Oxford University Press.
DOI: 10.1093/oso/9780190938635.001.0001

This negotiation has played out in many forms, some emphasizing the difficulties of the film medium itself (Maya Deren and Tony Conrad, for example), others the strictures of the "black box" and conventional film exhibition (e.g., the filmmakers associated with the London Filmmakers' Cooperative), still others the question of cinema's affinities with other art forms (Paul Sharits, projection performers like Bruce McClure and Kerry Laitala, or film quilters like Sabrina Gschwandtner and Richard Kerr). Expanded cinema, I have argued, plays out a dialectic of expansion and contraction, between the specification of cinema and the broadening of the field of materials and forms it can take. It thus enacted a principle of modernism—that of delimitation in the interest of "purity," as in Greenberg's writings—while simultaneously challenging some of modernism's core ideals. Kant, Greenberg's original modernist, "used logic to establish the limits of logic, and while he withdrew much from its old jurisdiction, logic was left all the more secure in what there remained to it."[2] Something like the inverse occurred in expanded cinema. The proliferation of new moving image and light-based media forms potentially expanded what cinema could be, but at the same time threatened its very existence, potentially dissolving it into so much undifferentiated "moving image media," "multimedia," or "intermedia." In its second and third historical waves, expanded cinema confronted this new problem, elaborating a conception of the cinematic that, while expanded across new terrain, retained its legibility and autonomy even in an era of "inter-" and "post-" everything: media, disciplinarity, film, cinema.

The interplay I have traced between the processes and logics of expansion and contraction, of liberation and limitation, has a corollary tension, one not unique to expanded cinema but applicable to all avant-garde film. This tension is in avant-garde cinema's relationship to mainstream film and media, and is perhaps felt more strongly in the classroom than in the field of professional academic writing. Introducing students to avant-garde cinema requires that a difficult balance be struck: one must acknowledge that cinema's radicalism and willful strangeness without "othering" or further marginalizing it in doing so. Teaching avant-garde film to uninitiated students or other newcomers (and most people in the world are newcomers) almost by necessity means confronting negative reactions shaped by unexamined assumptions not only of what constitutes a "good" film, but of what constitutes "a film" in the first place. My own students, for example, often report finding *Mothlight* "boring" despite its three-minute running time, and "not really a film" at all. Re-directing such responses toward a more considered critical reflection on students' own expectations about cinema entails pointing out that those expectations have been formed by conventional cinema, and that avant-garde films are only "strange," "bad," or "not actually cinema" when compared to that dominant. By this logic, experimental films are "films like any other," to reference Godard and Gorin's *Un film comme les autres* (1968). Seen from one perspective, Godard and Gorin's declaration is true: their film was written

---

[2] Greenberg, "Modernist Painting," p. 5.

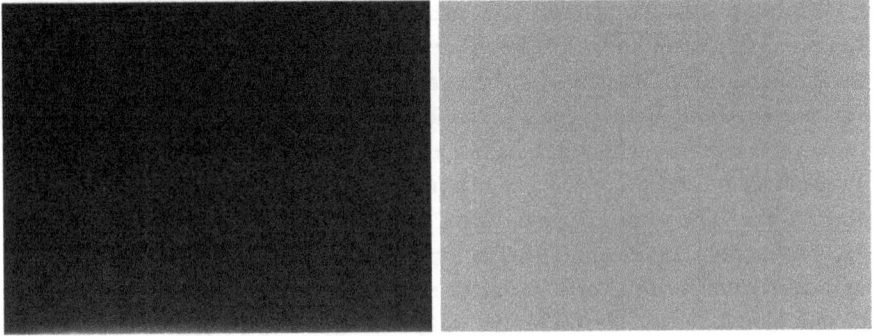

Fig. C.1. Tony Conrad, sequential frames from *The Flicker* (1966). 16mm film.
Courtesy the Tony Conrad Estate and Greene Naftali, New York.

and directed, shot on film, edited on the same devices used by Hollywood editors, and contained images, sounds, actions, and representations. From this egalitarian angle, which asserts the relativity of artistic standards and expectations, films like *Meshes of the Afternoon, Dog Star Man*, or *What the Water Said* are films like any other. Even *The Flicker* (fig. C.1) and *Line Describing a Cone* simply throw into relief necessary and sufficient conditions of all cinema.

This line of thinking is the equivalent of expanded cinema's act of contraction, of clarifying cinematic fundamentals even if these are realized in strange and unrecognizable forms. Beneath the unfamiliar surface of, say, a work of paracinema like *Cine-Matrix* or *Long Film for Ambient Light* is the DNA of all cinema. And historically, this link between avant-garde and expanded cinema and more traditional film has been bilateral, with filmmakers and critics in the popular film tradition at times articulating ideas about cinema that resonate with those of the avant-garde. The Academy Award–winning editor and sound designer Walter Murch has offered a model of film history that is plainly paracinematic, according to which the invention of cinema was predicated upon the formation of certain "cultural movements" during the 19th century. At the heart of cinema's invention was not just the invention of the film medium, but more importantly the presence of forces in the cultural *zeitgeist* that manifested across the arts—well before that invention. Murch summarizes these as "realism" and "dynamics":

> [T]here were cultural movements that matured in the 19th century—the idea of realism (from literature and painting), and dynamics (from music)—which are actually as much a part of cinema as the technical nature of film itself. And in 1787, realism and dynamics had not yet been born. And for film to be Cinema, you need three things: film, realism, and dynamics.[3]

---

[3] William Kallay, "The Three Fathers of Cinema & The Edison/Dickson Experiment (with Walter Murch), accessed May 14, 2017, http://www.fromscripttodvd.com/three_fathers.htm.

The establishment of these movements by the end of the 19th century, well in advance of even the most rudimentary filmic technology, explains the cinema's startlingly rapid maturation, Murch argues. "Realism" and "dynamics" coalesced in the new medium of film, providing the essence of an artistic form in what would otherwise have been merely a technological novelty.

On this basis, Murch identifies a rather surprising trio of men as the "Three Fathers of Cinema": Beethoven, Flaubert, and Edison. Edison, whom Murch takes as representative of film's multiple inventors, provided a medium in which Flaubert's meticulous observation of everyday reality and Beethoven's aggressively dynamic rhythms and orchestrations could merge. That is, Flaubert prefigures photographic realism, Beethoven envisions montage in musical form, and Edison provides the vehicle to propel these two cultural forces, now synthesized, into the 20th century as a new, quintessentially modern art form: cinema is in its essence "the dynamic representation of closely observed reality," Murch argues.[4] Hence, by a creative reversal of historical order, the film medium comes last rather than first in the chain of inventions prerequisite to the emergence of cinema.

Murch's account of the "three fathers of cinema" is not new, of course. It retells a story about cinema's origins told previously by Bazin, Frampton, and the early film historian Terry Ramsaye (who, like the researchers of the Prehistoric Picture Project, begins his account of film history in the stone age). Note that Murch's account also vacillates between two apparently opposing positions on cinema's ontology. One position is that cinema has an essence that distinguishes it from the other arts, thus securing its autonomy and validity as an art form. There is even an element of medium specificity in Murch's creative history: film is mechanical and chemical by nature, a physical medium, in his words, "ideally suited to the dynamic representation of closely observed reality."[5] The other ontological position, however, is a hybrid one, which has cinema drawing upon the essences of other arts forms. Cinema's essence is envisioned as an amalgamation of the essences of literature, painting, and music, making it a kind of trans-medium. Murch holds these two ontologies in a kind of generative tension, and in doing so unexpectedly articulates a major theoretical preoccupation that has been felt most acutely in avant-garde and expanded cinema: the charting of cinema's ontology in relation to the other arts. He also outlines, perhaps unwittingly, the very terms of expanded cinema's second and third waves, even implying a cinema beyond the bounds of moving image media.

The complex model of cinematic essentialism I have attributed to expanded cinema in this book is offered as a corrective to recent assaults upon notions of "specificity," which often point to the multiplication of moving image media forms in the 1960s and 2000s as evidence that beliefs in specificity are untenable and even counterproductive for art making. "Those were the days when we still spoke about 'the

---

[4] Ibid.
[5] Ibid.

cinematic,'" Noël Carroll has written.[6] "Those days" were the 1960s and 1970s, when formalist film criticism was at its height and, not by coincidence, cinema studies took shape as a discipline, with university film departments' existence validated by the fact that they had a unique object worthy of serious study. While recognizing that medium specificity may once have had utility, Carroll has been its most vocal critic, sustaining an assault upon the idea across a series of books and essays written over a period of more than three decades. Most recently he has exhorted us to "Forget the Medium!" He offers "the moving image" in place of a conception of an art form rooted in the physical materials of a specific medium (i.e., film). "The moving image" is a much more encompassing term, which acknowledges that art forms are not restricted to single physical materials.[7]

Carroll makes four major claims against what he calls "medium-specificity talk." The first is that conceptions of what counts as "a medium" are notoriously vague and slippery. Where is the medium of "film"? In a response to Murray Smith's defense of medium specificity, Carroll writes that

> apart from the various media, in the plural, that comprise the artform of the moving image, I don't know what that medium is. [Smith] can't, at this late date, be referring to film stock. So what does he have in mind? It is hard to evaluate claims on behalf of the medium when one does not know what it is. The terms of the argument become far too abstract.[8]

Carroll's second criticism, which flows logically from the first, is that all art forms are "multiple." They are realized in a variety of physical materials and share aesthetic traits with other art forms. Sculptures, for example, can be made of stone, metal, wood, plastic, and so on; cinema can be made in film (16mm, 35mm, IMAX), or in analog or digital video. Cinema also utilizes language, narrative, and performance, among other inter-arts forms. Contra medium-specificity theory, which differentiates art forms from one another, cinema shares the qualities of form, rhythm, narrative, juxtaposition of imagery, and so on, with other art forms.[9]

Carroll's third argument against medium specificity is that media are historically variable. Medium-specificity theory takes a medium—say, celluloid film—as an ahistorical absolute, Carroll claims, something akin to a natural kind.[10] From the essential physical structure of that medium, which medium-specificity theory treats like

---

[6] Noël Carroll, "Forget the Medium!," in *Engaging the Moving Image* (New Haven, CT: Yale University Press, 2003), p. 2.

[7] In addition to "Forget the Medium!," Carroll has written "Medium Specificity Arguments and the Self-Consciously Invented Arts: Film, Video, and Photography," "The Specificity of Media in the Arts," "Concerning Uniqueness Claims for Photographic and Cinematographic Representation," and "Defining the Moving Image," all of which are collected in Carroll's *Theorizing the Moving Image*. My summary of Carroll's anti-medium-specific arguments incorporates elements from all five of these essays.

[8] Noël Carroll, "Engaging Critics," *Film Studies* 8 (Summer 2006), p. 163.

[9] See especially "Defining the Moving Image," pp. 51–54 and "Forget the Medium," pp. 5–9.

[10] See "Defining the Moving Image," p. 53, for example.

DNA or molecular structure, the art form derives its aesthetic essence(s). But media change all the time, and new media, including new moving image media, appear frequently. Moreover, artists themselves often make modifications to media, adapting existing physical media to their aesthetic aims rather than accepting the limitations of some unchanging material structure that cannot be overcome. Arnheim provides an instance of medium specificity's ahistorical blindness, according to Carroll; his lifelong commitment to the idea that cinema reached its artistic peak in the mature silent period not only ignored technological changes that occurred during his lifetime, but also the fact that film at the time of its invention was silent and monochromatic merely by historical accident. "Clearly," Carroll concludes, "medium specificity arguments are not always on the side of either the angels or the future."[11]

Carroll's unveiling of medium-specificity theory's logical flaws and arbitrary limitations on artmaking are often astute and seem quite compelling. But ultimately, his critique, especially in its most recent incarnation ("Forget the Medium!") is plagued by a drastically reductive view of what medium-specificity theory is, not as some abstraction but as a historically dynamic discourse. And his alternative suffers from problems of its own. Carroll's blanket category of "the moving image" is so broad as to render any differentiation among art forms impossible, indeed meaningless, when such a task is eminently sensible. Just because cinema, television, video games, light shows, web art, and video installation have moving images in common is no reason to organize them under one all-encompassing rubric. Why? Because art forms are not defined merely by clusters of aesthetic traits, but by specific historical and institutional forces as well, wherein critical differences are to be found beneath surface similarities. As Carroll himself points out, both cinema and sculpture can be made with celluloid, but this doesn't make them the same art forms. *Something else* must determine whether we are to regard a work in celluloid as a sculpture, or a film, or a hybrid. Is it *really* beneficial to suggest a mega–art form, and related field of critical inquiry, that encompasses such diverse works as *Citizen Kane, Mothlight, Mary Tyler Moore, Stranger Things*, The Joshua Light Show, the work of Vito Acconci or Joan Jonas, internet art, YouTube videos, animated GIFs, flipbooks, Ms. Pac Man, and Fortnight? Carroll's variation on the theme of media convergence remains silent on this question. What's more, from a historical perspective, there is no unified historical tradition of "the moving image" but rather numerous traditions. These may be more or less interrelated but each has construed its objects and aims in quite different ways. Hence, Carroll's conglomerate category of "the moving image" is pitched at such a high level of generality as to leave significant differences among art forms unacknowledged, indeed unacknowledgeable.

I would argue that the source of the limitations of Carroll's critique of medium specificity is that he reduces it to a straw man, a greatly oversimplified, ahistorical abstraction that has never, in fact, existed. Who are these dogmatic, absolutist

[11] Noël Carroll, "Medium Specificity Arguments and the Self-Consciously Invented Arts," p. 19.

medium-specificity theorists Carroll has in mind? Nobody, even the artists and critics Carroll identifies as adherents to medium-specificity theory, characterizes either "cinema" or "the film medium" in such limited, simplistically physical terms. Medium specificity has always been more complex than Carroll's account would have us believe, and much more attuned to the philosophical quandaries of essentialism and medium-belonging Carroll rightly identifies.

Responding to this shortcoming of Carroll's position brings us to his fourth major criticism of medium-specificity theory, which is that proponents of the theory confuse empirical arguments about art forms and their media with analytical arguments. The former empirically—objectively—define art forms for all time, in the way that definitions of natural kinds do. The latter is a tool for "defining success," supporting evaluation of the artistry of individual films or filmmakers, or undergirding preferences for particular cinematic traditions or schools (as in Bazin's preference for long takes, deep focus, and camera movement over montage).[12] Carroll sums this point up neatly when we writes, "despite talk of purism, the so-called medium appears to turn out to have been the result of preferential stylistic gerrymandering."[13] By this, I take him to mean that those who claim to identify the essence of cinema in some specific physical component of a medium actually begin with presuppositions about cinema's essence, then verify those with reference to whatever facet of the physical medium seems best suited to doing so. In other words, they do not move from an objective, empirical view of the materials of the medium to a notion of the essence of the art form that logically follows from this, but in fact begin with covert a priori assumptions of what cinema as an art form *should* be, then retroactively yoke that conception to an obliging element of the physical medium. In this way, the *prescriptive* masquerades as the *descriptive*, as aesthetic values and tastes are covertly validated by empirical proof.

I believe Carroll is right that ontological claims about cinema made in the form of medium-specificity talk or other forms of cinematic essentialism are value laden. I don't agree with his claim that nobody is aware of this, nor that it is a liability. Artists in particular strike me as having been consistently aware that they are asserting values as much as neutral empirical descriptions of their medium. Experimental filmmakers assert a particular way of making cinema as much as they assert a particular definition of "cinema" (the art form) or "film" (the medium). Indeed, these are intertwined. Hence the value of a tripartite model of cinematic *specificities*, one of which is the specificity of a cinematic culture or what I have referred to as a mode of film practice. Filmmakers and critics strive, often knowingly, to validate their specific branch of cinematic practice, and the way avant-garde cinema conceives of cinema is distinct from the conceptions of Hollywood, art cinema, or moving image art in the gallery. Hence, in the medium-specific or essentialist claims of filmmakers and critics in the avant-garde two things occur at the same time: defining cinema and elevating a specific *kind*

---

[12] Carroll, "Forget the Medium!," p. 5.
[13] Ibid., p. 7.

of cinema to a privileged position. Carroll sees this as a theoretical flaw because it confuses objective and subjective accounts of the nature of cinema, when specifying the nature of something should proceed from empirical observations rather than a priori values. But while this makes sense in the case of natural kinds, things are much less clear cut in the case of an art form, which is a kind of collective, historically evolving invention via tacit and ongoing social contract. If this is accurate, then values are not out of place in defining art forms, nor physical media. More to the point, as I hope to have shown, at least within experimental film the aim has been as much to define *experimental* cinema as cinema itself, and values are rightly part of this activity. Carroll's call to "forget the medium" is thus simply untenable. We do not have to believe that physical media absolutely define artistic forms to believe that "remembering" them is an important component of understanding cinema. Anyone who believes that differences (or, for that matter, similarities) among physical media are not important has never made art. But, as should be clear, I am not arguing that the qualities of physical media define art forms in absolute senses, but that varying levels of specificity—of media, art forms, and artistic traditions—interact with one another as conceptions of "the cinematic" are formed, reconsidered, and reformed over time. Expanded cinema is a barometer of these changes and the forces behind them.

Without intending to, Carroll sets forth the major positive qualities of medium-specific theorizing of cinema as it has been practiced within the avant-garde and manifests most forcefully in expanded cinema. That is, Carroll's criticisms of medium-specificity talk can be reoriented from logical failings to positive assertions of expanded cinema's project vis-à-vis the definition of cinema. Expanded cinema acknowledges that a medium cannot be reduced to a single substance, object, material, or instrument; its models of the specificity of the medium recognize its complex component nature and deploy these components in diverse ways. There is no denial of cinema's historical hybridity and affinities with other art forms in expanded cinema, but an ongoing negotiation between specifying "the cinematic" and loosening that concept from a single medium or aesthetic form. And rather than isolating cinema from historical variability, expanded cinema engages with cinema history to trace out possibilities forgotten or marginalized by the standardization of physical media and exhibition formats, by no means taking cinema as anything like a natural kind. Finally, expanded cinema characterizes cinema as ultimately a conceptual phenomenon, which is not to say an imaginary or purely ephemeral one, but one shaped through discourse, ideas, ambitions, and imagined possibilities—a continuing reinvention. It is defined in part by knowledge structures: presuppositions, schemas, and conceptions of an art form's identity at any given time. Carroll's conception of "the moving image" is, like the definitions of expanded cinema initially offered by critics like Youngblood and Renan, overly expanded. It makes sense, then, that these critics also possess a notion of medium specificity that is overly contracted. For Carroll, medium specificity reduced to a simplistic materialism, while Youngblood and Renan saw it as the yoke of technological determinism thrown off in an act of liberation. All three are guilty of jettisoning the baby with the bathwater, as the saying goes. I hope to have shown that there is a very accommodating and fertile field between these two absolutes, which is where expanded cinema resides.

"[W]e stare at the pit in the earth and think we both do and don't know what sculpture is," Rosalind Krauss wrote in "Sculpture in the Expanded Field." "Yet," she countered:

> I would submit that we know very well what sculpture is. And one of the things we know is that it is a historically bounded category and not a universal one. As is true of any other convention, sculpture has its own internal logic, its own set of rules, which, though they can be applied to a variety of situations, are not themselves open to very much change.[14]

The "pit in the earth" was *Perimeters, Pavilions, Decoys* (1978), an earthwork by Mary Miss. But for Krauss it was also an emblem of the perils of artistic expansion, wherein something we thought we knew, something we even took for granted, has fallen away into a black hole of the unknown—the reassuring ground of tradition suddenly dropping out beneath us. The expansion of cinema, more or less coterminous with that of sculpture, into new, vast, uncharted space must have felt something like this at first. What I have shown in this book is how avant-garde film culture regained the familiar ground that seemed to have given way in this upheaval, while acknowledging, and even reveling, in the fact that it was—and to some extent always had been—contested.

But not lost. These are the days when we can still speak about "the cinematic."

* * *

November 14, 2018, the Wexner Center for the Arts in Columbus, Ohio. Richard Tuohy and Dianna Barrie close a program of their remarkable hand-made films with a projection performance entitled *Cyclone Tracery* (2018, a play on Cyclone Tracy, which destroyed the city of Darwin in northern Australia in 1974). *Cyclone Tracery* is performed on two side-by-side 16mm projectors. A single film print is threaded twice through each projector in a process called "bi-packing": threaded through the first projector, the film end is brought back to the front of the machine and coaxed through its film path once more, then pulled to the second projector to be loaded the same way. One reel of film thereby passes through four loops, two in each projector, before being wound onto the takeup reel of the second projector. The same imagery, then, is projected four times, multiplied across time in two variations of superimposition: each projector casts two images at once (each from a different section of the filmstrip), and the projectors are aimed at the same space on the screen. The imagery is of white concentric circles on a black background, "flicker printed," in Tuohy's words, meaning the circles are interrupted every other frame by a black frame.[15]

---

14 Rosalind Krauss, "Sculpture in the Expanded Field," *October* 8 (Spring 1979), p. 33.
15 Richard Tuohy, email to author, July 2, 2019.

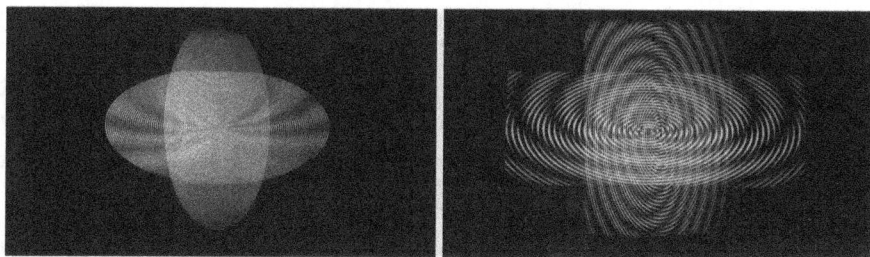

Fig. C.2. Richard Tuohy and Dianna Barrie, *Cyclone Tracery* (2018). Performance documentation. Two 16mm film projectors, one bi-packed 16mm film.
Courtesy Richard Tuohy and Dianna Barrie.

When projected, and furthermore superimposed in four layers, the film creates an especially powerful impression of rotation, while the overlay of multiple concentric circles produces illusory moiré patterns (fig. C.2). Tuohy and Barrie intensify these effects by fitting their projectors with anamorphic lenses, which stretch the circular images vertically into ovals, and by rotating one of the projectors onto its side during the performance, arranging the four overlapping cyclonic widescreen images into a rough cross form on screen.

The concentric circles have also been printed onto the film's optical soundtrack area, shifted from the center of each frame to the very edge of the filmstrip using an optical printer. The sound produced by the imagery combines the rapidly rising and falling pitches of Lis Rhode's *Light Music* and the throbbing electronic pulse of Bruce McClure's performances, what Touhy and Barrie aptly describe as "whaling sounds of tropical violence."[16] The greatly amplified sound thus complements the large scale of the images, the overall impression being one of immersion in a sense-overwhelming field of pulsating light and sound, the disorienting effects of which remain with the viewer for some time after the work concludes.

The complexities of *Cyclone Tracery*'s projection require that one of the filmmakers (Barrie in the iteration performed at the Wexner Center) "stand in between the two projectors and become part of the threading path in order to manage the flow of the film between the two projectors," in Tuohy's words (fig. C.3).[17] This is necessitated not only by the diabolical precariousness of this threading path, but also by the fact that film projectors run at slightly different speeds. Even a difference of only one frame per second between the work's two projectors will accumulate rapidly, and if the first projector runs slower than the second (i.e., if it cannot "keep up with" the second projector's consumption of film), the bi-packed loop will eventually contract to the point

---

[16] Richard Tuohy and Dianna Barrie, notes for *Cyclone Tracery*. See the online exhibition program for *Light Field*, presented at The Lab in San Francisco, March 15–17, 2019, http://www.lightfieldfilm.org/2019-program-7.

[17] Richard Tuohy, email to author, July 2, 2019.

Fig. C.3. Richard Tuohy and Dianna Barrie, *Cyclone Tracery* (2018). Performance documentation.
Courtesy Richard Tuohy and Dianna Barrie.

that tension on the film brings the entire infernal machine to a grinding halt. What's more, the person who massages the film through the two projectors is also working to prevent any tension from causing the strip to slip in either projector's gate; the print is carefully loaded into each projector so that two black frames are not projected simultaneously, on top of one another. As Tuohy explains:

> Since the film is bi-packed in the projectors, it is necessary to have the film fold back on top of itself such that you have image on top of image rather than image over black. If it was the latter, nothing would be projected. And the same goes for the sound heads of the projector—the film needs to be image over image and black over black at the sound head area or else you wouldn't hear any sound. This means there is always a risk of either projector dropping a frame in either the picture area or the sound area and thus loosing picture or sound from one or other projector. So it is actually rather tense![18]

Tuohy's description plays upon both meanings of "tense," referring to the physical tension upon the film necessary for all projection and to the emotional anxiety that

---

[18] Ibid.

attends any live performance, though greatly augmented in *Cyclone Tracery* by the willfully difficult process to which Tuohy and Barrie subject the film print, by the unpredictability in the cooperation of human and machine that standardized projection is designed to minimize. *Cyclone Tracery*, like so much of the expanded work in this book, is precisely about this relationship between filmmaker, medium, and moment. The acrobatics of the work are possible thanks to a long apprenticeship by Tuohy and Barrie to the film medium, which has allowed them to cultivate possibilities in that medium that would be unimaginable otherwise, making the film machine do not what it was intended to do but what it can do (albeit with great difficulty). Theirs is not a medium specificity or a reflexivity of the usual materialist sort—of filmic objects like framelines and emulsion grain—but of forces, energies, processes, and relations discovered in Tuohy and Barrie's tireless plumbing of the depths of their medium. Pavle Levi identifies a similarly objectless filmic energy in the Latham Loop, which is not a thing but "a *curvature of space* demarcated between the [projector's] spools, the gears, and the gate."[19] Levi refers to this as "a friendly 'ghost in the machine,'" bringing together thought and technology, conceptual and mechanized labor," a sign for "the inseparability of idea and matter."[20]

A similarly multivalent working model of cinema's essences is at the heart of Esperanza Collado's *We Only Guarantee the Dinosaurs* (2014–2015), a deliberately meandering and often opaque expanded cinema performance in which Collado, acting as both projectionist and performer, interacts with filmed images, exhibition space, projectors and filmstrips, and a variety of props (fig. C.4). Collado's statement about the work makes clear the way it is intended to trace out a range of cinematic essences, from the concrete to the conceptual:

> The starting point is the idea of projection as an experience linked to physics, geometry, spectacle, psychology, optics, and the collective inhabitation of a common space in the dark where the awareness of one's own body tends to disappear. In trying to invert this logic, degrees of visibility and presence are established while the existing tensions between the two-dimensionality of the projected image and the three-dimensionality of bodies and objects is negotiated.[21]

The "tensions" to which Collado alludes play out in an interchange between her real props and filmed images "specially conceived to dialogue" with the unfolding live spectacle.[22] For example, an image on screen of Collado, dressed in a white boiler suit, pulling a swath of bright red fabric into the frame until it covers the camera's field of view entirely is complemented by the real Collado stretching a length of red ribbon from one of two 16mm projectors to the surface of the screen

[19] Levi, *Cinema by Other Means*, p. xi.
[20] Ibid., pp. xi–xii.
[21] Esperanza Collado, unpublished notes for *We Only Guarantee the Dinosaurs*.
[22] Ibid.

Fig. C.4. Esperanza Collado, *We Only Guarantee the Dinosaurs* (2014–2015). Performance documentation. 16mm films, 8 × 1 m red carpet, palm tree, variable measure of ribbon, raincoat, kettle, cardboard box, dry ice, water, microphone, ostrich feather, tungsten lamp, 2 × 16mm film projectors on wheeled supports.
Image courtesy Esperanza Collado.

(fig. C.5). The ribbon imagery—real and filmed—figures into a motif of red objects: a red carpet unrolled then re-rolled during the performance and at times starkly illuminated by the beam of an empty projector, and a filmed closeup of Collado's hand holding a red card against the sky. Filmed images of glowing white smoke are echoed moments later by the steam from a bucket of dry ice, which Collado uses to illuminate the projector beam as it casts the image of a white circle against a black background (fig. C.6). A chintzy-looking palm tree in a pot, with which Collado dances at one point in the performance, resonates with filmed images of trees, which provide the backdrop for a series of shots of people eating figs.

Like Alex MacKenzie's film *The Wooden Lightbox* (see chapter 3), *We Only Guarantee the Dinosaurs* is an obscure catalog of filmic references ranging across different cinematic modes: the palm tree and red carpet hark back to the spectacle of classical Hollywood (as does Collado's use of Duke Ellington's 1937 recording of "Caravan," recorded in Hollywood and suggestive of the kinds of exotic locals on view in Joseph Cornell's *Rose Hobart*); the outlining of the projector beam with dry ice recalls *Line Describing a Cone*; the shots of people eating figs while looking into the

Fig. C.5. Esperanza Collado, *We Only Guarantee the Dinosaurs* (2014–2015).
Performance documentation.
Image courtesy Esperanza Collado.

Fig. C.6. Esperanza Collado, *We Only Guarantee the Dinosaurs* (2014–2015).
Performance documentation.
Image courtesy Esperanza Collado.

camera remind one of Warhol's *Eat* (1963); the interplay of Collado engaging in real and filmed actions is reminiscent of Guy Sherwin's work and is squarely within the London Filmmakers' Coop tradition of anti-illusionist film practice. The work's title is taken from "The Sound of Thunder," a short story by Ray Bradbury about a company that offers dinosaur-hunting safaris via time travel: "'We guarantee nothing,' said the official, 'except the dinosaurs.'" A participant terrified by the sudden appearance of a Tyrannosaurus Rex inadvertently tramples a butterfly and returns to a future that his actions have drastically altered. The implication of Collado's reference to this story is that avant-garde cinema returns to the film-historical past to explore—perhaps perilously—roads not travelled and alternate cinematic realities.

If the performance suggests a pile-up of film history references, it is also informed by a conception of cinema through which all manner of concepts, disciplines, and categories run. Collado's references to physics, geometry, and optics, and her incorporation of very deliberate, slow, and methodical actions with her props, implies that the "negotiation" of real and illusory film space at the center of *We Only Guarantee the Dinosaurs* is, in fact, a measurement of different kinds of distances and scales, understood both literally and metaphorically, or, in both material and ephemeral terms. Collado quotes Dominique Païni's 2004 essay "Should We Put an End to Projection?," in which Païni enumerates the meanings of the word itself, unearthing hidden associations that become the bases for Collado's essentialist investigation:

> Cinema's luminous resonance occupies a space and has the potentiality of turning it into a tactile, magnetic, and gaseous geometry from which projecting does not simply consist of creating optical and magnified images through a film and onto a screen. To project also relates to thought processes and bodily actions.[23]

That is, projection, according to Païni, is "a word that refers to activities of thought as much as of physical or bodily exertion," a phrase Collado cites approvingly in a statement accompanying the performance.[24] The notion links Collado's work to that of Paul Sharits, in its exhaustive cataloging of "filmic elements": "processes of intending to make a film; processes of recording light patterns on raw stock (films can be made which by-pass this mode); processes of processing; processes of editing; processes of printing; processes of projecting; processes of experiencing."[25] A film, or a cinematic work, is at the intersection of this nexus of objects, disciplines, thought processes, and energies.

[23] Dominique Païni, "Should We Put an End to Projection?," *October* 110 (Autumn 2004), pp. 23–48. The essay was translated and excerpted by Rosalind Krauss. The passage above does not appear in the *October* article, and so likely appeared in the original version of the text, which appeared in the catalog for "Projections: Les transports de l'image" at Le Fresnoy, Studio National des arts Contemporains in Tourcoing, France, November 1997–January 1998.

[24] Ibid., p. 23.

[25] Sharits, "Words Per Page," p. 37. See chapter 6.

Like the perplexed spectators gathered around Miss's *Perimeters, Pavilions, Decoys,* we might wonder where "the medium"—of film, of cinema—is in all this. Collado lists the materials of her work, in an almost comic aping of convention (e.g., "oil on canvas"): 16mm films, 8 × 1m red carpet, palm tree, variable measure of ribbon, raincoat, kettle, cardboard box, dry ice, water, microphone, ostrich feather, tungsten lamp, two 16mm film projectors on wheeled supports. Sally Golding's tech rider for *Light Begets Sound* (see chapter 3) is equally unwieldy: two film projectors with no film, motorized color shutters, camera flash units, various custom sound devices, mixing desk feedback, light-sensitive prepared screen, custom sound-light control software (figure C.7). She describes this ongoing, open-ended work as "A shifting project of generative feedback systems, amplified lighting, prepared screens and phasing projection beams." *Light Begets Sound* encompasses sound and image, digital and analog, mechanical and electronic, live action and recoded imagery; Golding describes it as "a durational performance" utilizing film and digital projectors, "custom software and custom built light sensitive instruments," and as "interrogating aural and optic as well as physiological senses." One could attempt to argue, à la Krauss, that Golding has invented her own medium that exists somewhere amid all the hardware and software, which indeed makes the work difficult to perform and a challenge for venues to accommodate. But as these materials are always changing, and as Golding's mechanical labors are ultimately aimed at a more ephemeral experience tied, in the final analysis,

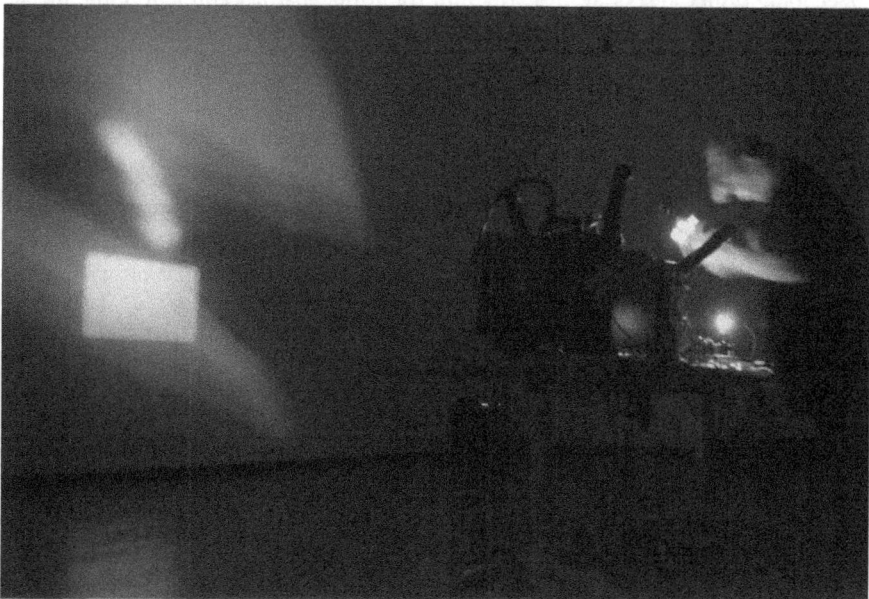

Fig. C.7. Sally Golding performing *Light Begets Sound* (2017–ongoing). Two 16mm projectors, light-sensitive prepared screen, flashlight, photo flash bulb, sound mixing equipment.

Photo courtesy of [S8] Mostra de Cinema Periférico. Image courtesy Sally Golding.

to her work as filmmaker and her ideas about cinema's nature, trying to identify a newly invented "medium" here seems beside the point. Like *Cyclone Tracery* and *We Only Guarantee the Dinosaurs*, Golding's work identifies "the cinematic" in the intersection of forces and materials, in Levi's words, "bringing together thought and technology, conceptual and mechanized labor."

To say that such works are typical of expanded cinema work is not to say they are average or mundane—far from it. I mean instead to take them as emblematic of expanded cinema as I have conceived of it in this book. They are decidedly filmic though not only so, not another expression of film about film, that meaning so often wrongly and unfairly attributed to a reflexive, medium-specific film practice. *Cyclone Tracery*, for instance, while plumbing the depths of a medium, in no way merely loops back to it exclusive of anything else, instead making reference to and indeed cinematically replicating natural forces (the tropical storm that is its namesake, and beyond that, space, time, energies), requiring both human action and human presence, creating illusion and multi-sensory effects, and trading in the aesthetic forms of music, performance, light and kinetic art, and, in its obdurate objecthood, sculpture. It is, in a word, manifestly *excessive*.

And let *Cyclone Tracery* also stand, in its specific visual content, as an emblem of expanded cinema's dialectic of expansion and contraction, of centripetal and centrifugal movement, its annexation of foreign artistic terrain and its grounding in a focused cinematic specificity both in its interplay of dematerialized materialism and its echoing of decades of avant-garde film tradition: abstract animation, the flicker film, hypnagogic imagery, structural film, and handmade D-I-Y craftsperson-ship. These works do not file away under the headings of intermedia, post-cinema, or post-medium art any more than they do under those of a simplistic pure film or pure cinema. Such terms and concepts might help us triangulate the position of expanded cinema in the landscape of modern art, but the ground it occupies within that landscape is its own. We neither need peg such work as manifesting an imagined purism nor an ill-defined interstitiality. Let us instead marvel at the distinct yet fantastically heterogeneous and endlessly surprising field of possibilities that avant-garde filmmakers find in cinema, expanded.

Index

For the benefit of digital users, indexed terms that span two pages (e.g., 52–53) may, on occasion, appear on only one of those pages.

Figures are indicated by *f* following the page number